THE SKI BOOK

THE SKI

Edited by

BOOK

Arbor House
New York

MORTEN LUND, ROBERT GILLEN *and*
MICHAEL BARTLETT

ALSO BY MORTEN LUND
Skier's World

Skier's Bible

Ski GLM

The Pleasure of Cross Country Skiing

ALSO BY BOB GILLEN
Winning Tennis: Strokes and Strategies of the World's Top Pros

The Tennis Book

ALSO BY MICHAEL BARTLETT
The New 1969 Golfer's Almanac

Bartlett's World Golf Encyclopedia

The Golf Book

The Tennis Book

Library of Congress Catalogue Card Number: 82-72066
ISBN: 0-87795-430-5
MANUFACTURED IN THE UNITED STATES OF AMERICA
10 9 8 7 6 5 4 3 2 1

This book is printed on acid free paper. The paper in this book meets the guidelines for permanence and durability of the Committee on Production Guidelines for Book Longevity of the Council on Library Resources.

Design by Antler & Baldwin, Inc.

Dedicated to those
writers who have
brought greater
recognition to, and
understanding of,
the sport of skiing
and to Robert B. McManus and
Eugene P. Gorman—two men
who know mountains

Contents

Part I THE PEAK EXPERIENCE

Part V   BREAKTHROUGHS

Part VI   RACER'S EDGE

Acknowledgments

—Mystery from *The Skier's World.* Copyright by Morten Lund. Reprinted by permission of VNU Books International

—The Onset from *The Poetry of Robert Frost,* edited by Edward Connery Lathem. Copyright 1923 © 1969 by Holt Rinehart and Winsten. Copyright 1951 by Robert Frost. Reprinted by permission of Holt, Rinehard and Winsten.

—Mont Blanc from *The Complete Poetic Works of Shelley* Copyright © by Percy Bysshe Shelley.

—The Skier and the Mountain from *Collected Poems 1930–1976* by Richard Eberhart. Copyright © 1960, 1976 by Richard Eberhart. Reprinted by permission of The Oxford Press, Inc.

—The Great Run from Ski Magazine. Copyright © by Ski Magazine. Reprinted by permission of Ski Magazine

—Skiing the Polar Snow from *Farthest North.* Copyright © by Fridtjof Nansen. Reprinted by permission of Harper Bros.

—Danger and Daring from *A Practice of Mountains.* Copyright © by Andrea Mead Lawrence and Sarah Burnaby. Reprinted by permission of Seaview Books

—The Oberland Glaciers from *The Bernese Oberland.* Copyright © by Arnold Lunn. Reprinted by permission of Eyre Metheun Ltd.

—Spring Fever on Skis from *Ski The Americas.* Copyright © by John Jay. Reprinted by permission of John Jay.

—Aspen's Greatest Day. Copyright © by Ski Magazine and Peter Miller. Reprinted by permission of the author and publisher

—At the Pole from *The South Pole.* Copyright © Roald Amundsen Foundation. Reprinted by permission of John Murray.

—Staib's Pole from Ski Magazine. Copyright © by Ski Magazine and John Henry Auran. Reprinted by permission of the author and publisher.

—With Skis On McKinley from *Pioneers on Skis.* Copyright © 1977 by Julian Cornell. Reprinted by permission of Smith Clove Press and Erling Strom

—I Skied Higher Than Any Man. Copyright © by Ski Magazine. Reprinted by permission of Ski Magazine

—In Pursuit of Pure Speed. Copyright © by Dick Dorworth. Reprinted by permission of the author.

—Skiing the Steeps. Copyright New York Times Magazine and Peter Miller. Reprinted by permission of the author and the publisher.

—Snow from *The Magic Mountain.* Copyright © by Alfred Knopf. Reprinted by permission of Alfred Knopf.

—There Is Never Any End to Paris from *The Movable Feast.* Copyright © Ernest Hemingway. Reprinted by permission of Charles Scribner's Sons.

—The Hartleys from *The Stories of John Cheever.* Copyright © by John Cheever. Reprinted by permission of Alfred Knopf.

—The Rescue from *The Music School.* Copyright © John Updike. Reprinted by permission of Alfred A. Knopf. This story originally appeared in *The New Yorker.*

—The Inhabitants of Venus from *Love on a Dark Street.* Copyright © Irwin Shaw. Reprinted by permission of Delacorte Press.

—An Alpine Pass on Ski from Strand Magazine. Copyright © Strand Magazine. Reprinted by permission of McClure's Magazine

11

—Pain and Pleasure on the Haute Route. Copyright Skiing Magazine. Reprinted by permission of Skiing Magazine

—This Could Be the Last Resort. Copyright © *by Time Inc.*. Reprinted by permission of Sports Illustrated.

—Schuss, Comerade by John Fry. Copyright Ski Magazine. Reprinted by permission of Ski Magazine.

—The Powder and the Glory. Copyright Playboy Magazine. Reprinted by the permission of Playboy magazine and the author.

—The Norse Started It All. Copyright Ski Magazine. Reprinted by permission of Ski Magazine and Jakob Vaage.

—A Way of Life. Copyright © 1941, 1971 The New Yorker. Reprinted by permission of The New Yorker.

—The Arlberg Technique from *World Ski Book.* Copyright Longmans, Greene. Reprinted by permission of the publisher.

—The Teaching Plan from *The New Official Austrian Ski System.* Copyright © 1959 Otto Mueller Verlag. Reprinted by permission of Stefan Kruckenhauser.

—The Ski Is a Tool from *How The Racers Ski.* Copyright © by W. W. Norton, Reprinted by permission of the author and W. W. Norton.

—No. "10" Powder. Copyright by *Powder* and Bob Jamieseon. Reprinted by permission of the author and the publisher.

—Working with Images from *The Centered Skier.* Copyright © 1977 by Denise McCluggage. Reprinted by permission of Denise McCluggage.

—One Minute Warning. Copyright Skiing Magazine and Betty Bell. Reprinted by permission of the author and the publisher.

—The Oldest Continuous Floating Ski Racer of Them All from Ski Magazine. Copyright © Burton Hersh. Reprinted by permission of Burton Hersh.

—He Went Straight In. Copyright Skiing Magazine and Nicholas Howe. Reprinted by permission of the author and the publisher.

—The Formative Years from *Skiing the Killy Way* by Jean-Claude Killy with Doug Pfeiffer. Copyright © 1971 by Jean-Claude Killy. Reprinted by permission of Simon and Schuster, a division of Gulf & Western Corporation.

—The Crash from *The 30,000 Mile Ski Race* by Peter Miller. Copyright © 1972 by Dial Press. Reprinted by permission of the author & publisher.

—Downhill. Copyright by James Salter and Paramount Pictures. Reprinted by permission of the author and Paramount Pictures.

—I Was the Irish Ski Team. Copyright Ski Magazine and Robert McKee. Reprinted by permission of the author and the publisher.

—The TV Watcher's Guide. Copyright *Powder* and Weems Westfeldt. Reprinted by permission of the author and the publisher.

—Resorting, The Sport of. Copyright © Art Buchwald. Reprinted by permission of Art Buchwald.

—Life with Stein, Leon and the Chilean Crazies. Copyright © Ski Magazine and Marti Sterling. Reprinted by permission of the author and the publisher.

—Heatherbedlam. Copyright Ski Magazine and Leon Uris. Reprinted by permission of the author and the publisher.

—Sun Valley Opens with a Bang and Skiing Hits Manhattan from *Sun* Valley. Copyright by Dorice Taylor. Reprinted by permission of Ex Libris Sun Valley.

—Social Climbing on the Slopes. Copyright Gay Talese. Reprinted by permission of Gay Talese.

—The Ski Bum as an Endangered Species. Copyright Jean Vallely. Reprinted by permission of Robert Finkelstein, Managment 3.

—Me and Truck. Copyright Skiing Magazine and Bob Jamieson. Reprinted by permission of the author and the publisher.

—The Two Million Dollar Ski Man. Copyright Ski Magazine and Morten Lund. Reprinted by permission of the author and the publisher.

—Suzy and Jill © Skiing Magazine. Reprinted by permission of the publisher and Dinah Witchel.

—Truman Capote, in Interview. Copyright Ski Magazine. Reprinted by permission of Ski Magazine.

—Records reprinted by permission of Ski Magazine.

—Special Acknowledgments to those who helped the editors in their task of searching out and picking the selections and pictures in this book to whom the editors owe a debt of gratitude: Dick Needham of Ski Magazine, John Auran and Dinah Witchel of Skiing Magazine, Jean King, Janet Nelson, Robert Redford, Robbi Miller, James Salter, Sandy Moore, Peter Wingle, Fletcher Manley, Peter Miller, Julia Rosenblatt, Carol Smith, Pat Cochran of Powder Magazine and Jack Hemingway.

The Editors' Preface

THE three of us want to record that we have had continual pleasure and astonishment in the pursuit of the pieces in this book. The men of letters who have at one time or another written about the sport of skiing are a unique group. No other sport, just for one instance, has evoked such interest as skiing has in not one but *two* Nobel prize winners, specifically Thomas Mann and Ernest Hemingway. And what other sport can list among the writers who have recorded their reactions to it names to compare with the following: John Updike, John Cheever, Conan Doyle, and Irwin Shaw? We dare say: no other sport.

It was an added delight to discover that there are among the great skier-explorers, like Fridtjof Nansen and Roald Amundsen, the conquerors of Greenland and the South Pole respectively, men who write as compellingly as they explore. And thirdly, we found an incredible variety of character, culture and style among those who had fashioned wondrously-wrought stories: the dark dreams of a Mann contrasted with the brightly lit tragedy of a Cheever, the stately pronouncements of a gentleman and knight, Arnold Lunn, with the wild, gothic irreverences of a Dick Dorworth. We found, as well, writers whose gift of the comic enhanced for us our experiences in the dangerous and ridiculous sport of skiing. The pages that follow are a veritable treasure store of sharp, gleaming personal perspectives by committed skiers who were just as committed as writers.

Our search was unobstructed, happily: this is the first-ever collection of previously published ski pieces covering the whole gamut of the sport. So this book is not only a first, but a long-overdue first.

May our readers have as magnificently rewarding a time in the reading of this collection as we, the editors, had in the gathering of it.

Morten Lund, Robert Gillen and
Michael Bartlett
New York, Fall 1982

Photo Credits

Foreword

by JEAN-CLAUDE KILLY

Jean-Claude Killy was twice world amateur champion, once world professional champion and one of two men in history to win all three gold medals in the alpine Olympic races—at Grenoble, France, in 1968. Today he is a leading ski industry businessman.

I have always striven in one way or another to create high standards for skiing; thus it is a particularly happy occasion for me to write the foreword for this collection of ski literature and journalism, selected for its high standards. The book stands as a tribute to the sport by the very finest writers on the subject, from literary men like Hemingway and Mann to journalists like Dorworth and Miller, tops in their field. It is obvious that the editors of the book spent an enormous amount of time and effort in making these selections.

I have always taken the sport seriously and it has always been a powerful influence on not only the physical circumstances of my life but on my philosophy and ethics. With the readers' leave, I would like to take them on a quick retrospective of my life to show just how deeply the values of the sport have become the values of my life, and the results that thereby accrued.

Pictures of me in my early days in Val d'Isère in the French Alps show something very interesting. As a young man, aged five to nine, I had managed—even though my parents were far from rich—to accumulate a ski outfit far more complete and grown up than my contemporaries wore: I had good boots, excellent skis, a fine ski jacket, visored hat, and a set of goggles. Right from the start, I set a high standard in all ways. I most desperately wanted to both look great and *be* great. Skiing was my passion. I was shy and it was the only way I could really express my drive, my courage, my cunning, my intelligence. For me it was winning or—exploding in some unfortunate way. I found I could win.

There were kids with more natural ability in Val d'Isère the same age as I was. I had to find ways of beating them. And I did. As ski racing became more and more important in my life, my father—a fine athlete and former member of the French national jumping team—allowed me to quit school to devote myself to ski racing. This gave me the time that I needed in order to create my "strategies for success." My real life began. I learned to discipline the wild fierce joy of bounding down the mountain that I had had as a kid and to channel it to carry me through the gates on the race course with an undeniable momentum. At 16, I was selected on the development squad of the most powerful French national ski team ever assembled. Three years later, I was skiing in no. 1 spot on the team, and in 1966 became world ski champon at Portillo, Chile. Two years later, I won all three alpine gold medals at the Grenoble Olympics. The elation of victory is the reward of the winner and I was fortunate in having more than my share of wins. I would not have traded a second of it for anything else.

In the years of struggle, I learned that you cannot be taught anything by anyone but yourself. I think that it is the single deepest philosophical rule I developed. I created my own technique. It was considered radical at the time but it worked, for me. I created my technique by endless experiment. I copied shamelessly and turned what others knew to my own ends.

The first world champion I had a chance to emulate was Guy Perillat of the French team. I shadowed him for days. I knew that in time it would not do just to be as good as Perillat, but I had to invent a way to be better than Perillat. I had no long range plan other than that. When I could finally beat Perillat, I knew I could beat anybody.

When, after my triple gold win in 1968, I turned to business as a way of continuing making a life, I found ways to teach myself as I had in ski racing. In the course of the years I have become if not a world champion businessman at least a good solid success. Today I own Jean-Claude Killy Skiwear, the largest firm of its kind in Europe and a number of smaller enterprises: the profits have never stopped increasing, year by year.

To teach oneself, one must have "success strategies." And mine—in racing and business— have been:

First: ask questions. It is the only way. I remember once that I was learning golf and happened to sit next to Arnold Palmer at dinner. I plied him with questions. More and more. Finally Palmer, a gentlemanly sort, turned and said, "Jean-Claude, would you *stop* asking me questions about golf, please?"

Second: investigate. Once when the ski company that I consult for was having trouble with the performance of some of its skis, I wondered if it was a question of differences in the skill with which the night shift and the day shift made skis. So I got up in the middle of the night, drove to the factory and inspected the skis being made. It was the beginning of the unraveling of the problem. We found that the night skis were colder in temperature and that when worked on they came out with slightly different—a crucial difference—bases than the "day skis." (I did not have to make that night trip—I would have been paid my fee anyway, but to me investigating is a compulsion.)

Three: learn from criticism. One writer once did an article on me which attacked my competence as a speaker, a public figure and my attitude—he left little unsaid. But I learned from it. I improved my English greatly. I learned to hold an audience with words. No one today hesitates to book me for a public appearance.

Four: get good help.

The success I had in racing owes a good deal to those who advised me, in particular Michel Arpin. He spent full time after an accident took him off the French team in helping me select and maintain my racing gear and picking race strategies. Some people are afraid of hiring bright, competent help. I feel that it is worth the risk of being overshadowed. You have to take that risk to get to the top.

Finally, get recreation: when I was racing, recreation was of course, anything *but* skiing. But now that I am not racing, I ski for recreation. I love to hire a helicopter and take myself and one or two others up to the deepest available powder. There is something unequalled about skiing deep powder. The pressure of the snow surging about the skis, the rush of the snow hitting in waves, the incredible high of feeling your skis riding on the balance point, cutting an arc at the slightest intentional movement of the legs. I am essentially and deeply an athlete. If am not skiing, I go biking at high speed through the countryside, or swim long distance off beaches, or run through the woods for miles. If I do not do something like this for three or four days every six weeks or so, I lose my edge as a businessman.

My approach to the sport, then, has been

emotional, but through a technical path. I write about skiing only very occasionally. This book says, in ways much better than I can, how rich, varied and rewarding is this sport for those who partake of it.

May this book add as much to your skiing as skiing does to your life.

Geneva 1982

PART I

THE PEAK EXPERIENCE

"In degrees of the ideal, all forces exist in balance. It takes only a feather to right the scale, to make all of the governing factors share equal tension. After long hours of technique, the ideal responds, and in such moments of deep joy I have truly moved bodiless as in flight."
Andrea Mead Lawrence and Sara Burnaby,
A Practice of Mountains

The Mystery

by MORTEN LUND

To be skiing is to be in a world not of man, but of light—an alternation of sun and shade, sparkling, evanescent, existing only in the moment.

To be skiing is to be in the sky's play of color on the snow, with azure going deep overhead, and magic shapes sailing and slipping high toward the sun, bright, billowing, and begetting, a shifting, unceasing, wondrous display.

To be skiing is to be in among peaks shimmering back to the horizon; other peaks lie beyond and other peaks beyond them. Always a beyond.

This is a skier's dream: a continent of mountains where the snow falls softly every day. Serrated escarpments frame a movement: skiers swiftly track down sculpted sides that shear like thundering cataracts far, far down. There is no sound in this world.

THERE is mystery here, the mystery of a different world, and the mystery of an inner world, too—of the body and its fabulous capacities for quickness and compound movement, a final gift of the gods. There is magic in instinctive responses to terrain flowing underfoot, and in the confidence to leave earth and to experience time expanding in indelible seconds of flight.

There is the mystery of partaking of an intimate, right, and destined relationship to a whole world of snow, rock, and sky—the skier as one with crystal, ice, and surging slope.

There are other mysteries.

There is the mystery of sport. The sport of animals preceded the sport of men; the playful survived and conquered; sport was preparation for survival. Now that sport no longer serves to sharpen survival skills, it serves to effect advantageous release of survival passions. Man today rides a current of unseen, impersonal, unpredictable changes and he himself is powerless. Yet continuing impotence is destructive to the psyche. In skiing man has an obvious, immediate challenge against which to exercise primitive power, to find release in hyperaction.

Skiers have thus found a way of releasing part of the human being so highly developed, so little expressed: the aggressive, adventurous, conquering self. This explains why people in large numbers will ski, in spite of the cost in time, money, and stress.

Skiing is no less challenging than high-wire walking. The skier has to control the tilt of his skis to within a part of an inch. The skier's precise footing at high forward speed equals the wire walker's precise footing at some distance from the ground. Challenges continually shifting in direction, subtlety, and kind call for total concentration. This demand of skiing makes it a su-

20

peraware state of being, with everything forgotten but sensation.

With other skiers, a good skier shares laughter, good humor under stress, the sense of adventure. He shares his pure, natural, uncivilized mastery. Every foot skied is a victory, every mountain conquered, an empire. First man into the deep nothingness of a white haze sets others following: down and down with him, sometimes fighting thick wayward snow, sometimes losing direction in white halos of light and blind in high-streaming snow.

There is mystery in the delight of the senses—the smell of the evergreen, sharp as a cutting edge, the touch of flakes, and the sting of driven snow. Wind records the plunge of the skier on every part of his body, an opposing torrent, now caressing and now ceasing as the skier stops.

There is the cold. The skier is warned by the sharp stab when he takes a deep breath. Nostrils close. Ears burn. Fingers grow leaden. The skier knows the cold.

There is warmth. The blood surges through the body as the skier warms to his own great, deep heat—a power from within, a volcano, an affirmation of power.

There is heightened awareness in skiing. In woods where aspen and spruce stand thick, the snow sifts through the trees, and branches bear a gift of ermine. Skis creak softly as they sink and glide through each glade. The only witness of the skier's presence is the skis' sibilance, cutting the crystal serenity of snow. The skier is aware of his world.

There's the mystery of pleasures, all equally sufficient—the pleasure of speed, the pulse of speed, the tremors of the skis vibrating in shock waves on resounding surfaces, the firecracker sound of cloth snapping in the air.

The absolute glee of the beginner when he finds he slides! It is no more stylish than a skidding on ice, and yet finally the weaving willfulness of the skis takes some direction—haltingly, comically, and successfully.

There is the mystery of forces, the straight line of the ski cleaving the curve of the turn, stabs of friction, the leverage, centripetal and centrifugal forces holding in and pulling out, inexorable gravity. The forces become the skiing itself.

There is the mystery of snow structure—that three atoms in one molecule carry the possibilities of glassy ice, of down feathers, of brilliant crystal. Snow falls as flakes lock with each other in a bushy bundle that settles slowly, draws in its ends, changes to a gem, and combines in clusters which spread and freeze in translucent sheets.

Finally, the mystery that snow exists. Water was created as vapor inside molten rock. The primordial Earth, a holocaust, cooled to a hard surface. The vapor escaped from inside Earth, rose to a cooling sky, and filmy crystals of airborne ice formed. Fine cirrus clouds appeared and fell toward Earth, the first snow.

The snow melted. Earth was not yet cold. But Earth cooled, and enormous devouring glaciers of hardened snow chased across entire continents, then retreated back to the heights to wait.

The snow ice is still in the high mountains. As winter comes on it spreads lower, reaches toward the temperate plain, spreads to meet the skiers, spreads on all continents to lower terrain: Vermont, California, the Great Lakes, Appalachia, Honshu and Carpathia and Hawaii, Kashmir and Lebanon, Algeria and Australia and Peru and Chile. In each of these places, bodies cool and warm and experiment with ecstasy as men forget the joys of summer and return to the mystery known as skiing.

The Onset

by **ROBERT FROST**

*The poet of winter par excellence is Robert Frost.
His feel for snow, how it bewitches the landscape, makes
him a poet whom skiers recognize as their own.*

Always the same, when on a fated night
At last the gathered snow lets down as white
As may be in dark woods, and with a song
It shall not make again all winter long
Of hissing on the yet uncovered ground,
I almost stumble looking up and round,
As one who overtaken by the end
Gives up his errand, and lets death descend
Upon him where he is, with nothing done
To evil, no important triumph won,
More than if life had never been begun.

Yet all the precedent is on my side:
I know that winter death has never tried
The earth but failed: the snow may heap
In long storms an undrifted four feet deep
As measured against maple, birch and oak,
It cannot check the peeper's silver croak:
And I shall see the snow all go down hill
In water of a slender April rill
That flashes tail through last year's withered
    brake
And dead weeds, like a disappearing snake.
Nothing will be left white but here a birch,
And there a clump of houses with a church.

The arrival of snow ushers in a delightful new world

Mont Blanc

by PERCY BYSSHE SHELLEY

The skiers' world is snow—and most often, a mountain. None have evoked with more bravura the spectacle of a mountain in winter than Shelley, who visited "the Vale of Chamouni" and walked across a crude bridge over the Arve Glacier in 1817. The powerful poem from which the lines below have been selected was the welcome outcome.

The everlasting universe of things
Flows through the mind, and rolls its rapid
   waves,
Now dark, now glittering, now reflecting
   gloom.

Now lending splendor, where from secret
   springs
The source of human thought its tribute
   brings
Of waters,—with a sound but half its own,
Such as a feeble brook will oft assume
In the wild woods, among the mountains lone,
Where waterfalls around it leap forever
Where woods and winds contend, and a vast
   river
Over its rocks ceaselessly bursts and raves.
. . . Far, far above, piercing the infinite sky,
Mont Blanc appears,—still, snowy and
   serene—
Its subject mountains their unearthly forms

Pile around it, ice and rock; broad vales
   between
Of frozen floods, unfathomable deeps
Blue as the overhanging heaven, that spread
And wind among the accumulated steeps;
A desert peopled by the storms alone,
Save when the eagle brings some hunter's
   bone,
And the wolf tracks her there. How hideously
Its shapes are heaped around, rude, bare and
   high,
Ghastly, and scarred, and riven.— Is this the
   scene
Where the old Earthquake-daemon taught her
   young
Ruin? Were these their toys? or did a sea
Of fire envelop once this silent snow?
None can reply—all seems eternal now.
The wilderness has a mysterious tongue
Which teaches awful doubts, or faith so mild,
So solemn, so serene, that man may be
But for such faith with Nature reconciled:
Thou hast a voice, great Mountain to repeal
Large codes of fraud and woe; not understood
By all, but which the wise, and great, and
   good,
Interpret, or make felt, or deeply feel.
. . . The glaciers creep
Like snakes that watch their prey, from their
   far fountains,

Moon over the Mont Blanc range: a symphony of shapes

Slow rolling on; there many a precipice
Frost and Sun in scorn of mortal power
Have piled—dome, pyramid and pinnacle,
A city of death, distinct with many a tower
And wall impregnable of beaming ice;
Yet not a city, but a flood of ruin
Is there, that from the boundaries of the sky
Rolls its perpetual stream . . .
Mont Blanc yet gleams on high: the power is
    there,

The still and solemn power of many sights
And many sounds, and much of life and death.
In the calm darkness of the moonless nights,
In the lone glare of day, the snows descend
Upon that Mountain; none beholds them there
Nor when the flakes burn in the sinking sun,
Or the star-beams dart through them, winds
    contend
Silently there and heap the snow with breath
Rapid and strong, but silently . . .

The Skier and the Mountain

by **RICHARD EBERHART**

The mystery of being one with the snow and the mountain: the altered state of mind that is the peak experience, caught by Richard Eberhart, one of poetry's modern masters.

The gods are too airy: feathery as the snow
When its consistency is just the imagination's,
I recognize, but also in an airy, gauzy way
That it will capture me, I will never capture it.
The imagination is too elusive, too like me.
The gods are the airiness of my spirit.
I have dreamed upon them tiptop dreams,
Yet they elude me, like the next step on the
　ski.
O pole along, push upward, I see the summit,
Yet the snow on which I glide is treachery.
The gods are too airy. It is their elusive
　nature

I in my intellectual pride have wished to know.
I have thought I knew what I was doing,
Gliding over the cold, resisting element,
Toward some summit all my strength could
　take.
The gods are the fascination of the place, they
　escape
The genius of the place they make. They
　evade
The blood of our question. Imagination is a
　soaring,
It never allows the firm, inevitable step.
The gods tantalize me, and the gods'
　imaginations.
I am thus the captured actor, the taken one,
The used, I am used up by the will of the
　gods,
I am their imagination, lost to self and to will.
In this impossibility is my humility.

The Great Run

by JAMES C. SPRING

The thoughts of a magazine editor can run to more than wordcounts and layout: Jim Spring, an editor of Ski Magazine when he wrote this, compares the heightened sensation of a marvelous descent to a soaring bird, an arching arrow in the sky.

I see the red thread emerging
Bobbing from white cloud to white cloud
A fiery arrow shot
From the great archer's perch
Now gliding through crests of snow.

The swell and toss
The turn and slight
Swaying. Faster and faster
Through great snowy rocks
Spreading white feathers
As some atavistic power charges
The skier's feet
With fragile wings.

He sings through the massive
Fields, now arrow, now bird
Always carving with perfection
The skier's calligraphy.

But the arrows slung up
Come back to die.
The archer who flung him through
The wax moth-stillness
Teased him with the heights
Now shoots him through the heart
And buries him on the mountain where
Even as the spring water rushes
And the butter-cold mud scums the snow
The skier lies content
With that great free-vaulting flying,
Trembling head-to-the-wind
Following the mountain down.
And finally the falling, falling arrow
Twitches one last time.

Skiing the Polar Snow

by FRIDTJOF NANSEN

Fridtjof Nansen was probably the most extraordinary skier in the history of the sport: in a time when skiing was primitive, he made mountain tours that would be exceedingly difficult with the best of equipment today. He was a consummate ski jumper as well, competing in the earliest Norwegian national championships. And he was the most intrepid explorer on skis the world has seen. Not only did he make the first crossing of the subcontinent of Greenland on skis but he also attempted to reach the North Pole on skis, and in so doing, went farther north than any man had before him: his plan of action was to let his specially-strengthened boat **Fram**, *which he had bought from his fellow explorer, Roald Amundsen after the latter's South Pole expedition, freeze in the Arctic ice and move with the ice movement until he was near enough to make the dash to the pole. His dash failed, and he and a companion spent two years skiing their way out of the Arctic, living by hunting and fishing. Nansen's survival would have been impossible for a less determined, hardy and skilled skier. His love of skiing never left him, even in the midst of the most frightful hardships. Here, sometime before he left* **Fram** *on his dash north, Nansen writes about a peak experience: a perfect day's skiing on the Arctic ice floe.*

TUESDAY, November 13. Thermometer −38° C. (−36.4° F.). The ice is packing in several quarters during the day, and the roar is pretty loud, now that the ice has become colder. It can be heard from afar—a strange roar, which would sound uncanny to anyone who did not know what it was.

A delightful snowshoe* run in the light of the full moon. Is life a vale of tears? Is it such a deplorable fate to dash off like the wind, with all the dogs skipping around one, over the boundless expanse of ice, through a night like this, in the fresh, crackling frost, while the snowshoes glide over the smooth surface, so that you scarcely know you are touching the earth, and the stars hang high in the blue vault above? This is more, indeed, than one has any right to expect of life; it is a fairy tale from another world, from a life to come.

And then to return home to one's cozy study-cabin, kindle the stove, light the lamp, fill a pipe, stretch one's self on the sofa, and send dreams out into the world with the curling clouds of smoke—is that a dire infliction? Thus I catch myself sitting staring at the fire for hours together, dreaming myself away—a useful way of employing the time. But at least it makes it slip unnoticed by, until the dreams are swept away in an ice-blast of reality, and I sit here in the midst of desolation, and nervously set to work again.

*"Snowshoes" was the American word for "skis." This usage no longer prevails.

28

The play of the wind creates designs in snow on an icefield

Wednesday, November 14. How marvelous are these snowshoe runs through this silent nature! The ice fields stretch all around, bathed in the silver moonlight; here and there dark cold shadows project from the hummocks, whose sides faintly reflect the twilight. Far, far out a dark line marks the horizon, formed by the packed-up ice, over it a shimmer of silvery vapor, and above all the boundless deep blue, starry sky, where the full moon sails through the ether. But in the south is a faint glimmer of day low down of a dark, glowing red hue, and higher up a clear yellow and pale green arch, that loses itself in the blue above. The whole melts into a pure harmony, one and indescribable. At times one longs to be able to translate such scenes into music. What mighty chords one would require to interpret them!

Silent, oh, so silent! You can hear the vibrations of your own nerves. I seem as if I were gliding over and over these plains into infinite space. Is this not an image of what is to come? Eternity and peace are here. Nirvana must be cold and bright as such an eternal star-night. What is all our research and understanding in the midst of this infinity?

Danger and Daring

by ANDREA MEAD LAWRENCE and SARA BURNABY

Andrea Mead Lawrence was America's first international superstar, the first competitor to prove that an American could not only be better but far better than European contemporaries. Capping a career when she was ranked first among the women skiers in the world, she won two gold medals in the 1952 Olympics at Oslo. Then she became team leader, and started raising a large family. She did not reach her 1952 level for the 1956 Olympics at Cortina; nevertheless she was an inspiration to her teammates. She has remained an extraordinary woman, deeply aware of her own needs and nature, something her collaborator was able to bring out in her autobiography, from which this selection is taken.

ACROSS Mono Lake's mirror, the last rails of light run east beneath first stars. It is summer 1976; all day I have followed and questioned the college students camping here. Biologists, limnologists, geologists, ornithologists, they are dedicated to a practice of judgment within the disposition of nature. No one in the group will receive academic credit for this study of the lake. They work for love and with a grant from the National Science Foundation. For many, this is the first long application of what they know. They test it beside the waters that hold us now, strangers, in the intimacy of a campfire and the evening meal. It is my turn to answer questions.

"What was it like," someone begins, "to win?" "How did you do it?"

I struggle for words.

Jeff, my questioner, insists: "I mean, what did you eat for breakfast?"

As we laugh I see the real question standing out in relief, the one unasked: what does it take to confront risk and the limits of your own daring? It is a question that suits us all, and Jeff's humor has brought it into perspective. He dares the ridiculous in favor of the specific, and with these students of natural law, I find a common ordering of edges. They know, as I do, that storms, slides of rock and snow, dawns and darks roll over the tops of mountains. All summer this eastern escarpment of the Sierra Nevada has confronted them with the base of an immense vertical plane, and if you stay there long enough, it absorbs your entire being: eyes, mind, body, and breath. I think of Simone Weil's remark: "Absolutely unmixed attention is prayer."

Skiing and mountain climbing are the ways in which I, too, absolutely engage the vertical slants of earth. In the seconds before the start of a race, the mountain is the ultimate landscape of a racer's mind. Sweeps of snow, cleared of competitors and officials, are pristine territory that for brief moments becomes entirely one's own.

That is how it feels to race my kind of human race. I know it as movement in time and instances of unmixed attention, binding ordinary activities and the ephemeral, in which to risk, to move, is the urge to transcend.

It is the way one lives by personal belief and according to the circumstances of a life where, in kinds and degrees, danger and daring appear as the true measurements to acknowledge in any practice. The bear goes over the mountain to see what he can see. We go, each in our own way, with humor, the senses, knowledge, and concentration. I see danger and daring as intrinsic to self-expression and the urge to excellence. I see them as flexible instruments shaped by resources of the mind, appearing upon each new threshold of awareness and achievement. I cannot fight or turn away from the narrow slot of forcing through which I pass toward gaining more space. It is inherent in all kinds of encounters: the kinds you must go through if you are to go on.

At Grindelwald, in Switzerland, I knew I would be up against the world's best women racers during my first international race, but I was not awed. By 1948 I had grown accustomed to racing against people older than I, and at fifteen all my enthusiasm went into that reach of distance without impediment. Out of sheer exuberance I tried to soar. Pumping, poling, leaping between the last gate and the finish, I felt I would get there faster with my feet off the ground. At the end of the slalom an older friend smiled at my grasshopper gyrations, and then quietly explained that the spirit was right but the body was wrong. As a resident of terra firma, one uses its friction for speed. In the drive to transcend limits, I had missed the connection. Skiing is a hydrofoiling action on a smooth surface, and only friction and thrust make it possible to achieve maximum speed. There is no bobsled, no thing, between a skier and the vertical plane.

On 210 centimeters of thin, carefully tuned skis, I have raced between 50 to 60 miles per hour; for men, the average is 70 to 80 miles per hour. In the 1980 Olympics the lap speeds for both men and women increased by another 10 miles per hour. In 1978, at the speed trials in Portillo, Chile, Steve McKinney skied at 125 miles per hour over a specially designed course. A prairie falcon swoops at 120 to 140 miles per hour, while a peregrine falcon, diving at 200 miles per hour, is the fastest creature on earth. Some of us are closing on the falcons. In attempts at speed, we continue to break barriers, thrusting danger and the limits of daring farther and farther out. A sky diver tells me that he uses the spread-eagle position to reach an average terminal velocity of 120 miles per hour; and an exceptional diver, exerting maximum thrust against air, reaches speeds of 180 to 200 miles per hour. These very great extensions do not occur by chance. They are not accident, or falling, or gliding, but a conscious effort in which all the factors governing speed must work together.

In 1948, as I trained the downhill course on the Galzig in Austria, I saw how long it was. Three and a half kilometers began rather deceptively and got steep in a rush. Knowing the course would take endurance and holding, I thrust against the mountain, feeling it press through my feet, and quite unexpectedly I was infused with a strange ease. I had felt my weight, balance, and gravity working separately for speed before, but that day they worked together and the entire dynamic seemed to gather in my solar plexus. I had no idea how this quickening and lightness occurred, but I recognized it as the essence of harmonious motion. In degrees of the ideal, all forces exist in balance. It takes only a feather to right the scale, to make all of the governing factors share equal tension. After long hours of technique, the ideal responds, and in such moments of deep joy I have truly moved bodiless as in flight.

What if I hadn't had skiing as a form of expression? A friend suggests that I might have chosen dance, for it can also be an expression of solo movement, of a self in a larger pattern. Like music, the mountain's line is my felt image of motion, and in it, dancer or skier, arms and hands are as important to balance as legs and feet. Yes, in dance, too, I could celebrate change as the only constant. Following the hand, a good dancer indicates what comes next; a gesture indicates the body's movement. How many times and turns since that day on the Galzig have I

Expert skiers have the ability to let caution go and drive downward

prefaced my direction in mountains—followed my own hand in sending movement out into space and with my other scooped the energy back into my embrace!

Release and scoop. I embrace the music of mountains, where balance is a rhythmic thrust against the vertical plane. From a springing floor of gravity and snow, I can thrust harder and speed up, but my rhythm remains the same; only my pace changes. At the end of sustained courses and speed or a long day of skiing, some part of this dynamic remains, electric and soaring. I feel as if I have covered the vast distances of wings. I project from this earth, my home, toward an essential nature where life approaches out of the vaporous air: hydrogen, water, the electric spark. Somewhere way back in the quiet half of time, these successful components of vitality grew into chains of molecules.

I see momentum as successful components: a deliberate gathering of rhythm and pace that ebbs very slowly, strengthens, and is born again. Like a sailor after voyaging long curves of the sea, I stand, still feeling mountains rock me. The relationship between my momentum and the forces of vitality extends and intertwines as I read that the rocks and stones of earth are pulled up by the moon and released at rates of up to 1 foot per day.

In separate sightings, fear is the recognition of danger; it is as strong and as true as the ideal that draws one on. Emerson writes that the ideal appears first like a toy or magnet, followed by the gleams and fragments in which one sees that it may be true, and finally by the austere ethic in which ones sees that it must be true. At fourteen, fear presented me with an ultimatum to rely on all the techniques I had gathered, and my physical thrust for speed began to deepen that belief in what I had chosen to do. I began to understand fear as a process through which I could extend the practice of my own daring. It was an opening on what must be true, on a system of possibility, desire, reward, and faith.

At Lake Placid, in my early racing days, downhill events were not usually served by ski lifts. We had to climb to the start on our skis, which is how we studied and memorized the course. At that time, prerunning the course was optional; today, training runs are mandatory because downhill races are dangerous. On Little Joe Mountain, I saw the course for the first time as I climbed to the starting gate. Approaching a huge crest near the middle, I realized that I would be racing over the top of it blind. I would be skiing as fast as I could go, with my carefully chosen path obliterated by a great white rise. At each step above the crest, the line I had worked out vanished beneath me until I could see it no more.

All the way to the top I thought about forcing myself through instinctive barriers, about natural inclinations for safety: to slow myself, to check, to stand up for one reassuring glimpse of the gap between trees that marked our eastern trails. It took an enormous and conscious daring to go through the fear pulling me back from what I was trying to accomplish. Its reward is judgment which is always arrived at on your own terms. Running fast and without hesitation, I raced in an undivided reliance on skills. I pushed my limits in an act of faith that carried me over the crest euphoric, yodeling, and laughing.

The Oberland Glaciers on Ski

by ARNOLD LUNN

Sir Arnold—he was knighted for his services to international skiing and ski tourism—was at once a competitor, recreational skier, international commissioner, inventor of new racing forms, internationally recognized authority on racing rules, foremost journalist and commentator on the sport and, when he chose, all-around celebrated gadfly, He invented the modern slalom, the modern ski meet, and he was the founder and editor of the influential British Ski Year Book. *Here we celebrate him for his deep sensitivity and love of the fundamental joy of skiing.*

THE Oberland glaciers are unrivaled not only for superb skiing but also for the splendor of the mountain scenery which each new glacier pass discloses. There is no corner of this glacier world in which I have not left tracks of my ski,* and in this—which is intended not only as a travel companion, but also as token payment for the infinite happiness which I have found among the peaks, passes, and glaciers of this glorious range, let me do what I can to encourage the skiers who know nothing of glacier skiing, to escape if only for a few days from overcrowded *pistes* and from the dictatorship of the skileteriat into the austere solitudes of

*Lunn follows the Norwegian usage, in which "ski" is both singular & plural form.

Lauteraar and Wetterkessel.

Inevitably I must write of things about which I have already written, a fact which raises an obvious problem. The late C. E. M. Joad was often criticized because he included long passages from earlier works in his later books. "Unfortunately," he replied, "it isn't enough to make a good point once. You will often need to make it again in different contexts, but when I have said something as well as I can say it, why rewrite it?" I am inclined to agree, but in general it is less irritating to the reader if the author makes it clear that he is quoting from an earlier book. It is of course only the exceptional reader who would remember that he had seen such passages before, for the average reader only retains the haziest general impression of a book that he has enjoyed; sometimes he will even forget the name of the author. I remember, for instance, being strongly urged by a priest to read a book which in point of fact I had written. He said it would do me good, as indeed it might have done had I not known the author. I hope therefore that the exceptional reader who has not only read but remembered my mountain books, will forgive the inclusion of two passages from *The Mountains of Youth* which I preferred to quote as written— in the mood of youth—rather than to rewrite, for if rewritten they would inevitably have been

Man crossing a glacier is a minuscule creature in the larger framework of nature

tinged by what Gibbon calls "the brown shade which colors the end of life."

I arrived in the Oberland exactly one year after the first pair of ski had appeared in Grindelwald. In my lifetime I have seen skiing evolve from the pursuit of a few eccentric individuals into the sport of the masses. Skiing today is so different in ideals and in practice from skiing at the turn of the century that it has become an almost completely different sport. It was the introduction of ski lifts and other methods of transporting a skier without effort to the heights, which has revolutionized skiing, a revolution which on the whole has been beneficial, for the modern skier averages ten to twenty times as much downhill skiing in the day as did the pio-

neers. In consequence, the novice learns more in a week than the pioneers in a month. Moreover, whereas fifty years ago there were many days when skiing was impossible either because the snow had not settled after prolonged snowfalls or because the snow had been ruined by *foehn* or rain followed by frost, there is no day on which the artificial snow of the *piste* is not skiable.

There has, however, been loss as well as gain. The pioneers were ski mountaineers and ski tourers who mastered the technique of skiing on *natural* snow, but the majority of modern skiers seldom deviate by 10 yards from the *piste,* and regard themselves as experts if they are fast on hard snow runs with every yard of which they are familiar, an illusion encouraged by the distribution of Olympic medals to ski racers who have proved themselves masters of *piste* skiing.

In my youth our conception of good skiing was very different, and no man would have been regarded as an expert who could not lead a party safely among the mountains, and who was not both fast and steady when skiing on natural snow over ground down which he had never skied before. The dull uniform surface of the modern *piste* varies little from day to day, but natural snow is never the same, and there is a subtle fascination in mastering the scholarship of snow as shaped by frost and thaw, sun and wind.

Ski racing is a great sport, but it is only one branch and by no means the most important branch of skiing. The highest form of skiing cannot, praise be to heaven, be tested competitively. Olympic medals are not and should not be awarded to ski mountaineers, for mountaineering is not a sport. It is a vocation.

The Glaciers in Winter

On January 8, 1897, a party of five Germans (if V. de Beauclair who came from Freiburg in Baden, and who though naturalized a citizen of the Argentine, may be reckoned as a German) left Guttannen near Meiringen to cross the Oberland on ski. Their names were W. Paulcke, V. de Beauclair, R. Monnichs, Dr. Ehlert, and W. Lohmüller. They crossed the Oberaar-Joch and Grunhorn-Lücke, attempted the Jungfrau, and descended to the Rhone valley via Bel Alp.

In the course of January, 1909, the present writer with a Genevese, F. F. Roget, and Kandersteg guides made the first end-to-end ski traverse of the Oberland from Kandersteg to Meiringen.

It may perhaps help the young skier to understand what Alpine skiing meant to the pioneers if I evoke some fugitive memories of that six-day tour among the Oberland glaciers in 1909. Neither the Lötschberg tunnel nor the Jungfrau railway was built, and the first link in our end-to-end traverse of the Oberland glaciers was the Petersgrat Pass, which we crossed from Kandersteg to the Lötschen-Tal on January 2–3.

Our equipment was primitive. Detachable sealskins had only just come into the market and I alone possessed them.* The guides tied knot-ted string round their skis. My own more primitive method before I acquired sealskins was, as I have already said, to dip the ski into a stream or water trough so that the running surface was covered with a thin film of ice which gave a grip on the ascent.

Our technique was as primitive as our equipment. We used the single stick, or two sticks held together, to help out our turns. None of us could have passed the modern Third Class Test, but owing to our mastery of stick technique we were quite as steady and not very much slower on really difficult snow than a modern Second Class runner. Our bindings gave ample play, and consequently in those days broken legs were exceptions. This was just as well, for whereas the modern *piste* skier finds himself on a rescue sleigh within a few minutes of breaking a leg, a broken leg in January in the High Alps might have had the most disastrous consequences.

On January 4, 1909, we left the little inn at Kippel long before the dawn. I remember Venus dipping behind the curve of the Lötschen-Lücke, and the Bietschhorn pyramid, an opaque shadow silhouetted against the transparent darkness of the star-pointed corridors of unending space. Ours was a reward denied to the modern skier who saunters out after a late breakfast, and hooks himself on to a ski hoist. A skier who is transported rapidly from the valley to the heights has neither the time nor the inclination to study and to enjoy the subtle transitions of tone and snow texture, the snows dechilled rather than warmed by the newly risen sun, and the same snows shot with incipient hints of color at noon.

I remember, after all these years, our first halt just after the sun had scattered the shadows on the slopes which we were ascending. The tracks of skiers who had crossed the pass in the opposite direction glinted in the young light. They were the only tracks in all that vast snow-scape.

It was to take us twelve hours from Kippel to

---

*For the benefit of the reader who does not ski I should explain that long strips of sealskin are attached by straps to the running surface of the ski to prevent back-slipping on the ascent.

the Lötschen-Lücke, but a modern skier can reach the Lötschen-Lücke in an easy two hours from the Jungfrau-Joch railway station. If he is energetic he can breakfast in Wengen, or the Scheidegg, take the train to the Jungfrau-Joch, cross the Lötschen-Lücke, catch the Lötschberg train at Goppenstein, and return to Wengen that same night. There have been days when as many as a thousand skiers have crossed the Lötschen-Lücke. Indeed, after a spell of fine weather there is often a well-defined *piste* down the pass. Not so in 1909. Between Paulcke's crossing of the Oberland in 1897 and ours in 1909, hardly a dozen ski parties crossed the Lötschen-Lücke, and we were the first to cross from West to East.

"In the first years of this century," my friend Othmar Gurtner once said to me, "I could put a name to almost every ski track which I saw between the Kleine Scheidegg and the Schiltgrat. So few people skied that one knew their different styles."

We could not identify the tracks of the skiers who had crossed the Oberland glaciers from east to west, tracks which we only lost four days later in the Grimsel Gorge, and I have never to my knowledge met them since, and yet this record of their adventures etched into the snow seemed gradually to create a fragile but definite link between us. Some afterglow from the flame of speed still seemed to linger in the spoor which dived down the slopes they had taken straight, some lingering echo of the hiss of powder snow in the banked curves thrown up by their ski as they linked their turns down the steeper slopes.

It is difficult if not impossible to convince a downhill-only skier that climbing can be enjoyable, and yet there is a very real enjoyment in a long steady ascent on ski which begins before the dawn and ends after the sun has set. There is indeed a growing sense of achievement as one watches the ever-widening horizon. I can remember after all these years the precise point at which on that January day in 1909, we first saw the distant range of Mont Blanc climb into the western sky above a minor buttress of the massive Bietschhorn.

Slowly the morning merged into the afternoon and the afternoon into the evening. Just below the final slope to the pass we made a last halt. Far away in the west the rose of sunset withered on the dome of Mont Blanc, and the cold austere light of the winter moon gradually triumphed over the fading twilight.

The Lötschen-Lücke is the one obvious exit from the long Lötschen valley. Throughout those long hours my eyes had returned again and again to the magnet of our pass, that gentle curve slung between the Sattelhorn and Aletschhorn. What lay beyond? As a boy I had explored the lesser Faulhorn range above Grindelwald, but had only seen the Aletschhorn glacier from the distant peaks. This was, indeed, my first big expedition in the central chain of the Oberland. I knew from photographs what to expect, but I was eager to translate anticipation into things seen, and as we approached the watershed my excitement rose. I remember looking up and calculating that two more long zigzags would carry me on to the pass. A final spurt, and the Finsteraarhorn lifted itself above the watershed and the pass was ours. The last webs of light, spun by the fading sunlight, were dissolving on the summit crests as we looked down onto the glacier valley to the Concordia Platz, where three great glacier rivers meet. This vast expanse of shimmering snow, bewitched by the magic of the moon, seemed less to reflect the moon than to radiate its own serene light from some secret source, as if the snowfields were indeed semitransparent. And suddenly our pass ceased to be a mere watershed between valleys and was transformed into a magic casement opening on to snow which no man would ever cross and revealing changeling peaks which no man would ever climb.

I wish I could find the words to describe or even faintly to suggest the luminous wonder of moments such as these. *"Si nemo ex me quaerit scio, si quarenti explicari vellim nescio."**

Two days later we climbed the Finsteraarhorn. I stripped to the waist and the sun poured its bounty onto my unsheltered body. A perfect hour of windless peace passed like five minutes. I made no attempt to record on the tablets of

*"If nobody asks me I know. If I wish to explain I do not know."—St. Augustine.

memory the details of a panorama which included every peak of importance from Mont Blanc to the Ortler, from the Dauphiny to the Dolomites, and what I still remember is less the individual aristocrats in this hierarchy of mountain majesty than the benediction of the Alpine sun insinuating iridescent color into a monochrome of black rock and white snow, and so long as life lasts I shall not forget the last moment of that memorable day.

We had finished supper in the Finsteraarhorn hut and before turning in for the night I stepped outside. The glorious pyramid of the Finsteraarhorn soared into the arch of heaven, where the stars had abandoned competition with the radiance of the moon. Facing the hut I could see the Grünhorn-Lücke, which we had crossed from the Concordia, the soft shimmer of its moonlit snows penciled by the pattern of our ski tracks, the snow thrown up by swings showing like the delicate burr of a silver point etching. Seldom have I known a happiness so unquestioning and so complete. Even if the weather broke, nothing could stop us completing our high-level traverse. All our anxieties were at end. We had done what we had set out to do.

In all achievement there is an element of self-satisfaction, but less in unambitious mountaineering than in most human activities. It needs an Everest expedition to make the headlines, for the desperate conquest of terrible cliffs, such as the North Faces of the Matterhorn and Eiger, only evokes a momentary ripple of interest outside the mountain brotherhood and even within that brotherhood. As I knew full well, few would know, and fewer still would care, whether the Oberland glaciers had or had not been traversed from end-to-end on ski.

The occasional flattering review of a book by a discerning critic or applause at the end of a lecture may feed the flame of vanity, but there is something impersonal and uncorrupted by egoism in the serene happiness of the hills. The late F. W. Bourdillon interpreted the quality of such moments in a paper read before the Alpine Club:

I suppose this ideal love of mountains—this love that we may almost call a platonic love, since it seeks no selfish gain—really exists in most or all of us; and is at the root of the instinct certainly of the climber, possibly even of the tourist. We have all of us had our "moments," either on the mountains, or perhaps in some distant view of them, when life and joy have assumed new meanings, and the world's horizons suddenly broken down and shown us realms of dream beyond and yet beyond. . . . However the moment of inspiration comes, it comes always twofold—half as a satisfying joy, half as a quickening impulse . . . the inmost moving impulse in all true mountain-lovers, a feeling so deep and so pure and so personal as to be almost sacred—too intimate for ordinary mention. That is, the ideal joy that only mountains give—the unreasoned, uncovetous, unworldly love of them we know not why, we care not why, only because they are what they are; because they move us in some way which nothing else does; so that some moment in a smoke-grimed railway carriage, when in the pure morning air the far-off cloud of Mont Blanc suddenly hung above the mists as we rounded the curves beyond Vallorbe, or, still fairer, from the slopes near Neuchâtel, the whole Bernese range slept dreamlike in the lake at our feet, lives in our memories above a hundred more selfish, more poignant joys; and we feel that a world that can give such rapture must be a good world, a life capable of such feeling must be worth the living.

Spring Fever on Skis

by JOHN JAY

John Jay has skied in more countries, on more slopes, and shot more film footage on skiing than any person in history: the record stands without challenge. Jay began shooting just before World War II broke out, went into the Tenth Mountain Division with so many other young skiers at the time. He came out, unlike so many, unscathed, and continued cranking out films, making at least one lecture film a year for the next thirty years. Today at sixty, his pace is down a bit, but he's still filming and still lecturing. Jay is also a proficient and occasionally inspired writer. It's notable that his best piece, taken from his Skiing the Americas, *is about a place most familiar to Americans, the Headwall at Tuckerman's Ravine in New Hampshire, a spot that has an almost compulsive fascination for American skiers in the early and middle years of the sport. Jay hasn't been back to the Ravine in a number of years: skiing the Headwall is a young man's game. But he's left us the single most powerful description of skiing it as seen by an ordinary skier.*

"HEADWALL!"

A thousand skiers pause in their tracks. Two thousand eyes gaze up to a familiar spot high on the northwest corner of Tuckerman's Ravine in New Hampshire. It is late afternoon in May; long blue shadows are already creeping across the 1,000-foot slope, leaving fro-zen corn snow in their wake. If anyone runs the headwall of Mount Washington now, he must realize that he is taking a chance. Who is this fellow?

"Headwall!"

Again the well-known cry rings out, echoing and reechoing from wall to wall of the vast snow bowl. A lone figure suddenly appears on the rim, a tiny silhouette against a blazing sky of blue. Calmly he leans on his poles, arms brown and bare in the warm sun, looking over the cliff that drops away from beneath the very tips of his skis. From his perch a mile above the ocean, he can see range after range of the White Mountains stretching almost to the Maine seacoast, 60 miles away. Though the surrounding peaks are bare, their woodlands green with the coming of spring, beneath his waxed boards lie many a foot of hard-packed snow. Blown over the summit of Mount Washington by fierce winter storms, it has settled a hundred feet deep in the glacial cirque yawning below him, creating an immense snow bowl half a mile or more in diameter—a spring skier's paradise.

"Headwall! HEAD . . . WALL . . . !"

Now a weird silence hangs over the ravine. Not a ski moves; the antlike skiers scattered below him seem frozen into the snow. The stage is set.

For the last time he carefully wipes the sweat from his tanned forehead. For the last time he stoops down to adjust the downpull steel cables of his Kandahar that will keep his heels pressed close to his skis. He will need all the control he can get for this run. Then he straightens up, tightens his grip on his poles, and slides his skis back and forth a few times, testing the klister. A moment later, he's off.

Skiing cautiously, within five seconds he reaches the narrow cleft between the outcropping rocks. Here, the steepest and most dangerous part of the descent awaits him: a nearly perpendicular wall of snow, sloping down from the rocky cliffs at an angle of 60 degrees. The slightest mistake means a 900-foot tumble.

He has a split second to pick his course. Leaning well downhill, he thrusts his poles firmly into the treacherous snow just to the right of his ski tips. Steel edges flash through the sun's rays as they swing around in a beautifully executed jump turn. His skis land with a crunch that sends a wave of snow surging down the face of the Headwall, to mushroom out on the floor far below.

Headed south across the ravine wall now, he starts a long traverse. On this icy snow, his skis pick up speed quickly. But some dark objects are looming up ahead; his stomach turns over inside him as he suddenly realizes what has happened. That beautiful jump turn he made was 10 feet too high! Instead of being above him, the rocks lie dead ahead, their jagged edges gleaming with tiny rivulets of melting snow. He has skied right into the trap.

While a fraction of time yet remains, he flexes his ankles ever so slightly and releases the biting grip of his steel edges on the slope. It is as if he had cut a rope holding him onto the mountainside. Instantly he plummets down like a lead weight, slipping sideways, skis wide apart, bobbling up and down, as he struggles to stay upright. Down, down—10, 25, 50 feet. The rocks seem to shoot up past him. He flexes his aching ankles again. The sharp steel bites into the corn snow once more, and his descent is checked temporarily.

Stunned by his narrow escape, he can only gasp for breath as he leans on one pole. But there is no time for rest. A small avalanche is bearing down upon him, dislodged by his plunging skis. Lowering his ski tips a few inches, he leans forward again, and the hickory boards respond to this opening of the throttle with a surge that speeds him up to 50 miles an hour in a few seconds.

As any eastern skier knows, the snow on the Headwall in May is liable to be rough and uneven from the scars of many small slides. Now, as he streaks along its tumbled, granular surface, high up on the face of the wall, our friend finds the going tough indeed. His skis are bouncing over ridges, chattering now and then over an icy spot. Tears well up in his eyes, to be whipped out instantly by the wind. Taut leg muscles begin to protest; his right knee pains him, bent almost double by the steepness of the slope, which forces his right ski to ride even with his left thigh. Useless and dangling from his uphill wrist is one ski pole, for what good are its 44 inches on snow that is racing by only 10 inches from his shoulder?

Halfway across the ravine wall, he strikes the edge of the great shadow. For a moment, his skis seem to shoot out from under him, so icy is this newly frozen corn snow. Gone temporarily is every semblance of form. For two fleeting seconds that seem hours, he struggles to throw his weight forward again where it belongs. Lunging, staggering, gyrating his free arm, by a miracle he makes it and recovers his balance, immediately leaning well forward once more until his chin is in a line with his knees and toes, his back almost parallel with his skis. With his center of gravity thus shoved forward to his lap, he is steadier and will have more control over his turns. And turn he must, for the end of the main Headwall is rapidly approaching.

Raising his stiff body out of its crouch for an instant, he brings his right shoulder forward and swings it around and downhill, leaning down into the slope with all his weight on his right ski. For a fraction of a second, the unweighted edge of the other ski seems about to catch in a ridge and throw him. He releases it just in time, and the narrow hickory blades swing around neatly

Sprinting down a steep Spring face, Toni Matt shows his mastery on skis

together, like twin booms coming about in a gale. He crouches down once more, and his edges shoot up hissing clouds of spray.

He heads back in another long traverse, losing altitude fast. Now the other knee is bent double, the other pole useless, but the relief of his cramped muscles feels good. Smoother snow lies ahead of him, packed by other skiers. Already some of the people who looked so antlike from the rim are growing to human size.

Blue shadows race by under his skis. The rushing wind blots out all sounds save the noise of his skis on the snow, the staccato flap-flap of his trousers.

At 60 miles an hour he bursts out of the shadow into the dazzling glare of sunlight again, and the sugary snow grabs at his skis. He had been expecting this and was ready for it. With a swift movement, he shoots his right ski forward and suffers no more than a sudden lurch. Bal-

ance assured, he swings into another wide turn amidst a glistening wave of snow, then points his tips straight down. For several seconds, he lets his flying boards ride free in a breathtaking schuss. Wind tears at his clothing. Faster and faster he races along the comparatively level floor of the ravine, riding the bumps like a surfboard, knees smoothing his ride with pistonlike efficiency.

Finally he finds room for a series of rhythmical linked turns, each a little shorter than the last, till he comes to a stop with one last christie, one last shower of spray, at the edge of the bushes guarding the end of the ravine. Knees trembling, eyes crying, every muscle in his body aching, he looks up to the faraway spot where he had stood only a few minutes before. The tracks of his descent gleam in the fading sunlight. Soon the shadow will swallow up the Headwall, and they, too, will be gone. . . .

Aspen's Greatest Day

by **PETER MILLER**

The most exhilarating experience the skier can have is to hit a marvelous resort on its most marvelous day. It happens a few times in a lifetime for most recreational skiers. Even skiing-surfeited residents of ski towns will admit to having had a "greatest day." Here is one of those as it happened at Aspen, by a writer whose talent is sufficient to capture the sensations.

ASPEN, Colorado. January 28, 1980. Monday was nasty. High winds and cloudy skies kept the skiers down and several lifts were closed. Only a trace of new snow had fallen. It had not been much of a season—a 34-inch base, just enough to get by. The mountain report for Monday cautioned skiers to watch for unmarked obstacles on the mountain.

January 29, Tuesday, was another gray day with no Aspenglow. The barometer dropped to 29.50 and the wind gusted but snow fell—11 inches at midstation—a biting snow, sharp bits of ice that sting the face when driven by wind. At 10 A.M. the temperature was 20 degrees but in the afternoon it moved down as the barometer began rising. By midnight large and incredibly delicate snowflakes were swirling and floating down and over the mall in Aspen, blotting out vision. "I have the sneaking suspicion," said one visitor, as he headed home, coated with snow-flakes, "that I ought to get up early."

January 30, Wednesday. Weather can be much like a lover's spat—mean, tempestuous, then quickly turning alluring, giving. In the predawn the barometer climbed into the thirties as the snow stopped and the temperature dropped to 6 degrees. A high pressure system scoured away the clouds. There was not a whisper of wind. Fog that hung in the valley below Walsh's Gulch was swirled about as the sun heated it. Clumps of snow lay precariously on the limbs of evergreens and every so often sifted down in a long stream, fine as gold dust. The cold pinched the nostrils and the snow squeaked underfoot. Smoke from a chimney rose straight up.

Ski instructor Scooter Lacouter was in Little Nel's, facing a dish of scrambled eggs and bacon. He looked up at the slope and lift. The line began building early. Several ski patrolmen danced through the new powder. Howie Mayer, who has skied Aspen since the fifties, was smiling. Erik Peltonen, his mustache covered with snow, stifled a giggle. Both did their best to look the part of two serious and bored patrolmen. They quickly cut the line and were lifted back up the mountain.

"Hmmmmm," mused Scooter. "Think they know something we don't know?" In the next fifteen minutes he had three calls, all pleas for an

42

early morning lesson.

"I think," Scooter said in his understated Yankee way, "that the skiing might be good."

Scooter collected his skiers for the morning: Jan Wenner, publisher of *Rolling Stone,* an aggressive, roly-poly man who over the past two winters had gone berserk over skiing; David Foster, a quiet, gentle man of intensity, the bartender at Jerome's; Robert Houston, a young Hollywood scriptwriter who learned to ski at Stratton, Vermont; and me, out in Aspen on assignment but taking this Wednesday off to ski.

The north face of the Ridge of Bell is Scooter's favorite powder run. It is steep and sprinkled with well-spaced aspens and pines. It is shaded in the morning, and the snow is the best on Aspen Mountain. This morning there was 16 inches of new snow, the snow of legends—light enough to blow a hole into.

"Well-l-l . . ." said Scooter, as we stood there, looking down the Ridge, nothing but untracked to stare at, and he pushed off and disappeared in a rooster tail of snow. Wenner skied down, hesitant on this first run, a serious look on his face. Then everyone let loose . . .

Oh, God, what is this . . . effortless, the skiing is so fluid, it moves inside you—the snow is so light, silky, it slips around and over, then suddenly the snow is not out there but inside, it sweeps through the feet, up, tingling the legs, touching the groin and settling in the gut. The head remains clear. Swirling around a tree, powder curls up from the tips and strokes parkas and faces, foils over in a soft satiny spray. Down, up, down, rhythmical, the Kiva—a move into the body's fourth dimension.

The skiers stop in the Gulch and look up at their tracks. They are giddy, laughing, bodies loose, spent but refreshed. They beat it down for another ride up . . .

This snow—it's unbelievable . . . 16 inches of ectoplasm on a 12-inch layer of granular that lies on a 44-inch base—72 inches of snow, of which 28 inches are new. The granular snow of Tuesday, hidden under 16 inches of smoke, acts like a trampoline, bouncing the skis up into the light snow of Wednesday, then down again. *A skier cannot make a mistake.*

In downtown Aspen the whoops of exhilaration from noisy skiers echo off the mountain. Anxiety grows in the gut of those who are deskbound. At noon the kids leave school. The sun sparkles, the air remains crisp. Freshness. Everyone hightails it to the mountain.

Mad. The skiers on Aspen Mountain are gleefully mad. Appetites for this powder turn feverish. Senses are sharpened. All want more and more of this effortless, silky fall through gravity.

At the end of the Ridge of Bell there is a steep bump run, hidden under the powder. Scooter takes it. All we can see is his flap-eared hat and snow-white mustache. His head moves down the mountain, disembodied, with no bounce, just moving through the powder, cutting a heavy spray. Suddenly the head disappears, then surfaces, disappears again in the trough of a powder-filled mogul, again breaks surface. A porpoise comes to mind, diving, leaping, cavorting, arching in the air, all done with effortless grace.

By noon almost everyone in Aspen who skis is on the mountain and locals are staking out their hidden runs—in the glades between Jackpot and Copper, in the tight aspens above Grand Junction. A cross-country skier three-pins it down Zaugg Park in slow-motion Telemarks.

A Chicago businessman and his son were the first to cut the powder on the Big Burn at Snowmass. "It was incredible," he said. "We just turned and our skis turned. There wasn't a track in front of us." He told us about his morning without boasting. He doesn't know that most people spend their whole ski life searching, hoping for such a moment.

By noon most of the powder is cut up and the insiders are over at Little Annie's or Walsh's Gulch, one of the best powder runs in the West.

By early afternoon most runs are skied out. When the lifts close, Little Nel's and the Tippler fill up. Faces have that relaxed look, as after a night of lovemaking. Words are few.

"I think," said Scooter to no one, as he looked into his beer, "that this is the second best day of skiing I've had in fifteen years." Scooter is not one to make overstatements.

Skiers whisk through a typical Aspen grove

The bars are quiet that night; most are in bed sleeping it off. Ed Cross, a ski patroller originally from Australia, is at the bar in the Mother Lode. A few shots and the tired bodies of the skiers turn one degree looser. Ed starts talking about the day. He is still slightly crazed by the experience. His eyes shine and he can't control his words very well. "The best ever! The very best ever, mate!" Then, without taking a breath he grabs the arm of his drinking friend and recites a poem he wrote two seasons ago:

Gray sky, no wind, brisk and clear
12 new inches, no need for fear
The snow waiting a virgin bride

The quiet calm of the chairlift ride
And now down the mountain turning
The snow billowing, churning
Chest high in the quiet of the trees
The only sound the carving of your skis
Left and right and always down
Diving, driving, seeking, experiencing
The closeness of nature
. . . Such is why I ski to live
and live to ski.

"Good night, mate," Ed says, and walks out the door. The snow is still crunchy underfoot and the night silent and relaxed on this Wednesday, January 30, 1980—the best day of skiing Aspen ever had.

PART II

THE OUTER LIMITS

''The mystical lure of tenter-hooking the hair's breadth between the devil and the deep blue sea has led men to drive the fastest, climb the highest and ski the steepest.''

Harvey Edwards, *To Ski the Eiger*

At the Pole

by ROALD AMUNDSEN

When Roald Amundsen was twenty-two, he and a companion set out on his first "expedition," a hike over the uncharted plateau from Oslo on the southeastern coast of Norway, 72 miles to the west coast near Bergen. They planned to ski it in two days but, trapped by a blizzard, went two days with only gruel for food, and four more without any food at all, finally getting out to civilization again when they were both very close to death. Twenty-two years later, still enamored of exploration, Amundsen with four companions reached the South Pole on skis, first men there December 14, 1911. Amundsen was forty-four years old. Without their skis, Amundsen's party would have taken much longer, have run into bad weather and would have run out of supplies. The English party, led by Scott, racing Amundsen to the pole, did not make good use of skis, did run into bad weather did run out of supplies and died there. Amundsen had luck, and skis—and, as he tells the story here, the triumph.

Apart of our equipment to which we gave special care was, of course, the skis; in all probability they would be our chief weapon in the coming fight. However much we might have to learn from Scott's and Shackleton's narratives, it was difficult for us to understand their statements that the use of ski on the Barrier was not a success. From the de-scriptions that were given of the nature of the surface and the general conditions, we were forced to the opposite conclusion, that skis were the only means to employ. Nothing was spared to provide a good skiing outfit, and we had an experienced man in charge of it—Olav Bjaaland. It is sufficient to mention his name. When, on leaving Norway, it was a question of finding a good place for our twenty pairs of skis, we found we should have to share our own quarters with them; they were all disposed under the ceiling of the forecabin. At any rate, we had no better place to put them. Bjaaland, who during the last month or two had tried his hand at the unaccustomed work of a seaman, went back to his old trade of ski maker and carpenter when we came into the trade winds. Both skis and bindings were delivered ready for use by Hagen and Co., of Christiania; it remained to adapt them, and fit the backstraps to each man's boots, so that all might be ready for use on arrival at the Barrier. A full skiing outfit had been provided for every man, so that those who were to be left on board might also have a run now and then during their stay at the ice edge.

Every day we had occasion to bless our skis. We often used to ask each other where we should now have been without these excellent appliances. The usual answer was: most probably at the bottom of some crevasse. When we first read the different accounts of the aspect and nature of the Barrier; it was clear to all of us, who were born and bred with skis on our feet, that these must be regarded as indispensable. This view was confirmed and strengthened every day, and I am not giving too much credit to our excellent skis when I say that they not only played a very important part, but possibly the most important of all, on our journey to the South Pole. Many a time we traversed stretches of surface so cleft and disturbed that it would have been an impossibility to get over them on foot. I need scarcely insist on the advantages of skis in deep, loose snow.

December 9 arrived with the same fine weather and sunshine. True, we felt our frost sores rather sharply that day, with −18·4° F. and a little breeze dead against us, but that could not be helped. We at once began to put up beacons— a work which was continued with great regularity right up to the Pole. These beacons were not so big as those we had built down on the Barrier; we could see that they would be quite large enough with a height of about 3 feet, as it was very easy to see the slightest irregularity on this perfectly flat surface. While thus engaged we had an opportunity of becoming thoroughly acquainted with the nature of the snow. Often—very often indeed—on this part of the plateau, to the south of 88° 25′, we had difficulty in getting snow good enough—that is, solid enough for cutting blocks. The snow up here seemed to have fallen very quietly, in light breezes or calms. We could thrust the tent pole, which was 6 feet long, right down without meeting resistance, which showed that there was no hard layer of snow. The surface was also perfectly level; there was not a sign of *sastrugi* in any direction.

Every step we now took in advance brought us rapidly nearer the goal; we could feel fairly certain of reaching it on the afternoon of the fourteenth. It was very natural that our conversation should be chiefly concerned with the time of arrival. None of us would admit that he was nervous, but I am inclined to think that we all had

a little touch of that malady. What should we see when we got there? A vast, endless plain, that no eye had yet seen and no foot yet trodden; or— No, it was an impossibility; with the speed at which we had traveled, we must reach the goal first, there could be no doubt about that. And yet—and yet—Wherever there is the smallest loophole, doubt creeps in and gnaws and gnaws and never leaves a poor wretch in peace. "What on earth is Uroa scenting?" It was Bjaaland who made this remark, on one of these last days, when I was going by the side of his sledge and talking to him. "And the strange thing is that he's scenting to the south. It can never be—" Mylius, Ring, and Suggen showed the same interest in the southerly direction; it was quite extraordinary to see how they raised their heads, with every sign of curiosity, put their noses in the air, and sniffed due south. One would really have thought there was something remarkable to be found there.

From 88° 25′ S. the barometer and hypsometer indicated slowly but surely that the plateau was beginning to descend towards the other side. This was a pleasant surprise to us; we had thus not only found the very summit of the plateau, but also the slope down on the far side. This would have a very important bearing for obtaining an idea of the construction of the whole plateau. On December 9, observations and dead reckoning agreed within a mile. The same result again on the tenth: observation 2 kilometers behind reckoning. The weather and going remained about the same as on the preceding days: light southeasterly breeze, temperature −18.4° F. The snow surface was loose, but skis and sledges glided over it well. On the eleventh, the same weather conditions. Temperature −13° F. Observation and reckoning again agreed exactly. Our latitude was 89° 15′ S. On the twelfth we reached 89° 30′, reckoning 1 kilometer behind observation. Going and surface as good as ever. Weather splendid—calm with sunshine. The noon observation on the thirteenth gave 89° 37′ S. Reckoning 89° 38·5′ S. We halted in the afternoon, after going 8 geographical miles, and camped in 89° 45′, according to reckoning.

The weather during the forenoon had been just as fine as before; in the afternoon we had some snow showers from the southeast. It was like the eve of some great festival that night in the tent. One could feel that a great event was at hand. Our flag was taken out again and lashed to the same two ski sticks as before. Then it was rolled up and laid aside, to be ready when the time came. I was awake several times during the night, and had the same feeling that I can remember as a little boy on the night before Christmas Eve—an intense expectation of what was going to happen. Otherwise I think we slept just as well that night as any other.

On the morning of December 14, the weather was of the finest, just as if it had been made for arriving at the Pole. I am not quite sure, but I believe we dispatched our breakfast rather more quickly than usual and were out of the tent sooner, though I must admit that we always accomplished this with all reasonable haste. We went in the usual order—the forerunner, Hanssen, Wisting, Bjaaland, and the reserve forerunner. By noon we had reached 89° 53′ by dead reckoning, and made ready to take the rest in one stage. At 10 A.M. a light breeze had sprung up from the southeast, and it had clouded over, so that we got no noon altitude; but the clouds were not thick, and from time to time we had a glimpse of the sun through them. The going on that day was rather different from what it had been; sometimes the skis went over it well, but at others it was pretty bad. We advanced that day in the same mechanical way as before; not much was said, but eyes were used all the more. Hanssen's neck grew twice as long as before in his endeavor to see a few inches farther. I had asked him before we started to spy out ahead for all he was worth, and he did so with a vengeance. But, however keenly he stared, he could not descry anything but the endless flat plain ahead of us. The dogs had dropped their scenting, and appeared to have lost their interest in the regions about the earth's axis.

At three in the afternoon a simultaneous "Halt!" rang out from the drivers. They had carefully examined their sledge meters, and they all showed the full distance—our Pole by reckoning. The goal was reached, the journey ended. I cannot say—though I know it would sound much more effective—that the object of my life was attained. That would be romancing rather too barefacedly. I had better be honest and admit straight out that I have never known any man to be placed in such a diametrically opposite position to the goal of his desires as I was at that moment. The regions around the North Pole—well, yes, the North Pole itself—had attracted me from childhood, and here I was at the South Pole. Can anything more topsy-turvy be imagined?

We reckoned now that we were at the Pole. Of course, every one of us knew that we were not standing on the absolute spot; it would be an impossibility with the time and the instruments at our disposal to ascertain that exact spot. But we were so near it that the few miles which possibly separated us from it could not be of the slightest importance. It was our intention to make a circle round this camp, with a radius of 12½ miles (20 kilometers), and to be satisfied with that. After we had halted we collected and congratulated each other. We had good grounds for mutual respect in what had been achieved, and I think that was just the feeling that was expressed in the firm and powerful grasps of the fist that were exchanged. After this we proceeded to the greatest and most solemn act of the whole journey—the planting of our flag. Pride and affection shone in the five pairs of eyes that gazed upon the flag, as it unfurled itself with a sharp crack, and waved over the Pole. I had determined that the act of planting it—the historic event—should be equally divided among us all. It was not for one man to do this; it was for *all* who had staked their lives in the struggle, and held together through thick and thin. This was the only way in which I could show my gratitude to my comrades in this desolate spot. I could see that they understood and accepted it in the spirit in which it was offered. Five weather-beaten, frostbitten fists they were that grasped the pole, raised the waving flag in the air, and planted it as the first at the geographical South Pole. "Thus we plant thee, beloved flag, at the South Pole, and give to the plain on which it lies the name of

Skier in the Antarctic faces enormous snow walls

King Haakon VII's Plateau." That moment will certainly be remembered by all of us who stood there.

One gets out of the way of protracted ceremonies in those regions—the shorter they are the better. Everyday life began again at once. When we had got the tent up, Hanssen set about slaughtering Helge, and it was hard for him to have to part from his best friend. Helge had been an uncommonly useful and good-natured dog; without making any fuss he had pulled from morning to night, and had been a shining example to the team. But during the last week he had quite fallen away, and on our arrival at the Pole there was only a shadow of the old Helge left. He was only a drag on the others, and did absolutely no work. One blow on the skull, and Helge had ceased to live. "What is death to one is food to another," is a saying that can scarcely find a better application than these dog meals. Helge was portioned out on the spot, and within a couple of hours there was nothing left of him but his teeth and the tuft at the end of his tail. This was the second of our eighteen dogs that we had lost. The Major, one of Wisting's fine dogs, left us in 88° 25′ S., and never returned. He was fearfully worn out, and must have gone away to die. We now had sixteen dogs left, and these we intended to divide into two equal teams, leaving Bjaaland's sledge behind.

Of course, there was a festivity in the tent that evening—not that champagne corks were popping and wine flowing—no, we contented ourselves with a little piece of seal meat each, and it tasted well and did us good. There was no other sign of festival indoors. Outside we heard the flag flapping in the breeze. Conversation was lively in the tent that evening, and we talked of many things. Perhaps, too, our thoughts sent messages home of what we had done.

Staib's Pole

by JOHN HENRY AURAN

Today there are few who would attempt to duplicate the polar explorations of Nansen or Amundsen. One who was willing to retrace Nansen's explorations was Bjørn Staib, also a Norwegian. Like Nansen, he succeeded, barely, in crossing Greenland and failed in his attempt to ski to the North Pole. John Auran, who has spent extended time on the staffs of both Ski and Skiing over the past generation, gives Staib recognition worthy of his feats.

BJØRN Staib is a hero in so old-fashioned a sense of the word that he is difficult to believe in A.D. 1965.

The ancients were only too well aware of man's limited capabilities, particularly in grappling with nature. The point of heroics was to grapple, not necessarily to succeed. The moderns, on the other hand, know that *someone* must succeed in the end and are only interested in the gimmick by which he will.

The latter point of view makes Staib, a twenty-seven-year-old Norwegian explorer-on-skis, highly suspect. Practically unknown to North Americans, Staib in 1962 duplicated Nansen's feat of crossing Greenland on skis. But when an attempt (also little publicized) to traverse the North Pole from Canada to Russia failed last year, he became the object of a great deal of derision in Europe. Not because he failed, but because he had no gimmick.

"That would have killed all sporting incentive," he replies to suggestions that it would have been possible to parachute men and supplies beyond the 25-mile nightmare of broken ice on Canada's Arctic coast, which decisively delayed the expedition for three weeks. "That would have been cheating. You either do it from coast to coast or do the best you can and if you don't make it, confess you are beaten. And, we were beaten."

Staib puts much emphasis on the last sentence. Obviously having done the best he could, he was not ashamed to admit that he was defeated by some of the most implacable elements on this planet. Having experienced them—and one has to experience them to understand the difficulties they pose—he realized that for all his accomplishments, man has yet to find a way to beat nature in direct contest. The only solution is to outwait it, and Staib now rates "patience to wait for an ideal winter" as one of the top prerequisites for a successful traverse of the Arctic Ocean.

Lonely feats which test the inner steel in man and bring him face to face with his mental, moral, and physical limitations have not been America's cup of tea. The objects of our admiration tend to be those who master great physical attributes with extraordinary coordination—Willie Mays, Sam Huff, and, at rare intervals, a Jesse Owens. Our long-distance runners and skiers, our mountaineers and adventurers have toiled in the luxury of virtual anonymity. It's one of the reasons why only an attentive few have heard of Bjørn Staib.

There's nothing about Staib that would make him stand out in a crowd. Although I had seen his picture in *National Geographic,* I didn't recognize him when we first met in the lobby of one of Denver University's dormitories and he had to introduce himself. The suspicion crossed my mind that he might be one of Willy Schaeffler's imports, one of those anonymous Scandinavian jumpers or langlaufers who year after year provide that little extra to make the Pioneers perpetual collegiate ski champions. Staib quickly and firmly set me straight when I asked.

"I realized that if I wanted to do a job in ski competition, I had to sacrifice so much else," he said as though the matter had come up at one time or another and he had made a conscious decision. "I have studied in Oslo, London, and Washington, D.C., and I realized I couldn't do both."

So he enrolled at DU to study finance and from the contents of his dormitory room it was obvious that he wasn't going off on any tangents. There were only a few hints of his two great adventures—and those only because he was taking his studies seriously.

If Staib's present dedication to the intricacies of finance seems incongrous against the background of his two great Arctic journeys, the incongruity is only in the eyes of the beholder. Success in both requires great amounts of bold dreaming.

That Staib should attempt to duplicate Nansen's accomplishments is really not too surprising. In his native Norway, Nansen is more than a shadowy historical figure; in fact he is something of a George Washington and is revered as much for his acts as statesman and humanitarian as for his work as scientist and explorer. "Since boyhood," Staib recalls, "I have heard and read about Nansen. He was a great sportsman and the

kind of man who could take a risk and run it through."

It was not the first time that Nansen inspired emulation. In 1888 he made the first successful traverse of the Greenland ice cap by using skis. The book he subsequently wrote, *Paa Ski over Grønland,* was published throughout Europe and fired the imagination of men like Bilgeri, Zdarsky, Iselin (Fred's father), and Sohm, who saw in skis a means to travel the mountains in winter. Their activities in turn started a boom which has shown no signs of leveling off after three-quarters of a century.

Staib's desire to duplicate Nansen's trip matured slowly. Like most Norwegians—"skiing is something we treasure very highly"—he toured outside of Oslo on weekends and on longer trips into the mountains during the holidays. Gradually he started to penetrate the wilderness. Northern Sweden and Lapland were added to his itinerary. And then came two years in the Norwegian army ski troops.

"It's there that I got the idea to do something unusual," he said. "I was in tremendous physical shape, better shape than I had ever been in before, and I enjoyed this. I wanted to take advantage of this before I deteriorated."

To duplicate Nansen's Greenland trek was a logical consequence. Although others had crossed the Greenland ice cap since Nansen, none had duplicated it. It is a good indication of the extreme difficulties under which Arctic expeditions labor that few "firsts" have been repeated.

Staib found a willing collaborator in a friend, Bjørn Reese, and between the two of them they put the expedition together. After more than three months of preparation, including a session at the Oslo school of navigation, the pair found themselves on their way to the east coast of Greenland aboard a Danish sealing ship. Not far from Angmagssalik fjord, from where Nansen approached the ice cap, they spent another month buying and training sled dogs and bringing themselves to peak condition.

The two-man expedition was completely self-contained, and once under way, cut off from civilization.

"We had no radio and we were entirely left to our own devices," Staib said. "We did have an arrangement whereby airplanes were to come out and look for us after fifty days. But after having gone through the expedition, I know how little they would have found."

Staib and Reese spent the first week working up the mouth of the glacier, a distance of about 25 miles. Although it was steep going, they stayed on skis most of the way. Crevasses were a constant danger and they encountered many treacherous snow bridges.

Once on the ice cap, they made good time—about 20 miles a day. Except for the occasional snow storm, they simply plodded along.

"On the ice cap there was perpetual drift snow," Staib said. "It's just like being on an ocean."

If there was little excitement on the ice cap, descending toward the mountains which make up Greenland's west coast more than made up for it. In the glacier falls, where the ice is being squeezed together, there is a constant sound like thunder. The ice resists the pressure for a while, then collapses and breaks with a tremendous burst. The air pressure from one of these bursts can flatten a man if he is too close.

"We had to be on our guard all the time day and night," Staib said, "because it was impossible to predict where the cracks would occur."

Reese and Staib had good reason to question the wisdom of their venture as they wandered among the broken ice. "We were like a couple of ants at the bottom of canyons of ice. We never knew whether the ice walls would stay in position. One time we walked a couple of days carrying a lot of equipment and ended up further away from the coast than when we started. This is sort of discouraging when food supplies are disappearing."

When they came within fighting distance of the west coast mountains, the ice formations were so bizarre, so broken, they had to abandon their sleds and destroy all of their dogs except the one who was willing to jump crevasses, and even he was considered a potential meal shortly before they reached the mountains.

"We were about as hungry as you can get,"

Staib said. "We almost came to an end with only about 5 or 6 miles to go. It was just pure luck that we came down alive."

The skis served them almost to the very end. "There were steep slopes in the west, but we never knew where the crevasses would be. So we zipped across as fast as possible—sometimes I wished we had slalom skis—and hoped that we were safe and wouldn't break through."

It took Staib and Reese thirty-one days to cross the almost 500-mile-wide ice cap. This success was hailed. To Staib it was only logical "to follow this up with a journey across the North Pole. No one had been there on foot since Peary did it in 1909 and no one had ever traversed the entire Arctic Ocean."

Organizing an Arctic expedition, as compared with the Greenland venture, was like getting an army on the move as opposed to taking a camping trip. Not only is a great deal more money and time involved, but the endless red tape is almost designed to discourage all but the most determined. During the more than twelve months of preparation, Staib made half a dozen trips to the United States and Canada; spent a couple of months on the two ice islands, T-3 and Arlis II, the ice-floe weather observation stations drifting around the Arctic Ocean; obtained General Curtis LeMay's cooperation in contributing a couple of C-130 transports for moving men, dogs, and supplies from Thule Air Force Base to Alert on Canada's Arctic coast opposite Greenland; and worked endless hours ironing out details of communication, navigation, and logistics. It makes the suggestion of one of Oslo's newspapers, *Dagbladet,* that the expedition was "simply improvised," somewhat ludicrous. Improvisation there was, but only after nature threw a curve ball of gigantic proportions.

Some time in the winter of 1963–64 (one of the worst in recorded Arctic history) an ice floe 11 miles long floated into Kennedy Channel between Greenland and Ellesmere Island and blocked the movement of ice out of the Arctic Ocean. This created a gargantuan ice jam as current, wind, and tide tumbled millions of tons of ice into an insane, labyrinthine barrier all along the coast and for 25 miles to the north. And even beyond the barrier was another 120 miles of rough ice.

Staib, standing on the shores of the Arctic, must have known that he was licked even before he got started. But there was also the awesome machinery he had set in motion.

"We couldn't just go back and say things are just too bad and we couldn't go," he said. "Irrespective of condition, you have to give it a crack!"

It was no problem to get the men through. But the dog-drawn sleds almost had to be lifted through—at the rate of about a mile and a half a day.

In truth, there is no ideal time for crossing the Arctic Ocean. Its ice covering, as Staib likes to say, "is like a layer of dust on a bucket of water." And although it looks solid enough from the air, it is constantly split asunder by irresistible storms and currents. In the winter the open water between the floes quickly freezes over, but during that time of the year the polar region is blacked out in a six-month-long night. Of course, in the so-called summer there is continuous daylight, but the leads stay open and there is no way to travel on the ice. The only time to go is in late winter or early spring, when the leads are still closed and there is daylight.

Above all, there is the cold, which defies adequate description. At 50 or more below, it isn't merely uncomfortable, it hurts. And traveling and living in the Arctic without permanent and adequate shelter can only be constant agony. It is almost impossible to draw a deep breath without feeling the ice form in your nose and throat. Even with the best cold-weather gear, there is the all-pervasive feeling of freezing. Yet exertion is dangerous, too, since the slightest perspiration turns to ice.

It was under such conditions that the expedition fought for three weeks in the Barrier. Their lightweight sleds, designed for rapid travel over the ice, broke up and they had to use heavy Eskimo sleds instead. Their supplies, supposed to last for a trip of about 1,300 miles, dwindled.

Staib must have felt despair and frustration, yet it appears that this is an emotion from which he freed himself. "At a time like this," he has said, "I believe in doing things rather than to stand still."

After breaking out of the Barrier—three weeks behind schedule—the expedition was able to take to skis and move across the ice at the pace originally scheduled. However, plans had to be drastically altered. The first target, instead of the North Pole, became Arlis II, about halfway to the North Pole, and the decision to go beyond it was postponed until it was reached. The logistics had to be changed, too. Provisions were cut to the point where they were adequate only for the dash to Arlis II. The rest of the supplies, including the plastic boats to be used on reaching the other side of the Arctic, were flown to the ice island by a U.S. Air Force supply plane.

If the pace gave rise to confidence, it was short-lived. Without seeming rhyme or reason, the ice can build into pressure ridges 40 to 50 feet high while you are watching—and disintegrate in a few minutes. To be near when this happens is like being in an earthquake. Chunks of ice the size of freight cars toss about and everything is in violent, heaving motion, including the place where you are standing. This is what happened to the Staib expedition a week after they broke out of the ice barrier and the day after that the six men were pinned down by a blizzard, which made it impossible to tell up, down, or sideways.

Skis, always essential for Arctic travel, now became indispensable. Crossing ice that sometimes was only the thickness of plate glass, the skis provided the essential distribution of weight which kept the men from breaking through. And they made speed, the other margin of safety, possible.

"Skiing in the Arctic," Staib said, "is not like skiing at home. There's no real variety, there isn't even any waxing. There is no wax for snow so cold and, anyway, there is no need for it. There are no hills to climb or descend."

Throughout the forty-one days their simple Norwegian touring skis with hardwood edges performed without difficulty.

With open water chasing them northward, Staib and his men arrived at Arlis II on May 8, 1964. There, after some heated debate, the decision was made to abandon the try for the North Pole, even though the expedition was only fourteen days from its goal.

The final decision was Staib's, and here is how he reasoned:

"You can take a heck of a lot of risks on a two- or three-man expedition that no one knows about. But when you're backed by the National Geographic Society and the leading papers in Scandinavia, you can't just sacrifice a man and come out the other side of the ocean as a daredevil hero and say, 'I made it and I am sorry one of the guys just died.' You should do everything you can and when circumstances are against you, pull out."

In Europe, where man-against-nature adventures are big news, every major exploit—Himalayan, Alpine or Arctic—is scrutinized for the slightest flaw and criticized with a ferocity that Americans reserve for politics. Staib's was no exception and his failure to reach the North Pole was bitterly derided in much of the European press.

In an age which prizes affluence and material comfort, it is rather ironic that those who venture beyond cozy certainty are most bitterly attacked when they fail—and, as Staib says, "You have to realize that you might be beaten all over again."

With Skis on Mt. McKinley

by ERLING STROM

Erling Strom was born in 1897 in the Norwegian mountains, served in the King's Royal Guard, then immigrated to the U.S. to become resident ski pro at the Lake Placid Club in 1927, the only fulltime paid instructor in the United States at the time; he pioneered cross-country ski trips in the then-liftless Rockies, was co-leader of the first ski ascent of Mount McKinley in Alaska, ran ski lodges at Stowe, Vermont and at Mount Assiniboine in British Columbia where he was the host and story-teller to thousands of skiers who became his friends and admirers. Here is Strom's own story of the 1932 McKinley ascent.

OUR trip to Mount McKinley was the last of the so-called pioneer expeditions, with no use of air transportation. It made one of the most amazing stories in the history of mountaineering because great success and terrible tragedy came to two different parties on the same mountain at the same time. With the help of a good memory and a carefully written diary I will therefore try to present as a main part of this book, and as accurately as possible, this most exciting ski trip I have ever undertaken.

It was on a hunting trip in Alaska in 1928 that I saw Mount McKinley for the first time, an enormously impressive giant, completely dwarfing its surroundings. The north side, where

there is nothing to obstruct the view, is particularly overwhelming. From the Yukon valley, no more than 1,500 feet above sea level, it rises to its great height of over 20,000 feet in one gigantic sweep of snow and ice. From Fairbanks, 150 miles to the northeast, it can be seen very plainly, and we were told that it can also be seen on very clear days from points on the Yukon River fully 300 miles away.

"Denali" it was called by Indian tribes in central Alaska, meaning "The Home of the Sun." Other tribes used other names, and so did the Russians when they owned it. Unfortunately, with the white man's usual lack of respect for colorful Indian names, it was changed to "Mount McKinley" in 1896 in honor of William McKinley, at that time candidate for president of the United States.

Due to its height and northerly location, McKinley is covered with snow and ice at all times. It was this snow that excited an old skier like me more than anything. The thought of standing on the top with skis on and 20,000 feet of downhill in all directions seemed so appealing that I decided to follow it up. Not that I really thought that a trip to McKinley would offer snappy downhill skiing. I knew too well what one can and cannot do with forty to sixty pounds on one's back. Yet, it would make a memorable ski tour and afford a good chance to compare skis with the cumbersome Indian snowshoes used on all previous expeditions.

I asked people in Fairbanks and elsewhere at what time of year the peak was most likely to be visible. The answer was always the same: "It is clear during April." Whenever climbing was discussed, however, I was immediately told that the month of April would be much too cold. One seemed to have the choice between being too cold then or snowbound later in the summer.

On return to Lake Placid that winter and for the next three years I talked about McKinley to anyone who would listen. I could probably pay my own part of the expenses, but I needed two or preferably three more who would be interested in a venture of this sort and could pay their share and at the same time were familiar with cross-country skiing. The combination was hard to find.

Meanwhile I learned what had happened on McKinley up to that time. In 1903 Judge Wickersham of Fairbanks, then a boom town, made an attempt to climb the North Wall, which to this day carries his name. With a party of four he packed in to the base, but was unfortunate in choosing an impossible route, and was soon turned back by unscalable walls of ice. It is told that he later, on various occasions, declared that the top of the mountain would never be reached without the use of balloons.

The same year Dr. Frederick Cook of Chicago approached the mountain from the south, but accomplished even less than Judge Wickersham. Three years later he returned, however, to win worldwide notoriety as the bogus conqueror of Mount McKinley. From a base camp some distance from McKinley he took one man with him, by the name of Edward Barrill, to make the final dash towards the top. He made the mistake of returning too soon. Among those left behind were two men, Belmore Browne and Herschel Parker. Of these two I came to know Belmore Browne very well. He was a small but powerful man, an artist who told me that he came along with Cook to draw animals for the Museum of Natural History. These two men agreed that Cook could never have reached the top in the short time he was away, in spite of his claim to

have done just that. After returning to civilization Dr. Cook wrote his fantastic book, *To the Top of the Continent.* The story was accepted and Dr. Cook became famous, but his fame was not to last very long.

In 1909 Dr. Herschel Parker and Belmore Browne started out again, for the purpose of checking on Dr. Cook. They followed the route as described in Dr. Cook's book as far as possible. Eventually the description became too vague and they figured that Cook had reached no farther. In exploring the surrounding country they succeeded in finding the place and were able to take an identical picture of the rock photographed by Dr. Cook as the top of the continent.

As I said before, I got to know Belmore Browne very well. He had a summer home in Banff and came to Assiniboine quite frequently. Before he passed away he gave me his copy of Dr. Cook's book. In it Belmore has made innumerable marginal notes. On one page an arrow points to the top of a rather small hump (small compared to the mountains around) indicating where the two pictures were taken. Beside it is written in ink: "The actual altitude of this rock is 5,300 feet above sea level. It is only 200 feet above the glacier and is 20 miles from McKinley." That put an end to the fame of one of the strangest figures in the history of exploration and mountaineering. Having faked the ascent of McKinley, the world would not believe him when he later claimed discovery of the North Pole.

The next thing to happen on McKinley was the so-called Sourdough Expedition of 1910. A Sourdough is any person who has spent twenty winters or more in Alaska. Four miners, who knew less than nothing about what they aimed to do, undertook the most haphazard venture in mountaineering history. They decided to plant a flag on the top of Mount McKinley that could be seen from the window of their favorite saloon in Fairbanks. They had luck and pluck and needed both.

Approaching from the northeast, and after weeks of struggle through one snow storm after another, they found a good route and actually reached the top of the North Peak. The account of the trip varies a great deal. One story has it that Peter Andersen, known as "The Indestructible Swede," climbed the 9,000 feet from the Muldrow glacier to the top alone in one day, carrying a 14-foot flagpole, typical result of a story being told and retold many times, gaining a little by each telling. The more generally accepted version is that both Taylor and Anderson reached the top and planted the flag on what they then thought was the top of the continent. Had they only known that the South Peak was 300 feet higher than the North, there is little doubt that they could have made the first ascent of America's highest mountain.

Realizing that the mountain was still unclimbed and with the South and highest peak in mind, Belmore Browne and Herschel Parker set out again in the summer of 1912, for the third time. They again started from the south, but after months of exploration they crossed the range and finally followed the route explored by the Sourdoughs, namely the Muldrow glacier and what later was named Karsten's Ridge. Seven different camps were used on the way up from a base camp on Cash Creek. At the highest one in the upper basin between the North and South Peaks they were snowbound for a couple of weeks. Then on the morning of June 29 the weather cleared, and with high hopes they tackled the last 3,000 feet. But luck was not with them. Clouds rolled in from the south, and before long they found themselves scarcely able to breathe and facing a howling blizzard. They still struggled on for another thousand feet. The wind velocity was such that it became impossible to stand upright, much less to move against the storm. Only 300 feet from the top they were forced to turn back.

A second try the following day was even less successful. That day they were stopped a thousand feet below the top. By then their supplies were exhausted and they had to start down. Just as well they did. No sooner were they off Karsten's Ridge and down the Muldrow glacier than the Katmai volcano, 400 miles away, erupted with such force that the shock was felt throughout a large part of central Alaska. In only a few seconds the ridge, which they had just descended, was shaken to pieces by the earthquake and transformed into an unscalable jumble of huge blocks of ice. Had the men remained an-

other day or two in the upper basin their bodies would have been there to this day. So, although defeated after having spent some twenty months of their lives on and around McKinley, luck after all was with them in the end.

The first ascent of McKinley was left finally to Archdeacon Stuck and his companions, Harry Karstens, at that time superintendent of McKinley Park, Robert Tatun, a missionary from Tennessee, and Walter Harper, a powerful young half-breed from Alaska, who, along with Harry Karstens, was responsible for the success of that expedition. These men found Karsten's Ridge still in very bad shape after the Katmai earthquake of the year before. It all but turned them back time and again. A regular staircase had to be hacked in the ice from 11,000 to 15,000 feet to make backpacking possible. Also, these men were stormbound in the upper basin at an elevation of 17,000 feet. Weatherwise they had reasonable luck, however, and after roughly two months of climbing, relaying supplies, and cutting ice steps, they reached the top of the South Peak.

This was in 1913. America's highest mountain had been conquered, and mountaineers looked elsewhere for new and unscaled peaks to climb. No more attention was paid to Mount McKinley until we arrived nineteen years later.

Not until 1932 did I have any luck, no matter how much I talked about McKinley.

Then one bright day a wire reached me at Kayenta, Arizona, at that time the remotest post office in the United States, when I was conducting a pack trip on the Navajo Indian Reservation.

"Would you still be willing to try McKinley?"

It was from my good friend Alfred Lindley, a young lawyer from Minneapolis, with whom I had just completed the Columbia Icefield trip. He was sightseeing in Alaska with his father, had flown out to McKinley to get a good look, and was as excited about the mountain as I was. I don't think he was much in doubt about my answer to his wire, but probably liked to have it in black and white.

From that moment on I must admit that I had little to do with the whole thing until we put on our skis at the McKinley station on the Alaska

Railway April 4, 1932. Lindley contacted the superintendent of McKinely Park, Harry Liek, who was eager to come along. So was one of the rangers in the park, Grant Pearson. With Liek on the trip we could make use of as many dogs and drivers as we needed from park headquarters and thereby eliminate the main expense.

There was one hitch. Those two Sourdoughs were used to snowshoes. While Liek had made some use of skis in Yellowstone Park, Pearson had not skied at all. Another long wire explained the situation and asked me if we could take a chance on including a nonskier. My answer was short and to the point: "We'll teach him on the way." That settled it.

Lindley, whose financial situation was such that he could produce the necessary supplies and equipment for those who did not have what was needed, became the organizer and natural leader of the expedition. Since Harry Liek, through his position as superintendent and supplier of the dog teams, was second in importance, our venture went down in history as the "Lindley-Liek Expedition of 1932."

On March 26 of that year I boarded a steamer in Seattle with my skis, sleeping bag, ice axe, climbing rope, etc., plus umpteen small cases of a special hardtack recommended by Admiral Byrd. This hardtack was meant to contain everything the body needs, from corned beef to castor oil, but proved utterly useless as it took too much energy to chew at high altitudes where it was intended to be our *pièce de resistance.*

The boat trip to Seward varied in its schedule, depending on the weather conditions and the amount of freight to be delivered along the coast. We arrived in Seward one day before the weekly train left for Fairbanks. This was perfect, as it gave me time to find my old friends from our hunting trip four years earlier, Hank Lucas and George Nelson, both famous hunting guides. Some celebration took place, but my hardtack and I appeared at the railroad station on time the next morning. As the northbound passengers were gathering the conductor came along and introduced everybody to everybody, as was the custom in Alaska at that time. Then someone mentioned a gentleman who had definite plans

to go north that morning but had been seen in such bad shape the night before that it seemed doubtful he could make the grade.

"We'd better see if we can find him," said the conductor, whereupon he and a number of locals departed for uptown while the train waited. The man was found within an hour and was practically carried to the station. We were ready to go.

Before passing Kenai Lake, the conductor came through and asked if anybody wanted to meet Nelly Niel (I could have the last name wrong). Along with a few others I held up my hand, although I had gone through this performance four years earlier. The train stopped and those of us who were interested piled out in the snow and climbed down a hill to the only house in sight, a good-sized cabin by a lake.

Nelly was a small woman, showing signs of a rather tough life. She had gained fame as a big game hunter, and had the most fabulous collection of trophies one could ever hope to find. The floor was covered with layers of bearskins, so that one sank inches when walking across. A world record moose with forty-nine points and a conglomeration of caribou, sheep, mountain goat, wolf and bear heads covered every inch of her walls. Nelly immediately began to tell stories. One good one was about a bear who left four claw marks down the back of her neck. They were still there and were exposed for all to see.

On the pretense of wanting a glass of water I went out into her kitchen. Even that had bearhides on the floor. By the back door, facing the lake, was a peculiar spring with a bell hanging from it. A thin string led out through a hole in the wall. The contraption looked like a regular doorbell, but something seemed wrong since the front door was at the other side of the house. My curiosity got the better of me so I had to ask, and I was told that the line went out into the lake and had a baited fishhook at the far end. That allowed Nelly to sit in her warm cabin and read a book while fishing. On departure we noticed an ashtray by the door with a couple of quarters in it. We all took the hint, presuming that Nelly and the conductor would divide the proceeds.

At the McKinley station I was met by Al

Lindley, who had come up a few days ahead, and by Harry Liek. Grant Pearson had left with his team and a load in order to set up a base camp on Cash Creek near the foot of the mountain. To my surprise I discovered two big lots of supplies and equipment in opposite corners of the station. One was our own. The other belonged to a party to be led by Alan Carpe, America's foremost mountaineer at that time. An almost unbelievable coincidence. For nineteen years no one had even thought of McKinley, and then suddenly two different parties, absolutely unaware of each other, planned to start for the mountain on the same day.

Carpe's expedition was for the purpose of studying cosmic rays, which was done in high places all over the world around that time. He had climbed Mount Logan, Canada's highest mountain (19,500 feet) a few years earlier and was well qualified for the job. Unfortunately for everybody concerned he had been delayed in the East, but had heard about us in time to catch us with a telegram before we started. We were asked to take another man with a team along, and bring his bunch of stuff as far as the dogs could pull it. This would enable him to regain lost time by flying out to the mountain. We were glad to give a helping hand, although it would mean more work for all of us. Eight hundred pounds were added to the eleven hundred we already had. It was much more than the one extra man could be expected to handle. Little did we then think that our help would indirectly be the cause of the tragedy on McKinley that year.

On April 4, we were ready to take off. Grant Pearson had come back from Cash Creek for another load. Two more rangers were to come along, John Rumohr, Norwegian by birth, and Whitey Pearson (no relation to Grant), each with a team of nine dogs. Somewhere along the line I had picked up a nasty cold and started out with a fever. I have always thought that hard work and free perspiration would kill a cold. It had worked before and it worked again.

On our way to the mountain we could use the various ranger cabins at Sanctuary, Igloo Creek, and Cooper Mountain, spaced roughly 25 miles apart. We crossed the Savage, Teklanika,

and Toklat rivers. For a time we followed the McKinley fork of the Kantishna and later the Clearwater, until finally on our fourth day we arrived where Grant had set up a large tent for our base camp on Cash Creek, supplied with stove and plenty of wood. This was the very spot where Parker and Browne had camped twenty years earlier.

Times had changed since then. The Alaska Railroad between Seward and Fairbanks had been built and the McKinley National Park established. The Parker-Browne Expedition had started from Cook's Inlet (named after Captain, not Doctor Cook), struggled through some of the wildest and roughest mountain country in America south of McKinley, finally crossed the main range and reached Cash Creek. They had used four months to get there, while we used four days, from the McKinley station.

Another change was not to our advantage. Previous expeditions had lived off the country, while we found ourselves in a national park where shooting was strictly prohibited. There was plenty to shoot at, caribou and white mountain sheep in great numbers. We once counted sixty-two sheep in one hour. Ptarmigan by the hundreds were cackling around the cabins at night keeping us awake, so we had to get up and chase them away. In spite of all this game around, even the least bit of poaching was out of the question with the park superintendent in our very midst.

Somewhere near Toklat River we had met the chief ranger, Louis Corbley, who turned around and joined us while John Rumohr went back to headquarters for a last load consisting of Carpe's belongings. We were glad to add Corbley's dogs to our own, and for good reason. It had been necessary to use part of a team that had been without food for eighteen days earlier that same winter. A trapper had become insane, killed his partner and disappeared, leaving his dogs tied up. They seemed to regain their strength within a short time, however, and before we were through with them they worked as well as the others.

At base camp we spent three very pleasant days in beautiful weather. We had various chores to do. Loads had to be rearranged and made smaller, since the climbing began at this point. Grant had to be taught a little about skiing, and as far as I remember he enjoyed his first lesson no end. In his book, *My Life of High Adventure,* he makes one slight mistake, however. He tells the world that I showed him how to use climbing skins. I have never used skins myself except once, and have been dead against them in mountainous country when there is the remotest chance of avalanches. I am sure Alfred Lindley was his teacher at this point. He had obtained four pairs of skins from Europe for us to use on McKinley. We shall soon see how that turned out.

We also tried on and compared our clothing for the high country. When Grant appeared in his parka with fluffy fur around his face he reminded me of pictures I had seen of Admiral Peary, so I made a remark to that effect. "Well, Mr. Amundsen, I ain't got nothing on you," said Grant, and with that we were nicknamed Peary and Amundsen for the whole trip. If anything resembled Amundsen, it might have been the fur parka I had borrowed from my good friend and countryman, the famous dog-driver, Leonard Seppala.

While at base camp we cut sixty willows to be used for marking the many crevasses we expected to encounter on the Muldrow glacier, not knowing that we really needed twice that many. Then, on the second day there we broke trail to McGonagall Pass. This is a low pass providing an entrance to the Muldrow. It had been discovered by one of the four Sourdoughs before their trip in 1912, and is surely the most practical approach to Mount McKinley. It was, of course, of great advantage to us that this route had been described by previous expeditions. We were never in doubt where to go. From camp to the pass was about 7 miles, the last 4 being a gentle climb up a rather narrow valley. Al and I went ahead on skis, carrying light packs. Harry and Whitey brought along a team with a small load while Grant and Louis went back to East Fork to fetch part of a load we had left there. John Rumohr was still on his way from headquarters with the last load for Carpe. This day gave Al and

myself a good chance to compare climbing skins with ski waxes, which we were both anxious to do.

At the beginning of the long valley where climbing actually began, we agreed to make an honest test. Each was to start up the hill when he was ready, and keep the same pace we had kept so far.

It took me no time to apply a little wax, which can be done without even removing the skis, provided one has cross-country equipment. Al's job was more complicated. He had to get off his skis, and in doing so he sank to the belt in deep snow. Knapsack had to come off too, so he could get hold of the skins. Tying these on is a major operation and takes time. When he finally got back on his skis and was ready to go, he had lost nearly ten minutes, and I was well on my way up the hill. The distance between us remained much the same for the next 4 miles. Al had thought the skins would help him to gain on me, but if anything it worked the other way. He was not in the best of humor when he found me, with a smug expression, no doubt, sitting waiting on the pass. He had to get off his skis once more, sinking to the belt a second time, in order to untie the skins for the return trip to camp. These were now miserably wet and heavy. When another five minutes were lost, his mind was made up. Instead of putting the skins back in his rucksack he rolled them into a neat bundle and threw them away as far as he could with a remark that pleased me very much: "That damned Norwegian is right again!" That is as much use as Al ever had of his skins. The ones brought for me never left base camp. Whether or not the other men used theirs on the steepest part of the glacier I can't remember. It is quite possible, as even uphill skiing on wax requires a little technique.

The next day was Sunday, April 10, and we declared a day of rest although Whitey Pearson insisted on taking one more load to the pass. Grant practiced skiing. Al took movies of the last living thing we saw on the way up, a very lonely porcupine in a cluster of willows. I made myself a pair of canvas overshoes, copying some I had bought from Oslo's famous shoemaker Peter

Andersen many years earlier. They prevented snow from getting in between the hairs on ski boots made of moose leather with the hair left on, and created a very valuable insulating air space. That night we heard a wolf howl, the only one we heard on this trip. Deep, powerful, eerie, one sound in nature I shall never forget.

With a good trail to the McGonagall Pass we could now go beyond that point and establish our first glacier camp a few miles up the Muldrow. This part of the glacier was flat and safe. We found it more difficult to keep warm at night with ice underneath, so clothes were put on instead of taken off when we crawled into our sleeping bags. It was interesting to notice that the dogs became aware of the same thing. Instead of digging a hole in the snow to get into, they now scratched snow together into a heap and curled up on the top of it to get as far away from the ice as possible.

The Muldrow glacier gave us about ten days of hard work due to the endless number of crevasses we had to cross. Al, Grant, and I would scout ahead, trying to find a way up while the others moved load after load from base camp. The three of us were always on a rope, with myself in the lead because I was the lightest and therefore the easiest to fish out if I fell into a crevasse. I also had had a bit more experience with glaciers than the others, although the Muldrow surpassed anything I had ever seen. Many crevasses were wide open and easy to avoid. Others covered by snow bridges could not be seen at all. Those were the ones to cause trouble. We had to feel our way slowly. I carried a long pole like a javelin with an iron point at one end. At the other end was fastened a long rawhide cord which again was tied to my wrist. When in doubt, which was most of the time, I would spear the pole into the snow a few feet ahead of my skis. Most often it would stop in the ice, but once in a while it would plunge right through and disappear, still hanging by the cord so I could retrieve it. On those occasions Al and Grant would keep the rope taut while I moved cautiously ahead, tramping hard with one ski and then the other as far forward as I could reach, trying to test the bridge. Then it could happen that a big hunk of

snow would fall in, right in front of me, and I would be standing at the edge with my ski points over a bottomless chasm of ice from 4 to 6 feet wide. Those were exciting moments. I would have to back up very carefully and move over one way or the other, hoping to find a narrower place to cross the crevasse.

Only twice on the whole trip did I slip in, and then no more than that my head was above the surface.

There were times when the bridges would carry us across because we were on skis, but when the dogs came pulling hard they would churn up the snow and fall right through. The three or four first dogs would be dangling by the harness, announcing their misfortune in no uncertain terms until they were out of breath and all but choking. When this happened, the driver would instantly tip the sled over on one side to hold everything. Usually two sleds were traveling together so there would be enough manpower around to pull the dogs back up. One might think this would dampen their enthusiasm for further pulling, but not at all. No sooner had they caught their breath than they were willing to try again in another place. My respect for the Alaskan sled dog has no limit. They actually like to work. When a team was harnessed in the morning, one by one, the last dogs would go wild for fear they would be out of a job.

On our scouting trips we found the skis to be of great advantage. For one thing, they carried us across crevasses much better than snowshoes would have done, because the weight is better distributed. Secondly, they gave us more time to scout ahead. During an eight-hour day we could work uphill for seven hours and return to camp the last hour. This saved time and would not have been possible on snowshoes.

Crevasses usually run crossways on a glacier. They are wide in the middle, but narrower near the mountains on each side. This meant that our best chance to cross would be uncomfortably near those mountain walls where overhanging glaciers could dislodge tons of ice at any moment. We both heard and saw such avalanches up and down the valley, and could expect to be caught in one at any moment. There were times when we skied from one side of the glacier to the other to find a suitable crossing, only to ski right back again for the next one. This made a zigzag trail at least 20 miles long to cover ten miles of glacier. Even more trouble was caused by the so-called seracs. They are formed where the glacier drops from one level to another. In such places the glacier is so broken up that it seems impossible to find a way, and hours of work with ice axes may be necessary. The weather was good most of the time. An occasional little snow storm gave us an excuse to rest for a few hours now and then.

Halfway up the Muldrow we had our second glacier camp, and on the tenth day after leaving base camp we were able to move to our third camp at the head of the glacier. Some of us by then had covered most of the distance at least six times. This was where Carpe's depot was placed as the dogs could go no farther. The following morning we said good-bye to Whitey Pearson and John Rumohr. Louis Corbley had left us earlier. I shall never forget the moment when the two teams headed down the glacier for the last time. The sudden stillness came as a surprise. We had not realized until that moment how much company our eighteen lively dogs had been. Our connection with the outside world came to an abrupt end. We had no radio of any kind, but were left in a cold bleak world, depending on our own strength and common sense to get us back out.

This, our third camp on the Muldrow, was 11,000 feet above sea level, jammed between high mountain walls. To our right we had the two peaks of Mount McKinley 9,000 feet above. Between them the so-called upper basin with Harper Glacier hanging over the edge and continually discharging tons of ice, thundering down a rock wall of several thousand feet and waking us all too frequently during the night. In front of us we had Karsten's Ridge coming off Mount Brooks at our left and dipping down to a saddle only 500 feet above our camp; from the saddle it climbed up and up to our right, subsequently reaching Browne's Tower, which can be called a shoulder of the South Peak itself.

This saddle was our next goal, and at no time were our skis of greater advantage. With packs of no more than forty pounds we could climb a switchback trail in about an hour and return to camp in two minutes.

It is said that "time will heal all wounds," and so it was with Karsten's Ridge. There were no longer any visible signs of the damage done by the Katmai earthquake, which gave the Stuck party their greatest difficulties. Although steep and sharp, the ridge had regained its original smooth form, much as the Sourdoughs found it when they first came. This ridge was to bring us up from 11,000 to 15,000 feet. More experienced mountaineers might have handled it better than we did.

We debated whether or not to use a climbing rope on the way up. The idea was that if one of us slipped off one way, the nearest man would jump to the opposite side. This would work if we could remember to jump, but none of us would guarantee that. Better each man for himself and no one else to blame if anything happened. However, we did feel it necessary to cut steps so as to be sure that our crampons would grip the ice and not clog up with snow and slip off.

While Al and Harry were backpacking from camp to the saddle, Grant and I started to cut steps, not knowing at that time that we would need between six and seven thousand of them. We would work all morning, go down to the camp for a bite of lunch, and then up again to work some more. One-third of the way up we came to a place where the ridge leveled off and gave us a chance to dig out a shelf for our two tents. Once that was done we moved camp again. Tents, sleeping bags, caribou hides, lath mats, cooking utensils, primus stoves, kerosene, everything we needed was divided among the four of us. As soon as the tents were set up we went down to the saddle for a load of grub, as our new ridge camp was no place to be caught without food.

We were now about 12,000 feet up and had the most tremendous view towards the east, a jumble of peaks separated by glaciers running in all directions as far as the eye could reach. No wonder the Parker-Browne Expedition had used four months from Cook's Inlet traveling through country like this. This camp was the most interesting on our whole trip. When a tin can was thrown out of the tent door, it dropped a mile.

So far we had enjoyed wonderful weather most of the time, with a few little snowstorms not worth mentioning. Our one and only real storm came the second day on the ridge. For thirty-six hours we had to stay inside if for no other reason than to hold the tents down so they would not blow away. Fortunately we had all packed up the one load of grub which gave some extra weight on the tent floors. It was blowing so hard that moving up or down the ridge would be impossible. We could well see how we could be trapped in the upper basin, and were glad we were prepared, grubwise, to ride out a sizable storm such as previous expeditions had been forced to do. Rather than to cut steps farther up the ridge when the storm was over, we took time to bring all our supplies up from below so as to have them with us.

We all worked hard. Grant and I had a friendly agreement that neither of us should ever carry more than the other. This became serious business. We weighed our loads on a small spring scale, brought for that purpose, and I don't think they varied more than an ounce or two on the whole trip.

From time to time we made a rather interesting observation, although it was nothing new. Various accounts of Himalayan expeditions had told us that a normally slow heartbeat is an advantage in high climbing. Our only contribution to science was that we did check on this once in a while. It so happened that Grant and I had equally slow pulse. Our hearts beat fifty-two per minute at rest before the trip started. Lindley's heart beat normally close to seventy, while Harry's best was well over eighty under the same circumstances. There was no doubt that we could do work on the entire trip exactly in proportion to our heartbeats. Lindley kept up rather well for most of the time. Liek, however, was allowed lighter packs throughout. Furthermore, he was troubled with dizziness, so we made him the cook and left him in camp while working on the ridge. After all, I am not sure that he is not the one to be admired the most. He was six years

older and by nature not as well equipped for what we were doing as the rest of us. Yet he got to the top.

Karsten's Ridge took us twelve days. It meant endless trips up and down, first for cutting steps and then for backpacking. The upper part became very steep in spots and so sharp that we had to cut steps for the left foot on the left side and for the right foot on the right side of the ridge. The Muldrow was now 4,000 feet below us on one side while a glacier on the other side was at least half again that far below. Had anyone slipped off there would be no stopping, and the body would probably never have been found.

To get off the ridge we had to traverse a particularly steep section and work our way around a tricky ice corner and onto some rocks, the first ones we had seen since we left McGonagall Pass. After half a day's work we were able to fasten a rope to one of the rocks, stretch it around the corner and fasten the other end to a sack full of ice. For this we dug a hole where we could pack it with snow and let it freeze to the glacier. None of us was particularly fond of this place. Al became a little sick when he first went by and we actually worried about whether or not Harry would make it at all. But as the days went by he also became more used to the heights, and everybody managed in the end.

After several trips Grant and I began to feel at home and did not mind the backpacking once we had learned to arrive at the corner with the correct foot first. Climbers will understand why this is necessary in very tight places. From this point it was a long way back down to camp. Although we had good weather, there was enough wind to fill our steps with snow each night. This we had to scoop out with our hands the first trip up the next morning. Since here we are talking about thousands of steps, one can imagine the work involved. From the rock where the rope was fastened there was a chimney to climb up and above that another seven hundred steps to cut before we reached a more moderate slope leading over to Parker Pass, the site of our next camp.

One of the last days on the ridge became quite exciting. We spotted two dots moving on the Muldrow glacier. With binoculars we could see two men coming up the glacier along our trail. Later we saw them arrive at the depot we had left for them and put up their two tents. We were surprised that only two men came, but figured they had been sent ahead to have camp in readiness for the rest of the party. With our good and well-used trail to follow there was not much danger in splitting up.

On Saturday, April 30, we were ready to move our camp from Karsten's Ridge to Parker Pass. Why that place is referred to as a pass I do not know. It is really no more than a low ridge with a large rock on top, sticking out of the snow and providing an excellent landmark in an otherwise totally white world. From this ridge one gets a good view of the Upper Basin with Harper glacier coming down through it.

By now we had moved all our supplies to a cache above the rock chimney. Most of that work had fallen on Grant and myself. Al felt half sick at that time, and Harry was unable to negotiate the ice corner with a pack on his back. We got an early start that day. After dividing our camping equipment according to our abilities to carry, we started up for the last time. All went well. We could help each other around the ice corner and up the chimney. By our cache we had a good rest. With all our equipment and supplies brought to this point, we had a feeling of achievement and great satisfaction. We knew that only a long spell of bad weather could stop us now.

Since the day was yet young we tackled the seven hundred steep steps we had cut out two days earlier. From this time on, the lack of oxygen began to slow us down. We had to stop more frequently to catch our breath, and we moved slowly between stops. In the end this turned out to be one of our most exciting days. We knew that Archdeacon Stuck had left a maximum-minimum thermometer by a large rock on Parker Pass at an elevation of 16,000 feet, more or less. He contended that Denali, as he called the mountain, with its great height and northerly location might get lower temperatures than any other place on earth. In his book, *The Ascent of Denali,* there is a picture of that rock. As we moved into the Grand Basin with Harper glacier on our right and Browne's Tower above us on

the left we suddenly spotted and recognized the rock half a mile ahead of us. We could only approach it slowly but knew full well that something very interesting was in store for us. It was Grant who first walked around the rock and instantly called to the rest of us: "Here she is!" Placed in a horizontal position and with a stone holding it down could be seen the end of a small weather-beaten wooden box. There it was, just as Hudson Stuck had left it nineteen years earlier.

We decided to postpone the historic moment of opening and reading the thermometer until the next day. It was more important to set up camp, and while Al and Harry attended to that, Grant and I went down to our cache for a load of grub. In fact, we brought up two loads before evening. That made this our toughest day so far. We had climbed 7,000 feet all told between eight in the morning and nine o'clock in the evening, and with packs weighing forty pounds, carefully weighed on our spring scale. Our usual rum toddy tasted particularly good that night.

The spot we had chosen for camping this time was a bad one. We were too close to the rock, and the wind whipping around it would wake us up every so often. But before moving again we wanted to bring up the rest of our cache. That meant two trips to the rock chimney for everybody. We found that everything took more time now. Scouting out and preparing the next camping place became a major operation, not to speak of moving most of our belongings once more. We were glad to have our skis at this point, but had we known that they would be of little or no value from now on, we would have left them on the Muldrow glacier. We moved only a short distance this time to a sheltered spot near the Harper glacier. Part of the supplies were cached by the big rock. Since we now were above the difficult parts we knew we could always drop down this far and get what we needed no matter what the weather did to us. As it happened, we never came to touch this cache again and were pleased to learn that Bradford Washburn found it ten years later and had a chicken dinner on us.

Not until the morning of the third of May

did we attend to the thermometer. We had purposely waited for clear weather so as to take some pictures before we disturbed it. That done, we all gathered around for the big moment. Ceremoniously we removed the rock holding the thing down. Then we carefully opened the lid of the box without shaking it and keeping it in the same horizontal position. A small visiting card appeared and we read: "Please read carefully and return to Archdeacon Stuck, 281—4th Ave., New York City." The card was dated June 7, 1913. The thermometer was now exposed and we could see that the little float or indicator was tipped over in the bulb. It had hit the bottom. The scale of the thermometer went to 95 below zero, but the indicator had gone half an inch below that where it could go no farther. It is fair to say that the temperature had been 100 below zero or more at least one time during the past nineteen years. It was a pity that Archdeacon Stuck did not live to see his thermometer retrieved. He had passed away only a few years earlier. We used his thermometer throughout the rest of our trip and found it in perfect order.

In the afternoon of this same day we had the most unique experience of the whole trip. We suddenly heard an airplane and lost no time getting out of our tents. Instinctively we looked up until Harry said he did not think any plane in Alaska could fly higher than we were at the moment. Then we ran down to a point below us from which we could see the Muldrow glacier. After much searching with binoculars we discovered a plane circling over Carpe's camp. It looked like a dragonfly, and a small one at that, and yet the noise was terrific, surely due to the mountains all around forming a tremendous megaphone directing the noise right up to us. There we sat, 4,000 feet above, looking straight down upon an airplane flying 11,000 feet above sea level. Few people in this world will ever get into the same situation.

The Grand Basin with Harper glacier was a more livable place than the Muldrow. We used a rope the first trip up, but found good going and the few crevasses caused us no trouble. The snow was so hard that it paid to use crampons instead of skis. These were brought along in case

snow should fall while we were up there. Our main problem now was altitude. We cut our loads to half and could take only forty steps at one time without stopping. We never sat down to rest as it took too much effort to get up again, but just leaned arm and forehead on our ice axes until we had caught our breath.

At 17,000 feet we picked our last campsite. Shoveling out a place for our two tents was quite a job at this altitude. Each man could shovel no more than two minutes. Then the shovel was passed on. Everything was brought to this point before we moved our camp on the afternoon of May 6 to this highest camping place in North America. It was also one of the coldest. At least Grant insisted that the 30 below we had here felt as cold as 60 below on the Yukon.

Answering normal nature calls became very complicated. We had to get all ready and unbuttoned inside the tent, rush outside for as few moments as possible and be back in with the last part of the job undone, that last part being four pairs of pants to be relocated. These necessary quick movements completely exhausted us. Even turning over in our sleeping bags was an effort. A tin can was opened in two installments with a rest in the middle. In fact, we opened few tins but settled for oatmeal with plenty of sugar and milk of the powdered variety, called Klim, thereby eliminating the effort of chewing. Commander Byrd's hardtack had been discarded long ago. It took a long time to melt snow, and we had no trouble picking up a teaspoon from the bottom of a boiling kettle.

The nights were cold now but we devised a system that can be highly recommended. We buttoned our sleeping bags all around and slept inside, head and all. Too much heat would have been lost having the head outside, drawing in cold air and blowing it out again at a much higher temperature. I must admit that although I am no fresh air fiend, I felt the need of more oxygen after an hour or two. That called for poking a finger out between two buttons (fortunately no zippers in those days), making a blow hole in front of the mouth. That solved the problem until one moved and the hole closed up. The performance was then repeated after another hour or two. Boots were kept inside the sleeping bags so as not to be stiff in the morning. All the clothes we had were kept on day and night. Washing was out of the question. One cup of water was passed around. Into that we dipped a corner of a handkerchief and washed our eyes. That was all, and plenty, since there is really not much to make you dirty at 17,000 feet.

We were now in the upper end of the Grand Basin where the two previous expeditions had been stormbound for weeks during June and July. Had we really chosen the right time, and would our luck hold? When we woke up the next morning there was no doubt. The sun was already shining from a clear blue sky, and there was no wind. The temperature had been 35 below that night. Although we needed a day of rest, we could not afford to let a day like this go by. With some nuts, raisins and chocolate bars we tackled the last 3,300 feet, all full of hopes and enthusiasm. At no time this day were we in doubt about making it, but what we had not quite counted on was the time and effort it would take. We soon found that twenty-five slow steps were all we could take at one time. Then we rested by leaning on our ice axes, and each rest took longer than the time we had used making the twenty-five steps.

Halfway up a strap broke on one of my crampons. While fixing it I told the other boys to go ahead whenever they were ready, so as not to start freezing. They had made twenty-five steps three times when I took up the chase some fifteen minutes later. We all started together and my only chance to catch up was to add a few steps each time. Because I had rested I was able to add three steps the first time, but after that it took all my strength and willpower to do twenty-seven steps to their twenty-five. By doing that I caught up with the others in two and a half hours, and yet we had been within speaking distance all the time.

The top of McKinley forms a wide horseshoe with the middle of the shoe as the highest point. From below it seemed simple enough to climb the nearest end of the horseshoe and then follow the ridge to the top. This is what previous expeditions had done, but

to me that route looked rather exposed and I suggested working around the corner and up the middle of the horseshoe, thereby being sheltered until the very top in case a sudden storm should come up. Fortunately no storm came. The sun kept shining, not that we benefited directly because we were in the shade almost all the time. The higher we came the more we realized how terribly lucky we were with the weather. Only the altitude bothered us. It took all our strength and willpower to make the last thousand feet.

At five o'clock, exactly nine hours after we had left camp, we gathered a few feet below the top and walked up together. In that one glorious moment we were repaid for all our struggles. Nothing in the world is as satisfying as reaching the top of a mountain, and the tougher the trip the better the feeling. No other job can be so definitely completed. One can do no more. The fact that this was the highest point in all North America added to the thrill of the moment.

The view was tremendous but to me no more impressive than the one we had from the camp on Karsten's Ridge. This was like the view from a plane when even high mountains below seem to flatten out. Even so, the country southeast of McKinley was a jumble of peaks and glaciers such as we had never seen before. Only Mount Foraker to the west, with its 17,000 feet, was big enough really to hold its own. The sun right behind gave it the most beautiful brilliant halo. Toward the north the Yukon Valley stretched endlessly. The horizon was so far away that we could not distinguish between heaven and earth.

We spent about fifteen minutes on the top. I managed to freeze five fingers in an attempt to take pictures. My mittens were off for no more than three minutes when the fingers turned white. I called to the others not to remove mittens, and the result was not a single picture on the South Peak, although Al made a feeble attempt to take movies with mittens on.

It may seem ridiculous to spend thirty-three days getting to a place and then only fifteen minutes in the place when you get there, but even that was almost too much at 25 below zero. We took a last look at the views we would never see again, and were very happy and pleased with ourselves as we started down. It is customary to leave some sort of a record on a mountain and we had brought a small metal tube with paper and pencil inside for this purpose. From the top we had seen an outcrop of rocks just 200 feet below us on the opposite side from the one we came up. It was the logical place to deposit our record. While Al and I attended to that, Grant climbed down through the rocks to see what was below. I will never know why we had not written our names on the paper before this. Maybe we had not wanted to take things for granted. The proper thing would have been for each of us to write his own name, but under the circumstances no one seemed particularly interested. Grant had left us saying, "You do it, Al, you know our names as well as we do." With very large wolf mittens and a short pencil Al did a remarkable job. Not that the names can ever be deciphered, but we let that be the least of our worries. The chance of it being found is very small, since the rocks are not on the logical route up and down from the Grand Basin. We wondered why Archdeacon Stuck had not chosen this place for his thermometer rather than 4,000 feet lower on Parker Pass. My guess would be that the rocks were not exposed at the time he was there. The glacier may build up to cover them again.

We had decided to continue down this way as it seemed no farther than the way we had come up. Meanwhile Grant seemed to have disappeared. We looked right and left but no Grant. Just where had he gone? There was no place to hide. Then we spotted a black dot where the glacier flattened out between 800 and 900 feet below. There he stood, waving his arms and seeming very excited. He had slipped just below the rocks and had sailed down the 800 feet much too fast to stop en route. As we climbed down after him we picked up his ice axe, cap, mittens and even his knapsack. He had crossed a lot of hard-blown ridges on his way and was banged up considerably. When we reached him we found him in bad shape. His face was covered with blood. One eye was so swollen that he could not see out of it, one ear partly torn, and otherwise

he was hurting all over. But Grant was not one to let minor details like that bother him. He never detained us one minute on the way down to camp in spite of complete blindness in one eye.

Our trip this day had taken us twelve hours and we were too tired to eat but had our usual rum toddy with some powdered milk added to give it body, much like our Assiniboine "cougar milk."

Early the next morning I heard Grant groaning in his bag, and when he woke up he told me that one place hurt more than all the others. It was his lower arm. We rolled up the sleeves of three sets of underwear, one shirt, two sweaters and a parka and found that the sharp point of the ice axe had gone through all that and made a deep gash in the thick part of his arm. We melted some snow, washed it off as best we could and tied a handkerchief around it. Since there is nothing to infect a sore at that altitude we did not take the doctoring very seriously.

Grant's mishap prompted us to take a rest this one day. We all needed it, even after the exhilaration of that beautiful clear day on the top of McKinley, which was more than we had hoped for. If the weather broke now we had no kick coming. Although these were cold nights we slept well. Our thermometers read 30 below in the morning, but Grant kept insisting it was colder than that. He had experienced nearly 60 below on the Yukon and did not think that had felt any colder. One thing is certain, that I froze my fingers much more quickly on top of this mountain than I would have in Stowe with the same temperature. I theorized that with lack of oxygen the heart cannot pump blood to the fingertips and toes as effectively as it can at lower altitudes.

Al and I put on skis this afternoon. The reason was no other than to be able to say that we had skied above 17,000 feet. We even took a movie to prove it. I realized now that I had made a bad mistake. Al had ordered from the Northland Ski Manufacturing Co. in Minneapolis (his home town) four pairs of short skis to be used in this upper basin and then discarded. I had my own ideas. From the Muldrow glacier I had seen the most beautiful snow-covered slopes high between the two peaks, promising wonderful skiing which I did not want spoiled by some miserable short skis. For this reason I had brought up my regular skis, but discovered later that the "damned Norwegian" had been wrong this time. I was the only one in the party who had to bring his skis down again for use on the trip back to the station, and must admit they were no help going down the Karsten's Ridge a few days later.

Much discussion went on that day about whether or not we should try to climb the North Peak. We had planned to do that provided our food, the weather, and strength held out. Grant and I realized that this was not the time to press that question too much. I suggested we should sleep on it until morning and then see what the weather would do.

The next morning we all felt better, but was that to be good enough? Grant and I were just getting out of our bags when we overheard a remark from the other tent. It was Harry, who already was making the oatmeal: "I don't see no reason for climbing a peak that is lower than the one we just have clumb."

Grant nearly exploded. "Did you hear that, Amundsen? Harry doesn't want to climb the North Peak. We want to, don't we?" With one eye still closed and the rest of him hurting all over, he could have been expected to fall in with Harry's idea, but nothing was further from his thoughts. "You tell 'em, Amundsen, won't you?" So I promised to do my best. The reason for my being the one to say something was simply that Harry Liek was the superintendent of McKinley National Park and Grant was one of his rangers. He was in no position to tell his boss what he ought to do.

The subject came up the minute we entered the other tent. Al asked me what I thought. I could only say that there was no reason for not going. We had fine weather and plenty of food. I reminded them that nobody had done both peaks, so it would be fun to make that a kind of "first." But if the two of them wanted to have another day of rest, Grant and I could certainly get up alone. That fixed it. Al immediately wanted to come along, and Harry naturally did not want to be the one unsuccessful member, so off we all went again.

Rather than starting straight up for the top we went to the head of Harper glacier and from there doubled back on a long, fairly moderate grade. We agreed that the two trips are equal. The North Peak is 300 feet lower, but in one place we had to cross a draw and lose a bit of altitude so the final result seemed the same. We made it in a little less time but that came from being better acclimated. This time we managed to take some pictures on the top. We, of course, looked for the famous Sourdough flagpole but really did not expect to find any trace of that as a considerable amount of hard snow covered the whole top.

Luck was still with us the next morning as we made ourselves ready for the trip down. Every little move was an effort, and this time everything had to be brought along. All the sleeping gear, bag, caribou hide, and wooden mat made of inch-thick sticks tied together one inch apart so they could be rolled in a bundle. This mat was a most valuable piece of equipment. It gave air-space underneath the caribou hide and kept us away from the snow and ice. Then our camera equipment, two primus stoves, shovel, climbing rope, ice axes, tent, and ski boots since we preferred to use Laplanders (boots of reindeer hide) at this altitude, plus some food. Our second tent we left right there with all the provisions we had brought up to carry us through one of those storms we had read about in accounts of earlier expeditions. We also left one rope, which later proved to be a mistake, and half a bottle of rum. The reason for leaving all this was that we wanted to limit our loads to sixty pounds.

At twelve o'clock we were ready to take off. Since no snow had come we still used Laplanders with untold numbers of socks. All skis but mine were left behind. At no time has the difference between going up and down hill been as noticeable as this morning. We found we could practically run down where we had crawled up. Stopping for rests was not necessary. We passed our cache on Parker Pass shortly after noon, having had a quick bite at our old campsite near Harper glacier, and tackled the difficult part of the descent right away. Going down proved no easier than coming up. All our steps were blown in and had to be opened up. This could now only be done with the shovel.

Getting down Karsten's Ridge became quite an ordeal. It was impossible to stand in two steps of different height and shovel out the third one below, with a sixty-pound knapsack on one's back. A system had to be developed. Each man shoveled one hundred steps. Then he made a place on one side of the ridge so he could step aside and another place on the other side of the ridge for the next man's load to go into. That done, the shovel could be turned over to the second in line. Once they all had passed the first man he had to go up the one hundred steps he had dug to fetch his sack. The nights of Alaska are fortunately light enough at that time of year so one can work outside. We could therefore keep going all night and arrived at the Muldrow glacier at six o'clock in the morning after eighteen hours of steady going.

We had been looking forward to a day's rest and a good visit with the cosmic ray party whom we expected to find asleep in their tents at this time of morning. This was not to be. As we approached their tents we were unhappily surprised to find fresh snow covering their tents and obliterating all tracks around them. That immediately caused us to worry. Some clouds we had seen from above but paid no attention to had brought 2 or 3 inches of snow to the Muldrow. When passing an old campsite on the ridge we had noticed a rope and an ice axe which, having been brought up that far, indicated that the men intended to climb the mountain.

Something obviously had gone wrong. We hardly dared open the tents. When we did, nobody was there, but we found two empty sleeping bags and some mulligan in a pot on the stove in one tent. The other tent had the cosmic ray equipment set up making a slight ticking noise. It seemed obvious that the men had left camp with the intention of returning but had not returned. Under their pillows we found the two diaries. These revealed that the two men we had seen coming up the glacier were Alan Carpe (the leader) and Theodore Koven, and that three more men were expected but were now overdue. No doubt the two men had gone down the glacier to meet their companions. But why had they not taken their sleeping bags along? And why were two skis used as tent-poles?

We took time for a very quick meal before we hurried down the glacier in case there was trouble somewhere and we could be of help. Again we made use of the rope as the trail was so nearly obliterated it was very difficult to follow. Under the most recent few inches of snow we could see some ski tracks going down, which was what we expected. But these tracks did not follow our old trail accurately. Since these men had gone up the trail only once they had not memorized it in detail and were now unable to follow it. We knew this could mean disaster, and only too soon did we find that to be the case.

One mile and a half below the camp I heard Al, who was close behind me, saying, "Oh, oh, look there!" I was in the lead and paying attention to the trail so I had missed it. Far over to the left was a little black spot where no black spot should be. We swung over, being pretty sure of what we would find. Partly covered with snow lay the frozen body of a man, face down. We did not know whom we had found until we read the name Theodore Koven on a medicine bottle in his pocket. Nearby was a hole in a snow bridge. On the edge of it was planted an ice axe, probably left there to mark the hole. Koven had fallen in, had probably broken his skis in the fall, as he had ski boots on, but had been able to climb out again. He had been bleeding on one side of a knee and seemed to be slightly injured on one side of the head also. It might have been snowing at the time, and without skis to carry him over crevasses he had not dared to go very far. We could see where he had walked back and forth to keep warm, but had finally succumbed at one end of his little trail. We noticed that he had opened his clothing in front as much as possible. His chest was quite bare. This led us to think that while freezing to death the last sensation is that of great heat. I believe that to be right.

Our first thought was to bring the body with us down the glacier to where the airplane could land. In order to do this Lindley and I went back up that mile and a half to camp where a dogsled had been left so the men could bring back with them the very expensive cosmic ray apparatus.

By the time Al and I came down again, Grant and Harry had tried to reconstruct the accident. There were some almost obliterated tracks right near the hole where someone had taken a few sidesteps up to the edge. Could it mean that one man had fallen in, and that the other had tried to look for him, gone too close to the crevasse and fallen in himself? That seemed a possibility. With the rope tied on, we approached the hole and called into it, without really expecting to get an answer. From the diaries we knew that too much time had elapsed since the accident. If Koven, who had been free to move back and forth to keep warm, had not been able to stay alive, Carpe, jammed between two walls of ice, would have had no chance whatsoever. On the other hand, the man who made the sidesteps could have backed away and continued down the glacier, so we could still hope to find him alive in a camp below, with the other three men.

We loosened the rope again and used it for tying Koven's body to the sled, thereby making our only mistake on the whole trip, one we would regret within the next twenty minutes. Grant's and Harry's skis were tied on with the body. These two men were more used to snowshoes, and as Grant put it when he threw his skis aside: "I don't want them there things when I am not on the rope. They take me places I don't want to go."

We arranged it so that I had one end of the rope in front to pull the sled, while Al had the other end behind the sled so that he could hold it from running into my heels. With the two snowshoers behind we started to move over to the trail.

No more than five minutes later and a couple of hundred yards ahead we heard a little "whoof" from Harry. Grant had disappeared right in front of his face. There was just a big hole in the snow, and for the second time on the trip Grant was gone.

At no time on the trip did the skis prove their superiority to snowshoes as dramatically as here. The snow bridge had carried both Al and myself plus the sled with its long runners, but when Grant came on snowshoes where all the weight goes on one foot at a time he went right through. This time we were really frightened. We called Grant but got no answer. Then Al moved as near the hole as he dared. Not knowing how deep Grant had fallen and hoping he was still alive, Al had to be very careful as an ever so little hunk of ice broken off the edge could be the end of Grant. When he then called again he got a faint answer: "I am all right but I need the rope."

Leave it to Grant to fall 40 feet into a crevasse and tell us he is all right. We measured that distance on the rope later. His good luck was that he happened to be carrying the tent. It made a big roll crossways on his back and extended well out beyond his hips and shoulders. As the crevasse narrowed towards the bottom, the roll caught both sides and jammed. In fact it got stuck, the shoulder straps broke and Grant went on another foot or two, but now at greatly reduced speed. No doubt he needed the rope.

The body had to be untied and the rope lowered. Grant could reach the sack above his head and tie the rope to it and we started pulling. By the time we had it almost up, the rope had cut into the edge of the ice and the sack got stuck. For reasons already mentioned we could not step close enough to the hole to lift the sack up onto the ice, so we had to let it down again and find another method. With Harry still on the other side of the crevasse we could let Grant tie with the middle of the rope, keep one end ourselves and give the other to Harry. That way we could pull the sack up in the middle and once it was above the surface Al and I yanked it over to our side.

Now the rope went down for Grant. This time the pulling was harder. I was nearest the edge now and when Grant got up to where I could see him he was making signs to let him down again quickly. Somehow the rope was tightening around his middle so he could not breathe. We all but dropped him again. After a few frightening minutes came the next faint message. All we could hear of it was the one word: "Crampons." They were strapped onto his sack, and soon lowered down with the rope. This time we got somewhere. With crampons on his feet Grant could help a good deal. When the crevasse got wide enough he could walk up one wall with his back against the other. When we had him near the top and in plain sight, I asked him how he felt.

"Just fine," said Grant.

"Then you better brace yourself so we can get a picture," said I.

There he sat until we got a movie camera out of one of the sacks and threw it over to Harry, who took the picture while Al and I did the last bit of pulling. Grant had been in the crevasse for just an hour but was none the worse for the wear. With one eye still closed, and jammed in the bottom of a V-shaped crevasse, he had found it difficult to tie on his crampons. That was his only complaint. Skis were now thrown over to Harry and with the help of the rope we pulled him across a little distance from the hole.

Grant's accident had shown us that we needed the rope between us for our own safety. The body had to be left behind. We were now pretty tired, to put it mildly. Thirty hours had passed since we started the day before. Why we did not camp right then and there I cannot remember. We may have been too tired to think very clearly. We may have expected to find the other men at any moment, and I know we were anxious to know whether or not Carpe had shown up. Whatever was our reason we wrapped the body in the tent, put the sled up on end as a marker, tied the rope between us and started once more. It was now six o'clock the second afternoon and it began to snow. The nine following hours became the worst and most nerve-wracking I have ever had to go through.

Since I had been on the lead of the rope coming up the glacier it was natural that I took the lead going down. We knew we had at least one hundred crevasses to cross and an obliterated trail we had to follow accurately. Sixty of these crevasses had been marked on the way up but by the time we got to them the markers were snowed under. Only an occasional one could be seen. I soon realized that the three men behind me depended entirely on me to find our

way down. It had to be done almost entirely by feeling. Low-hanging clouds made it darker than on Karsten's Ridge the night before, and the falling snow made it almost impossible to see anything. I felt as if I could just as well have been blindfolded. It became a slow trip. Only some open crevasses could be recognized and in relation to those I could remember bits of the route up. I would continually get off the trail, but could then feel the snow becoming softer underneath. With a ski pole I would find where it was the hardest underneath and move over to it.

To complicate matters, Harry, who was at the end, kept falling. He no longer had strength enough to get up himself so we had to back up and help him. The language we then used was not pretty. He had given up completely and just asked us to cut the rope and leave him. Grant, however, kept in good spirits: "Amundsen, I am sure going to use you for a lead-dog after this trip!"

On two occasions Al, who was second in line, thought I had made a turn in a wrong place. I said I didn't think so and that there should be a marker a few feet ahead of us. Next second I swished the snow away from in front of my skis and the marker popped up right there.

In writing these things I may sound as though I am bragging but I can afford that. If I have anything to brag about in this life it is those nine hours down the Muldrow glacier.

We got off by McGonagall Pass where we had come on the glacier more than four weeks earlier. The feeling of solid ground underneath can hardly be described. The rope was taken off, and with tears streaming Al shook my hand, saying: "I didn't think it possible." Later, he wrote in the *Canadian Alpine Journal* that "with the uncanny instinct of a born mountaineer, Strom found his way down without mistake." In the *New York Times* he made an even more flattering remark. On May 17, 1932, he wrote: "The ability of Erling Strom, who led the entire way, to remember the location of concealed crevasses undoubtedly saved us."

Here on McGonagall Pass we found a tent with two of the three men who had been expected up the glacier. We immediately asked if they had seen anything of Carpe. When the answer was no, we could tell them that both Carpe and Koven had lost their lives at the upper end of the Muldrow, and that we had found Koven's body. We were surprised at a remark made by one of the men at that moment: "I told Carpe he shouldn't try to beat those boys up the mountain." He really shouldn't have, inasmuch as we had brought most of his equipment halfway up the mountain.

These men had been flown out to the Muldrow but had gotten no farther because an elderly gentleman by name Beckwith had taken ill right away. A younger man, Percy Olton, was staying with him, while the third member, whom we did not meet, had taken off in hope of finding a cabin with a telephone. He was to phone Fairbanks to have the plane come back and pick up the sick man. His idea was to follow our trail as he knew we had passed the various cabins. Too much snow had obliterated our trail, however, so he had lost it very soon. His plan was to keep going for five days in search of a phone. If he had not found one by that time he would backtrack and return to McGonagall Pass on the tenth day.

Since we had left our last tent with the body, and these men had only one tent with no room for the four of us, there was not much for us to do but to go on down the remaining 7 miles to our original base camp on Cache Creek, where we had left a big tent standing with a tin stove, plenty of wood, food, and everything. We were so happy to be off the glacier and out of all danger that we decided we might as well have it over with. We agreed to phone Fairbanks as soon as we got to a phone and then said good-bye.

Less than two hours later we staggered into our tent at base camp, forty and one-half hours after we had left our highest camp, and still with over fifty pounds on our backs. Harry Liek was then so exhausted that he fell asleep on the floor before getting his knapsack off. Al Lindley got his off but fell asleep right after. Grant, however, threw his sack down and turned to me: "Amundsen, there ain't no heroes without food. Let's eat."

He started building a fire while I opened some tin cans. We concocted some sort of a soup with pork sausage cut up in it. Then we woke up

the others, or should I say we tried to. Al could come alive and enjoy the soup, but Harry was too far gone, probably as nearly dead as a human being can get without actually dying. We took his sack off and got him up in a sitting position, and I shall never forget Grant standing behind his boss, holding both his ears to keep the head straight up, while I was trying to feed him a little soup with a spoon. We had no luck because he could not even swallow, so we put him in his sleeping bag and rolled him over to one side and out of the way. The rest of us had our meal and then crawled in to sleep for the next twelve hours. Then when we woke up we all had a real meal, but we crawled right back into the bags again and slept for another twelve hours.

It was now the twelfth of May. Spring had come to the low country. Bits of bare ground were showing here and there, with pussywillows ready to bud, and ptarmigans cackling everywhere. We felt as if life had begun again.

On the way back to the railroad we traveled at night on hard crust and slept on the bare spots during the day when the sun made the snow too soft for good skiing. These were four beautiful days and nights. I was continuously reminded of my birthplace above the timberline in Norway, where I spent the first eight years of my life in the same kind of country. Particularly exciting to me was the ever-present ptarmigan. It was the first bird I ever knew and has been my favorite ever since. The tremendous number of white mountain sheep we had seen on the way out also seemed to be around to bid us good-bye. They probably were the last ones that Alfred Lindley and I would ever see.

On May 16, we reached the McKinley station exactly six weeks after we had started, and a truly great adventure had come to an end.

By then we had telephoned Fairbanks and a plane was sent out to pick up the three men on McGonagall Pass. A problem faced the pilot inasmuch as there was no snow in Fairbanks to take off from on skis although these were needed for landing on the Muldrow glacier. So the fire department got busy, sprinkling enough water on the airstrip to enable the plane to take off from the mud. A few hours later it splashed down safely in the same place. With that the Cosmic

Ray Expedition of 1932 also came to its end.

It has been natural to think back and try to figure out how it can come about that one group can be successful while another can fail so completely on the same mountain at the same time. As I said in the beginning, I do think that our helping hand was, in an indirect way, at least part of the cause of the tragedy on McKinley that year. By bringing eight hundred pounds of their supplies and equipment halfway up the mountain, we enabled the other party to fly out. Thereby they lost the five or six days of hard training that we had in reaching McGonagall Pass. Then, we provided them with a good trail up the glacier, the result of another ten days of hard work on our part. This trail gave Carpe and Koven a chance to start up alone, which they never would have attempted without it. Fortunately for us, we had learned the trail in detail through our many trips up and down, while they couldn't possibly remember very many of the hundred switchbacks between dangerous crevasses, after walking the trail just once. When it then became obliterated by inches of new snow a few days later they became trapped. Had they only realized this and remained where they were, nothing much would have happened. Attempting to go down the glacier and meet their companions was their big mistake.

Later, we realized that Carpe did not even use skis, which I discovered when in New York at the Explorers Club I met the gentleman whom we had found sick in the tent on McGonagall Pass. I asked him if Carpe had brought more than one pair of skis up the glacier. His answer was definitely "No." That gave a new slant to the whole picture. We had seen a pair of skis in the cosmic ray camp on the Muldrow used as tent poles. These were Carpe's only skis. It means that he had gone down the glacier to meet his companions in boots, possibly with crampons but nothing else. The ski tracks we found, where someone had sidestepped to the edge of the hole, must have been Koven's, who could have had no other reason for getting near the crevasse but to look for Carpe, whom he probably had seen disappear.

To complete the McKinley story I should relate that Koven's body was retrieved later that summer. We had wired the family and offered to go back after a few days of rest if it was felt important enough to have him brought out and buried, but an answer came, insisting that no more lives be risked on McKinley. Later that summer there was a change of mind. Merle Lavoy, Belmore Browne's old companion, and Grant Pearson with some helpers made the trip in. The sled that we had put up on end as a marker was then barely showing above the snow.

As a reducing exercise a trip to McKinley can be highly recommended. Harry Liek lost twenty-four pounds before it was all over. Lindley lost slightly above ten, while I lost a little under ten pounds. Grant Pearson lost one single pound. He told us he had been running purposely behind his dogsled all winter long instead of riding it. In this connection I would like to sidetrack and tell a little story about Grant to complete my readers' picture of the toughest little man I have ever known.

When I went through Seattle on my way from Alaska, I was tackled by the Seattle Mountaineering Club and taken along to some gathering at Paradise Inn on Mount Rainier where I had to tell about our trip. In the audience happened to be a landscape painter named Ziegler. During the evening he told me that he had painted a great deal around McKinley and had enjoyed hearing me talk about his old friend Grant Pearson, for whom he had great respect. I soon found out why. Grant had once come into his camp and stopped for a cup of tea. He had discovered that Ziegler had run out of sugar.

"Think I better bring you some," Grant said. "I have lots of it in my cabin down the river." When he took off a little later he said, "I'll be back as soon as I can."

Ziegler fixed up a little supper that evening but no Grant appeared. Then when he arrived before breakfast the next morning Ziegler made some remark about having expected him back for supper.

"Where the hell do you think I live?" said Grant. "My cabin is 28 miles down the river."

On the steamer between Seward and Seattle I met a doctor who had practiced in Alaska for a long time. My frozen fingers had turned black by this time and were hard as ebony. Several would-be "experts" had told me I would have to have them amputated. Therefore I asked the doctor what I could do to save the fingers. He took a very good look, shook his head and told me I would have to amputate three fingers at the first joint and the two worst ones at the second. I thanked him but said I could have thought of that myself and decided to do nothing of the kind. Three months later the black flesh began to peel off by itself. I carried a pair of nail scissors and cut off bit by bit as it loosened from the healthy part. The last black fingertip came off as a thimble with nail and all. It was big enough to hold a few drops of water. Underneath appeared a small pink finger with the beginning of a new nail. By the time that finger and nail had grown to full size exactly six months had passed since it froze on the top of McKinley. Aside from freezing more easily, the fingers are as good as they ever were. This unique experience has led me to think that during the years there might have been amputations made in Alaska that have not been absolutely necessary.

It had been my hope that the trip would give a boost to cross-country skiing in America. That might have been the case had not what we call Alpine skiing, with its lifts and tow-ropes, come in with full force just at that time. The fact that we had used considerably less time from base camp to top than previous expeditions (Stuck and Parker-Browne) was never mentioned. We had proven the value of skis on glaciers and their superiority to snowshoes in no uncertain way, but also that was lost, largely because the tragedy naturally became the most important news item at that particular time. I have always maintained that a completely successful expedition of any sort makes a poor story. Something must go wrong or there is little to tell about. Grant Pearson added a bit of flavor to our trip by slipping off the South Peak and getting himself thoroughly banged up; also by falling into a crevasse. Without that and the finding of Hudson Stuck's thermometer, plus the freezing of a few fingers, our story contained little drama.

As so often in this world, history had repeated itself. Roald Amundsen made a quick trip of his discovery of the South Pole by using dogs and skis, the time-tried method of transportation in the Arctic. The English explorer, Captain Scott, thought that Shetland ponies and motorsleds would be an improvement. As a result he and his men also reached the South Pole but never returned. Alan Carpe and Koven might have been alive today had they stuck to dogs and skis instead of trying to save time by making use of the most modern form of transportation, the airplane.

I Skied Higher than Any Man

by FRITZ STAMMBERGER

Today there have been ski descents higher than the one described by Fritz Stammberger but his was the first from above 20,000 feet in the Asian mountains and was made under such life-and-death conditions that it still ranks as one of the most courageous high descents in the annals of ski exploration. In March, 1964, Stammberger—then a ski instructor at Aspen—became one of a four-man German expedition to attempt Cho Oyu, a 26,750-foot peak in the Hindu Kush,. The challenge was to reach the top without use of oxygen. Only Stammberger retained the strength necessary to reach the peak. On the descent, one of the four became unable to continue: Stammberger skied down from 24,000 feet to base camp for help, a 7,300-foot vertical run over crevasses whose snow bridges could give way at any moment. The rescue party returned to find one of Fritz's climbing companions dead and the other dying, unable to resist the incredible cold of nights in bivouac. In later years, Stammberger continued to climb, mostly solo, on expeditions that were high in risk. He failed to return from a 1975 second solo attempt on 25,230-foot Tirich Mir in Pakistan, a sector of the Hindu Kush; his body was never found. Here in his own words, the Cho Oyu climb and ski descent.

IN the specialized languages of Himalayan mountaineers, Cho Oyu is the easiest *achttausender* to climb. While a peak of 8,000 meters is never really "easy," Cho Oyu does lend itself to mountaineering adventures not yet practical on any other of the world's fourteen mountains which are 26,300 feet or higher. It is not very difficult to approach and its technical problems decrease as the altitude increases. That is why we selected it for the first ski assault on an *achttausender*.

The idea for the expedition was Rudi Rott's. He is a veteran Himalayan climber and has made a solo trip to the *Marchenwiese* of Naga Parbat. Rott was aware that the American Everest expedition had attempted to use skis, but these had been employed only for transportation at altitudes below 20,000 feet. The Cho Oyu expedition was to be an attempt not only to get skis to the 26,600-foot summit, but also to make active use of them in climbing and in the descent. Rott justified the expedition to the German Alpine Club on the grounds that major ski ascents had been made in most major mountain ranges of the world except in the Himalayas. Now that all *achttausenders* had been climbed, it was time to open the Himalayas to skis.

Our expedition was a small one by Himalayan standards. In addition to Rott there was Sepp Geschwendtner, the camp manager; Dr. Alois Thurmayr, a doctor with some mountaineering experience; Georg Huber, conqueror

75

of the north walls of the Eiger and the Matterhorn, the latter in the winter; and myself.

My participation was an unusual stroke of luck. I have climbed on four continents. I reached 19,000 feet on Annapurna and 21,500 feet on the 25,300-foot Trich Mir in Pakistan in solo attempts. But at the time the Cho Oyu expedition was being formed, I was a ski instructor in Aspen and was not even aware that such an adventure was being planned. It had always been my dream to be on a big ski adventure and to climb an *achttausender*. Rott, perhaps because he himself had a predilection for solo climbing, had remembered me, even though I was over 5,000 miles away.

I met the expedition on March 22, 1964, about halfway on the twenty-day march from Katmandu to the main camp. It was there that I learned that Thurmayr had been included in the summit party despite his lack of experience in high-mountain climbing. Although I was talked out of my objection to him, I remained skeptical.

There were other problems on the approach. Rott got sick and lost his memory for five days. Just as disturbing was the trouble with the Sherpas as we approached the site of our main camp. They wanted to stay as far away from the Chinese border as possible. When they finally balked altogether we were still some distance from the main campsite. As a result we had to put up our main camp at a spot not exactly of our choice.

Nevertheless, these problems were soon forgotten as we started our training climbs. We were very successful as we recorded a first ascent of the 21,050-foot Jasamba Himal, which we named Peak Zlatnik, in honor of a German climber who was to be a member of our expedition, but who was injured shortly before his departure for Nepal. We also made a successful assault of Napche Himal (21,650 feet) over the previously unclimbed west ridge.

The conditioning period over, we started our assault on Cho Oyu on April 15. It was necessary first to establish a base camp since our main camp was over 3 miles from the foot of the mountain because of the Chinese border problem. This trip to the new camp presented no great difficulties with the help of three Sherpas,

the mail runner and the kitchen boy.

We experienced most of our difficulties in establishing Camp I and Camp II. The afternoon storms were ferocious, the crevasses treacherous, and the skis an incredible extra burden in addition to the tents, sleeping bags, and other supplies we had to carry.

At Camp I we experienced a three-day delay. Sherpa Aila became sick and had to return to the main camp. Supplies, including Huber's and Thurmayr's skis, had to be brought up from base camp by the Sherpas. In the process of finding a shorter route, the Sherpas lost their way in the rock barrier.

We used the delay for acclimatization to the higher altitude. On one of the days I went on a little ski tour to the base of the ice fall for which I was rewarded with a magnificent downhill run. But during this run it became apparent that I had to ski strictly by the book at such an altitude, with a technique as highly economical of effort as possible if I was to conserve my strength. I was well served by the American Technique which we teach at Aspen.

After struggling up to Camp II at 20,340 feet we decided to make a nonstop assault on the summit. It meant that we would take our tents and supplies with us, dispensing with permanent support camps. This arrangement had the advantage of allowing us to proceed more rapidly and with only one Sherpa, Fudorje, who had proved himself a courageous and rugged mountaineer in the tough going to Camp II. The decision enabled us to reach Camp IV at almost 24,000 feet, only ten days after leaving the main camp.

We decided the summit assault should be made by two groups. Huber and Thurmayr formed one team and Fudorje and myself the other. Huber urged our team on. *"Geh nur zu"* (Go to it), he said.

Not long after the start it was apparent that the distance between our two teams was widening. Our being ahead of Huber and Thurmayr, however, was not unusual since it had been the situation daily. I fully expected to meet them at the summit.

Less than 3,000 feet of relatively easy climbing lay between Camp IV and the top of Cho

Ascending great heights on skis involves dangers equally great

Oyu. Except for the quartzband at 24,000 feet, there's little of any technical difficulty. In the Alps the distance could have been climbed in a couple of hours. But here, in the Himalayas, it took us eight hours. Whether you are successful in climbing Cho Oyu in the final analysis is a matter of condition and the ability of your heart and lungs.

About four o'clock in the afternoon, Fudorje and I stood on Hillary Peak, about 175 feet below the summit. This was enough for Fudorje. But I struggled on another hour to reach the top where I photographed the United Nations flag while awaiting the arrival of my companions.

I don't remember exactly my feeling on reaching the top. There was a little triumph and the feeling that everything is beneath you. It seems now that it was all quite primitive, probably the sort of thing prehistoric man felt when he killed a buffalo.

Although the rocky conditions encountered after reaching 25,000 feet made it apparent that skiing from the summit was impossible, I had, almost unconsciously, carried my skis to the top. It was apparent that Huber and Thurmayr weren't going to make it that day. I carried the skis back down again.

At 24,000 feet we found Huber and Thurmayr huddled in their sleeping bags. They were planning a summit assault for the next day and were already boldly building themselves a totally inadequate bivouac for the night in order to save themselves the effort of climbing the additional 300 meters they had already made that day. Although weather conditions were almost ideal, I managed to persuade them to return to Camp IV. On the descent Thurmayr showed signs of altitude sickness as he stumbled and occasionally fell on the way to the tent.

At Camp IV, within the so-called death zone, the doctor attempted to assure us of the harmlessness of his state. After a day of complete rest, Huber and I undertook a second attack on the summit. But it consisted of not much more than putting on our high altitude boots and crampons. My friend desperately tried to make some steps, but then admitted that he couldn't. We ordered Sherpa Fudorje to descend to the base camp and bring reinforcements in the form of six Sherpas, food, and equipment.

Our last refill of gas finally was exhausted. The night that followed, without water, when each of us tried to melt snow with his body warmth, has gone into my memory as the most frightful of my life. The cosmic cold made our attempts useless. Sleep was not to be thought of. Only Huber, with the merciful help of some sleeping pills, managed a few hours of rest.

The night brought decisive changes in Huber's ambitions. In the morning he had but one desire: down.

Putting on boots and crampons was a painful and exhausting process. As I helped the doctor out of the tent, I fully realized the seriousness of our situation. Unable to stand on his own legs, he would now fall right, now left . . . all in the immediate proximity of deadly crevasses. Finally, I made an attempt to carry or drag Thurmayr, but the latter's unconscious refusal to cooperate made all effort fail.

Since Fudorje had gone down earlier for fresh supplies, it was now up to me to get help. I could have gone on foot—about a two-day trip. There was also the risk of breaking into one of the numerous snow-covered crevasses. It was the time element and the risk which prompted me to use my skis.

Considering that this was to be the first major ski mountaineering expedition in the Himalayas, the decisions on skis and bindings had been remarkably casual. Without any particular concern for individual preferences, Erbacher metal combination skis were chosen and they were 185 centimeters long for all members of the party. The skis were absolutely standard, and no attempt was made to modify them in any way.

Since I am 6 feet, 3 inches tall and weigh one hundred and eighty pounds, I would have much preferred longer skis. The extra length wouldn't have bothered my turning but could have materially helped in distributing my weight. Every centimeter is appreciated when crossing crevasses.

Nevertheless, in the course of my ski descent from almost 24,000 feet on Cho Oyu, I had no reason to fault the skis. They worked perfectly, the edges held when they had to (a crucial consideration) and the Marker bindings gave me no trouble whatsoever.

In the course of the downhill run, I encountered almost every conceivable condition from deep powder to blue ice and I had to be prepared for changes of conditions within a ski length. The most hazardous parts of the run were the ice fields, which covered the mountain in vertical strips of about 100 feet in width. I had to enter these fields and traverse them without too much sideslipping so that I could reach the other side to turn.

Although I have skied many of the more difficult runs in the world, I have never encountered anything so continuously steep or hazardous as I did on the 7,300-foot run down Cho Oyu. The only thing I can compare it with is to imagine a 3-mile long Corkscrew (on Aspen Mountain), but with blue ice instead of groomed trails. Aside from the difficulty of the terrain itself there was the mental strain of getting through the crevasses, yet skiing without fall.

There was no margin for error. The entire descent required a precise, efficient technique, as if I were demonstrating in front of a class in Aspen. Anything different would have quickly exhausted my strength and would have greatly increased the risk of falls. As far as I was concerned, my skiing at these extreme altitudes was the ultimate proof of the effectiveness of modern technique. That I was able to pass this test of making the world's highest ski descent, I attribute to the thousands of hours I have spent on skis each winter.

I was able to reach the main camp in two hours, and a rescue party of four Sherpas was underway by daybreak. Unfortunately only one of these men was able to reach Camp IV and was only able to relieve Huber's and Thurmayr's terrible thirst before returning to base camp. Then, with the help of six Sherpas from a Japanese expedition, we made a second rescue attempt. Fudorje, myself, and a third Sherpa managed to reach Camp IV.

But inside the tent Georg Huber already had been dead for two days. I saw Dr. Thurmayr lying in the arms of Fudorje, who fed him patiently with soup. He muttered incessantly that he had done everything he could . . . everything. Night was falling and it was necessary to hurry. Using skis, air mattresses, and ski poles, we quickly constructed a sled on which we moved the doctor with indescribable efforts to a camp established a thousand feet below. Given soup and coffee, the condition of the doctor improved. His voice grew stronger and stronger. It gave us hope that his life could be saved if moved to a lower altitude.

But the next morning we found ourselves in the center of a frightful storm, which didn't subside until noon the following day. During that time Fudorje was able to improve the sled and once we were under way we were able to make rapid progress. But it was not rapid enough. At the ice fall just above Camp II, Alois Thurmayr died.

It is difficult to talk of accomplishments when men have died, but accomplishments there were on the Cho Oyu expedition. Despite extreme conditions, skis are useful in the Himalayas for reconnaissance, for moving supplies, for rapid retreats (except in very poor weather), and for making sleds in emergencies. And, of course, there will always be the sporting aspect of skis at these altitudes. Despite the tragedy of Georg Huber and Alois Thurmayr, the Cho Oyu expedition has brought skis to the Himalayas to stay.

In Pursuit of Pure Speed

by DICK DORWORTH

Of the ski journalists now writing, none have had a closer acquaintance with the outer limit of speed than Dick Dorworth; during a break in the training as a member of the U.S. national Alpine team in Portillo, Chile, Dorworth became the co-holder of the world speed record. He is currently an instructor at Squaw Valley, California, as well as being a member of first-ascent ski expeditions, including the recent first-ascent expedition in the Chinese Pamirs. Dorworth as well is a formidable writer, having grown up in the 1960s counterculture that was the norm in that decade, and having been able to embody that ethic in essays whose depth and power give them a place among the most evocative of their era. Dorworth is also a principal organizer and force behind the current international speed-run circuit which is steadily gaining recognition. Dorworth's story starts with the first record attempt in which he participated, at Portillo in 1963.

THE process of detachment—of viewing myself abstractly—had reached an astonishingly intricate, fragile state. I was in an incredible state of mind. Fear, desire, frustration, the scope of our attempt, and pure physical and mental exhaustion had combined to wind me up so tight, so fast, that the contest was not as much with time as whether the record or the human mechanism would fall first.

The next day, the twenty-ninth, was the last day Portillo would be open, the last possible chance for the record. Accordingly, we decided to go up early in the morning and run while the track was still ice. We were sure ice would make the difference. With one day, perhaps only one run left and in us, it was necessary to extend ourselves. Sleep, the night of the twenty-eighth, was restless and unfulfilling. Fatigue sleep of a job undone.

We rose early, ate, and were out on the hill while most of the hotel slept. It was cold and clear. The shaded track was rock hard. Springtime frozen corn; it would remain firm for several hours. We had prepared the track perfectly at the end of the previous day. For the first time, every condition was in our favor.

We took a practice run to test the timing from 20 yards above the measured area. We averaged more than 100 kilometers per hour, and I knew in the center of my spine our track was as ready as we. I would not allow the thought that it was more ready. I remembered what Reddish had told me many months before.

The sun began to climb the track. C. B. Vaughan and I went with it. Because of the steepness, 400 meters takes great amounts of time and energy, and I was very tired. We climbed slowly, planning to reach the top before the sun exposed the entire track. I felt C. B. had more energy than I, but that may have been hypersensitivity to my own state.

We talked and joked, but the next day we could not remember any of it. When we got to the top the sun was on the track. Portillo was awake. Far below—an impassable distance—people came out to watch. On the hotel porch many had binoculars. Skiers came down the plateau and stood off to one side near the bottom of the track. Spectators of a play in which the actors had not learned their parts, an audience removed, but only on the surface of action. They feared and hoped as did we. Difficult to realize at that moment, but we needed and used their positive energy, for it is true that each is a part of the main.

In that critical state and time, reality was C. B., the gigantic track below, the feeling of vertigo, and the hard knowledge that the next few minutes were the culmination of all that was behind, the determinant of much of what lay ahead. Funk, Purcell, the timers, other racers and many friends were down there watching with varying degrees of interest and involvement; our friends; warm human beings with whom we had formed close and not so close relationships, laughed, danced, drank, gotten angry, forgave and were forgiven; our immediate companions in eating, sleeping, working, relaxing—life; but at the top of the Portillo speed track, those people might as well have been on another planet. All living, except my reality, was suspended. They could not really understand the high degree of control we had made from the chaos of our feelings, nor our predicament, nor the mind which equates self-abstraction with being near God. They could only see us as tiny figures on a white wall of snow, but the least thoughtful could not help but realize our commitment.

I was nearly sick with vertigo and fear. We did warm-up exercises (a delicate task on a slope of 80 percent steepness), and in those last minutes I discovered a bit of the structure of action.

The months of discipline, work, self-abstraction and the winding-up process, honed to a fine, sharp edge by the last run on the last day under the iciest, most difficult, most perfect conditions enabled me to see myself marvelously clear.

I nearly laughed and would have but for physical fear. A great calm and confidence (not in *success*, but in my *self*) filled me. "Duped again," I would say in a later time. I was at the precipice of the fastest skiing ever done, the fastest a human body had moved without free-falling or mechanical aids, hanging on the side of a snow-blasted cliff, stinking with fear and the stubbornness not to be beaten by it, when I saw the absurdity of my position. Many things had put me up to where I was—whatever it was in my inherent personality that caused me to recognize skiing as my form of expression when a young boy had put me there, and a racing potential which eluded my best efforts. And a public school education with its accent on grade rather than content. And the power of the great yellow lie called journalism which warps the world's mind with its pretension and shallowness. And the Hollywood ethic upon which I was weaned, an ethic preaching that what matters is coming through in the end—a barely disguised belief in a better life after death which makes lightheaded excuses for lifetimes of misery. And people like Number 7 who wage war on the past with inverted minds. And all the sweet experiences that had gone to hell. And Beattie with his clumsy feet and blind assurance. And all the teams I and others would never make. And all the old racer friends like Marvin Moriarity and Gardner Smith and Jim Gaddis who had been caught by the sharp, sly, double-edged axe of politics, wielded by the universal soldiers of my particular way of life . . . but there was also the strength that learning about those kinds of things gives. And there were the good examples of how a man should be; I had once categorized them according to three fine competitors—Werner, Miller, and Beuk. There was Funk down there taking pictures; broken leg and all his hopes. There was Marcelle, dying the hard way. And Barnes, Lyder, and Tiger, already gone.

And my parents, who never understood but took pleasure when it reached newsprint. There was the good life and people of La Parva. And there were all the friends right there at Portillo. Somewhere in the world was a guy I didn't know named Plangger, and he had something I wanted. And with me was my comrade, C. B. Vaughan. All the people and times and places I had known, and all the shades of emotions I had ever felt, and all the work I had ever accomplished came with me to Portillo. Pushed, pulled, or just came along as disinterested observers. Hard to know, but assuredly there.

And every one of them copped out at the last minute, leaving me entirely, flat alone. Duped again. Abandoned by my own illusions, leaving *just* me to do whatever was necessary.

The essential education.

The territory my mind had chosen as its battling ground—my place to wage war on all the inequity, hypocrisy, stupidity, and frustration I had ever known; and my time to justify myself for Marcelle, Ken, Tiger, Brett, Brunetto, Funk, Lewellen, and to my particular friends in Reno, Ron the Mustache, and Joan the Potter, and to a few others for their faith, friendship, and a smile at the right time—was an icy precipitous piece of snow on the side of an Andean mountain, useful in nature only for the tiny bit of water it would hold a little longer. Absurd. Pathetic in its attempt. Yet, something would be saved. Something communicated all around. Duped again, but not entirely for nothing.

I could have laughed.

Inside, where action begins, I was peaceful, confident, and supremely happy. Calm, because preparation gives self-control, and I had come prepared. Confident, because confidence is the only possible state of mind under such circumstances; to be where we were without believing in ourselves would be suicidal, and, while life *is* richer and more poignant when it is risked (an effect carrying over and preceding the act of risking), it is so through a deep desire to go on living. And happy, supremely so, I say, to discover in that structure mentioned earlier, that life was okay, and so was I; the important thing was commitment, and I found in myself the ability to give everything, to lay the whole show on the line. In that ability is hidden happiness, and all men have it, lurking somewhere amidst neuroses, education, experience and belief, centered in the heart. Success, while certainly not unimportant, is a problematical (mathematical?) afterthought.

While in that delicate, beautiful state, I adjusted my goggles one more time, and signaled my readiness to the timers, feeling more than usual action in the center of things. Far below *(like looking through the wrong end of a telescope)* the signal pole waggled back and forth. I wished C. B. luck, said I'd see him at the bottom. I felt a sentimental reluctance to leave the big redhead up there alone.

"Good luck, Boy," he said. C. B. called his friends "Boy."

I planted my left pole below and to the back of my skis, the right above and to the front, executed a quick jump turn, pulled my poles out in midair, and landed in a full tuck, headin' down.

Acceleration like a rocket launched in the wrong direction. The sound of endless cannons, moving closer. Irreversible commitment.

The soles of my feet said this was the one. My eyes saw the transition and peaceful flat, far, far away. My body, appalled at the danger in which it had been placed, acted automatically, reluctantly perhaps, but with an instinct and precision that preceded the mind which put it there. My naked mind had finally gotten ahold of the big one that had always gotten away.

Jesus, it is fast.

After 100 meters I estimate the speed at over 150 kph. That left 200 meters to the timing and 100 meters in the trap before the longed for landing. Never have I wanted more to be finished with something. A few seconds, less than ten . . . a long way, more than time can record. More than anything, I wanted not to fall. Probably there is little difference in the end result of a fall at 150 kph and one at 170 kph, but the ice that morning accentuated everything that was happening. Acceleration. Sound. The beating against the legs. The texture feeling. The thin line of error.

In big speeds the skis make peculiar movements. On ice they make them faster, harder. Tremendous air pressure pushes the tips up, the skis want to become airborne. You push forward with everything you have. The air pushes up the tips; you push forward; there is a continuous change of pressure from tip to tail of the skis. Continuous and violent. On a good run your body absorbs both change and violence. On a bad run your body demonstrates them. The tips tend to make a curious, fishtail motion, which, combined with the tip to tail pressure change, cause the ski to pivot slightly underneath the foot. These things are happening to the skis you are riding. Happening as fast as a vibration and with as much power as the speed you are carrying.

While this is happening at the feet the rest of the body is trying to hold a stable, compact, tuck position. Air pressure tries to push you over backward, with a continuous, ever mounting force. If you break the tuck the pressure tries to rip your arm off. If you stood up at those speeds, your back would hit the snow before the thought could come of what a mistake you had just made.

About a hundred yards above the trap, my right arm, as it had the previous day, flew out to the side for some inexplicable reason of balance. It is tremendously unsettling. (The next time you are ripping along one of America's scenic highways at 100 miles per hour, stick an arm out the window.) I jammed both hands forward and down—a high-speed version of what, in another age, was known as the "Sailer crouch," the stablest position in skiing—and rocketed through the trap and into the transition.

Each mile per hour after 95 feels like a difference of 10 miles per hour at half that speed. When I reached the transition I felt more like a Ferrari than a human, and I knew before the timers that no one had skied that fast before.

The run-out was easy—gradually extending the arms and raising the body for air drag, and a long left turn entered at about 60 mph until I was able to stop. It took a couple of hundred more feet than any previous run.

I stopped. I took off my helmet and goggles. I was alive. The most alive I had been in my twenty-four years. I felt the sun and saw the beauty of Portillo in the Andes as never before. My spirit was clean. My mind could rest content. I had discovered my own structure of action, and I had acted. For the time, the illusions had been stripped away, and I was completely alive. Also, successful.

I walked back around the corner and halfway up the flat. Up on the hill, Funk was jumping up and down with his cast like a club-foot chimpanzee.

"One-seven-one," he yelled. "Wahoooo," hopping about like mad, arms waving.

I stood in the flat waiting for C. B. The calm joy I was experiencing was tempered by anxiety for the big redhead. I was safe in a giant, flat expanse of snow; I was alive; I was happy; I was tuned to a very high plane; but it wasn't over until C. B. was safely down, so I waited a little longer.

Despite fatigue, the aftereffects of hyperadrenalation, anxiety and realization of the world record with all its attendant hoopla, those few minutes were the most peaceful, satisfying moments I had ever known. I knew they would be few, and I knew they were enough.

In ten minutes, the diplomatic "Bobby" Muller and Chalo Dominquez, the timers, had reset the watches. The pole waved for "Ceb." He came in his yellow-black racing tights like a tiger falling off a white cliff. The sound—skis rattling against ice, wind rippling skin-tight clothes, and the impact of a body moving through air at 100 mph—carried clear to the flat; a unique sound impossible to forget, and not a reassuring one. C. B. rode a tight but high tuck. Twice his arms broke position, flashing out to his sides and immediately returned. Then, quite literally, he thundered into the transition and past me on the flat and around the corner to a stop.

It was all over.

I stood within my peace wondering about C. B.'s time and looking to see if it was in me to go up again that day, in case his time was faster than mine. Almost two years later I was to remember that moment; I remembered it because it took that long to understand what that moment, that question, that impetus in myself was. As luck would have, it was a catechism I was not to face that day.

C. B. was still around the corner, experiencing, discovering, and questioning on his own when Tito Beladone, the Grand Ambassador of Chilean skiing and friend of several years, skied down the outrun to me. "You and C. B. have the same time," he said. The moment was inordinately formal to Tito's vision of skiing, but he gave me a hug, a pat on the back, a kiss on the check, Chilean fashion, and his congratulations. He was elated and proud; I felt humble to have a part in giving him that moment.

I thanked Tito and skied down to C. B. I told him what had happened and we had a few minutes together. During those minutes we knew what we had accomplished, and it was a fine time.

Then the backwash of success arrived. The friends, the ones with faith, the interested, the incredulous, and even the cynical and weak doubters, came to say what we already knew. And it was wonderful to hear.

1964: First Year at Cervinia: The Wreck

The Cervinia speed run is both objectively and subjectively different from Portillo's. The Chilean track measures 400 meters to the transition and up to 80 percent steepness; Italy's is a kilometer long and 62 percent at the steepest point. It starts nearly flat and falls off to about 20

World record holder Steve McKinney on his way at one hundred mph plus

percent for 400 meters; on a good run the competitor is traveling about 60–70 mph at the end of this relative flat; then the contour changes abruptly and drastically, and the rest of the track is a consistent 60 percent. This contour change coincides with a crevasse which is boarded over and covered with snow to allow a crossing. It is impossible to resist being thrown in the air where the track changes. Depending on the individual run, conditions of the track, and, of course, the competitor, seekers of speed fly anywhere from 20 to 120 feet. How the racer masters that obstacle will have an appreciable effect on his time. As in downhill racing, it is faster to be in the air 20 feet than 100 feet; but the most important factor is one's ability to hold the extremely low, tight, body position before the bump, in flight and after landing. Opening the arms slightly for balance will cost you the race. A serious alienation from the thread of balance at this point results in one of those struggling runs that brings awareness of the depth of the will to survive, a realization that casts a glow of understanding on the terror and struggle of rising from the swamp to open air. After landing, the big speeds commence. Up to then, speed is acquired gradually; the racer has time to get into a comfortable, compact position, time to get accustomed to speed, time to get acquainted with the muscles he will need, time to think. In elapsed time, measured in seconds, the racer is on the Cervinia track three to four times longer than in Portillo; they are tracks of different temperaments arriving at the same conclusion. Commitment. Concentration. Freedom. Or the struggle of terror.

There is another crucial difference between Cervinia and Portillo: the transition, in terms of safety, the most important part of a speed run. In the transition, speed begins to diminish. The transition is like the first touchdown of a jet, except this jet lands at full speed. It is where the potency of speed, the consequence of commitment, the gyroscope of balance show their hands. It is where gravity, always tiptoeing in your shadow, adds its weight to your passing. As if to see that your legs are as strong as you have committed them to be.

The transition in Portillo goes from a 52 percent slope to a 15 percent slope. You must accept and adapt to a 37 percent change in grade. Gravity does not hit you very hard; it tiptoes slightly behind.

In Cervinia, the transition holds you the way a jet taking off forces you into your seats; except this jet reaches top speed much faster. The transition is from a 60 percent slope to a 15-yard flat to a 12 percent slope, but the 12 percent is in the other direction. Uphill. You are confronted with a 72 percent change at over 100 mph. It is a transition that would like to suck you down and break you into a million pieces and spit them out in China. Gravity romps upon your head.

There is a difference between Cervinia and Portillo which manifests itself more in psychology than objective reality. After the racer in Cervinia has gone 200 meters he disappears from the vision of the competitors on top. More than thirty seconds pass before an impersonal loudspeaker on a post at the start announces the racer's time and *"La Piste e Libre,"* the track is free. Sometimes the track is not free. This can mean several things, including a fallen racer. But you do not know because you cannot see; and the starters, in radio contact with the bottom, are arbitrary about what they tell you. Aside from his announced time, you do not know how it went for the previous racer. This can weigh heavy upon the mind.

July 15, 1964. A day I must always remember. A day that expanded the horizons of my experience, showing me something of myself that only such a day could reveal.

Good weather. The best track we had seen. C. B. had a good run the day before and was hungry for more. I, too, had banished my discouragement and felt confident. I remember, distinctly, abundant happiness; to be in Cervinia doing this was, as I told the Peace Corps girl, the *best* thing I could do with myself; nothing was so important to my progress as a man than getting my body down a mountain on a pair of skis, just as fast as I could go. I don't know why, but I know it was so.

But that superb bitch, Fate, had a fickle lesson I hadn't learned. We were all at the top. The first run began. The timing was not functioning perfectly, and the times of several racers had been missed. C. B. was growling about the timers not missing him. Alberti and I posed for photographs. DiMarco had an early starting number; mine was several numbers later; he went, but I was not watching. Bruno and I were talking when the starters and the speaker on a post simultaneously silenced us and changed the mood of the day.

DiMarco had gone 173.493 kph. The record was his, once again.

I felt empty; I did not want to talk or look anyone in the eye. It was a private moment. I think it was a private moment for every competitor who was consciously and seriously ready to win. The others, the Italians, cheered and shouted for their countryman's success; it was not a good position for the Americans.

I went to C. B. We encouraged each other and readied ourselves to get the record back. He had served his apprenticeship, and when he went a few minutes later he was prepared. He went 168.145, a run beaten only by DiMarco, Plangger, and he and I in all of skiing history, but far short of what was necessary.

Then came my turn. I moved out to the track, acutely aware of that interpersonal pressure I have always hated. What had once been an attempt on my part was now expected of me. That was my feeling, as if a heavier load than I ever intended to carry was, suddenly, mine. But I knew the work well, and I had faith in my will.

"La Piste e Libre."

I began. In relative terms, it does not seem much to build up to 20-30-40 and 50 mph when, in a few seconds, you will be hurtling along at more than 100 mph. But you must pay close attention at those relatively slow speeds; your mind is absorbed in technical details, and there can be no abstract thoughts like records or the game. Your attention must be total.

Perhaps, on that run, my attention was strained.

I rolled my body into the most aerodynamic cone I knew how to make, working the terrain changes with a flat ski to get every wave of speed before the jumps and the steep hill, velocity at the jumps helping determine the eventual speed through the timing trap. I focused down, doing my best.

I flew off the jump but held position and landed with no problem. The big speeds rolled in upon me and I aimed along the right side, the fastest line.

About a hundred yards above the trap, the inexpressible happened. That thing you must never dwell upon, that point in space and time to which Perillat referred—"You must not think too much"—had coincided with my run. The thread of balance had broken. It was apparent and inescapable that I was going to fall. I was convinced. There was no fear, only a clinical, sure knowledge. All the time I was trying to avoid the inevitable fall, and all the while I was falling there was no fear. Only a (detached?) cool observation of the fastest flow of events I had ever witnessed. There is an infinitely fragile line of balance at 100 mph because you are more like a projectile than a skier, and once that line is broken it does not mend easily. About 200 yards remained to the transition; it takes slightly over four seconds to travel that far that fast. It seemed like five minutes, and I tried every conceivable adaptation to regain balance—and the line is so thin that spectators didn't know I was in trouble until I actually fell; even C. B., watching closely, didn't know—but only a forgiving God could have saved me, and the forgiving gods were busy elsewhere that day. I knew it would expose me defenselessly once I fell, but I was not scared; I tried a hundred positions and a thousand thoughts, but I would not be forgiven inattention. Experience breeds a slight contempt for the forces in speed. When I reached the transition it sucked me down, just like I knew it would; but I thought I'd try for Iraq in two or three pieces rather than China in a million. As I went down I tried to get on my back and bottom. Perhaps I could ride it out in a long skid; I'd seen ski jumpers do that. Now I know that strange things happen to your body when it meets the snow at 100 mph, no matter what the position. In the twinkling of hitting the snow I regained a proper respect for speed. If you are inattentive, as well as somewhat stupid, you may breed a contempt for big speeds, forgetting respect through the grace of being atop your skis each run. No one on his back at 100 mph will ever after have contempt for speed. Something caught—a hand, perhaps—and then came one of those falls skiers have bad dreams about. Eighty yards up that hill rising out of the transition, in every conceivable body position, including upside down and backward and 5 feet off the snow. A memorable fall. Visually a blur of snow and sky and an occasional form moving faster than focus. Too fast for the eye, but not for the mind. The films of the fall pass much more quickly than the memory impression left with my mind, for the mind registers feelings, the eye only illusion. The left ski went away as the binding meant it to, and was last seen on the way to Zermatt. The right ski loyally stayed, and halfway through the fall the leg broke. The fall and I finished our relationship and it left me in a pile. Alone. I hurt everywhere and I began to review my scant knowledge of physiology. Not until then did I fear (*feel* fear) that I may have destroyed my body. I once broke a leg that took two years to put back in shape. I flashed on those years. Bad years. I knew my good leg was broken, and my body was a pulsing pain. I undid the binding, which meant I would move, and fear gave way to the objective mind. My fall deposited me apart from people, and it took a little time for them to arrive. My left ski, poles, gloves, goggles, and glasses were no longer with me, and the sleeves of the ultra tight Japanese speed suit were somehow shoved up and over my elbows in a wad. C. B. was the first person to reach me; I was happy for that, and grateful that he came so fast. He supervised the first-aid men, and I was touched by his concern.

Italians are really prepared for accidents; I was fascinated by the first air splint I had seen, used on my own leg. People were swarming around, and by then it was decided that in the relative world of injuries I was all right; there were the smiles and relief of the silence of disaster giving way to the movement of life.

There was no fear, only a clinical, sure knowledge . . . all the time I was trying to avoid the inevitable fall, and all the time I was falling there was no fear. Only a (detached?) cool observation of the fastest flow of events I had ever witnessed.

A few years later I came to realize what it is to have your mind and the rest of your existence so far out of harmony. It is one thing to be intelligent, objective, aware, hip to your surroundings; it is something else, entirely, to observe your own impending destruction with the clinical eye of a research technologist in his laboratory, with no more feeling than the scalpel of a Dachau bone surgeon.

The mind was designed to keep body and soul (and mind) together. It was not intended to be so powerful as to block out the natural emotion of fear. If the mind can obliterate fear when there is every reason to feel fear then what can the mind not obliterate? Love? Compassion? The sight of blood? If you are not afraid when you *should be* afraid, then you stand accused of stupidity. Your mind has sold you down a stream flowing nowhere.

In time, that fall gave to me a fear—not fear of broken bones or the impact after speed stops or even death, for you accept those possibilities in the act of commitment; no, not that; but a fear of a mind so delighted with its own capabilities and power that it has neglected the basics—doing what it is supposed to do—keeping body and soul and mind together.

My mind failed in allowing no fear to me as I was falling up a hill at 100 mph, but valuable lessons are locked up within your failures. I learned that my natural feelings are friends, not enemies to be crushed and avoided and suppressed by a mind gone mad with power. I learned that from my fall, but I didn't learn immediately.

1965: Second Year at Cervinia: The Death
The morning of July twenty-sixth the track was ice

down to the blue disc (the one Gasperl hit), about 100 meters above the trap. Solid, wind-blown ice. Below that, the track was covered with soft, new snow, about 8 inches deep, blown there by the laws of terrain and wind. Those in charge prepared it in the same, masterly fashion. We were two days without skiing and this day was added to the schedule; it was an extension of our time. We went up to the Plateau Rosa early. The weather was beautiful, a slight bit cold.

At the top we joked, wished each other luck, did warm-up exercises, adjusted equipment—just like always. I was completely absorbed in what had to be done. The two days off skis were noticeable.

Mussner went first. His time came back up as 172.084. I was really excited when I heard that. The first time over 170 this year! The record was in sight! I ran fifth or sixth and held my position. It was a wonderful, free run; but I felt the change going off the ice onto soft snow. My time was 170.373, but I, and everyone else on the outrun, thought they announced 173. I hurried back up thinking I had the best run of the round, and I was full of getting the record back. I don't know what it is about that bloody record.

When I got to the top Ninni told me I was fourth behind Mussner, Siorpaes, and Leitner. That seemed logical because I had been surprised to hear my time as 173. It hadn't felt so fast. The slight disappointment filled me even more with desire for the the record. I kept saying to myself—"I'm gonna get that bastard back." I talked a little with Mussner and congratulated him for his fine first run. I spoke to Siorpaes. I observed the rituals. I remember grinning because I was sure Mussner and Siorpaes were as full of the record as I.

Then there came a time when no one wanted to go. There was no particular reason. One hadn't finished waxing. Another was cold. Still another was tuning his mind. I was still tired from climbing up too fast. Mussner appeared ready, but he didn't want to go; I don't know why—nerves probably. (I'm sure now that he had a premonition.) I jumped into the breach and said I was ready. Actually I was still tired, but I was so excited and anxious about finally breaking into the 170s that it didn't matter. I went anyway, and I held my position over both jumps. I put my head down just before the soft

part of the track, and immediately pulled it back up. The track was a monstrous mess. It hadn't even been side-slipped between rounds. I lost my position. It was like driving a car across a furrowed field at 100 mph.

I didn't know how fast I was, but I knew it wasn't very good. Now I know that my time was 168.539 kph. I was mad about the track and I skied to a stop in front of Egon. I said "The track is really bad, Egon, why don't they work on it?" He knew what I meant and felt just about like I did, and he said something like, "I don't know, you can't talk to these fucking Italians." Then I said, quote, "Well, someone's going to get hurt up there." Unquote.

Egon took my skis and began waxing them. A few were still getting into the 170s, and I was full of—with luck—the record.

Then Mussner came.

On Sunday night, the twenty-fifth, Mussner saw a photo of Luigi taken on the first day. In this photograph Luigi's head is completely down and all you can see is the top of his helmet. It is the most fantastic Lanciato photo I've seen. Walter studied the photograph for a few minutes. "Tomorrow I will do that," he told Luigi. Luigi grinned, as any champion will whose disciples are trying to imitate him. It is the grin of pride and of being flattered, but it is also a grin of awareness of the difficulties in the refinements of any champion's technique, the refinements which all disciples try for and hardly any ever achieve. In this case, the refinement of putting one's head between one's knees and skiing blind at more than 105 mph.

Mussner came and his head was down. I have the impression that when I was on top and Walter didn't want to go he was forcing himself to be able to put his head down. (Perhaps also fighting a premonition.) This is what I think, but there is no way to know. Later, Franca told me that Mussner nearly didn't go again; I don't know why, nor does anybody. Then he said something like, "Well, there's still the record." And he left the top.

He came and I saw him from above the blue disc, just before where the track was bad. His head was already down, his position was good, and he held it like that all the way. Many things went into the sequence of what happened then, and no one will ever know exactly what they were, but this is what I think:

At the top of the timing area he began to veer right. I saw immediately that he was on his way off the track. A cold electric shock passed through me like a tidal wave of fear. My heart went numb and my blood disappeared. Walter went off the track just at the end of the timing, just missing the electric eye pillar. He went through a little post and that ridiculous net they had fanned out on each side. When he hit that post the world changed.

At that speed many things could cause a slight deviation of direction. It is impossible to have more than an opinion as to why he went off the course. It was obvious from watching how he held this position, and from what he said afterward, that he was unaware he was off course until he had already fallen. I believe two things killed Walter Mussner, not one more than the other. I think the bad track caused him to veer to one side against the natural slope of the track, and I think Walter's head being down made him unaware of what was happening, and, therefore, unable to correct it. I think if the track had been properly groomed he wouldn't have veered off course; and if he had kept his head up he would have known what was happening, and he would have been able to correct it. But—and Walter Mussner is dead.

What happened when Walter hit that post and fell is something I don't think I will forget as long as I live; and it will be more than a few days before the image leaves my mind, allowing me easy sleep at night and to write and read and be naturally of this life the rest of the time. He clocked a time of 170.132 kph just as he fell; but, to the naked eye, it appears that the racers in the last 30 meters of the 100-meter trap accelerate to a much greater speed. I would not be surprised if the racer who clocks 170 for 100 meters is traveling at 190 for the last 10 or 20 meters. Right there, where there is that little boost of acceleration that anyone can observe, Walter fell. With incredible force and speed he went end over end, feet and then head hitting the snow, and each turn wrenching his body unbelievably. Afterwards, eleven holes were counted in the snow, feet, head, feet, head, feet, head, and, at the end, everything. It was difficult to believe it was a human body undergoing such gyrations, such speed, such force. The only thing I have ever seen like it were movies of Bill Vukovich's car at Indianapolis when he was killed in 1955. It was similar to that.

For a few seconds that seemed like minutes after he stopped in a motionless pile in the transition, everyone was frozen still with astonishment and fear. There was—I am sure in everyone because it was there in me— the hope of a miracle that Walter Mussner would get up and that no one would have to go pick him up. At the same time, I don't think there was a doubt in anyone's mind that he wasn't going to move by himself. I have seen some bad falls, and I have even had a few myself; but this wasn't like a skiing fall anyone had ever seen before. No one has ever fallen like that.

Then Rico was screaming over the loudspeaker. That snapped people out of their trance. Dozens of people were suddenly all around Walter, about 30 yards from where I stood. I started to go, but instinct told me not to; and I am glad I didn't. Ivo (Mahlknecht) and Felice (DeNicolo) were there, and they were closer comrades than I; so he wasn't alone when he shouldn't be alone.

It took about half an hour to get him off the hill. During that time not one person even sideslipped the track, though competition was obviously to continue as soon as possible. I was mad and sick with the knowledgeable suspicion that if Walter wasn't dead he was an agonizing pile of broken bones. Egon was furious the way the German temperament gets furious when unhappy.

I stared at the group around Walter. Egon finished waxing my skis. I was, however, finished psychologically and spiritually, and I knew it. I told Egon I would run again if the track began to be fast enough for a record. I would go up and wait and listen to the times. If they got close I would go; if not, not. Egon said it was finished, but I went up and waited anyway; but I never came down on the track.

Just before I went up to wait, Hans Berger broke away from the group around Walter and came my way. Hans, who lives in Kufstein, is small, with tiny, delicate features and an expressive face. He usually looks about eighteen years old, though he is thirty. When he came up to me, he looked a hundred years old and there were tears in his eyes.

"Ist es schlecht?" I asked.

"Ja," he said in a strange way.

"Sehr schlecht?"

"Sehr schlecht," he answered in a way that made me know it was.

I went up to the top and waited with that in the pit of my stomach. Probably, it was best the track never got fast enough to make me think a record was possible.

They took Walter to Aosta and he lived a little more than five hours. Unfortunately, he was conscious most of that time. He fractured his skull, broke two vertebrae in his neck, pulverized his entire pelvic region, broke one femur and tore loose the femoral artery, and he tore himself open from the anus to the navel. He had acute hemorrhages of the brain, stomach, and leg. Toward the end he went blind. If he had lived he would have lost one leg, he wouldn't have been a man any longer, and he probably would have been paralyzed. Kiki went with him to Aosta and held his hand until he died. She is only twenty and has never seen a dead person before, and she was still in shock and sometimes hysterics the next night when she and her mother told me about it.

The Italian and Swiss papers are full of stupid things about it. The people of Cervinia all say that the track was "perfetto," and they put the whole blame on a mistake of Walter's. They've gone on at some length why it's not the fault of the Lanciato committee, the organization, or anyone's. That is not quite true. Some say there is nothing dangerous about the Lanciato. That, too, is not quite true. Others call the Lanciato stupidly insane. Nor is that true. If I uttered to the press what I think about the track, they would interpret it as blaming those responsible for track maintenance for Walter's death. That, also, is not the truth; and it would do infinitely more harm than good. And it would not help Walter. There is no prevention (except abstention, which is ridiculous) for such accidents, and there is no blame. It is part of skiing that fast.

I was the only one competing that day who saw Walter fall, and I returned to the top with a different perspective on our endeavors. The racers and officials asked about the delay. Why was the track closed so long? I said Walter had a bad fall that tore up the track a bit; the delay was necessary for repairs. I had neither desire nor right to elaborate.

I sat at the top for a long time. Some racers got in six runs, nearly everyone got four or five. Only Mussner and I ran just twice. Visions of his fall tumbled through my brain. I could not make them leave. (They entered my dreams and woke me in the night for the next two years.) It was the same clear day, but a grainy, colorless filter had descended on the world.

Leitner, leading with 172.744, decided not to run again unless his time was beaten. It never was. My time dropped from fourth best to eighth. Luigi, suffering badly from a strep throat and cold, took five runs before breaking into the first ten. My place on the result sheets, the race itself, winning or losing no longer mattered. What importance has the race alongside life itself? What game do we play in which the loser forfeits life? What type of men play this game? For it was obvious from the beginning that one of us would die because of some human failing, neglecting, for a billionth of eternity, the rules of the game. Is human failure cause to die? If it is, are we not playing with the rules and stakes of Neanderthal Man? I never meant to play a game in which one of the players would inevitably, through mathematical laws as sure as those governing Russian roulette, smash his body beyond repair; yet I played and watched it happen, and I felt deep in my innards that I had always known it was going to happen. I remembered waiting for C. B. at the bottom of Portillo's track, wondering about the game's next move if he beat my time. The questions would not disappear. I had no answers.

My friend Franca Simondetti gave Leitner and me some Sangria. We drank it over small talk and silence. Strange to drink the sweet Sangria, to feel its wonderful vapors fill your body and your brain, exploding your taste buds as you sit in the sun—sweet Sangria—all the while trapped with death in a vision of the boyish face of Walter Mussner and a fall unlike any other. Strange to sit like that with Ludwig Leitner, the big German who exudes toughness and confidence and plays the game hard, drinking and healthy. Life's mysteries unfold through everyday functions.

Tiring of Sangria, small talk, and waiting for a run I neither wanted nor would ever make, I skied down alongside the track. Racers were still coming, about one a minute. As a competitor, I was allowed to stand close to the track, and I watched the big speeds from about 30 feet away. For the first time in three years of playing with eternity, I viewed it with a new realization of flesh and blood men, mere mortals, at play with the forces of the universe; it was wondrous that we dared, but never again would I view another man as a rival whose mistakes or refinements I must note and use to my advantage. I could hardly believe what I saw. I knew these men. We had joked, laughed, eaten, drunk, and skied together. We had entered into freedom and struggled with terror, and together we had ignored our common reality. Walter Mussner reminded us of our negligence. I watched my friends like children in a play yard; proud, arrogant, innocent. We had accomplished great things, but, when all was done and spoken, we were just men; probably we could be better men, for we had not put away childish things.

When I got down to Cervinia, the word was around that Mussner was badly hurt. Only those who saw him fall had any idea what that meant. Most of the racers didn't think that Walter would not be back with them. I returned to my hotel, changed clothes, and packed my ski bag for Egon to take to Kufstein. Walter was in Aosta and I had heard he was alive when he reached the hospital; that is usually a good sign for the chances of survival. I put my thoughts with Walter Mussner and packed my bag.

After, I was carrying the heavy bag of skis up the street to Egon's hotel when something happened I cannot define but only describe. It came in what I have come to know as a "flash." Suddenly I knew Walter Mussner was dead. It was sure; it was something I *knew.* Walter was dead, and I no longer felt the hard sadness that had been with me since the fall. What I felt was something like intense peace and joy and relief, all together, I do not know if that feeling arose because Walter was out of his suffering, or because what had happened had happened to him and not to me, or if there was another reason. I set down my big, red Kneissl ski bag and rested. I did not question the fact of his death nor the quality or means of my knowledge, but I wasn't *supposed* to feel what I felt. For I felt better and more alive than I had since Walter began veering right.

An hour later Kalevi told me Walter Mussner was dead.

Diary, July 4, 1965
From now on every man who tries seriously and truly for a record carries death in his hind pocket. I think that this year everyone will make it, but after this it will get too fast, too tough, and eventually someone will buy the farm no one ever wants but everyone gets.

Skiing the Steeps

by PETER MILLER

There are four dimensions of "outer limits." The first is distance, as in skiing to the Pole. The second is height, as in skiing above twenty thousand feet. The third is speed, as in setting the world speed record. Here is the fourth: sheer steepness.

THE Headwall of Tuckerman's Ravine on Mount Washington in New Hampshire is shaped like the inside of a teacup—and it is just about as steep, relatively speaking. A person standing on the rim of the Headwall with skis on looks down and sort of under him to the "lunch rocks" and the outrun 4 miles below.

Tuckerman's is the steepest accessible ski run in North America. On a lean snow year, a skier can drop half a mile at a 45- to 50-degree angle. And every spring, when the danger of avalanche has abated and the surface has turned to the icy granules known as corn snow, enthusiasts make their way to Mount Washington, some just to watch, but most to make the climb up (there is no lift) and the slide down.

On Memorial Day weekend, the most popular time on the Headwall, skiers in various stages of paralysis, bravado and skill dot the slope. My own initial descent, despite the overwhelming urge to crouch into the mountain and hold on with all toes, featured what might be called a spectacular aerial eggbeater turn, a 30-foot drop and a 25-mile-an-hour skid to the bottom of the mountain. Litter marked my progress down the fall line: a hat, wallet, camera with the case ripped in half, a glove, a red handkerchief. When I came to rest, I found the abrasive corn snow had ripped open my hand, I had a gash in my forehead and one of my skis was coming apart, but I was otherwise unscathed. And I was exhilarated. I had become a devotee of skiing steeps.

Skiing the steeps, or, as it is called in France, where it originated, "ski extreme" has radically changed over the past two decades. Once just a way of seeking thrills and spills, it has become a sophisticated specialty within the sport of skiing.

In it simplest form, skiing the steeps means searching out and skiing down a slope that has a pitch of more than 45 degrees. The breakthrough, like the four-minute mile, is 60 degrees.

Ski resorts don't have pitches this steep that are open to the public. A slope of 45 degrees, for instance, means for every 10 feet of length the slope drops 10 feet. According to Jim Branch of Sno-engineering, a leading ski resort planning company, most top expert trails are slanted at 40 degrees. The average advanced intermediate slope at most ski areas is about 29 degrees, which

92

Sylvan Saudan making a first descent of the deadly Eiger

is also the incline of the Lake Placid Men's Olympic Downhill trail.

"When you ski down a slope of 45 degrees or more," said Branch, "you are making a controlled free fall. Give a little kick with your skis and you can drop 150 feet down the mountain—in the air."

As it is involving, skiing the steeps is more than skiing a couloir or cirque that is 45 degrees or more. Steep skiers leave behind the lifts and crowds and manicured trails of today's ski areas and climb a mountain, and ski down terrain that is not only steep but often has changeable snow conditions. The purist steep skier climbs up to ski down (no lifts, no helicopters, no oxygen) and carries what he needs for his descent on his back. Many, in this quest for steepness, search out runs or mountains that have never been skied before. They are adventurers who have climbed and skied mountains in Peru, Pakistan, the Himalayas, and Alaska besides those muscular mountains with massive shoulders that form those deep valleys in the North American and European mountain country.

Often the steep skier's feats are unpublicized; he is usually a loner and shares the experience with a few close friends. Some have died in their pursuit of new descents. Fritz Stammberger of Aspen, Colorado, a quiet, tough mountain man who made an incredible descent down the north face of the Maroon Bells, a 55-degree slide that drops 2,500 feet into a pile of rocks, disappeared on Tirich Mir, a 25,300-foot peak in Pakistan. He was last seen on his way up, soloing, without oxygen. A French skier, Jean Moran, recently died on Annapurna, reportedly from exhaustion, and there have been reports of other recent deaths. All were on quests to climb and ski mountains using solo technique, no oxygen assists and no large support teams.

The traceable roots to skiing the steeps lead back to 1939, when André Tournier, a legendary French mountain man, skied down the middle glacier of the Aiguille d'Argentière near Chamonix in the French Alps. Today it is skied by many, but at that time, with the equipment available—7-foot wooden skis, leather boots that gave very little control and front-throw cable bindings with "beartrap" toe pieces—it was a stunning achievement. The following year, Emile Allais and Etienne Livacic skied the north face of the Dôme du Goûter on Mont Blanc, Europe's highest mountain. In 1946, Louis Lachenal and Maurice Lenoir skied the 40-degree pitch of the south face of the Col des Droites, also in Chamonix.

In the United States, Sig Buchmayr, a small, bouncy Austrian who had come to this country in 1934 to teach skiing at Sugar Hill in New Hampshire, astounded skiers by doing a jump turn on Mount Washington, landing 50 feet below, then wiggling easily to the bottom.

These men performed their feats with what is now considered primitive equipment, using the techniques their heavy equipment dictated. The modern steep skier uses the same lightweight skis that an expert skier would use—slightly stiff and about 190 centimeters long. Most steep skiing is done in the spring, when there is little danger of avalanches, and longer skis might slip or chatter on the firm spring snow. Steep skiers use good commercial bindings and they set them tight—no steep skier wants to lose a ski.

The steep skier, like any good skier, tries to keep his weight right over the skis. This may take a strong will: on a 50-degree slope, the skier is making what amounts to a dive through space between every turn. The impulse, familiar to practically all skiers, to sit back on the skis and stay close to the mountain rather than to thrust out and down into the turn, is even harder to resist on steep slopes. But, as practically all skiers can imagine, sitting back and trying to drop anchor can be a serious mistake on the steeps. Turns are continuous, providing the only braking action of the fall. On steeps, the skier must also remember to lift the tails of his skis high enough so they do not catch on the slope.

The forerunners of the modern European steeps specialists were two Austrians, Gerhart Winter and Herbert Zacharias, who skied successfully down the 45-degree Couloir Pallavicini of the Grossglockner, south of Salzburg, Austria, on July 7, 1961. They had climbed up, using ice axes and crampons, and skied down with short skis. The most famous of these early skiers was Heini Holzer, from the South Tyrol. A man of incredible strength, and about as wide as he was tall (5 feet 3 inches), Holzer made numerous first descents on steep couloirs in the Italian Dolomites and in the French and Swiss Alps. He was the first to ski the north face of the Piz Roseg in Switzerland, south of St. Moritz. Years later, the same north face took his life when Holzer was making a routine descent.

Sylvain Saudan, a Swiss in his early forties who now lives in Chamonix, was one of the first to make a profession of steep skiing. He gives illustrated lectures, called "Ski the Impossible," showing his incredible descents—down the west face of the Eiger in Switzerland, from just below the summit of Mount McKinley in Alaska, and additional descents in Europe, South America and the Himalayas. Short, compact, with thighs and arms the size of a professional football lineman's, he developed a unique turn for skiing the steeps that the French dubbed "the windshield-wiper turn." Using long ski poles, Saudan plants one pole downhill, then lifts both his skis off the snow in what appears to be a jump turn. But the tails of his skis are anchored in the snow, and, arcing the tips from side to side, he makes one turn after another in a rhythmic, 180-degree, windshield-wiper motion.

Saudan's leading rival for new steep descents is Patrick Vallençant, thirty-five. A lean French mountain guide, he has made more than fifty descents of 45 degrees or more, first near his home in Chamonix, then in Peru, where he claims to have broken the 60-degree barrier by skiing the 21,817-foot Yerupaja in 1979. On one stretch of this massive and steep mountain, Vallençant says, he skied down a 65-degree pitch.

Vallençant is the skier who now sets the standards. He climbs alone, with no ropes, up the steeps he plans to descend. Depending on weather and location, a climb may take as much as three weeks. A descent can be done in a few hours. He climbs in spiked mountain-climbing boots and carries an ice axe in each hand. On his back is a pack with food, clothes, rescue equipment, his skis and his poles. He claims the only way to have a true steep descent is to climb up, by yourself, without oxygen, then to ski down the route that was climbed.

"To arrive at the top of a steep pitch by lift or helicopter," said Vallençant, "is like drinking an *eau-menthe* (the French equivalent of a Shirley Temple). It's a pleasant drink, but it does not charge you up." For Vallençant, the climb up is not only part of the challenge, it is also practical, for on the way up he becomes acquainted with the steepness of the slope, the condition of the snow, the wind, the hidden crevasses.

Vallençant, like most serious steep skiers, does not focus on the danger inherent in his sport. He is mystical about the descent. In his book, *Ski Extrême,* published in 1979 in France, Vallençant describes his thoughts. "At the beginning of any steep descent," he writes, "concentration of incredible intensity fills me. I make one or two turns with my eyes and mind. I plot to the centimeter where my skis will track. Sometimes a few centimeters is all there is; there is no space for error.

"When I concentrate so, the world disappears. The universe becomes a pair of skis and life is their passage on a steep slope. The direction of the skis isolates me. There is man, and a slope of snow, in unison. . . .

"To ski a very steep slope is completely beautiful; it is pure, hard, vertical, luminous in a dimension that, by its nature, is foreign to us, yet I become a part of this cosmic dimension. When I turn, there is a fraction of a second when I lose contact with the snow and remain suspended in air. The skis cut through space and I perceive the steepness of the slope with extraordinary acuteness. It is a marvelous phenomenon and I gain a fullness far beyond what we normally comprehend. I see this with such intensity that I have made skiing the steeps the goal of my life.

"I know of no feeling of freedom that is more powerful than to stand on a summit and look down past my ski tips at a wall of snow, almost vertical. It is freedom, and yet pride is there, the sensation of ruling the world from the height of my solitude."

Vallençant, for all his Saint Exupéry style of romantic mysticism, is also, like Saint Exupéry, a very good pilot. He developed a turn to control his speed and conserve his strength while skiing the steeps. He calls this turn the lifted-jump, or pedal-jump, turn. Breaking the rules of ordinary skiing, Vallençant pushes off with his uphill ski, then lifts his downhill ski and, rotating it in midair, jumps onto it, changing direction and finishing the turn. He refers to it as "jumping into the void." (In the average Alpine ski turn, both skis are usually on the snow.)

Vallençant continually searches for new mountains to descend. He went to Kashmir, to the Karakoram Range, and, without oxygen, skied down Broad Peak from an altitude of 25,425 feet—the mountain is 26,400 feet high, but the top 975 feet were not skiable. (It is reported that Sylvain Saudan plans to ski the same peak, but from the very top and thus set a record for unassisted ascent and descent.) Vallençant lost twenty-six pounds in his effort. Next he intends to climb and descend Mount St. Elias in Alaska.

Vallençant supports himself by lecturing on his expeditions and instructing skiers in steep skiing at Chamonix; he is also a professional mountain guide. This professional approach to steep skiing is definitely European. In the United States, though there are some ski celebrities like Rick Sylvester at Squaw Valley and Bill Briggs at Jackson Hole, skiing steeps is a casual affair. A few friends get together and decide to climb a peak and ski some perpendicular couloir, and they just do it. No fanfare.

Most American ski resorts frown on out-of-bounds skiing and some revoke the lift tickets of those who go beyond the boundaries. In some states, going out of bounds is a misdemeanor. What worries resort and forest-service personnel are the search and rescue problems. There are no hard statistics on the number of injuries or fatalities the increase in steep skiing has produced, and there are some who claim that, because it is so difficult, only very strong skiers are tempted to try and there are fewer accidents than might be expected. But National Forest Service officials at Mount Washington's Tuckerman Ravine estimate that, depending on conditions, there are at least half a dozen serious skiing injuries annually. Since the 1930s, when skiers began

climbing up to Mount Washington, five deaths have been attributed to skiing accidents.

Despite the risks and restrictions, steep skiing is attracting new disciples every year. They find niches of steep skiing known only to local skiers—the Maroon Bells and Mount Hayden near Aspen, in the San Juan Mountain range of southern Colorado, the mountains in British Columbia. But the most popular steep skiing remains on the Headwall of Mount Washington in the East and the longer scarier couloirs at Jackson Hole, Wyoming, in the West.

The most famous steep at Jackson Hole is Corbet's Couloir. It is a narrow chute near the top of the mountain that slices obliquely through two rock faces. It is about 300 yards long and 45 degrees, if there is not too much snow. A skier must jump into the couloir from an overhanging ledge of snow; the smart ones jump and turn in midair, so they land with their first turn under control.

Victor Gerdin expresses the flavor of Jackson Hole in his approach to skiing. A tall, drawling, understated ski school supervisor, he knows the couloirs as well as anyone. "Sometimes," he said to me last spring, as we searched out some of the area's inbound steep runs, "I just got to get away from people and remind myself what skiing is all about.

"I've skied the steeps with some who don't have the ability to ski well," he continued, "and I almost have a heart attack when I see them fall and slide into the rocks. They think if they sit down, they'll stop, but if you take 30 percent of your body weight off your ski edges there's nothing else to do but wash out."

When skiing on his own, Gerdin voluntarily gets himself into situations where mistakes are not allowed. There are two steep runs in Cody Bowl, to the southwest of the ski resort; they are reached by a traverse, some downhill and some uphill. (If you use the lift to get up at Jackson Hole, you must get permission from the ski patrol to go out of bounds.) They are called Once Is Enough and Twice Is Nice. Gerdin first skied Once Is Enough on a Memorial Day about five years ago. Because of rocks and steepness at the top, he lowered himself into it on ropes—with his skis on.

"It was well over 55 degrees," Gerdin said. "I took some slack off the rope to see if I could just stand on the slope, but I couldn't hold an edge. Without the rope, my legs would have been shaking so bad I could not have made it." Gerdin moved down the slope, to where it was only about 50 degrees, and skied down.

"You have only 2 or 3 inches of edge on the snow when you turn," he said. "You swing your skis, and you're on the tips and tails, bouncing around, and it's pretty scary.

"When you stand at the top of Twice Is Nice and look down this 50-degree slope," continued Gerdin, "it looks like an elevator shaft. There is a severe dogleg in it, and you know you don't have a prayer if you fall because you'll bang into the rocks.

"I was nervous and shaking," he said, "feeling the adrenaline. I started the first turn, pulling up my tails so they wouldn't catch on the slope, turning my skis 180 degrees for each turn, looking down at the rocks. In my first turn, as I looked down, I suddenly realized, 'Holy smoke! I really can't screw up on this one!' You feel like that all the way down, until it's finished. Once is enough on Twice Is Nice."

After my first ignominious run down Tuckerman Ravine, I returned to Mount Washington and skied down the Headwall; this time, I beat the mountain. It is indeed sensational to force yourself over your skis, to see the bottom of the slope under your ski tips, to feel the wind and light and snow within as you effortlessly drop 20 or more feet from turn to turn. The rhythm builds up, time slows down. Here, there is fierce joy and freedom, an exultation that Vallençant puts so well:

"There is something better in us because of our feats in these mountains; we become more at peace with ourselves. There is a passion of denial, of struggle, that the mountain teaches us. I have the impression, after a descent, of dropping all restraints—my heart is open and free, my head is clear . . . all the beauty of the world is within the mad rhythm of my blood."

PART III
THE MAGICAL MOUNTAIN

". . . and then there was perfect cover on the lower trails and after an hour there was perfect cover everywhere, perhaps four inches that fanned like spume when we turned, a gift, an epiphany, an unaccountable improvement on our mastery of those snow-buried slopes and falls. Then we went up and down, up and down, our strength inexhaustible, our turns snug and accomplished. The clinicians would say that we were skiing down every slope of our lives back to the instant of our birth; and men of good will and common sense would claim that we were skiing in every possible direction toward some understanding of the triumph of our beginnings and our ends."

John Cheever, *Falconer*

Snow

by THOMAS MANN

Nobel Prize–winner Thomas Mann is best known for Death in Venice *and* The Magic Mountain: *the last, from which this selection, "Snow," is taken, is set with heady intellectual themes for which Mann is renowned. Hans Castorp, Mann's hero, has gone to spend a few weeks in a high-altitude sanitarium, a most widely used treatment—in those days—for tuberculosis. Castrop, intending to stay only a few weeks, remains there indefinitely, trapped by his fascination with the struggle between life and death in the highly civilized atmosphere of the sanitarium. In a gesture, prompted perhaps by his unconscious desire to escape to the "normal" world, Castrop learns to ski. He almost loses his life in a storm, and while waiting for it to subside, has his "dream of humanity," a paradox of paradise and brutality.*

D AILY, five times a day, the guests expressed unanimous dissatisfaction with the kind of winter they were having. They felt it was not what they had a right to expect of these altitudes. It failed to deliver the renowned meteorological specific in anything like the quantity indicated by the prospectus, quoted by old inhabitants, or anticipated by new. There was a very great failure in the supply of sunshine, an element so important in the cures achieved up here that without it they were dis-

tinctly retarded. And whatever Herr Settembrini might think of the sincerity of the patients' desire to finish their cure, leave "home" and return to the flatland, at any rate they insisted on their just dues. They wanted what they were entitled to, what their parents or husbands had paid for, and they grumbled unceasingly, at table, in lift, and in hall. The management showed a consciousness of what it owed them by installing a new apparatus for heliotherapy. They had two already, but these did not suffice for the demands of those who wished to get sunburnt by electricity—it was so becoming to the ladies, young and old, and made all the men, though confirmed horizontalers, look irresistibly athletic. And the ladies, even though aware of the mechanico-cosmetical origin of this conquering-hero air, were foolish enough to be carried away by it. There was Frau Schönfeld, a red-haired, red-eyed patient from Berlin. In the salon she looked thirstily at a long-legged, sunken-chested gallant, who described himself on his visiting card as *"Aviateur diplomé et Enseigne de la Marine allemande."* He was fitted out with the pneumothorax and wore "smoking" at the midday meal but not in the evening, saying this was their custom in the navy. "My God," breathed Frau Schönfeld at him, "what a tan this demon has—he gets it from the helio—it makes him look like a hunter of eagles!"

"Just wait, nixie!" he whispered in her ear, in the lift, "I'll make you pay for looking at me like that!" It made goose-flesh and shivers run over her. And along the balconies, past the glass partitions, the demon eagle-hunter found his way to the nixie.

But the artificial sun was far from making up for the lack of the real one. Two or three days of full sunshine in the month—it was not good enough, gorgeous though these were, with deep, deep velvety blue sky behind the white mountain summits, a glitter as of diamonds and a fine hot glow on the face and the back of the neck, when they dawned resplendent from the prevailing thick mantle of gray mist. Two or three such days in the course of weeks could not satisfy people whose lot might be said to justify extraordinary demands from the external world. They had made an inward compact, by the terms of which they resigned the common joys and sorrows proper to flatland humanity, and in exchange were made free of a life that was, to be sure, inactive, but on the other hand very lively and diverting, and carefree to the point of making one forget altogether the flight of time. Thus it was not much good for the Hofrat to tell them how favorably the Berghof compared with a Siberian mine or a penal settlement, nor to sing the praises of the atmosphere, so thin and light, well-nigh as rare as the empty universal ether, free of earthly admixture whether good or bad, and even without actual sunshine to be preferred to the rank vapors of the plain. Despite all he could say, the gloomy disaffection gained ground, threats of unlicensed departure were the order of the day, were even put into execution, without regard for the warning afforded by the melancholy return of Frau Salomon to the fold, now a "life member," her tedious but not serious case having taken that turn by reason of her self-willed visit to her wet and windy Amsterdam.

But if they had no sun, they had snow. Such masses of snow as Hans Castorp had never till now in all his life beheld. The previous winter had done fairly well in that respect, but it had been as nothing compared to this one. The snowfall was monstrous and immeasurable, it made one realize the extravagant, outlandish nature of the place. It snowed day in, day out, and all through the night. The few roads kept open were like tunnels, with towering walls of snow on either side, crystal and alabaster surfaces that were pleasant to look at, and on which the guests scribbled all sorts of messages, jokes and personalities. But even this path between walls was above the level of the pavement, and made of hard-packed snow, as one could tell by certain places where it gave way, and let one suddenly sink in up to the knee. One might, unless one were careful, break a leg. The benches had disappeared, except for the high back of one emerging here and there. In the town, the street level was so raised that the shops had become cellars, into which one descended by steps cut in the snow.

And on all these lying masses more snow fell, day in, day out. It fell silently, through air that was moderately cold, perhaps ten to fifteen degrees of frost. One did not feel the cold, it might have been much less, for the dryness and absence of wind deprived it of sting. The mornings were very dark, breakfast was taken by the light of the artificial moon that hung from the vaulted ceiling of the dining room, above the gay stenciled border. Outside was the reeking void, the world enwrapped in gray-white cotton-wool, packed to the windowpanes in snow and mist. No sight of the mountains; of the nearest evergreen now and again a glimpse through the fog, standing laden, and from time to time shaking free a bough of its heavy load, that flew into the air, and sent a cloud of white against the gray. At ten o'clock the sun, a wan wisp of light, came up behind its mountain, and gave the indistinguishable scene some shadowy hint of life, some sallow glimmer of reality; yet even so, it retained its delicate ghostliness, its lack of any definite line for the eye to follow. The contours of the peaks dissolved, disappeared, were dissipated in the mist, while the vision, led on from one pallidly gleaming slope of snow to another, lost itself in the void. Then a single cloud, like smoke, lighted up by the sun might spread out before a wall of rock and hang there for long, motionless.

At midday the sun would half break through, and show signs of banishing the mist.

In vain—yet a shred of blue would be visible, and suffice to make the scene, in its strangely falsified contours, sparkle marvelously far and wide. Usually, at this hour, the snowfall stopped, as though to have a look at what it had done; a like effect was produced by the rare days when the storm ceased, and the uninterrupted power of the sun sought to thaw away the pure and lovely surface from the new-fallen masses. The sight was at once fairylike and comic, an infantine fantasy. The thick light cushions plumped up on the boughs of trees, the humps and mounds of snow-covered rock-cropping or undergrowth, the droll, dwarfish, crouching disguise all ordinary objects wore, made of the scene a landscape in gnome-land, an illustration for a fairy tale. Such was the immediate view—wearisome to move in, quaintly, roguishly stimulating to the fancy. But when one looked across the intervening space, at the towering marble statuary of the high Alps in full snow, one felt a quite different emotion, and that was awe of their majestic sublimity.

Afternoons between three and four, Hans Castorp lay in his balcony box, well wrapped, his head against the cushion, not too high or too low, of his excellent chair, and looked out at forest and mountain over his thick-upholstered balustrade. The snow-laden firs, dark green to blackness, went marching up the sides of the valley, and beneath them the snow lay soft like down pillows. Above the tree line, the mountain walls reared themselves into the gray-white air: huge surfaces of snow, with softly veiled crests, and here and there a black jut of rock. The snow came silently down. The scene blurred more and more, it inclined the eye, gazing thus into woolly vacuity, to slumber. At the moment of slipping off one might give a start—yet what sleep could be purer than this in the icy air? It was dreamless. It was as free from the burden—even the unconscious burden—of organic life, as little aware of an effort to breathe this contentless, weightless, imperceptible air as is the breathless sleep of the dead. When Hans Castorp stirred again, the mountains would be wholly lost in a cloud of snow; only a pinnacle, a jutting rock, might show one instant, to be rapt away the next. It was absorbing to watch these ghostly pranks; one

needed to keep alert to follow the transmutations, the veiling and unveiling. One moment a great space of snow-covered rock would reveal itself, standing out bold and free, though of base or peak naught was to be seen. But if one ceased to fix one's gaze upon it, it was gone, in a breath.

Then there were storms so violent as to prevent one's sitting on the balcony for the driven snow which blew in, in such quantity as to cover floor and chair with a thick mantle. Yes, even in this sheltered valley it knew how to storm. The thin air would be in a hurly-burly, so whirling full of snow one could not see a hand's breadth before one's face. Gusts strong enough to take one's breath away flung the snow about, drew it up cyclone-fashion from the valley floor to the upper air, whisked it about in the maddest dance; no longer a snow storm, it was a blinding chaos, a white dark, a monstrous dereliction on the part of this inordinate and violent region; no living creature save the snow-bunting—which suddenly appeared in troops—could flourish in it.

And yet Hans Castorp loved this snowy world. He found it not unlike life at the seashore. The monotony of the scene was in both cases profound. The snow, so deep, so light, so dry and spotless, was the sand of down below. One was as clean as the other: you could shake the snow from boots and clothing, just as you could the fine-ground, dustless stone and shell, product of the sea's depth—neither left trace behind. And walking in the snow was as toilsome as on the dunes; unless, indeed, a crust had come upon it, by dint of thawing and freezing, when the going became easy and pleasant, like marching along the smooth, hard, wet, resilient strip of sand close to the edge of the sea.

But the storms and high-piled drifts of this year gave pedestrians small chance. They were favorable only for skiing. The snowplow, laboring its best, barely kept free the main street of the settlement and the most indispensable paths. Thus the few short feasible stretches were always crowded with other walkers, ill and well: the native, the permanent guest, and the hotel population; and these in their turn were bumped by the sleds as they swung and swerved down the slopes, steered by men and women who leaned

The snow buries the ice and rock of the Alps' risky terrain

far back as they came on, and shouted importunately, being obsessed by the importance of their occupation. Once at the bottom they would turn and trundle their toy sledges uphill again.

Hans Castorp was thoroughly sick of all the walks. He had two desires: one of them, the stronger, was to be alone with his thoughts and his stock-taking projects; and this his balcony assured to him. But the other, allied unto it, was a lively craving to come into close and freer touch with the mountains, the mountains in their snowy desolation; toward them he was irresistibly drawn. Yet how could he, all unprovided and foot bound as he was, hope to gratify such a desire? He had only to step beyond the end of the shoveled paths—an end soon reached upon any of them—to plunge breast-high in the snowy element.

Thus it was Hans Castorp, on a day in his second winter with those up here, resolved to buy himself skis and learn to walk on them, enough, that is, for his purposes. He was no sportsman, had never been physically inclined to sport; and did not behave as though he were, as did many guests of the cure, dressing up to suit the mode and the spirit of the place. Hermine Kleefeld, for instance, among other females, though she was constantly blue in the face from lack of breath, loved to appear at luncheon in tweed knickers, and loll about after the meal in a basket-chair in the hall, with her legs sprawled out. Hans Castorp knew that he would meet with a refusal were he to ask the Hofrat to countenance his plan. Sports activities were unconditionally forbidden at the Berghof as in all other establishments of the kind. This atmosphere, which one seemed to breathe in so effortlessly, was a severe strain on the heart, and as for Hans Castorp personally, his lively comment on his own state, that "the getting used to being up here consisted in getting used to not getting used," had continued in force. His fever, which Rhadamanthus ascribed to a moist spot, remained obstinate. Why else indeed should he be here? His desire, his present purpose was then clearly inconsistent and inadmissible. Yet we must be at the pains to understand him aright. He had no wish to imitate the fresh-air faddists

and smart pseudo-sportsmen, who would have been equally eager to sit all day and play cards in a stuffy room, if only that had been interdicted by authority. He felt himself a member of another and closer community than this small tourist world; a new and a broader point of view, a dignity and restraint set him apart and made him conscious that it would be unfitting for him to emulate their rough-and-tumble in the snow. He had no escapade in view, his plans were so moderate that Rhadamanthus himself, had he known, might well have approved them. But the rules stood in the way, and Hans Castorp resolved to act behind his back.

He took occasion to speak to Herr Settembrini of his plan—who for sheer joy could have embraced him. "*Si, si, si!* Do so, do so, engineer, do so with the blessing of God! Ask after nobody's leave, but simply do it! Ah, your good angel must have whispered you the thought! Do it straightway, before the impulse leaves you. I'll go along, I'll go to the shop with you, and together we will acquire the instruments of this happy inspiration. I would go with you even into the mountains, I would be by your side, on winged feet, like Mercury's—but that I may not. May not! If that were all, how soon would I do it! That I cannot is the truth, I am a broken man.—But you—it will do you no harm, none at all, if you are sensible and do nothing rash. Even—even if it did you harm—just a little harm—it will still have been your good angel roused you to it. I say no more. Ah, what an unsurpassable plan! Two years up here, and still capable of such projects—ah, yes, your heart is sound, no need to despair of you. Bravo, bravo! By all means pull the wool over the eyes of your Prince of Shadows! Buy the snowshoes, have them sent to me or Lukaçek, or the chandler below-stairs. You fetch them from here to go and practice, you go off on them—"

So it befell. Under Herr Settembrini's critical eye—he played the connoisseur, though innocent of sports—Hans Castorp acquired a pair of oaken skis, finished a light brown, with tapering, pointed ends and the best quality of straps. He bought the ironshod staff with the little wheel, as well, and was not content to have his purchases sent, but carried them on his shoulder to Settembrini's quarters, where he arranged with the grocer to take care of them for him. He had looked on enough at the sport to know the use of his tools; and choosing for his practice-ground an almost treeless slope not far behind the sanatorium, remote from the hubbub of the spot where other beginners learned the art, he began daily to make his first blundering attempts, watched by Herr Settembrini, who would stand at a little distance, leaning on his cane, with legs gracefully crossed, and greet his nursling's progress with applause. One day Hans Castorp, steering down the cleared drive toward the Dorf to take the skis back to the grocer's, ran into the Hofrat. Behrens never recognized him, though it was broad day, and our beginner had well-nigh collided with him. Shrouded in a haze of tobacco smoke, he stalked past regardless.

Hans Castorp found that one quickly gets readiness in an art where strong desire comes in play. He was not ambitious for expert skill, and all he needed he acquired in a few days, without undue strain on wind or muscles. He learned to keep his feet tidily together and make parallel tracks; to avail himself of his stick in getting off; he learned how to take obstacles, such as small elevations of the ground, with a slight soaring motion, arms outspread, rising and falling like a ship on a billowy sea; learned, after the twentieth trial, not to trip and roll over when he braked at full speed, with the right Telemark turn, one leg forward, the other bent at the knee. Gradually he widened the sphere of his activities. One day it came to pass that Herr Settembrini saw him vanish in the far white mist; the Italian shouted a warning through cupped hands, and turned homewards, his pedagogic soul well pleased.

It was beautiful here in these wintry heights: not mildly and ingratiatingly beautiful, more as the North Sea is beautiful in a westerly gale. There was no thunder of surf, a deathly stillness reigned, but roused similar feelings of awe. Hans Castorp's long, pliant soles carried him in all directions: along the left slope to Clavadel, on the right to Frauenkirch and Glaris, whence he could see the shadowy massif of the Amselfluh, ghostlike in the mist; into the Dischma valley, or up behind the Berghof in the direction of the wooded Seehorn, only the top of which, snow-covered, rose above the tree line, or the Drusatscha forest, with the pale outline of the Rhätikon looming behind it, smothered in snow. He took his skis and went up on the funicular to the Schatzalp; there, rapt six thousand feet above the sea, he reveled at will on the gleaming slopes of powdery snow—whence, in good weather, there was a view of majestic extent over all the surrounding territory.

He rejoiced in his new resource, before which all difficulties and hindrances to movement fell away. It gave him the utter solitude he craved, and filled his soul with impressions of the wild inhumanity, the precariousness of this region into which he had ventured. On his one hand he might have a precipitous, pine-clad declivity, falling away into the mists; on the other sheer rock might rise, with masses of snow, in monstrous, Cyclopean forms, all domed and vaulted, swelling or cavernous. He would halt for a moment, to quench the sound of his own movement, when the silence about him would be absolute, complete, a wadded soundlessness, as it were, elsewhere all unknown. There was no stir of air, not so much as might even lightly sway the tree boughs; there was not a rustle, nor the voice of a bird. It was primeval silence to which Hans Castorp hearkened, when he leaned thus on his staff, his head on one side, his mouth open. And always it snowed, snowed without pause, endlessly, gently, soundlessly falling.

No, this world of limitless silences had nothing hospitable; it received the visitor at his own risk, or rather it scarcely even received him, it tolerated his penetration into its fastnesses, in a manner that boded no good; it made him aware of the menace of the elemental, a menace not even hostile, but impersonally deadly. The child of civilization, remote from birth from wild nature and all her ways, is more susceptible to her grandeur than is her untutored son who has looked at her and lived close to her from childhood up, on terms of prosaic familiarity. The latter scarcely knows the religious awe with which the other regards her, that awe which conditions all his feeling for her, and is present, a constant, solemn thrill, in the profoundest depth of his soul. Hans Castorp, standing there in his puttees and long-sleeved camel's-hair waistcoat, on his *skis de luxe,* suddenly seemed to himself exceedingly presumptuous, to be thus listening to the primeval hush, the deathlike silence of these wintry fastnesses. He felt his breast lightened when, on his way home, the first chalets, the first abodes of human beings, loomed visible through the fog. Only then did he become aware that he had been for hours possessed by a secret awe and terror. On the island of Sylt he had stood by the edge of the thundering surf. In his white flannels, elegant, self-assured, but most respectful, he had stood there as one stands before a lion's cage and looks deep into the yawning jaws of the beast, lined with murderous fangs. He had bathed in the surf, and heeded the blast of the coast guard's horn, warning all and sundry not to venture rashly beyond the first line of billows, not to approach too nearly the oncoming tempest—the very last impulse of whose cataract, indeed, struck upon him like a blow from a lion's paw. From that experience our young man had learned the fearful pleasure of toying with forces so great that to approach them nearly is destruction. What he had not then felt was the temptation to come closer, to carry the thrilling contact with these deadly natural forces up to a point where the full embrace was imminent. Weak human being that he was—though tolerably well equipped with the weapons of civilization—what he at this moment knew was the fascination of venturing just so far into the monstrous unknown, or at least abstaining just so long from flight before it, that the adventure grazed the perilous, that it was just barely possible to put limits to it, before it became no longer a matter of toying with the foam and playfully dodging the ruthless paw—but the ultimate adventure, the billow, the lion's jaws, and the sea.

In a word, Hans Castorp was valorous up here—if by valor we mean not mere dull matter-of-factness in the face of nature, but conscious submission to her, the fear of death cast out by irresistible oneness. Yes, in his narrow, hyper-civilized breast, Hans Castorp cherished a feeling of kinship with the elements, connected with the new sense of superiority he had lately felt at sight of the silly people on their little sleds; it had made him feel that a profounder, more spacious, less luxurious solitude than that afforded by his balcony chair would be beyond all price. He had sat there and looked abroad, at those mist-wreathed summits, at the carnival of snow, and blushed to be gaping thus from the breastwork of material well-being. This motive, and no momentary fad—no, nor yet any native love of bodily exertion—was what impelled him to learn the use of skis. If it was uncanny up there in the magnificence of the mountains, in the deathly silence of the snows—and uncanny it assuredly was, to our son of civilization—this was equally true, that in these months and years he had already drunk deep of the uncanny, in spirit and in sense. Even a colloquy with Naphta and Settembrini was not precisely the canniest thing in the world, it too led one on into uncharted and perilous regions. So if we can speak of Hans Castorp's feeling of kinship with the wild powers of the winter heights, it is in this sense, that despite his pious awe he felt these scenes to be a fitting theater for the issue of his involved thoughts, a fitting stage for one to make who, scarcely knowing how, found it had devolved upon him to take stock of himself, in reference to the rank and status of the *Homo Dei.*

No one was here to blow a warning to the rash one—unless, indeed, Herr Settembrini, with his farewell shout at Hans Castorp's disappearing back, had been that man. But possessed by valorous desire, our youth had given the call no heed—as little as he had the steps behind him on a certain carnival night. *"Eh, Ingegnere, un po' di ragione, sa!"* "Yes, yes, pedagogic Satana, with your *ragione* and your *ribellione,"* he thought. "But I'm rather fond of you. You are a windbag and a hand-organ man, to be sure. But you mean well, you mean much better, and more to my mind, than that knife-edged little Jesuit and Terrorist, apologist of the Inquisition and the knout, with his round eyeglasses—though he is nearly always right when you and he come to grips over my paltry soul, like God and the Devil in the medieval legends."

He struggled, one day, powdered in snow to the waist, up a succession of snow-shrouded terraces, up and up, he knew not whither. Nowhither, perhaps; these upper regions blended with a sky no less misty white than they, and where the two came together, it was hard to tell. No summit, no ridge was visible, it was a haze and a nothing, toward which Hans Castorp strove; while behind him the world, the inhabited valley, fell away swiftly from view, and no sound mounted to his ears. In a twinkling he was as solitary, he was as lost as heart could wish, his loneliness was profound enough to awake the fear which is the first stage of valor. *"Praeterit figura huius mundi,"* he said to himself, quoting Naphta, in a Latin hardly humanistic in spirit. He stopped and looked about. On all sides there was nothing to see, beyond small single flakes of snow, which came out of a white sky and sank to rest on the white earth. The silence about him refused to say aught to his spirit. His gaze was lost in the blind white void, he felt his heart pulse from the effort of the climb—that muscular organ whose animallike shape and contracting motion he had watched, with a feeling of sacrilege, in the x-ray laboratory. A naïve reverence filled him for that organ of his, for the pulsating human heart, up here alone in the icy void, alone with its question and its riddle.

On he pressed; higher and higher toward the sky. Walking, he thrust the end of his stick in the snow and watched the blue light follow it out of the hole it made. That he liked; and stood for long at a time to test the little optical phenomenon. It was a strange, a subtle color, this greenish-blue; color of the heights and deeps, ice-clear, yet holding shadow in its depths, mysteriously exquisite. It reminded him of the color of certain eyes, whose shape and glance had spelled his destiny; eyes to which Herr Settembrini, from his humanistic height, had referred with contempt as "Tartar slits" and "wolf's eyes"—eyes seen long ago and then found again, the eyes of Pribislav Hippe and Clavdia Chauchat. "With pleasure," he said aloud, in the profound stillness. "But don't break it—*c'est à visser, tu sais.*" And his spirit heard behind him words of warning in a melliflu-

ous tongue.

A wood loomed, misty, far off to the right. He turned that way, to the end of having some goal before his eyes, instead of sheer white transcendence; and made toward it with a dash, not remarking an intervening depression of the ground. He could not have seen it, in fact; everything swam before his eyes in the white mist, obliterating all contours. When he perceived it, he gave himself to the decline, unable to measure its steepness with his eye.

The grove that had attracted him lay the other side of the gully into which he had unintentionally steered. The trough, covered with fluffy snow, fell away on the side next the mountains, as he observed when he pursued it a little distance. It went downhill, the steep sides grew higher, this fold of the earth's surface seemed like a narrow passage leading into the mountain. Then the points of his skis turned up again, there began an incline, soon there were no more side walls; Hans Castorp's trackless course ran once more uphill along the mountainside.

He saw the pine grove behind and below him, on his right, turned again toward it, and with a quick descent reached the laden trees; they stood in a wedge-shaped group, a vanguard thrust out from the mist-screened forests above. He rested beneath their boughs, and smoked a cigarette. The unnatural stillness, the monstrous solitude, still oppressed his spirit; yet he felt proud to have conquered them, brave in the pride of having measured to the height of surroundings such as these.

It was three in the afternoon. He had set out soon after luncheon, with the idea of cutting part of the long rest-cure, and tea as well, in order to be back before dark. He had brought some chocolate in his breeches pocket, and a small flask of wine; and told himself exultantly that he had still several hours to revel in all this grandeur.

The position of the sun was hard to recognize, veiled as it was in haze. Behind him, at the mouth of the valley, above that part of the mountains that was shut off from view, the clouds and mist seemed to thicken and move forward. They looked like snow—more snow—as though there were pressing demand for it! Like a good hard storm. Indeed, the little soundless flakes were coming down more quickly as he stood.

Hans Castorp put out his arm and let some of them come to rest on his sleeve; he viewed them with the knowing eye of the nature lover. They looked mere shapeless morsels; but he had more than once had their like under his good lens, and was aware of the exquisite precision of form displayed by these little jewels, insignia, orders, agraffes—no jeweler, however skilled, could do finer, more minute work. Yes, he thought, there was a difference, after all, between this light, soft, white powder he trod with his skis, that weighed down the trees, and covered the open spaces, a difference between it and the sand on the beaches at home, to which he had likened it. For this powder was not made of tiny grains of stone; but of myriads of tiniest drops of water, which in freezing had darted together in symmetrical variation—parts, then, of the same anorganic substance which was the source of protoplasm, of plant life, of the human body. And among these myriads of enchanting little stars, in their hidden splendor that was too small for man's naked eye to see, there was not one like unto another; an endless inventiveness governed the development and unthinkable differentiation of one and the same basic scheme, the equilateral, equiangled hexagon. Yet each, in itself—this was the uncanny, the anti-organic, the life-denying character of them all—each of them was absolutely symmetrical, icily regular in form. They were too regular, as substance adapted to life never was to this degree—the living principle shuddered at this perfect precision, found it deathly, the very marrow of death—Hans Castorp felt he understood now the reason why the builders of antiquity purposely and secretly introduced minute variation from absolute symmetry in their columnar structures.

He pushed off again, shuffling through the deep snow on his flexible runners, along the edge of the wood, down the slope, up again at random, to his heart's content, about and into this lifeless land. Its empty, rolling spaces, its dried vegetation of single dwarf firs sticking up through the snow, bore a striking resemblance to a scene on the dunes. Hans Castorp nodded as he stood and fixed the likeness in his mind. Even his burning face, his trembling limbs, the peculiar and half-intoxicated mingled sensations of excitement and fatigue were pleasurable, reminding him as they did of that familiar feeling induced by the sea air, which could sting one like whips, and yet was so laden with sleepy essences. He rejoiced in his freedom of motion, his feet were like wings. He was bound to no path, none lay behind him to take him back whence he had come. At first there had been posts, staves set up as guides through the snow—but he had soon cut free from their tutelage, which recalled the coast guard with his horn, and seemed inconsistent with the attitude he had taken up toward the wild.

He pressed on, turning right and left among rocky, snow-clad elevations, and came behind them on an incline, then a level spot, then on the mountains themselves—how alluring and accessible seemed their softly covered gorges and defiles! His blood leaped at the strong allurement of the distance and the height, the ever profounder solitude. At risk of a late return he pressed on, deeper into the wild silence, the monstrous and the menacing, despite that gathering darkness sinking down over the region like a veil, and heightening his inner apprehension until it presently passed into actual fear. It was this fear which first made him conscious that he had deliberately set out to lose his way and the direction in which valley and settlement lay—and had been as successful as heart could wish. Yet he knew that if he were to turn in his tracks and go downhill, he would reach the valley bottom—even if some distance from the Berghof—and that sooner than he had planned. He would come home too early, not have made full use of his time. On the other hand, if he were overtaken unawares by the storm, he would probably in any case not find his way home. But however genuine his fear of the elements, he refused to take premature flight; his being scarcely the sportsman's attitude, who only meddles with the elements so long as he knows himself their master, takes all precautions, and prudently yields when he must—whereas what went on in Hans Castorp's soul can only be described by the one word challenge. It was perhaps a blameworthy, presumptuous attitude, even united to such genuine awe. Yet this much is clear, to any human understanding: that when a young man has lived years long in the way this one had, something may gather—may accumulate, as our engineer might put it—in the depths of his soul, until one day it suddenly discharges itself, with a primitive exclamation of disgust, a mental "Oh, go to the devil!" a repudiation of all caution whatsoever, in short with a challenge. So on he went, in his seven-league slippers, glided down this slope too and pressed up the incline beyond, where stood a wooden hut that might be a hayrick or shepherd's shelter, its roof weighted with flat stones. On past this to the nearest mountain ridge, bristling with forest, behind whose back the giant peaks towered upward in the mist. The wall before him, studded with single groups of trees, was steep, but looked as though one might wind to the right and get round it by climbing a little way up the slope. Once on the other side, he could see what lay beyond. Accordingly Hans Castorp set out on this tour of investigation, which began by descending from the meadow with the hut into another and rather deep gully that dropped off from right to left.

He had just begun to mount again when the expected happened, and the storm burst, the storm that had threatened so long. Or may one say "threatened" of the action of blind, nonsentient forces, which have no purpose to destroy us—that would be comforting by comparison—but are merely horribly indifferent to our fate should we become involved with them? "Hullo!" Hans Castorp thought, and stood still, as the first blast whirled through the densely falling snow and caught him. "That's a gentle zephyr—tells you what's coming." And truly this wind was savage. The air was in reality frightfully cold, probably some degrees below zero; but so long as it remained dry and still one almost found it balmy. It was when a wind came up that the cold began to cut into the flesh; and in a wind like the one that blew now, of which that first gust had been a forerunner, the furs were not bought that could protect the limbs from its icy rigors. And Hans Castorp wore no fur, only a woolen waistcoat,

which he had found quite enough, or even, with the faintest gleam of sunshine, a burden. But the wind was at his back, a little sidewise; there was small inducement to turn and receive it in the face; so the mad youth, letting that fact reinforce the fundamental challenge of his attitude, pressed on among the single tree-trunks, and tried to outflank the mountain he had attacked.

It was no joke. There was almost nothing to be seen for swimming snowflakes, that seemed without falling to fill the air to suffocation by their whirling dance. The icy gusts made his ears burn painfully, his limbs felt half paralyzed, his hands were so numb he hardly knew if they held the staff. The snow blew inside his collar and melted down his back. It drifted on his shoulders and right side; he thought he should freeze as he stood into a snowman, with his staff stiff in his hands. And all this under relatively favoring circumstances; for let him turn his face to the storm and his situation would be still worse. Getting home would be no easy task—the harder, the longer he put it off.

At last he stopped, gave an angry shrug, and turned his skis the other way. Then the wind he faced took his breath on the spot, so that he was forced to go through the awkward process of turning round again to get it back, and collect his resolution to advance in the teeth of his ruthless foe. With bent head and cautious breathing he managed to get under way; but even thus forearmed, the slowness of his progress and the difficulty of seeing and breathing dismayed him. Every few minutes he had to stop, first to get his breath in the lee of the wind, and then because he saw next to nothing in the blinding whiteness, and moving as he did with head down, had to take care not to run against trees, or be flung headlong by unevennesses in the ground. Hosts of flakes flew into his face, melted there, and he anguished with the cold of them. They flew into his mouth, and died away with a weak, watery taste; flew against his eyelids so that he winked, overflowed his eyes and made seeing as difficult as it was now almost impossible for other reasons: namely, the dazzling effect of all that whiteness, and the veiling of his field of vision, so that his sense of sight was almost put out of action. It was nothingness, white, whirling nothingness, into which he looked when he forced himself to do so. Only at intervals did ghostly-seeming forms from the world of reality loom up before him: a stunted fir, a group of pines, even the pale silhouette of the hay-hut he had lately passed.

He left it behind, and sought his way back over the slope on which it stood. But there was no path. To keep direction, relatively speaking, into his own valley would be a question far more of luck than management; for while he could see his hand before his face, he could not see the ends of his skis. And even with better visibility, the host of difficulties must have combined to hinder his progress: the snow in his face, his adversary the storm, which hampered his breathing, made him fight both to take a breath and to exhale it, and constantly forced him to turn his head away to gasp. How could anyone—either Hans Castorp or another and much stronger than he—make head? He stopped, he blinked his lashes free of water drops, knocked off the snow that like a coat of mail was sheathing his body in front—and it struck him that progress, under the circumstances, was more than anyone could expect.

And yet Hans Castorp did progress. That is to say, he moved on. But whether in the right direction, whether it might not have been better to stand still, remained to be seen. Theoretically the chances were against it; and in practice he soon began to suspect something was wrong. This was not familiar ground beneath his feet, not the easy slope he had gained on mounting with such difficulty from the ravine, which had of course to be retraversed. The level distance was too short, he was already mounting again. It was plain that the storm, which came from the southwest, from the mouth of the valley, had with its violence driven him from his course. He had been exhausting himself, all this time, with a false start. Blindly, enveloped in white, whirling night, he labored deeper and deeper into this grim and callous sphere.

"No, you don't," said he, suddenly, between his teeth, and halted. The words were not emotional, yet he felt for a second as though his heart had been clutched by an icy hand; it winced, and then knocked rapidly against his ribs, as it had the time Rhadamanthus found the moist cavity. Pathos in the grand manner was not in place, he knew, in one who had chosen defiance as his role, and was indebted to himself alone for all his present plight. "Not bad," he said, and discovered that his facial muscles were not his to command, that he could not express in his face any of his soul's emotions, for that it was stiff with cold. "What next? Down this slope; follow your nose home, I suppose, and keep your face to the wind—though that is a good deal easier said than done," he went on, panting with his efforts, yet actually speaking half aloud, as he tried to move on again: "but something has to happen, I can't sit down and wait, I should simply be buried in six-sided crystalline symmetricality, and Settembrini, when he came with his little horn to find me, would see me squatting here with a snow-cap over one ear." He realized that he was talking to himself, and not too sensibly—for which he took himself to task, and then continued on purpose, though his lips were so stiff he could not shape the labials, and so did without them, as he had on a certain other occasion that came to his mind. "Keep quiet, and get along with you out of here," he admonished himself, adding: "You seem to be wool-gathering, not quite right in your head, and that looks bad for you."

But this he only said with his reason—to some extent detached from the rest of him, though after all nearly concerned. As for his natural part, it felt only too much inclined to yield to the confusion which laid hold upon him with his growing fatigue. He even remarked this tendency and took thought to comment upon it. "Here," said he, "we have the typical reaction of a man who loses himself in the mountains in a snow storm and never finds his way home." He gasped out other fragments of the same thought as he went, though he avoided giving it more specific expression. "Whoever hears about it afterwards, imagines it as horrible; but he forgets that disease—and the state I am in is, in a way of speaking, disease—so adjusts its man that it and he can come to terms; there are sensory appeasements, short circuits, a merciful narcosis—yes, oh yes, yes. But one must fight against them, after all, for they are two-faced, they are in the highest degree equivocal, everything depends upon the point of view. If you are not meant to get home, they are a benefaction, they are merciful; but if you mean to get home, they become sinister. I believe I still do. Certainly I don't intend—in this heart of mine so stormily beating it doesn't appeal to me in the least—to let myself be snowed under by this idiotically symmetrical crystallometry."

In truth, he was already affected, and his struggle against oncoming sensory confusion was feverish and abnormal. He should have been more alarmed on discovering that he had already declined from the level course—this time apparently on the other slope. For he had pushed off with the wind coming slantwise at him, which was ill-advised, though more convenient for the moment. "Never mind," he thought, "I'll get my direction again down below." Which he did, or thought he did—or, truth to tell, scarcely even thought so; worst of all, began to be indifferent whether he had done or no. Such was the effect of an insidious double attack, which he but weakly combated. Fatigue and excitement combined were a familiar state to our young man—whose acclimatization, as we know, still consisted in getting used to not getting used; and both fatigue and excitement were now present in such strength as to make impossible any thought of asserting his reason against them. He felt as often after a colloquy with Settembrini and Naphta, only to a far greater degree: dazed and tipsy, giddy, a-tremble with excitement. This was probably why he began to color his lack of resistance to the stealing narcosis with half-maudlin references to the latest-aired complex of theories. Despite his scornful repudiation of the idea that he might lie down and be covered up with hexagonal symmetricality, something within him maundered on, sense or no sense; told him that the feeling of duty which bade him fight against insidious sensory appeasements was a purely ethical reaction, representing the sordid bourgeois view of life, irreligion, Phlistinism; while the desire, nay, craving, to lie down and rest, whispered him in the guise of a comparison between this storm and a sandstorm on the desert,

before which the Arab flings himself down then draws his burnous over hid head. Only his lack of a burnous, the unfeasibility of drawing his woolen waistcoat over his head, prevented him from following suit—this although he was no longer a child, and pretty well aware of the conditions under which a man freezes to death.

There had been a rather steep declivity, then level ground, then again an ascent, a stiff one. This was not necessarily wrong; one must of course, on the way to the valley, traverse rising ground at times. The wind had turned capriciously round, for it was now at Hans Castorp's back, and that, taken by itself, was a blessing. Owing, perhaps, to the storm, or the soft whiteness of the incline before him, dim in the whirling air, drawing him toward it, he bent as he walked. Only a little further—supposing one were to give way to the temptation, and his temptation was great; it was so strong that it quite lived up to the many descriptions he had read of the "typical danger-state." It asserted itself, it refused to be classified with the general order of things, it insisted on being an exception, its very exigence challenged comparison—yet at the same time it never disguised its origin or aura, never denied that it was, so to speak, garbed in Spanish black, with snow-white, fluted ruff, and stood for ideas and fundamental conceptions that were characteristically gloomy, strongly Jesuitical and anti-human, for the rack-and-knout discipline which was the particular horror of Herr Settembrini, though he never opposed it without making himself ridiculous, like a hand-organ man for ever grinding out *ragione* to the same old tune.

And yet Hans Castorp did hold himself upright and resist his craving to lie down. He could see nothing, but he struggled, he came forward. Whether to the purpose or not, he could not tell; but he did his part, and moved on despite the weight the cold more and more laid upon his limbs. The present slope was too steep to ascend directly, so he slanted a little, and went on thus a while without much heed whither. Even to lift his stiffened lids to peer before him was so great and so nearly useless an effort as to offer him small incentive. He merely caught glimpses: here clumps of pines that merged together; there a ditch or stream, a black line marked out between overhanging banks of snow. Now, for a change, he was going downhill, with the wind in his face, when, at some distance before him, and seeming to hang in the driving wind and mist, he saw the faint outline of a human habitation.

Ah, sweet and blessed sight! Verily he had done well, to march stoutly on despite all obstacles, until now human dwellings appeared, a sign that the inhabited valley was at hand. Perhaps there were even human beings, perhaps he might enter and abide the end of the storm under shelter, then get directions, or a guide if the dark should have fallen. He held toward this chimerical goal, that often quite vanished in mist, and took an exhausting climb against the wind before it was reached; finally drew near it—to discover, with what staggering astonishment and horror may be imagined, that it was only the hay-hut with the weighted roof, to which, after all his striving, by all his devious paths, he had come back.

That was the very devil. Hans Castorp gave vent to several heartfelt curses—of which his lips were too stiff to pronounce the labials. He examined the hut, to get his bearings, and came to the conclusion that he had approached it from the same direction as before—namely, from the rear; and therefore, what he had accomplished for the past hour—as he reckoned it—had been sheer waste of time and effort. But there it was, just as the books said. You went in a circle, gave yourself endless trouble under the delusion that you were accomplishing something, and all the time you were simply describing some great silly arc that would turn back to where it had its beginning, like the riddling year itself. You wandered about, without getting home. Hans Castorp recognized the traditional phenomenon with a certain grim satisfaction—and even slapped his thigh in astonishment at this punctual general law fulfilling itself in his particular case.

The lonely hut was barred, the door locked fast, no entrance possible. But Hans Castorp decided to stop for the present. The projecting roof gave the illusion of shelter, and the hut itself, on the side turned toward the mountains,

afforded, he found, some little protection against the storm. He leaned his shoulder against the rough-hewn timber, since his long skis prevented him from leaning his back. And so he stood, obliquely to the wall, having thrust his staff in the snow; hands in pockets, his collar turned up as high as it would go, bracing himself on his outside leg, and leaning his dizzy head against the wood, his eyes closed, but opening them every now and then to look down his shoulder and across the gully to where the high mountain wall palely appeared and disappeared in mist.

His situation was comparatively comfortable. "I can stick it like this all night, if I have to," he thought, "if I change legs from time to time, lie on the other side, so to speak, and move about a bit between whiles, as of course I must. I'm rather stiff, naturally, but the effort I made has accumulated some inner warmth, so after all it was not quite in vain, that I have come round all this way. Come round—not coming round—that's the regular expression they use, of people drowned or frozen to death.—I suppose I used it because I am not quite so clear in the head as I might be. But it is a good thing I can stick it out here; for this frantic nuisance of a snow storm can carry on until morning without a qualm, and if it only keeps up until dark it will be quite bad enough, for in the dark the danger of going round and round and *not* coming round is as great as in a storm. It must be toward evening already, about six o'clock, I should say, after all the time I wasted on my circular tour. Let's see, how late is it?" He felt for his watch; his numbed fingers could scarcely find and draw it from his pocket. Here it was, his gold hunting-watch, with his monogram on the lid, ticking faithfully away in this lonely waste, like Hans Castorp's own heart, that touching human heart that beat in the organic warmth of his interior man.

It was half past four. But deuce take it, it had been nearly as much before the storm burst. Was it possible his whole bewildered circuit had lasted scarcely a quarter of an hour? " 'Coming round' makes time seem long," he noted. "And when you *don't* come round'—does it seem longer? But the fact remains that at five or half past it will be regularly dark. Will the storm hold up in time to keep me from running in circles again? Suppose I take a sip of port—it might strengthen me.''

He had brought with him a bottle of that amateurish drink, simply because it was always kept ready in flat bottles at the Berghof, for excursions—though not, of course, excursions like this unlawful escapade. It was not meant for people who went out in the snow and got lost and night-bound in the mountains. Had his senses been less befogged, he must have said to himself that if he were bent on getting home, it was almost the worst thing he could have done. He did say so, after he had drunk several swallows, for they took effect at once, and it was an effect much like that of the Kulmbacher beer on the evening of his arrival at the Berghof, when he had angered Settembrini by his ungoverned prattle anent fish-sauces and the like—Herr Ludovico, the pedagogue, the same who held madmen to their senses when they would give themselves rein. Hans Castorp heard through thin air the mellifluous sound of his horn; the orator and schoolmaster was nearing by forced marches, to rescue his troublesome nursling, life's delicate child, from his present desperate pass and lead him home.—All which was of course sheer rubbish, due to the Kulmbacher he had so foolishly drunk. For of course Herr Settembrini had no horn, how could he have? He had a hand-organ, propped by a sort of wooden leg against the pavement, and as he played a sprightly air, he flung his humanistic eyes up to the people in the houses. And furthermore he knew nothing whatever of what had happened, as he no longer lived in House Berghof, but with Luckaçek the tailor, in his little attic room with the water-bottle, above Naphta's silken cell. Moreover, he would have no right nor reason to interfere—no more than upon that carnival night on which Hans Castorp had found himself in a position quite as mad and bad as this one, when he gave the ailing Clavdia Chauchat back *son crayon*—his, Pribislav Hippe's, pencil. What position was that? What position could it be but the horizontal, literally and not metaphorically the position of all long-termers up here? Was not he himself used to lie

long hours out of doors, in snow and frost, by night as well as day? And he was making ready to sink down when the idea seized him, took him as it were by the collar and fetched him up standing, that all this nonsense he was uttering was still inspired by the Kulmbacher beer and the impersonal, quite typical and traditional longing to lie down and sleep, of which he had always heard, and which would by quibbling and sophistry now betray him.

"That was the wrong way to go to work," he acknowledged to himself. "The port was not at all the right thing; just the few sips of it have made my head so heavy I cannot hold it up, and my thoughts are all just confused, stupid quibbling with words. I can't depend on them—not only the first thought that comes into my head, but even the second one, the correction which my reason tries to make upon the first—more's the pity. *'Son crayon!'* That means her pencil, not his pencil, in this case; you only say *son* because *crayon* is masculine. The rest is just a pretty feeble play on words. Imagine stopping to talk about that when there is a much more important fact; namely, that my left leg, which I am using as a support, reminds me of the wooden leg on Settembrini's hand-organ, that he keeps jolting over the pavement with his knee, to get up close to the window and hold out his velvet hat for the girl up there to throw something into. And at the same time, I seem to be pulled, as though with hands, to lie down in the snow. The only thing to do is to move about. I must pay for the Kulmbacher, and limber up my wooden leg.''

He pushed himself away from the wall with his shoulder. But one single pace forward, and the wind sliced at him like a scythe, and drove him back to the shelter of the wall. It was unquestionably the position indicated for the time; he might change it by turning his left shoulder to the wall and propping himself on the right leg, with sundry shakings of the left, to restore the circulation as much as might be. "Who leaves the house in weather like this?" he said. "Moderate activity is all right; but not too much craving for adventure, no coying with the bride of the storm. Quiet, quiet—if the head be heavy, let it droop. The wall is good, a certain warmth seems to come from the logs—probably the feeling is entirely subjective.—Ah, the trees, the trees! Oh, living climate of the living—how sweet it smells!"

It was a park. It lay beneath the terrace on which he seemed to stand—a spreading park of luxuriant green shade-trees, elms, planes, beeches, birches, oaks, all in the dappled light and shade of their fresh, full, shimmering foliage, and gently rustling tips. They breathed a deliciously moist, balsamic breath into the air. A warm shower passed over them, but the rain was sunlit. One could see high up in the sky the whole air filled with the bright ripple of raindrops. How lovely it was! Oh, breath of the homeland, oh, fragrance and abundance of the plain, so long foregone! The air was full of bird song—dainty, sweet, blithe fluting, piping, twittering, cooing, trilling, warbling, though not a single little creature could be seen. Hans Castorp smiled, breathing gratitude. But still more beauties were preparing. A rainbow flung its arc slanting across the scene, most bright and perfect, a sheer delight, all its rich glossy, banded colors moistly shimmering down into the thick, lustrous green. It was like music, like the sound of harps commingled with flutes and violins. The blue and the violet were transcendent. And they descended and magically blended, were transmuted and re-unfolded more lovely than before. Once, some years earlier, our young Hans Castorp had been privileged to hear a world-famous Italian tenor, from whose throat had gushed a glorious stream to witch the world with gracious art. The singer took a high note, exquisitely; then held it, while the passionate harmony swelled, unfolded, glowed from moment to moment with new radiance. Unsuspected veils dropped from before it one by one; the last one sank away, revealing what must surely be the ultimate tonal purity—yet no, for still another fell, and then a well-nigh incredible third and last, shaking into the air such an extravagance of tear-glistening splendor, that confused murmurs of protest rose from the audience, as though it could bear no more; and our young friend found that he was sobbing.—So now with the scene before him, constantly transformed and transfig-

ured as it was before his eyes. The bright, rainy veil fell away; behind it stretched the sea, a southern sea of deep, deepest blue shot with silver lights, and a beautiful bay, on one side mistily open, on the other enclosed by mountains whose outline paled away into blue space. In the middle distance lay islands, where palms rose tall and small white houses gleamed among cypress groves. Ah, it was all too much, too blest for sinful mortals, that glory of light, that deep purity of the sky, that sunny freshness on the water! Such a scene Hans Castorp had never beheld, nor anything like it. On his holidays he had barely sipped at the south, the sea for him meant the colorless, tempestuous northern tides, to which he clung with inarticulate, childish love. Of the Mediterranean, Naples, Sicily, he knew nothing. And yet—he *remembered*. Yes, strangely enough, that was recognition which so moved him. "Yes, yes, it's very image," he was crying out, as though in his heart he had always cherished a picture of this spacious, sunny bliss. Always—and that always went far, far, unthinkably far back, as far as the open sea there on the left where it ran out to the violet sky bent down to meet it.

The sky-line was high, the distance seemed to mount to Hans Castorp's view, looking down as he did from his elevation onto the spreading gulf beneath. The mountains held it embraced, their tree-clad foothills running down to the sea; they reached in half-circle from the middle distance to the point where he sat, and beyond. This was a mountainous littoral, at one point of which he was crouching upon a sun-warmed stone terrace, while before him the ground, descending among undergrowth, by moss-covered rocky steps, ran down to a level shore, where the reedy shingle formed little blue-dyed bays, minute archipelagoes and harbors. And all the sunny region, these open coastal heights and laughing rocky basins, even the sea itself out to the islands, where boats plied to and fro, was peopled far and wide. On every hand human beings, children of sun and sea, were stirring or sitting. Beautiful young human creatures, so blithe, so good and gay, so pleasing to see—at sight of them Hans Castorp's whole heart opened in a responsive love, keen almost to pain.

Youths were at work with horses, running hand on halter alongside their whinnying, head-tossing charges; pulling the refractory ones on a long rein, or else, seated bareback, striking the flanks of their mounts with naked heels, to drive them into the sea. The muscles of the riders' backs played beneath the sun-bronzed skin, and their voices were enchanting beyond words as they shouted to each other or to their steeds. A little bay ran deep into the coastline, mirroring the shore as does a mountain lake; about it girls were dancing. One of them sat with her back toward him, so that her neck, and the hair drawn to a knot above it smote him with loveliness. She sat with her feet in a depression of the rock, and played on a shepherd's pipe, her eyes roving above the stops to her companions, as in long, wide garments, smiling, with outstretched arms, alone, or in pairs swaying gently toward each other, they moved in the paces of the dance. Behind the flute player—she too was white-clad, and her back was long and slender, laterally rounded by the movement of her arms—other maidens were sitting, or standing entwined to watch the dance, and quietly talking. Beyond them still, young men were practicing archery. Lovely and pleasant it was to see the older ones show the younger, curly-locked novices how to span the bow and take aim; draw with them, and laughing, support them staggering back from the push of the arrow as it leaped from the bow. Others were fishing, lying prone on a jut of rock, waggling one leg in the air, holding the line out over the water, approaching their heads in talk. Others sat straining forward to fling the bait far out. A ship, with mast and yards, lying high out of the tide, was being eased, shoved, and stead-ied into the sea. Children played and exulted among the breaking waves. A young female, lying outstretched, drawing with one hand her flowered robe high between her breasts, reached with the other in the air after a twig bearing fruit and leaves, which a second, a slender-hipped creature, erect at her head, was playfully with-holding. Young folks were sitting in nooks of the rocks, or hesitating at the water's edge, with crossed arms clutching either shoulder, as they tested the chill with their toes. Pairs strolled along the beach, close and confiding, at the maiden's ear the lips of the youth. Shaggy-haired goats leaped from ledge to ledge of the rocks, while the young goatherder, wearing perched on his brown curls a little hat with the brim turned up behind, stood watching them from a height, one hand on his hip, the other holding the long staff on which he leaned.

"Oh, lovely, lovely," Hans Castorp breathed. "How joyous and winning they are, how fresh and healthy, happy and clever they look! It is not alone the outward form, they seem to be wise and gentle through and through. That is what makes me in love with them, the spirit that speaks out of them, the sense, I might almost say, in which they live and play together." By which he meant the friendliness, the mutual courteous re-gard these children of the sun showed to each other, a calm, reciprocal reverence veiled in smiles, manifested almost imperceptibly, and yet possessing them all by the power of sense associ-ation and ingrained idea. A dignity, even a gravity, was held, as it were, in solution in their lightest mood, perceptible only as an ineffable spiritual influence, a high seriousness without austerity, a reasoned goodness conditioning every act. All this, indeed, was not without its ceremonial side. A young mother, in a brown robe loose at the shoulder, sat on a rounded mossy stone and suckled her child, saluted by all who passed with a characteristic gesture which seemed to comprehend all that lay implicit in their general bearing. The young men, as they approached, lightly and formally crossed their arms on their breasts, and smilingly bowed; the maidens shaped the suggestion of a curtsy, as the worshipper does when he passes the high altar, at the same time nodding repeatedly, blithely and heartily. This mixture of formal homage with lively friendliness, and the slow, mild mien of the mother as well, where she sat pressing her breast with her forefinger to ease the flow of milk to her babe, glancing up from it to acknowledge with a smile the reverence paid her—this sight thrilled Hans Castorp's heart with something very close akin to ecstasy. He could not get his fill of looking, yet asked himself in concern whether he had a right, whether it was not perhaps punishable, for him, an outsider, to be a party to the sunshine and gracious loveliness of all these happy folk. He felt common, clumsy-booted. It seemed unscrupulous.

A lovely boy, with full hair drawn sideways across his brow and falling on his temples, sat directly beneath him, apart from his companions, with arms folded on his breast—not sadly, not ill-naturedly, quite tranquilly on one side. This lad looked up, turned his gaze upward and looked at him, Hans Castorp, and his eyes went between the watcher and the scenes upon the strand, watching his watching, to and fro. But suddenly he looked past Hans Castorp into space, and that smile, common to them all, of polite and brotherly regard, disappeared in a moment from his lovely, purely cut, half-childish face. His brows did not darken, but in his gaze there came a solemnity that looked as though carved out of stone, inexpressive, unfathomable, a deathlike reserve, which gave the scarcely reassured Hans Castorp a thorough fright, not unaccompanied by a vague apprehension of its meaning.

He too looked in the same direction. Behind him rose towering columns, built of cylindrical blocks without bases, in the joinings of which moss had grown. They formed the façade of a temple gate, on whose foundations he was sitting, at the top of a double flight of steps with space between. Heavy of heart he rose, and, descending the stair on one side, passed through the high gate below, and along a flagged street, which soon brought him before other propylaea. He passed through these as well, and now stood facing the temple that lay before him, massy, weathered to a gray-green tone, on a foundation reached by a steep flight of steps. The broad brow of the temple rested on the capitals of powerful, almost stunted columns, tapering toward the top—sometimes a fluted block had been shoved out of line and projected a little in profile. Painfully, helping himself on with his hands, and sighing for the growing oppression of his heart, Hans Castorp mounted the high steps and gained the grove of columns. It was very deep, he moved in it as among the trunks in a forest of

beeches by the pale northern sea. He purposely avoided the center, yet for all that slanted back again, and presently stood before a group of statuary, two female figures carved in stone, on a high base: mother and daughter, it seemed; one of them sitting, older than the other, more dignified, right goddesslike and mild, yet with mourning brows above the lightless empty eye-sockets; clad in a flowing tunic and a mantle of many folds, her matronly brow with its waves of hair covered with a veil. The other figure stood in the protecting embrace of the first, with round, youthful face, and arms and hands wound and hidden in the folds of the mantle.

Hans Castorp stood looking at the group, and from some dark cause his laden heart grew heavier still, and more oppressed with its weight of dread and anguish. Scarcely daring to venture, but following an inner compulsion, he passed behind the statuary, and through the double row of columns beyond. The bronze door of the sanctuary stood open, and the poor soul's knees all but gave way beneath him at the sight within. Two gray old women, witchlike, with hanging breasts and dugs of finger-length, were busy there, between flaming braziers, most horribly. They were dismembering a child. In dreadful silence they tore it apart with their bare hands—Hans Castorp saw the bright hair blood-smeared—and cracked the tender bones between their jaws, their dreadful lips dripped blood. An icy coldness held him. He would have covered his eyes and fled, but could not. They at their gory business had already seen him, they shook their reeking fists and uttered curses—soundlessly, most vilely, with the last obscenity, and in the dialect of Hans Castorp's native Hamburg. It made him sick, sick as never before. He tried desperately to escape; knocked into a column with his shoulder—and found himself, with the sound of that dreadful whispered brawling still in his ears, still wrapped in the cold horror of it, lying by his hut, in the snow, leaning against one arm, with his head upon it, his legs in their skis stretched out before him.

It was no true awakening. He blinked his relief at being free from those execrable hags, but was not very clear, nor even greatly concerned, whether this was a hay-hut, or the column of a temple, against which he lay; and after a fashion continued to dream, no longer in pictures, but in thoughts hardly less involved and fantastic.

"I felt it was a dream, all along," he rambled. "A lovely and horrible dream. I knew all the time that I was making it myself—the park with the trees, the delicious moisture in the air, and all the rest, both dreadful and dear. In a way, I knew it all beforehand. But how is it a man can know all that and call it up to bring him bliss and terror both at once? Where did I get the beautiful bay with the islands, where the temple precincts, whither the eyes of that charming boy pointed me, as he stood there alone? Now I know that it is not out of our single souls we dream. We dream anonymously and communally, if each after his fashion. The great soul of which we are a part may dream through us, in our manner of dreaming, its own secret dreams, of its youth, its hope, its joy and peace—and its blood-sacrifice. Here I lie at my column and still feel in my body the actual remnant of my dream—the icy horror of the human sacrifice, but also the joy that had filled my heart to its very depths, born of the happiness and brave bearing of those human creatures in white. It is meet and proper, I hereby declare that I have a prescriptive right to lie here and dream these dreams. For in my life up here I have known reason and recklessness. I have wandered lost with Settembrini and Naphta in high and mortal places. I know all of man. I have known mankind's flesh and blood. I gave back to the ailing Clavdia Chauchat Pribislav Hippe's lead pencil. But he who knows the body, life, knows death. And that is not all; it is, pedagogically speaking, only the beginning. One must have the other half of the story, the other side. For all interest in disease and death is only another expression of interest in life, as is proven by the humanistic faculty of medicine, that addresses life and its ails always so politely in Latin, and is only a division of the great and pressing concern which, in all sympathy, I now name by its name: the human being, the delicate child of life, man, his state and standing in the universe, I understand no little about him, I have learned much from 'those up here,' I have been driven up from the valley, so that the breath almost left my poor body. Yet now from the base of my column I have no meager view. I have dreamed of man's state, of his courteous and enlightened social state; behind which, in the temple, the horrible blood-sacrifice was consummated. Were they, those children of the sun, so sweetly courteous to each other, in silent recognition of that horror? It would be a fine and right conclusion they drew. I will hold to them, in my soul, I will hold with them and not with Naphta, neither with Settembrini. They are both talkers; the one luxurious and spiteful, the other forever blowing on his penny pipe of reason, even vainly imagining he can bring the mad to their senses. It is all Philistinism and morality, most certainly it is irreligious. Nor am I for little Naphta either, or his religion, that is only a *guazzabuglio* of God and the Devil, good and evil, to the end that the individual soul shall plump into it head first, for the sake of mystic immersion in the universal. Pedagogues both! Their quarrels and counter-positions are just a *guazzabuglio* too, and a confused noise of battle, which need trouble nobody who keeps a little clear in his head and pious in his heart. Their aristocratic question! Disease, health! Spirit, nature! Are those contradictions? I ask, are they problems? No, they are no problems, neither is the problem of their aristocracy. The recklessness of death is in life, it would not be life without it—and in the center is the position of the *Homo Dei*, between recklessness and reason, as his state is between mystic community and windy individualism. I, from my column, perceive all this. In this state he must live gallantly, associate in friendly reverence with himself, for only he is aristocratic, and the counter-positions are not at all. Man is the lord of counter-positions, they can be only through him, and thus he is more aristocratic than they. More so than death, too aristocratic for death—that is the freedom of his mind. More aristocratic than life, too aristocratic for life, and that is the piety in his heart. There is both rhyme and reason in what I say, I have made a dream poem of humanity. I will cling to it. I will be good. I will let death have no mastery over my thoughts. For therein lies goodness and love of humankind, and in nothing else. Death is a great power. One takes off one's hat before him, and goes weavingly on tiptoe. He wears the stately ruff of the departed and we do him honor in solemn black. Reason stands simple before him, for reason is only virtue, while death is release, immensity, abandon, desire. Desire, says my dream. Lust, not love. Death and love—no, I cannot make a poem of them, they don't go together. Love stands opposed to death. It is love, not reason, that is stronger than death. Only love, not reason, gives sweet thoughts. And from love and sweetness alone can form come: form and civilization, friendly, enlightened, beautiful human intercourse—always in silent recognition of the blood-sacrifice. Ah, yes, it is well and truly dreamed. I have taken stock. I will remember. I will keep faith with death in my heart, yet well remember that faith with death and the dead is evil, is hostile to humankind, so soon as we give it power over thought and action. *For the sake of goodness and love, man shall let death have no sovereignty over his thoughts,*—and with this—I awake. For I have dreamed it out to the end, I have come to my goal. Long, long have I sought after this word, in the place where Hippe appeared to me, in my loggia, everywhere. Deep into the snow mountains my search has led me. Now I have it fast. My dream has given it me, in utter clearness, that I may know it forever. Yes, I am in simple raptures, my body is warm, my heart beats high and knows why. It beats not solely on physical grounds, as fingernails grow on a corpse; but humanly, on grounds of my joyful spirits. My dream word was a draught, better than port or ale, it streams through my veins like love and life, I tear myself from my dream and sleep, knowing as I do, perfectly well, that they are highly dangerous to my young life. Up, up! Open your eyes! These are your limbs, your legs here in the snow! Pull yourself together, and up! Look—fair weather!''

The bonds held fast that kept his limbs involved. He had a hard struggle to free himself—but the inner compulsion proved stronger. With a jerk he raised himself on his elbows, briskly drew up his knees, shoved, rolled, wrestled to his feet; stamped with his skis in the snow, flung his arms about his ribs and worked his shoulders violently, all the while casting strained, alert glances about him and above, where now a pale blue sky showed itself between gray-bluish clouds, and these presently drew away to discover a thin sickle of a moon. Early twilight reigned: no snowfall, no storm. The wall of the opposite mountain with its shaggy, tree-clad ridge stretched out before him plain and peaceful. Shadow lay on half its height, but the upper half was bathed in palest rosy light. How were things in the world? Was it morning? Had he, despite what the books said, lain all night in the snow and not frozen? Not a member was frostbitten, nothing snapped when he stamped, shook and struck himself, as he did vigorously, all the time seeking to establish the facts of his situation. Ears, toes, fingertips, were of course numb, but not more so than they had often been at night in his loggia. He could take his watch from his pocket—it was still going, it had not stopped, as it did if he forgot to wind it. It said not yet five—it was in fact considerably earlier, twelve, thirteen minutes. Preposterous! Could it be he had lain here in the snow only ten minutes or so, while all these scenes of horror and delight and those presumptuous thoughts had spun themselves in his brain, and the hexagonal hurly vanished as it came? If that were true, then he must be grateful for his good fortune; that is, from the point of view of a safe homecoming. For twice such a turn had come, in his dream and fantasy, as had made him start up—once from horror, and again for rapture. It seemed, indeed, that life meant well by her lone-wandering delicate child.

Be all that as it might, and whether it was morning or afternoon—there could in fact be no doubt that it was still late afternoon—in any case, there was nothing in the circumstances or in his own condition to prevent his going home, which he accordingly did: descending in a fine sweep, as the crow flies, to the valley, where, as he reached it, lights were showing, though his way had been well enough lighted by reflection from the snow. He came down the Brehmenbühl, along the edge of the forest, and was in the Dorf by half past five. He left his skis at the grocer's, rested a little in Herr Settembrini's attic cell, and told him how the storm had overtaken him in the mountains. The horrified humanist scolded him roundly, and straightway lighted his spirit-kettle to brew coffee for the exhausted one—the strength of which did not prevent Hans Castorp from falling asleep as he sat.

An hour later the highly civilized atmosphere of the Berghof caressed him. He ate enormously at dinner. What he had dreamed was already fading from his mind. What he had thought—even that selfsame evening it was no longer so clear as it had been at first.

There Is Never Any End to Paris

by ERNEST HEMINGWAY

Young Ernest Hemingway left America to write in Europe, arriving with his new bride Hadley in 1922, settling in Paris. Almost immediately they started taking ski lessons, at Chamby-sur-Montreux, Switzerland. The next year, they skied Cortina d'Ampezzo in Italy: there were no lifts there, then; they climbed up and skied down. Then the young couple began spending every winter from the end of November to the Easter at Schruns in the Vorarlberg, the Austrian province nearest to Switzerland. The two enrolled in the local ski school, run by Walter Lenz, a well-known mountain guide and business partner of Hannes Schneider (whose Arlberg Ski School was located on the other side of the Arlberg Pass). Hemingway became so familiar with the Schruns mountain country that he sometimes hired out as a ski guide. Hemingway divorced Hadley and skied no more until 1936 when he was invited to Sun Valley, Idaho, for the opening week by Steve Hannagan. He returned the next winter to write For Whom the Bell Tolls *while in residence. He returned ten years later with his fourth wife, Mary, and they bought a house in Sun Valley in 1958. Hemingway died there in 1961.*

WHEN there were the three of us instead of just the two, it was the cold and the weather that finally drove us out of Paris in the wintertime. Alone there was no problem when you got used to it. I could always go to a cafe to write and could work all morning over a *café crème* while the waiters cleaned and swept out the cafe and it gradually grew warmer. My wife could go to work at the piano in a cold place and with enough sweaters keep warm playing and come home to nurse Bumby. It was wrong to take a baby to a cafe in the winter though; even a baby that never cried and watched everything that happened and was never bored. There were no baby-sitters then and Bumby would stay happy in his tall cage bed with his big, loving cat named F. Puss. There were people who said that it was dangerous to leave a cat with a baby. The most ignorant and prejudiced said that a cat would suck a baby's breath and kill him. Others said that a cat would lie on a baby and the cat's weight would smother him. F. Puss lay beside Bumby in the tall cage bed and watched the door with his big yellow eyes, and would let no one come near him when we were out and Marie, the *femme de ménage,* had to be away. There was no need for baby-sitters. F. Puss was the baby-sitter.

But when you are poor, and we were really poor when I had given up all journalism when we came back from Canada, and could sell no stories at all, it was too rough with a baby in Paris in the winter. At three months Mr. Bumby had crossed the North Atlantic on a twelve-day small Cu-

120

narder that sailed from New York via Halifax in January. He never cried on the trip and laughed happily when he would be barricaded in a bunk so he could not fall out when we were in heavy weather. But our Paris was too cold for him.

We went to Schruns in the Vorarlberg in Austria. After going through Switzerland you came to the Austrian frontier at Feldkirch. The train went through Liechtenstein and stopped at Bludenz where there was a small branch line that ran along a pebbly trout river through a valley of farms and forest to Schruns, which was a sunny market town with sawmills, stores, inns and a good, year-round hotel called the Taube where we lived.

The rooms at the Taube were large and comfortable with big stoves, big windows and big beds with good blankets and feather coverlets. The meals were simple and excellent and the dining room and the wood-planked public bar were well heated and friendly. The valley was wide and open so there was good sun. The pension was about two dollars a day for the three of us, and as the Austrian schilling went down with inflation, our room and food were less all the time. There was no desperate inflation and poverty as there had been in Germany. The schilling went up and down, but its longer course was down.

There were no ski lifts from Schruns and no funiculars, but there were logging trails and cattle trails that led up different mountain valleys to the high mountain country. You climbed on sealskins that you attached to the bottoms of the skis. At the tops of mountain valleys there were the big Alpine Club huts for summer climbers where you could sleep and leave payment for any wood you used. In some you had to pack up your own wood, or if you were going on a long tour in the high mountains and the glaciers, you hired someone to pack wood and supplies up with you, and established a base. The most famous of these high base huts were the Lindauer-Hütte, the Madlener-Haus and the Wiesbadener-Hütte.

In back of the Taube there was a sort of practice slope where you ran through orchards and fields and there was another good slope behind Tchagguns across the valley where there

was a beautiful inn with an excellent collection of chamois horns on the walls of the drinking room. It was from behind the lumber village of Tchagguns, which was on the far edge of the valley, that the good skiing went all the way up until you could eventually cross the mountains and get over the Silvretta into the Klosters area.

Schruns was a healthy place for Bumby, who had a dark-haired beautiful girl to take him out in the sun in his sleigh and look after him, and Hadley and I had all the new country to learn and the new villages, and the people of the town were very friendly. Herr Walther Lent, who was a pioneer high-mountain skier and at one time had been a partner with Hannes Schneider, the great Arlberg skier, making ski waxes for climbing and all snow conditions, was starting a school for Alpine skiing and we both enrolled. Walther Lent's system was to get his pupils off the practice slopes as soon as possible and into the high mountains on trips. Skiing was not the way it is now, the spiral fracture had not become common then, and no one could afford a broken leg. There were no ski patrols. Anything you ran down from, you had to climb up. That gave you legs that were fit to run down with.

Walther Lent believed the fun of skiing was to get up into the highest mountain country where there was no one else and where the snow was untracked and then travel from one high Alpine Club hut to another over the top passes and glaciers of the Alps. You must not have a binding that could break your leg if you fell. The ski should come off before it broke your leg. What he really loved was unroped glacier skiing, but for that we had to wait until spring when the crevasses were sufficiently covered.

Hadley and I had loved skiing since we had first tried it together in Switzerland and later at Cortina d'Ampezzo in the Dolomites when Bumby was going to be born and the doctor in Milan had given her permission to continue to ski if I would promise that she would not fall down. This took a very careful selection of terrain and of runs and absolutely controlled running, but she had beautiful, wonderfully strong legs and fine control of her skis, and she did not fall. We all knew the different snow conditions and everyone knew how to run in deep powder snow.

We loved the Vorarlberg and we loved Schruns. We would go there about Thanksgiving time and stay until nearly Easter. There was always skiing even though Schruns was not high enough for a ski resort except in a winter of heavy snow. But climbing was fun and no one minded it in those days. You set a certain pace well under the speed at which you could climb, and it was easy and your heart felt good and you were proud of the weight of your rucksack. Part of the climb up to the Madlener-Haus was steep and very tough. But the second time you made that climb it was easier, and finally you made it easily with double the weight you had carried at first.

We were always hungry and every mealtime was a great event. We drank light or dark beer and new wines and wines that were a year old sometimes. The white wines were the best. For other drinks there was kirsch made in the valley and Enzian *Schnapps* distilled from mountain gentian. Sometimes for dinner there would be jugged hare with a rich red wine sauce, and sometimes venison with chestnut sauce. We would drink red wine with these even though it was more expensive than white wine, and the very best cost twenty cents a liter. Ordinary red wine was much cheaper and we packed it up in kegs to the Madlener-Haus.

We had a store of books that Sylvia Beach had let us take for the winter and we could bowl with the people of the town in the alley that gave onto the summer garden of the hotel. Once or twice a week there was a poker game in the dining room of the hotel with all the windows shuttered and the door locked. Gambling was forbidden in Austria then and I played with Herr Nels, the hotelkeeper, Herr Lent of the Alpine ski school, a banker of the town, the public prosecutor and the captain of Gendarmerie. It was a stiff game and they were all good poker players except that Herr Lent played too wildly because the ski school was not making any money. The captain of Gendarmerie would raise his finger to his ear when he would hear the pair of gendarmes stop outside the door when they made their

rounds, and we would be silent until they had gone on.

In the cold of the morning as soon as it was light the maid would come into the room and shut the windows and make a fire in the big porcelain stove. Then the room was warm, there was breakfast of fresh bread or toast with delicious fruit preserves and big bowls of coffee, fresh eggs and good ham if you wanted it. There was a dog named Schnautz that slept on the foot of the bed who loved to go on ski trips and to ride on my back or over my shoulder when I ran down hill. He was Mr. Bumby's friend too and would go for walks with him and his nurse beside the small sleigh.

Schruns was a good place to work. I know because I did the most difficult job of rewriting I have ever done there in the winter of 1925 and 1926, when I had to take the first draft of *The Sun Also Rises,* which I had written in one sprint of six weeks, and make it into a novel. I cannot remember what stories I wrote there. There were several though that turned out well.

I remember the snow on the road to the village squeaking at night when we walked home in the cold with our skis and ski poles on our shoulders, watching the lights and then finally seeing the buildings, and how everyone on the road said, *"Grüss Gott."* There were always country men in the *Weinstube* with nailed boots and mountain clothes and the air was smoky and the wooden floors were scarred by the nails. Many of the young men had served in Austrian Alpine regiments and one named Hans, who worked in the sawmill, was a famous hunter and we were good friends because we had been in the same part of the mountains in Italy. We drank together and we all sang mountain songs.

I remember the trails up through the orchards and the fields of the hillside farms above the village and the warm farmhouses with their great stoves and the huge wood piles in the snow. The women worked in the kitchens carding and spinning wool into gray and black yarn. The spinning wheels worked by a foot treadle and the yarn was not dyed. The black yarn was from the wool of black sheep. The wool was natural and the fat had not been removed, and the caps and sweaters and long scarves that Hadley knitted from it never became wet in the snow.

One Christmas there was a play by Hans Sachs that the schoolmaster directed. It was a good play and I wrote a review of it for the provincial paper that the hotelkeeper translated. Another year a former German naval officer with a shaven head and scars came to give a lecture on the Battle of Jutland. The lantern slides showed the movements of the two battle fleets and the naval officer used a billiard cue for a pointer when he pointed out the cowardice of Jellicoe and sometimes he became so angry that his voice broke. The schoolmaster was afraid that he would stab the billiard cue through the screen. Afterwards the former naval officer could not quiet himself down and everyone was ill at ease in the *Weinstube.* Only the public prosecutor and the banker drank with him, and they were at a separate table. Herr Lent, who was a Rhinelander, would not attend the lecture. There was a couple from Vienna who had come for the skiing but who did not want to go to the high mountains and so were leaving for Zurs where, I heard, they were killed in an avalanche. The man said the lecturer was the type of swine who had ruined Germany and in twenty years they would do it again. The woman with him told him to shut up in French and said this is a small place and you never know.

That was the year that so many people were killed in avalanches. The first big loss was over the mountains from our valley in Lech in the Arlberg. A party of Germans wanted to come and ski with Herr Lent on their Christmas vacations. Snow was late that year and the hills and mountain slopes were still warm from the sun when a great snowfall came. The snow was deep and powdery and it was not bound to the earth at all. Conditions for skiing could not be more dangerous and Herr Lent had wired the Berliners not to come. But it was their vacation time and they were ignorant and had no fear of avalanches. They arrived at Lech and Herr Lent refused to take them out. One man called him a coward and they said they would ski by themselves. Finally he took them to the safest slope he could find. He crossed it himself and then they followed and the whole hillside came down in a rush, rising over them as a tidal wave rises. Thirteen were dug out and nine of them were dead. The Alpine ski school had not prospered before this, and afterwards we were almost the only members. We became great students of avalanches, the different types of avalanches, how to avoid them and how to behave if you were caught in one. Most of the writing that I did that year was in avalanche time.

The worst thing I remember of that avalanche winter was one man who was dug out. He had squatted down and made a box with his arms in front of his head, as we had been taught to do, so that there would be air to breathe as the snow rose up over you. It was a huge avalanche and it took a long time to dig everyone out, and this man was the last to be found. He had not been dead long and his neck was worn through so that the tendons and the bone were visible. He had been turning his head from side to side against the pressure of the snow. In this avalanche there must have been some old, packed snow mixed in with the new light snow that had slipped. We could not decide whether he had done it on purpose or if he had been out of his head. He was refused burial in consecrated ground by the local priest anyway, since there was no proof he was a Catholic.

When we lived in Schruns we used to make a long trip up the valley to the inn where we slept before setting out on the climb to the Madlener-Haus. It was a very beautiful old inn and the wood of the walls of the room where we ate and drank were silky with the years of polishing. So were the table and chairs. We slept close together in the big bed under the feather quilt with the window open and the stars close and very bright. In the morning after breakfast we all loaded to go up the road and started the climb in the dark with the stars close and very bright, carrying our skis on our shoulders. The porters' skis were short and they carried heavy loads. We competed among ourselves as to who could climb with the heaviest loads, but no one could compete with the porters, squat sullen peasants who spoke only Montafon dialect, climbed steadily like pack horses and at the top, where the

Climbing up the ski high country demands both stamina and courage

Alpine Club hut was built on a shelf beside the snow-covered glacier, shed their loads against the stone wall of the hut, asked for more money than the agreed price, and, when they had obtained a compromise, shot down and away on their short skis like gnomes.

One of our friends was a German girl who skied with us. She was a great mountain skier, small and beautifully built, who could carry as heavy a rucksack as I could and carry it longer.

"Those porters always look at us as though they looked forward to bringing us down as bodies," she said. "They set the price for the climb and I've never known them not to ask for more."

In the winter in Schruns I wore a beard against the sun that burned my face so badly on the high snow, and did not bother having a haircut. Late one evening running on skis down the logging trails Herr Lent told me that peasants I passed on those roads above Schruns called me "the Black Christ." He said some, when they came to the *Weinstube*, called me "the Black Kirsch-drinking Christ." But to the peasants at the far upper end of the Montafon where we hired porters to go up to the Madlener-Haus, we were all foreign devils who went into the high mountains when people should stay out of them. That we started before daylight in order not to pass avalanche places when the sun could make them dangerous was not to our credit. It only proved we were tricky as all foreign devils are.

I remember the smell of the pines and the

sleeping on the mattresses of beech leaves in the woodcutters' huts and the skiing through the forest following the tracks of hares and of foxes. In the high mountains above the tree line I remember following the track of a fox until I came in sight of him and watching him stand with his right forefoot raised and then go carefully to stop and then pounce, and the whiteness and the clutter of a ptarmigan bursting out of the snow and flying away and over the ridge.

I remember all the kinds of snow that the wind could make and their different treacheries when you were on skis. Then there were the blizzards when you were in the high Alpine hut and the strange world that they would make where we had to make our route as carefully as though we had never seen the country. We had not, either, as it all was new. Finally towards spring there was the great glacier run, smooth and straight, forever straight if our legs could hold it, our ankles locked, we running so low, leaning into the speed, dropping forever and forever in the silent hiss of the crisp powder. It was better than any flying or anything else, and we built the ability to do it and to have it with the long climbs carrying the heavy rucksacks. We could not buy the trip up nor take a ticket to the top. It was the end we worked for all winter, and all the winter built to make it possible.

During our last year in the mountains new people came deep into our lives and nothing was ever the same again. The winter of the avalanches was like a happy and innocent winter in childhood compared to the next winter, a nightmare winter disguised as the greatest fun of all, and the murderous summer that was to follow. It was that year that the rich showed up.

The rich have a sort of pilot fish who goes ahead of them, sometimes a little deaf, sometimes a little blind, but always smelling affable and hesitant ahead of them. The pilot fish talks like this: "Well, I don't know. No, of course, not really. But I like them. I like them both. Yes, by God, Hem; I do like them. I see what you mean but I do like them truly and there's something damned fine about her." (He gives her name and pronounces it lovingly.) "No, Hem, don't be silly and don't be difficult. I like them truly. Both of them I swear it. You'll like him (using his baby-talk nickname) when you know him. I like them both, truly."

Then you have the rich and nothing is ever as it was again. The pilot fish leaves of course. He is always going somewhere, or coming from somewhere, and he is never around for very long. He enters and leaves politics or the theater in the same way he enters and leaves countries and people's lives in his early days. He is never caught and he is not caught by the rich. Nothing ever catches him and it is only those who trust him who are caught and killed. He has the irreplaceable early training of the bastard and a latent and long-denied love of money. He ends up rich himself, having moved one dollar's width to the right with every dollar that he made.

These rich loved and trusted him because he was shy, comic, elusive, already in production, and because he was an unerring pilot fish.

When you have two people who love each other, are happy and gay and really good work is being done by one or both of them, people are drawn to them as surely as migrating birds are drawn at night to a powerful beacon. If the two people were as solidly constructed as the beacon there would be little damage except to the birds. Those who attract people by their happiness and their performance are usually inexperienced. They do not know how not to be overrun and how to go away. They do not always learn about the good, the attractive, the charming, the soon-beloved, the generous, the understanding rich who have no bad qualities and who give each day the quality of a festival and who, when they have passed and taken the nourishment they needed, leave everything deader than the roots of any grass Attila's horses' hooves have ever scoured.

The rich came led by the pilot fish. A year before they would never have come. There was no certainty then. The work was as good and the happiness was greater but no novel had been written, so they could not be sure. They never wasted their time nor their charm on something that was not sure. Why should they? Picasso was sure and of course had been before they had ever heard of painting. They were very sure of another painter. Many others. But this year they were sure and they had the word from the pilot fish who turned up too so we would not feel that they were outlanders and that I would not be difficult. The pilot fish was our friend of course.

In those days I trusted the pilot fish as I would trust the Corrected Hydrographic Office Sailing Directions for the Mediterranean, say, or the tables in *Brown's Nautical Almanac.* Under the charm of these rich I was as trusting and as stupid as a bird dog who wants to go out with any man with a gun, or a trained pig in a circus who has finally found someone who loves and appreciates him for himself alone. That every day should be a fiesta seemed to me a marvelous discovery. I even read aloud the part of the novel that I had rewritten, which is about as low as a writer can get and much more dangerous for him as a writer than glacier skiing unroped before the full winter snowfall has set over the crevices.

When they said, "It's great, Ernest. Truly it's great. You cannot know the thing it has," I wagged my tail in pleasure and plunged into the fiesta concept of life to see if I could not bring some fine attractive stick back, instead of thinking, "If these bastards like it what is wrong with it?" That was what I would think if I had been functioning as a professional although, if I had been functioning as a professional, I would never have read it to them.

Before these rich had come we had already been infiltrated by another rich using the oldest trick there is. It is that an unmarried young woman becomes the temporary best friend of another young woman who is married, goes to live with the husband and wife and then unknowingly, innocently and unrelentingly sets out to marry the husband. When the husband is a writer and doing difficult work so that he is occupied much of the time and is not a good companion or partner to his wife for a big part of the day, the arrangement has advantages until you know how it works out. The husband has two attractive girls around when he has finished work. One is new and strange and if he has bad luck he gets to love them both.

Then, instead of the two of them and their child, there are three of them. First it is stimulating and fun and it goes on that way for a while. All things truly wicked start from an innocence.

So you live day by day and enjoy what you have and do not worry. You lie and hate it and it destroys you and every day is more dangerous, but you live day to day as in a war.

It was necessary that I leave Schruns and go to New York to rearrange publishers. I did my business in New York and when I got back to Paris I should have caught the first train from the Gare de l'Est that would take me down to Austria. But the girl I was in love with was in Paris then, and I did not take the first train, or the second or the third.

When I saw my wife again standing by the tracks as the train came in by the piled logs at the station, I wished I had died before I ever loved anyone but her. She was smiling, the sun on her lovely face tanned by the snow and sun, beautifully built, her hair red gold in the sun, grown out all winter awkwardly and beautifully, and Mr. Bumby standing with her, blond and chunky and with winter cheeks looking like a good Vorarlberg boy.

"Oh, Tatie," she said, when I was holding her in my arms, "you're back and you made such a fine successful trip. I love you and we've missed you so."

I loved her and I loved no one else and we had a lovely magic time while we were alone. I worked well and we made great trips, and I thought we were invulnerable again, and it wasn't until we were out of the mountains in late spring, and back in Paris that the other thing started again.

That was the end of the first part of Paris. Paris was never to be the same again although it was always Paris and you changed as it changed. We never went back to the Vorarlberg and neither did the rich.

There is never any ending to Paris and the memory of each person who has lived in it differs from that of any other. We always returned to it no matter who we were or how it was changed or with what difficulties, or ease, it could be reached. Paris was always worth it and you received return for whatever you brought to it. But this is how Paris was in the early days when we were very poor and very happy.

The Hartleys

by JOHN CHEEVER

The late John Cheever began to ski in the 1930s, when one of his acquaintances came back from St. Anton after having taken lessons from Hannes Schneider at the Arlberg Ski School. Cheever skied enthusiastically off and on through his life until he hurt his knee and switched from alpine to cross country skiing. "When you ski," he told Ski Magazine editor Janet Nelson, in an interview some time before his death, "it is the thrill of living. It is an end in itself. Skiing has no more significance than blowing a feather off your knee." Cheever wrote only a single short story with a skiing background but he wrote some superb paragraphs on the sport in his best-selling Falconer, *a quote from which opens the "Magical Mountain" section of this book.*

Skiing is often used by writers as a metaphor for the dangers of life—in spite of the fact that skiing is slightly less likely to do you in than riding in the family car. But the element of risk is more obvious in skiing than in driving: your body is speeding along without any shield between it and the snowy icy reaches down which one skis. Here, Cheever capitalizes on the drama of skiing, to illustrate the vulnerability of the human condition.

MR. and Mrs. Hartley and their daughter Anne reached the Pemaquoddy Inn, one winter evening, after dinner and just as the bridge games were getting under way. Mr. Hartley carried the bags across the broad porch and into the lobby, and his wife and daughter followed him. They all three seemed very tired, and they looked around them at the bright, homely room with the gratitude of people who have escaped from tension and danger, for they had been driving in a blinding snow storm since early morning. They had made the trip from New York, and it had snowed all the way, they said. Mr. Hartley put down the bags and returned to the car to get the skis. Mrs. Hartley sat down in one of the lobby chairs, and her daughter, tired and shy, drew close to her. There was a little snow in the girl's hair, and Mrs. Hartley brushed this away with her fingers. Then Mrs. Butterick, the widow who owned the inn, went out to the porch and called to Mr. Hartley that he needn't put his car up. One of the men would do it, she said. He came back into the lobby and signed the register.

He seemed to be a likable man with an edge to his voice and an intense, polite manner. His wife was a handsome, dark-haired woman who was dazed with fatigue, and his daughter was a girl of about seven. Mrs. Butterick asked Mr. Hartley if he had ever stayed at the Pemaquoddy before. "When I got the reservation," she said, "the name rang a bell."

"Mrs. Hartley and I were here eight years ago February," Mr. Hartley said. "We came on

127

the twenty-third and were here for ten days. I remember the date clearly because we had such a wonderful time." Then they went upstairs. They came down again long enough to make a supper of some leftovers that had been kept warm on the back of the stove. The child was so tired she nearly fell asleep at the table. After supper, they went upstairs again.

In the winter, the life of the Pemaquoddy centered entirely on cold sports. Drinkers and malingerers were not encouraged, and most of the people there were earnest about their skiing. In the morning, they would take a bus across the valley to the mountains, and if the weather was good, they would carry a pack lunch and remain on the slopes until late afternoon. They'd vary this occasionally by skating on a rink near the inn, which had been made by flooding a clothes-yard. There was a hill behind the inn that could sometimes be used for skiing when conditions on the mountain were poor. This hill was serviced by a primitive ski tow that had been built by Mrs. Butterick's son. "He bought that motor that pulls the tow when he was a senior at Harvard," Mrs. Butterick always said when she spoke of the tow. "It was in an old Mercer auto, and he drove it up here from Cambridge one night without any license plates!" When she said this, she would put her hand over her heart, as if the dangers of the trip were still vivid.

The Hartleys picked up the Pemaquoddy routine of fresh air and exercise the morning following their arrival.

Mrs. Hartley was an absent-minded woman. She boarded the bus for the mountain that morning, sat down, and was talking to another passenger when she realized that she had forgotten her skis. Her husband went after them while everyone waited. She wore a bright, fur-trimmed parka that had been cut for someone with a younger face, and it made her look tired. Her husband wore some navy equipment, which was stenciled with his name and rank. Their daughter, Anne, was pretty. Her hair was braided in tight, neat plaits, there was a saddle of freckles across her small nose, and she looked around her with the bleak, rational scrutiny of her age.

Mr. Hartley was a good skier. He was up and down the slope, his skis parallel, his knees bent, his shoulders swinging gracefully in a half circle. His wife was not as clever but she knew what she was doing, and she enjoyed the cold air and the snow. She fell now and then, and when someone offered to help her to her feet, when the cold snow that had been pressed against her face had heightened its color, she looked like a much younger woman.

Anne didn't know how to ski. She stood at the foot of the slope watching her parents. They called to her, but she didn't move, and after a while she began to shiver. Her mother went to her and tried to encourage her, but the child turned away crossly. "I don't want *you* to show me," she said. "I want daddy to show me." Mrs. Hartley called her husband.

As soon as Mr. Hartley turned his attention to Anne, she lost all of her hesitation. She followed him up and down the hill, and as long as he was with her, she seemed confident and happy. Mr. Hartley stayed with Anne until after lunch, when he turned her over to a professional instructor who was taking a class of beginners out to the slope. Mr. and Mrs. Hartley went with the group to the foot of the slope, where Mr. Hartley took his daughter aside. "Your mother and I are going to ski some trails now," he said, "and I want you to join Mr. Ritter's class and to learn as much from him as you can. If you're ever going to learn to ski, Anne, you'll have to learn without me. We'll be back at around four, and I want you to show me what you've learned when we come back."

"Yes, daddy," she said.

"Now you go and join the class."

"Yes, daddy."

Mr. and Mrs. Hartley waited until Anne had climbed the slope and joined the class. Then they went away. Anne watched the instructor for a few minutes, but as soon as she noticed that her parents had gone, she broke from the group and coasted down the hill toward the hut. "Miss," the instructor called after her. "Miss . . ." She didn't answer. She went into the hut, took off her parka and her mittens, spread them neatly on a table to dry, and sat beside the fire, holding her head down so that her face could not be seen. She sat there all afternoon. A little before dark, when her parents returned to the hut, stamping the snow off their boots, she ran to her father. Her face was swollen from crying. "Oh, daddy, I thought you weren't coming back," she cried. "I thought you weren't ever coming back!" She threw her arms around him and buried her face in his clothes.

"Now, now, now, Anne," he said, and he patted her back and smiled at the people who happened to notice the scene. Anne sat beside him on the bus ride back, holding his arm.

At the inn that evening, the Hartleys came into the bar before dinner and sat at a wall table. Mrs. Hartley and her daughter drank tomato juice, and Mr. Hartley had three Old-Fashioneds. He gave Anne the orange slices and the sweet cherries from his drinks. Everything her father did interested her. She lighted his cigarettes and blew out the matches. She examined his watch and laughed at all his jokes. She had a sharp, pleasant laugh.

The family talked quietly. Mr. and Mrs. Hartley spoke oftener to Anne than to each other, as if they had come to a point in their marriage where there was nothing to say. They discussed haltingly, between themselves, the snow and the mountain, and in the course of this attempt to make conversation Mr. Hartley, for some reason, spoke sharply to his wife. Mrs. Hartley got up from the table quickly. She might have been crying. She hurried through the lobby and went up the stairs.

Mr. Hartley and Anne stayed in the bar. When the dinner bell rang, he asked the desk clerk to send Mrs. Hartley a tray. He ate dinner with his daughter in the dining room. After dinner, he sat in the parlor reading an old copy of *Fortune* while Anne played with some other children who were staying at the inn. They were all a little younger than she, and she handled them easily and affectionately, imitating an adult. She taught them a simple card game and then read them a story. After the younger children were sent to bed, she read a book. Her father took her upstairs at about nine.

He came down by himself later and went into the bar. He drank alone and talked with the bartender about various brands of bourbon. "Dad used to have his bourbon sent up from Kentucky in kegs," Mr. Hartley said. A slight rasp in his voice, and his intense and polite manner, made what he said seem important. "They were small, as I recall. I don't suppose they held more than a gallon. Dad used to have them sent to him twice a year. When grandmother asked him what they were, he always told her they were full of sweet cider." After discussing bourbons, they discussed the village and the changes in the inn. "We've only been here once before," Mr. Hartley said. "That was eight years ago, eight years ago February." Then he repeated, word for word, what he had said in the lobby the previous night. "We came on the twenty-third and were here for ten days. I remember the date clearly because we had such a wonderful time."

The Hartleys' subsequent days were nearly all like the first. Mr. Hartley spent the early hours instructing his daughter. The girl learned rapidly, and when she was with her father, she was daring and graceful, but as soon as he left her, she would go to the hut and sit by the fire. Each day, after lunch, they would reach the point where he gave her a lecture on self-reliance. "Your mother and I are going away now," he would say, "and I want you to ski by yourself, Anne." She would nod her head and agree with him, but as soon as he had gone, she would return to the hut and wait there. Once—it was the third day—he lost his temper. "Now, listen, Anne," he shouted, "if you're going to learn to ski, you've got to learn by yourself." His loud voice wounded her, but it did not seem to show her the way to independence. She became a familiar figure in the afternoons, sitting beside the fire.

Sometimes Mr. Hartley would modify his discipline. The three of them would return to the inn on the early bus and he would take his daughter to the skating rink and give her a skating lesson. On these occasions, they stayed out late. Mrs. Hartley watched them sometimes from the parlor window. The rink was at the foot of the primitive ski tow that had been built by Mrs. Butterick's son. The terminal posts of the two looked like gibbets in the twilight, and Mr. Hartley and his daughter looked like figures of contrition and patience. Again and again they would circle the little rink, earnest and serious, as if he were explaining to her something more mysterious than a sport.

Everyone at the inn liked the Hartleys, although they gave the other guests the feeling that they had recently suffered some loss—the loss of money, perhaps, or perhaps Mr. Hartley had lost his job. Mrs. Hartley remained absent-minded, but the other guests got the feeling that this characteristic was the result of some misfortune that had shaken her self-possession. She seemed anxious to be friendly and she plunged, like a lonely woman, into every conversation. Her father had been a doctor, she said. She spoke of him as if he had been a great power, and she spoke with intense pleasure of her childhood. "Mother's living room in Grafton was forty-five feet long," she said. "There were fireplaces at both ends. It was one of those marvelous old Victorian houses." In the china cabinet in the dining room, there was some china like the china Mrs. Hartley's mother had owned. In the lobby there was a paperweight like a paperweight Mrs. Hartley had been given when she was a girl. Mr. Hartley also spoke of his origins now and then. Mrs. Butterick once asked him to carve a leg of lamb, and as he sharpened the carving knife he said, "I never do this without thinking of dad." Among the collection of canes in the hallway, there was a blackthorn embossed with silver. "That's exactly like the blackthorn Mr. Wentworth brought dad from Ireland," Mr. Hartley said.

Anne was devoted to her father but she obviously liked her mother, too. In the evenings, when she was tired, she would sit on the sofa beside Mrs. Hartley and rest her head on her mother's shoulder. It seemed to be only on the mountain, where the environment was strange, that her father would become for her the only person in the world. One evening when the Hartleys were playing bridge—it was quite late and Anne had gone to bed—the child began to call her father. "I'll go, darling," Mrs. Hartley said, and she excused herself and went upstairs. "I want my daddy," those at the bridge table could hear the girl screaming. Mrs. Hartley quieted her and came downstairs again. "Anne had a nightmare," she explained, and went on playing cards.

The next day was windy and warm. In the middle of the afternoon, it began to rain, and all but the most intrepid skiers went back to their hotels. The bar at the Pemaquoddy filled up early. The radio was turned on for weather reports, and one earnest guest picked up the telephone in the lobby and called other resorts. Was it raining in Pico? Was it raining in Stowe? Was it raining in Ste. Agathe? Mr. and Mrs. Hartley were in the bar that afternoon. She was having a drink for the first time since they had been there, but she did not seem to enjoy it. Anne was playing in the parlor with the other children. A little before dinner, Mr. Hartley went into the lobby and asked Mrs. Butterick if they could have their dinner upstairs. Mrs. Butterick said that this could be arranged. When the dinner bell rang, the Hartleys went up, and a maid took them trays. After dinner, Anne went back to the parlor to play with the other children, and after the dining room had been cleared, the maid went up to get the Hartleys' trays.

The transom above the Hartleys' bedroom door was open, and as the maid went down the hall she could hear Mrs. Hartley's voice, a voice so uncontrolled, so guttural and full of suffering, that she stopped and listened as if the woman's life were in danger. "Why do we have to come back?" Mrs. Hartley was crying. "Why do we have to come back? Why do we have to make these trips back to the places where we thought we were happy? What good is it going to do? What good has it ever done? We go through the telephone book looking for the names of people we knew ten years ago, and we ask them for dinner, and what good does it do? What good has it ever done? We go back to the restaurants, the mountains, we go back to the houses, even the neighborhoods, we walk in the slums, thinking that this will make us happy, and it never does. Why in Christ's name did we ever begin such a wretched thing? Why isn't there an end to it? Why can't we separate again? It was better that way. Wasn't it better that way? It was better for Anne—I don't care what you say, it was better for her than this. I'll take Anne again and you can live in town. Why can't I do that, why can't I, why can't I, why can't I . . .'' The frightened maid went back along the corridor. Anne was sitting in the parlor reading to the younger children when the maid went downstairs.

It cleared up that night and turned cold. Everything froze. In the morning, Mrs. Butterick announced that all the trails on the mountain were closed and that the tramway would not run. Mr. Hartley and some other guests broke the crust on the hill behind the inn, and one of the hired hands started the primitive tow. "My son bought the motor that pulls the tow when he was a senior at Harvard," Mrs. Butterick said when she heard its humble explosions. "It was in an old Mercer auto, and he drove it up here from Cambridge one night without any license plates!" The slope offered the only skiing in the neighborhood, and after lunch a lot of people came here from other hotels. They wore the snow away under the tow to a surface of rough stone, and snow had to be shoveled onto the tracks. The rope was frayed, and Mrs. Butterick's son had planned the tow so poorly that it gave the skiers a strenuous and uneven ride. Mrs. Hartley tried to get Anne to use the tow, but she would not ride it until her father led the way. He showed her how to stand, how to hold the rope, bend her knees, and drag her poles. As soon as he was carried up the hill, she gladly followed. She followed him up and down the hill all afternoon, delighted that for once he was remaining in her sight. When the crust on the slope was broken and packed, it made good running, and that odd, nearly compulsive rhythm of riding and skiing, riding and skiing, established itself.

It was a fine afternoon. There were snow clouds, but a bright and cheerful light beat through them. The country, seen from the top of the hill, was black and white. Its only colors were the colors of spent fire, and this impressed itself upon one—as if the desolation were something more than winter, as if it were the work of a great conflagration. People talk, of course, while they ski, while they wait for their turn to seize the rope, but they can hardly be heard. There is the exhaust of the tow motor and the creak of the iron wheel upon which the tow rope turns, but the skiers themselves seem stricken dumb, lost in the rhythm of riding and coasting. That afternoon was a continuous cycle of movement. There was a single file to the left of the slope, holding the frayed rope and breaking from it, one by one, at the crown of the hill to choose their way down, going again and again over the same surface, like people who, having lost a ring or a key on the beach, search again and again in the same sand. In the stillness, the child Anne began to shriek. Her arm had got caught in the frayed rope; she had been thrown to the ground and was being dragged brutally up the hill toward the iron wheel. "Stop the tow!" her father roared. "Stop the tow! Stop the tow!" And everyone else on the hill began to shout, "Stop the tow! Stop the tow! Stop the tow!" But there was no one there to stop it. Her screams were hoarse and terrible, and the more she struggled to free herself from the rope, the more violently it threw her to the ground. Space and the cold seemed to reduce the voices—even the anguish in the voices—of the people who were calling to stop the tow, but the girl's cries were piercing until her neck was broken on the iron wheel.

The Hartleys left for New York that night after dark. They were going to drive all night behind the local hearse. Several people offered to drive the car down for them, but Mr. Hartley said that he wanted to drive, and his wife seemed to want him to. When everything was ready, the stricken couple walked across the porch, looking around them at the bewildering beauty of the night, for it was very cold and clear and the constellations seemed brighter than the lights of the inn or the village. He helped his wife into the car, and after arranging a blanket over her legs, they started the long, long drive.

The Rescue

by JOHN UPDIKE

The experience of suburbia, John Updike's special literary territory, certainly includes skiing, which draws a great part of its practitioners from there. Thus, it is more than natural in the course of things for Updike characters to be seen at a ski resort. The story that follows concerns the emotional interplay between people living in the same town, a description that could be applied to almost any Updike novel, including his recent popular Couples *and* Rabbit Is Rich.

HELPLESSLY, Caroline Harris found herself paired with Alice Smith, struck in the backs of their knees by an onrushing, rumbling chair, and hurled upward. When she had been a child her father would toss her toward the ceiling with the same brutal swooping lurch. Alice snapped the safety bar, and they were caged together. It was degrading for both of them. Up ahead, Norman and Timothy roosted smugly, having, on this first run to the top, greedily seized the first chair. From the rear, hooded and armed with spears, they were two of a kind, Timothy only slightly smaller than his father; and this, too, she felt as a desertion; a flight from her womb. While she was dragged through the air, joggled at each pier, the whiteness of the snow pressed on the underside of her consciousness with the gathering insistence of a

headache. Her boots weighed; her feet felt captive. Rigid with irritation and a desire not to sway, she smoked her next-to-last cigarette, which was cheated of taste by the cold, and tried to decide if the silent woman beside her were sleeping with Norman or not.

This morning, as they drove north into New Hampshire, there had been in the automobile an excessive ease, as if the four of them knew each other better than Caroline remembered reason for. There had been, between Alice and Norman, a lack of flirtation a shade too resolute, while on sleepy, innocent Timmy the woman had inflicted a curiously fervent playfulness, as if warm messages for the father were being forwarded through the son, or as if Alice were seeking to establish herself as a sexual nonentity, a kind of brotherly sister. Mrs. Harris felt an ominous tug in this trip. Had she merely imagined, during their breakfast at Howard Johnson's, a poignance in the pauses, and a stir of something, like toes touching, under the table? And was she paranoid to have felt this morning a deliberate design in the pattern of alternation that had her and her son floundering up the T-bar together as the other two expertly skimmed down the slope and waited, side by side, laughing vapor, at the end of the long and devious line? Caroline was not reassured, when they all rejoined at lunch, by

A fall of snow turns an ordinary slope into a descent of adventure

Alice's smile, faintly flavored with a sweetness unspecified in the recipe. Alice had been her friend first. She had moved to their neighborhood a year ago, a touching little divorcée with preschool twins, utterly lost. Her only interest seemed to be sports, and her marital grief had given her an awkward hardness, as if from too much exercise. Norman had called her pathetic and sexless. Yet a winter later he rescued his skis from a decade in the attic, enrolled Timmy in local lessons, and somehow guided his wife in the same dangerous direction, as irresistibly as this cable was pulling them skyward.

They were giddily lifted above the tops of the pines. Caroline, to brace her voice against her rising fear, spoke aloud: "This is ridiculous. At my age Tahitian women are grandmothers."

Alice said seriously, "I think you do terribly well. You're a natural dancer and it shows."

Caroline could not hate her. She was as helpless as herself, and there was some timid loyalty, perhaps, in Norman's betraying her with a woman she had befriended. She felt, indeed, less betrayed than diluted and, turning with her cigarette cupped against the wind she squinted at the girl as if into an unfair mirror. Alice was small-boned yet coarse; muscularity, reaching upward through the prominent tendons of her slender throat, gave her face, even through the flush of windburn, a taut sallow tinge. Her hair, secured by a scarlet ear-warmer, was abundant but mousy, and her eyes were close-set hazel, and vaguely, stubbornly inward. But between her insignificant nose and receding chin there lay, as if in ambush a large, complicated, and (Caroline supposed) passionate mouth. This, she realized, as the chair swayed sickeningly, was exactly what Norman would want, a mouse with a mouth.

Disgust, disgust and anger, swept through her. How greedy men were. How conceited and heedless! The sky enlarged around her, as if to receive the immensity of her condemnation. With deft haste Alice undid the safety bar. Caroline involuntarily transposed inaction into an undoing of Norman's clothes. Icy with contempt for her situation, she floated onto the unloading platform and discovered, slipping down the alarming little ramp, that her knees were trembling and had forgotten how to bend.

Of course, they were abandoned. The men had gone ahead, and beckoned, tiny and black, from the end of a tunnel tigerishly striped with the blue shadows of birches. On whispering skis held effortlessly parallel Alice led, while Caroline followed clumsily struggling against the impulse to stem. They arrived where the men had been and found them gone again. In their place was a post with two signs. One pointed right to GREASED LIGHTNING (EXPERT). The other pointed left to the LIGHTNING BUG (INTERMEDIATE-NOVICE). "I see them," Alice said, and lightly poled off to the right.

"Wait," Caroline begged.

Alice christied to a stop. A long lavender shadow from a mass of pines covered her and for a painful instant, as her lithe body inquisitively straightened, she seemed beautiful.

"How expert is it?" The Harrises had never been to this mountain before; Alice had been several times. Caroline envisioned her surrounded by tan and goggled men, and abruptly saw her own ineptitude at skiing to be a function of her failure to be divorced. She glimpsed, in the corner of her eye, like a gleam flowing obliquely through a door left ajar, a peculiar possibility of freedom.

"There's one mogully piece you can sideslip," Alice said. "The Bug will take you around the other side of the mountain. You'll never catch the men."

"Why don't you follow them and I'll go down the novice trail? I don't trust this mountain yet." It was a strange mountain, one of the lesser Presidentials, rather recently developed, with an unvarnished cafeteria and very young boys patrolling the trails in naïvely bright jackets striped in yellow and green. At lunch, Norman said he twice had seen members of the ski patrol fall down. His harsh laugh, remembered at this bare altitude, frightened her. The trembling in her knees would not subside, and her fingertips were stinging in their mittens.

Alice crisply sidestepped back up to her. "Let's both go down the Bug," she said. "You shouldn't ski alone."

"I don't want to be a sissy," Caroline said, and these careless words apparently triggered some inward chain of reflection in the other woman, for Alice's face clouded, and it was certain that she was sleeping with Norman. Everything, every tilt of circumstance, every smothered swell and deliberate contraindication, confirmed it, even the girl's very name, Smith— a nothing-name, a prostitute's alias. Her hazel eyes, careful in the glare of the snow, flickeringly searched Caroline's and her expressive mouth froze, it seemed, on the verge of a crucial question.

"Track!"

The voice was behind them, shrill and young. A teen-age girl, wearing a polka-dot purple parka, and her mother, a woman almost elderly, who looked as if she had rouged the tip of her nose, turned beside them and casually plunged over the lip of Greased Lightning.

Caroline, shamed, said, "The hell with it. The worst I can do is get killed." Murderously stabbing the snow, she pushed off to the right, her weight flung wildly back, her uphill ski snagging, her whole body burning with the confirmation of her suspicions. She would leave Norman. Unsteady as a flame she flickered down the height, wavering in her own wind. Alice carefully passed her and, taking long traverses and diagrammatically slow turns, seemed to be inviting her not to destroy herself. Submitting to the sight, permitting her eyes to infect her body with Alice's rhythm, she found the snow yielding to her as if under the pressure of reason; and, swooping in complementary zigzags, the two women descended a long white waterfall linked as if by love.

Then there was a lazy flat run in the shadow of reddish rocks bearded with icicles, then another descent, through cataracts of moguls, into an immense elbow-shaped stage overlooking, from the height of a mile, a toy lodge, a tessellated parking lot, and, vast and dim as a foreign nation, a frozen lake mottled with cloud shadows and islands of evergreen. Tensely sideslipping, Caroline saw, on the edge of this stage, at one side of the track, some trouble, a heap of dark cloth. In her haste to be with the men, Alice

would have swept by, but Caroline snowplowed to a halt. With a dancing waggle Alice swerved and pulled even. The heap of cloth was the woman with the red-tipped nose, who lay on her back, her head downhill. Her daughter knelt beside her. The woman's throat was curved as if she were gargling, and her hood was submerged in snow, so that her face showed like a face in a casket.

Efficiently, Alice bent, released her bindings, and walked to the accident. The prints of her boots in the snow were each perfect intaglios. "Is she conscious?" she asked.

"It's the left," the casket-face said, not altering its rapt relation with the sky. The dab of red was the only color not drained from it. Tears trickled from the corner of one eye into a fringe of sandy hair.

"Do you think it's broken?"

There was no answer, and the girl impatiently prompted, "Mother, does it feel broken?"

"I can't feel anything. Take off the boot."

"I don't think we should take off the boot," Alice said. She surveyed the woman's legs with a physical forthrightness that struck Caroline as unpleasant. "It might disturb the alignment. It might be a spiral. Did you feel anything give?" The impact of the spill had popped both safety bindings, so the woman's skis were attached to her feet only by the breakaway straps. Alice stooped and unclipped these, and stood the skis upright in the snow, as a signal. She said, "We should get help."

The daughter looked up hopefully. The face inside her polka-dot parka was round and young, and a secondary face, the angular face of a woman, had been stenciled over its features. "If you're willing to stay," she said, "I'll go. I know some of the boys in the patrol."

"We'll be happy to stay," Caroline said firmly. She was conscious, as she said it, of frustrating Alice and of declaring, in the necessary war between them, her weapons to be compassion and patience. She wished she could remove her skis, for their presence on her feet held her a little aloof; but she was not sure she could put them back on at this slant, in the middle of nowhere. The snow here had the same eerie un-visited air of grass beside a highway. The daughter, without a backward glance, easily snapped herself into her skis and whipped away, down the hill. Seeing how easy it had been, Caroline unfastened hers and went and stood beside Alice. Her own boots also made exquisite prints, total and sharp. Alice looked at her wristwatch. The hurt woman moaned.

Caroline asked, "Are you warm enough? Would you like to be wrapped in something?" The lack of an answer left them no choice but to remove their parkas and wrap her in them; her body felt like an oversize doll sadly in need of stuffing. Caroline, bending low, satisfied herself that what looked like paint was a little pinnacle of sunburn.

The woman murmured her thanks. "My second day here, I've ruined it for everybody—my daughter, my son . . ."

Alice asked, "Where is your son?"

"Who knows? I bring him here and don't see him from morning to night. He says he's skiing, but I ski every trail and never see him."

"Where is your husband?" Caroline asked; her voice sounded lost in the acoustic depth of the freezing air.

The woman sighed, "Not here."

Silence followed, a silence in which wisps of wind began to decorate the snow-laden branches of pines with out-flowing feathers of powder. The dense blue shadow thrown by the woods grew heavy, and cold pressed through the chinks of Caroline's sweater. Alice's thin neck strained as she gazed up at the vacant ridge for help. The smothered sobbing made a trickling undercurrent. At last, Caroline thought to ask, "Would you like a cigarette?"

The body sat right up. "I'd adore a weed." The woman pulled off her mitten, and hungrily twiddled her fingers. Her nails were garishly polished. She did not seem to notice, in taking the cigarette, that the pack became empty. Gesturing with stabbing exhalations of smoke, she became chatty. "I say to my son, 'What's the point of coming to these beautiful mountains if all you do is rush, rush, rush, up the tow and down, and never stop to enjoy the scenery?' I say to him, 'I'd

rather be old-fashioned and come down the mountain in one piece than have my neck broken at the age of fourteen.' If he saw me now, he'd have a fit laughing. There's a patch of ice up there and my skis crossed. When I went over, I could feel my left side pull from my shoulders to my toes. It reminded me of having a baby."

"Where are you from?" Alice asked.

"Melrose." The name of her town seemed to make the woman morose. Her eyes focused on her inert boot.

To distract her, Caroline asked, "And your husband's working?"

"We're separated. I know if I could loosen the laces it would be a world of relief. My ankle wants to swell and it can't."

"I wouldn't trust it," Alice said.

"Let me at least undo the knot," Caroline offered, and dropped to her knees as if to weep. She did not as a rule like self-pitying women, but here in this one she seemed to confront a voluntary dramatization of her own inner grief and sprain. She freed the knots of both the outer and inner laces—the boot was a new Nordica, and stiff. "Does that feel better?"

"I honestly can't say. I have no feeling below my knee whatsoever."

"Shock," Alice said. "Nature's anesthetic."

"My husband will be furious. He'll have to hire a maid for me."

"You'll have your daughter," Caroline said.

"At her age, it's all boys, boys on the brain."

This seemed to sum up their universe of misfortune. Nothing was left to say. In silence, dark as widows against the tilted acres of white, they waited for rescue. The trail here was so wide skiers could pass on the far side without spotting them. A few swooped close, then veered away, as if sensing a curse. One man, wearing steel-framed spectacles and a raccoon coat, and smoking a cigar, waved to them and shouted in what seemed a foreign language. But the pattern of the afternoon (the sun had shifted away from the trail) yielded few skiers. Empty intervals of minutes went by. The bitterly cold air had found every loose stitch in Caroline's sweater and now was concentrating on the metal bits of brassiere that touched her skin. "Could I bum another coffin nail?'' the injured woman asked.

"I'm sorry, that was my last."

"Oh, dear. Isn't that the limit?"

Alice, so sallow now she seemed Oriental, tucked her hands into her armpits and jiggled up and down. She asked, "Won't the men worry?"

Caroline took satisfaction in telling her, "I doubt it." Looking outward, she saw only white, a tilted rippled wealth of colorlessness. Her private loneliness she now felt in communion with the other two women; they were all three abandoned, cut off in this penumbral world, wounded, unwarmed, too impotent even to whimper. A vein of haze in the sky passingly dimmed the sunlight. When it brightened again, a tiny upright figure, male, in green and yellow stripes, stood at the top of the cataracts of moguls.

"That took eighteen minutes," Alice said, consulting her wristwatch again. Caroline suddenly wondered if such a finicky tomboy could be seriously loved.

The woman in the snow asked, "Does my hair look awful?"

Down, down the tiny figure came, enlarging, dipping from crest to crest, dragging a sled, a bit clumsily, between its legs. Then, hitting perhaps the same patch of ice, the figure tipped, tripped, and became a dark star, spread-eagled, a cloud of powder from which protruded, with electric rapidity, fragments of ski, sled, and arm. This explosive somersault continued to the base of the precipitous section, where the fragments reassembled and lay still. The women had watched with held breaths. How they yearned for that limp puppet to become erect! Obediently, it did. The boy (he was close enough now to be a boy, with lanky legs in swankishly tight jeans) scissored his skis above his head (a miracle, they had not popped off), hopped to his feet, jerkily sidestepped a few yards uphill to retrieve his hat (an Alpine of green felt, with ornamental feathers), and skated toward them, drenched with snow, dragging the sled and grinning.

"That was a real eggbeater," Alice told him.

"Who's hurt?" he asked. His red ears protruded and his face swirled with freckles; he was so plainly delighted to be himself, so clearly somebody's son, that Caroline felt herself share, by a kind of parturition, his absurd pride.

And as if with this clown there entered into vacuity a fertilizing principle, more members of the ski patrol sprang from the snow, bearing from several directions blankets and bandages and brandy, so that Caroline and Alice were pushed aside, as it were, from themselves. They retrieved their parkas, refastened their skis, and tamely completed their run to the foot of the mountain. There, Timmy and Norman, looking worried, were waiting beside the lift shed. Her momentum failing, Mrs. Harris actually skated—what she had never managed to do before, lifted her skis in the smooth alternation of skating—in her haste to assure her husband of his essential innocence.

The Inhabitants of Venus

by IRWIN SHAW

The modern writer most closely associated with skiing through the past two decades has been Irwin Shaw, who spent a good deal of his seventy years on skis, having owned a house in the resort of Klosters in Switzerland for many years, and spent his morning writing and his afternoons skiing. Somewhat slowed down today by knee injury, Shaw nevertheless maintains a keen interest in the sport. One of his last novels, Top of the Hill *is set in a Vermont resort, with the hero leaving his job in Manhattan to become a ski instructor while he sorts out what he wants to do in the future—a recurrent urban fantasy. Here, in a story written over a dozen years ago, Shaw works with a typical international ski scene, and pulls out of it a riveting tale.*

H E had been skiing since early morning, and he was ready to stop and have lunch in the village, but Mac said, "Let's do one more before eating," and since it was Mac's last day, Robert agreed to go up again. The weather was spotty, but there were occasional clear patches of sky, and the visibility had been good enough to make for decent skiing for most of the morning. The teleferique was crowded and they had to push their way in among the bright sweaters and anaracs and the bulky packs of the people who were carrying picnic lunches and extra clothing and skins for climbing. The doors were closed and the cabin swung out of the station, over the belt of pine trees at the base of the mountain.

The passengers were packed in so tightly that it was hard to reach for a handkerchief or light a cigarette. Robert was pressed, not unpleasurably, against a handsome young Italian woman with a dissatisfied face, who was explaining to someone over Robert's shoulder why Milan was such a miserable city to live in in the wintertime. *"Milano si trova in un bacino deprimente,"* the woman said, *"bagnato dalla pioggia durante tre mesi all'anno. E, nonostante il loro gusto per l'opera, i Milanesi non sono altro volgari materialisti che solo il denaro interessa,"* and Robert knew enough Italian to understand that the girl was saying that Milan was in a dismal basin which was swamped by rain for three months a year and that the Milanese, despite their taste for opera, were crass and materialistic and interested only in money.

Robert smiled. Although he had not been born in the United States, he had been a citizen since 1944, and it was pleasant to hear, in the heart of Europe, somebody else besides Americans being accused of materialism and a singular interest in money.

"What's the Contessa saying?" Mac whispered, across the curly red hair of a small Swiss

138

woman who was standing between Robert and Mac. Mac was a lieutenant on leave from his outfit in Germany. He had been in Europe nearly three years and to show that he was not just an ordinary tourist, called all pretty Italian girls Contessa. Robert had met him a week before, in the bar of the hotel they were both staying at. They were the same kind of skiers, adventurous and looking for difficulties, and they had skied together every day, and they were already planning to come back at the same time for the next winter's holiday, if Robert could get over again from America.

"The Contessa is saying that in Milan all they're interested in is money," Robert said, keeping his voice low, although in the babble of conversation in the cabin there was little likelihood of being overheard.

"If I was in Milan," Mac said, "and she was in Milan, I'd be interested in something else besides money." He looked with open admiration at the Italian girl. "Can you find out what run she's going to do?"

"What for?" Robert asked.

"Because that's the run I'm going to do," Mac said, grinning. "I plan to follow her like her shadow."

"Mac," Robert said, "don't waste your time. It's your last day."

"That's when the best things always happen," Mac said. "The last day." He beamed, huge, overt, uncomplicated, at the Italian girl. She took no notice of him. She was busy now complaining to her friend about the natives of Sicily.

The sun came out for a few minutes and it grew hot in the cabin, with some forty people jammed, in heavy clothing, in such a small space, and Robert half-dozed, not bothering to listen anymore to the voices speaking in French, Italian, English, Schweizerdeutsch, German, on all sides of him. Robert liked being in the middle of this informal congress of tongues. It was one of the reasons that he came to Switzerland to ski, whenever he could take the time off from his job. In the angry days through which the world was passing, there was a ray of hope in this good-natured polyglot chorus of people who were not

threatening each other, who smiled at strangers, who had collected in these shining white hills merely to enjoy the innocent pleasures of sun and snow.

The feeling of generalized cordiality that Robert experienced on these trips was intensified by the fact that most of the people on the lifts and on the runs seemed more or less familiar to him. Skiers formed a kind of loose international club and the same faces kept turning up year after year in Mégève, Davos, St. Anton, Val d'Isère, so that after a while you had the impression you knew almost everybody on the mountain. There were four or five Americans whom Robert was sure he had seen at Stowe at Christmas and who had come over in one of the chartered ski club planes that Swiss Air ran every winter on a cut-rate basis. The Americans were young and enthusiastic and none of them had ever been in Europe before and they were rather noisily appreciative of everything—the Alps, the food, the snow, the weather, the appearance of the peasants in their blue smocks, the chic of some of the lady skiers and the skill and good looks of the instructors. They were popular with the villagers because they were so obviously enjoying themselves. Besides, they tipped generously, in the American style, with what was, to Swiss eyes, an endearing disregard of the fact that a service charge of fifteen percent was added automatically to every bill that was presented to them. Two of the girls were very attractive, in a youthful, prettiest-girl-at-the-prom way, and one of the young men, a lanky boy from Philadelphia, the informal leader of the group, was a beautiful skier, who guided the others down the runs and helped the dubs when they ran into difficulties.

The Philadelphian, who was standing near Robert, spoke to him as the cabin swung high over a steep snowy face of the mountain. "You've skied here before, haven't you?" he said.

"Yes," said Robert, "a few times."

"What's the best run down this time of day?" the Philadelphian asked. He had the drawling, flat tone of the good New England schools that Europeans use in their imitations of upper-class Americans when they wish to make fun of them.

"They're all okay today," Robert said.

"What's this run everybody says is so good?" the boy asked. "The . . . the Kaiser something or other?"

"The Kaisergarten," Robert said. "It's the first gully to the right after you get out of the station on top."

"Is it tough?" the boy asked.

"It's not for beginners," Robert said.

"You've seen this bunch ski, haven't you?" The boy waved vaguely to indicate his friends. "Do you think they can make it?"

"Well," Robert said doubtfully, "there's a narrow steep ravine full of bumps halfway down, and there're one or two places where it's advisable not to fall, because you're liable to keep on sliding all the way, if you do. . . ."

"Aah, we'll take a chance," the Philadelphian said. "It'll be good for their characters. Boys and girls," he said, raising his voice, "the cowards will stay on top and have lunch. The heroes will come with me. We're going to the Kaisergarten. . . ."

"Francis," one of the pretty girls said. "I do believe it is your sworn intention to kill me on this trip."

"It's not as bad as all that," Robert said, smiling at the girl, to reassure her.

"Say," the girl said, looking interestedly at Robert, "haven't I seen you someplace before?"

"On this lift, yesterday," Robert said.

"No." The girl shook her head. She had on a black, fuzzy, lambskin hat, and she looked like a high-school drum majorette pretending to be Anna Karenina. "Before yesterday. Someplace."

"I saw you at Stowe," Robert confessed. "At Christmas."

"Oh, that's where," she said. "I saw you ski. Oh, my, you're *silky.*"

Mac broke into a loud laugh at this description of Robert's skiing style.

"Don't mind my friend," Robert said, enjoying the girl's admiration. "He's a coarse soldier who is trying to beat the mountain to its knees by brute strength."

"Say," the girl said, looking a little puzzled.

"You have a funny little way of talking. Are you American?"

"Well, yes," Robert said. "I am now. I was born in France."

"Oh, that explains it," the girl said. "You were born among the crags."

"I was born in Paris," Robert said.

"Do you live there now?"

"I live in New York," Robert said.

"Are you married?" The girl asked anxiously.

"Barbara," the Philadelphian protested, "behave yourself."

"I just asked the man a simple, friendly question," the girl protested. "Do you mind, monsieur?"

"Not at all."

"*Are* you married?"

"Yes," Robert said.

"He has three children," Mac added helpfully. "The oldest one is going to run for president at the next election."

"Oh, isn't that too bad," the girl said. "I set myself a goal on this trip. I was going to meet one unmarried Frenchman."

"I'm sure you'll manage it," Robert said.

"Where is your wife now?" the girl said.

"In New York."

"Pregnant," Mac said, more helpful than ever.

"And she lets you run off and ski all alone like this?" the girl asked incredulously.

"Yes," Robert said. "Actually, I'm in Europe on business, and I sneaked off ten days."

"What business?" the girl asked.

"I'm a diamond merchant," Robert said. "I buy and sell diamonds."

"That's the sort of man I'd like to meet," the girl said. "Somebody awash with diamonds. But unmarried."

"Barbara!" the Philadelphian said.

"I deal mostly in industrial diamonds," Robert said. "It's not exactly the same thing."

"Even so," the girl said.

"Barbara," the Philadelphian said, "pretend you're a lady."

"If you can't speak candidly to a fellow American," the girl said, "who can you speak

The skier in silhouette looks like a kind of extraterrestrial being

candidly to?'' She looked out the Plexiglas window of the cabin. "Oh, dear," she said, "it's a perfect monster of a mountain, isn't it? I'm in a *fever* of terror." She turned and regarded Robert carefully. "You *do* look like a Frenchman," she said. "Terribly polished. You're definitely *sure* you're married?"

"Barbara," the Philadelphian said forlornly.

Robert laughed and Mac and the other Americans laughed and the girl smiled under her fuzzy hat, amused at her own clowning and pleased at the reaction she was getting. The other people in the car, who could not understand English, smiled good-naturedly at the laughter, happy, even though they were not in on the joke, to be the witnesses of this youthful gaiety.

Then, through the laughter, Robert heard a man's voice nearby, saying, in quiet tones of cold distaste, *"Schaut euch diese dummen amerikanischen Gesichter an! Und diese Leute bilden sich ein, sie wären berufen, die Welt zu regieren."*

Robert had learned German as a child, from his Alsatian grandparents, and he understood what he had just heard, but he forced himself not to turn around to see who had said it. His years of temper, he liked to believe, were behind him, and if nobody else in the cabin had overheard the voice or understood the words that had been spoken, he was not going to be the one to force the issue. He was here to enjoy himself and he didn't feel like getting into a fight or dragging Mac and the other youngsters into one. Long ago, he had learned the wisdom of playing deaf when he heard things like that, or worse. If some bastard of a German wanted to say, "Look at those stupid American faces. And these are the people who think they have been chosen to rule the world," it made very little real difference to anybody, and a grown-up man ignored it if he could. So he didn't look to see who had said it, because he knew that if he picked out the man, he wouldn't be able to let it go. This way, as an anonymous, though hateful voice, he could let it slide, along with many of the other things that Germans had said during his lifetime.

The effort of not looking was difficult, though, and he closed his eyes, angry with himself for being so disturbed by a scrap of overheard malice like this. It had been a perfect holiday up to now, and it would be foolish to let it be shadowed, even briefly, by a random voice in a crowd. If you came to Switzerland to ski, Robert told himself, you had to expect to find some Germans. Though each year now there were more and more of them, massive, prosperous-looking men and sulky-looking women with the suspicious eyes of people who believe they are in danger of being cheated. Men and women both pushed more than was necessary in the lift lines, with a kind of impersonal egotism, a racial, unquestioning assumption of precedence. When they skied, they did it grimly, in large groups, as if under military orders. At night, when they relaxed in the bars and *stublis,* their merriment was more difficult to tolerate than their dedicated daytime gloom and Junker arrogance. They sat in red-faced platoons, drinking gallons of beer, volleying out great bursts of heavy laughter and roaring glee-club arrangements of students' drinking songs. Robert had not yet heard them sing the Horst Wessel song, but he noticed that they had long ago stopped pretending that they were Swiss or Austrian or that they had been born in the Alsace. Somehow, to the sport of skiing, which is, above all, individual and light and an exercise in grace, the Germans seemed to bring the notion of the herd. Once or twice, when he had been trampled in the teleferique station, he had shown some of his distaste to Mac, but Mac, who was far from being a fool under his puppy-fullback exterior, had said, "The trick is to isolate them, lad. It's only when they're in groups that they get on your nerves. I've been in Germany for three years and I've met a lot of good fellows and some *smashing* girls."

Robert had agreed that Mac was probably right. Deep in his heart, he wanted to believe that Mac was right. Before and during the war the problem of the Germans had occupied so much of his waking life, that V-E Day had seemed to him a personal liberation from them, a kind of graduation ceremony from a school in which he had been forced to spend long years, trying to solve a single, boring, painful problem. He had reasoned himself into believing that their defeat had returned the Germans to rationality. So, along with the relief he felt because he no longer ran the risk of being killed by them, there was the almost as intense relief that he no longer had especially to *think* about them.

Once the war was over, he had advocated reestablishing normal relations with the Germans as quickly as possible, both as good politics and simple humanity. He drank German beer and even bought a Volkswagen, although if it were up to him, given the taste for catastrophe that was latent in the German soul, he would not equip the German army with the hydrogen bomb. In the course of his business he had very few dealings with Germans and it was only here, in this village in the Graubunden, where their presence was becoming so much more visible each year, that the *idea* of Germans disturbed him anymore. But he loved the village and the thought of abandoning his yearly vacation there because of the prevalence of license plates from Munich and Dusseldorf was repugnant to him. Maybe, he thought, from now on he would come at a different time, in January, instead of late in February. Late February and early March was the German season, when the sun was warmer and shone until six o'clock in the evening. The Germans were sun gluttons and could be seen all over the hills, stripped to the waist, sitting on rocks, eating their picnic lunches, greedily absorbing each precious ray of sunlight. It was as though they came from a country perpetually covered in mist, like the planet Venus, and had to soak up as much brightness and life as possible in the short periods of their holidays to be able to endure the harshness and gloom of their homeland and the conduct of the other inhabitants of Venus for the rest of the year.

Robert smiled to himself at this tolerant concept and felt better-disposed toward everyone around him. Maybe, he thought, if I were a single man, I'd find a Bavarian girl and fall in love with her and finish the whole thing off then and there.

"I warn you, Francis," the girl in the lambskin hat was saying, "if you do me to death on this mountain, there are three juniors at Yale who will track you down to the ends of the earth."

Then he heard the German voice again. *"Warum haben die Amerikaner nicht genügend Verstand,"* the voice said, low but distinctly, near him, the accent clearly Hochdeutsch and not Zurichois or any of the other variations of Schweizerdeutsch, *"ihre dummen kleinen Nutten zu Hause zu lassen, wo sie hingehören?"*

Now, he knew there was no avoiding looking and there was no avoiding doing something about it. He glanced at Mac first, to see if Mac, who understood a little German, had heard. Mac was huge and could be dangerous, and for all his easy good nature, if he had heard the man say, "Why don't the Americans have the sense to leave their silly little whores at home where they belong?" the man was in for a beating. But Mac was still beaming placidly at the Contessa. That was all to the good, Robert thought, relieved. The Swiss police took a dim view of fighting, no matter what the provocation, and Mac, enraged, was likely to wreak terrible damage in a fight, and would more than likely wind up in jail. For an American career soldier on duty in Frankfurt, a brawl like that could have serious consequences. The worst that can happen to me, Robert thought, as he turned to find the man who had spoken, is a few hours in the pokey and a lecture from the magistrate about abusing Swiss hospitality.

Almost automatically, Robert decided that when they got to the top, he would follow the man who had spoken out of the car, tell him quietly, that he, Robert, had understood what had been said about Americans in the car, and swing immediately. I just hope, Robert thought, that whoever it is isn't too damned large.

For a moment, Robert couldn't pick out his opponent-to-be. There was a tall man with his back to Robert, on the other side of the Italian woman, and the voice had come from that direction. Because of the crowd, Robert could only see his head and shoulders, which were bulky and powerful under a black parka. The man had on a white cap of the kind that had been worn by the Afrika Corps during the war. The man was with a plump, hard-faced woman who was whispering earnestly to him, but not loudly enough for Robert to be able to hear what she was saying. Then the man said, crisply, in German, replying to the woman, "I don't care how many of them understand the language. Let them understand," and Robert knew that he had found his man.

An exhilarated tingle of anticipation ran through Robert, making his hands and arms feel tense and jumpy. He regretted that the cabin wouldn't arrive at the top for another five minutes. Now that he had decided the fight was inevitable, he could hardly bear waiting. He stared fixedly at the man's broad, black-nylon back, wishing the fellow would turn around so that he could see his face. He wondered if the man would go down with the first blow, if he would apologize, if he would try to use his ski poles. Robert decided to keep his own poles handy, just in case, although Mac could be depended upon to police matters thoroughly if he saw weapons being used. Deliberately Robert took off his heavy leather mittens and stuck them in his belt. The correction would be more effective with bare knuckles. He wondered, fleetingly, if the man was wearing a ring. He kept his eyes fixed on the back of the man's neck, willing him to turn around. Then the plump woman noticed his stare. She dropped her eyes and whispered something to the man in the black parka and after several seconds, he finally turned around, pretending that it was a casual, unmotivated movement. The man looked squarely at Robert and Robert thought, If you ski long enough you meet every other skier you've ever known. At the same moment, he knew that it wasn't going to be a nice simple little fistfight on the top of the mountain. He knew that somehow he was going to have to kill the man whose icy blue eyes, fringed with pale blond lashes, were staring challengingly at him from under the white peak of the Afrika Corps cap.

It was a long time ago, the winter of 1938, in the French part of Switzerland, and he was fourteen years old and the sun was setting behind another mountain and it was ten below zero and he was lying in the snow, with his foot turned in that funny, unnatural way, although the pain hadn't really begun yet, and the eyes were looking down at him. . . .

He had done something foolish, and at the moment he was more worried about what his parents would say when they found out than about the broken leg. He had gone up, alone, late in the afternoon, when almost everybody else was off the mountain, and even so he hadn't stayed on the normal *piste,* but had started bushwacking through the forest, searching for powder snow that hadn't been tracked by other skiers. One ski had caught on a hidden root and he had fallen forward, hearing the sickening dry cracking sound from his right leg, even as he pitched into the snow.

Trying not to panic, he had sat up, facing in the direction of the *piste,* whose markers he could see some hundred meters away, through the pine forest. If any skiers happened to come by, they might just, with luck, be able to hear him if he shouted. For the moment, he did not try to crawl toward the line of poles, because when he moved a very queer feeling flickered from his ankle up his leg to the pit of his stomach, making him want to throw up.

The shadows were very long now in the forest, and only the highest peaks were rose-colored against a frozen green sky. He was beginning to feel the cold and from time to time he was shaken by acute spasms of shivering.

I'm going to die here, he thought, I'm going to die here tonight. He thought of his parents and his sister probably having tea, comfortably seated this moment in the warm dining room of the chalet two miles down the mountain, and he bit his lips to keep back the tears. They wouldn't start to worry about him for another hour or two yet, and then when they did, and started to do something about finding him, they wouldn't know where to begin. He had known none of the seven or eight people who had been on the lift with him on his last ride up and he hadn't told anybody what run he was going to take. There were three different mountains, with their separate lifts, and their numberless variations of runs, that he might have taken, and finding him in the dark would be an almost hopeless task. He looked up at the sky. There were clouds moving in from the east, slowly, a black high wall, covering the already darkened sky. If it snowed that night, there was a good chance they wouldn't even find his body before spring. He had promised his mother that no matter what happened, he would never ski alone, and he had broken the promise and this was his punishment.

Then he heard the sound of skis, coming fast, making a harsh, metallic noise on the iced snow of the *piste*. Before he could see the skier, he began to shout, with all the strength of his lungs, frantically, *"Au secours! Au secours!"*

A dark shape, going very fast, appeared high up for a second, disappeared behind a clump of trees, then shot into view much lower down, almost on a level with the place where Robert was sitting. Robert shouted wildly, hysterically, not uttering words anymore, just a senseless, passionate, throat-bursting claim on the attention of the human race, represented, for this one instant at sunset on this cold mountain, by the dark, expert figure plunging swiftly, with a harsh scraping of steel edges and a *whoosh* of wind, toward the village below.

Then, miraculously, the figure stopped, in a swirl of snow. Robert shouted wordlessly, the sound of his voice echoing hysterically in the forest. For a moment the skier didn't move and Robert shook with the fear that it was all a hallucination, a mirage of sight and sound, that there was no one there on the beaten snow at the edge of the forest, that he was only imagining that he was shouting, that with all the fierce effort of his throat and lungs, he was mute, unheard.

Suddenly, he couldn't see anything anymore. He had the sensation of a curtain sinking somewhere within him, of a wall of warm liquid inundating the ducts and canals of his body. He waved his hands weakly and toppled slowly over in a faint.

When he came to, a man was kneeling over him, rubbing his cheeks with snow. "You heard me," Robert said in French to the man. "I was afraid you wouldn't hear me."

"Ich verstehe nicht," the man said. *"Nicht parler Französisch."*

"I was afraid you wouldn't hear me," Robert repeated, in German.

"You are a stupid little boy," the man said severely, in clipped, educated German. "And very lucky. I am the last man on the mountain." He felt Robert's ankle, his hands hard but deft. "Nice," he said ironically, "very nice. You're going to be in plaster for at least three months. Here—lie still. I am going to take your skis off. You will be more comfortable." He undid the long leather thongs, working swiftly, and stood the skis up in the snow. Then he swept the snow off a stump a few yards away and got around behind Robert and put his hands under Robert's armpits. "Relax," he said. "Do not try to help me." He picked Robert up.

"Luckily," he said, "you weigh nothing. How old are you?—eleven?"

"Fourteen," Robert said.

"What's the matter?" the man said, laughing. "Don't they feed you in Switzerland?"

"I'm French," Robert said.

"Oh," the man's voice went flat. "French." He half-carried, half-dragged Robert over to the stump and sat him down gently on it. "There," he said, "at least you're out of the snow. You won't freeze—for the time being. Now, listen carefully. I will take your skis down with me to the ski school and I will tell them where you are and tell them to send a sled for you. They should get to you in less than an hour. Now, whom are you staying with in town?"

"My mother and father. At the Chalet Montana."

"Good." The man nodded. "The Chalet Montana. Do they speak German, too?"

"Yes."

"Excellent," the man said. "I will telephone them and tell them their foolish son has broken his leg and that the patrol is taking him to the hospital. What is your name?"

"Robert."

"Robert what?"

"Robert Rosenthal," Robert said. "Please don't say I'm hurt too badly. They'll be worried enough as it is."

The man didn't answer immediately. He busied himself tying Robert's skis together and slung them over his shoulder. "Do not worry, Robert Rosenthal," he said, "I will not worry them more than is necessary." Abruptly, he started off, sweeping easily through the trees, his poles held in one hand, Robert's skis balanced across his shoulders with his other hand.

His sudden departure took Robert by surprise and it was only when the man was a considerable distance away, already almost lost among the trees, that Robert realized he hadn't thanked the man for saving his life. "Thank you," he shouted into the growing darkness. "Thank you very much."

The man didn't stop and Robert never knew whether he had heard his cry of thanks or not. Because after an hour, when it was completely dark, with the stars covered by the cloud that had been moving in at sunset from the east, the patrol had not yet appeared. Robert had a watch with a radium dial. Timing himself by it, he waited exactly one hour and a half, until ten minutes past seven, and then decided that nobody was coming for him and that if he hoped to live through the night he would somehow have to crawl out of the forest and make his way down to the town by himself.

He was rigid with cold by now, and suffering from shock. His teeth were chattering in a frightening way, as though his jaws were part of an insane machine over which he had no control. There was no feeling in his fingers anymore and the pain in his leg came in ever-enlarging waves of metallic throbbing. He had put up the hood of his parka and sunk his head as low down on his chest as he could, and the cloth of the parka was stiff with his frosted breath. He heard a whimpering sound somewhere around him and it was only after what seemed to him several minutes that he realized the whimpering sound was coming from him and that there was nothing he could do to stop it.

Stiffly, with exaggerated care, he tried to lift himself off the tree stump and down into the snow without putting any weight on his injured leg, but at the last moment he slipped and twisted the leg as he went down. He screamed twice and lay with his face in the snow and thought of just staying that way and forgetting the whole thing, the whole intolerable effort of remaining alive. Later on, when he was much

older, he came to the conclusion that the one thing that made him keep moving was the thought of his mother and father waiting for him, with anxiety that would soon grow into terror, in the town below him.

He pulled himself along on his belly, digging at the snow in front of his face with his hands, using rocks, low-hanging branches, snow-covered roots, to help him, meter by meter, out of the forest. His watch was torn off somewhere along the way and when he finally reached the line of poles that marked the packed snow and ice of the *piste* he had no notion of whether it had taken him five minutes or five hours to cover the hundred meters from the place he had fallen. He lay panting, sobbing, staring at the lights of the town far below him, knowing that he could never reach them, knowing that he had to reach them. The effort of crawling through the deep snow had warmed him again and his face was streaming with sweat, and the blood coming back into his numbed hands and feet jabbed him with a thousand needles of pain.

The lights of the town guided him now, and here and there he could see the marker poles outlined against their small, cozy Christmasy glow. It was easier going, too, on the packed snow of the *piste* and from time to time he managed to slide ten or fifteen meters without stopping, tobogganing on his stomach, screaming occasionally when the foot of his broken leg banged loosely against an icy bump or twisted as he went over a steep embankment to crash against a level spot below. Once he couldn't stop himself and he fell into a swiftly rushing small stream and pulled himself out of it five minutes later with his gloves and stomach and knees soaked with icy water. And still the lights of the town seemed as far away as ever.

Finally, he felt he couldn't move anymore. He was exhausted and he had had to stop twice to vomit and the vomit had been a gush of blood. He tried to sit up, so that if the snow came that night, there would be a chance that somebody would see the top of his head sticking out of the new cover in the morning. As he was struggling to push himself erect a shadow passed between him and the lights of the town. The shadow was very close and with his last breath he called out. Later on, the peasant who rescued him said that what he called out was "Excuse me."

The peasant was moving hay on a big sled from one of the hill barns down to the valley, and he rolled the hay off and put Robert on instead. Then, carefully braking and taking the sled on a path that cut back and forth across the *piste,* he brought Robert down to the valley and the hospital.

By the time his mother and father had been notified and had reached the hospital, the doctor had given him a shot of morphine and was in the middle of setting the leg. So it wasn't until the next morning, as he lay in the gray hospital room, sweating with pain, with his leg in traction, that he could get out any kind of coherent story and tell his parents what had happened.

"Then I saw this man skiing very fast, all alone," Robert said, trying to speak normally, without showing how much the effort was costing him, trying to take the look of shock and agony from his parent's set faces by pretending that his leg hardly hurt him at all, and that the whole incident was of small importance. "He heard me and came over and took off my skis and made me comfortable on a tree stump and he asked me what my name was and where my parents were staying and he said he'd go to the ski school and tell them where I was and to send a sled for me and then he'd call you at the chalet and tell you they were bringing me down to the hospital. Then, after more than an hour, it was pitch dark already, nobody came and I decided I'd better not wait anymore and I started down and I was lucky and I saw this farmer with a sled and . . ."

"You were very lucky," Robert's mother said flatly. She was a small, neat, plump woman, with bad nerves, who was only at home in cities. She detested the cold, detested the mountains, detested the idea of her loved ones running what seemed to her the senseless risk of injury that skiing involved, and only came on these holidays because Robert and his father and sister were so passionate about the sport. Now she was white with fatigue and worry, and if Robert had not

been immobilized in traction she would have had him out of the accursed mountains that morning on the train to Paris.

"Now, Robert," his father said, "is it possible that when you hurt yourself, the pain did things to you, and that you just *imagined* you saw a man, and just imagined he told you he was going to call us and get you a sled from the ski school?"

"I didn't imagine it, papa," Robert said. The morphine had made him feel hazy and heavy-brained and he was puzzled that his father was talking to him that way. "Why do you think I might have imagined it?"

"Because," said his father, "nobody called us last night until ten o'clock, when the doctor telephoned from the hospital. And nobody called the ski school, either."

"I didn't imagine him," Robert repeated. He was hurt that his father perhaps thought he was lying. "If he came into this room I'd know him right off. He was wearing a white cap, he was a big man with a black anarac, and he had blue eyes, they looked a little funny, because his eyelashes were almost white and from a little way off it looked as though he didn't have any eyelashes at all. . . ."

"How old was he, do you think?" Robert's father asked. "As old as I am?" Robert's father was nearly fifty.

"No," Robert said. "I don't think so."

"Was he as old as your Uncle Jules?" Robert's father asked.

"Yes," Robert said. "Just about." He wished his father and mother would leave him alone. He was all right now. His leg was in plaster and he wasn't dead and in three months, the doctor said, he'd be walking again, and he wanted to forget everything that had happened last night in the forest.

"So," Robert's mother said, "he was a man of about twenty-five, with a white cap and blue eyes." She picked up the phone and asked for the ski school.

Robert's father lit a cigarette and went over to the window and looked out. It was snowing. It had been snowing since midnight, heavily, and the lifts weren't running today because a driving wind had sprung up with the snow and there was danger of avalanches up on top.

"Did you talk to the farmer who picked me up?" Robert asked.

"Yes," said his father. "He said you were a very brave little boy. He also said that if he hadn't found you, you couldn't have gone on more than another fifty meters. I gave him two hundred francs. Swiss."

"Sssh," Robert's mother said. She had the connection with the ski school now. "This is Mrs. Rosenthal again. Yes, thank you, he's doing as well as can be expected," she said, in her precise, melodious French. "We've been talking to him and there's one aspect of his story that's a little strange. He says a man stopped and helped him take off his skis last night after he'd broken his leg, and promised to go to the ski school and leave the skis there and ask for a sled to be sent to bring him down. We'd like to know if, in fact, the man did come into the office and report the accident. It would have been somewhere around six o'clock." She listened for a moment, her face tense. "I see," she said. She listened again. "No," she said, "we don't know his name. My son says he was about twenty-five years old, with blue eyes and a white cap. Wait a minute. I'll ask." She turned to Robert. "Robert," she said, "what kind of skis did you have? They're going to look and see if they're out front in the rack."

"Attenhoffer's," Robert said. "One meter seventy. And they have my initials in red up on the tips."

"Attenhoffer's," his mother repeated over the phone. "And they have his initials on them. R.R., in red. Thank you. I'll wait."

Robert's father came back from the window, dousing his cigarette in an ashtray. Underneath the holiday tan of his skin, his face looked weary and sick. "Robert," he said, with a rueful smile, "you must learn to be a little more careful. You are my only male heir and there is very little chance that I shall produce another."

"Yes, papa," Robert said. "I'll be careful."

His mother waved impatiently at them to be quiet and listened again at the telephone. "Thank you," she said. "Please call me if you hear anything." She hung up. "No," she said to Robert's father, "the skis aren't there."

"It can't be possible," Robert's father said, "that a man would leave a little boy to freeze to death just to steal a pair of skis."

"I'd like to get my hands on him," Robert's mother said. "Just for ten minutes. Robert, darling, think hard. Did he seem . . . well . . . did he seem *normal?*"

"He seemed all right," Robert said. "I suppose."

"Was there any other thing about him that you noticed? Think hard. Anything that would help us find him. It's not only for us, Robert. If there's a man in this town who would do something like that to you, it's important that people know about him, before he does something even worse to other boys . . . "

"Mama," Robert said, feeling close to tears under the insistence of his mother's questioning, "I told you just the way it was. Everything. I'm not lying, mama."

"What did he *sound* like, Robert?" his mother said. "Did he have a low voice, a high voice, did he sound like us, as though he lived in Paris, did he sound like any of your teachers, did he sound like the other people from around here, did he . . . ?"

"Oh . . . " Robert said, remembering.

"What is it? What do you want to say?" his mother said sharply.

"I had to speak German to him," Robert said. Until now, with the pain and the morphine, it hadn't occurred to him to mention that.

"What do you mean you had to speak German to him?"

"I started to speak to him in French and he didn't understand. We spoke in German."

His father and mother exchanged glances. Then his mother said, gently, "Was it real German? Or was it Swiss-German? You know the difference, don't you?"

"Of course," Robert said. One of his father's parlor tricks was giving imitations of Swiss friends in Paris speaking in French and then in Swiss-German. Robert had a good ear for languages, and aside from having heard his Alsatian grandparents speaking German since he was an infant, he was studying German literature in school and knew long passages of Goethe and Schiller and Heine by heart. "It was German, all right," he said.

There was silence in the room. His father went over to the window again and looked out at the snow falling in a soft blurred curtain outside. "I knew," his father said quietly, "that it couldn't just have been for the skis."

In the end, his father won out. His mother wanted to go to the police and get them to try to find the man, even though his father pointed out that there were perhaps ten thousand skiers in the town for the holidays, a good percentage of them German-speaking and blue-eyed, and trainloads arriving and departing five times a day. Robert's father was sure that the man had left the very night Robert had broken his leg, although all during the rest of his stay in the town, Mr. Rosenthal prowled along the snowy streets and in and out of bars searching among the faces for one that answered Robert's description of the man on the mountain. But he said it would do no good to go to the police and might do harm, because once the story got out there would be plenty of people to complain that this was just another hysterical Jewish fantasy of invented injury. "There're plenty of Nazis in Switzerland, of all nationalities," Robert's father told his mother, in the course of an argument that lasted weeks, "and this will just give them more ammunition, they'll be able to say, 'See, wherever the Jews go they start trouble.'"

Robert's mother, who was made of sterner stuff than her husband, and who had relatives in Germany who smuggled out disturbing letters to her, wanted justice at any cost, but after a while even she saw the hopelessness of pushing the matter any further. Four weeks after the accident, when Robert could finally be moved, as she sat beside her son in the ambulance that was to take them both to Geneva and then on to Paris, she said, in a dead voice, holding Robert's hand, "Soon, we must leave Europe. I cannot stand to live anymore on a continent where things like this are permitted to happen."

Much later, during the war, after Mr. Rosenthal had died in occupied France and Robert and his mother and sister were in America, a friend of Robert's, who had also done a lot of skiing in Europe, heard the story of the man in the white cap, and told Robert he was almost sure he recognized the man from the description Robert gave of him. It was a ski instructor from Garmisch, or maybe from Obersdorf or Freudenstadt, who had a couple of rich Austrian clients with whom he toured each winter from one ski station to another. The friend didn't know the man's name, and the one time Robert had been in Garmisch, it had been with French troops in the closing days of the war, and of course nobody was skiing then.

Now the man was standing just three feet from him, his face, on the other side of the pretty Italian woman, framed by straight black lines of skis, his eyes looking coolly, with insolent amusement, but without recognition, at Robert, from under the almost albino eyelashes. He was approaching fifty now and his face was fleshy but hard and healthy, with a thin, set mouth that gave a sense of control and self-discipline to his expression.

Robert hated him. He hated him for the attempted murder of a fourteen-year-old boy in 1938; he hated him for the acts that he must have condoned or collaborated in during the war; he hated him for his father's disappearance and his mother's exile; he hated him for what he had said about the pretty little American girl in the lambskin hat; he hated him for the confident impudence of his glance and the healthy, untouched robustness of his face and neck; he hated him because he could look directly into the eyes of a man he had tried to kill and not recognize him; he hated him because he was here, bringing the idea of death and shamefully unconsummated vengeance into this silvery holiday bubble climbing the placid air of a kindly, welcoming country.

And most of all he hated the man in the white cap because the man betrayed and made a sour joke of the precariously achieved peace that Robert had built for himself, with his wife, his children, his job, his comfortable, easygoing, generously forgetful Americanism, since the war.

The German deprived him of his sense of

normalcy. Living with a wife and three children in a clean, cheerful house was not normal; having your name in the telephone directory was not normal; lifting your hat to your neighbor and paying your bills was not normal; obeying the law and depending upon the protection of the police was not normal. The German sent him back through the years to an older and truer normality—murder, blood, flight, conspiracy, pillage, and ruins. For a while Robert had deceived himself into believing that the nature of everyday could change. The German in the crowded cabin had now put him to rights. Meeting the German had been an accident, but the accident had revealed what was permanent and nonaccidental in his life and the life of the people around him.

Mac was saying something to him, and the girl in the lambskin hat was singing an American song in a soft, small voice, but he didn't hear what Mac was saying and the words of the song made no sense to him. He had turned away from looking at the German and was looking at the steep stone face of the mountain, now almost obscured by a swirling cloud, and he was trying to figure out how he could get rid of Mac, escape the young Americans, follow the German, get him alone, and kill him.

He had no intention of making it a duel. He did not intend to give the man a chance to fight for his life. It was punishment he was after, not a symbol of honor. He remembered other stories of men who had been in concentration camps during the war who had suddenly confronted their torturers later on and had turned them in to the authorities and had the satisfaction of witnessing their execution. But whom could he turn the German over to—the Swiss police? For what crime that would fit into what criminal code?

Or he could do what an ex-prisoner had done in Budapest three or four years after the war, when he had met one of his jailers on a bridge over the Danube and had simply picked the man up and thrown him into the water and watched him drown. The ex-prisoner had explained who he was and who the drowned man was and had been let off and had been treated as a hero. But Switzerland was not Hungary, the

Danube was far away, the war had finished a long time ago.

No, what he had to do was follow the man, stay with him, surprise him alone somewhere on the slopes, contrive a murder that would look like an accident, be out of the country before anyone asked any questions, divulge nothing to anyone, leave the body, if possible, in an isolated place where the snow would cover it and where it would not be found till the farmers drove their herds high up into the mountains for the summer pasturage. And he had to do it swiftly, before the man realized that he was the object of any special attention on Robert's part, before he started to wonder about the American on his tracks, before the process of memory began its work and the face of the skinny fourteen-year-old boy on the dark mountain in 1938 began to emerge from the avenging face of the grown man.

Robert had never killed a man. During the war, he had been assigned by the American army as part of a liaison team to a French division, and while he had been shot at often enough, he had never fired a gun after arriving in Europe. When the war was over, he had been secretly thankful that he had been spared the necessity of killing. Now he understood—he was not to be spared; his war was not over.

"Say, Robert . . . " It was Mac's voice finally breaking through into his consciousness. "What's the matter? I've been talking to you for thirty seconds and you haven't heard a word I said. Are you sick? You look awfully queer, lad."

"I'm all right," Robert said. "I have a little headache. That's all. Maybe I'd better eat something, get something warm to drink. You go ahead down by yourself."

"Of course not," Mac said. "I'll wait for you."

"Don't be silly," Robert said, trying to keep his tone natural and friendly. "You'll lose the Contessa. Actually, I don't feel much like skiing anymore today. The weather's turned lousy." He gestured at the cloud that was enveloping them. "You can't see a thing. I'll probably take the lift back down. . . ."

"Hey, you're beginning to worry me," Mac

said anxiously. "I'll stick with you. You want me to take you to a doctor?"

"Leave me alone, please, Mac," Robert said. He had to get rid of Mac and if it meant hurting his feelings now, he'd make it up to him some way, but later. "When I get one of these headaches I prefer being alone."

"You're sure now?" Mac asked.

"I'm sure."

"Okay. See you at the hotel for tea?"

"Yes," Robert said. After murder, Robert thought, I always have a good tea. He prayed that the Italian girl would put her skis on immediately and move off quickly once they got to the top, so that Mac would be gone before Robert had to start off after the man in the white cap.

The cabin was swinging over the last pylon now and slowing down to come into the station. The passengers were stirring a bit, arranging clothes, testing bindings, in preparation for the descent. Robert stole a quick glance at the German. The woman with him was knotting a silk scarf around his throat, with little wifely gestures. She had the face of a cook. Neither she nor the man looked in Robert's direction. I will face the problem of the woman when I come to it, Robert thought.

The cabin came to a stop and the skiers began to disembark. Robert was close to the door and was one of the first people out. Without looking back, he walked swiftly out of the station and into the shifting grayness of the mountaintop. One side of the mountain dropped off in a sheer, rocky face next to the station and Robert went over and stood on the edge, looking out. If the German, for any reason, happened to come over near him to admire the view or to judge the condition of the *piste* of the Kaisergarten, which had to be entered some distance farther on, but which cut back under the cliff much lower down, where the slope became more gradual, there was a possibility that one quick move on Robert's part would send the man crashing down to the rocks some hundred meters below, and the whole thing would be over. Robert turned and faced the exit of the station, searching in the crowd of brightly dressed skiers for the white cap.

He saw Mac come out with the Italian girl. He was talking to her and carrying her skis and the girl was smiling warmly. Mac waved at Robert and then knelt to help the girl put on her skis. Robert took a deep breath. Mac, at least, was out of the way. And the American group had decided to have lunch on top and had gone into the restaurant near the station.

The white cap was not to be seen. The German and the woman had not yet come out. There was nothing unusual about that. People often waxed their skis in the station, where it was warm, or took time to go to the toilets downstairs before setting out on their runs. It was all to the good. The longer the German took, the fewer people there would be hanging around to notice Robert when he set out after him.

Robert waited on the cliff's edge. In the swirling, cold cloud, he felt warm, capable, powerful, curiously light-headed. For the first time in his life he understood the profound, sensual pleasure of destruction. He waved gaily at Mac and the Italian girl as they moved off together on the traverse to one of the easier runs on the other side of the mountain.

Then the door to the station opened again and the woman who was with the German came out. She had her skis on and Robert realized that they had been so long inside because they had put their skis on in the waiting room. In bad weather people often did that, so that they wouldn't freeze their hands on the icy metal of the bindings in the biting wind outdoors. The woman held the door open and Robert saw the man in the white cap coming through the opening. But he wasn't coming out like everybody else. He was hopping, with great agility, on one leg. The other leg was cut off in mid-thigh and to keep his balance the German had miniature skis fixed on the end of his poles, instead of the usual thonged baskets.

Through the years, Robert had seen other one-legged skiers, veterans of Hitler's armies, who had refused to allow their mutilation to keep them off the mountains they loved, and he had admired their fortitude and skill. But he felt no admiration for the man in the white cap. All he felt was a bitter sense of loss, of having been deprived, at the last moment, of something that had been promised to him and that he had wanted and desperately needed. Because he knew he was not strong enough to murder a cripple, to punish the already punished, and he despised himself for his weakness.

He watched as the man made his way across the snow with crablike cunning, hunched over his poles with their infants' skis on the ends. Two or three times, when the man and the woman came to a rise, the woman got silently behind the man and pushed him up the slope until he could move under his own power again.

The cloud had been swept away and there was a momentary burst of sunlight and in it, Robert could see the man and the woman traverse to the entrance to the run, which was the steepest one on the mountain. Without hesitation, the man plunged into it, skiing skillfully, courageously, overtaking more timid or weaker skiers who were picking their way cautiously down the slope.

Watching the couple, who soon became tiny figures on the white expanse below him, Robert knew there was nothing more to be done, nothing more to wait for, except a cold, hopeless, everlasting forgiveness.

The two figures disappeared out of the sunlight into the solid bank of cloud that cut across the lower part of the mountain. Then Robert went over to where he had left his skis and put them on. He did it clumsily. His hands were cold because he had taken off his mittens in the teleferique cabin, in that hopeful and innocent past, ten minutes ago, when he had thought the German insult could be paid for with a few blows of the bare fist.

He went off, fast, on the run that Mac had taken with the Italian girl, and he caught up with them before they were halfway down. It began to snow when they reached the village and they went into the hotel and had a hilarious lunch with a lot of wine and the girl gave Mac her address and said he should be sure to look her up the next time he came to Rome.

PART IV

THE SKI COUNTRY

"The fact is that it is easier to climb an ordinary peak, or to make a journey over the higher passes, in winter than in summer, if the weather is only set fair. In summer you have to climb down as well as to climb up, and the one is as tiring as the other. In winter your trouble is halved, as most of your descent is a mere slide."

—Arthur Conan Doyle, *An Alpine Pass on Ski*

An Alpine Pass on Ski

by ARTHUR CONAN DOYLE

The creator of Sherlock Holmes was an intrepid sportsman and outdoor enthusiast who spent several winters in Davos, Switzerland, long before it became fashionable to take winter vacations in the Alps. Inspired by Nansen's The First Crossing of Greenland, *Conan Doyle had Norwegian skis sent to him at his hotel and went out with guides to learn the sport. He prevailed upon two guides to retrace their daring high mountain traverse to the town of Arosa. Doyle's sprightly remarks on the trip hide the fact that the trip was risky. No guides today will undertake to retrace Doyle's route over Meyerfelder Furka because of the avalanche danger inherent in the terrain. But Doyle survived and his advocacy of the sport had great impact: in Davos, today, there is a tablet memorializing Doyle for "... bringing the new sport and the attractions of the Swiss Alps to the attention of the world."*

THERE is nothing peculiarly malignant in the appearance of a pair of skis. They are two slips of elm wood, 8 feet long, 4 inches broad, with a square heel, turned-up toes, and straps in the center to secure your feet. No one, to look at them, would guess at the possibilities which lurk in them. But you put them on, and you turn with a smile to see whether your friends are looking at you, and then the next moment you are boring your head madly into a snowbank, and kicking frantically with both feet, and half-rising, only to butt viciously into that snowbank again, and your friends are getting more entertainment than they had ever thought you capable of giving.

The Surprises in a Pair of Skis

This is when you are beginning. You naturally expect trouble then, and you are not likely to be disappointed. But as you get on a little, the thing becomes more irritating. The skis are the most capricious things upon the earth. One day you cannot go wrong with them; on another, with the same weather and the same snow, you cannot go right. And it is when you least expect it that things begin to happen. You stand on the crown of a slope, and you adjust your body for a rapid slide; but your ski stick motionless, and over you go on your face. Or you stand upon a plateau which seems to you to be as level as a billiard table, and in an instant, without cause or warning, away they shoot, and you are left behind, staring at the sky. For a man who suffers from too much dignity a course of Norwegian snowshoes would have a fine moral effect.

Whenever you brace yourself for a fall, it never comes off. Whenever you think yourself absolutely secure, it is all over with you. You come to a hard ice slope at an angle of 75 degrees, and you zigzag up it, digging the side of your skis into it, and feeling that if a mosquito settles upon you, you are gone. But nothing ever happens, and you reach the top in safety. Then you stop upon the level to congratulate your companion, and you have just time to say, "What a lovely view is this!" when you find yourself standing upon your two shoulder blades, with your ski* tied tightly round your neck. Or, again, you may have had a long outing without any misfortune at all, and, as you shuffle back along the road you stop for an instant to tell a group in the hotel veranda how well you are getting on. Something happens—and they suddenly find that their congratulations are addressed to the soles of your skis. Then, if your mouth is not full of snow, you find yourself muttering the names of a few Swiss villages to relieve your feelings. "Ragatz!" is a very handy word, and may save a scandal.

But all this is in the early stage of skiing. You have to shuffle along the level, to zigzag, or move crab fashion, up the hills, to slide down without losing your balance, and, above all, to turn with facility. The first time you try to turn, your friends think it is part of your fun. The great ski flapping in the air has the queerest appearance—like an exaggerated nigger dance. But this sudden whisk round is really the most necessary of accomplishments; for only so can one turn upon the mountain side without slipping down. It must be done without ever presenting one's heels to the slope, and this is the only way.

The Ski Makes Mountain Climbing Easy

But granted that a man has perseverance, and a month to spare, in which to conquer all these early difficulties, he will then find that skiing opens up a field of sport for him which is, I think, unique. This is not appreciated yet, but I am convinced that the time will come when hundreds of Englishmen will come to Switzerland for the skiing season in March and April. I believe that I may claim to be the first, save only two

*Doyle alternates between "ski" and "skis" as the plural form

Switzers, to do any mountain work (though on a modest enough scale) on snowshoes; but I am certain that I will not, by many a thousand, be the last.

The fact is that it is easier to climb an ordinary peak, or to make a journey over the higher passes, in winter than in summer, if the weather is only set fair. In summer you have to climb down as well as to climb up, and the one is as tiring as the other. In winter your trouble is halved, as most of your descent is a mere slide. If the snow is tolerably firm, it is much easier also to zigzag up it on ski, than to clamber over boulders, under a hot summer sun. The temperature, too, is more favorable for exertion in winter; for nothing could be more delightful than the crisp, pure air on the mountains, though glasses are, of course, necessary to protect the eyes from the snow glare.

A Ski Mount of Over 9,000 Feet

Our project was to make our way from Davos to Arosa, over the Furka Pass, which is over 9,000 feet high. The distance is not more than from 12 to 14 miles as the crow flies, but it has only once been done in winter. Last year the two brothers Branger made their way across on ski. They were my companions on the present expedition, and more trustworthy ones no novice could hope to have with him. They are both men of considerable endurance, and even a long spell of my German did not appear to exhaust them.

We were up before four in the morning, and had started at half past for the village of Frauenkirch, where we were to commence our ascent. A great pale moon was shining in a violet sky, with such stars as can only be seen in the tropics or the higher Alps. At quarter past five we turned from the road, and began to plod up the hillsides, over alternate banks of last year's grass, and slopes of snow. We carried our ski over our shoulders, and our ski boots slung round our necks, for it was good walking where the snow was hard, and it was sure to be hard wherever the sun had struck it during the day. Here and there, in a hollow, we floundered into and out of a soft drift up to our waists; but on the whole it was easy going, and as much of our way lay through fir woods, it would have been difficult to ski. About half past six, after a long, steady grind, we emerged from the woods, and shortly afterwards passed a wooden cowhouse, which was the last sign of man which we were to see until we reached Arosa.

Over Rolling Snowfields

The snow being still hard enough upon the slopes to give us a good grip for our feet, we pushed rapidly on, ever rolling snowfields with a general upward tendency. About half past seven the sun cleared the peaks behind us, and the glare upon the great expanse of virgin snow became very dazzling. We worked our way down a long slope, and then coming to the corresponding hillside with a northern outlook, we found the snow as soft as powder, and so deep that we could touch to bottom with our poles. Here, then, we took to our snowshoes, and zigzagged up over the long white haunch of the mountain, pausing at the top for a rest. They are useful things the ski; for, finding that the snow was again hard enough to bear us, we soon converted ours into a very comfortable bench, from which we enjoyed the view of a whole panorama of mountains, the names of which my readers will be relieved to hear I have completely forgotten.

The snow was rapidly softening now, under the glare of the sun, and without our shoes all progress would have been impossible. We were making our way along the steep side of a valley, with the mouth of the Furka Pass fairly in front of us. The snow fell away here at an angle of from 50 to 60 degrees; and, as this steep incline, along the face of which we were shuffling, sloped away down until it ended in absolute precipice, a slip might have been serious. My two more experienced companions walked below me for the half mile or so of danger, but soon we found ourselves upon a more reasonable slope, where one might fall with impunity. And now came the real sport of snowshoeing. Hitherto we had walked as fast as boots would do, over ground where no boots could pass. But now we had a

pleasure which boots can never give. For a third of a mile we shot along over gently dipping curves, skimming down into the valley without a motion of our feet. In that great untrodden waste, with snowfields bounding our vision on every side, and no marks of life save the track of chamois and of foxes, it was glorious to whiz along in this easy fashion. A short zigzag at the bottom of the slope brought us, at half past nine, into the mouth of the pass; and we could see the little toy hotels of Arosa, away down among the fir woods, thousands of feet beneath us.

The Ski, a Shoe or a Sled at Your Pleasure

Again we had a half mile or so, skimming along with our poles dragging behind us. It seemed to me that the difficulty of our journey was over, and that we had only to stand on our skis and let them carry us to our destination. But the most awkward place was yet in front. The slope grew steeper and steeper until it suddenly fell away into what was little short of being sheer precipices. But still that little, when there is soft snow upon it, is all that is needed to bring out another possibility of these wonderful slips of wood. The brothers Branger agreed that the place was too difficult to attempt with the ski upon our feet. To me it seemed as if a parachute was the only instrument for which we had any use; but I did as I saw my companions do. They undid their ski, lashed the straps together, and turned them into a rather clumsy toboggan. Sitting on these, with our heels dug into the snow, and our sticks pressed hard down behind us, we began to move down the precipitous face of the pass. I think that both my comrades came to grief over it. I know that they were as white as Lot's wife at the bottom. But my own troubles were so pressing that I had no time to think of them. I tried to keep the pace within moderate bounds by pressing on the stick, which had the effect of turning the sledge sideways, so that one skidded down the slope. Then I dug my heels hard in, which shot me off backwards, and in an instant my two skis, tied together, flew away like an arrow from a bow, whizzed past the two Brangers, and vanished over the next slope, leaving

Skiers en route to an Alpine pass string out single file on a mountain

their owner squattering in the deep snow.

It might have been an awkward accident in the upper field, where the drifts are 20 or 30 feet deep. But the steepness of the place was an advantage now, for the snow could not accumulate to any very great extent upon it. I made my way down in my own fashion. My tailor tells me that Harris tweed cannot wear out. This is a mere theory, and will not stand a thorough scientific test. He will find samples of his wares on view from the Furka Pass to Arosa, and for the remainder of the day I was happiest when nearest the wall.

However, save that one of the Brangers sprained his ankle badly in the descent, all went well with us, and we entered Arosa at half-past eleven, having taken exactly seven hours over our journey. The residents at Arosa, who knew that we were coming, had calculated that we could not possibly get there before one, and turned out to see us descend the steep pass just about the time when we were finishing a comfortable luncheon at the Seehoff. I would not grudge them any innocent amusement, but still I was just as glad that my own little performance was over before they assembled with their opera glasses. One can do very well without a gallery when one is trying a new experiment on skis.

Pain and Pleasure
on the Haute Route

by AL GREENBERG

The classic European mountaineering tour is the "Haute Route," stretching from Mont Blanc on the French-Swiss border to the Matterhorn on the Italian-Swiss border, a well-traveled track which nevertheless has the everlasting dangers of ski mountaineering at sufficiently frequent intervals to make any trek along it more than routine: danger, hardship and the sheer wildness of the mountain country make one cognizant of the question of one's own survival. Al Greenberg, an experienced skier but inexperienced mountaineer, has led Skiing Magazine, as editor in chief, through arduous and rewarding ascents of the high routes of publishing.

M Y wife was a little shaken. "Are you sure you want to go on this?"
What unnerved her was a form Walter Bruderer of the Swiss National Tourist Office had sent over for my signature. Walter had proposed this trip and had been besieging me with information on things like the ski-mountaineering programs at Martin Epp's Alpine Sportschule Andermatt or the list of equipment I would need.

But at the last minute came this paper for me to sign, agreeing not to hold the Swiss National Tourist Office or Swiss-Air liable "for any injury, damages, or other inconveniences I may suffer as a result of my travels."

Never, in over a decade of European skiing, had anyone suggested signing such a form. But then again, never before had I set out to ski the famed Haute Route, the high road across the Alps from Chamonix to Saas-Fee (or, in this case, vice versa). I was indeed sure I wanted to go and, had it been required, would probably have signed away more than that for the opportunity.

It was the list of equipment that gave me pause. Skis, touring bindings, skins—not too much of a problem. "Unbreakable ski sticks" were not the kind of poles I'd ever used, but it seemed a reasonable enough requirement, I figured it wouldn't be easy to get ski boots that were "not too high or stiff for climbing," yet with "enough support for skiing," but I had lots of friends with helpful advice to offer on this score.

The "Harscheisen" confounded me a bit. These are crampons, that attach to the skis. Walter told me to forget those: just take regular crampons and an ice axe—plus some silver wax, a rucksack, of course; extra socks, knickers, warm-up pants, a down parka, a lightweight wind parka, a couple of light sweaters, a track suit for sleeping and wearing in the huts, hut slippers, extra gloves, goggles, sunglasses, a Swiss army knife, a flashlight, suncream, hats, toilet articles . . . it was quite a list.

"When you get to Saas-Fee, your guide,

Lucky Imboden, will go over what you have. Since you'll want to send your street clothes on to Geneva, you can arrange to send back anything he says is superfluous.'' Walter advised. So I brought everything on the list—plus.

The train from Geneva, first along the lake to Lausanne and Montreux, then down to Martigny and east to Sion, Sierre, Visp, and Brig, was roughly the valley route paralleling the high road we would shortly undertake. The train sped along in its smooth, efficient Swiss way, but still the trip was taking hours.

"We're going to have to do this same distance on skis with all this gear?'' I asked photographer Del Mulkey, who had met me in Geneva. Del, even with all his camera gear, was not as weighed down as I, but then Del is an experienced ski mountaineer.

"Wrong,'' he reminded me. "The distance we have to travel is up and down, not just across.'' A sobering thought.

At Brig, where we caught a bus to Saas-Fee, we met others in ski clothes, packs, mountaineering gear in tow—including an elderly Japanese couple who wanted to know if we were headed for the Britannia hut that night, which we knew to be our first destination. It was reassuring to see that this adventure was being attempted by other than hardy, ruddy-faced mountain boys, though we later learned that many weekenders made it up to one of the huts without doing much more than strolling around for the view.

The folly of my excessive packing became apparent on the hike from the bus terminal to the Hotel Mistral, the inn where we were to rendezvous with our guide. This was clear on the other side of town, by the lift station, and I was still in street clothes, carrying pack, skis, boots, poles, and a duffel bag filled with all those extras. For the first time, I began to doubt my fitness for this venture.

At the inn, there was no Lucky Imboden, nor had anyone ever heard of him. Later, another guide arrived who knew him and gave us his phone number. No answer. We tried the tourist office, but it was closed—Saturday afternoon. Nothing to do but wait in the warm May sun, which would have been pleasant enough had we

been less anxious about a possible mixup.

Finally, Lucky arrived—and gruffly dismissed as absurd half of what I had brought. My skis, boots, and bindings passed inspection, but the poles, he assured me, would break, the skins were too narrow, the crampons and ice axe unnecessary; as for the track suit and hut slippers, they brought guffaws. The wax, he said scornfully, tossing it back in my duffel bag, would make it impossible for my skins to stick (alas, I had prewaxed my skis, though in my dry-run use of the skins, they *had* stuck). By the time we had bundled half my gear for shipment back to Geneva, I no longer felt encumbered. This would be a lark.

Needless to say, I had also taken an immediate dislike to Lucky. As the trip went on, I got over this—replacing it with a deep, abiding hatred.

Having kept us waiting for so many hours, he now rushed us, lest we get to the hut too late. First, though, he introduced us to the other member of our group, a diminutive, shy young Japanese woman, Mari Goto, who had been spending the year as a ski instructor in Zermatt. She diffidently informed us that she thought she would be the first Japanese woman to complete the Haute Route. We hoped she was right.

The two best-known peaks of the Alps are Mont Blanc, on the French-Italian border, and the Matterhorn, on the Swiss-Italian border. The path between them was mapped out over a hundred years ago by English mountaineers, mostly as a summer climbing route which crosses glaciers, traverses steep ice walls, and includes technical climbs up rocky spires. Today, it is the classic ski mountaineering trek which hundreds attempt every year—possibly thousands, if you include those who ski only a portion of the route. I confess, it had long been a dream of mine.

Saas-Fee, this first week in May, was still operating for limited lift skiing, and the cable car was running, primarily, it seemed, for ski mountaineers. Though purists might consider it cheating, apparently the use of whatever uphill transportation you can get is considered proper by ski mountaineers. In fact, from the top of the cable-car station, Lucky tried to negotiate a ride up an additional section, where a T-bar normally operated, on a snow-cat. When it seemed that he had failed, we donned our skins, only to be told at the last minute that we could ride after all. When we got off, we could dimly make out our destination off on a high ridge—the Britannia hut. From there, we were to start on the Haute Route before dawn the next morning.

But first, there was a short stretch to ski (during which I hit a rut and came out of my bindings more easily than I wanted to), and then about an hour's hike, skis on our shoulders. This didn't present any problems, except that I slowly became aware that I was developing a couple of blisters on the insides of my feet in the heel areas.

I was wearing Kastinger's special Messner Himalaya ski mountaineering boots. I had discovered when I first tested them that they were about a size too large for me, but several mountaineering friends whose judgment I respected had advised me to keep them and wear extra socks. I was to discover that this was very bad advice. By the time I got to the Britannia hut, the blisters had already burst. It was not an auspicious beginning.

The hut was jammed with people. Lucky wanted to make sure that we had all our gear packed so we could bolt out of there as soon as we got the wake-up call at 4 A.M., least we should have to wait for the crowds along the route. I was bewildered. This was the lonely serenity of ski mountaineering?

The huts consist of a large dining area and adjoining kitchen, and rooms with banks of beds. These were wooden pallets with rolled-up mattresses and blankets. The food served was *"haute cuisine"*—which literally means "high kitchen," and kitchens don't come much higher than these except in airplanes, where the quality is roughly comparable. But it was hot, healthy, and plentiful.

I had a fitful night, not because of the altitude, but because two beer-drinking teen-agers were playing a radio and wouldn't shut up until the man in the bunk adjoining mine spoke sharply to them in what sounded like reprimanding German. The man turned out to be a sur-

geon from Heidelberg whose path kept meeting ours for the next week—but at that moment, I was simply grateful that some of that old Teutonic discipline was still around.

When the wake-up came, my flashlight failed, slowing me down enough to irritate Lucky no end. Breakfast was very hard bread and jam and awful coffee which I probably wouldn't have wanted at any time, let alone at four in the morning. Del was wise enough to take tea, with which we filled our canteens.

We managed to be among the first to set out, though why this was important escaped me. We followed Lucky on a gentle downhill stretch for five or ten minutes, at which point we joined a group of shadowy figures who had taken their skis off and were putting their skins on. The Ramer skins I was using warned that the skis must be dry, so I took some time making sure the skins would stick—again to the annoyance of an impatient guide.

And then the real experience began. Climbing skins—so-called because they used to be made of sealskin, but are now either of mohair or synthetic fur like nylon or polypropylene—permit one to glide forward in the smooth direction of the fibers, but hold the snow in the opposite direction so there is no sliding backward. A good skin is supposed to provide traction on slopes of up to 35 degrees.

We never climbed anything that steep. On that first day, I had some problems getting used to the technique. The only previous times I had used skins, it was for short hauls where a step at a time was adequate. I soon realized that a step here had to include a glide or the progress would be painfully slow, but it took several days to get the hang of it.

The action is much like cross-country skiing—not just shuffling the skis forward, but pressing the knee ahead and driving forward while the heel of the rearward foot comes well off the ski. I learned later that it is a help on steep climbs to put on the attachment that permits the heel to be raised relative to the ski at all times. With this in place, your foot starts at the horizontal, which means less stretching of the Achilles' tendon and is therefore less tiring.

Between the pain from my blisters and my inexpert stride, my progress was embarrassingly slow. Several groups passed us, and Lucky grew visibly more irritated. With daylight, it grew warm, though the weather was hazy. When we stopped to shed our down parkas and I took a swig from my canteen, he became greatly perturbed, admonishing me that I would get sick. I was more concerned about dehydration than stomach cramps and ignored his warnings, which did nothing to cement our relations.

It takes a couple of seconds to read, "after five hours of climbing, we reached the top." But what an eternity five hours of actual climbing can seem—and many mornings, we climbed for six or seven hours. Six months after the fact, the pain and exertion no longer stand out. What remains is the recollection of repeated expectation followed by disappointment. You focus on a crest that just *has* to be the summit, only to get there and see yet another crest and another, cascading on the horizon.

On the gentle slopes, we'd head straight up, taking in the rock formations about us. On the steeper ones, we'd traverse a series of Z's. My poles were adjustable-length Ramers, and it was an advantage to have the uphill pole short, the downhill pole long on these steep traverses, though Lucky would snarl every time I took the extra seconds to adjust the length. He insisted you could accomplish the same thing by holding one pole mid-shaft, the other by the grip, which was true, but the additional push I got from holding both poles by the grip was a comfort and, with my poor technique, much needed.

That first day, I was too self-absorbed to pay much attention to the surroundings, though even through my blistered discomfort and slow motion. I was always aware of the glacial formations surrounding us. The Britannia hut was at an altitude of just under 10,000 feet. Our ascent was along the Holaub and Allalin glaciers up to the Adler pass at 12,550 feet—which is not really a very impressive vertical to have accomplished in a morning, but when we took off our skins to start down the Findeln glacier, it felt like a well-merited reward.

The top was steep; the powder was deep and

Mountain refuge hut on Haute Route almost disappears in a blizzard

a bit on the heavy side, but manageable. My inclination would have been to get into the fall line and just go, but Lucky gave us a sharp warning to follow his tracks, and off he went in a series of long, traversing turns. My skis—Kästle Tour Randonnee 190s— were responsive, though my boots were still too loose. Before leaving the States, I had skied with them and found that with tight buckling, they gave fine control, but now my blisters objected to overtightening. Soon, however, we were out on an endless stretch of downhill, and, as we turned and turned and turned, I forgot equipment problems, thinking only that I would gladly endure climbs twice as tough for payoffs like this.

We were all alone on this immense slope. The others were off in another direction. Lucky informed us that he had been unable to get us hut reservations for that night, and that we would have to spend the night in Zermatt. He assured us we would not lose time, since we would take the cable car up on Monday, then climb to the Schönbiel hut, where we would have been Monday night in any event. Besides, he had business in neighboring Täsch.

Since this interruption meant an opportunity to buy better first-aid materials for my feet, stock up on dried fruit and nuts for snacks, get a stronger spring for my bindings, a better flashlight, etc., it was not unwelcome. We would also get to ski Zermatt's lift-served glaciers that afternoon and Monday morning, Lucky said, so it didn't sound bad at all.

But a hitch developed. At the bottom of the Findeln glacier, Lucky had expected us to take a lift up to join the main runs down to Zermatt, but neither this lift nor another one lower down was operating. We had to ski out, following a narrow path along the Findeln stream—a boring run-out that finally brought us to town, after skiing down the outrun of a ski jump. By the time we finished lunch, there was no question of further skiing.

We spent the next morning shopping and sightseeing in Zermatt, not hastening to get extra skiing in because of flat light. We lunched at the Schwarzee-cable-car restaurant, and when Lucky showed up, two hours later, we skied down a short way and then started a long traverse, not using skins, but not losing any altitude either. For a while, the sun peeked through, and we became quite warm. Down in the valley, we could see bare ground.

On our left was a fairly steep wall, and we passed repeatedly over slide areas, but Lucky did not seem concerned, and I trusted his judgment. I was following directly in his tracks. Mari Goto seemed to be having a slower time of it, and Del fell back every now and then to take pictures. So when it came time to don our skins, for a change I was in the lead, and Lucky suggested I go on while he awaited the others. There was no question of their being able to overtake me.

It was eerie. Lucky had told me to follow the tracks, which seemed easy, but now it was lightly snowing, and it was hard to distinguish climbing tracks from downhill tracks. Though west to east is the more popular way to follow the Haute

Route, we rarely saw either skiers or tracks coming from the west. But here, tracks seemed to go every which way, and inevitably, I headed off in the wrong direction. Fortunately, the others saw me before I was hopelessly lost.

This time, the climb was only a couple of hours, though some sections were so steep, we had to take off our skis and shoulder them, kick-stepping our way up. We had gone out of hazy sunlight into the clouds, and at close to 9,000 feet, it was beginning to get a bit chilly, even with the exertion of the climb.

The woolen Woolrich knickers I had been advised to take were serviceable in all kinds of weather, though I'm not sure that a regular Alpine suit wouldn't have done as well. I had a flannel shirt and, for when it was really cold, a bulky down parka—which saw action mostly as a pillow. My most useful garment was a Gore-Tex Terrashell from Early Winters, which had venting zippers to let out heat, yet when zipped tightly all around, especially with a sweater underneath, was very nearly as warm as the down parka. It folded up into its own little carrying bag when not in use.

I had a pair of lightweight cross-country gloves, a pair of Aris Alpine ski gloves, and a pair of down mittens (which I never used). I had both goggles and mountaineering sunglasses (with side protection) and needed both. A wool hat and a sun-visor cap completed the picture, plus Duofolds and lightweight Angostar tops and bottoms. From the point of view of dress, I had what I needed.

But up to that point, I wasn't quite sure what all this effort was for. The run down the Findeln glacier was superb, and I suppose that there was a satisfaction in having enjoyed it after so much effort instead of after a lift ride or a helicopter trip. But I wondered if that alone could explain the legend of this experience.

As the Schönbiel hut came into view, I had my answer. Not the sight of the hut itself, but another sight, almost religious in the depth of feeling it inspired. For just at that moment, there was a break in the clouds and, out of the grayness around us, the sun's rays picked out the tip of the Matterhorn.

Yes, there it was, seemingly close enough to touch. You could no doubt get similar, equally impressive closeups on various cable car rides around Zermatt. But the climb up for this somehow made it seem a special reward, not really attainable without the sacrifice.

Later in the week, we were to see all about us the panoramas of awesome Alpine peaks that have attracted pilgrims to this part of the world for so long. Again, similar views could be seen from any high place in that region, no matter how you reached it. I'd gasped at such spectacles before, without having suffered for the privilege. But this time, there was a difference.

For one thing, we were out there in the middle of this white wilderness with no signs of civilization to obstruct the view, and our communion with nature was total. Then again, perhaps the degree of suffering I had endured made me rationalize the rewards, projecting relief into mystical satisfaction. At any rate, several times that week, the beauty of the spectacle was overwhelming, almost to the point of tears—a depth of emotion I had never experienced from a similar view seen from a lift terminal or a helicopter window.

Most of those in the Schönbiel hut were on the last leg of the Chamonix-to-Saas-Fee trip. Most of those we had encountered at the Britannia hut had been weekenders. My bunkmate from Heidelberg, who had spent the previous night at the Monte Rosa hut, and his companion and their guide were the only ones we met who were planning to do the Haute Route east to west, as we were.

A professor of surgery at the University of Heidelberg, Dr. Michael Trede was a slim, agile-looking man: his lawyer companion, Reinhart Freidenberg, was a bit stockier but just as fit. Dr. Trede confided that he was in his fifties and wanted to accomplish this before he grew too old. I had had the impression, watching him move along on his skis, that he had taken this kind of jaunt every year since his youth.

Next morning, we were up at four again and out by five, donning skins, taking them off for a downhill stretch, putting them back on. My map shows that we climbed over 2,500 vertical feet to the Col d'Herens, skied on the upper Tsa de Tsan glacier, through the Col du Mont Brulé onto the Arolla glacier. At that point, we still had four or five hours more of climbing to reach the Cabane de Vignettes. The weather was threatening, and Lucky decided it would be best to ski down to the town of Arolla for the night. On the way down, we ran into our Heidelberg friends who had started out for the Vignettes, but the weather above was as Lucky suspected, and they had to give it up.

We had some wide-open, easy skiing for most of the way down, till suddenly the snow changed. At this lower altitude, it was totally rotten. I ended up traversing and kick-turning, which is what our Heidelberg friends were doing, too. But Lucky, the other guide, Del, and Mari were able to turn in the stuff after a fashion. My attempts led to falls, and getting up with a pack on my back became harder and harder. At one point, I used my poles to get up and snapped one, proving Lucky's prediction about my poles correct. The adjustable feature required having holes in the shaft, which of course does weaken the shaft. Fortunately, I had brought some fiberglass tape, and was able to repair the pole.

We skied out past some Swiss army soldiers on maneuvers; hiked to a small hotel, leaving our skis at the base of a T-bar we passed; and spent a delightful afternoon cleaning up, eating, and resting. It was cheating, for Haute Route purists, but again I was grateful for it.

Next morning, we started out well after sunrise, having had breakfast at the hotel's normal hour, took a long T-bar up past the rotten snow, then started climbing. At one point, it was snowing and visibility was just about zero. Lucky got out his compass, map, and altimeter and headed us off into what was an absolute whiteout. Without a guide who knew the terrain, with its cliffs, crevasses, and avalanche dangers at every step of the way, it would have been pure suicide. But whatever feelings I had about Lucky's personality, I had the utmost confidence in his competence. It proved to be well placed.

Sure enough, after hours of climbing, the Cabane de Vignettes loomed in sight. Perched on the side of a cliff, it was a very imposing stone structure. Outside, sitting on a wall beyond which the drop was all the way down to nowhere, was a young man reading a book, and as we came back from the ski storage room where Del and I had been chatting, he asked if we were Americans—which he himself quite clearly was, the first we'd encountered. Was he with an American group? Not exactly. He was a friend of a French guide who used to be a K2 racer-chaser in the States.

"Not Lionel Wibault?" I asked in amazement. Indeed, it was. I didn't actually know Lionel. The reason I was familiar with the name—and amazed at running into him—was that a few days before leaving the States, I had had dinner with some Vermont friends, Chris and Marilyn Brown. Marilyn is the former Marilyn Cochran, and when she heard I would be on the Haute Route, she told me to be sure to say hello to her old racer-chaser if I should run into him. Though I took his name, the prospect seemed as likely as running into someone's friend in New York City.

Lionel proved to be a charming and knowledgable guide who, on this trip, was just taking some friends on the Haute Route for the fun of it—no fee (when arranged through the Swiss National Tourist Office, a seven-day trip such as ours, including guide, hut meals, and lodging, is about $345: four days on the Haute Route costs about $230). He was delighted to hear news of Marilyn, delighted to know she had married a skier (Chris, an engineer, is also a ski coach), and was himself so full of enthusiasm that he livened up the whole hut. It was he who put me wise to using the raised heel attachment for my bindings for easier climbing on the steep.

Had we made it to the Vignettes the previous night, we might have headed for the Cabane de Chanrion, and then, reversing the classic route, on to the Cabane de Valsorey, from where we'd have made our way to Bourg St.-Pierre, thence by bus to Orsières and Champex for the climb to the Refuge d'Argentière, with the final day's long run down to the Argentière end of the Chamonix valley—all very difficult going. Instead, we now had a relatively easy morning's climb to the Cabane des Dix, hitting the Cabane de Chanrion next day in the midmorning.

Lucky's plan was to ski from there into Italy, get a taxi to Courmayeur for the night, and the next day take the cable to the Pont Helbronner for the spectacular Vallée Blanche run down to Chamonix.

As it turned out, that route had us covering more terrain by wheel and cable than the more traditional route, and also eliminated some of the most difficult climbing. But I was in no mood to object. Neither my nor Lucky's nursing methods had done my feet any good. I now had raw flesh across both insteps and on the insides of each heel. The physical exertion was not really a problem for me. I was not slowed down by exhaustion nearly so much as by pain. As for the skiing, except for my inability to cope with rotten snow, I hadn't run into anything more intimidating than many slopes I'd skied at places like Jackson Hole, Taos, or Stowe.

The next-to-last day, for instance, we encountered a rather steep wall that Lucky had warned us might require negotiating by rope. Instead, we sidestepped it for a while, then realized we could ski it.

The toughest section came as we made our way down to the Italian village of Balme. We crossed the frontier at the Fenètre de Durand in the shadow of 11,600-foot Mont Gelé, rapidly losing altitude and snow. The final section was over a small trail of snow that weaved in and out of trees and rocks, requiring some very quick turns to avoid ruining the ski bottoms. I negotiated this somewhat cautiously, with Lucky urging me to move faster because of the danger of icefalls and avalanches as the sun got warmer. I knew he was right, but couldn't speed up my pace. At one point, I was no more than 100 feet beyond a point where he had indicated an ice overhang that was about to give way—when suddenly it did. It didn't fall exactly on the trail, but close enough to underscore the seriousness of his warnings.

When we ran out of snow, collapse was total—and the taxi to Courmayeur was most welcome.

For our final day, we awoke to a clear blue sky, the first we'd seen all week. There had been new snow during the night, and the cable car was packed with weekend skiers who would probably take the run several times.

The powder was marvelous. Del commented that he'd never seen me ski so badly, and Lucky insisted on taking my pack to ease my way (with two packs, he still put down perfect tracks). No matter, I enjoyed the run, knowing it was the last.

Then there was the long walk out. I was shuffling along, unable to take a normal stride, dosing myself with pain pills, and when Lucky offered to take my skis, too, I exploded that my problem had nothing to do with what I was carrying but with the shape my feet were in. Finally, he understood, studied the problem a moment, and suggested I try carrying my outer boots, walking in the inners.

It worked! I ended the Haute Route whistling through the forest path to Chamonix.

This Could Be the Last Resort

by WILLIAM OSCAR JOHNSON

When the resort of Beaver Creek, Colorado, finally opened in 1981, it was the first large ski complex to do so in five years. Sports Illustrated's William Johnson thought it could be the last big one. That brings up the question of why what was once routine—starting a new resort in America—has become rare and risky.

LAST summer the mountain looked like a benign Colorado version of Mount St. Helens. Toppled trees were everywhere, their trunks scattered like Vulcan's own matchsticks over great slashes of raw dirt. There was no steam, no underground thunder, no acres of gray ash, but still the devastation seemed final, the damage irrevocable. Now a blanket of snow has fallen over the mountain and the transformation is miraculous. Summer's ravages have changed into winter's glories, and the harshly barbered mountainside of July has become a network of ski trails, beautifully groomed, gracefully sculpted. It's a place of authentic splendor: Beaver Creek, long awaited and often despaired of, North America's latest major ski resort—and, just possibly, its last.

The last resort? Forever? Well, there are plans for a few others, hopes for a few more—dreams. But there is no guarantee that there will be another laid out on the scale of Beaver Creek—a first-class "destination resort" (travel-agent jargon for a resort that offers lodging) to rival the country's best and biggest: Aspen, Vail, Sun Valley.

Of course, the saga of Beaver Creek has been climaxed by success: the area will open on December 15 with 25 miles of trails and six chair lifts strung over some 450 acres of the rugged Rockies. But reaching this happy point involved such a long, painful, expensive, exhausting, frustrating process that sane men may well be discouraged from trying ever again to create something like Beaver Creek. Cal Conniff, executive director of the National Ski Areas Association, is paid to be optimistic about the future and fortunes of the ski business. Yet he says, "I'm not suggesting that it's flat-out impossible to develop another major destination ski resort. It's not, but there are obstacles now that tend to scare away investment capital. It's a cumbersome process, full of roadblocks and inherent risks, and terribly slow. From the first conception of a new area it will take five years at least before you can even start the first lift running. The process tends to tie up a lot of money. And the cost of a full-blown destination ski resort is at a minimum $100 million, which means that only large corporations can afford to get involved. Individuals simply don't have that kind of money. Besides, a

166

ski area is a long-term investment. You have to figure that you'll be in operation five years before you begin to get a true return on your money."

So it seems we've reached the end of an era in skiing; no longer can we look forward to the opening of new, better and bigger ski areas, at least certainly not at the frenetic pace that has typified new development over the past three or four decades. Even now, Beaver Creek itself is nowhere near completion. What will open for the 1980–81 season is a $30 million fraction of the entire project, including a mountain full of lifts and trails, an architecturally superb "grandiose rustic"-style restaurant at the 10,208-foot level and a one hundred and seventy-seven car parking garage at the foot. Period. This year there will be nothing else at Beaver Creek—not so much as a single bed to sleep in.

An estimated $500 million will be spent over the next few years—no one knows how many— to produce an 80-acre village with restaurants, shops, bars and taverns, plus six thousand beds in hotel rooms and condominiums. In addition to the village, there will be two hundred and forty-five homesites (original price from $250,000 to $450,000; now as much as $600,000) tucked in among the trees, streams, and beavers and along an eighteen-hole, par-70 Robert Trent Jones Jr. golf course. The homes are expected to be enormously expensive, at least $1 million each, and will be built by such insatiable devotees of retirement recreation as former President Jerry Ford, who bought the first lot at Beaver Creek, valued at $300,000, to add to the luxurious spread he already owns in Palm Springs.

Brian Rapp, thirty-eight, an ex-Yale quarterback, has zigged and zagged through a variety of careers since he engineered the 1964 defeat of Harvard—Presidential Executive Interchange Fellow at the State Department, assistant county executive of Santa Clara County, California, and, most recently, president of the Beaver Creek Resort Company. "To live here is something few people will be able to afford," Rapp says. "We expect it to be in the class of Pebble Beach, Sea Pines, Aspen—even St. Moritz or Zermatt. This

Skiers descending Peregrine trail at Beaver Creek draw snaking tracks

will be a planned community, rigidly and carefully designed, a true new town, in its way. But it isn't going to be Columbia, Maryland. We are planning to make Beaver Creek better than the best."

Beaver Creek village will be located 10 miles west of Vail and 110 miles west of Denver, in a valley 2 miles from Interstate 70. In all, there will be 4,901 acres devoted to skiing, golf, the village, and homesites; 2,126 of those acres will be privately held, and 2,775 others, which are federally owned, will be used under permit from the U.S. Forest Service. The sugar daddy for the whole $500 million shebang is Vail Associates, which, of course, owns the Vail ski area. But Vail Associates isn't generating that kind of money from skiing. About 80 percent of the firm's stock is owned by one Harry Bass, whose family fortune springs from the vast resources of the Goliad Oil Company of Texas. The Bass family has been in skiing for years—Harry's brother, Dick, underwrote the building of Snowbird in Utah in 1972—even though it certainly isn't the kind of investment hard-headed businessmen ordinarily seek out. Vail Associates has had quite a few millions tied up in Beaver Creek, but until next week, when the first trickle of skiers arrive to enjoy the resort's "preview season," Beaver Creek won't have generated a dime of income.

"For four years, Vail Associates has been pouring money into the development of the mountain, and there has been no cash coming in at all," says Rapp. "This is one reason people aren't being facetious when they talk about this as being the 'last resort.' Money men are reluctant to get involved in skiing because there's more risk than ever involving more money than ever. The downside is steeper than it's been before."

It wasn't always this way. Once upon a time, risk in the ski resort business referred to possible broken legs among guests, and downslides—the steeper the better—were covered with snow. That wasn't very long ago, but then, nothing is really very long ago in the story of ski resorts. Indeed, as recently as 1930 there was no organized skiing in the entire U.S., not a rope tow, not a stumpless hillside, not a single tanned, handsome, grinning Austrian expatriate to utter that favorite phrase of ski instructors, "Bend zee knees; two dollars pleez."

In Europe, the Alps had drawn winter vacationers from England since the late nineteenth century, but few were skiers. Most were upper-class "toffs" who skated in top hats and played hockey in shirts and ties. It wasn't until the early 1900s that "plank-hoppers" or "skeesters," as they were rather contemptuously called, were commonly seen at the better European winter resorts. Sir Arnold Lunn, founder of the famed Kandahar slaloms and an early British disciple of skiing for fun, described the sport as he found it in 1898 at the French resort of Chamonix:

About four or five Englishmen at Chamonix skied, but I cannot remember seeing any of the locals do so, with the exception of our instructor, who regarded his skis with obvious distaste and terror. He slid down a gradual slope, leaning on his stick and breathing heavily, while we gasped our admiration for his courage. Somebody asked him whether it was possible to turn. He replied in the negative, but added that a long gradual turn was just possible if one dragged oneself round on the pole. He claimed to have seen an expert perform this difficult maneuver but modestly added that he was unable to demonstrate it himself.

Perhaps the single most influential force in producing the ski boom was the invention of a method for moving skiers up hills without climbing. A few Alpine areas were ahead of the game: Davos with its Parsenn railway (completed in 1933), Zermatt with its groaning old ratchet train nicknamed Grannie (1890) and Wengen with its *Jungfraujochbahn* (1912). These uphill-transportation systems were all built for use by summer visitors, but later proved useful for hauling winter vacationers, too. Thus these lucky towns became the first "in"—or, rather, "up"—ski resorts.

But it wasn't until 1932 that skiing's true revolutionary genius appeared. He was a Swiss engineer and weekend skier named Gerhard Müller, who also happened to be the owner of an old motorcycle. Müller invented and patented the world's first rope tow. It consisted of a length of 1-inch hemp rope and parts from his motorcycle, geared and connected in such a way that a skier gripping the rope would be dragged uphill by the snarling motorcycle engine. The process was slightly less painful and a lot more frightening than climbing under one's own power. Nonetheless, Müller's invention was a success, and mountains and ski resorts have never been the same since.

In the U.S., the great-great-granddaddy of Beaver Creek was born in 1934 at Woodstock, Vermont. It was created by the unlikely combination of a former Dartmouth ski team captain (colleges in northern climes had had such teams since 1909), the owner of a hostelry called the White Cupboard Inn, and a sawmill mechanic.

They arranged to pay ten dollars to a farmer named Clinton Gilbert to rent a steep section of sheep pasture for the winter of '34. The place was called Gilbert's Hill and as John Jay wrote in his book *Ski Down the Years*, "Gilbert's Hill became the Kitty Hawk of the American ski scene."

The rope tow on Gilbert's Hill was an Erector Set arrangement of grooved wheels, wooden supports, and thick ropes, all powered by a sturdy Model T motor that drove a tire-less rear wheel. The tow on Gilbert's Hill offered a 500-foot uphill pull that resulted in increasingly intense pain and fatigue the closer one got to the top. Use of the tow cost one dollar a day and allowed the skier perhaps ten times more downhill runs than he would've been able to make had he had to climb the slope unassisted.

Tows soon appeared everywhere—from Mount Rainier in Washington to Mount Mansfield in Vermont, from Norfolk, Connecticut (where snow trains brought passengers the 140 miles from New York City at two dollars a head, round trip), to Wilmot Hills, Wisconsin, where a man named Walt Stopa put in no fewer than eleven rope tows, creating the then-famed "Alps of Chicago," which had a nice suburban vertical drop of 198 feet.

But all of this was primitive stuff, only the dimmest rumblings of the American ski resort boom. It was, writes Jay, "a time when everyone yodeled and smelled like a tossed salad (pure olive oil was the thing for a tan)," a time when skiers rented beds in drafty New England farmhouses, where they slept "stacked like layer cakes in four-decker bunks . . . and lined up for everything from the bathtub to the rope tows."

The first American ski resort worthy of the name was built in 1936 on a sweep of sheep-ranching land at the foot of Idaho's magnificent Sawtooth Mountain Range by the Union Pacific Railroad, then headed by W. Averell Harriman. The name of the resort was Sun Valley, and its original reason for existence was to create a destination in the West to lure passengers onto the railroad. The Lodge at Sun Valley was as luxurious as any resort hotel in the world—equipped with a glass-walled, heated outdoor swimming pool and a dining room where the strains of Eddie Duchin's orchestra sounded nightly. The skiing was terrific and the slopes boasted the world's first chairlift, which was patterned after a banana-loading device used on docks in the tropics. But none of these attractions was as important to the success of Sun Valley as the mind of a public-relations genius named Steve Hannegan. His most notable previous coup was publicizing a bleak stretch of sand in Florida, which became a thriving settlement of waterfront homes called Miami Beach. A devout cold-weather hater, Hannegan denounced Sun Valley at first sight as "a godforsaken field of snow." He then went to work to make it seem to be something quite different. First he persuaded Harriman to name the place Sun Valley. Hannegan then created a famous poster that showed a young man skiing in the sun while stripped to the waist. He also arranged for Hollywood to discover the resort. Mountain scenes for *She Met Him in Paris*, starring Claudette Colbert, were filmed in Sun Valley, and from the moment it opened, the Lodge glittered with celebrities, including such high-voltage luminaries as Tyrone Power, Clark Gable, and Gary Cooper.

Nothing quite like Sun Valley ever happened again, but the publicity that Hannegan generated for it spilled over everything that had to do with skiing. The sport suddenly took on a glamour that Model T-driven rope tows on farmers' hills simply couldn't give it. Although World War II forestalled the boom, no sooner was the war over than the ski business began to grow into a national industry. The postwar growth was nourished by (1) a vast supply of army surplus equipment, which gave thousands of people an opportunity to buy inexpensive skis, boots, and bindings, and (2) a cadre of enthusiastic young civilian entrepreneurs recently mustered out of the elite Tenth Mountain Division, America's only unit of ski troopers. They spearheaded the opening of some of the country's grandest resorts, including Vail, Jackson Hole, and Aspen.

The power behind Aspen, Colorado's premier ski resort, was a Tenth Mountain man named Friedl Pfeifer. With the money of an enlightened Chicago industrialist named Walter

Paepcke as backing, Pfeifer & Co. built the "world's longest ski lift," a then-startling 13,800 feet in length, with a vertical drop of 3,295 feet. The lift opened for business in January, 1947—and business immediately went from bad to worse. First the Rio Grande Railroad shut down the town's connection with the main line, a disaster for Aspen, which is even more remote than Sun Valley. Worse, the skiing proved far too dangerous to attract average skiers. Not only was the mountain breathtakingly steep, but another unnerving hazard was the mine shafts that appeared suddenly before unwary skiers and threatened to send them tumbling several hundred feet down a hole. The town of Aspen had once had a thriving population of twelve thousand and an annual production of $15 million worth of silver from its mines, but by the time the world's longest ski lift opened, the place had only a few hundred residents. And there was no Steve Hannegan to promote it. But in 1950 Aspen attracted the Fédération Internationale de Ski world championships, and that same year Paepcke brought such superstar intellectuals as Dr. Albert Schweitzer, Thornton Wilder, and José Ortega y Gasset to Aspen for the Goethe Bicentennial Celebration. These things put Aspen on the map, and the ski boom in Colorado at last began in earnest.

The 1950s saw new resorts in every part of the U.S., and the early sixties produced an all-out explosion in skiing. From 1960 to 1965, a total of three hundred and eighty-six new areas opened, among them some of the nation's first: Crested Butte, Steamboat Springs, Vail. Where previously there had been nothing but rocks and eagles and avalanches, there were now lift lines and fast-food cafeterias and people parading in new stretch pants. Ski industry income ballooned from an estimated $125 million in 1960 to $750 million in 1970 and $3.5 billion in 1980. Downhill skiers increased at the rate of 15.4 percent a year in the 1960s, from a doughty handful of 2.1 million in '60 to 6.5 million in '70 and 15 million in '80. The proliferation of new areas continued at the stunning rate of more than thirty per annum well into the seventies. In 1972, a vintage year, thirty-five areas opened, including three superb major-league resorts—Copper Mountain in the Rockies, just one and a half hours out of Denver; Telluride in the San Juan Mountains in the southeast corner of Colorado; and Snowbird in the power-packed Wasatch Mountains, forty-five minutes from Salt Lake City.

But after 1972 the boom slacked off, the beginning of the end had occurred. The last truly major area—Mary Jane, 70 miles west of Denver—opened in 1975. Between 1973 and 1980 an average of only eight new areas have started up in the U.S. each year. This season there are but three. Beaver Creek is one—*the* one, really. The other two are comparative anthills: Ski Starlite in southern Indiana not far from that well-known winter-sports paradise, Lewisburg, Kentucky, and Ski Scaley in western North Carolina.

Now people in the ski business are quick—very quick—to say that growth in their industry hasn't been completely snowed under. They claim that the number of skiers and ski dollars continues to increase at a rate of close to 10 percent a year. But the pattern of prosperity hasn't been uninterrupted. There have been some killing seasons indeed.

There were a few bizarre winters in the seventies that left either the East or the West or both lacking the one commodity without which there is no point for a skier to get up in the morning—snow. During these years of brown disasters, ski area operators prayed, complained, tried to get along exclusively on expensive manmade snow, filed for bankruptcy, changed their religion and prayed some more. In the season of 1976–77, the worst of these winter droughts, almost no snow fell in either the East or the West until March. Sun Valley had to hold the World Cup ski races on an entire run of manmade snow. Most areas shut down weeks before they ordinarily would have, and ski area industry profits fell 20 percent between 1975 and 1977.

Then, in the winter of 1977–78, the U.S. was blessed with blizzards, and ski areas racked up their highest average profits ever. As the Ski Areas Association's Conniff says, "The ski business is just as vulnerable and volatile as agriculture. We are totally dependent on the weather—over which we have no control at all. You never know. The vintage year it was perfect from Maine to Oregon, but last season it was excellent in some areas in the West, a disaster in some in the East. It's totally unpredictable."

But it isn't just the weather that lends a boom-or-bust air to the ski business. The industry is also a potential victim of the energy crisis. In 1974, a massive shortage of gasoline resulted in long lines at service stations and short lines at ski lifts, particularly at those belonging to the more remote resorts. "What happens in the Middle East is critical to our industry," says Conniff. "A gasoline shortage could practically snuff us out. Skiers rely on the automobile. There's no mass transit to most resorts. I think that if there's a supply of gasoline—no matter what the cost—skiers will go skiing. But if the time comes when there's *no* gas, we're in big trouble."

So there the business dangles, caught between the two most unpredictable and uncontrollable forces in the world: the weather and Middle East politics.

Still, the riskiness of it all isn't the main reason that we have come to a relatively static period in the growth of ski resorts. The primary problem is one of money and time. About the money: to create a ski mountain, be it on the scale of Sun Valley or Ski Starlite, the costs are astronomical. Jim Branch, a ski area design consultant and president of Sno-Engineering in Franconia, New Hampshire, estimates that it costs $3,500 per acre to prepare a new trail (Beaver Creek has 450 acres in trails for its premier season). Branch says you cannot install a new lift line for less than $100 per linear foot (Beaver Creek has 26,287 linear feet of lifts), and he guesses that the installation of a trustworthy snow-making system will run from $10,000 to $20,000 an acre.

About money and time: millions will be tied up for years before an area earns a dime of ski revenue. From the moment the land is purchased until the first skier buys a lift ticket, half a dozen violent economic cycles might occur—from high interest rates to low, from massive inflation to modest and back to massive, from recession to boom. And during all that, the money invested in a ski mountain is doing about as much good as if it were stuck in a mattress. It's not a situation that your average gimlet-eyed banker is eager to involve himself with. Beaver Creek went through years of all this and, amazingly, succeeded anyway.

Bob Parker, the senior vice-president of Vail Associates, is a lanky, bearded man who was in the Tenth Mountain Division and, along with Pete Seibert, another Tenth Mountain man, was for all practical purposes the creator of the Vail ski area. Seibert is no longer at Vail, having departed four years ago after a series of management disagreements; he now runs a small operation in Utah called Snow Basin. Parker remains at Vail, and most observers give him the credit for having wrought the success of Beaver Creek. Parker's expertise lies in public relations and marketing, not technical mountain-making, which was Seibert's speciality, and therein lies the truth of how one must proceed in creating a ski resort these days: the science of persuasion—not engineering and finance—is the essence of the game.

Before selecting the site at Vail, which opened in 1962, Seibert and his cohorts had searched the mountains from Canada to Mexico for several years, looking for a suitable place to build a dream ski area. As Parker puts it, "Damned few mountains in the Rockies have skiable terrain *and* developable real estate at the bottom. Vail did. But so did Beaver Creek, and Pete liked it better."

Unfortunately, at the time key sections of Beaver Creek were the property of a crusty old rancher named Willis Nottingham, who didn't want to sell. Seibert and Parker developed Vail instead, but Seibert began an annual ritual with old man Nottingham that went on for ten years. The two of them would share a bottle of whiskey every Christmastime, on which occasions Seibert would casually bring up the subject of buying Nottingham's land. Finally, in 1970, Nottingham said, "All right, I'm older and I've got arthritis and it's tough to get around. I'd like to leave the mountains. If I can find me another ranch, I'll talk about Beaver Creek." In the summer of 1971 Seibert found some property in another section of Colorado and persuaded Nottingham that it was made for him, and the deal was concluded.

It was at this point that the ill-fated drive to bring the 1976 Winter Olympics to Colorado began gathering steam. In the winter of 1972 the Colorado organizing committee came to Vail Associates to discuss using Vail as the site for the Olympic Alpine events, but Vail Associates sold the committee on using the still-virginal Beaver Creek instead.

However, around that time a new political force came to the fore in Colorado—an angry and idealistic crowd of environmentalists. They began the move against holding the Olympics in the Rockies. The crusade was led by a state legislator named Richard Lamm, who rode his white charger into the Colorado governorship in 1974. On the way, Lamm and an increasingly concerned public overturned the Olympic project with a referendum vote in November 1972. The battle was bitter and even now there are angry echoes of those days of conflict.

"Lamm and his people managed to create the impression that there would be negative environmental impact at Beaver Creek and other venues," Parker says. "That and their claim that the Olympics would cost too much are what beat the Games. However, I like to make the point these days—eight years after Lamm and his group shot the Olympics down—that all the environment impacts they projected as likely to happen because of the Games have happened anyway. There was a very carefully conceived land-use plan that would have gone into effect as a protective measure if the Olympics had been held here. When the Olympics were rejected, that plan was automatically out. And no similar plan has been enacted in its place; in fact, there has been no meaningful environmental legislation passed in Colorado since then. It's a small point I like to repeat whenever I can."

Governor Lamm, a Democrat, replies that there has been less pressure for this kind of legislation in recent years and also that both houses of the Colorado legislature have been controlled by the Republicans for the entire 1970s with the

exception of 1975–76, and have been relentlessly hostile to such ideas.

Richard Lamm was sworn in as governor on January 15, 1975, and almost his first act was to file an objection to the approval his predecessor had given Beaver Creek. "It is very clear that this is a lame duck type of action, precipitously done," said Lamm. Ten days later the U.S. Regional Forester for the area approved Beaver Creek's designation as a winter sports site, and Lamm countered by asking for a review of that decision. Two weeks later, on February 11, 1975, the Sierra Club also requested a review.

Lamm points out that the bitterness and intensity of the opposition to Beaver Creek was based to some extent on conditions unique to the time. "We needed some rational way to deal with some one hundred applications for ski areas that were pending at that time, some systematic way of having state input," he says. "In recent years, the economic climate has changed and most of those requests to build new areas have withered away."

But in 1975 the future of Beaver Creek was very much in doubt. There were arguments over virtually every aspect of the development: water supply, population density, air quality. Not until March, 1976, was the area granted the essential Forest Service special-use permit, and even then some environmentalists were angered that it was given. The Environmental Defense Fund sharply criticized the Forest Service for not preparing a statement on a broader geographical basis that would have included Beaver Creek's environmental impact on the entire Upper Eagle Valley—an area that had been scarred with an unsightly sprawl of condominium town houses and apartments in recent years. The environmentalists were also very concerned because the ski area bordered on the proposed Holy Cross Wilderness Area, and they wanted a study on what the impact might be on wildlife there.

The battle was joined, but instead of attacking with anger and vindictiveness, Parker and Vail Associates embarked on an enlightened strategy of patience and forebearance. It was a time-consuming and costly approach that, despite its success, is fraught with discouraging echoes for future Beaver Creeks.

Says Parker: "Quite simply, rather than fighting or habitually refuting the environmentalists' concerns, we made a concerted effort to demonstrate either that the negative impacts they predicted would not—*could not*—happen, or we came up with mitigations that corrected anything they felt would go wrong. Instead of bitching back and forth, letting our emotions guide us, we tried to answer their concerns reasonably. To do that, we had to have the facts."

Vail Associates had earlier hired the Rocky Mountain Center on Environment (ROMCOE) to produce some of the most detailed impact studies ever done. "We wanted to anticipate the environmental opposition, and the ROMCOE study gave us all the basic building blocks for understanding the ecology of the area," says Parker. "Then, for example, when the environmentalists came along and said, 'You're going to ruin the range for the elk herds,' we'd say, 'No, we're not,' and we had a precise and accurate statistical basis for saying so."

The impact study for Beaver Creek is a masterpiece of its type. It included voluminous information on how the ski resort would affect everything from bird migration to soil erosion, from the mating habits of elk to the preservation of some decrepit old pioneer cabins. It examined the effect of the ski area on water flow volumes in Beaver Creek and the Eagle River, on the life of fish and pollywogs and beavers there. It went so far as to measure the amount of air pollution that might be caused by smoke from fireplaces. The ROMCOE findings resulted in Vail Associates' promising that there would be a local ordinance requiring residents to snuff out their fireplace fires if smoke levels reached a point of irritation. Depending on air quality, Beaver Creek could be limited to as few as one thousand fireplaces. The survey examined the possible impact of loose dogs on the elk, and Vail Associates proposed to implement strong leash laws—or, if that wasn't enough, to prohibit dogs from the place.

"We designed our surveys to avoid confron-

Base lodge at Beaver Creek has subdued appearance

tation," says Parker. "And we thought up our own standards sometimes if we didn't think the environmentalists were tough enough. We wanted to head off all litigation; we wanted everyone as satisfied as possible. In the long run, we left them no substantial issues to pin an appeal on."

It cost a lot of money—the surveys, legal fees, engineering studies and analyses involving everything from transportation routes on the mountain to the visual impact of the ski area as seen from Interstate 70, the superhighway at the foot of Beaver Creek Valley. Vail Associates spent $7.25 million before any construction work began on the mountain.

It was probably worth it, because even opponents of the project now feel pretty good about how things worked out. Clif Merritt, executive director of the American Wilderness Alliance, says, "We're basically happy with what we got, and Vail Associates has been quite sensitive over the years to wilderness and environmental values."

"I think this is one of the best resorts in the world from an environmental standpoint," says Governor Lamm. "I'm disappointed they went back on the transportation plan we'd agreed on, but I understand the reasons." (The governor refers to the fact that in June, 1977, after having gotten approval for Beaver Creek, Vail Associates summarily announced that, rather than entirely banning the use of private automobiles as had been proposed, it would permit the people who rented or owned property in the village to enter with their cars—a change which Lamm at that time defined as a breach of contract. "We never planned to ban all vehicles," says Parker.)

By the time the Beaver Creek ground-breaking ceremony was held in July, 1977, five years had passed since Vail Associates acquired the land. The construction of the first road up the mountain was to be completed the following summer, but it still wasn't clear skiing. Each additional step of the construction had to be preceded by another round of hearings and approvals by various federal, state, county and local agencies. In all, Beaver Creek had to receive fifty-two separate official stamps of approval. Some ski trails were finally cut in the summer and fall of 1979, and in the winter of 1980 the mountain was available via snowcats and trucks to a handful of VIP skiers. In April, 1980, the first chairlift tower was put up; all last summer the mountain was alive with the construction of everything from ski trails to sewage facilities.

Dean Kerkling, the man in charge of designing Beaver Creek's trails, has used computerized projection drawings that display topographical characteristics and tree density to lay out the ski runs. "We're trying to fine-tune our design," says Kerkling. "Trails used to be laid out like stripes on a mountainside, harsh straight lines. Skiability was the first order of business; visual esthetics were beside the point. We're trying to break up the harshness, to soften the effects of

our trails. We're leaving islands of trees in the middle of some. We've selected individually the trees we want to keep and those we'll drop. If we see a particularly beautiful aspen, we'll tie it with a ribbon, which means it has to be saved. We've even tied chicken wire around the base of some particularly good trees to save them from the beavers."

Beaver Creek will have an uncommon amount of glade skiing, which is the best kind available. As an unusual bonus for non-tree-skiing novices, the top of the mountain, with its stunning view of the Gore Mountain Range, will be given over almost totally to beginners' slopes. Kerkling says that the mountain—which he refers to as "the product"—will be laid out so that roughly 30 percent of the slopes will be intermediate in difficulty, with the remaining 70 percent about evenly split between beginner and expert runs. "This is the best mix from a marketing standpoint," he explains.

The mix and the market of "the product" will be only mildly tested this winter, because the number of skiers will be limited to thirty-three hundred a day. But still the mountain, which has a vertical drop of 3,340 feet, will at last be available to those skiers who are excited by the idea of trying the first major resort to open in five years—and possibly the last for some time to come. The trail names are unfamiliar, but they may soon become part of the sport's lore—classics that every skier will want to challenge at least once. The steepest are named after birds of prey—Golden Eagle, Goshawk, and Peregrine, which is among the steepest and longest runs extant. The run called Centennial is a certified FIS downhill course and, when not set for a race, is a good intermediate trail. The names of it and the other middling trails are of historical or western origin. There are also historical names for those beginners' runs at the top—Mystic Island, Booth Gardens, Sheephorn.

It has been a long, long time coming, but finally Beaver Creek is with us; it will be around for a much longer time than it took to get it started. All in all, it was probably worth the wait.

Schuss, Comrade

by JOHN FRY

The perks of the top editor of a ski magazine include the pick of the places in ski country. John Fry, former college racer, inventor of NASTAR, co-instigator of the World Cup and longtime editor-in-chief of Ski, and then of Cross Country, has made the most of his opportunities. The results were, as here, often splendid. Fry tours us through the intricacies of skiing in the two major Communist countries of the world, Russia and China. Fry's story begins with his visit to Russia in 1966.

IF you have skied the sophisticated Andean resorts in summer and chased the Shah down the mountains of Iran, there are, I suppose, few places left to go. The rarely visited Caucasus region of the Soviet Union, however, would be one. Its particular attraction is to the Westerner who wants to see Russia but who would like to avoid the tourist-packed borscht belt of summer. A winter trip costs about 40 percent less, and the skier can slice a portion of Russian life that is largely inaccessible to most Western tourists. True, travel in Russia is complex and often frustrating. But with a mind free of prejudice and an itinerary mapped out with the precision of a battle campaign, the experience becomes a life's memory. Authority for these findings is a group of us who traveled to the Soviet Union to ski and sightsee last winter.

As with most Americans, the first leg of our trip to Moscow was from New York to Paris. (In 1967, Air Canada will introduce direct Montreal-Moscow flights over Greenland.) "We" includes my wife, Marlies, daughter, Leslie, and her Stowe schoolfriend Katy Kellogg, both eleven. At Orly, we meet by two months' prearrangement with Don Brolin. Don is Warren Miller's vice-president in charge of taking much of the commendable film footage which appears in Warren's annual ski movie. He has just flown in from Tokyo. Three hundred and sixty degrees around the globe have brought us together.

Eastward, Europe is obscured by a carpet of clouds that billows from the Atlantic on over France, Germany, Czechoslovakia, Poland, Byelorussia, to Moscow. As we break through the clouds we glimpse the endless, flat, snow-covered forests that stretch out beyond Moscow, bleak and unredeemed by warmth, color or sun. Inevitably, the mind calls up the image of Napoleon's and Hitler's armies paralyzed in this vast frozen tract.

At the airport, our mountain of ski equipment draws curious glances, but surprisingly, no one asks to inspect the contents of our bags. Once equipped with the necessary visa, it is easier for a man to pass through the portals of Moscow than it is to get through the needle's eye of Kennedy Airport customs.

Three Zim limousines are commandeered to carry us over the snow-covered roads into Moscow. With newly exchanged rubles and kopeks (one dollar approximately equals one ruble, the official rate) I tip the porter. Later I attempt to tip our driver, but it is refused. This is the first of many confusing adventures in the mysterious art of the Soviet gratuity.

At dinner that night at the Metropole Hotel, we have our first experience with the meal coupons issued by Intourist to foreign visitors. (Coupons, not cash, are the universal currency of the foreign tourist in the Soviet Union. You buy them in a lump sum from your Intourist-franchised travel agent in America before leaving.) Carefully, we tear out the coupons marked "supper" to pay the bill. As it happens, this is totally unnecessary. Any combination of breakfast, dinner, tea, and supper coupons equal to the amount of the bill, will do.

The cupola'd magnificence of the Kremlin can hardly have caused more awe among our two little girls, Leslie and Katy, than the main dining room of the Metropole, a cross between the Plaza Hotel and a Kansas City ballroom. It is International Ladies' Day in Moscow, and a thousand Russian swains have escorted their ladies to dinner at the Metropole. The orchestra is playing. I have heard it all a score of years before, dancing to a bad copy of Glenn Miller's band. A neighboring Muscovite asks Marlies to dance, a customary and delightful table-hopping practice in Russia. Dinner takes three hours. We retire to our suite of rooms, as big as our New York apartment. Incongruously, skis, boots, and poles are stacked in a corner of a barren dining room. It is snowing outside. Leslie is delighted with her cot. It's like the beds at Camp Hochelaga.

Our plan is to stay in Moscow for three days before flying south to ski in the Caucasus. With a pretty Moscow University student, Natalya, as our Intourist guide, we find most of the traditional landmarks—St. Basil's, the Kremlin, and Tretyakov art galleries, GUM department store, and a walk in Sokolnyki Park which is popular with hundreds of cross-country skiers on Sundays. For ordinary hill skiing, Muscovites have the Lenin Hills, a stretch of escarpment that lies between the Moscow River and the University. There are no tows on the Lenin Hills, but the slope swarms with youngsters running slalom or using the two jumps. Looking out over the City of Moscow and the flat plains stretching away to the south and east, one begins to understand why the Russians have developed so little Alpine skiing: for in addition to the absence of an affluent society to support it, the nearest major mountains are 700 miles away in the Caucasus and the Urals.

At the U.S. Embassy, I talk with Al Logan, an enthusiastic Aspen and Squaw Valley skier, who is serving his last few months as a cultural attaché in Moscow. He would like to accompany us to the Caucasus, but cannot because of the official chill on Vietnam. This points up the interesting contrast of Soviet relations between foreign governments and foreign individuals: as private citizens we are heartily welcomed; as a U.S. official, Logan is not. Our puzzlement is only further increased later, when Intourist officials blandly assure us that Logan's visit would be welcome.

There are only three major Alpine ski resorts in the Soviet Union. The most remote is at Alma Ata, to the east of Tashkent in the Trans-Ili Alatau Mountains near the Chinese border. The best known and most often skied by Westerners is Bakouriani in the Georgian Caucasus, visited by Roland Palmedo ten years ago. (Two American friends currently are at Bakouriani, later report that they enjoyed the skiing in Czechoslovakia better.) Finally, there is Itkol (meaning "cold water") in the northern Caucasus. Logan believes that we and a just-departed American photographer, Ross Wagner, are the first Americans ever to visit Itkol.

Three days in Moscow without sun, the great March thaw filling the streets with slush, and we are ready to leave for the mountains. Roudolf Kalantarov, an executive of Intourist, will accompany us on the trip. Since Roudolf has appeared on the scene, all of our problems previously insoluble by minor functionaries—a change of itinerary to include Tbilisi (Tiflis), a visit to an Orthodox church service, difficulties in contacting Russian Ski Federation officials—

have suddenly evaporated. It should be said that the foreigner in Russia is afflicted by the same bureaucratic snarl that afflicts the Soviet citizen. Russians manage to get through it all with a marvelous sense of humor, and we find it works too. Rather than get angry, we invariably meet with sympathy and success when we joke about difficulties. To wit, when we are told that it is impossible to book tickets to see the Bolshoi Ballet Company, I ask the girl at the theater desk: "What about tickets for the student ballet in Rostov next year?" She breaks into a broad grin, lifts the phone, and tries to do something about our problem.

To reach Itkol from Moscow in one day, as we will do, involves a jet flight to Mineralne Vody (literally, "Mineral Water") one of the famous watering spas in the northern Caucasus, made popular by wealthy Leningrad families in the nineteenth century. These spas are still popular with the workers, and medical practitioners of the Socialist Republics still believe firmly enough in the curative powers of the mineral waters to send thousands of patients there annually. The Moscow-Mineralne Vody flight is about 800 air miles, and the cost is merely fifty dollars round trip. Air travel is extremely cheap in the Soviet Union, one reason perhaps being that it is subsidized by defense needs. The passenger planes with their glass nose-cones could be converted overnight into bombers.

At 33,000 feet we still have our overcoats on. The Aeroflot hostess delivers information about the flight in Russian, *sans* loudspeaker system. She concludes by giving her name and home city, and asks if anyone has any questions. "Yes," cries a mustachioed Georgian wag from the back of the plane, "what's your address?"

At Mineralne Vody, our mountain of baggage and people—Roudolf, Don Brolin, a second Intourist guide, a driver, two children, my wife, and I—are met by a Chevrolet Greenbrier-type transporter which will take us to Pyatigorsk (pronounced Pitygorsk), another mineral spa, and our departure point for the three-hour drive into the mountains to Itkol. From the heights of Pyatigorsk, where the famous Russian poet Ler-

montov was slain in a duel, we can see the immense snow-plumed crest of Elbrus, the highest mountain in Europe, and our destination.

From Pyatigorsk, we enter the autonomous republic of Kabardina Balkari. This is not one of the fifteen republics of the Soviet Union, but is a part of the Russian Federation which, in turn, counts as one of the fifteen, as does Georgia, which we will visit later. Our officially atheistic guides point out with libertarian pride that this mountainous republic is almost entirely Moslem in religion.

The country now grows mountainous. We are entering the rocky, arid foothills of the northern Caucasus, not unlike the country outside Denver. We are also driving back in years, it seems. The farms grow more primitive. Small burros carrying huge fagots or pulling water carts, appear along the roadside. Old people, shy, their faces leathered and wind-etched, wear the same clothes their great grandfathers wore a century ago—somber blacks with an occasional hand-woven shawl rich as a royal diadem in hues of red, green, and orange. Whenever the road appears blocked by a group of these people, our driver begins sounding his horn from a hundred yards off, and hand still pressed to the horn, roars through in a cloud of dust without diminishing speed in the slightest. This sort of road conduct, which would merit a curse or a twenty-five-dollar speeding ticket in America, apparently is commonplace here. I am reminded of our visit to a crowded Moscow restaurant. Despite a long queue of hungry Muscovites outside, we are shepherded to the head of the line where our escort cries at the maitre d'—"Amerikanski! Amerikanski!"—and we immediately are admitted to a free table. Privileged dining and road hogging are favors freely bestowed on Westerners and high Party officials, even if they offend egalitarian sensibilities.

Dusk falls. The children sleep. We trundle through a major industrial center, a strategic molybdenum mining town whose existence I am now disclosing as my sole contribution to the CIA from this trip. The road grows steeper and bumpier. Snow appears in the forests. Suddenly in a blaze of light, the five-story, Disney-at-

Squaw-Valley hotel of Itkol comes into view. We have arrived.

The entrance floor of the hotel is crowded with ski racers waxing and filing edges. This is the time of the annual Winter Competitions of the Peoples of the Soviet Union. We are led to a big, modern dining room. Supper consists of caviar, fried eggs, and champagne. Altogether, a pleasant surprise. So is our suite of two rooms— comfy, neatly furnished, with an outside balcony. Only the bathroom leaves us puzzled, considering the modernity of the rest of the hotel. It is a tiny, ill-lit cubicle with an unenclosed shower and a drain in the middle of the floor. Turn the shower on and everything—you, the john, washbasin, and anything else you have been foolish enough to leave in the bathroom—gets doused.

The next morning, Don Brolin and I head for the slalom hill on Mount Cheget and our first look at Itkol's ski facilities. The single chair on Cheget, perhaps three-quarters of a mile long, probably has no peer for slowness in the world. The result is a long lift line, but our guide and our new-found disrespect for queuing up, propel us to the front of the line. The ride up (thirty kopeks or about thirty-three cents), however slow, is blessed by scenic beauty. To the left is a dazzling hanging glacier, to the right a vista of the enormous flank of Elbrus. It is hard to realize that this 18,500-foot giant is at least a full 4,000 feet higher than any of the surrounding mountains. We can see the pylons in place for construction of a forty-passenger aerial tramway which will go to about the 15,000-foot level on Elbrus, the future major attraction of Itkol as a year-round resort. Elbrus will be skiable all year.

Despite poor wind exposure, Cheget offers some fine skiing from above timberline down into steep, tree-lined slopes. Don and I photograph the slalom action. The men, representing teams from many parts of the Soviet Union, appear to ski well, but cautiously. Later I am asked by one of the Russian coaches what I think of the racers. I diplomatically remark that the men ski well, but lack aggressiveness. "They don't attack the course enough," I say. He nods a kind of sad acknowledgment. But as in so many Russian sports, the girls present a different story. With a little more exposure to European racing, two or three of them look as though they could break into the first ten in world competition.

The equipment and clothing used by the racers are almost entirely imported from Austria. There is a preponderance of Kästle and Kneissl skis, Marker toes and turntables. At the bottom, we take off our Head skis, and immediately a group of about ten Russians gathers around to inspect our equipment. The Sputnik-like appearance of the Grand Prix heel release is a special object of heated discussion.

Our girls are off with Itkol's head instructor, who insists on giving them a lesson. After years of drill in the Stowe school program, Leslie is told that all is wrong with her American technique. She must learn to get in a crouch and hold out her arms propeller fashion when turning. The unkind fact is that underneath the top echelon of racers, Russia has little instruction and few competent recreational skiers. The untutored skiers we see at Itkol, however, get full marks for *plain guts*. They'll go down any slope—often in a bathing suit.

After dinner in the evening, there is dancing to guitar and saxophone, and much enjoyable exchanging of pins, a favorite Russian pastime. (I would advise anyone going to ski in Russia to take along a gross of U.S. Ski Team pins. The effort will be rewarded with a harvest of every conceivable kind of Russian pin—from gymnastic expert to mountain climber.) As a special honor, we are presented with first degree Alpinist pins by Zalihanov, seventy-eight, on behalf of his one-hundred-and-twelve-year-old father, one of the oldest men in this region of the Caucasus renowned for the longevity of its people. Incredibly, the elder Zalihanov is reputed to have climbed to the top of Elbrus only two years ago. He sired his youngest son at the age of eighty-three.

At the bar, the president of the Russian Ski Federation, Vassily Zakchartchenno, buys us a bottle of champagne. There is a lively discussion with a cameraman from the Urals who sadly confesses that he doesn't know what to do on his vacation. What he does know is that he wants to do something "challenging," something "tough," not stay in a luxurious hotel like Itkol. Vassily has brought a friend from Moscow, the painter Ilya. Ilya goes to phone his girlfriend in Moscow. He smokes Kents. Everyone looks at a copy of *Ski* magazine. They admire the pictures, point at the advertisements. "There's a lot of advertising," I volunteer in the miscast role of commercial advocate. "Yes," nods Vassily, "that is your style, you Americans."

With Vassily, we speak almost entirely in French. Clearly, this disconcerts our assigned Intourist guides who can understand none of it. Clearly, too, Vassily does not seem enamored of their presence. Very tall, elegant and mannered, Vassily bears all the marks of the cultured intellectual. By vocation, he is a Moscow editor. I discern his role in Russian skiing to be like that of a Palmedo or a Lowell Thomas who has joined with some of his gentlemen friends to further the interests of Alpine skiing, hitherto a somewhat *recherché* sport for Nordic-oriented Russians. This, in fact, proves to be the case. Vassily's Russian Ski Federation has split off from the Nordic end of the sport in order to advance the interests of Alpine skiing and to aid in the creation of more resorts like Itkol.

The next day, Vassily takes us to the Roundhouse at the top of the Cheget chairlift. A glorious spot for sunning. In glowing terms. Vassily describes a wonderful New Year's Eve party in the Roundhouse. "No one but the best sort of people in the Soviet Union were invited," he relates; a famous doctor from Moscow, a physicist, writers, "all top people." As delicious black coffee is served to us, we wish we had been there. Vassily also describes the fierce battles fought with the Germans, the elite Edelweiss division, in these mountain valleys during the war. Only two years ago, corpses of two German soldiers were found atop Elbrus, perfectly preserved by the cold and absence of bacteria after more than twenty years.

In the afternoon, back at the hotel, I spot children from the local village selling woolen sweaters and hats. I approach them, camera in hand. Immediately, they stow their handicrafts in bags and run off into the woods. Vassily coaxes them out. It is apparent what has happened.

Even in this remote mountain resort, private enterprise is forbidden. The children, dispatched on this vending errand by their parents, have been instructed to flee when anyone attempts to photograph them. But now they're back and smiling the incredibly radiant smiles of Russian children. Katy buys a handsome woolen hat for five rubles.

In the evening, the children tucked in bed, we are invited to the home of Yuri, the ski area manager, for coffee and champagne. Yuri is the prototype of the disenchanted exurbanite, in love with the mountain, who one day says, "To hell with it all," chucks his job as a well-paid engineer in Moscow, divorces his wife, and takes off for the ski hills to live happily ever after. He has a swinging new wife and a ski life.

Yuri proudly shows his complete taped library of American jazz, the Azerbaidzhan carpet is rolled up and soon we are all twisting like crazy.

Later, we talk about resort skiing. *How much does it cost to ski at Itkol?* Answer: if you come like an atomic physicist we met at the hotel, a lot. If you're like Ruth, a Moscow computer engineer who is staying with Yuri and his wife and working as a ski bum, virtually nothing. *How much does it cost to ski at Squaw Valley?* Answer: relatively, the same as at Itkol. Under the comprehensive Intourist plan, we are paying about twenty dollars a day which includes private car and translator. *How do Americans get to ski resorts?* Answer: they drive 200 miles on Friday night, ski two days, drive 200 miles back. *But in Moscow, we have hills right in the city.* Retort: and so do many American cities, but people want the bigger mountains. All present nod in accord.

The next day, it snows and skiing is limited. We meet an American who has just arrived at Itkol, an engineer engaged in defense work in California. He insists on having his Intourist guide with him at all times, but this proves impossible when he dons skis. His pale, unathletic guide, assigned at Pyatigorsk, cannot ski.

That evening, we are invited to the home of the Itkol ski lift engineer, Alexei Maleinov—a drab apartment in one of those drab cement block buildings that sprout like ant heaps over the Russian landscape, even into this remote Caucasian mountain valley. But, as in so much of Soviet life, the warmth and vivacity of our new Russian friends quite obscures the surroundings. We have skied hard all day in the brilliant sun that bathes the palms and grapevines of the Black Sea spas only a hundred miles away. The evening's reward is a rare dinner: wild boar cooked Caucasian style. A few days before, hunters have killed a boar in another valley. Now Alexei has charcoaled it and added a mouth-watering sauce. We sit around the table eating with our hands out of a communal pot. With fine Georgian wine we toast one another in a babel of French, German, and English translated by our Intourist guide. Later there is talk about what skiing is like in America, a sort of boisterous Khrushchev-Nixon kitchen debate, but with friendly, gracious banter.

Present at Alexei's is a middle-aged woman who heads the most important trade union of Kabardina Balkari. In this case, trade union money is helping to build the resort and lifts at Itkol. Vassily and our host Alexei are specially ingratiating in talking to this gruff, stolid lady whose funds Itkol needs. She seems suspicious of this whole crazy ski business. I am reminded of a wary Vermont banker being coaxed for a loan by an impoverished ski area operator. Later, Vassily confides to me the difficulties of raising money from the State to build lifts and promote Alpine skiing. The fact is that Russia is a flat country with about 8 million cross-country ski enthusiasts. The esoteric, expensive sport of Alpine skiing probably numbers only a few thousand adherents. Funds are lacking to train racers and buy ski equipment. Many Russian racers, too, are students who, like their American counterparts, must train and compete while trying to keep up with stiff academic programs.

Don Brolin has left us now, and it is our last night in Itkol. From here we will go on to visit the colorful, ancient Georgian capital of Tbilisi (Tiflis) and to savor the fine shashlik, cheese, and wines of southernmost Russia. Then it will be back to Moscow for an evening at the ballet, and our return to Paris.

Curiously, Vassily, after inviting us to spend the night in the Roundhouse on Cheget, is evading us. I run over possible reasons why: his rudeness to Roudolf of Intourist whom we have wholeheartedly befriended; a social slight; possibly it even has something to do with a Russian girl who has been skiing with us and has indiscreetly talked of coming to the United States. It is all very peculiar, and we shall never know why.

Roudolf, an immensely charming Armenian who handles North American and British travel for Intourist, invites me to join him in a drink. With a bottle of vodka and a bowl of fruit between us, we drink into the morning's small hours. The conversation runs over every conceivable topic from Roudolf's in-laws to the Soviet Jewish question. At 1 A.M. a snowball fight erupts outside the hotel. People on the balconies are hurling snowballs on comrades below who return the fire. A special target seems to be a noisy gallery of East Germans. One, stripped to his waist, bursts into our room with a fresh supply of snowballs to replenish our dwindling snow pile. Everywhere, snowballs are exploding on the hotel's windows and bursting into the rooms of sleeping skiers. One of the Russian women's coaches emerges and shouts at the snowballers to stop, her voice trailing off into the deep, snowy Caucasian night.

But the battle has ended.

China 1980

There are two ways to appreciate the early history of skiing—say, as it existed at the turn of this century. One is to visit a ski museum. The other is to travel into the farther hills of northeastern China in the region once known as Manchuria.

On the ski hill near Shangzhi, a drab, flat agricultural and woodcutting town of twenty thousand people about 700 miles northeast of Peking, a teenager stared in wonder at my gleaming red Fischer cross-country skis. I stared in wonder at the primitive hand-carved wooden skis strapped to his boots with rope thongs. Weatherbeaten and knotted, they were clones of those antique skis mounted as treasures above the fireplaces of expensive ski chalets in Europe and America. Here in China, however, a youngster was actually skiing on them.

I was reminded of an aboriginal boomerang from Australia I once saw in a museum: how much richer the experience to see it hurled at a wild rabbit which, downed, is roasted and eaten near the campfire. In China, the ski that is a museum artifact to Westerners is still in use.

"*Ke-yi*" (it is possible) said our hosts when we asked to visit a woodworking shop where skis are made. The cold and dimly lit, stone-floored shop normally produces school furniture, but for one month a year the woodworkers turn their efforts to making several hundred pairs of skis for the town's children.

To make a ski, a 2-meter block of walnut typically is shaved down and shaped at the tip and tail. The wood is steamed and bent at the tip to form the shovel, then blocked at the midsection to give it a rudimentary camber.

A drawknife and plane are the basic tools of ski making. A hammer is used to fashion the binding toepiece from a piece of brass plate, and pliers are used to shape and attach the bail on the binding.

The woodworking shop at Shangzhi is one of several efforts to "mass produce" skis in China. They sell for about four yuan ($2.50) a pair. Elsewhere, ski making seems to be an art that has been practiced a long time by rural people, who use the same tools. In a couple of hours, a father or affectionate uncle can crudely shape a pair of skis for a youngster. The youngster can then practice *huaxue* ("skiing," pronounced "hwah-shoo").

That afternoon at Shangzhi, we skied cross-country and practiced downhill skiing and Telemark turns with local youngsters. Back at the hostel in the evening, Ned, Jan, Tim, and I dined with our hosts Coach Pi, Mr. High, and Captain Friendship, along with local, county and sports officials. The county leader offered a formal toast—a traditional one evidently—to the health of persons who have just borne a child. Although no one at the table quite fit the toast, we nevertheless quaffed our *mou-tai,* a fiery schnapps. Mine shot like a lightning bolt to my stomach.

After dinner, we gathered for a formal conference. The Chinese officials sat uneasily in a row as Coach Pi, head of sports training and competition in Heilongjiang Province, led the discussion.

"There are about two thousand young people who are engaged in organized competitive skiing in China," he told us. "A youngster who shows promise has the opportunity to ski almost every afternoon after school. Other selected skiers train and compete under coaches during school vacations, such as the lunar New Year's break which is now taking place. We have some two hundred officials who are engaged during winter in organizing skiing.

"The government's new emphasis on China's need to succeed in international sports means that more money will be invested in skiing in the years ahead—several hundred thousand yuan (about $200,000) annually."

Coach Pi surrendered the floor to Mr. Li, the man in charge of skiing in the region. Tall and serious—"a political spokesman," Tim whispered to me—he told us that skiing would be more advanced in China today had it not been for the Gang of Four.

Many of China's current ills are blamed on the infamous Gang of Four now in jail, including the wife of former Chairman Mao Tse-Tung. The Cultural Revolution, which they fomented, scorned bourgeois Western pursuits. Skiing was perceived as an unimportant activity in the mid-1970s.

"Are you saying the Gang of Four suppressed skiing in China?" I asked.

The officials nodded vigorously and I glanced above their heads at the portraits of Chairman Mao, the current Party Chairman Hua Guofeng, Lenin, Marx, and Stalin, wondering what *they* would think.

Our discussion moved on to questions about skiing in America.

"We have about 10 million people who ski," I said, then paused to hear the officials gasp with expressions of astonishment on their faces. Recalling the evident disapproval of skiing by Chairman Mao's wife, I noted that President Carter likes to ski cross-country, Vice-President Mondale and former President Ford are both strong skiers, and that the Kennedy family are longtime ski enthusiasts.

The Chinese showed no further curiosity about Western skiing, so we adjourned the conference to discuss plans for the next few days of skiing.

Finding a place to stay is the principal limitation on backcountry travel in China, and the officials had determined that where we were staying now—a gloomy, two-story hostel flanked by a cement factory—was inadequate. We tended to agree. The toilet was a hole in the floor and facilities for showering were nonexistent.

Coach Pi proposed a trip to Yabuli, the second highest mountain (4,000 feet above sea level) in Heilongjiang Province. Here, also in Shangzhi County and close to train service from Harbin, China's first major ski area, may soon be built complete with lifts and hotels. But when we discovered it would take five hours to drive to Yabuli for an inspection, we declined. We would go instead to Yangshou (a name meaning "long life"), where the hotel would be superior and the skiing better organized. Food, too, we were assured, would be good. But then the meals served in China seem appetizing no matter where one travels. As in France, where you can eat well in the farthest reaches of the countryside, the traveler in China benefits from a tradition of culinary art that is everywhere.

Our van rolled out of Shangzhi in the morning, its interior redolent of the garlic that had laced our 7 A.M. breakfast, but inoffensive since, as they say, when everyone eats garlic, no one seems to notice. Our van roared powerfully ahead over the dirt road. Bicycles, pedestrians and horse-drawn carts and sleighs edged to the side, blasted away by the unrelenting horn-blowing of our driver.

The country around us would not be out of place in New Hampshire. At the same latitude, the winter days are similar in length, the hills rising a thousand or more feet in height, colored gray and dun by the leafless trees of winter. Prevailing westerly winds bring little moisture to northeastern China from the Mongolian Desert and the hills do not rise high enough to catch the snow; consequently, snowfall is limited to a couple of feet each winter. Only when the same cold air, traveling eastward from China, crosses the Pacific does it pick up the ocean's moisture and drop it in prodigious snowfalls on Sapporo and the northern Japanese island of Hokkaido. But in Manchuria, the sun shines with Colorado consistency.

At Yangshou, we settled comfortably into the county hostel, a tidier, cement block carbon copy of the place we had left in Shangzhi. Such "hotels" are used by traveling officials from the central government, or by technicians posted to the country to oversee a construction project.

After lunch at the hostel, we drove 20 miles to a small range of hills surrounding a frozen reservoir. This is one of the prime centers for cross-country ski training. The youngsters were brightly dressed, wore gloves and were racing on the kind of skis we had seen being made in the shop at Shangzhi. Their coach, Li Zhanting, an athletic forty-year-old former cross-country racer, introduced us to two members of his team. Wu Mingshu, fifteen, Chinese junior women's champion, learned to ski by borrowing skis and boots from older racers.

Zhang Dongrang is an athletic seventeen-year-old who earns top marks in school. From Yangshou, he began skiing when he was ten and became China's junior cross-country champion in 1979.

Racing against the Chinese youngsters across the reservoir and into the surrounding hills, Ned and Jan set a hot pace that left the Chinese skiers two or three minutes behind after 3 kilometers. Afterwards, Ned and Jan organized games of tag and ball on cross-country skis, and the Chinese joined in enthusiastically. Such games teach agility and quickness on skis.

On most evenings we were in bed by 9 P.M. The absence of bars and entertainment means there is no après-ski in China. In fact, our liveliest moments often were reserved for the morning. One *avant-ski* activity consisted of sneaking out of the hotel at 6 A.M. to inspect homes and visit informally with residents of Yangshou without attracting the attention of our officials who, while not opposed to such visits, were anxious to preselect whom we should see. One afternoon,

Ned and Jan tried the same trick. They were followed by two officials.

"Are you sure you don't want to return to the hotel for a rest?" they asked. The Chinese word for "rest" is *xiu-xi* (pronounced "shoo-shee") and we were to hear it often on our trip. Suggestions that we take a *xiu-xi,* we found, could mean one of three things: (1) a genuine concern for our health, (2) here's something we don't particularly want you to do or see, or (3) we (your guides) are tired and don't feel like taking you to another damned house/shop/landmark.

Consideration for guests is a virtue, in moderation, but with the Chinese it can be excessive. The next day we had planned to ski on the hill at Chang Shan ling Chang, a woodcutting village about three-quarters of an hour away. Concerned for our comfort, the officials planned to drive us back to the hotel in Yang-shou for lunch, an hour-and-a-half round trip. We resisted.

"Let's take some bread and thermos bottles of tea with us. We can spend more time skiing," I said. A long discussion ensued.

"In the West," I proposed, "people are accustomed to eating at the ski hill. It needn't be a special meal." This last remark was prompted by an event of the day before. We had similarly resisted returning to town from the cross-country ski center to eat, so the officials had brought the chef and maid from the hotel to serve us a full luncheon. It was a scene that recalled the picnics once served to British aristocracy on the hunting field.

At length, we won the argument, and at noon we all sat in the minibus eating braided crullers (a kind of twisted doughnut). Even our hosts seemed to concede that a Western-style ski lunch was not such a bad thing.

Out on the hill, a crowd had gathered. The munchkins—five- to eight-year-old children—were schussing the hill on their ski shoes as the village looked on. One munchkin soared off a bump and fell forward on his face. The crowd laughed uproariously. The youngster looked up, his face and bare hands covered with snow, not knowing whether to cry or to laugh with the crowd. Unable to decide on either emotion, he

picked himself up and resumed sliding down the hill.

So far no one had exhibited any desire to make a turn. But now a brightly dressed girl from the village descended the hill, making a series of cautiously skidded christies. She was followed by a boy I assumed to be the local champion. Of Korean descent, he had managed to obtain a pair of Japanese factory-made skis, leather boots of 1960s vintage and beartrap bindings. Although the skis lacked steel edges, he linked a respectable series of turns. His technique, neither modern nor wedeln, was reminiscent of the turns taught by Emile Allais in the 1950s. We were quick to congratulate him on his prowess.

Clearly, the Chinese are light-years away from becoming an Alpine ski power. Lack of money puts lifts, fiberglass racing skis, and plastic boots out of reach of Chinese skiers. But with the continued dedication of the coaches we met, proper track-setting equipment and modern touring skis, they can make rapid progress in cross-country. The incentives are enormous for a Chinese youngster. Simply being selected for the cross-country ski team means obtaining a pair of gloves to protect his hands from Manchuria's sub-zero temperatures.

At a formal ceremony at the reservoir, we presented provincial authorities with ten pairs of Kastle, Trak and Rossignol skis, Dolomite boots, and cross-country bindings. We also supplied them with waxes, literature on modern cross-country ski design and how to build a track-setting sled.

We returned to Harbin to a series of banquets. The final day, I had played hockey at the insistence of Coach Pi, who learned that I had grown up with skates on my feet in Montreal. Aching and sore, I arrived at the banquet to find *mou-tai,* beer, and wine waiting on a table covered with spiced chicken, sea slugs, pressed duck, fresh trout and *shan-yao* (mountain medicine), which is a potato covered with sugar and banana. Thanks to the frequent toasts that are a fixture of the Chinese banquet, my pain was quickly eased. Dish followed dish, fifteen in all, as I counted. We ate monkey head mushrooms (so-called because of the shape of the mushroom), Flying Dragon grouse, and bear's paws. The latter are a delicacy, boiled and sliced very thin, tasting like delicately flavored ham. The banquet concluded with Mongolian hot pot, a Chinese form of fondue. Chunks of beef, chicken, pork, muskrat, and shrimp are held with chopsticks and dipped into a boiling pot of broth placed at the center of the table. Each guest is free to mix his own sauce from a selection of ginger, sesame, red bean curd, chopped garlic, pureed pickle curry powder, and red pepper sauce, mixed into a base of soy sauce and vinegar. At the end, the rich broth is poured into soup dishes and served to everyone at the table.

Holding my *mou-tai* glass high, I proposed a final *gam-bei* (toast): "Good snow, a good future for skiing in China." Outside, the bus was waiting to take us up to the train for our overnight return to Peking.

The Powder and the Glory

by JOHN SKOW

Giving vent to the powder pig in him, John Skow, essayist, film critic and serious skier, chases the airy stuff down by helicopter and skins. Heaven and hell are inches apart here deep in the Canadian Rockies' ever-ample supply of the deep stuff.

THE temperature in the room has passed 195 degrees. The rim of the sawed-off wine bottle is hot enough to hurt the lips. Surprisingly, the beer inside it is still cool, but the heat in the room is now solid and important. Respectful attention must be paid to it. We sit there in our skins, paying attention. We have begun to glisten and turn pink: two or three men in our late thirties or early forties, tennis players, handball bulldogs and 3-mile joggers, by the look of us; a boy of about fourteen; and a couple of chunky college girls. Nobody is wearing anything, except for one of the girls, who has a towel turbaned around her hair. She is the blonder of the two and has turned pinker. Sing ho for chunky college girls. Our mood is light and uncluttered, as far as I can tell. Each of us has wandered separately to the sauna, whose door lists no rules and no hours, poked his head in and thought, well, sure. The trace of sexuality in our happenstance is pleasant, partly because it is so faint as to be weightless. The white-pine chunks burning in the iron wood stove rule the room. I lie back on the hot cedar. The heat enters my shoulders and thighs and reads the day's history.

Seven A.M.: a profound breakfast, stretched to the limits of meaning. Then out to the helicopter for stupidity drill. Don't wander around the back of the aircraft, Ed Pruss, the pilot, is saying, because the tail rotor will kill you. Don't carry your skis on your shoulder, nor hold them vertically, because the main rotor of the big Bell 204 will hit them and they will fly around and kill you. He goes on to mention something else that will solve all your problems suddenly, but I miss it, because I am mooning about snow. I have been mooning all winter about the snow in this place. But we can't fly. Above 8,000 feet, the mountains are socked in. I sidestep up a hundred yards and run some slalom gates, moodily and not well.

A cathedral-like lunch, then back out to the helicopter. This time, although conditions look no better, the thing is going to fly. Nine of us pack into its abdomen. Leo, who is running things, sits up front. We swing up into the weather. White, defined by dark green and shades of gray. Then, as we rise beyond the tree line, nothing at all but luminous white for seconds at a stretch. Astonishingly close, the gray of a rock wall. The gray drops behind again.

What is there for Ed Pruss to brace his sight against? I strain to see through the fogged Plexiglas of the door and discover that I am looking at a motionless floor of snow a few feet away. We have landed. The door pops open; a shock of cold. Blown snow. Out into it, running crouched, the blades whuffing overhead. Kneel, the noise level rises, there is a blast of air. Blink, straighten, the copter is gone, a small diminishing noise in a light fall of snow.

Now no sound.

Leo yells. He has dumped the skis from the chopper rack and is sorting them. No time. The next team will be here in three or four minutes. We stamp out standing places in the new powder that has fallen. My legs are stiff. I can feel the chill through my down parka. I clamp my bindings and fall into line behind one of the other skiers as we shuffle up a slight rise.

Jumping off: Leo picks his line and yells for us to stay to the right of it. I have been in the mountains enough to know why: our pitch is the uppermost fall of a glacier and the gentle shadow barely visible through the falling snow on the run-out to the left is a big crevasse. Leo drops down the hang, curling slowly. He has thirty-five pounds of survival gear in a rucksack on his back and his skiing is strong, rather than beautiful. He handles the slope like a carpenter guiding a plank through a table saw.

Someone goes. Someone else. My turn: I am a tower of rust. Adrenaline has begun to work, but the effects have not yet reached my knees, where the joint mice play. One of the skiers ahead of me catches an edge and windmills, and it is obvious that the crusted ruts of last week's wretched weather lie under the softness of today's pretty powder. I revert to survival skiing and blast through my turns with too much force. I am still perpendicular when I reach Leo, a quarter of a mile below, but my track, as I look back to criticize it, is not a linking of smooth curves but a ridiculous jitter of zigzags.

By now, however, enough cold air has passed through my lungs to set my machinery in motion and skiing begins to look possible. *"Gemma weiter,"* says Leo—Austrian mountain dialect for "Let's move it." Leo Grillmair and his partner, Hans Gmoser, emigrated twenty years ago from Linz, Upper Austria. They arrived in Calgary on top of a logging truck, frostbitten and broke. It is a matter of opinion, of course, but for several years now, a growing number of opinions have run in the same direction, toward the belief that this nest of mountains in Canada's Bugaboos, where Grillmair and Gmoser have set up their helicopter operation, is the best place in the world to do powder skiing.

We track down after Leo. Looser now, swing free, accept the snow. To some extent, we do. And don't. Most of us are fairly good skiers, but the mystery the amateur athlete never manages to solve has nothing to do with technique, which he knows cold. It is how to find and keep his edge. We ski tentatively. Each of us is waiting to hear a single sound, the beat of great wings as grace descends.

The helicopter waits at about 7,500 feet. It has been warm all week, with a snow-eating Chinook blowing out of the west, and below this level what covers the ground is unskiable mashed potatoes. The helicopter freights us back into the snowfall and we scuttle out into it, better now at the guerrilla routine.

Some orderly soul asks where we are. "Groovy's Ass," Leo says. He is not joking. There is another run here called Holy Shit. Groovy's Ass, although not especially fearsome, figures in one of the great guest-book inscriptions of the Western world: "I left my teeth in Groovy's Ass." Yah, says Leo, somebody wrote that in the Bugaboo lodge book last week, after cracking up on the run and breaking off a couple of teeth.

Everyone is mightily cheered by this information, and although grace cannot be said to have descended, the group experiences a lively attack of competence. It is a mild version of a reaction I have noticed before in the mountains: the bells of hell go ting-a-ling-a-ling for you but not for me. Mountaineers are mostly decent types and they are no less empathetic than valley people, but there are so many opportunities to get into bad trouble that even the news of some other party's fatal accident, if heard during a climb, sometimes releases an odd shudder of en-

The most glorious ski experience is spending a day in light, dry powder snow

ergy that is almost exhilaration: I am not dead, therefore I feel very, very quick.

We run with some style for an hour or so. No one minds that what we are doing is not true powder skiing—only about 6 inches of new stuff has fallen so far and it is still possible to ski on the snow, as if it were a floor, instead of in the snow, as if it were a sea. We splash about in the shallows. At just the point at which first-day fatigue would tatter our elegance, snow and fog interpose tactfully and Ed tells Leo that flying is finished for the day. We ski down to the lodge out of what is now the beginning of a true storm.

The sauna has driven me out. My feet tingle. Their heat melts the snow I am standing on and it re-forms as ice under my toes. Snow grains blow on the wind. They sting the skin of my belly and thighs. My head feels clear and sharp and a little crazy. The storm is going to blow all night and there must be a foot of new snow now up at 10,000 feet. Tomorrow morning there will be 2 feet, 30 inches, a full yard. We are rich.

Let us say that it is storming now at Zermatt, or Zürs, or Vail. Fine, light snow fills the streets to the height of a boot top and more of it is sifting down. Skiers hunching through the storm on their way to drinks at Gramshammer's or *Rehrücken* at the Walliserhof think about how it will be in the morning and their riches make them lightheaded. Yet there can be no knowledgeable skier at any of these great stations who would not prefer to be transported instantly to this small lodge in the Bugaboos, west of Banff.

The explanation lies mainly in numbers. The Bugaboos are spectacular, but they are not higher nor more splendid nor more snowed upon than the great peaks of the Rockies or the Alps. They are a good deal more private, however. Something like 300 square miles of the Bugaboos are easily reachable by helicopter from Hans Gmoser and Leo Grillmair's lodge. Beyond these miles are more miles, and in all of this vast area, in any given week, there are only forty souls to make tracks in the powder. If you cross another skier's trail, it is because you want to.

There are other numbers bound up with the uniqueness of this place. The Bell 204 has places for a pilot, a guide, nine other skiers, ten pairs of skis tied outside the cabin in a rack on the landing gear, and enough survival equipment and freeze-dried food to last two weeks. The price of so much lifting power is close to half a million dollars. It costs $9 a minute, or $540 an hour, or far too much, to run this most sophisticated of all ski lifts.

The high-season price of a week of skiing, with 70,000 vertical feet of helicopter transport included, is $610. This means that a skier from the East Coast, paying something more than $300 for his air fare to Calgary, must lay out at least $900 for his amusement. If he skis more than 70,000 vertical feet—and he can do that in two days if his knees and the weather are good—his expense can run to around $1,300. It is senseless to pay this much and use second-rate equipment, so he buys a good pair of powder skis and a set of bindings for $225. Maybe—what the hell—he buys a pair of new, high-rise, plastic superskier boots for $175. This hemorrhage of cash is so absurd that the last bite seems almost sane. The Easterner hears that the only goggles that will not fog up when he is ear-deep in powder are a double-lens model turned out (as it happens) by a powder-skiing dentist named Smith. Smith's good goggles cost $20—cheap.

Disbursement on this scale limits the Bugaboos to the prosperous and the fanatic. Most of my companions this week are successful business *honchos* in their forties, old jocks. Several of the rest are orthopedic surgeons, cheerful, healthy men, slightly less fit than the *honchos,* amiably determined to complete the circle of their lives by plowing their bonesetting profits back into the snow. But not everyone here is loaded: a citizen whose mental moorings have been loosened by fantasies of powder skiing will cash in his life insurance or sell his car to get to where the powder is. There are men here, I am certain, who have made promises to their wives and their banks that can't be kept, and one or two women who have abandoned their men with a kiss and instructions for operating the drier.

With this assortment of hard cases I pass the evening. Yesterday morning, waiting in the lobby of the Calgary Inn, we went through the squint-eyed routine with which every expedition begins, inspecting one another without delight and wondering which unrevealed character would be the casualty, which the complainer. Now everything is friendly and uncritical. We have agreed that we are splendid people. As the week progresses there will be minor modifications of this view, but now we apply Bushmill's superior Irish liniment to unadmitted aches and exchange the comfortable fribble of ski talk. Smugness carries the night.

If it is agreed that the triple forward flip is a baroque excess, outside the classic canon, then the most spectacular maneuver in recreational skiing is undoubtedly the great-circle route by which a beginner at powder skiing gets down a mountain. The great circle offers speed, terror, unpredictable action, heartbreaking displays of courage, and blood on the sand. It is as stirring as a good train wreck. A New Hampshire friend of mine, upon being excavated after his first great circle, which he performed on Bell Mountain at Aspen, said it all: "That was a pissah."

Picture your beginner, then, at the top of a big *Steilhang.* The German word means "steep-hang" and is expressive; the snow does not lie on the ground, it hangs on what is almost a cliff face and now and then lets go in an avalanche. Powder skiing is done on *Steilhangs,* because when the powder is really deep, the pressure of it on the skier's thighs and waist would bring him to a stop on a normal slope. The powder skier needs steepness for the same reason that a water skier needs a fast boat.

So the beginner, who is not a beginner but something of a hot-shot back home on the packed-down trails he is used to, adjusts his goggles and his white silk scarf, brings his right thumb and forefinger together gallantly and steels his nerve. In addition, he steels his arms, his backbone, legs and feet, and clenches his jaw. Thus, he is totally rigid as he launches on the great circle. The reason is panic, for his instincts and training tell him that snow is a solid. This solid now entangles his feet and skis (he believes with fear and trembling) and will catch his edges

and cause him to capsize over his ski tips, ripping out all the tendons in both legs. The only turn that can be made in deep snow in a condition of total rigidity is the stem. Given the steepness of the slope, the arc of the stem turn made by the desperate beginner is fantastically large. It is, in fact, the dreaded great circle. The physics of a large arc on a steep slope mean that the beginner is moving at a sickening rate by the time he starts to pull out of the downhill phase of his dive.

At this point, the most insensitive onlooker turns away. Any variation in slope, snow texture, light, or wattage of terror will cause the beginner to lose the balance he is fighting to keep and he will, as pilots used to say in World War II, auger in. A high-speed fall in powder is not always disastrous, since the stuff is soft, but it is always messy and always tiring. It is incredibly hard, on a steep slope at 9,000 or 10,000 feet, to find and dig out skis and poles, clean and reset bindings, scrape snow off boot bottoms, clamp the bindings and take a swipe at smeared sunglasses with the thumb of a wet ski glove. It is even hard to stand up before starting this salvage operation, because the powder offers no floor to push against. The capsized beginner rages. If his control is steady, he rages silently, and if not, he shrieks ragged curses. He apologizes when he reaches his friends, who are waiting in disgust on the flat below, but what is in his heart is murder.

As it happens, I am past all this, although one or two sufferers in our group are not. I no longer perform my celebrated interpretation of the great circle, because I have realized, after augering in more times than now seem necessary, that powder snow is not a solid but a fluid. I respond to it with whatever fluidity I can squeeze from a gristly, awkward body, and make uncalamitous turns. My skiing is workmanlike.

Workmanlike is not good enough, however. Look here: Sepp Renner, a big, laughing kid from Andermatt, one of the Swiss guides, is going down a *Steilhang.* He carries the usual guide's rucksack, packed with a tent, stretcher, food, stove, and jointed probe to use when someone is caught in an avalanche. I have skied with a rucksack enough to know that it limits what you can do, no matter how strong you are.

But watch Sepp. He could ski like a stone, schuss the hang at flat-out speed, and in complete control, but that is not what is on his mind. What he does is to swash from side to side down the fall line, so slowly that it does not seem possible for a motion to be arrested to that degree. It is a dance. He has filmed himself in slow motion.

The rest of us follow. Those who imitate well throw themselves down the hang without thought. The rest, and I am one of these, try to explicate the poetry with close textual analysis. Observe: this exceptionally strong man uses no strength at all, and no quickness, only balance and serenity. Watch now: he rises, falls . . . I build serenity from these Tinkertoys of technique.

Beer in the sauna. An inordinate dinner. Chess. I have cased the talent, know I can win and do win—my kind of gamble. I ascend to my upper bunk at 10:01 and am asleep by 10:02.

Hans Gmoser has appeared. He has been skiing to the north, in the Cariboo Mountains, where he runs a second helicopter operation. He is thin, fairly tall; a tough, loose, acute man whose manner is quiet. He has a quality I have seen before in one or two other Austrian mountaineers I know, several race-car drivers and not many others. It is hard to say what this quality is. Perhaps it is that he and his conception of himself are more nearly congruent than is true of most men.

Gmoser (pronounced Gmoser; there is a run here called Gmadness) runs a climbing school in the summer here in the Bugaboos. He has never done any Himalayan climbing, but he did put a new route up Mount McKinley a few years ago. He tells a long, amusing, self-deprecating story about bivouacking on McKinley in an igloo whose tunnel entrance eventually stretched to several yards, because snow fell without letup for four days. Several of us are sitting after supper in the dining room of the Bugaboo lodge. It is warm and cheerful and someone has ordered more wine. It is very funny to think of Gmoser and his partner crawling farther and farther each day to get outside, and of the snow whistling past their bare bottoms at 100 miles an hour as they squat to relieve themselves. (The humor of mountain stories is a matter of viewpoint. Once some friends and I spent one night, not four days, in an emergency igloo that we had built to keep ourselves from freezing to death on a glacier in Switzerland. Not one of us thought that it was funny at the time.)

Heading out to the helicopter at 7:15 A.M., I stop, unzip my kidney pack and look inside. The Skadi is there. I take it out and hold it to my ear. It is beeping, as it should be. I knew it was in the kidney pack, beeping correctly, because I had checked both things ten minutes before. But the Skadi is comforting. It is the single most effective piece of survival gear ever developed for skiing or climbing in avalanche country.

The next-best safety measure, after a Skadi, is the forlorn system generally used in the Alps and in the rest of North America: you tie a long red string around your waist, let it trail behind you and hope that part of it shows after the avalanche has buried you. The Skadi is a little radio sender-receiver. If you are carrying one and are buried, your friends switch their Skadis to receive and track you down. The method is fast and accurate to about 6 inches. We proved this one morning by exhuming Sepp, whom the other guides had buried with snow shovels while we ate breakfast. Afterward Sepp mentioned, laughing and yelling insults in Schweizerdeutsch at his friends, that this was the second time he had been dug up by a party using Skadis. "Yes?" *"Ja,"* said Sepp; the other time was last year. He was buried not by snow shovels then but by an avalanche, here in the Bugaboos.

I think I have it. We are at the bottom of an amiable escarpment named Ego by someone who turned around, looked at his tracks and found them good. Hot damn, I think, finding my track good, it looks just like the ski magazines!

It even feels that way: straight down the face, a kind of dancing fall, astonishingly slow, with never a surface to touch. I have heard the beat of great wings.

For the rest of the run it works, and for a few pitches here and there throughout the morning. Flight is not in my nature, nor physical grace, but for a short time I am an aerial being.

The gods smile. As a reward for skiing good snow more or less correctly, they send me a mountainside crusted with mean, ridged, rackety bad snow. I am an eastern skier and this is the sort of briar patch I know and love. A few boulders and some frozen mud would make me feel even more at home, but the deep white-pine forest through which we are running is a good substitute. I run the big pine trunks as if they were slalom poles, then hare off on a wild series of jumps. One of the women skiers, a pretty westerner with wind crinkles at the corners of her eyes, has fallen on the evil crust and is sliding down the hillside on her slick nylon parka and wind pants. She is helpless; her speed is not increasing, but it is not diminishing, either. Will she slide on until she is arrested by the Bugaboo lodge 1,500 feet below? Will she miss the lodge and slide to the town of Spillimacheen, worn to a few nylon threads and a couple of eye crinkles? Not at all; the Green Hornet is at hand. He pulls jauntily out of a jump and stops her with his sinewy body, unhurt but angry and swearing like hell. There is no end to my splendor.

Ed, the pilot, is a mild, square-shaped man in his forties. When he is not flying skiers in the Bugaboos, he flies oil geologists and drilling crews in the Arctic. The drillers, he says, are a hairy-eared bunch, big-*macho* types, and some of them, on their first tours in the Arctic, tend to think that safety rules are a bit candy-assed. "I had told this new guy," says Ed, "that you don't throw things near a helicopter. But he was a type who hadn't listened to anyone yet in his life and he wasn't going to start with me. What he threw, when we were unloading a drilling rig, was a five-pound package of dynamite. The package hit the rotor and detonated. The blast knocked a big piece of rotor off and the machine just about vibrated itself to pieces before I could get it shut off."

Ed does no downhill skiing, but he handles the helicopter the way a downhill racer would. Control is better at speed, he says. "I like to brake to a landing with a flare, because it uses less power. It looks flashy, but there's a reason. At sea level the Bell has 1,100 horsepower, but

at 12,000 feet it only turns about 800, and if you try to lower it straight down on nothing but the engine, you don't have much left to handle a wind gust."

It is Friday evening. Tomorrow is getaway day. The group is drawing apart and, by way of apology, its members are exchanging addresses. We have flown five and a half days out of a possible six, which is unusually good, and at least three of these days have been spectacular, unimprovable-on. Gmoser's reckoning is that I have skied 116,000 vertical feet, which is about average for the group.

It has been a good week, but the New England conscience—yes, thanks, another Scotch, and some more of those hummingbirds' tongues—worries about the huge cost of helicopter skiing. Is the Bugaboo circus merely a particularly excessive instance of the suburbanization of skiing? A sport that once was clean and hard and fairly simple is cheapened—thanks, just a touch more, and some ice—by glitter and glut. There are too many credit-card machines in ski country, and the rule holds: anything you can buy with plastic is plastic. Is it organic to pay $825 for a week of helicoptering?

It's not an easy question and I am inclined to leave it open. Gmoser, who is a tasteful man, has taken the curse off conspicuous consumption by avoiding any egregious luxury in the lodge. His food is imaginative and good, but it is eaten on simple plank tables. The beds are comfortable, but they are bunks. You shave in a communal bathroom.

Gmoser, who grew up in thin times in Austria to a job as an electrician's apprentice, feels that the costs are out of proportion. He would like to run his operation without the helicopter, he says, but U.S. and Canadian skiers just won't walk up mountains with skis and skins in any great numbers. And, as I know well enough from ski-mountaineering in the Alps, if you climb 7,000 feet in four active hours, you have very little energy left to spend on improving your deep-snow technique. If it is bad, it stays that way. The helicopter skier can ski like a Holstein for two runs and still have energy left to analyze his mistakes and ski like a Thomson's gazelle on the third.

I assuage the New England conscience—rare, please, and some of the Bordeaux—by meditating in this swampy fashion for fifteen minutes and by going off in the morning with Gmoser on one of the ski-and-skin tours he runs each year, mostly to keep himself honest.

We start from Banff, where Gmoser's firm. Canadian Mountain Holidays, has its office, and ride a bus to Sunshine, a ski area nearby. It is tremendously satisfying to be climbing on skis again and to leave the prepared, mashed-down slopes of Sunshine in the direction of Mount Assiniboine, 20 miles away over a couple of passes. The day skiers watch us leave in horror.

We are a very mixed group of fourteen climbers and among us is a beginner who has gone trustfully to the camping store. In mild weather, he wears a down-stuffed vest, down parka and down wind pants. He carries a large variety of splendid gear, including a big still camera, a big movie camera and a bottle of whiskey. Within 250 yards of easy upward plodding, he is soaked with sweat and has turned dangerously red. We do what we can. We peel off his feathers and that night we lighten his pack by drinking his whiskey.

The journey to Assiniboine takes two days at our easy pace. Halfway there, we stop at a trapper's cabin. It is crowded and I decide to sleep in the snow. Since I have a bivouac sack with me—a large plastic bag, waterproof and windproof—the decision involves no risk, and no more discomfort than sleeping on the cabin floor and having my colleagues step on my face. But the beginner is much impressed. In the morning, he puffs out of the cabin, banging his hands together to keep from freezing, to view my frozen corpse.

Gmoser, it develops, admires Scandinavian cross-country wax. For an Austrian, this is heresy, but he is encouraged by a couple of old Norwegian Resistance fighters, now Canadian businessmen, who are making the trip on narrow cross-country skis. (The rest of us, of course, are using normal ski-mountaineering equipment—downhill skis, with bindings that let the heel rise when we walk.) The wax functions magically for Gmoser and the Norwegians but not for me. I do not believe, and to walk uphill with wax, you must be a true believer. I am used to skins—fibrous nylon pads that allow even skeptics to climb with ease. I slip back 2 feet for every 3 I ascend, like the frog in the riddle.

A warm log lodge, a frozen lake, a big, sharp-spired mountain. Assiniboine, rising on the opposite shore. We spend three days there, climbing for a couple of hours in the morning and a couple in the afternoon, and skiing what we climb. It is just strenuous enough to justify a lot of pleasant laziness.

On the walk out, at 8,000 feet in Allenby Pass, I hear a wild humming that puzzles me. After a time, I understand. The wind has set the magnesium struts of my pack frame to vibrating.

For almost an hour one morning, we follow the fresh tracks of a running cougar and a rabbit. Then the tracks veer off. We never learn who won the race. A mile or so farther, crashed in Brewster Creek and weathered to scraps, is the carcass of an elk that did not survive the winter.

On our last night, a tough, elderly chemist who has made the trip produces a bottle of overproof Canadian rum. He is a hero; he has packed it all the way to Assiniboine and halfway back. He mixes it with lemon juice and magic herbs. We call the resulting potion the Allenby Pass, in honor of our stiff thighs, and we celebrate, of course, the Allenby Passover.

PART V

BREAKTHROUGHS

"... Always it takes time. A winter out of your life. A time without money, or a lover; even the wine and song must be subdued. ... It's a martial art, you know, an esoteric science for fools, played out on the fluted ridges ... a gentle karate of the ridges, a flashing of blades in soft snow. Not the death snap of combat karate, but the gentle pull and soft release of the Samurai archer; a warm, loving oscillation of life, like the afterburn of sex in a hot, Moroccan afternoon; a rowing through long waves, the playing of an old and mellow violin."

—Bob Jamieson, *Number "10" Powder*

The Norse Started It All

by JAKOB VAAGE

Norway's Jakob Vaage, the world's preëminent ski historian, has traced back to Norway, without notable exception, the first instances of sport skiing in the Alpine countries of Europe and as well in the United States. Here he sketches in broad strokes the first hundred years of skiing, distinct from its prehistoric use in transport and hunting: the breakthrough of skiing into the realm of sport.

THE ski, as a utilitarian tool, is very old. As old as the Pharoahs, in fact. Among the mute relics of precivilized northern Europe is a series of partially preserved pieces of wood from Finland, Russia, Sweden, and Norway. They are unmistakably skis. The oldest are more than forty-five hundred years old. Supporting the dates of such finds was the discovery of a typical Stone Age cave drawing at Rodøy near the Arctic circle in Norway. It shows an easy rider on what appears to be a pair of 12-foot skis headed downhill, schussing neatly with the help of a balance pole, knees slightly bent: date 2000 B.C.

Such a proto-Norwegian may have used skis for pleasure—but he built them out of necessity. It is likely a human would have had an impossible time negotiating life in the Arctic without over-the-snow transport of some sort. The American Indian had his snowshoes, the Eskimo his sled, the Norseman his skis.

The first references to skis in writing were in the Norse sagas that came out of the mists of history along with the Upanishads and the Old Testament. The Norse tradition gave us Ull, god of the hunt and of skiing, activities which were very likely synonymous in winter.

Egil Skallagrimsson's saga in A.D. 950 tells how King Haakon the Good sent his tax collectors out to his fiefdoms on skis. A couple of centuries later there were regulation bow-and-arrow ski troops: King Sverre sent out his ski troops under Päl Belte as scouts before the feudal battles that took place in A.D. 1200 near what is now Oslo. From then on, for the next five hundred years, frequent allusions to ski troops in military maneuvers emanate from Norway.

Just about the time George Washington and his men were being plagued by snow at Valley Forge, the Norwegians (under their Danish king) were thanking Ull for the snow that enabled them to better defend their country against the Swedes. By 1776, the Norwegians already had fifteen hundred ski troops under arms and had written the world's first ski book, a nice little handwritten job put out in 1733 by a Norwegian ski troop commander, Captain Jens Emahusen. It was written in German (the military language) and it not only designated the length of skis—270 centimeters for the left foot and 210 centimeters for the right—but also outlined a complete seventy-two-step military rifle drill on skis. A copy of the book, *Skiloperegglement,* is extant in the Holmenkollen Ski Museum in Oslo.

The *Skiloperegglement* went through two handwritten revisions before a printed and illustrated rival came out. In 1765, *Geteichnete Figuren* was run off the newfangled printing press, with hand-colored illustrations of red-coated ski troops performing a series of drills—including the first illustration of the kick-turn. Two years later, in 1767, an early drawing from life of civilian skiing appeared when Father Knud Leem's observations and sketches on the Lapps in Norway were published. One of his drawings shows two Lapp skiers with clubs. One is going downhill, in much the same posture as the Rodøy man. The other Lapp, however, seems to be making a crude Telemark.

But sport means fun. There wasn't much of that in trekking after reindeer in Lapland or being shot at while on skis. However, in 1779, as the Revolution was having its ups and downs in the United States, Father Nicolay Jonge's *Geographie* (World Description) was published in Denmark, a sort of Baedekker of its time. It notes that "In Norway, it is common for kids to practice skiing so extensively that even along the coast of Norway, where there is no practical need for them, skis are used for fun."

Thus, we can pinpoint the decade when the sport was born—the same decade in which the United States saw light of day.

Obviously grown-ups, too, got interested in the fun of it all. In 1787, a chaplain, Jens Lassen, noted piously in his diary that he skied cross-country to four churches in the Sogn district to save money he would have had to spend hiring horses for the circuit.

An early mention of ski jumping as such came in a military memoir written in 1808, the diary of Major Jens Hjorth which recalled how General Olav Rye made a jump of 15 *alen,* about 30 feet (not bad), from an improvised snow jump, much like the ones used in freestyle aerial contests today. Rye was from Telemark. (Evi-

dently a peasant farmer population of strong skiers was in the making in Telemark.)

By 1800, the two main forms of the Nordic sport had thus been established: jumping and cross-country.

Now for a slight detour to set the perspective for the spread of the sport. The early 1800s embraced the War of 1812, in which the Americans brought the British fleet to its knees in the Atlantic, and the era in which the British fleet helped bring Napoleon to his knees by blockading the entire coast of Europe from Norway to the boot of Italy.

Norway, in consequence, was reduced to a state of starvation. Norwegian blockade runners, when caught, were thrown into English dungeons for the duration. The only people who treated such prisoners humanely were the English Quakers. By the time the Norwegian prisoners had been repatriated in 1814, a number of them had converted.

A boatload of disaffected Norwegian Quakers set off on July 4, 1825, in the good ship *Restauration,* for New York—forty-nine years to the day after the Declaration of Independence. The ship was a 54-footer and carried fifty-three people to New York. The emigrants went up the Hudson and the Erie Canal to the forestland of Ontario. This land proved, in the long run, too hard to work and so they marched off to Illinois in 1835. Here they founded Fox River, the first all-Norwegian settlement in U.S. territory, harbinger of eight hundred thousand Norwegians to come.

Back in Norway, two years after Fox River was settled, a couple of Norwegians from Numedal traversed the Telemark region—headed for Fox River. The brothers Ole and Knut Nattestad were embarking at Bergen. They overnighted along the way in the small Rue farmhouse in Tinn. Here they held spellbound a ten-year-old named Jon Tostensen with tales of the new country. The Nattestads, on reaching Fox River, wrote glowing accounts back to the Tostensens who then and there decided to make the move. Jon was then only eleven, but of course he was already an accomplished skier, as befitted a proper Telemark male at that age. The Tosten-

A mid-1800s ski meet in Norway with skiers using a long balance pole

the slow modes of communication in those times.

In 1853, the first Norwegian, H. Müller, recorded as having skied in Europe, toured across the snows of northern Germany. As the century wore on, more and more Norwegians and later the Germans, Swiss and British, copying the Norwegians, began to use the Alps as ski terrain.

Back in Norway, the sport was becoming demilitarized. In 1843, the first big meet *without* military events was held, a simple thirty-minute cross-country event in Tromsø. In 1820 the first advertisements for skis appeared in newspapers in Oslo (then Christiania)—so the world's first ski dealers were on the scene. In 1849, the first commercial ski tour was advertised in the Trondheim papers. Although skiing had spread, it was a national sport only in Norway.

The forms of competition were often invented on the spot. A challenge would be issued and accepted. It might be to take off one's vest between the top and the bottom of a given hill, or carry a full mug of beer to the bottom without spilling a drop.

Racing in the 1840s resembled a freestyle contest of today. The premium was on inventiveness, skill and finesse, strength and controlled turns, cutting fine figures. A standard figure was the full 360-degree turn at the end of the course. It was wild, it was fun—qualities lost in modern competition until American freestyle skiers reinvented it.

Almost, or perhaps even more, remarkable than the rapidly rising popular interest in skiing as a national sport was the contribution to the sport made in the 1840s by a single Norwegian, Sondre Norheim of Morgedal, the best skier in Telemark. Norheim not only invented the first modern binding, and the first modern ski, but the first two recognizably repeatable controlled ski turns. Truly, Norheim fathered the sport of skiing.

Norheim in his twenties not only outskied his accomplished fellow Telemarkers but came upon the idea of a much-improved binding to replace the traditional toe-and-underfoot strap configuration. Norheim's was a combination of toe and stiff heel straps, the latter made out of

sens made it to Fox River and took up farming again, not knowing that in a few years they would be headed west where Jon would take a new name—and with that name become the most famous skier in American history: Snowshoe Thompson.

Norwegian skis, of course, were already being used in the midwestern United States fairly regularly. But it wasn't until 1841 that the first ski trip in America was actually recorded. It took place near Beloit, Wisconsin, northwest of Chicago. Then came a memorable growth period. Within a generation, the use of skis for sport had spread in the United States, carried by Norwegians from coast to coast, to New Hampshire and to the Rockies as well as to the better-known mining town racing hills of the Sierra. It was remarkable mobility for a new sport, considering

Ski jumping at Huseby in late 1800s preceded Holmenkollen jump meets

birch-root shoots, two shoots spiraling about each other, going around the heel and fastened to the ski at each end. This binding was supple in the forward direction so you could tour with it, but had enough lateral rigidity for downhill skiing to transmit the motions of the skier's feet to the skis without a lot of slack and wobble. As a result of his bindings, Norheim was able, in the 1840s, to standardize his hitherto crude turns and make them maneuvers of precision and beauty.

Morgedal became, with Norheim's fame and leadership, a hotbed of skiing, but skiing was gaining all over in Norway. The Christiania papers were full of ads for "Land skis," skis made in the district of Land. Evidently they were the Head skis of their day. (Within a generation, close copies of the Land would be used in the first recorded race in Colorado.) In 1861, the first ski club in the world was formed in Norway.

Telemark held the first big invitational jump in 1866 and Norheim won. In 1867, the first invitational national Nordic-downhill meet was held in Christiania.

A year later, in 1868, Norheim came to the annual Christiania touring-jumping meet (points were scored for style then) and swept the field. He was forty-two, but he outskied the field, which averaged twenty years his junior. Contestants had never even seen a controlled turn. A Christiania newspaper said: "Sondre Norheim could come down like lightning and suddenly stop in a second . . . A new era has risen in skiing."

Norheim developed two turns which were given a name later. The first was called "Telemark" in honor of the inventor's home district. The second was called "Christiania" in honor of the capital of the inventor's country.

The Telemark was a long sweeping turn in

which Norheim went into a one-foot lunge, stuck one ski out ahead of the other, and edged it until it started to carve around the turn. This split the tails apart, so they pointed away from each other and the tips toward each other. The Telemark was really the forerunner of the varied stem turns of the classic Austrian school.

The Norwegian Christiania was a move we would today call "a scissors christie" or "racing step turn." Norheim split the inside ski away, angled it in the direction of the turn to come, and leaned on it. When this ski started to pull into the turn, Norheim brought the other ski around parallel during the slide. It was the first skidded turn. And it was a true "christy" turn in that the skis were swung in the same direction throughout the turn. This, after its migration to Europe, became the famous christie of Hannes Schneider's Arlberg school.

There remained only one element to complete the essentials of modern skiing, and that was a modern ski with "sidecut"—that is, a ski narrow in the middle underfoot and wider at the ends. Refining an older Telemark pattern, Norheim created the first modern sidecut in a pair of skis he made in 1870. The ski was light enough to be flexed by the force of the turn; the sidecut facilitated the carving action of the ski. With this, the career and accomplishments of Norheim had capped the first one hundred years of skiing as sport.

What has come in the second one hundred years of skiing has, in a sense, been an extension of the first one hundred years.

The later bindings of Schou, Hagen, and Huitfeldt—not to mention Look, Marker, and Salomon—are extensions of the Norheim principle of a rigid binding connection. You can call a carved racing turn an extension of the Telemark. The modern ski has a sidecut very close to Norheim's 1870 ski. The wedeln is an extension of the scissors christie. Even freestyle was previewed a century ago by Telemarkers who flew off "kickers" with abandon.

There were still great developments to come. Nordic skiing and downhill, still intermingled in competitive runs, would go their own way, and ski competition would become international. Still, it was an interesting first one hundred years.

A Way of Life

by C. LESTER WALKER

The first modern ski technique, the direct ancestor of today's technical teaching, was invented by an Austrian, Hannes Schneider, of St. Anton. His technique began in an imitation of Norwegians and then was powerfully shaped by his own passionate character and love of teaching and mountains. His breakthrough was teaching a series of steps that brought the skier from a slow and safe "snowplow" through the faster stem and christie forms, a progression encouraged by a class rather than a "guide" atmosphere. Walker interviewed Schneider in 1946.

IT was a Dartmouth ski instructor who coined the feverish aphorism "Skiing is a way of life." Undoubtedly this is a little too sweeping, though in justice it must be admitted that for a *Skimeister* talking about skiing, he was not being unusually high-flown. Hannes Schneider, however, is one man to whom these words are literally applicable; skiing *is* the way of his life, no question about it. Schneider is the originator of skiing as this generation knows it. Before the popularization of the Arlberg Technique (named after the Tyrolean hamlet of St. Anton am Arlberg, where from 1919 until the *Anschluss* Schneider maintained his famous school) there were, to be sure, people who used skis, but they found it as perilous and uninviting a sport as bicycling cross-country without a coaster brake. The deep crouch characteristic of modern skiing is Schneider's invention; before that skiers slid downhill grandly erect, hoping they wouldn't fall. Schneider was also the first man to perfect a turn which was equally revolutionary, the stem-Christiania,* to supersede the old-fashioned turn called the Telemark, in which hardy athletes took corners on too steep slopes in a flurry of churned-up snow and snapping anklebones.

However, there would today be no ski equipment department at Abercrombie & Fitch or Saks, no weekend snow planes out of La-Guardia Field, if Schneider had merely discovered a way of negotiating the headlong slopes of the Tyrolean Alps at no great personal risk. The important thing is that he learned how to teach it, painlessly and with a high degree of efficiency. When he started out as a teacher in the Austrian Tyrol, there was only a handful of ski instructors, and they had no particular method. *"So macht man es"* ("That's the way you do it"), they would say to their pupils, performing a turn. Single-handed, Schneider raised ski instruction to a point where it was feasible for the Austrian government to give written examinations in the sub-

*The modern term is stem-christy.

199

Hannes Schneider fathered modern ski techniques and teaching

ject. He developed exercises for beginners based on the "snowplow" and the "snowplow turn," in which the skis are toed in to form a V. The current furor among skiers over the teaching method of Ernest Loosli, of the Château Frontenac, in which the snowplow turn and the snowplow are dispensed with, is a left-handed tribute to Schneider. Schneider's method is so firmly established that it is possible to make a career of defying it.

Schneider is now *Skimeister* at the Eastern Slope Ski School, at North Conway, New Hampshire. A refugee, he has fared better than many of his countrymen. The school is owned, and run as a kind of hobby, by Harvey Gibson, president of the Manufacturers Trust Company, who helped Schneider get out of Austria before the war started. Schneider draws a modest salary and is able to show his sponsor a satisfactory return.

Schneider, whose wife died a year ago, lives with his son, Herbert, and his daughter, Herta, in a frame house on Grove Street, North Conway, next door to Father Belford, the parish priest. Father Belford has adopted the Tyrolean custom of blessing his flock's skis once every year, and Schneider has relaxed his old-country principles to the extent of giving ski instructions on Sunday. He never did this in the Arlberg.

On the ski slopes, Schneider is now assisted by his son, half a dozen instructors whom he trained in the Tyrol, and some promising North Conway boys, mostly under draft age. He has got over being appalled at the American notion that the whole trick of skiing can be mastered in one weekend, but he still maintains the iron discipline that characterized the Arlberg school. A pupil who shows up late for a morning session is told, with severe politeness, "I think better you come again this afternoon. No?" He rarely speaks to pupils while they are on the skiing slopes, confining his activities to supervising the instructors, but occasionally, in the lobby of the Eastern Slope Inn, he will single out some novice for a friendly word. "You see, it is better the knees to bend. No?" The pupils, born and bred in the national tradition of inferiority to athletic coaches, love it.

Schneider tactfully conducts his social life with the fact in mind that in North Conway he is still somewhat a "foreigner." But with his tall, slightly stooped figure, his sun-browned, aquiline face, and his grizzled hair, he fits well into the New Hampshire scene. He has learned to play golf, he drives a Dodge, and he drinks quantities of canned fruit juices. Although the government has ruled that Austrians are not enemy aliens, his naturalization was interrupted by our entrance into the war, on the technical ground that he came into the country on a post-*Anschluss* German passport. For the moment, at least, even when he or one of his foreign-born instructors merely wants to make a lengthy ski run which takes them out of the township, they have to notify the authorities. The main reason Schneider regrets his ambiguous status is that he would like to volunteer as an instructor of ski troops.

Schneider was born fifty-one years ago in Stuben am Arlberg, a village of fifty-six inhabitants. His father owned a dozen or so head of cattle and grew potatoes. "Even now I can eat potatoes three meals a day," Schneider says. His parents planned to apprentice him to a cheesemaker. All that was changed by the fact that he saw a pair of skis just about as early as he saw the inside of a dairy. Next door to the Schneider home was an inn which took in city people who from time to time came up to try skiing in the mountains. The villagers thought they were touched in the head. For sport, the natives hunted chamois, and they considered skis, which had been introduced in the Alps by visiting Norwegians only a few years before, manifestly unsafe. Little Hannes got a bad case of hero worship, however, and hung around the visitors. "From Vienna, from Salzburg they come," he recalls. "Students, professors, army officers from the great world outside, and to me they are like gods. Sometimes I stop outside the inn and just reverently touch the skis. Other times I listen while they talk around the big tile stove indoors. Always the skiers they argue. I am aware there is some kind of a fight going on."

Hannes soon understood that most of the arguments were about whether skiing, a sport that is believed to have originated on the comparatively gentle hills of Norway, could ever be adapted to the choppy, precipitous Alpine country. An Austrian army officer named Mathias Zdarsky had written a highly theoretical book to prove that it could, and the city people were sustaining all sorts of contusions in the course of testing his theories. Hannes fashioned himself a pair of skis out of wood begged from the local sledmaker, made toe irons out of an old sieve, and practiced in the moonlight by himself until he was a pretty fair skier. By the time he was twelve, he was the best in his village, and the people who came up from the cities to ski took an interest in him. One of them, a serious skier named Victor Sohm, taught him the Norwegian technique, and he won every formal competition he entered.

A race he won at the nearby village of Bödele bei Dornbirn decided his future when he was only seventeen. A group of enthusiasts from Les Avants, in Switzerland, offered him three francs a day to go there as instructor, and a somewhat similar offer was made by the Hotel Post in St. Anton am Arlberg. Schneider, after dutifully consulting his parents, decided to go to St. Anton, because it was just over the pass from his native village and because the Austrian pay was a bit higher. In December, 1907, he crossed the mountains to St. Anton, a place he was to make famous all over the world.

At first, Schneider hardly earned his small salary. Winter visitors were few, pupils fewer, and as a result he spent a good deal of time skiing by himself. One day, after taking a couple of particularly nasty falls, Schneider, without thinking much about it, finished the rest of his run in a deep crouch. This, of course, had the effect of lowering his center of gravity, and no more falls resulted. He tried the crouch again the next day, and this time discovered what was apparently a new way to turn. This turn, refined, is today's stem-Christiania, one of the distinguishing features of the Schneider technique.

For over a year Schneider practiced his new technique under all possible conditions. In the *Bierstube* of the Hotel Post, he analyzed it with his mentor, Victor Sohm. Finally, in the winter of 1910, he came out into the open with it, entering several of the big slalom competitions. (Slaloms are what you see in newsreels—racing against time on downhill courses staked out so that the skiers are compelled to make a series of sharp turns.) His rivals, who had laughed when Schneider sat down, or nearly sat down, on his skis, were mortified and amazed when he carried off first place in every slalom.

After this, Schneider's way was clear. More and more pupils came to St. Anton am Arlberg to learn the sensational new technique. Schneider now had the problem of learning how to teach them. The *"So macht man es"* system was repugnant to his orderly mind, and he gradually developed his own method. "I told myself," he says, "that I would make each pupil learn the fundamentals properly. Then he would by himself become a good skier. First we make control,

Schneider retained his superb skiing ability to the end of his life

then style. Then speed will come by itself." The acid test of this theory came during the First World War. Hannes, who was serving with the Austrian army on the Russian front, was transferred to a plateau 2½ miles up among the glaciers on the Italian frontier. He and one assistant were put in charge of a hundred and twenty artillerymen, with instructions to make skiers of them. Each took sixty men and applied the St. Anton system. From the point of view of a *Skimeister,* this pupil-teacher relation was ideal, since the pupils were under military discipline. "In private courses the wishes of the pupil must be considered somewhat," Schneider points out in recalling this golden moment. At any rate, after three weeks of instruction, the artillerymen were all doing stem-christies on a 28-degree slope while carrying full packs. Schneider had a bad moment when several staff officers descended upon him, having heard that he was

disregarding the army instruction code for teaching skiing; the results, however, were so plainly satisfactory that he was let off without a court-martial.

After the war the great European ski vogue began with the rush of an Alpine snowslide. Schneider returned to St. Anton, married his childhood sweetheart, the daughter of the town roadmaster, borrowed $400, built himself a house, and started his own ski school. Seven years later he had twenty-four assistant instructors, all of them village boys, and with them was giving four hundred lessons a day. St. Anton, with its enormous transient population of skiers, was like an E. Phillips Oppenheim dream. Kings, maharajas, princes, and American millionaires and their womenfolk, gorgeously dressed for their adventure with the great outdoors, lined up every day for their beginners' lessons. One of Schneider's present instructors remembers hearing him mutter, as he surveyed a new class, *"Guten Morgen,* Chanel, Patou, Houbigant, Caron . . .''

Classes began at ten in the morning, on the dot. If a pupil was late, he lost his lesson; if an instructor was late, he lost his day's pay. If a duke skied before his turn, his peasant instructor dressed him down sharply. New pupils were judged on ability and assigned to classes by Schneider, who permitted no quarrelling with his decisions. "I can tell by the way they walk toward me carrying their skis," he used to say. One rainy morning, when Schneider went outdoors to meet his classes, he found several pupils holding umbrellas; without a word he seized the umbrellas and beat them into wreckage with a ski pole. Another morning, when the rain was really too heavy for skiing, Schneider found one single, sodden pupil waiting for him on the slope. It was Albert, king of the Belgians.

The discipline was like a breath of clean, cold air in the lungs of Schneider's wealthy clientele. The sterner he was, the more they liked it. The authority he delegated to his assistant instructors was as absolute as his own. During one especially crowded season he took a green lad employed part time at a local butcher shop and put him in charge of a beginners' class that included, in addition to some minor European nobility, a couple of American Stotesburys. The young instructor showed up one fine morning with some unfinished business—several packages of chops and *Schnitzel* that had to be delivered. He told his class that if they would wait until he had made his deliveries, the instruction would begin. Then, waving *auf Wiedersehen,* he started off. The class swung into line and started off after him, because nobody had understood a word of what he had said. The blue-blooded little procession made its way down the hills and through the back yards of St. Anton, dodging happily under the clotheslines, "My dear," one of the ladies said afterward, "it was wonderful. We skied *right* through a pigpen."

One maharaja, when he came to St. Anton, insisted on a private tutor. Schneider, who had already pretty thoroughly absorbed the manpower of the village, finally got him an instructor fully equipped to teach him the fundamentals, a youngster who had just turned thirteen. The maharaja was delighted with his lessons and when he left St. Anton he gave the lad a tip of $2,000 and a motorcycle.

Schneider had a dreamlike interlude in Japan, significant, perhaps, in the light of later events. In 1930, the Japanese government telegraphed him an offer of $10,000 for four weeks of his services. Placing his St. Anton school in charge of his assistants, Schneider packed up and left for the Orient. He found that the Japs had planned to get their money's worth in ski instruction; every moment of his four weeks in their country was scheduled, even his hours of sleep. His first assignment was to lecture to thirty-five hundred students, with the aid of an interpreter. "I—in my tuxedo—to talk of ski!" Schneider says, still horrified.

The Japanese, Schneider soon learned, had implicit faith in the power of indoctrination. Many ski students had memorized, word for word, a book he had written, *Wunder des Schneeschuhs.* Moving pictures and still photographs were made of Schneider in every position. Arriving at a mountain near the town of Takata, he found five hundred eager pupils waiting for the single lesson they happily assumed would make skiers of them. Schneider had to fall back on *"So macht man es."* He crouched, slid, and turned for their benefit, and they crouched, slid, and turned in obedient and quite successful imitation. "Like on a string, all together," he recalls. "It is comic." His visit—and probably his entire career as *Skimeister*—reached a climax the day he found himself perched far up on Fujiyama, the slopes below crawling with thousands of enthusiastic novices. He gave his instructions through a megaphone. Below him, interpreters with megaphones passed the word on. Below them, the pupils skied.

Leading a party of several hundred relatively advanced Japanese students over the snows of a mountain named Neko Tokky, Schneider had his first encounter with Japanese "face." A fog set in, and Schneider advised seeking shelter for the night. Very well, the Japanese told him, they would find Neko Tokky's ski shelter. It seemed to Schneider, who had noticed the shelter on the way up, that they were heading in the wrong direction, and he was bold enough to say so. His pupils assured him, with many a hiss and grin, that their way was the right way. Schneider, who has a solid confidence in his own judgment, insisted on leading the party in what his instinct told him was the right direction, and, sure enough, there was the shelter. In a moment the Japs were plunged into gloom; they looked at Schneider and muttered. The interpreter explained, when Schneider finally asked what was wrong, that they had lost face in mistaking their way on their own mountain. "Tell them that I often lose the way in *my* mountains," Schneider said. Everybody cheered up immediately.

Back in St. Anton with the proceeds of his Japanese expedition, Schneider built himself the biggest house in the village, with thirteen rooms and two baths. He became a patron of the town band and other municipal projects. Not only did he have twenty-four full-time assistants but his Arlberg Technique was being taught by disciples all over the world, wherever there were snow and hills. His popularity was fabulous. He was the hero of half the great men of Europe. Meanwhile, in Germany, Hitler was getting his start.

Schneider knew Kurt Schuschnigg, the Austrian chancellor, though he didn't give any thought to politics; he used his acquaintance with the statesman solely in an attempt to get him interested in financing a ski tow at St. Anton. He skied in *The Ski Chase,* a ski film which Leni Riefenstahl, the actress who was or was not Hitler's lady friend, made at St. Anton, but he heartily disliked her, and so did his assistants. The high spot of Fräulein Riefenstahl's sojourn in St. Anton, as far as Schneider and his staff were concerned, came when she was bitten in the seat of her all-white ski suit by Friedl, a St. Bernard belonging to one of Walter Damrosch's daughters. Before long, the *Roter Adler,* a pro-Nazi newspaper in Munich, began attacking Schneider. There are all sorts of stories why, but a man who has relatives still within Hitler's reach can't be questioned too closely on the subject. One story says that he fired an instructor who

was a Nazi. At any rate, his feelings about the Third Reich seem to have been obvious. In March, 1938, a few hours after the Germans entered Austria, Schneider was arrested and taken to jail in another town.

A howl of wrath arose from skiers everywhere. It happened that Europe's biggest ski event, the Arlberg-Kandahar meet, was scheduled for the following week at St. Anton. The race committee solemnly convened there and canceled the meet. "We have no heart in an Arlberg-Kandahar without Hannes," the official announcement said. In New York, Harvey Gibson, who had already imported five or six of Schneider's best young assistants to teach at Eastern Slope, went into action; he assigned a man in the London office of the Manufacturers Trust to the mission of getting Schneider released. Gibson's representative hammered at officials of the Nazi Party for ten months, during which the ski bloc stirred up such an anti-Nazi sentiment in the foreign press that finally Schneider was released and given permission to leave the country, with the understanding that the incident was to be given no undue publicity and the first press releases on the subject were to be dictated by the Nazis. In February, 1939, Schneider and his family sailed for the United States. Seven days later he was in North Conway, walking under an arch of skis made by one hundred and fifty local schoolchildren, while the church bells of the town rang in welcome.

Schneider, in addition to his salary, is provided with his house and living by the school, and he gets the usual fees for permitting the use of his name by manufacturers of skiing equipment. Summers he works as boss of the gang that is gradually enlarging the open slope on Cranmore Mountain. Last fall he took an automobile trip out to the Coast and, like a born American, came back with opinions about everything; he thought California overrated and liked the plains of Nebraska best of all he saw. He was also slightly wonderstruck. His Shell credit card, which enabled him to charge gas and oil in any state, seemed miraculous to him. In Idaho he went hunting and fulfilled a boyhood dream by shooting an elk.

People ask him sometimes if he plans to go back to St. Anton after the war. "Perhaps I go back just to visit," he tells them. "I am a little afraid of the changes that there may be in the place and the people. So, likely for good I settle here." As far as his friends know, he would be perfectly happy at North Conway if only he had a supply of snow equal to that of the Tyrol. "In all the years, only three days there without snow!" he will exclaim, looking indignantly at a bare April slope near North Conway. There is a story about a party given for him at the Harvard Club of Boston when he was here in 1936 on a brief visit. Somebody had brought along photographs of the White Mountain ski country—Mount Cranmore, Mount Washington, the dizzy Headwall of Tuckerman's Ravine. Schneider looked at them politely, then spoke to his interpreter. "He wants to know," the interpreter said, "where the mountains are."

The Arlberg Technique

by HANNES SCHNEIDER

Hannes Schneider is to modern skiing what Einstein was to modern physics. Here, as head of the Arlberg Ski School, Schneider writes about his key discovery, the stem-christy. This was essentially a faster turn than the basic Arlberg stem turn, The skis skid very slowly in the stem turn: in the stem-christy, they skid much faster, resembling the old Norwegian Christiania, or "christy," but more stable and teachable. Schneider found that when he sprang up and forward in the turn and threw his arm and shoulders in the direction of the turn, this novel and fascinating stem-christy took the place. Thus, the stem-christy became the "third rung" of the Arlberg Ski School "ladder," the first two being the stem brake and the stem turn. From the stem-christy later evolved a fourth rung the "tempo christy," or "parallel christy," the first modern parallel ski turn.

ONE morning in December, 1948, I closed the Bildstein springs on my skis and ran from the halfway station on Cranmore Mountain, North Conway, New Hampshire. That run marked the opening of my fiftieth season on skis, fifty years of skiing and teaching in all parts of the world—Austria, Switzerland, Germany, Japan, Canada, France, and the United States. In those fifty years I have witnessed an astonishing change in skiing. From the days when it was hardly more than an indispensable means of transportation, it has developed into a tremendously popular international sport that has brought hundreds of thousands of vacationists and serious skiers to the ski centers of the world. The passage of these exciting years has served to confirm my faith in the Arlberg Technique. Perhaps it would be fitting to tell something of its history and development.

It was on December 7, 1907, that the Hannes Schneider Ski School opened in St. Anton am Arlberg with one instructor—myself. The teaching technique was rather simple, judged in the light of later developments. A great deal of time was spent in practicing the straight schuss, using small hills. This gave the novice a sense of balance and confidence. For control, I taught then, as I do now, the snowplow. Using this means of braking, the novice was able to run down an easy slope in control and stop at any given point. At this stage, it was simple for him to start the snowplow turn. Shifting his weight by swinging shoulders and hips, he was able to negotiate fairly steep slopes in control.

Just as the snowplow turn evolved naturally from the snowplow, so the stem turn developed out of the snowplow turn. It happened in this way. While traversing with the skis together, I stemmed the lower ski and swung into the fall line, turning from the shoulders and hips. The turn was done crisply without waste motion. It had all the satisfying characteristics of a natural evolutionary maneuver. I practiced it assiduously and by the next season I had perfected the stem turn to the point where it could be incorporated into my system of teaching. Members of my advanced classes who used the stem turn showed immediate improvement in their negotiation of difficult slopes. Their control was better than that of skiers using the Telemark, which at that time was the last word in skiing finesse.

By 1909, word-of-mouth recommendation had drawn a large number of skiers to my school, of which I was still the lone instructor. It was during that season that I developed the turn that is now called the stem-christie. Like most inventions, it was born of necessity, in the following way.

While skiing alone on the Galzig in St. Anton, I encountered a dangerous stretch of breakable crust. Traversing in the crouch always associated with the Arlberg Technique, I started the normal stem turn. My skis stuck in the fall line impeding forward progress. To turn the skis back to the traverse, I was forced to pick up both skis and force them around in a jumping turn. On the next corner I repeated the maneuver, and continued the descent of the treacherous terrain in this manner. Next morning, I went out on the practice slope and tried an experiment. Stemming slightly with the downhill ski, I shifted my weight around, using shoulders and hips. The turn was completed smoothly without lifting the skis off the surface of the snow. The faster I went, the less stem, or opening, was needed to make the turn. I returned to the top of the slope and made several linked turns in this manner. I had discovered a natural series of turns, each evolving into a faster one and culminating in the stem-christie. This led eventually to the tempo-christie, now called the parallel turn. I found that I could now travel at higher speeds than racers who used Telemarks.

I hesitated to include the stem-christie in the regular classes that winter despite my belief that it was a part of the technique. Most of the students who watched it were reluctant to try it themselves. Speed was essential in executing this turn and, to the novice, speed was his natural enemy. Very few pupils attempted it on their own. For proper performance of the turn, the skier must swing the body from the shoulders and hips when the skis are in the fall line, coming forward at the same time. In completing it, the skier resumes his crouching position. I had complete faith in the turn, but since it was more or less experimental, I did not want to rush anyone into it.

During the 1910 season I attended the Swiss championships at Grindelwald. This meet consisted of jumping, cross-country, and a form of giant slalom. I had never competed in any downhill or slalom events, but I could not help wondering how my style would stand up against the top-flight racers in the slalom.

I have always believed and still do that on that day at Grindelwald the beginning of the skiing revolution was established on an international scale. Using stem-christies for almost the entire length of the course, I improved on the winners' time by several seconds. Except for the great Swiss champion Ed Capite, the competitors all used Telemarks. My run was witnessed by several hundred people, few of whom had ever seen a racer using this new technique. But although it was announced that my time was the best, I was regarded as some sort of freak or exhibitionist. Many of those who witnessed it, however, were tremendously excited by this new style of skiing.

In the winter of 1911, the championships took place at St. Moritz. Not long after my arrival there, I discovered that my "revolutionary" technique had preceded me. In the slalom, several racers were using the stem-christie, but months of grueling practice had given me confidence and speed. I bettered all times and took first-place honors.

During that week I visited Davos. Ed Capite was there, and we skied together and talked. He too had been experimenting. Except for the stem-christie, our styles were much alike. My turns were faster than his, however, as I skied more in the fall line. One afternoon while out skiing with him, I demonstrated the tempo turn on all types of terrain, and on our last trip down, he followed closely behind me through the woods. Neither of us knew then that we were being watched by Dr. Arnold Fanck, the man who, nine years later, was to be largely instrumental in making the technique internationally famous through his motion picture production *Wunder des Schneeschuhs.*

By the following year, the revolution had slowly begun to gain momentum. There were now three instructors at my school to teach the increasing number of students who wanted to learn what had come to be called the Arlberg Technique. A class was established for teaching the stem-christie. Later, a more advanced class was taught the tempo or parallel turn. There was

Basic Arlberg position was wide-straddling pigeon-toed snowplow

every reason to believe that each season would show an expanding interest in the technique. But in 1914 Austria went to war, and my instructors and I entered the service.

During the war years I was given an opportunity to develop novices into mountain-type skiers. The teaching, of course, was nothing like that of a regular ski school, but I did achieve interesting results with these men. They were in good physical shape and were able to devote seven hours a day to skiing. On this basis, really skillful skiers could be turned out after two weeks of instruction—men who could negotiate steep mountain country while carrying their field equipment. It was a gratifying achievement.

Until 1920, skiing as a sport lay fallow. In that year, however, Dr. Fanck started production on a ski movie in Germany. But the skiers he employed did not satisfy him, and he asked me to join him at Garmisch-Partenkirchen. It was then that I learned that he had witnessed my descent with Ed Capite through the woods at Davos. After watching a few runs in that magnifi-

cent mountain country, he told me that my technique was ideal for his film, and offered me the job. During the next two years we made *Wunder des Schneeschuhs, Fox Hunt in the Engadine,* and *The White Art.*

Although more than a quarter of a century has elapsed since it was made, the first of these films is still considered a perfect example of spectacular skiing and mountaineering. With the worldwide exhibition of these three films, the last of which demonstrated the Arlberg Technique, the skiing revolution became an accomplished fact, and the experts of the various nations were compelled to accept it as such. Austria was first to adopt my teaching pattern. Germany followed. German experts came to St. Anton to study at my school and took what they had learned back to their own country. Shortly afterwards, the Swiss Ski School was formed and patterned itself on my technique with a few minor variations. Next came France, which invited me to go to Chamonix and supervise the first Ski Instructors' Examination to be held there. Japan followed with an invitation to teach my technique to skiers in the Japanese Alps. While I was there, some of my instructors went to Australia and New Zealand to teach the Arlberg Technique to the members of several of their ski clubs. In addition to the international publicity that the Arlberg Technique thus received, Dr. Fanck and I wrote a book entitled *Wunder des Schneeschuhs* describing the technique of my school. We illustrated each phase with strips from the film. The book sold well over a million copies throughout the world.

Interest in the Arlberg Technique was so greatly heightened by the movies and the book that between 1922 and 1927 the number of instructors at the school increased from four to thirty. In 1938, my last year at St. Anton, there were forty-one instructors at the school, and we were turning out large numbers of accomplished skiers.

In recent years, my system of teaching has been criticized as being too slow. I do not consider this to be a valid criticism, for the following reasons.

Today in North Conway, just as in St. Anton before the last war, my instructors are up against the very real problem, common to all ski schools, of turning the soft novice, essentially terrified by skis, into the finished skier, who, as I see him, is a skier who can run downhill using linked christies.

It is my firm belief that more pupils have mastered skiing through the use of the Arlberg Technique than by any other known teaching method. This has been achieved by adhering to a logical system of teaching, proceeding by natural stages from the straight schuss to the snowplow, the snowplow turn, the stem turn, and the stem-christie. Each class learns as a group. Group teaching helps pupils to learn by watching each other's mistakes. Pupils who are above average and who quickly grasp the fundamentals of a class are promoted to the next class at the end of the lesson. The time spent in that class has not been wasted by the above-average pupils. He has not only perfected that phase of the technique, but has also gained strength through the exercise.

The individuality of the skier can be developed only when he has become a finished skier.

I do not mean by this that other schools have not been successful in teaching downhill skiing. Some of the schools whose technique I have observed are excellent, but to my mind they are more suited to the further progress of the finished skier than to the development of the beginner. As a result their success with new pupils is uneven.

This article would not be complete without a description of the basic principles of the Arlberg Technique. A complete explanation of the system is obviously not possible here, but I believe the reader will grasp the essentials of the technique from the discussion that follows.

Since its inception forty-two years ago, the Arlberg Technique has been based on four essential principles. They are: control, safety, form, and speed. Of these, control is most important, for once this is learned the others follow naturally.

A beginner learning to ski at an Arlberg school goes through a natural series of classes. Each class is designed to develop his ability without impairing his confidence. After a few walking exercises on level ground, he is taught the downhill run. Next the snowplow for control. This is followed in natural stages by the snowplow turn, the stem turn, and the stem-christie. With confidence the beginner skis faster and his turns become easier.

The snowplow is the cornerstone of the entire technique. It is so basic that even topflight racers depend on it in difficult situations. The safety a novice feels when he uses this maneuver gives him courage to advance and go faster. The snowplow turn is taught next. Using his old friend, the snowplow, the pupil learns that he can change direction down the slope in full control at all times.

Up to this point, control and safety are emphasized. Thereafter, form is taught—the ability to swing the body in making the turn and the need to develop coordination and timing. Relaxation is the secret of mastering these two skills. A pupil must not be pushed along too quickly on slopes too steep for his ability or he will "freeze," and his capacity for quick learning will be retarded.

My school has always taught the fundamentals on easy slopes. The snowplow is taught preferably on a hill with a small ridge where the pupil can assume the snowplow position. A gully, if it is available, is the ideal place to teach the snowplow turn. Terrain of this type makes it easier to teach the pupil his first turns. After a few runs under these conditions, he can duplicate the maneuver on any other type of slope.

When the pupil begins to get the feel of swinging his snowplow turns, he is taught the traverse and stem turn. He runs across the slope, skis together, and changes direction by using the stem turn instead of the snowplow. Proficiency in the use of this turn means that a skier can handle almost any trail or slope in any snow condition with perfect safety and control. It can be taught in a short time, thus enabling the majority of skiers who have only a week or two available for skiing to get out and enjoy their brief ski vacations almost anywhere.

But, to be good, a skier must also develop a sense of timing and coordination. These are the two basic factors of good skiing form. Without them, a skier cannot become expert. Therefore, after mastering the stem turn, the pupil concentrates on his form. Practice develops his natural coordination and sharpens his sense of timing. In areas with rolling hills, pastures and easy trails, local ski schools should plan cross-country jaunts for pupils who have reached the stem-turn class. In this type of country, the intermediate skier may practice all the exercises he has learned in school—walking, climbing, and running downhill with linked turns. A trip of this sort pleases the intermediate skier as much as a steep hill delights the expert, giving him a glowing sense of achievement. As master of his skis, he can control them, and make them go anywhere.

When the intermediate skier finds that he has enough control to increase his speed, he is ready for the stem-christie class. This is taught on a fairly easy slope that does not frighten him. It is in this class that the skier learns why he has spent so much time in the earlier classes mastering his coordination and timing: for the stem-christie, the first of the speed turns, depends on split-second timing. When he has done a few of these turns successfully, the pupil discovers that he can go faster and faster, allowing his skis to run closer to the fall line. In other words, he lets his skis run almost straight downhill. It is then that he is gradually promoted to steeper hills depending on his ability to learn. At this point he can be said to ski safely with control and form and be ready for the fourth principle of the Arlberg Technique—speed.

Speed in skiing takes courage. It cannot be taught like the rest of the system. Nor can it be acquired until the other principles have been mastered. A skier who has control is safe. A skier who has form will not make errors that cause him to fall. Mastery of these two principles permits the skier to attempt speed. With speed, the skier runs in the fall line. He finds himself making parallel turns and skiing the steepest slope in perfect control and safety in any snow condition. The pupil who reaches this stage by the Arlberg Technique is a really finished skier.

The time it takes to produce a finished skier varies naturally with the individual. A young athlete of college or high-school age advances through the classes rapidly. Most pupils, however, are office workers, housewives, and the like, all of whom are in soft physical condition. Furthermore, they can devote only a short time to skiing each winter. It is with these people that I find personal satisfaction in my teaching system. If I can teach them to run down a hill with control and safety during their brief vacations, I know I have achieved something. What a pleasure it is to see the average recreational skier's face light up when he finishes a run down a good-sized slope in absolute control and without fear!

Although the Arlberg Technique was designed primarily to teach average recreational skiers, it was also intended for the development of racers. Once the individual learns control, speed takes care of itself. One need only check the names of past winners of the FIS world championships, the Kandahar, or the U.S. National Championships to find many exponents of the Arlberg Technique.

The system is as sound today as it has always been in its objective of developing the individual skier naturally. It teaches the recreational skier to ski safely, yet at the same time produces fine finished skiers and top-flight racers. I attribute this to the four basic principles of the technique mentioned previously: control, safety, form, and speed.

Introduction to the Teaching Plan

by STEFAN KRUCKENHAUSER

The most important step forward after Schneider's discovery of the stem and parallel christies was the discovery of the Austrian and French racing skiers that they could link short, quick skidded turns, one right after the other, to create a much more controlled descent in a confined space than they could with the wide-swinging Arlberg turns. The new racing turn was made by turning the skis with the legs and letting the upper body do nothing but balance the motion of the lower body, (as opposed to swinging the upper body in the direction of the turn). The balancing motion of the upper body tended to turn the upper body away from, rather than toward the turn, a "reverse" motion. The new turns were at first called "reverse," or "the Austrian reverse," in this country. A connected series of short reverse turns was known, and still is today, as "the wedel," or "wedeln," the German verb and noun, respectively, meaning "wagging" as a dog wags his tail. Prof. Stefan Kruckenhauser, Schneider's successor as the chief Austrian theorist, laid out a precise teaching plan for instructing pupils in the reverse turns, in a book which was translated to English by Roland Palmedo as The New Official Austrian Ski System, *published in the United States in 1958. Within a few years, every ski school in the United States was teaching "wedel" and the largest technical breakthrough in ski history had taken place.*

In Palmedo's translation, swing means "skid" and thus the stem-swing is the skidded-stem or stem-christy:

Kruckenhauser's teaching plan built from the stem-christy (skidded stem) to the skidded parallel, just as does the American Teaching Method today.

WE waited a long time for our plan of teaching. May it not seem immodest, but here a good thing really took time. The struggle to find the right way took us almost ten years.

To properly understand our plan of teaching, a review of the developments which led to its creation is in order.

The three great Austrian ski pioneers—Zdarsky, Bilgeri, and Schneider—who worked out our Alpine skiing in long years of competition and success, gave us two turns: the stem turn and the stem-swing (Christiania). From 1922 to 1930, ski technique stood still, with these two turns, as did the way of teaching in all Austrian ski schools.

In instruction, traversing was given a place, but sideslipping was accorded little value. This is understandable, for downhill running at that time meant mostly running in untouched snow. Traversing involved no particular difficulties. Because there were no *pistes,* sideslipping was of little usefulness.

211

About 1937, a considerable number of the outstanding skiers were distinguished by an especially smooth manner of swinging, the elegance of which invited imitation, but whose finely coordinated movements appeared to be difficult to master and could not be precisely explained by the skiers themselves. The talk was of "hip-swing"—this vague concept meant little and helped still less. Today we know that these very skiers ran with today's technique, even though in an undefined way. The stem-swing taught by good ski teachers as early as 1937 already had the characteristics of a light and relaxed sequence of movements,

A few young skiers who had an elegant and relaxed style carried out their swings with leg action, meanwhile holding their shoulders still or turning them counter to the direction of the turn, and these young men coined a name for these swings (even though the term is not entirely appropriate), namely "counter-shoulder turns" (or inside shoulder turns).

The significant thing was that no one had taught these young men this technique (and no one had forbidden them it). Although this extraordinarily agile method was noticed, no one at first asked what it led to. Even when expert runners like Nogler and Franz Gabl won noteworthy victories with this technique, its significance was not yet recognized. Only when the Arlberger, Toni Spiss, and the Kitzbühler, Christian Pravda won decisively with it, Spiss especially with an agility that gave him the name "Rubber-Spiss," was it gradually recognized that in these cases not only the condition, competitive spirit and luck of the competitors brought victory, but also to a noteworthy extent their ski technique. The chief reason for the success of our master skiers is their ski technique, the technique which one includes under the term "wedeln."

In the French book, *Ski 1957*, no less an authority than Emile Allais wrote the foreword. The first sentence of this preface said much, perhaps everything: *"A livre vient a son heure . . ."* ("This book comes at the right moment . . .")

In two hundred and forty pages, the two authors, G. Joubert and Vuarnet, analyze the ski technique which is now influencing the whole world; almost half of the book is concerned with the problem of wedeln.

It is no great step from the more-or-less stemmed swing, which almost every young skier has to get behind him in his development, to swinging with "leg action" alone, that is, swing turns which result almost entirely from the work of the legs, and especially, it is no break in the whole sequence of movements.

That was decisive for us. We reached the conclusion that the study of the relaxed and efficient manner of swinging of the many master skiers would produce many gains for the further development of popular skiing, since both have the same roots. More than four years of experience in teaching have now fully confirmed this. Only then did we come out with our plan of teaching.

Two important areas of training are basic in our ski instruction:

Sideslipping forward
Stem turn and stem-swing

Those are the chief goals, that is the basic program.

Sideslipping forward is for us the very "key" to Alpine skiing. How this sideslipping forward is to be carried out did not come to us immediately, but our ultimate deductions were all the more productive. The proper body position for it is the firm foundation of today's ski technique.

Sideslipping forward as well as the turns and swings brought us to an important means of turning the skis: "turning pressure of the heels" (also called "heel pressure" for short). This "heel pressure" also is a characteristic of our technique and of our teaching . . .

Most skiers will be able to perfect their stem-swings on the trails, constantly reducing the angle of stem, and in time try swinging parallel, in accordance with their aptitude and condition; and even (I venture to write this as experience justifies it) to get acquainted with wedeln—out of pure pleasure in new movements.

First "wedel" skier was Austrian racer Toni Spiss

The Ski Is a Tool

by WARREN WITHERELL

The third great technical development after Arlberg and wedel was the development of carving turns, in which the ski, rather than being skidded, is set on edge, bent in an arc by a downward pressure, and thus enabled to "carve" the turn without any turning impetus given to the skis by the skier. A ski in a carved turn, of course, will not skid, but make a definite curved "cut" in the snow. Carving is a much more difficult turn to initiate and control than is the skidded stem-christy or parallel christy. But the carved turn has great advantages in speed, precision and stability. It was the genius of an American, Warren Witherell, to make the first definitive statement of carving technique; he was the first to perceive that when the top racers turned, the turn was something done largely by the ski—not the skier. Witherell, the highly successful ski coach and headmaster at Burke Academy in Vermont, taught a generation of young racers to carve and his book How the Racers Ski *was enthusiastically received as a breakthrough. Less enthusiasm, however, was generated by Witherell's idea that the carving turn should be taught from the beginning to all recreational skiers. The speed and coordination required seemed to make it, in the eyes of most instructors, much more difficult to learn than the traditional skidded turns—the stem-christy and parallel christy. Today serious carving is usually taught after the skier learns to christy.*

SNOW skis are not two-by-fours. They are carefully designed tools with controlled camber, flex, side-cut, torsion, etc. The most advanced skis have been developed through racer-oriented testing programs. The skis have thus been engineered to respond precisely to the techniques outlined in this book. Stated simply—the skis are designed to carve an arcing path through the snow when they are sufficiently rolled on edge, and when sufficient pressure is applied to bend them into reverse camber.

The most basic concept in modern racing technique is this: *If you stand correctly on your skis, they will turn for you. If you apply correct edge angle and pressure to a ski, the ski itself will provide most of the required turning forces.*

If you wish to ski as the best racers do, you must learn to *carve* turns—i.e., turn without skidding or sideslipping. When a racer turns, he "feels" the texture of the snow and the shape of the terrain; he is sensitive to the flex and shape of his skis; he applies correct edge angle and pressure to his skis in the snow—and then he stands loose and flows with them. His upper-body movements are completely natural and relaxed. His body is free to maintain balance in response to terrain.

By contrast, most recreational skiers, including many instructors, constantly assume forced and self-conscious body positions. They try to change the direction of their skis through upper-body movements (rotation, counter-rotation, split-rotation, etc.)—and after achieving a desired line, they worry anew about a "proper" stance for each following traverse. They are concerned with final forms rather than fluid motion. To verify this observation, watch the public carefully next time you ride a chairlift. Or watch a group of ski instructors at a certification exam. Or watch instructor and class during a ski lesson. They're incredibly self-conscious and constrained.

Many ski technicians argue that all turns must be started with some upper-body movement. In a sense they may be right. Certainly racers learn to initiate turns—but they do so as naturally as a child learns to turn a bicycle. Racers don't think about body movement. How you *think* about skiing is important. Most skiers *think* their upper bodies control each turn—so their body motions are self-conscious. Racers *think* their skis control each turn—so their body motions are more natural. A racer may move his body to change edge or pressure on his skis, or to anticipate changes in balance, but he does not think about moving his body. He thinks about the different feel of his ski edges in the snow, or about the line in the snow he wants his skis to follow.

The superior balance that racers exhibit results from their lack of self-consciousness about body positions. Most recreational skiers are frequently out of balance because they assume particular body positions learned from ski schools or ski magazines. These defined positions restrict a skier's natural reaction to terrain changes. Whenever the upper body is consciously used to create rotational forces, it is restricted from seeking natural balance. As balance adjustments are particularly required during periods of edge and direction change, it is desirable to provide maximum freedom to the upper body at these times. By disengaging the upper body from an active role in creating turning forces, a racer frees his hands, arms, and torso to make relaxed, natural balance adjustments in response to terrain variations.

It is not possible to ski like a racer until you are completely convinced that conscious upper-body motions are as unnecessary in ski technique as in walking. Most traditional ski technicians will choke over this idea. It is, however, a central idea to the thesis of this book. Let's pursue the argument.

Consider running down a dry stream bed—one consisting of variously shaped boulders and rocks. Think for a moment how difficult this activity is. The boulders are unevenly spaced. Some are round, some pointed. A few have flat tops, but most are tilted. Each requires a different angle of attack and departure. This physical activity is extremely complex. How do you progress down the stream? Do you consciously angulate? Do you think about unweighting or leading with your outside arm? Do you employ reverse shoulder because Stein Erikson does? Of course not. You just run. Your body balances quite naturally, though each step is a different length, and each landing place on a different angle.

What do you *think* about when running in a stream bed? *You think about your feet*—specifically about placing your left foot on a green rock, then your right foot on a gray rock. You pick a point with your eyes, and your foot goes to it. As your foot moves to a rock, every other part of your body follows in perfect balance. If you must land on a slippery rock, you feel the rock with the soles of your feet or sneakers—just as racers feel the snow. You use the nerves in your feet and the muscle tension in your legs to sense whether you will grip on the rock or slide off. If you feel you are sliding, you "edge" more. You edge by rolling your ankle and knee "into the hill." To balance that lateral movement, your upper body instinctively tilts (angulates) away from the hill. Throughout this exercise, you think mostly about the surface on which you are standing, or about the next point on which you will land. When skiing, a good racer picks a spot on the snow with his eyes, and his skis go instinctively to it. His body follows as naturally as your body follows your foot to a green rock.

What this comparison shows is that *body mo-*

tions are no more difficult in skiing than in stream-bed-running. In fact, balance is simpler when skiing—almost constant contact can be maintained with the snow (as opposed to being airborne between rocks); and a skier can often stand on two feet simultaneously (while a runner is limited to one foot at a time). What makes skiing difficult for most people is that they can-

Racer pressures skis to carve through the snow

not direct their feet as easily with skis attached as with sneakers attached. The goal is to teach you the art of directing your skis as easily as you direct your feet. When you learn this art, skiing becomes as natural as walking.

Modern skiing is a process of standing correctly on your skis—of applying to your skis varying edge angles and pressures to achieve a desired performance.

If you roll a ski on edge, and apply sufficient pressure to create reverse camber, [bend the skis] the ski will turn. As you increase the amount of edge angle and/or pressure, the ski will turn more sharply. The sharper turn results from an increase in reverse camber. Once a turn is begun and the ski is carving, additional pressure is applied to the ski by centrifugal force—the skier's mass trying to drift outside in the turn while the carving edge provides resistance.

The arc of a turn remains constant as long as the same pressures and edge angle are applied to the ski, and the terrain remains the same. Any change in edge angle, pressure, or terrain will change the turning radius of the ski.

Forward, neutral, or back *pressure distribution* on a ski influences the arc a ski carves in the snow.

Forward *pressure distribution* bends the front of a ski more than the back. This helps to initiate turns, or to shorten the radius of a turn in progress.

Neutral *pressure distribution* bends a ski on an even arc. This is ideal for sustained turns of a constant radius.

Back *pressure distribution* bends the back of a ski more than the front. This can be useful at the end of quick turns, or for turns of minimal direction change on relatively easy terrain.

A ski will stop turning when the edge assumes a straight line—i.e., when the reverse camber that sustains the turn is neutralized. I call this "neutralizing a ski," or "neutralizing a turn." For any given traverse, there is a combination of edge angle, pressure, and pressure distribution which causes a ski edge to carve a straight path.

It is always a delicate balance between changes of edge angle, pressure, and pressure distribution that neutralizes the turning power of a ski. The exact movements required to *neutralize* a ski vary with every turn. They depend on the terrain, snow condition, speed, type, and condition of ski—almost infinitely changing variables. Only by experimentation can a skier learn the *many* ways a turn can be neutralized. It is a fine art—one mastered by experience and experiment. A skier's "feel" for the snow is especially important at this point where turns end and traverses begin.

It is difficult to picture the carving action of a ski simply by reading about it. You must *feel* it. Go out on the snow and experiment. The simplest carving action of a ski can be experienced on relatively flat terrain and at medium speed by spreading your skis about 2 feet apart, still parallel, and putting most of your weight on one ski—let's use the right. (Carry some weight on your left or inside ski to maintain balance and directional control). Roll your right ski 30 to 45 degrees on edge by moving your knee to the inside. If you just stand on your ski—with enough pressure to bend it into reverse camber—your ski will carve a long arc in the snow. Don't push the tail out or thrust the ski laterally in any way. Make long, gradual turns left and right close to the fall line by shifting your weight alternately from one ski to the other. Keep both skis parallel but 2 feet apart throughout this exercise. Your inside ski, which is lightly weighted and just providing balance, should drift easily as the downhill ski carves each turn.

To vary the radius of your turns, experiment with different edge angles and pressure applications. Vary forward and back pressure distribution. Explore the reactions you can get from a nonskidding, edged ski. You will note that a little forward pressure helps initiate a sharper turn. Most carved turns begin with forward pressure distribution and are characterized by a forward push of the feet in the middle of the turn. Experiment with this pushing ahead of your feet to bring your skis to a position of neutral pressure distribution. Turns can be ended by reducing pressure at this point.

Obviously this kind of turn is of too long a radius to be useful on steeper terrain, but it is a *pure carved turn.* It will help you to feel your ski turn without skidding. Study the track you leave in the snow. There should be a definite line left by the edge of your ski. If there is enough loose snow, the groove of your ski will leave a raised track as well.

This wide-stance, pure-carve exercise is useful for teaching carved turns even to very accomplished racers. It helps them learn to initiate turns with no lateral push to edge or change the direction of their skis. To make a properly carved turn, a ski must be edged first, then have pressure and leverage applied to initiate its change of direction.

If you try to change the direction of a ski while it is still flat on the snow, some lateral skidding of the ski will occur. To prevent skidding, the carving edge must be in the snow before direction change occurs. Remember: *to make a pure carved turn—you must edge your ski first, then apply pressure and let it turn.*

No. "10" Powder

by BOB JAMIESON

If there's a bard of powder, it is Bob Jamieson, who can write not only inspired lyric description but inspired technical description: a soaring "how to break through the powder barrier."

DEEP snow begins, as all things do, in waking. The champagne pop of consciousness. The fetal warmth of a heavy quilt. The room is dark, outside it is snowing. Four days now. In the pale winter night snowflakes dance, tumbling down the sky, each flake lost in its private dance with gravity. Muscles stretch and groan, sore from yesterday's turns. Cold floor. Sweaty ski clothes, the sweet stench of stale beer. An early morning O.J., stiff boots, a breakfast of sorts, then out into the astounding silence of falling snow. Shin deep. We wade through it, boots crunching, skis on shoulder slipping sometimes, grating in anticipation.

The lift is silent, immobile, snow-covered. We are early. And so, with cold feet and impatience we share the falling snow and coming morning with a few others, stomping and waiting. A company elf arrives and soon is bouncing here and there with a broom. Fluff scatters in clouds revealing dark, greasy metal. A mechanical cough, a hum, gears clank and the chairs lurch into motion, beginning their daily, endless journey. The elf nods and we slide into place.

"Have a good ride," he says with a jealous, knowing smile. We nod and smile in reply, the chair comes and we glide upwards into the still descending snow. He returns to his dance with the broom, we tip up on one cheek each and sweep the snow from beneath us. Cold bum. Admission price to the greatest snow on earth.

TIME. Always it takes time. A winter out of your life. A time without money, or a lover, even the wine and song must be subdued, for deep stuff demands all of you. It's a martial art, you know, an esoteric science for fools, played out on the fluted ridges of the Rockies; a gentle karate of the ridges, a flashing of blades in soft snow. Not the death snap of combat karate, but the gentle pull and soft release of the Samurai archer; a warm, loving oscillation of life, like the afterburn of sex in a hot, Moroccan afternoon; a rowing through long waves, the playing of an old and mellow violin.

The silent spruce slip by, violet against the somber sky. There is a hint of blue. The snow is thinner now, single cloud sparks drifting down. I watch a single crystal fairy dance down the sky. Another taps me on the nose.

SNOW. The Pacific is the beginning of it all. In its warm, empty reaches tropical squalls gather the equatorial dampness and carry it, as the planet turns, to the Sierras, the Wasatch, and the Rockies. There, in the wind howling over the

219

ridges, a lattice collects, molecules holding hands, and empty chattering space becomes a blossom in tiny, frozen lines. Unique, exquisite, a trillion tiny mandalas form and on those special 4-foot days, they join together, then join again in inch wide asteroids tumbling silently to the mountain slopes below. It is there, like hawks with quick eyes, that we wait.

Such stuff this snow. Upon your cuff it hesitates a second, then blows away, feathers. A day or two and it becomes an airy, fluid crystal drooping from a winter roof. A few centuries and it becomes a glacier, blue and groaning, carving new mountains. Mutable, unique stuff. But for you and me, just now it is virgin, newborn, waiting.

The sky is blue now, the distant peaks etched silver against its utter depths. Three more towers and we are in the sun. Crystals of snow still descend, scattered now, each a diamond translating sunshine into tiny, iridescent rainbows. The last tower passes, the ramp arrives. Our skis cut the drifts that rib the ramp and we slide off, down into 3 feet of snow. We struggle through the drift, then begin working our skis through the wind-pack down around toward the mountain lip. We look down, then up. The quick and easy ones are below, of course, but it is only 2 feet deep there and packed underneath. Above us lie the biggies, the long and wild ones, the unpacked, their beginnings still lost in the tattered patches of cloud that remain in the lee of the peaks. We begin, crawling upwards. The track is gone so we guess a line and begin the upward angling journey to the top. It will be an hour at least.

PLACES. You will always have to work for it. Like so many things, deep snow retreats before you. But you won't understand that until you have tried it, so to begin, we will provide a few distant hints. The secret really, is the storm tracks. Storm tracks, jet streams and mountain ranges in the way. In Africa on the vast Serengeti Plains at the end of the dry season, you can watch the first storms coming in off the equator, vast, dark things, laying a swath of life-giving moisture across the plains. The next day you will see the animals on the move, heading across the dusty distance toward the storm track where they know, in a few days, there will be fresh, green grass. So also in the western states. A different kind of animal, in VW vans, can be seen heading across the desert steppes, heading for distant ranges of peaks recently storm-tracked. They are not looking for green grass.

Morning sweat. Beer oozing out of your pores. Grunts and four-lettered words of wisdom. The sky is dazzling blue, the last wisps of cloud are retreating over the ridges. The snow sparkles. We go slowly, picking up a ski one at a time, stomping down a place for it, then shifting upward one step. Below us there is shouting and howling as the others cut up. Laughter, turns, and sunshine for everyone but us.

CRASHING. How to spend the night. Cheap. Jackson, Hostel X, hot sticky rooms, but lots of friends and the price is right. Other than that, the trailer courts in town or the little summer shacks up Wilson way. Alta. The Gold Miner's Daughter has dorms and a management that understands. And up at the end of the road there is the Snow Pine Lodge. Home once long ago. Snowbird? Hah! Stay at Alta. In Banff years ago Mrs. White used to give us a bed for a buck a night and serve tea and muffins in the morning. You have to sleep in the flowerpots now. Sun Valley, Ketchum, Rossland, Schweitzer, Telluride, just walk down the street and say "Hi" to someone with funny eyes. They will fill you in. And in Ta Ta Creek, B.C., if you can ever find it, just ask for me.

Still slogging. The lower slopes are distant now, but the top still hides. Sweat, sunglare, muscle ache. This is no way to start the day. But on we go, thrashing upwards, fools that we are.

GEAR. Just as western man does not understand that technology is only an adjunct to the art of life, so western skiers do not realize that ski gear is but an appendage to the art of skiing. Hot gear cannot make you ski.

Poles. Sticks with hands attached. Nothing special, some fellows like a bit more length, for reach, though for the life of me I can't figure out what they are reaching *for*. They also tend to run your arms up a bit high. In deep snow you are not planting into anything anyway, you just sorta put it out there and turn. Baskets, of course, are essential. They give you a little back pressure to play with, especially when you are trying to get out of a divot.

The most delightful powder is so light it hovers cloudlike over skiers

Boots. You know those guys who water-ski on bare feet? I've always wanted to try that, winter style. Except that I have ticklish feet. But until we can work that one out, we gotta wear boots. There are two schools. Old boots and plastic boots. And there is an essential difference. Over the last ten years in the change from funny old leather boots to bananas, we have reduced our options by one joint. Which makes things a lot easier and more precise and probably better on hard pack. Not so in deep snow. Take a look at some tracks laid down in '65 and compare them to some of today's tracks. The old turns were round, the new ones are variations on going straight downhill. They aren't completed turns, they never really get out of the fall line. Why?

Okay. But listen carefully, because words don't explain this very well. Remember the "coma" position? Like from the history books? Some dude with a funny hat, one arm high, the other (downhill) reaching out like he is gonna stab a bull, his body like a sickle moon over the mountain. Okay. Take a white pencil and put him in 4 feet of snow. Guess what, classic deep snow technique. A little more knee and hip flexion, but the position is right on. The essential control from this position is a *heel* push and a twist of about 25 degrees in the ankle to put the skis at almost 90 degrees to the slope. In deep snow what transpires in this position is a gentle downhill drift through the snow with your skis against the grain. Several things happen. You have excellent control, your turns get very round and, if you are right on and in a very steep place, the blast from the previous turn will come cruising over your head. Good turns, good fun. But try that essential heel push in your bananas. Guess what? It doesn't work. And that is why the modern powder heavies can't quite make the pretty turns the old boys could. All we are doing these days is a sort of outrageous compression turn which does not provide control, does not slow you down and makes your tracks look like a snake in a hurry. The essence of the entire matter, however, is that it doesn't matter as long as you are turning and digging it. It is kinda like the difference between making love on a Caribbean beach when it is 110 in the shade, and doing the bumpity-bumpity in the back seat of a '55 Chevy in Michigan in January.

Skis. Flat sticks. Any ski will do if you ski it hard enough and long enough. Like the old Head Vector, a downhill ski from the early sixties. Get 70,000 miles on them and they are one of the finest powder skis there is. The old Head Standard is a classic of course, the Head Powder is the same ski with things softened up a bit inside. And there is the Miller Soft. If you want to ski just deep stuff, it is the one. And then there are the new boys in town, Fischer Fats and Fischer Deeps, Haute Routes (Rossignol) and others. They all work, but I'd like to see a little more spontaneous combustion in the ski design business. Let's hear it for single skis, but let's get really wild. How about round bottoms? Fluted bottoms? Hydro-foils, fins, how about a 3-inch side cut and shovels 5 inches wide?

Bindings. For keeping the sticks on. Anything will do, the problems arise when you fall down. It had better be easy to put back on.

The top approaches, bending slowly closer. Sweat has collected in a wet band around my middle. Clothing half off, half on, goggles up, squinting into the glare and distance. The final 50 feet takes forever. We collapse, panting, wasted, in the sun.

TECHNIQUE is not a proper word to describe our gentle dance in snow, nor are words fit tools for dissection. But we will try. Find a good, old-fashioned rocking chair. Sit on the edge of it and put your feet, wide-stance, on the front edges of the rockers. Get someone to start you rocking. It is as close to deep snow as one can get in your living room. All it requires is balance. *But,* don't sit back. In powder your tips ride higher, in relation to your solar plexus, than they do on hard-pack, so your point of balance is back a bit, closer to the mountain, that's all this sitting back nonsense is. The point is to balance yourself against the snow.

In deep snow, a ski turns only because it wants to. Your problem is simply to balance it, to direct it in such a way as to allow it to turn. One provides the balance and the shifting of weight along the ski, the torque that lays an edge, but the ski and the ski alone can turn.

To understand this it helps to understand a few things about your body. Your body is a great big spring. If you let it be. The rocking chair posture is not a sitting back and relaxing, but a flexing and bending of muscles and sinews that depresses your lower body into a compression spring. Standing straight you are solid, stiff, in the army. Fully crouched, ankles, knees, and hips bent full you are a Slinky toy in a heap, no elasticity, no nothing. But, somewhere in between, when your muscles and bones and tendons come together in balance, they become utterly sensitive to pressure against your feet, and they can balance you against the snow world outside and, poof, you get that gentle, Cadillac ride that it is all about.

The trick in all of this is to turn around your center, your solar plexus. In order to turn around your center you have to know about your outer centers. The head. Obvious. Tuck your head in, keep your neck and back straight (they do the same in karate), and look straight down the mountain. Then there is the axilla, the armpit, the chakra of skiing. Don't ask me why. Anyway, why not? Something as clean as skiing deep snow ought to have its origins in the pits, right? Third, the crotch, the vortex, the infolding, outfolding center between your legs. These are the balance points for the sine curves of muscle and bone that are your legs and arms. Your skis come off your legs at 90 degrees; so also your poles off your arms. So what you have is an energy spiral with the tools on the edges. The controls for tip and tail balance are in your toes; for left and right balance in your knees, your turn initiators are in your wrists. Your head has to handle what the astronauts call yaw. Now the only problem is getting everything to work together, but when you do, when you get the sine curve sliding through, you create a sine curve in another dimension. We call 'em tracks.

On the ridge the wind cuts, chopped snowflakes sandpaper our faces. We dance along. Chaplin figures, hurrying chop-chop to the end of the ridge, to where the mountain drops away. A single turn and we are there, suddenly out of the wind, looking down on the source of our foolishness.

Before moguls, preparation is physical, a stretching and twisting of muscles; before deep snow it is spiritual, a stretching and twisting of the mind. And so, amid the silver minarets of the Rockies, we wail a silent white Moslem chant and contemplate that first turn, that first soft sifting of snow and body and mind.

BREATHING is essential, or you will fall down. And sometimes it is very hard to remember to do this simple thing. So a mantra. Breathe in a figure eight, breathe out a figure eight. Dance through the loops in your mind that make you breathe and ski.

On the very edge we hesitate, lost in mountains, snow, and sky. We zip up, goggles come down, buckles click tighter. No words. We are ready.

FIRST TURN. It is essential, that first turn. It defines your run. Don't ask me why, but somehow that first soft slipping in snow locks you into a certain dance step. Begin with a long sweeping turn and that's where you are at for the rest of the mountain. Begin slowly, tight, swinging back around on that first turn, and the rest will be the same, a minuet with yourself. So forget the distance, the plunging slope, concentrate on just that first pole plant and turn.

The squirrel routine begins:
"After you, sir, you broke trail, you deserve first turns . . ."
"Oh, no, no. . . . I insist, you are the guest today . . ."
"Oh, no, no. . . . I insist . . ."
"Oh, no, no. . . . I insist . . ."

Softly I am away. Soft, inky, smoothness engulfs me. I turn, gently, slowly, then turn again before I see the sun, sparkling through a million dancing diamonds. My beard is full of snow, a tiny bridge of snow remains, a perfect half-moon

across my nose and goggles. I breathe carefully, through my nose, and smile.

CONTROL, a kind of loose control, a control, with ecstasy before, a thinking with the third mind, is what is needed. If you must be rational, expend it on understanding your body and do it at night, in bed, alone. Think out every body motion, correct it, smooth it, then finish and go to sleep and forget it. In the morning go skiing, not thinking. Let the rational energy work on your lower brain centers, let the synapse pulses rearrange how your body moves, then in the snow, just let it move. No last second corrections please.

Third turn, running down the up elevator in the department store called the Rocky Mountains. In each turn I descend a step, yet return immediately to where I began. I attempt to descend, to alter my relationship to this dancing albino world, but remain the same. Time and place are but pole plants, the vortex infolding of snow under pressure. Reality is crystalline. My heart pumps.

MUSIC is the point of all this. Racing is music, the music of speed. Freestyle is modern music, the rock and roll of the mountain and it is no wonder that the violin players on their downhills don't like it. Powder, of course, is the dark jazz of skiing and when you are cooking, watch over your left shoulder and you'll see a little guy with a big drum, a very big drum, beat slowly.

People ask me sometimes, when I am telling tales and remembering times in Africa and I get a distant, crazy look in my eye, what it was really like . . . And I can answer only with a parable, a story I heard from an old Greek war hero turned elephant hunter called Eliopolis: over a bottle of Ouzo in a little Accra bar called the Twasan d'Or, the Golden Fleece.

"Picture, my friend, the biggest, ugliest, blackest whore in the world," says he, "Ten gallon tits, lips like ripe peppers, a face like moldy Jell-O and an ass like a Taureg camel. Imagine being trapped in a Lagos dive with her for a week. Then picture, friend, that old bitch throwing you the wildest night ride of your life. That, amigo, is Africa."

And so for you, my deep snow friends, picture for yourselves the grandest, softest white whore in the world, lean and mean, with dark and distant eyes, throwing you the longest, gentlest bit of loving that you will ever know. That is deep snow. But I digress.

Turns, more turns, each one a waltz in a streaming white gown. When I come out I can see the force wave of my presence rippling before me in the snow, when I go down, I can almost feel it. The hill stretches behind me, compresses before me. My breath comes in gunshots, slamming out of my lungs. I watch the slow arc of my arm and pole plant, feel the flex and torque and twist of muscles and tendons as I come out over a little roll, my skis free, arcing around and down into snow again, folding the snow inward, creating a turbulent wave that washes up and over me.

WHY do we do this thing? Because it feels good. Why does it feel good? Because it makes us resonate. Most of our time we spend running around in the infinity loop of ordinary existence, going nowhere. But sometimes on a mountain you can bend the loop from its course and make of it a sine curve. You know, tracks. Also rhythm, music, and dance. So dance. Dance like a madman, like a shaman, or dance a ballroom dance in tails, it doesn't matter. Just dance. Let the curve stride through you. And that, my friends, is the meaning of all the dipping and weaving, the turning and churning, the whispers and shouts. You gotta just let it all hang out.

I crank a turn and plunge into the trees, poling high through the branches, cruising down over a lip, blowing through air full of snow, landing a millisecond, then going off into air again.

One final steep pitch, I break over and land in an explosion of snow. This time the snow is very deep and I am seconds coming up. When I finally do I am lopsided in the snow and going very fast. The surface of snow around me is fluid. A hiss, a roar wells up. Whiteness again. Where is up? Where is down? Where am I going? Will I survive? Am I alive?

THE STEEPER the deeper and the deeper the better and when it's moving it adds a further dimension. Of course, you may die. But one can, contrary to popular belief, survive the length of a breath in outer space, if you keep your mouth shut. So also for white space. The Virgin at Sunshine Village in Canada, is about a breath-length

long. It is aptly named, for after a dump it is hard to find, tight, sweet and blocked with snow. It is a narrow chute, too steep to be called a run. When you ski it, it slides immediately with you and you are gone in a white, slipping world, dark shadows of rocks rushing by, then pop, it tosses you out below with a boggled mind and a new respect for snow and gravity. A respect that some call fear.

Just as it slowed this one also tossed me out and I turned again, down and down, through the last few turns to the bottom. The last turn I made wide and slow, coming around to look back up the mountain. And then I fell on my face, looking deep into the meaning of the snow crystals sticking to my eyeballs.

Soon the others arrived and we knocked off our skis and walked across the flat and into the crowd. There in the midst of the mechanical and biological madness of a big-time ski resort I stopped for a moment, skis on shoulder, and forgot for a moment where I was.

HEROES? There are none in deep snow, only greater fools. And only fools can know the way of it. The ancient sages of China walked in the mountains with staves only because they did not have skis. Now modern man has created the plastic wands essential for perfect understanding. Pure contemplation is needed, but it is not enough. So also for menial labor. China abounds in both of these, but lacks the wild soul fire of the African night, the simple, mindless rapture of an Aspen spring night chemical binge. Now, with the mixing of the races and modern high tech we have the essentials for a new generation of mystics. Mountains peopled by those with the time to contemplate, who partake of menial labor and rejoice in the wild dance of skiing. Watch for them, friends, wise men on the ski patrol, gurus in the kitchen, and the leaders of the *jhad*, directing traffic in the parking lot.

The bar, the end. We are hot, sweaty, dripping snow from hats and beards. We smile too much. I look around at the madding crowd, then turn to watch the bubbles dancing in my beer, carbon dioxide doing its thing in the alcoholic beverage of choice, west of the Rocky Mountains.

Working with Images

by DENISE MC CLUGGAGE

A final breakthrough in modern skiing concerns the psychological side of skiing. Some teachers, in many cases inspired by the Eastern disciplines of Zen and Tao- ist Buddhism, began to find mental techniques that led to fast learning and high performance—mental tech- niques quite as specific and effective as "body techniques" aimed at the same goals. Zen had infiltrated sports as early as the 1920s with the publication of Zen and the Art of Archery. *But the impact of Tim Gallwey's ran like* The Inner Game of Tennis *(1970) was much greater: it broke like a wave over the sports world, and was followed by Gallwey's "inner" books on skiing and golf. A dozen books on mental ap- proaches to the sport were subsequently written on ski- ing alone. The most persuasive of these was* The Cen- tered Skier *by Denise McCluggage, sometime race driver and weekly newspaper publisher. McCluggage is Taoist rather than Zen but in common with Gallwey, she focuses on the process of learning and performing rather than the bottom line result to keep tension within functional bounds; and she uses images, feelings and deep focus to achieve results both more quickly and per- manently than those achieved by verbal detailed direc- tions and exhortations. McCluggage's theories were tested and refined in cooperation with the ski school at Sugarbush, Vermont, where The Centered Skiing Work- shop is still going.*

What you see is what you get, honey!
                    —Geraldine (Flip Wilson)

THE BMW team sits in silence, eyes closed, in a semicircle around the team manager. On this sunny motel terrace the men are "driving" the Watkins Glen race course, mentally practicing their lines through the turns and their shift points. As each raises his hand to signal the completion of a lap, the team manager clicks his stop watch and notes that the times done in the head are comparable to the times done on the track.

The player at the free-throw line methodi- cally bounces the ball, draining excessive tension from his shoulders and arms. Bounce, bounce. Centering. He settles his eyes on the flat ellipse that is the entry to the basket's netting. When he sees a ball there, flowing over the rim like a leaf riding a torrent down a drainpipe, he takes the ball which he holds, scoops it low, Rick Barry style—and gently launches it on the stream to follow its image. Swoosh.

The skier closes the chairlift bar and sighs, brushing from the full length of her right side the evidence that her just-completed run was not accomplished entirely on her skis. She lets her eyes close and turns on the replay mechanism in her head. She sees herself leaving her weight shift too late into the turn and the ski tips crossing; she feels her stiffened expectation and watches the fall. Stop. Reverse. Abruptly she whisks herself backwards out of the instantly healing sitzmark, back around the turn to the point where the offending sequence began. Stop. Mark it.

As the chairlift carries her up the mountainside she shoots Turn 1, Take 2 in her head. This time, she watches the timely transfer of weight, the pole plant, her body moving minimally, her edged skis pressed into a carving arc. Okay. That's a print. And in the Moviola of her mind she splices the new footage in place and continues with her run—reshooting, recutting as she rides. At the summit, she slides off the chair with a smile appropriate for a skier with such a fine first run behind her.

The golfer on the practice tee pauses after each drive and closes her eyes. In her head she is watching an instant replay of her last shot, courtesy of the muscles that have just experienced it. They play it back for her faithfully. One section she returns to again and again, slowing it, stopping. There it is—in clear frozen-frame evidence; her shoulders are starting to unwind ahead of her hips. She nods in recognition and tees up another ball.

These are examples of how different techniques of visualization can be used in sports. The motor racing team is using *Mental Practice,* the basketball player is using what could be called *Instant Preplay,* the skier is involved in *Recut Your Movie,* and the golfer is her own video equipment in *Instant Replay.* These all work because of the interdependence of muscle movement and imagery.

There is increasingly clear evidence that imagery and muscles are inseparable. The "split-brain" studies of Robert Ornstein and others have demonstrated as much. These experiments involve the differing functions of the right and left hemispheres of the brain. It comes to this: Any movement needs an accompanying image,

however unconscious we are of the existence of the image. In short, no image, no movement.

Any thought, in word or image, has a bodily accompaniment also, however subtle. Perhaps the movement is discernible only on a sensitive, graph-tracing machine, but it is there.

You can demonstrate to yourself on a more obvious level how muscle activity accompanies thought. Think now of a tennis match. "Watch" the action from high up in the stands on a line with the net as two good players rally from the baseline. Settle your fingers lightly on your closed eyelids as you watch the ball go back and forth. Hit . . . hit . . . hit. Perhaps your fingers sense very little movement in the eye. Now transfer your vantage point down to net level where the ball boys crouch, and watch another exchange. Hit . . . hit . . . hit. See if you notice a difference.

Mental Practice

In the 1920s, the physiologist Edmund Jacobsen conducted experiments in which subjects imagined themselves doing certain actions, such as running. He found that the muscles germane to those tasks showed definite contractions, small but measurable. It was clear that the appropriate neural paths were being traversed as surely as if the person were actually doing the action.

Jacobsen's findings became the basis for a number of experiments out of which emerged the fact that *mentally practicing a motor skill can be as valuable as actual practice of the skill.* One such experiment was in Australia with basketballs. In the project three groups were randomly selected, one of which practiced free throws with an actual ball each day for twenty days. The other two groups handled the real ball only on the first and twentieth days, but one of those groups, on the intervening days, had twenty minutes of mental practice—throwing free throws in their imaginations. Come the showdown: the group with no practice had not improved; the group with actual practice and the group with mental practice showed almost the same improvement.

Nearly everyone who has tried to learn a skill

The mind has a powerful image-making capacity to control action

has some experience with the uses of mental practice. My first discovery of its value came by chance long ago when I was taking fencing lessons from Hans Halberstadt in San Francisco. One evening he was working with me on an intricate sequence with the foil involving beats, disengages, feints, parries, and counters—a veritable salad of artifice. My spirit was enthusiastic, but my hand was a stubborn puppy. I could not get it to do what it was meant to do. Hans, as was his wont when exasperated, picked up his mini-baseball bat, but even the threat of a clout could not change my doughy performance—much to my puzzlement. I was usually a quick study.

But the puzzlement proved helpful. During the week it turned my thoughts again and again to the elusive sequence, running it through my mind. Came the next session with Hans. *Salut . . .* on with the mask. *En garde.* And there it all was. Slick as soap. Perfect. And astonishing.

Looking back, I realize I had an accurate mental picture of the parts of the action all laid out like an easy-to-make plastic model. As I put the parts together slowly in my mind, over and over, my body was "moving," too. It was being programmed; a muscle memory was being created. Then, when my body was called upon to respond with actual movement, it did. The whole of the action was produced out of its mentally assembled parts.

But the whole of such an action cannot be treated as merely an aggregate of its parts. We know better than that about sums and wholes. The whole is, as well, *an expression of the relationship of the parts to each other.* The whole is somehow latent in each part—complete and entire—like a hologram. I had not learned a linear progression. I had tuned into a system.

In some teaching approaches that are aimed at the so-called "inner" skier or tennis player or golfer, improvement in the pupil is dramatic and almost mystical. ("Did *I* do that?") But some of that drama and mystery goes along with the charismatic presence of the teacher. Call it the Guru Effect. ("I can only do it when you are around.") The Centered Skiing workshops at Sugarbush do not depend on any individual's personality or on

heightened experience for their effectiveness, although the energy level does indeed run high. Rather than a mere five-day turn-on, what we hope for in the workshops is to plant a seed that will grow in the individual skier without dependence on any of us. That we have been successful has been attested to by most of our workshop skiers. Bill Berry, who wrote about the program for *Ski* magazine, told us the following season that it was the most enduring ski instruction he had ever experienced. It lasts because it stems from a process, a means of doing. *It is a path, not a destination.*

Means is the critical idea here. We speak of *ordering* processes (in the sense of establishing a sequence), not of *ordering* results (in the sense of demanding an outcome). These processes *do* lead to desirable results, but not results that are lusted after with an intensity that slurs the means. There is a fine interplay between wholes and parts that a fixation on outcome destroys; the too-desired outcome is then lost as well.

We speak, too, of wholes/parts and ends/means—relationships within systems. We do not mean wholes *and* parts or ends *and* means—separated and individual, as if the names named *things.* The names name *relationships,* just as the names of subatomic particles name relationships. (Do not count on actually meeting a quark one day, however charming you may be.) Wholes/parts and ends/means are named one way or the other depending on which of their Janus faces* is most important in the system *at the moment*—their particle nature or their holistic aspect.

In skiing, for instance, the pole plant is a whole action (one on which we spend a full two-hour session in the Sugarbush workshops). It is a part, too, of the turn initiation. And it has parts: the flexion of the wrist, the awareness of Center. The whole of which it is a part is in turn a part. Thus the system flows. The names we use— whole, part, pole plant, turn—are simply a way of commenting on specific aspects of the intercon-

---

*Arthur Koestler in *The Ghost in the Machine* also draws on the Roman god Janus to describe the two-way facing aspects of wholes/parts—which he calls "holons"—in his investigation of hierarchies.

nectedness of the action at any one moment. The risk is, as the risk always is, in *getting stuck* there. The risk is in putting on a capital letter, listing it in the index, and thinking of it as a noun, a thing, a Pole Plant, instead of going with the process—flowing with that unnameable which is named the Tao.

(If all this is more puzzling to you than enlightening, don't be concerned—it's only a small part of the whole.)

The Gap in the Film

When an action is imaged**—not just *thought about* sequentially, but actually *experienced* in the imagination—the same obstacles appear that appear in doing the action itself. If you really *image* a trip to the post office, it will take you as long to get to the mail box in your head as it would in actuality, unless, of course, you choose to work in distorted time (either condensed or stretched). In that case you can run a cross-country course of several hours' duration, for instance, in a minute; or you can stretch a fleeting action into attenuated slow motion.

If you image taking something off a shelf, and the shelf is too high, you will not be able to reach it in your image any more than you can in actuality. You can then call on fantasy to fly you to the shelf or stretch you there like Alice in Wonderland. Or you can stick with mundane possibility and image a stool to stand on.

When using imagery for learning a skill, it is important to be meticulously detailed in the picturing. Make the action continuous—as whole, as complete, as you can with as much sensory dimension as you can summon. Texture your image; hear the sounds and feel what is there to feel, taste, smell. *Be* there. Be with the whisper of the skis, the blue shadows, the cold. Hear the snow rattle on your parka; take its sting on your cheeks.

If, however, you have trouble seeing part of your action—if the film judders in the mind's

---

**There is a subtle distinction between *imagining* and *imaging*. Maybe because *imagine* is used more often in its meanings of to *ponder*, *suppose* or *think about* and less often in its meaning *to form mental pictures* its edge for visualization has been dulled. *Image* is used as a verb, then, to emphasize the sensory replication of an event or situation in the mind.

projector, rips, skips, or gets stuck, that can also be instructive. *It can point up a gap in your knowing.* The message is: your body is not completely informed (by either image or emblazoned neural path) about what it is meant to be *doing* at that particular point. To switch metaphors, it doesn't know the lyrics, so it hums.

Since the tendency is not to notice these aberrations in the film, just as you politely overlook a minor social gaffe by a friend, I ask my workshop visualizers to be particularly watchful for "missing frames"—those jumps in action in an otherwise smooth and continuous mental picturing of an action. Some important information is hiding in the miss. The missing frames are clue enough that there's a muddled message in the motor nerves—a kink in the feedback loop. There is no grooved response, just a catch-as-catch-can improvisation each time.

The frames are missing in your inner movie because your body is not clear as to what the script calls for in that sequence. It neither knows, for instance, what you *usually* do in your right turn (because you don't usually do the same thing), nor what you *should* do for a proper right turn (because you don't know). So your mental movie skips.

During a visualization exercise with a Centered Tennis group at a summer clinic, I asked both the pros and the pupils to run through their various strokes mentally. The results were instructive to all of us. "My backhand's the only stroke I can visualize all the way through," one young man said. His pro verified what I suspected: his backhand was the only stroke he made the same way twice.

The head pro came out of his reverie slowly. "I can't believe it, but that must be it," he said. In playing the movie of his serve in his head, the film kept slowing down in one place, moving frame by frame, unbidden, as if to draw his attention to something. "I could see the wrist was breaking okay, but the arm was not whipping," he said. In a tournament the weekend before he had felt his serve was off but hadn't pinned it on anything specific. "I can see and feel now that's what I've been doing lately. Actually pushing my serve." We were appropriately solemn over the vehicle of the discovery.

Some of the pros there saw their strokes as if from a camera positioned in their eyes, an entirely subjective shot. Others saw themselves as they were used to seeing themselves on videotape, an objective camera at a straight-on, medium distance. One saw his movie from a point about 20 feet over his head looking straight down on him. As you get more proficient with your built-in audio-visual equipment, you will find yourself, without conscious intent, mixing up your shots—close-ups, boom shots, tracking shots, p.o.v. instructor, the works. You may even produce otherwise impossible shots from below snow level looking up—a fish-eye curve to your skis, your boots gargantuan, and your head a tiny dot in the distant blue. Ah, yes, it can all get deliciously out of hand.

Words and Images
Knowing in words what you are "supposed" to do in a ski turn can be useful, but it is certainly not sufficient. *The weight is transferred to the uphill ski as the ski tips are eased toward the fall line, the wrist flexes to plant the pole, the body center moves laterally downhill to the inside of the turn . . .* For one thing, words can never describe all that goes on in the simplest actions, never mind something as complicated as sliding downhill—a process of directing and redirecting a quiverful of vectors so that the results are aesthetically satisfying as well as physically secure.

For another thing, words are left-brain dwellers, and movement in space is right-brain territory. "The part of you that can talk about it is not the part of you that can do it," my friend Gene Coghill, a talking/doing golf pro, has told me.

But words can be useful if you can translate them into the stuff of right-brained communication—images, feelings. Words are handy freeze-dried things to carry with you, but to use them you must add dimension, and swell them into space-filling wholes suitable for your purpose.

The body needs images, sensations, to act upon. Words couched in metaphors serve the purpose admirably. Metaphors are at once words and images on which the body can act. A metaphor is a bilinguist for the brain, as it were; it speaks to both hemispheres at once, verbal for the left and imagery for the right.

The architect who designed your turn may be able to describe it in precise terms; but if your body has no working drawings, no images, the muscles and tendons with hard hats and hammers will not know what to *do*. Give it an image; give it a metaphor.

Mental Practice for Racers
Every ski racer I have known uses visualization to a lesser or greater degree. Ski racing lends itself particularly well to mental practice because of the comparatively short times involved in even the longest downhill, and because of the relatively few variables. That is, the course is known and there are only one person's responses—your own—to deal with. There are no erratically bouncing balls, no teammates, and no immediate competitors. Dr. Richard Suinn, a Denver psychologist, has worked with ski racers, notably Olympic cross-country skiers Bill Koch and Tim Caldwell, using mental practice. He calls his technique *visual motor behavior rehearsal* (VMBR). Other psychologists also use mental practice or mental rehearsal effectively in skiing and other sports.

Visualization, and thus mental practice, is easier for some than for others. Imagery, our first language, usually fades as we grow up because of the social emphasis on words. The precociously verbal tots are probably the poobahs of the playground ("You be this, *I'll* be that") because they are most like the ultimate authority—adults—with their words, words, words.

Words become demonstrably powerful and useful in dealing with others—in overwhelming peers and in delighting adults with early evidence of socialization. Our Image Makers, in the face of this apparently superior technology, gradually fall into disuse.

Words, the noisy residents of our logical left brain, can overwhelm our quieter right-brain tenants if our consciousness is not alert. Words, so successful in dealing with the exterior world, can take over running things inside, too.

A leaf, a spiky kite, floats down to join its image on a pond. (Words inside say, "Hey, look at that leaf. Isn't that beautiful?") The moon is a gauze of ice crystal. (Words inside say, "Wow! Some moon!")

Though it is impossible to measure the grip words have on us, and appreciate their ability to obfuscate the silent dance of images, it is important to recognize their hegemony. Skiers in thrall to words, for instance, can believe themselves to be practicing mentally, or learning a race course, when they are only *thinking about it* in words. "Now here I must remember to keep a flat ski. Here I must keep my body low."

Remember, *images* are what instruct the body. Talk to yourself in words if you want to, but be sure that the words are translated into sight images, sound images, feeling images. That totality of sensation is what gets the race course into your body, bones, and brain—especially in a slalom course where you cannot practice or even shadow the course directly.

Slalom racers, walking up the edge of the course to memorize its path, should be certain that they *see* themselves whole in the gates: their skis where they want them to be, and their shoulders where *they* will be (if their skis are where they want them to be). Some skiers pick a line through the gates for their skis *only,* failing to visualize their entire body in action. They fail to take into account the room their body (leaning at high speeds) needs to clear the poles. Then, on their run, they are thrown off by having to adjust to a wider line—or else scatter bamboo like pickup sticks.

In memorizing the course, slalom racers should make sure they are seeing the gates in a pattern, not in a verbal lineup: "and after the flush comes an open hairpin," etc. They must recognize the difference between *talking or thinking about* and *seeing.* They must *image.*

Instant Preplay

Instant Preplay is a little different from Mental Practice because it happens, as the name suggests, immediately preceding the action, rather like follow-the-leader. The image does something and then you do it. The golfer watches the image ball to the cup, looks back at the palpable version and strokes it in. The weight lifter waits within his allotted time to see the lift, then instantly imitates it.

High jumper Dwight Stones is more articulate about his experience with Instant Preplay than most athletes: "I see a translucent image of myself coming out of myself. I watch to see if it will make it. Many times it doesn't. I have to concentrate harder . . . . The last time I set the record I could see two steps before I jumped that I had made it. I could see that so clearly that I even quit on it a little—almost too much."

Tim Gallwey, of *The Inner Game of Tennis* fame, whose excellent books have had major impact on the way tennis is taught and thought about, uses Instant Preplay with telling effect, although he doesn't call it that. In the serve his students "aim" at a target of a tennis ball can by visualizing the ball hitting the can. Then they allow their bodies to put their vision into effect. If they miss the can, they take note of exactly how much they missed, allow that information to be fed into their cybernetic body mechanism, and serve again, with no conscious effort to correct for their error. Within a few attempts the ball they actually serve will be following the path of the ball they visualize, and knocking over the can.

This is the essence of Instant Preplay in all its simplicity. But to say it is simple is not to say it is easy.

The problem lies in the difference between (1) *seeing* the desired result and then attending to the process that will achieve that result, and (2) *striving* for the desired result. It is the difference between attending to the *means whereby* and *end-gaining,* to use the terms of F. M. Alexander. It is the difference between *letting it happen* and *making it happen.* And we seem, sadly, to have a cultural bias toward the more effortful way.

Instant Preplay is most useful in those self-starting moments in sports—the tennis serve, the free throw, the place kick, the golf swing, the high jump, bowling. It is valuable in skiing, too.

In skiing, think of the turn as already existing in space in its powerful eloquence and simplicity. All you have to do is see it, ski into it, and put it on. See it, ski into it, and put it on, rhythmically, down the hill, shadowing with your flesh-and-blood body the vision that precedes it. (It's a game to play with space and time. But then, it all is.)

Again, putting on an existing ski turn which you *see* ahead of you is simple, but not always easy. The seeing will come and go. Suddenly it is there; grasp at it and it is gone. Even acknowledging its presence can dissipate it. Don't despair. Give it space to be there and it will be there. *Wanting* to see the turn can lead you to *imagining* that you see the turn, but that is not the same. You'll realize the difference when you actually *see* the turn.

Let go. Images are elusive and fragile and shatter from direct left-brained demands. Look soft, and you will see your turn. Then ski into it and put it on.

Recut Your Movie

The film you recut can be a very old "movie" from childhood when you *always* struck out, *never* caught the ball, or it can be as recent as our chairlift rider correcting her first run of the day—immediately after the fact.

You can go back to those moments in your memory and reexperience the emotions that accompany the pictures. Enjoy them; suffer them. You know that. You do that. But do you know that you can also *change* those moments? You can go back along that corridor and close some doors left ajar or held ajar, and reclaim the energy now kept there as the doorstop.

How can that be? To accept the possibility of reediting something as sacrosanct as Truth—"I mean all that is the way it actually *happened*"—is not easy for most of us. As a journalist I have an investment in the notion that there is a "really" which can be uncovered and reported. Facts, after all, are facts, and opinions about facts cannot change them. It's a belief system in which I function as a good reporter.

But there is, too, "a Rashomon effect" in which facts *are* as they are *remembered*, and how they are remembered depends on the rememberer's point of view—the matrix through which

he perceived it at the time and the one that now filters his recall. Consider, if you've the stomach for it, all the versions of Watergate that we have had, and all that are yet to come. "Memory," Julian Jaynes says, "is the medium of the must-have-been."*

The past, then, is not *what* is remembered, but is *memory itself.* The past exists, not "back there" somewhere, but in the reconstructing and reordering in people's minds *now.*

As John O. Stevens puts it: "It is really difficult to bring home the realization that everything exists in the momentary now. The past exists only as parts of present reality—things and memories *I think about* as being 'from the past.' The idea of the past is sometimes useful, but at the same time it is an idea, a *fantasy* that I hold *now.* Consider the following problem: 'Prove to me that the world was not created two seconds ago, complete with artifacts and memories.' "**

Well . . . I just *know* it *wasn't.* . . .

See, it's difficult. But the nice thing about it all is that you can if you want—like the more linear-minded in the skiing workshops—agree to act *as if* there is nothing but the *now,* and as if the past can be edited. We are, after all, not out to change recorded history, airbrushing from archival photographs the likenesses of those no longer in favor; we are just ridding ourselves of some emotional residue that clouds our view of the way we, personally, live now.

In recutting your movie, even if you cannot change what "happened," whatever that is, you can change your *feeling* about what happened. Whatever happened, happened *then;* whatever we feel about it, is happening *now.* And the *feeling* is what is important in collecting the energy you've invested in a memory.

Recutting your movie of a distant afternoon may not, then, change the "fact" that you slipped rounding second base and got thrown out at third, rather than scoring the winning run as

*Julian Jaynes, *The Origin of Consciousness in the Breakdown of the Bicameral Mind.*
**John O. Stevens, *Awareness: Exploring, Experimenting, Experiencing.*

your recut version has it; but it will change your feeling of klutzy failure that you carry with you over that incident, a feeling that colors your present. ("I have a record of failing in the clutch." "I've always been clumsy.")

Memory erasing is the term Ruth Carter Stapleton uses for her version of movie recutting in her book *Gift of Inner Healing.* "Imagination is so powerful it can really implant the experience in you," she says.

It can. It does. In so doing it exorcises those demons of failure, turns off the power of the programming words like *always* and *never,* and allows you to reclaim energy, fragmented of old, for present use.

In a workshop called "The Tao of Sports" that I conducted one summer, the group went into their memories to recut some childhood movies. Stretched out on the floor, they relaxed the tensions in their bodies, attended to an easy breathing, and settled into a receptive state. I asked them all to reach into their memories for an incident in their childhood in some sport or game in which they had failed miserably—come in last, missed a gate, fallen, struck out, let down the team, disgraced their school, dishonored their family, etc. (The intense pressures of competition on children in our society and the natural hyperbole of childhood do not make these terms appear extreme.)

I asked the group to play their movie through slowly, experiencing it all, feeling again whatever they felt at the time—usually a string of "dis-es": disappointment, dismay, disgrace, disgust, dislike . . . dismal. Then I asked them to replay their movie, only this time cutting in new footage in which they changed disaster to triumph. In this footage they make the catch, hit the ball, win the race. I asked them to feel the feelings that go with that—reveling in the success and approbation, and bring it all back with them.

There was some good energy reclaimed, and some surprises for a few. One young woman said she had always hated softball, was always chosen last, was always relegated to the least active field, and was always expected to drop every ball that came her way, anyhow, and usually did. In her reverie, she went back and replayed a game; and this time she caught every fly, deftly fielded hard grounders, threw clotheslines to the right bases, and was cheered and made to feel part of the team.

On this revisiting, too, she noticed how much fun the others were having, fun she now felt capable of sharing. "It looks like a pretty good game after all," she said. "I think I'll give it another chance."

Instant Replay

The visualization technique I call *Instant Replay* can be like having your own video equipment with you. You do something; stop; ask your inner playback mechanism what did I do and it shows you. Sometimes it shows you directly, as if copied by the latest Sony equipment; and sometimes it shows you symbolically. And *that* can be fun.

I had just returned to Vermont from Big Sur in California where I had attended an Esalen workshop called "Energy Awareness" led by Bob Nadeau, the *aikido sensei.* As usual, working with Bob had pushed open not only doors, but walls, and repatterned some of my bland, blind ways of being. For one thing my Image Maker went delightfully berserk, rather like the broom in *The Sorcerer's Apprentice.* It was nearly unstoppable and I was awash in unbidden images, some as fleeting and acceptably unreal as those in the hypnagogic world we inhabit just short of sleep. Some were simply vivid everyday pictures.

I was used to "seeing" words, often as the word itself in print (Helvetica type, quite black on shiny paper) and sometimes in cliché picture images. But now I was seeing startling pictures called up by the words—outrageous puns and nonsense images. It was like having my own personal B. Kliban drawing in my head. (He's the one responsible, if that's the word, for such mania in book form as *Cat, Don't Eat Anything Larger than Your Head,* and *Whack Your Porcupine.*)

There were memory images loosed, too. My mind was a film editor's bin with strips of unrelated footage hanging from the pins. Every so often I was treated to a quick segment of an Antonioni or Altman movie, a little Kubrick, Buñuel, Bergman, of course, and even Maya Deren! There were paintings by Magritte, Chagall, Rousseau. Klee drawings. Twyla Tharp floated by. A slam-dunk by Dr. J. and a quick forty-eight frames of a section of the Nürburgring race course called the Fox Röhe. It was a right-hemisphere garage sale and I thoroughly enjoyed it.

I was also at the peak of discovering the value of my Instant Replay images. And in the midst of this, golf pro John Callahan and I put together a workshop in Centered Golf at the Sugarbush course. I am not a golfer, although I have a moderately good swing—probably because it has never been under the pressure of scoring. John and I worked at the practice tee to check out the validity of my Instant Replay. I would hit a ball, "replay" it, describe what I saw—what flaws were revealed—and he would check me on the accuracy of my picture.

As it turned out there were several different ways that the inner messages were revealed in Instant Replay. One time I had a close-up, stop-frame picture of my wrists midway through the downswing. They were uncocking, straightening. I said to John, "I see I'm dissipating my power by snapping my wrists too early." He nodded. I played the mental tape through again, this time watching to see whether my wrists stayed properly cocked. When they did, I made another swing.

That was typical of one way I got the message: direct and straightforward. Sometimes that way was in close-up as it was with the wrists. Most often it was a straight-on view, as if seen by John. Sometimes, when appropriate, the view was directly overhead. I did not consciously specify the format, I just closed my eyes and took what I got.

Other messages were sent more symbolically. After one swing I saw in my interior Instant Replay an image of my legs, particularly my left leg from the knee down, as a wood carving. That was it: a still picture of a rather nice carved leg (not in the least bit bowed). The grain in the calf was lovely, like contour lines on a map, and the

whole thing was finished in a soft matte glow. I admired it. The message was clear, too. "My legs are dead," I said. John nodded, increasingly intrigued by this replay mechanism I had plugged into.

The wooden leg image directed my awareness to the excessive tension just above my knee. I had blocked the flow of *ch'i*. I worked on breaking that energy dam: Centering, attending to the wholeness of my breathing, and letting go the tension in my legs. Immediately I felt a downward rush of warmth through my lower legs, down through the cotton soles of my *kung fu* shoes (I said I was not a golfer) to deep in the ground. I was newly aware of the ground's texture and temperature. I was now grounded.

On the next shot my legs felt alive. The difference was astonishing. I could sense my left heel trigger the whole unwinding of the swing, the lower legs leading the way to a solid *whonk* of the ball. That was one fine feeling. I began to understand the appeal of the game.

So that was yet another sort of image. My Instant Replay equipment provided an obvious symbol—dead wooden leg in place of an alive flesh-and-blood energy conduit.

But the topper was yet to come. I worked my way through the bucket of balls, hitting, instantly replaying, correcting. I was getting a little cocky now. Then I hit such a hit! It had to be the largest single collection of everything that can be wrong with a golf shot. It was up and down and pushed and forced and the ball zipped off sideways into the parking lot. I went to my Instant Replay. Image Maker, what do you make of *that!*

The Image Maker was up to it. There greeting my mind's eye was a bright green plastic twenty-gallon trash can full to the gunnels with garbage! Grapefruit rinds (pink and squeezed into half moons). Melon remains. Eggshells. Coffee grounds . . . Garbage. I laughed out loud. "John, you won't believe this!" He could not deny it was a singularly succinct description of the shot he had just witnessed.

What to do about it? Back to the Image Maker, and instantly—thinkable but unthought of, quite on its own volition—there appeared in all its massive, bristly pink splendor a *pig*, scarfing up the garbage. What better way to get rid of it. My reasoning left brain, given time, might have come up with the same solution, but this was a completely spontaneous message from the Image Maker.

It was perfect because there was nothing salvageable in that swing, nothing to "correct." The best way to keep its ghost from haunting future swings was to get rid of it entirely. I had. The next shot was probably the best I hit all day—any day. Clean as a pig's whistle, you might say.

Ask Your Energy

The Centered Skiing workshop instructors thought I had really slipped over the edge this time. It was a preseason session and I had something to share with them. John looks at me with his mouth slightly agape. Martin's head is cocked to one side. Peter has that look that says we must be having language difficulties. And Bucky, who had rented my studio to live in the season before, seems to have decided that he had been right all along: the landlady is dingy. Still, they are going along with it.*

I ask them to "settle" into their energy body and take hold of the chair they were standing behind as if to lift it. "Set-t-tle, set-t-tle." I could hear Bob Nadeau's soothing sibilance suggest the same thing in my memory of the workshop with him. At Esalen, in the hall called Huxley, we all held one of the ubiquitous giant cushions which are the furniture of that realm and, settling into ourselves, had "asked our energy" how to lift them. And most of us had after a time been rewarded by mental images which directed our bodies to the least effortful way to complete the task; i.e., lift the cushions. What came were symbols of easy lifting that were messages both from and to our bodies—images which are always there, like television signals in the air, but unnoticed unless we tune in to them.

*The instructors whose bare first names, like the names of saints (which they are in their way) are scattered throughout this chapter, have last names too. They are: Peter Forsthuber, Bucky Makowski, Martin Marnett, John Nyhan.

Bob's workshop involved practice in tuning into the myriad of images, full of information and direction, which surround us and to which we are usually oblivious. The "off" button is perennially pushed.

In the Wunderbar at Sugarbush, where we hold the morning sessions of the Centered Skiing workshops, there are sturdy captain's chairs, not cushions, so I ask the four instructors to each stand behind a chair ready to lift it, and set-t-tle into his energy, into his Center, and notice any image that comes to him.

Don't look for an image, don't either expect one or not expect one. Don't *do* anything; just *be* there. Images are shy, reticent. They are dubious, now, after years of being ignored in favor of the talkative left side of the brain, which quickly pipes up with: "Flex your knees. Lift with the large muscles of the leg. Protect your back from strain."

Set-t-tle.

Breathe into your Center. When the image comes, you will notice it more in the having-been-there. Trust it. Let it sidle into your ken without having to bear the brunt of your full attention. A stray dog will ease to your quiet hand and shy away from the slapped thigh and the "Here, boy!"

Nothing.

The looks.

The four instructors are standing, slowly lifting the chairs and setting them down, lifting and down. Then the expectancy and the watchfulness start to shift subtly to simple receptivity. They are waiting now, just waiting the way mountains wait.

Martin's face lights up. "CO_2 cartridges!" he says. He is pleased. "There was suddenly a CO_2 cartridge in each leg of the chair. When I lifted, pow! They fired!" And when they fired the chair was easier to lift; it rose with less muscling, less effort.

Now the images are more readily noticed. We are all visited by them and offer them for discussion: forklifts, derricks, helium balloons, hydraulic jacks. All spontaneous images to help in the given task, here, now, of lifting a chair. And the lifting *is* easier. Everyone agrees to that, even in the regular workshop sessions later in the season: if you have an image, the task is easier. The pooh-poohers wave it off. Ah, that's just your imagination.

Precisely!

In search of an explanation one might suggest that the image of assistance has allowed us to cut back on the excess of effort we usually assemble when faced with a task. Since we have "outside" help, we have cut our own input back to bare necessity. Lifting the chair *seems* less effortful because it *is* less effortful; we have put less effort into it. We have differentiated out the superfluous and the redundant muscularity, accepting in its stead the generous aid of imaged forklifts, and CO_2 cartridges.

We can experience a similar feeling of ease in action when arising from a chair, for instance, if we image a large balloon attached to our heads lifting us up. Give your body an image to act on and allow your body freedom to act on it, and you will be more economical in your moving.

However, there is an important difference between a consciously created image and an image that appears spontaneously when we settle into our Center and "ask our energy."

What is the difference? I think it is that the conscious image is a message *to* our bodies, whereas the spontaneous image is a message both *from* and *to* our bodies. It is a more knowing image, a more complete metaphor. With the conscious image we impose on our bodies an order from central headquarters, the brain. With the spontaneous image we incorporate into it feedback from the distant outposts of the nervous system as well. The spontaneous image knows what's going on in the hinterlands.

I think you'll be happier with an example.

I noticed in the workshops that the lifting images that were reported were always particularly appropriate for that person's body and body condition. One man, whose image was of a weight lifter doing curls, had powerful biceps and forearms and could easily raise the chair by curling it. A young woman, slightly built, had been struggling to lift her chair with bent arms and upper body tension. She reported no image;

no, no image yet. Suddenly she relaxed and the chair seemed just to swell off the floor. She looked astonished. "What was your image?" I asked her. "Nothing, really," she said. "Well, wait a minute. There was this balloon thing under the chair . . . ." She had exhaled to fill it, her body had eased, and the chair was lifted.

There was one skeptic, proudfully logical, who believed well enough that you could *image* an image, but to have one appear unplanned for? Nevertheless, he agreed to make room for it. He, too, suddenly changed the way he was lifting. He had been tentatively moving the chair about, but now his knees bent and straightened with his upper body perfectly erect, and the chair rose authoritatively. "A large worm gear right under the seat," he said sheepishly. I suggested that the straight up-and-downness of his image might be telling him that there was a potential weakness in his lower back. He shot me a look. "I do have a bad lower back."

Thus, workshop after workshop, I became increasingly convinced that a spontaneous image—being in touch with your entire body—can not only bring a possible trouble spot to your awareness, but it can also direct you around it to the completion of your task. It's a built-in how-to-do-it-better guide with a self-protection feature. It's a handy gadget to have.

Indeed, I used mine again a few minutes ago. Having decided to avoid finishing this chapter by pruning the apple tree, I managed to get myself, literally, out on a limb. The excitement of the chase had worked me out too far, and getting back wasn't going to be easy. The terrain dropped away rather sharply below. Getting down, I realized, was not going to be as simple as it would have been a quarter century earlier. There is that way of placing your hands beside you on the limb, pivoting and swinging down to drop to the ground. But, that would mean going from a bent arm to a straight arm rather abruptly, and my right elbow had been paining me for months (an excess of improper use having caught up to me).

So. "Ask your energy."

There were several rapid images all telling me to keep my elbow straight throughout. In one version, my arm was in a heavy cardboard tube, like a mailer. In another it was baked in a crust like a Beef Wellington. But the operative image was one of those hanging wooden monkeys that Danish furniture stores import by the windowful: straight arm, cupped hand, and articulated shoulder. Monkeys know more about trees than anyone. I acted on it; leaning far out to a limb opposite, hooking my (wooden) hands over it (with unopposed thumb, I noticed) I swung down on my straight arms. I felt not the slightest elbow twinge. And here I am, back at the typewriter, smug as hell.

The capacity to visualize is in all of us—recapturable by practice, if you refuse to let words and linearity limit your gallery. *Seeing with the Mind's Eye* by Mike Samuels and Nancy Samuels, and Robert H. McKim's *Experiences in Visual Thinking* are good places to begin widening your internal vision. So is *Put Your Mother on the Ceiling* by Richard de Mille.

But look, all I want to do is stop stemming on my right turn!

Believe me, it helps to open yourself to images. See red Frisbees, glockenspiels and gold velvet chairs, Popsicles, winged horses and needle-nosed pliers, striped spinnakers, winged serpents, thick-pile carpets, and toasted marshmallows. See things—real things, fanciful things; even a right turn without a stem. There are continuous showings in the magic theater of the mind. And there's *always* a cartoon.

PART VI

RACER'S EDGE

"Rudd subconsciously knew he was overshooting the bump, and the automatic reflexes that a downhiller develops started to function. Again he stood up on his skis, making a windcheck of his body to slow him down. But he remained airborne, hit the top of the next bump and, like a stone skipped across a trout pool, was scaled higher into the air, over the hill, straight over the flat, twenty-five feet over the ground. His speed still produced the whistling swish as he hurtled through the air. He was no longer a ski racer in control of the mountain, he was a projectile."

Peter Miller, *The 30,000 Mile Ski Race*

One-Minute Warning

by **BETTY BELL**

The skiing equivalent of diving's "rapture of the depths" is "rapture of the starting line," when everything is heightened and everything is possible, especially winning.

CAREFULLY I edge forward into position, try not to disturb my wax, stop with the toes of my boots just behind the electronic start. The tips of my skis hang over the edge of this phone-booth world, and the rest lie in the shallow grooves worked and worried into the hard-packed snow by those who have gone before. I arch forward and lean on my extended poles. There is nothing that interests me above my elbows, which frame the run that lies below.

I shall be here one minute—a world of time ticking away in slow motion. I move my skis back and forth; there is an ever-so-slight reluctance on their part to slide, to break, but I think the wax is right for farther down the course where I shall need it. The snow squeaks in the January cold, and the sun in the pale sky offers little warmth.

I take a great interest in my breath—studied and forced. I suck the air into my chest and expel it in visible, audible bursts, my lips held as though to blow smoke rings, the sound a repetitious *whoo, whoo, whoo* which would embarrass me under any other circumstances.

I study my boots and their mating with their toe pieces. There is no trace of snow on them. It has not snowed here in weeks, and the single buckle on each boot gleams store-shiny on the clean black. I raise my toes and feel the impulse to rise travel along the fronts of my skis. We are wedded, my skis and I.

I flex my ankles against the holding pressure of my boots, feel the minute difference in snugness, and put down the impulse for further adjustment.

Behind me, I hear the thirty-second warning. A splurge of adrenaline explodes in my body, courses everywhere—my groin, fingertips, toes, even my ears feel the fleeting warmth—and I am calm in its wake. Confident. Strong. Super-honed.

I feel everything: my kneecaps against the snug pull of my pants; my ribs against the skin-like top; the extra pressure of the number which stretches across my chest and back and ties beneath my arms; the straps of my poles pulling down at the bases of my thumbs and wrists; each finger within my gloves secure around the grips.

My mind starts down the course. I see myself as though I am a spectator . . . the initial thrust with my poles . . . the quick skate . . . the folding into a tuck down this first, steeply falling-away traverse.

Starting gun frees skier to dance his way down the flagged course

A hand falls on my right shoulder, and I am given the fifteen-second warning. The hand infringes on my mind's run, and there is a resulting flash of resentment; then I am back on my line, back on the 6-inch width my mind has drawn down this mountain. My body must do as my will directs: enter the first blind turn exactly abreast of the snag pine at the right edge of the course; come through the second gate in the meadows above the trough; swallow the camel's back with my legs at the base of the little roll 10 yards before its apex.

The ten-second warning has gone by and now I am part of the five-second countdown, my body picking up its rhythm—*four*—a slight sway forward with each intonation—*three*—a building momentum—*two*—timed to explode with—*one*—the signal that shall let me—GO!

The Oldest Continuous Floating Ski Racer of Them All

by **BURTON HERSH**

Old ski racers never die, they go on living their victories over and over in bars and other off-slope arenas. Here Burton Hersh, biographer of Teddy Kennedy and the Mellon family, and a devoted skier, tells of Chris Pravda as the erstwhile idol of millions finds old age shading him at the finish line.

FOR an enterprising group of people whose only business is, by reputation, business, Americans seem to share a horror of watching almost anything begin to turn out-and-out professional. We extracted poor Jim Thorpe's hard-earned medals from him. We hated it when the golfers set up money tournaments. We fought pro tennis. So when a crowd of the world's really top-notch skiers started up a professional ski racing circuit a few years back, the surprise was that it survived—even fitfully.

One person for whom the off-again, on-again pro tour was a really congenial way of life, and who misses it sorely, is Christian Pravda.

Pravda was one of the masters. By 1954, at the midpoint of a decade of Alpine racing presided over almost exclusively by an oligarchy of Austrians, Pravda was world downhill champion. He won the Austrian—i.e., the European—national championship nine times. When that bored him, he came to the United States and over-

whelmed whatever talent was available. Then Pravda retired to the eminence of a Sun Valley instructorship—semi-retired, really. In 1959, when he was thirty-two, he won the Harriman Cup for the third time and took it home with him.

All of which may suggest why, when professional racing started, Pravda was along, too. More than along: in 1960–61 he snapped up over $1,200 in prize money and became the man all the others intended to plow under. By early 1962, the second time around, it was clear that the plow was catching up with him: he had slipped noticeably from a regular winner to an infrequent one.

As his luck soured, weekend after weekend, he became obsessed with detail. I remember a Saturday race that year in upper New York State; I found him wandering through the basement of the main lodge, wholly given over to what seemed to be a central fixation: filing sharper the steel edges of the skis that he races on. He was going at it in the rigorously controlled frenzy of a man sharpening his soon-to-be-needed bayonet. A wiry and increasingly balding troll in indifferently puckered stretch pants, he stood humped almost angrily over the bottoms of his skis on a workbench. At each stroke of the file, he half shuddered. He was as nervous as a lynx on Benzedrine.

242

Methodically he began to lay wax on in streaks. For an out-of-doors-career-man, Pravda sported an astonishingly sophisticated face: beneath what was left of the hairline all the rest was umber pouches, cut by two tiny triangular brown eyes that almost met at the wrap-around nose and the smile twisting downwards at the corners. Out of a private rucksack of jumbled equipment, Pravda jerked free a 2-inch-long electric flat-iron, plugged it in and began to iron the wax smooth to the bottoms.

Anderl Molterer, fellow professional, strolled up listlessly. Molterer—at the time perhaps the world's finest all-around skier—ran an indifferent hand over his canary-white forelock, yawned and sat down. Obviously he didn't understand why *der Pravda* was so incurably intense about these matters. He gazed down sleepily for a moment longer and sauntered away.

Some American skiers entered. Collectively taller, offhandedly heckling each other with the kind of joyless wisecracks Americans favor, they swept over to the other side of the ski shop. Bindings clattered. Christian Pravda paused and looked up, and then stared coldly. He returned to buffing wax with a cork block: a moment later, for no practical reason that anyone could imagine, he returned to sharpening his edges.

Pravda got a beer upstairs. He continued working. He is an incessant gum-chewer and chainsmoker, sometimes both at once, and his pupils shuttle incessantly. Hovering at a permanent age of forty, he has been racing since 1943.

A reporter came up. Pravda nodded through a low-key questioning. Yes, the Olympic medals . . . and the Austrian, and the North American . . . He confessed to a great racing career . . . well behind him. Twirling the grips of a new pair of poles somebody had just given him, he suddenly began to explain why he hadn't been winning: "Because, you see, I was out too long teaching all zose years at Zun Falley." Pravda's eyes snapped into focus.

"So for me it's much harder to race. And too damn much traveling. Espechially after Aspen. You don't know that? That I race in the schampionships this year mit 101 fever? Fantastic, I don't even see the gates as I am running through

them. Still, I ski all right again, but . . . I don't know, maybe my reflexes are going or zumzing. The last two races I missed gates too, you know. Chust missed them, chust didn't see them.

"Still," Pravda insisted grimly, "it's fun." He finished his beer and ignited another cigarette. "You see, the kits, they want to take the chances. I'm too old for that. I rather figure it out always to be in the money." Pravda plumed smoke. "I wish I would be five years younger. I could take these kits easy."

Pravda first came to the United States in 1950 from the resortiest of the Austrian resorts, elegant Kitzbühel, where The Duke had romanced Wally Simpson not too many years earlier. And there were those glamour-charged days at Sun Valley, when eastern seaboard debutantes competed for the waitress slots in Harriman's cafeterias, and the livin' was uncommonly easy. Secretaries to vacationing highnesses, the ladies were primed for the twelve-point buck of all après-ski performances: the European professionals. American women appreciated Christian whole-heartedly.

During the 1960–61 season, while awaiting a race at the clubby Sugarbowl resort out in California, Pravda disappeared. There was a general canvass of the area, and in the end Christian was found in the bar, one hand around the waist of his romantic interest that weekend and the other pushing aside the remains of a double whiskey sour. Pravda's friends steered him in the direction of the slope. Racing, he came down within perhaps one-tenth of a second of the winner.

Inspired performances like this became increasingly rare. After a season or so, it was evident that Pravda would be lucky to hold third position at best. "NOW ON THE HILL," the announcer would say, tossing out a tidbit of characterization on each skier for the crowd, "WE HAVE THE GENTLEMAN OFTEN REFERRED TO AS THE GRAND OLD MAN OF SKIING, THE WORLD FAMOUS CHRISTIAN PRAVDA." The grand old man certainly looked it as he pumped across the finish line: wheezing, eyes watering uncontrollably into a puffy red face.

Pravda's 1950 slalom style has typical "reverse shoulder" position

It became routine to overhear Pravda's explanation as to why he hadn't won that afternoon: his bindings had not been set right, the slalom poles had been much too close, the course wasn't steep enough, the heavier men had definite advantages when the surface was that icy, and he was racing at one hundred and forty-five pounds, fifteen below his normal weight. The other Austrian racers began to work him over in quick little jabs of insidious Tyrolese. Clearly, they were getting to him.

"I didn't go so good, huh?" Pravda decided, but without meeting anyone's gaze. "I chust took it too easy. But I mean, how close can you get, one-tenth of a second. I don't know . . ." He began to grind the faces of a pair of coins together in his fingers. "You know, a lot of the

times lately it's like . . . I don't know, like I don't care anymore, like I don't want to win really zumtimes. Like it is in a dream." He looked a little embarrassed. "For me it's better to play golf," Christian said, finally.

"Are you much of a golfer?"

"I play golf a lot, especially since the last couple of years," Pravda said. "All summer, that's why I stay in Aspen, because I love so much to play golf. And to visit my little boy." Pravda suddenly had to look away and pluck hard on his long curl of nose, and devote himself to drinking coffee. He had been married to a girl from an excellent Houston family, and the marriage had been brief and very turbulent. Almost all of the other Austrians put their earnings into *pensions* in the Vorarlberg. Christian spent his. In

Pravda's life there simply wasn't any old country to go back to.

As a promising schoolboy athlete during the late Thirties, Pravda had been selected by the government for special training in the *Heiot* camps of the mountains. The camp regimen was brutal; each of the trainers was equipped with an air rifle high powered enough to drive pellets so deep into the hindquarters of any slacker than a surgeon was often required to extract them. The camps were unparalleled for conditioning. A wild boy and something of a troublemaker, alternating moodiness with flashes of vehemence, Pravda showed the temperament of a competitor. With Toni Speiss, Christian evolved the "reverse shoulder," a technique dependent on the fact that a racer can run with his knees slung hard into a hill while his chest is cocked away, and then abruptly reverse this position around a pole. The torque/counter-torque effect of this reversal turns the skier twice as fast and with half as much effort as the older "rotation" ever could. The high-speed refinement of this maneuver, known as wedeln or wag, involved an up-and-down bobbing that would make swerving still easier. The whole technique succeeded as only true success can: the Austrians who perfected it came to dominate international racing. By the mid-fifties just about everybody who could ski was back in ski school to be "converted," and worldwide ski instruction became, for the time, an Austrian cartel.

After that things became deceptively simple. Those vast, warmed, glassed-in swimming pools at Sun Valley could probably have been depended on to rust the iron out of anybody's backbone. Still, there is one recorded instance of Pravda's endeavoring to get back to the *Heiot* values. For reasons nobody has since been able to get quite straight, Christian accepted the position of head of the ski school on an obscure Canadian mountain. It was a cold and blustery winter on the fringes of the Arctic circle that year, and Pravda's mountain remained deserted. Every day at ten and two, Pravda donned his ski school parka and tramped out to the meeting place: nobody else did. The season passed extremely slowly. People refer to that time, half in admiration and half in amusement, as "Christian Pravda's winter in exile." As it happened, it was not his last: in 1966, Pravda forsook Sun Valley for the comparative obscurity of the Sun Bowl at Flagstaff, Arizona. This season he is at the Park City Resort in Park City, Utah.

Pravda raced one last round on the pro circuit. In the 1966 season he pulled out a third in an important race. Then the pro circuit died again, and he went back to Sun Valley to coach a new generation of youngsters who seemed born to bedevil him.

One telling anecdote survives. Sitting around an empty midmorning cafeteria with Christian, one of his momentary blond camp followers noticed how nerved up the racer seemed. Without speaking, she pulled out a vial of black and chartreuse capsules from her purse and rolled it across the table. He knitted his eyebrows at it.

"Why don't you take one, Christian?" she said. "Librium. A mild tranquilizer. It'll just take the nervous edge off. Most of the others use them. Go ahead."

"I don't need nothing like that," Pravda almost barked. "Look, see. My hands." He extended his weathered and wrinkling fingers, knuckles up. "See, look, very calm, not even shaking or nothing. See? Feel my pulse, go on, feel it . . ."

"Christian, I certainly didn't mean to imply—"

"—because, like I said, I been racing twenty years anyhow. You think I need a . . . a medicine or something so I can ski? With little kits like these? You just watch. Today I take the chiant slalom. Because it's a long enough race so that more than chust go-go-go is a part of it."

Indignation steeped within him; hardly an hour afterwards, he poured himself through the first run of the afternoon and won it.

It left him calmed. "You know, if you do really good, really fantastic, chust one time, it can give you lots of confidence," he told the well-wishers who surrounded him. "Once it goes like it ought to, then you know you can win it anozer time."

He Went Straight In

by NICHOLAS HOWE

Out of the past, the specter of Dick Buek haunts the ski runs of the world. On their best day, most world champions could never have touched Buek down Exhibition. His personality, a wonderful, whacky wild legend, lives on. Nicholas Howe knew him when.

PARTWAY down the Cold Springs run at Sun Valley, the roof of a small house stuck up through the snow. It was early in the season, and the crowds on Baldy were still so small that only the center of the run was skied out. The first time I came up the Cold Springs chairlift, I saw the roof and figured this was probably a pumphouse. The snow had already buried it to the eaves.

The second time I came up the lift, I saw that someone had traversed over to the little house and written a short message on the snow-covered roof: O.K. BUEK.

The third time up, I saw a single straight track coming all the way down the run. The track ran into the unbroken snow, aiming straight at the house. Clean as an arrow the track went up the short, steep ramp of the roof. It cut the words in two and ended at the ridge pole. A long way down below, the snow showed the impact of a heavy landing, and the track continued straight on down the run. Dick Buek had seen that short message in the snow.

I had been at Sun Valley only a few weeks, that December of 1952. Previously I had spent five years in a classy prep school in Massachusetts, hating every minute of it. All through prep school, I worked for Joe Dodge in the AMC hut system. Joe's daughter Ann was the perennial crew boss at the headquarters in Pinkham Notch, and his son Brookie seemed to be the gravitational center of most of what went on in the rest of the system. Both were about five years older than I, close enough to be friends, distant enough to be heroes. Both were great skiers— world-class skiers.

I was not a great skier. During those years, I was heading with disconcerting rapidity toward my eventual height of 6 feet 5 inches, a process that does not lend itself to athletic greatness. Nevertheless, I skittered down the icy foothills of the Berkshires during the winter term at school, and during the Christmas and spring vacations and whatever weekends I could squeeze out of the complex prep-school parietal rules, I would head north and fling my ungainly adolescent bones down the old Wildcat trail or the fearsome precipice of Tuckerman's Ravine.

In the endless study halls at school, my despised classmates would pass notes describing

246

their triumphs during the Christmas season in Westchester County or the spring vacation in Bermuda. I hid ski magazines behind my textbooks and studied the race results. I treasured the idea that no one in the Westchester crowd even suspected that I knew most of the Eastern Class A racers who appeared in those listings—much less that I had met them through my famous friends Ann and Brookie Dodge, up on the freezing Wildcat trail in December, or in the glorious spring sunshine sitting on Lunch Rocks in Tuckerman.

As those prep school years dragged on, the A racers moved into the ranks of the FIS and Olympic teams, which included such solid New England names as George Macomber, Malcolm McLane, Ralph Miller, Bill Beck, Gale Shaw, Dave Lawrence, and Brooks Dodge. But they were joined in the magazine articles by new names from the Rockies and the Sierra.

I pored over the pictures of these western skiers. Here, indeed, was a new world to ponder. They didn't even sound like the kind of people we had in the East: Jack Reddish, Pinkie Robinson, Yves Latreille, Yvon Tache, Katy Rodolph, Jannette Burr, and—standing at the end of a women's team picture—the stunning Brynhild Grasmoen.

From time to time, a name would appear in a downhill race, a name I never recalled seeing in any position but first place in those western circuits. In the accompanying article, the writer always made a point that in this race, Dick Buek had *not* crashed.

In the spring of my last year of prep school, I decided, almost without realizing it, that I would not go to college the next year. I'd go out West to ski.

Sun Valley in the winter of 1953 was flood tide in the good life for ski bums. I got a job, but it was not really clear to me what the job was *for*. There were employees everywhere, hundreds and hundreds of them, all working for the Union Pacific Railroad even though no trains came near the place. There were lifts reserved exclusively for the use of employees. There were dining halls and chalets for employees. There were em-

ployees whose only job was to be convivial in the bars at night. There were employees whose only function was to serve other employees—wait on them at meals and change the linen in their rooms. There were fresh flowers and insurance and railroad retirement benefits for employees. There were large paychecks and lift tickets for everyone in this dreamland of carefully antiqued Alpine architecture and Hollywood movie stars, and suddenly I realized what it was—a three-dimensional travel poster, a place whose main reason for existence was to enable the Union Pacific to say that it existed. It was the world's most sumptuous write-off. In the world of the tax loss, overhead is king, and we were the overhead.

The first thing a newly hired employee had to do was take a physical for the railroad—hardly more than a finger-prick blood test. I was waiting outside the doctor's office with two lovely girls. They looked vaguely familiar, but I thought that was because in a place where you don't know anyone, almost everybody looks vaguely familiar. They included me easily in their conversation, and the taller of the two reached over and smoothed a flap on my parka where my mother—years of private-school reflexes behind her—had sewn a name tape. "Oh, Nicholas Howe," said this stunning apparition. "Hi, I'm Brynhild Grasmoen, and this is Katy Rodolph." I lost my breath for a minute.

In those years, there was no World Cup competition, and with the Olympics and FIS World Championships on a four-year cycle, there was an off-year between each international meet. In 1953 the big American resorts vied to employ the medalists and team members from the Olympics of the previous year. Sun Valley had won a resounding victory at this competition, and as the season opened I realized that I had stumbled into the pages of last year's *Ski Annual*.

In the next few weeks, Brynhild effortlessly moved me through the gathering of her friends. It was nothing less than an Olympic pantheon. Almost everyone I had ever heard of was there. I half expected them to come to breakfast in chariots, or at least to call down thunderclaps at will, but they were just skiers after all. On his first day after getting to Sun Valley, Stein Eriksen rode up the top lift on Baldy a few chairs ahead of me. He skated away from the lift, and fell on his first turn. But a consummately graceful fall.

In those first days, a thread ran through conversations all over the Valley, as if trying to pull anticipation into being. On lift lines and lunch lines, in ski shops and saloons, everywhere people turned to each other and asked, "Is Buek here yet?"

Then one day there were those tracks on Cold Springs. That evening at supper, I heard someone say, "I was sure Buek would do it." Sitting across the table, another person said, "Yeah, he always does."

Brynhild was working up at the restaurant on Baldy the next day, and I stopped by to say hello. I did this a lot; shy, uncertain of myself, and struggling with western powder, I felt in need of a friend. Unbelievably, this superb woman of world renown, the one I had so admired through those years of glowing press releases, had become my pal. Now a stranger came over and flicked an oyster cracker at her. She batted it back and said, "Dick, this is my friend Nick Howe." Nodding at him, she said, "Dick Buek." Buek said, "Hi, Nick. You got your sticks?" He hopped down off the porch and, as he put on his skis, he turned back to me and said, "C'mon, Nick. Don't sweat it. Just point 'em down."

I was completely floored. This was the person everyone had been waiting for. Olympic team members from four countries had been waiting for him. He was a team member himself. *Medal winners* had been waiting for him to get to Sun Valley. Now, less than twenty-four hours after he got there, he was waiting for *me* to go skiing with *him*. Me, the greenest nobody in the Valley. As I struggled with my bindings, I wondered what was happening to me. Whatever it was, Buek had done it.

People often seem to be a different size from what they ought to be. Expectations tend to warp this sense, and even people you know well can sometimes seem to be the wrong size. Some people seem too small for themselves, some too big. I could never get a clear idea of Buek's size. He

was much shorter than I was, but I couldn't really tell how much shorter. It seemed to vary. He was very strong, but lean to the point of being skinny. Part of this ambiguity was due to the peculiar way he moved. A lot of the time he sort of hopped and hitched himself around, very tight and restless. Then in an instant he would drop into a relaxation so complete that it seemed as if, were some seen or unseen prop removed, he would fall to the ground. He seemed to project a curious double image as these qualities shifted. Watching him, I often thought of a raccoon.

In the popular view, he was a dog. There were quite a number of dogs among the luminaries of skiing that year, most notably Jack Reddish, captain of the Olympic team and known, of course, as "Red Dog." And Pinkie Robinson, still trying to live down the loss of his pants in an important race the year before. He was "Pink Dog."

Buek was "Mad Dog." He was an enthusiastic—even mindless—slave of gravity. As far back as the stories traced him, his life was one of screaming descents. If he stayed on his feet, the word went out that another impossible slope had finally been schussed. If he crashed, there would be a maelstrom of violence that the spectators would never forget. He liked, as he put it, to point 'em down. He had bets out that he would outlive everyone he knew. If such were not to be the case, however, he had thought about that, too. "When I go," Buek would say, "I want to go straight in."

Buek's skiing was something else. He was hardly a stylist, but everyone would stop whatever they were doing when he pushed off. The galvanizing quality of many great skiers lay in the knowledge that no matter what conditions or circumstances might be, they would master them with the same superb ease. With Buek it was the opposite: people would watch with the lurking apprehension that *anything* might happen. At times, he had the sleek art of a ski school instructor, but this could instantly give way to a hesitant wobbling as though on tiptoe on his skis, as if trying to decide what to do next. Then he would drop into a loose crouch and bash off down the fall line. People often became anxious when they saw him coming down a slope above them—and with good reason. Almost every skier past stem turns tries to perfect an elegant maneuver to thrill onlookers when he stops. Buek had no such move. In fact, it was often touch-and-go whether he would stop at all, and people downslope learned to be cautious.

There was another thing, perhaps more disconcerting and more revealing than any other. From time to time, as he skied on Baldy, he would seem to disappear, replaced by a succession of characters, by turns mincing, overly mannered, braggadocious, haughty, or staggering. He would be playing out a skiing caricature of the members of a ski school class he had just passed, self-inflated by their home addresses and the grandeur of the big-name instructor at their head. Then he might stop and spend ten minutes teaching me some advanced racing secret with all the seriousness and patience that a coach would lavish on some elite racer. Me, who was still fumbling around on my heavy old ridge-top Northlands. An eastern kid on his ice skis.

I got some softer skis, and broke them. I got another pair, and broke those, too. Then Dick decided I should do it right, and he took me to get a pair of Eriksens. I was dazzled by the bright red top edges and deep white grooves on the top surfaces front and back of the foot. After that, he took me down to Ed Scott's shop in Ketchum to have the right kind of bottom put on, and Parsenn GS edges. The complex geometry of those edges had carried me through many a dreary hour in study hall the previous year, and that was as close as I had ever thought I'd come to them.

Scottie's shop was a magnet for the real insiders. It was so small that only a few people could come in at one time. Miracles of repair were performed there on all the wood skis, but the principal product were Scottie's famous longthong bindings. The leather straps started at about 6 feet, and then slowly stretched to incredible lengths as you used them. But they never broke, another of Scottie's secrets. (The secret was rumored to be fermented whale urine.) This shop was also the source for the small brass name plates that I had seen on the skis of the mighty. Buek asked Scottie to make

Dick Buek was one part joy, one part insouciance, one part madness

some marked NICK HOWE—SKI PATROL—SUN VALLEY. Two pairs.

Dick's own equipment looked, more than anything else, lived in. In this mecca of what was the latest style sensation, razor-creased Bogner stretch pants, he wore baggy old gabardines and shapeless sweaters. His skis were hacked and gouged from his violent eggbeaters, with pieces of adhesive tape stuck over the worst places. Before a minor race, he once looked down at them and told the person starting next after him that he didn't think they'd make it to the bottom. This may have been a psych, but it seemed likely that they wouldn't.

He had a pair of Allais Racer boots, the outer layer made of leather that had about the same flex as quarter-inch plywood. Dick had somehow reduced his to the homey look of bedroom slippers. The outer layer normally had a space down the instep an inch and a half wide, but he had tightened his so often and so hard that there was almost no space left at all. He said he was having a zipper put in. It would save lac-

Buek's technique was the headlong attack on the racing course

ing time, and that way they would also look better for après-ski wear. He also had a plan to save wear and tear on his longthong bindings by screwing the boots to his skis, and most people thought he would.

Dick gave up this idea, however, when it occurred to him to mount the toe irons off-center so he stood on his skis pigeon-toed. He had two theories about this idea. For one thing, it would let him put more pressure on the inside edges in turns. Furthermore, he said, since he walked pigeon-toed anyway, it was probably unnatural to have his feet straight when he skied. Word of this technological breakthrough spread, and soon every upwardly mobile striver in Sun Valley had

his bindings so far off center that he stood practically crossways on his skis.

Waxing was another touchy subject. Everyone had formulas of incredible complexity, and alcohol stoves burned far into the night as new melts were prepared in search of a slippery edge over one's roommate. A persistent but unconfirmed rumor had it that Stein Eriksen's preternatural skills were due to a tiny sliver of wax added to each of his melts, a wax that he alone in the world possessed.

All of these marvelous elixirs were painted on in shingled steps which were themselves subject to arcane formulas. Finally, the whole job was carefully buffed with crumpled newspaper on the theory that microscopic amounts of graphite transferred from the printing and added the essential finishing touch. Some advanced specialists argued the merits of the inks different publishers used.

One day Buek put on his boots, and after he had laced them up, he painted them with a thick coat of shiny silver wax. His arrival at the mountain created a sensation. To all the eager questioners, he explained that everyone had missed the point about waxing, and let it go at that.

Stein Eriksen seemed to live in a world beyond the reach of the rest of us. Even the greatest skiers were daunted by Stein's flips—the calm approach run, the enormous impact as he hit the steep pitch of the take-off he built in the snow, the soaring swan dive through the air, the precise pike for the somersault, and the perfect touchdown.

One day up on Ridge Run, Stein was doing flips for some *Life* photographers and the inevitable crowd. When he was through, several skiers of certifiable genius tried it, lurching off the ramp, sprawling awkwardly through the air, and crashing in disarray into the snow.

Suddenly there was a yell from way up the mountain, far above Stein's starting place. It was Buek, poling and skating for extra speed. He hurtled into the ramp and catapulted into the air. He was halfway through his second somersault when he hit. His tips went in first, and one ski broke halfway to the binding, buckling upward. Dick smashed down onto this, and half buried himself in the snow. He bounded up, blood spurting from his face. Digging the snow out of his nose, he muttered, "Jesus Christ, I've been murdered." The broken ski had gone into his mouth when he landed on it, and had broken some dental relic of an earlier disaster. There was something sharp sticking out through a large tear in the side of his face. He pulled this shard out through his cheek and stuck it in his pocket. Then he went on down the mountain on the unbroken ski and got himself sewed up. Before the end of the afternoon, he was back up on Ridge, trying the somersault again.

What drove him to these improbable feats seemed to be an almost unreasoning faith in his own body and a limitless capacity for hope. That winter, this was never more evident than at the Harriman Cup downhill.

The Harriman Cup was the climax of the Sun Valley season, and a centerpiece of the national circuit. That year, it was also a try-out race for the 1954 FIS team. Heavy snow fell for two days before the races began. On the ski patrol, we worked endlessly boot-packing and shoveling bumps on the fearsome "Exhibition" section of the course, a wall that dropped away under the lift with a menacing row of steel towers along the side. The bumps had built up so high that a person standing in a trough could reach out and touch the uphill crest at shoulder level.

There was a control gate set at the top, and all the other racers studied Exhibition closely, trying to find a single line that would get them through the terrifying bumps, some miracle of surveying and luck that would give them a chance of getting through.

Buek stood at the top of Exhibition, this entrance itself an immense roll that could throw a racer 50 yards down the slope if he hit it wrong. Dick was hanging languidly in the straps of his poles with a quizzical half-smile on his face, his eyes idly sliding down the slope. Then he would give a little shuffle and slip over the edge. A few minutes later he would be back, sometimes matted with snow, sometimes not. I was working on the course nearby and suddenly I realized what he was doing. He was skiing out a fan of lines from the top gate, trying every possible angle from top to bottom so that in the race, it wouldn't matter how he bounced around or how out of shape his line might be. There'd be nothing on Exhibition that would surprise him.

A week or so after this he gave another lesson in how to prepare for a race. Some college students had set a slalom on the slope just below the porch at the Roundhouse restaurant. They were splendid, with all the newest equipment, and several were wearing knickers with expensive Norwegian knee socks. This was a daring affectation—at that time, only Andrea Mead Lawrence, with two golds in last year's Olympics, was wearing knickers. They were her trademark.

These hotshots spent most of the morning out there, each one climbing up and down the course again and again, closing his eyes and making complex hand signals to himself as he struggled to memorize this demanding seven-gate slalom. Finally these taxing exercises overwhelmed the fashion plates of the Roundhouse slope, and they retired to the porch for lunch. Then Dick slipped the straps of his ski pants out from under his feet and bloused the pants at the knee. His red long johns were left in place to serve as knicker socks. A pair of huge old nineteenth-century skis decorated the wall above the fireplace in the restaurant, and Dick took these out on the course. With his boots stuck into the rotting leather toe loops, he soberly sidestepped up and down the course, squinting his eyes and making delicate hand maps as he prepared his line for each gate. Then he ran the course. It was the last run of the day. The college hotshots did not resume their practice.

The April thaw scattered the denizens, great and small, of that Sun Valley winter. I went back to New Hampshire for the spring skiing season in Tuckerman's Ravine, and in June, I headed west again to look for work on the Coast.

Dick had been in an appalling crash in May. Riding his motorcycle, he hit a swerving car head-on. The reports were that he had totaled the car with his body, and was in a hospital near San Francisco.

Brynhild was taking summer courses at Stanford, and when I got to the Coast I stopped to visit her. The next day we went over to the hospital, and I found Buek lying on a therapy table while a nurse gingerly massaged his leg with her fingertips. If he had been slender before, he was wasted now. There seemed to be nothing left of him under the sheet. With the nurse dabbling at his leg, so gently that she seemed afraid if she touched it any harder it might come apart in her hands, Dick gleefully gave me a running account of the most recent devastation, and showed me several feet of new scars where, as he said, "the docs were looking around to see if there were any good parts left." Evidently, the doctors hadn't found much, but,

Dick said, "You should have seen the car."

The doctors thought the rest of his body would eventually be returned to at least minimal serviceability, but they had little hope for his left knee. I lost track of Dick's enumeration of the explorations and operations, but I gathered that the medical staff had done everything they could. He said they were quite pleased that they had kept him alive, and had promised him that with a few years of careful rehabilitation he might be able to get out of his wheelchair and walk a little. The nurse murmured something soothing about being a good patient as she slid the leg back under the sheet. There was so little flesh left you could almost see the texture of the bones underneath; laced and knotted with scars, it looked like the dead limb of an old apple tree.

Buek made the appropriate grimaces of pain that the nurse seemed to expect—he had countless times explained the importance of "playing the role"—and as soon as the nurse was out of the room, he hopped down off the table and started doing knee bends on his good leg. Or, at least, his less bad leg. "You'll have to excuse me for a minute, Nicker. I want to be in hard training by August, and I'm a little behind schedule."

I was aghast. Surely the spindly remains of his legs would break in two. "In training for what?"

"The FIS," he said. "1954 is an FIS year, ya know."

After this regimen, he got back on the table and said, "There's just one problem." He dropped the bad leg over the edge of the table. Flopping down, it straightened to about 110 degrees and stopped with a loud *click*. "No further. That's it. There's something in there that stops it, and the docs can't fix it." Feeling slightly giddy, I mumbled something about that being a pretty tough break.

"Are you kidding? This is the big break I've been waiting for. Look here." He showed me some sketches he had made on the back of an envelope. "See, these two rods end in discs that are held together by a bolt through the middle. See these things around the edges?" There was a row of holes near the rim of the saucer-shaped end of the rods. "When you get the plates rotated right, a kind of peg goes through the holes that match up. I've got a bud that can make this out of stainless steel, and I'll tell the docs to cut that bad knee right out of my leg and put this in. They can hammer the rods into the sawed-off ends of the bones, and there'll be this little window where I can reach in and set the crouch I need for a downhill. It'll be strong as hell . . . I'll put a cotter pin on the axle nut so it won't fall apart on the big bumps." He was delighted. It was even better than the pigeon-toed bindings.

I studied the sketch. "Won't it be tricky changing the setting during a race . . . like for turns?"

"That's the whole point," he said, really excited now. "I'll never have to run slalom again . . . all that up and down. Won't be able to make all those turns. I always hated slalom."

There must have been technical problems he hadn't anticipated, because Buek stayed with the old knee, even though he couldn't get it within 70 degrees of straight. He didn't make the FIS team the next winter, but he did win the National Downhill Championship at Aspen. As a concession to the doctors, he raced with his leg in a cast.

Buek was drafted and, incredibly, accepted for service. He got leave and made it to some races in 1955. The North Americans were at Cannon Mountain that year, designated tryouts for the '56 Olympic team. The weather was terrible—rain, freeze-up, and a blizzard.

Waiting for the start of the slalom, all the racers were doing their fretful prerace calisthenics: jumps, squats, knee-drops, and the like. Buek hobbled around in a sort of bearlike shuffle; since one leg never straightened, he kept the other always bent. He stared at these warm-up antics as if he had never seen such a thing. Chiharu Igaya was there, the superb slalom specialist from Japan, nimble as a cat. As Igaya went through his exotic warm-up drill, Buek stopped in front on him and studied his exercise with a mixture of anxiety and solicitude. Finally he said, "Jeez, Chicky, aren't you afraid you'll fall down on the course. I mean, look how loose your knees are. I wouldn't dare ski on legs like that. Might

lift for a turn and fall right over on your face. You ought to get this kind. . . . He kicked his left leg and the knee stopped short in a semi-crouch. "Big improvement. Can't ever stand up straight, much less wind resistance. Keeps you closer to the ground . . . easier to keep your balance."

The downhill was on the day of the freeze. The lower part of the course went over the steepest part of the mountain. The run was gated through the precarious connections of ice between expanses of frozen mud yawning like sand traps on either side. I had to chop steps with my poles to make a place to stand beside the course.

When Buek came over the top of the last steep pitch, I could see ribbons of leather flapping behind his right boot. A ring on the bindings had broken partway down the course, and for the rest of the race he had only the toe iron to keep control of the ski. That was the one on his good leg.

He finished second, a tick behind the winner.

The next weekend was the Internationals, at Stowe. While Buek was making a training run for the downhill, a spectator had pushed out onto the course. Dick swerved to avoid a collision, hit a bump, and smashed into a tree. He broke his back.

Since he was in the service at the time they took him to the air force hospital near Burlington, Vermont. A few days after the races, I drove over to see him. The guard at the desk was incredulous. "You know him? Christ, we couldn't keep him. He was hurt real bad—back in a cast and everything—but he said he was leaving. Said he had something to do out West. Said he was army and we were air force and we had no authority. Said the only man who could give us both orders was the president, and unless we got an order from Eisenhower he was going out the window."

Buek was gone. The next weekend was the Harriman Cup downhill at Sun Valley.

In the summer of 1957 I decided to go West again. I had a vague plan to see if there was any work at the site of the 1960 Olympics at Squaw Valley. I wrote to Dick and said I'd drop by if my car made it, but it was chancy, because the car was a heap. He wrote back and told me to travel light. If my car crapped out, I should call him and tell him where I was. If I had only a few things, he would come and pick me up in his plane. The typewriter he used seemed to have been stripped for speed. There were no capitals and almost no punctuation. The signature was a typed "md."

The car made it, but not by much. It wheezed up Donner Pass in first gear. Dick was sitting in the sun on the porch of his house in Soda Spring, deeply tanned and shaggy, and wearing only an absurd pair of Bermuda shorts. He'd had another crash, and he showed me the new scars. He joked about this, and although he looked hard and fit, it seemed to me he was smaller than I remembered. I wondered how many parts were left that he could still afford to lose.

He hopped off the porch to show me around his place, his gait and posture now so modified to compensate for the accumulation of injuries that I couldn't be sure which direction was his true heading. There was an old motorcycle that looked as if it had been thrown through a stone wall. I asked him if it ran, and he said, "Sure,

everything runs." I asked him, hesitantly, if that was the one that hit the car. "Naw," he said, twisting the throttle grip, "this is my mom's bike."

He was filled with enthusiasm for his new project. Hopping around, he explained about his plane. He was putting a new engine in the Piper, and he'd figured out a way he could pack the whole thing in a crate 20 feet long and less than 5 feet in cross-section. He talked about it as if it were a lunch box. "I'll just put the plane in that box and throw in my sticks and my toothbrush and go to Europe on a steamer. I can make the whole circuit next winter. That's all you need, isn't it—your plane and your toothbrush and your sticks?"

I stayed around for a while, but there weren't any jobs, so I went back East. In the fall, I heard that Buek had nearly drowned in a sailing accident. I felt relieved. That should be his accident for the year.

In November, I heard that something had happened to Dick's plane while he was flying over Donner Lake. He went straight in.

Formative Years and Victorious Years

by JEAN-CLAUDE KILLY with DOUGLAS PFEIFFER

The most famous of modern racers, Jean-Claude Killy, turned a triple Olympic gold into the largest fortune ever amassed by a ski champion, rose to the top from a childhood that was characterized by compulsive skiing, a broken home, and a complete dedication to winning. Here Jean-Claude takes us back to the very beginning of the most renowned career in the history of sport. His collaborator, Doug Pfeiffer, former editor of Skiing, now a free-lance ski writer, is an authority on every phase of the sport.

I am often asked, was there not one special moment when I decided to be a ski racer. No, it was more that a series of experiences throughout my early life cast the mold for me. Ski racing had to become my world.

For almost as long as I can remember I have loved to ski. I was just three when my family moved to Val d'Isère where my father was to start a ski club. It was 1946. I have few recollections of my birthplace, Saint-Cloud, a small town west of Paris. Our new life in the mountains made me happy right from the beginning. Skiing was as normal to the children of Val d'Isère as eating and drinking, and I played around on borrowed skis until I was five. Then finally I received a pair of my own, and from that moment on I was rarely seen without them. My parents nicknamed me Toutoune—I guess because I was like a crazy dog, obsessed with my skiing.

Val d'Isère was a very different place in those days. The roads were narrow and dangerous and there were only six hundred beds in the town (today there are eight thousand). Most of the buildings were rather rustic. I vividly recall one in particular because it concerns my early skiing. There was a roof covered by drifting snow. Smooth white drifts reached from the peak of the roof to the ground on one side and formed a perfect mountain for skiers my age and size.

When a teleferique was installed in town—Le Solaise—my friends and I would always make one or two runs after school. In fact, I believe I did my first racing then because of a school teacher. He loved to ski also, so every Monday he'd take us out to the mountain, and one after another, we'd race each other down. Our equipment wasn't very fancy; in fact, I remember once my sister fell down and came out of her skis and boots! They went down the hill while she stood in the snow in stocking feet.

There weren't many instructors at Val in those days, and my friends and I devised an excellent technique for getting a free *Mont-Blanc*—a delicious dessert we loved made of cream, chestnuts, and chantilly sauce. We would offer to teach the tourists to ski for the price of one cake, and generally we would end up with the cake, sometimes without having to give the lesson.

I skied as much as possible, making twelve or so long runs every day, yet I was only eight or nine. My father cautioned me that I was skiing too much, using up all my energy so that I had none left over to grow tall and strong. But, though I remained small for my size, I won my first victory about that time. It was for a slalom, and a cup was offered by Queen Juliana of Holland who was vacationing in Val d'Isère. Before the race, feeling very important, I went up to the race officials and demanded a *bossard*. How embarrassed I was when they laughed, and I found the right word for the racing bib I wanted was *dossard!* My first one, donned at the age of eight, was shaped like a heart.

My eighth year was also marked by my first ski trip to a race away from Val d'Isère. What an incredible discovery it was for me to find skiers on the other side of the mountain! In 1953, when I was ten, I won all three Alpine events in the Critérium des Jeunes, even beating the twelve- and thirteen-year-olds. For the first time my name made the regional papers, and this had a strange effect on me. I think that the competitive urge deep within me began to crystallize.

These were the sort of experiences that rooted me in skiing competition for good: seeing my name in the papers; having a special team sweater that not all my friends could have; going places they didn't go; and seeing how proud my parents were of me. There is a pleasant taste to victory, and soon I was thinking, Why not try for a bigger cup, a longer trip, a more important victory? Ski racing chose me—I was thrown into it as a way of life because it was all around me. And, because I discovered that I had a strong, competitive spirit, I stayed with it. I was a timid, secretive child, and not much of a scholar, so it was through skiing that I could express myself. How casual fate is in deciding who will make it, who won't. I skied with so many kids in Val, some that showed more promise than I, but none of them continued skiing. Somehow, I had the right circumstances and the passion to carry out what was started for me—the life of a ski champion.

At a young age I discovered I had the ability to imitate other skiers' styles. I have guarded this gift, for it served me well in developing my own technique, a do-it-yourself one, for I never took a lesson. I had great fun imitating French ski stars like Henri Oreiller, the first French Olympic champion. I learned a lot from him because he skied with a style years ahead of his time. Later, when I trained with the French team, I was especially influenced by the downhill form of Adrien Duvillard. He stayed low in the turns while the rest of the racers kept their bodies high. By watching many skiers and copying their styles, keeping some things, discarding others, I gradually developed a sense of what I wanted to achieve on skis—a style free of mannerisms, allowing for independent action of the legs, the lateral play of the knees and ankles controlling turns precisely and handling sudden checks and accelerations smoothly. I think most skiers lose the spontaneity they had as children. I didn't. I have kept loose on skis and trusted my own intuition, and though I made many mistakes along the way, my best-from-everything style worked magic for my last few racing years.

I have missed only two years of skiing in my life. When I was eleven I was sent to school at a place called Chambéry. Actually, in those days this was only a three-hour drive from Val d'Isère, but to me it might have been the other end of the world. I couldn't understand why my parents would do such a thing to me, although later I learned it was because they were separating. I felt abandoned, robbed of the people and mountains I cherished, and I seemed very different from any of the children at the school.

I would look out through the dusty classroom windows and dream about Val d'Isère, my friends, the snow-covered mountains. I lost my appetite, had no interest in my studies. I became more and more unhappy and shut myself off completely from the people around me. I was still very short for my age as well as frail, and gradually my health became worse until I contracted a severe pulmonary infection. I was packed off immediately to a hospital at Saint Gervais and, during the four months there, I became more and more withdrawn. After I had partially recovered, the doctors forbade any skiing for at

Jean-Claude Killy topped his meteoric career with a triple gold

least a year so I was sent to a second school in Voiron, even farther away from the mountains. Here skiing was out of the question. Kept away from the sport which I loved and which represented freedom and happiness to me, I was miserable. I vowed to make up for lost time when I got out.

After these two school years, my next school was much closer to skiing. It was at Saint Jean de Maurienne. I was thirteen, and that summer I trained with the French B Team. Early in the school year, I was invited to compete in the Ilio Colli Cup at Cortina d'Ampezzo. Nothing could prevent me from going on that trip, so without the necessary permission from my school (which it would have been impossible to get) I headed for Italy with the team. The results? A broken leg and a dismissal from school! The world was at an end for me, I thought. But as he was often to do in the future, my father called me and said, "Don't worry, Toutoune, I'm here." Our family

was one of few words, but it was always a safe, good feeling to know that despite this, we were very close and warm. That broken leg of mine had another effect on me which underlines how I feel about the chances of fate. I was bedridden only a few months, but when I got up an amazing thing happened! I had grown 15 centimeters (6 inches). I believe all my growing years had been too active, as my father always said, so I had no time to grow. So breaking my leg, one of the most upsetting experiences in my life, in a way made my future victories possible. Now I had the size and strength to be a championship contender.

Within three months I was racing again—academia had lost out. In 1959 I won a number of victories including the Critérium des Jeunes. When I was fifteen I made the "hopefuls" for the French Ski Team, and in the winter of 1960 I trained with the team itself. I traveled and skied with them all—Adrien Duvillard, Guy Perillat, Charles Bozon, Michel Arpin, François Bonlieu. I was the youngest, and I listened and watched carefully to learn all I could.

The first international competition I won was a slalom, the Grand Prix de Morzine in 1961. I beat Léo Lacroix and Adrien Duvillard, who fell. That night I received the rooster, the emblem of the French team. The same week Guy Perillat, then only twenty-one, suddenly soared to international recognition with a series of incredible victories at Wengen and Kitzbühel.

My skiing at this time had a lot of punch and spontaneity. My mistake was in trying to sustain the straightest, fastest line throughout the course. This was to attain speed, but in the end I lost more time than I gained because of the terrible falls I took. In the slalom my attack was too strong, and I lost precision and control. Physically I wasn't able to handle the problems my great acceleration created. I hit the ruts, went out of control and lost my balance. But I was only seventeen. There was still time.

My excitement over the Morzine victory and my admittance to the French team were overshadowed by a terrible automobile accident a few days later. We skidded on a gravel section of the road and, while I came out with a few scratches, my friend and passenger was killed. It was a tragedy that matured me and affected me deeply. To pull myself out of deep depression I dedicated my life entirely to skiing, going at it with more force and determination than ever before.

The 1961–62 season opened at Val d'Isére with the Critérium de la Première Neige. I fell in the slalom, and in the giant slalom I was given the number 39, which meant the course would be pretty rutted by the time I ran it. It looked as if luck was not with me that day, but I have never fought as hard as I did on that GS (giant slalom) course. It was worth it for I won, beating Adrien Duvillard and Michel Arpin by more than a second. The old order was changing—the newspapers heralded me as the future French ski champion. More important was my father's happiness and the reward he gave me—a chronometer he had had as a pilot during the war. I had always hoped to earn it.

In two months the World Championships at Chamonix were to be held and it was not clear who would be chosen to race. Perhaps it was fate, though I was pressing too hard for speed, but at the Ilio Colli at Cortina I once again broke my leg. Soon after, the team for Chamonix was announced, and our coach, Honoré Bonnet, came to see me in the hospital with the news that he had intended to use me in the championships! I was terribly disappointed and, though I was at Chamonix, it was on crutches.

At this time I spent six months in the mountains of Algeria with the French army. By virtue of early leave I got out in the fall of 1963, but as soon as I reached home I came down with jaundice. That whole season, though I struggled through, I was never myself. My skiing had lost its punch and I was scrambling all the time to improve my point standing to qualify for the 1964 Olympics at Innsbruck. I accomplished this, and assured myself I could race among the first fifteen in all three events.

My performance at the Olympic Winter Games was a disaster: I placed fifth in giant slalom and I was eliminated in the slalom and the downhill. One of the problems: I had allowed an inexperienced technician to prepare my skis. I felt the time spent waxing was time wasted, and

I had no talent for deciding which wax to use. I preferred to use that time studying the course or relaxing before the race. After Innsbruck, two ski men traveled with the team to take care of the equipment. Later Michel Arpin worked with me developing and caring for my equipment.

I was severely criticized for my performance at Innsbruck. A friend, noting my lack of strength, suggested a complete checkup as he thought I might not have recovered from my bout with jaundice. How right he was! I had been treated incorrectly and was suffering from amoebic dysentery. So I again spent the first half of that summer recuperating, and then in August went to Portillo, Chile, to train for the 1964–65 season.

There was one race I'll never forget during 1965. It was at Kitzbühel. So far the French team had been thoroughly dominated by the Austrians, especially in downhill. We blamed our French-made equipment, but the manufacturers said we were just looking for excuses for our inability. Encouragingly, our downhill at Kitzbühel wasn't bad. Léo Lacroix placed fourth and I tenth. In the slalom the next day that indomitable Austrian, Karl Schranz, won the first run, ahead of everyone by 1.38 seconds. I wanted more than anything to give him a run for his money in the second run. I memorized the course thoroughly, studying the positions of the flags, the difficult spots, changes in snow conditions. Standing in the starting gate, I looked over to where Schranz was standing. He looked nervous, so I made an effort to look relaxed, flashing a confident smile his way. I was going to hit hard, to win. Skiing that slalom I found my style. All that I had been striving for actually happened—and worked! I didn't concentrate on the next gate, but on the fourth or fifth one ahead of me. This gave me time to anticipate the difficulties, to play with time. I was playing; I felt I could run through the course, my skis and I were so in tune. When I crossed the finish line, even the Austrians cheered, something they usually reserve for their own heroes. Schranz came in three seconds behind me. I won not just the slalom, but the combined, too. Only three French skiers had ever attained the same record at Kitzbühel before me. Moments like this make me forget the unhappy, bad times.

Two days later at the Megève downhill, I raced on Austrian skis and won. This proved to my country's equipment manufacturers that the French could win with the right skis. We became more determined than ever to catch up to and surpass the Austrians. That summer I went to Australia, racing and testing French skis with Léo Lacroix. We worked on fiberglass technology, an effort that eventually paid off for it was on the perfected model of a ski we developed that I won the World Championship downhill. Léo and I wanted a 230-centimeter downhill racing ski, longer than most skiers were using. We were sure it would work, but eventually we found out differently.

We also worked to improve our English that summer. I had come a long way from the narrow valley of Val d'Isère and now realized that an athlete, especially a skier, can become very closed off from life. I didn't want to forget about the realities of life, to become dependent on the French racing system—it's so easy to do. You have someone to make all the decisions for you; people are assigned to take care of both you and your equipment, and racing occupies you ten months of the year. When your racing days are over, you suddenly don't know what to do. I wished to avoid this sad situation.

When the 1966 season began I felt great. I had gained some weight and was stronger. My first race was a victory at Adelboden. The Lauberhorn was next, and I expected to place high, especially since I had the new long downhill skis I believed in. It was not to be, I was shattered. The long ski was a failure. Léo placed fifteenth; I was in the thirties! The team was attacked from all sides. Honoré Bonnet, our own coach, said we would never do well in downhill. The tension caused among us by his lack of confidence was incredible. But most of all we were angry. Léo Lacroix had given ten years of his life searching for one major victory. The team felt abandoned and it was not fair, since we were good skiers and fearless men, not the cowards Bonnet had pictured. We went on to prove him wrong. In the next few years I won many downhills, and La-

croix won that season as well. I never quite forgot that insult from Bonnet, even though I respect him greatly for creating a French team at the time he did. Although a champion makes himself a winner, he develops better in a close community with a team that has good spirit.

About this time, I learned a new, very beneficial method of relaxation—yoga. Georges Coulon taught me to understand it, and it left me relaxed and ready to fight in the French Championships at Courchevel. Although I left there without a win but with morale much improved, for Léo Lacroix had his downhill victory. Two events remained before the World Championships—I won the coveted diamond "K" in the Kandahar and the Giant Slalom title on the American circuit.

Portillo, 1966. I will never forget it. The French walked away with sixteen out of twenty-four medals! In the men's downhill I felt good. My skis were performing well, and Michel Arpin, my ever faithful friend, was in Portillo to care for them. An auto accident had kept him off the team and he was with us as a technical advisor. He had taken me under his wing and we worked together to perfect the team's skis. The day of the downhill was beautiful. I kept my line on the course—one different from anyone else's—and took the turns to the outside, keeping my style smooth. At the finish Arpin ran up to me. "You won," he shouted. "You're crazy!" I answered. "There are all the others still to come!" But it was true. Lacroix had second place. Most exciting, I was the world champion. THE CHAMPION OF THE WORLD! my mind shouted. Even two years later, winner of three Olympic gold medals, I didn't feel as happy, as elated, as I did at that moment.

For two nights after my victory, I didn't sleep a wink. When I lose, I sleep soundly, but it's always the same—when victorious, I relive the course a thousand times.

The Austrian press tried to minimize the French sweep at Portillo. They claimed the time of year was wrong, the altitude too great. My downhill was called insignificant because the run at Portillo was too short to count. They wanted to see me on a tougher course, and I was ready for them.

I began to think seriously about winning at the 1968 Olympic Winter Games only after I won the World Cup in 1967. That victory was terribly important for me because it gave me tremendous confidence and assured me I could win in all three disciplines—giant slalom, slalom, and especially downhill, my weakest event. That 1966 FIS World Championship in Portillo, Chile, was the beginning, and the continued victories I put together in 1967 proved to me that I could do it.

During the many major races that counted toward the 1967 World Cup, many journalists and friends talked to me about the forthcoming Olympics, wondering if I could do what Toni Sailer had done in 1956—win all three gold medals. I put such questions aside at the time because I wanted to concentrate on getting a perfect score in the season-long events for the World Cup. I knew later on there would be time to think of the Olympics.

Preparation is everything to winning. It is easy to say, "I am going to win," but it is hard to convince yourself that it's really possible. After all the other racers are thinking the same thing. So I don't think about it; instead I concentrate on my training and my equipment, which really determine who will make it. Then, on the day of the race, whether it is an Olympic contest or not, I can say with confidence, "I am ready."

I think I had a slight advantage over the others in preparing for the Olympics because they were the only challenge left to me in ski racing. I'd dream about winning, think how fantastic it would be, but never did I tell myself I would win. However, I did decide not to try for the combined title at Grenoble, partly because the medal for it is an FIS one, not an Olympic one, and partly because that's what I did at Portillo. After I won the downhill, I didn't ski as hard as I could have in the other races just to make sure I wouldn't fall. I was a disappointment to myself.

When I returned home in the late spring of 1967 after the World Cup, I did a little car racing because I enjoyed the excitement, but mostly I trained to keep in condition. I'd ride my bicycle up the Col de l'Iseran, a steep pass outside Val d'Isère, going as fast as I could both up and downhill. Going downhill fast on a bike is something like downhill racing, and is very good for the nerves.

In July, Michel Arpin came up with many pairs of skis for me to try out. There were skis with a great variety of flexes and bases, some for hard snow and ice, some for soft snow—skis for everything that might happen at Grenoble. It was at that time we decided that I would use 220-centimeter downhill skis. The longer ones we'd experimented with hadn't been so good for me and also I knew the downhill at Grenoble would be won in the turns—nine important ones—and shorter skis would be easier to turn. Michel and I worked for four days high in the mountains that July. He clocked me on every run and kept a chart on how well I did on every pair of skis in all kinds of snow conditions. Then we picked the ten best pair and Michel went back to the factory to try to make even better ones.

Michel has always skied with much the same style as I do, and we used the same size skis and boots. He had always known that I didn't like to prepare skis—mounting bindings, filing edges and waxing—although my loss at Innsbruck had convinced me of its importance. So, from the Portillo races, Michel took care of everything concerning my skis. All I had to do was race. It was fabulous. We understood each other perfectly. When everybody was up in the morning preparing their skis for the race or for practice, I could stay in bed and sleep a couple of hours longer because I knew Michel would do a good job on my equipment.

He did more than take care of my skis. In addition he acted like a coach, timing me and the other racers during practice and during the races. And he was always picking up information that would be useful to me. Besides that, Michel was great fun and relaxing for me to be with.

At Christmastime 1967, Michel once again came to Val d'Isère with another load of skis. By that time we had had the first big race of the season, the Critérium de la Première Neige in Val d'Isère. I won one of the two giant slaloms, but the downhill was canceled due to lack of snow. It was very odd, but when we tested the new skis here that Michel had brought, the ones we picked in July still remained the best.

My results in the big January races were disappointing. I had good runs and beat one of the top Swiss, Edi Bruggmann, in the Adelboden giant slalom, but I couldn't really get anything going. I think I was trying too many things. Every day, new skis. And the weather was very bad. That may have thrown me off a bit. It was a good thing I didn't have to prove anything in those races. Even though I wasn't winning very much, I never lost my confidence. But I must admit, when you don't win and don't win, you start to think. And this is not good. When you think too much, you become conscious of what you are doing and you get into trouble. You must be spontaneous—like a cat, just move fast, without thinking.

At Kitzbühel, the last big race before the Olympics, I got off my line in the downhill—a bad mistake—and yet I came in second. It was unbelievable. I said to myself, "Without that mistake you would have been the winner for sure. So now you are back in tune and you should be okay for Grenoble."

Another important thing happened at Kitzbühel. Toni Sailer told me how he won his three Olympic gold medals at Cortina d'Ampezzo. He said what helped him most was staying off skis for several days just before the Olympics. "You have to relax and not try too hard," he told me, and I could believe him because I knew he always was a great sportsman. He didn't try to press me, or really encourage me. The way he gave me that hint was in a very matter-of-fact way, and I decided to follow his advice.

The next week was the last race before the Games. It was at Megève. I went up the mountain for the slalom, then decided I didn't want to race. It was the first time in my life that I ever did that. I told Bonnet that I wanted to go away for a few days and not ski.

"That's all right," he said. "Do what you want. I'm sure you know what's right for you."

Within an hour I was on my way (I had my car with me) and I went to the home of Louis Jauffret at Montgenèvre in France's southern Alps where there is always sun. It was a relief to do nothing but lie on the sundeck, just relaxing, after all the bad weather we had in the races before the Olympics. Louis was really fantastic to me, hiding his disappointment over not qualifying for the team in slalom. "That's okay, I don't care," he said, "But I care for you and I want to put you in a good mood to win." I told him I didn't want to think about skiing at all, and that's what happened. While I was at his house, for over a week, we didn't talk skiing once.

I rejoined the team when the Olympic courses opened for training. Michel had arrived before me and had everything ready. I decided to concentrate completely on the downhill because it was the first and most difficult of the races. I knew if I did well in it I would do well in slalom and giant slalom.

It felt good to get back on skis again after my rest, but on the first day of training my times were quite slow. Michel was timing me against the other racers, but he told me not to worry. Sure enough, by the second day I was as good as everybody else, and by the third, I was really becoming the master of the course. My times over the important sections were much faster than those of the others. This was psychologically important. I began to feel very confident. Bit by bit, all my little concerns began to drop away so that the only thing I had to do was to go to the starting gate and run the course.

Michel was tremendous in getting me into this mood. He kept coming up with bits of information that put my mind at ease. He would scout around in the training rooms and the nightclubs to get intelligence on wax and equipment and then he would study his graphs of the times so that we knew exactly how we stood. One day he heard that Gerhard Nenning, who had won the downhills at Wengen and Kitzbühel and was one of my big rivals, had trouble with his skis and was trying to find a new pair. This was good for me because I knew I had prepared better than he had and also when you don't have the right skis before a race you start to worry, especially if it's the race of your life, as it was for him. Even before the nonstop training run, I reached the point where I knew I was in the best physical condition possible, my equipment was ready, and I knew every inch of the *piste* by heart. There was nothing else I could do except relax and wait for the day of the race.

But it wasn't going to be as easy as all that. I felt right on the morning of the downhill, but I made a mistake. I always take a run of a mile or so before each race so that my wax is adjusted to the snow conditions. To do this at Grenoble I went to a slope I thought had powder snow on it. But the wind had blown off the snow, and all that was left was scratchy ice. By the time I got to the bottom, I had practically no wax left, and when I got back to the starting hut, there was no time left to rewax.

I met Michel at the start and told him what had happened. I said, "I think I am going to lose the race." Funny, but I didn't feel panicky. All I could think was, "Too bad I will not win because of an unlucky accident."

But Michel remained very confident.

"That's okay," he said. "There is no problem. I've been down the course and you will win without wax. Just get a good start."

I always concentrate on a good start and push very hard out of the starting gate. But in the Olympic downhill, when the starter said, *"Allez,"* I don't think I ever pushed so hard in my life. *Formidable!* I shot out of the gate and picked up lots of speed in the first section of the course. By the second gate I felt very, very fast—fast enough to win. So I completely forgot about the wax and concentrated on the course, particularly the two bumps at Col de la Balme. Everything had to be timed just right if I was going to land high on the second bump—necessary if I were to be able to carry plenty of speed across the flat. The last part of the course was quite rutted by the time I came through—the winner by eight-hundredths of a second. Unbelievable! I am sure I won the race at the top, by the time I had reached the second gate.

There was a tremendous excitement at the finish line, and I can't remember all that happened. When everything quieted down I asked Michel, "Were you really sure about my winning without the wax?"

"Not at all," he said, laughing very hard.

"But up top I didn't think was the place to tell you that."

After I had won that downhill gold medal, I did begin to think seriously about the other two golds. The giant slalom was the next race, and I knew it was my best event. I said to myself, "This is the week for me. Nobody can stop me."

And nobody did. My winning the gold medal in giant slalom looked very easy to everybody because I won the race by over two seconds, but there were some important reasons for it. First of all I had not practiced giant slalom since I had won it at Adelboden, so when I started training again at Grenoble I was fresh and eager. More important was a belief I held about two-run giant slaloms, which by the way, I am not in favor of. I've always raced the two runs as two separate races. For the first run at the Olympics, it was a beautiful, sunny day and the course was hard and almost icy. I went all out in the first run, attacking each gate very aggressively as though there were no tomorrow. I think the other racers were holding back a bit, trying to save something for the next day. Well, the next day was very foggy and the *piste* had softened during the night, and the chances of anyone catching up with me by making a fantastic run went out of the window. All I had to do was run the course smoothly. I didn't have to risk anything. Billy Kidd made a beautiful run under these bad conditions and managed to beat me, but he was so far behind from the first run that he couldn't make up the difference. This was a very unlucky Olympics for him.

It was an easy victory, but I was still happy about it. After the close call in the downhill, it was good to be way out in front. I felt I had great momentum, great confidence, and, as it turned out, I needed it in the slalom.

The slalom turned out to be a long, drawn-out race and very controversial. Since I was in the center of those controversies, I can give you only my version of what went on.

There was only one gold medal at stake, but actually we racers had to run three races for a chance to win it. First there was the elimination race. The skiers raced in groups of six, with half of each group being eliminated and the other half advancing to the classification race to determine the starting order for the final slalom. I believed these races were terribly unfair, but I went along with the elimination slalom. Then when I realized that I had to race again only to establish my starting number, I was very bitter. I made up a petition to the FIS (Fédération Internationale de Ski) asking that the classification race be canceled. Nearly all the first-group racers signed it and I presented it to Marc Hodler, president of the FIS. "I am sure you are right," he said, "but the race was approved by the FIS and it is too late to change anything." But he did assure me that if the weather were bad and if there were danger to the racers, the jury would consider canceling the race. This is what happened when the fog didn't lift. I never at any time threatened to strike, but some of the racers may have felt that way about the classification race. I am sure they wouldn't have done it though, even if the race had been run.

Of course, the next day the weather was just as bad, perhaps worse. I thought it stupid to hold the slalom under those conditions, but I didn't think the jury could do anything about it. The Tenth Winter Olympic Games were to come to an end after this Sunday, and if the slalom had been postponed it would have created a big mess in Grenoble.

With the weather the way it was, it was a very difficult course. Most of the time I couldn't see more than a gate in front of me as I was climbing up for the first run. I had number 15, ordinarily not good, but this time it was a help because, as I got into the starting gate the fog lifted a little bit so I could see the gates. I thought that a sign, a good omen.

I made a good run, a very strong run under the conditions, and it gave me a half-second lead over the strongest field ever to race in the Olympics. Fourteen racers were within less than a second of my time, and most of them closer than that. But it didn't bother me to have the lead. Some racers get nervous when they are out in front, but I don't. I think it is good to have a lead because the others have to press very hard to catch up, and, when one presses, it is easy to make a mistake.

For the second run, the fog was solid. I tried very hard to make another fast run. I'm sure I could have done better if the weather had been clear, but under the circumstances I felt pretty good. Still there was a chance for someone to beat me if he took wild risks.

When Haakon Mjoen of Norway came down, he was more than a second faster and beat my combined time, but I wasn't worried. I felt it was possible for someone to be faster than I, but not by that much. Sure enough, the word came down that he had missed some gates and was disqualified.

Karl Schranz was something else again. His time for the first run was closer to mine than Mjoen's, and he had beaten my second run by a little more than half a second.

Nevertheless, I had a feeling that everything would turn out all right. My brother was with me and he was very anxious to know what was going on. I told him, "There was some trouble on top. Just wait and don't make any comments. It could be that he was disqualified." But then I added for insurance, "Maybe not. Maybe he is the Olympic champion." But I didn't really think so.

It was funny that day seeing Schranz. He had a big, wide smile as he posed for photographers, but it wasn't an Olympic smile. He wasn't smiling with his eyes, and I felt he was acting. I am sure he knew the jury was not going to recognize his claim that he missed the gates because of interference.

When, after a long meeting, the jury disqualified Schranz and named me the winner, I was very, very happy. The three gold medals were an impossible dream come true. I was only sorry that there would always be a question about my medal in slalom, at least in the minds of some people.

But that's ski racing. There's no way of telling exactly why you win or why you lose. There are a lot of little things that make a difference: your mood, the weather, the courses, your equipment, and maybe what you eat. For me, the rest I got with Louis Jauffret beforehand, and the help I got from Michel Arpin were the secret weapons that played a big role in my Olympic victories.

Immediately after the Games, of course, I felt something of a letdown. For some time Mark McCormack, an American who had helped golfers like Arnold Palmer and Jack Nicklaus earn more than a million dollars each, was urging me to consider the possibility of coming to America to capitalize on my fame. But I did not feel quite ready to give up ski racing. Since the events at the Olympics counted toward the World Cup, and I already had a clear-cut point advantage toward winning this trophy, I decided to continue racing for the balance of the 1968 season. After all, I could always decide to turn professional later, couldn't I? And my name would be even more important, I thought, if I were to win the World Cup for a second consecutive year.

The next two months of racing passed slowly for me. My concentration was not entirely on racing. However, I did manage to insure that I would win the World Cup again. Much of the time I was thinking of my future. I had neglected school in my passion for skiing, I was not trained for business or trade, and I didn't want to become a guide or a ski instructor.

At the end of the season I decided to follow Mark McCormack's advice—and ever since I have been busier than ever making ski movies, doing "The Killy Challenge" for TV, doing personal appearances, helping design skis and boots, consulting with editors, and of course making money and seeing the world. I only hope that you who follow in my tracks will have as much success as I, and make as many real friends along the way as I have. Good luck!

The Crash

by PETER MILLER

In the winter of 1970–71 Peter Miller followed an entire World Cup race circuit from beginning to end, and wrote the remarkable The 30,000 Mile Ski Race, *an evocation of the life of the racers that has never been equalled. The racer's life is one of ups and downs. Here is a description of one of the "downs," a fall so spectacular that they still talk about it in Val d'Isère, Killy's home town, where it happened.*

IT was a bright day, warm in the sun, and on the terraces in the center of Val d'Isère indolent skiers and the other people who did not work during the day were absorbing the warmth into their bodies, hoping it would last into the night. From their seats they could gaze at the mountains that loom around the village. To the north the mountains were snow covered and laced with ski trails and lifts. To the south and east the sun had melted the snow from them and obscenely exposed their brown, shaley sides. Parapets were built into those mountains, and roads zigzagged up their slopes, seeming, at first glance, to lead to a high-altitude mining operation. But the road and parapets acted as retainers to keep the town from being showered by avalanches.

On December 15 there was not enough snow to avalanche, just enough to ski on, and to

race. Val d'Isère is France's most sportive ski resort, and a large troupe of racers, coaches, trainers, and racer-chasers—ski equipment representatives, technicians, officials, public relationists, journalists, race fans, relatives, groupies and other hangers-on—had driven to the resort to race, to watch the race, to be watched, to make some money, to have fun.

Although the first race of the season had been in Sestriere, Italy, the traditional and unofficial opening of the World Cup ski racing and social scene was here in Val d'Isère. Here grouped the caravan that would travel throughout the winter sports spas of Europe and America, ostensibly to see who were the best racers in the world. The Val d'Isère event is known as the Critérium International de la Première Neige and Coupe Henri Oreiller. One reason for the excitement and anticipation is that the latter race, the Coupe Henri, is held on one of the more exciting downhill trails in Europe, and nearly everybody likes to watch a skier going 70 miles per hour down a mountain and maybe obliterating himself in a crash.

Of the two hundred and eight racers and fifty-odd coaches and trainers on hand—representing sixteen countries, including Japan and Liechtenstein—twenty-four were American: three coaches, two managers, one doctor, nine girl racers, nine men, all traveling on a $40,000 budget from the United States Ski Association. On the afternoon of the fifteenth at the finish of the downhill, they lined up for a team photograph. The sun had just sunk behind the summit of the Bellevarde, high over their heads, where the downhill trail begins. It had been a day of training on the downhill, as required by the rules, so that the racers would be familiar with the speed and dangers of the course. The training was finished for the day, and the Americans' thoughts had not yet turned to tomorrow's program—a slalom race for the girls, more downhill training for the men. They smiled easily for the photographer—a new team, new coaches, and forty-five races to go. New places to see and the excitement, perhaps, of victory. The racers came from similar backgrounds, raised within a middle-class society in small towns near the mountains and ski slopes; half were from the Rockies and the Sierras, half were from the Adirondacks, the Green and White Mountains of New England. Their parents had started them on their racing careers, driving them to the ski slopes, buying them tickets and equipping them with several hundred dollars' worth of skis, boots, poles, and clothes. Most of the racers were attending college or had recently graduated. They were young, the girls averaging nineteen years, the men slightly under twenty-one.

At fifty-four, their head coach, Willy Schaeffler, was a good generation gap older. His hair is gray, thin and combed straight back, close to his skull. Part of his face seems to be paralyzed, so that his smile stops in the middle. Willy is a neat dresser and walks erect, almost stiffly. His blue eyes are appraising and sometimes appear quite cold. He spent the first half of his life in Germany, where he was born.

He had told the team earlier, when they were training in Aspen, Colorado, that he was the team hatchet man and that if someone had to be kicked off the team, he would do it, and he would be the scapegoat for all the difficulties. He had also told them that he was going to discipline their minds and bodies, and that although skiing is an individual sport, everyone must work together. And that meant schedules. He planned to run a tightly regimented organization. He wanted to develop winners.

Willy has been a winner all his life. In his twenty-two years as the coach at the University of Denver his ski teams won one hundred out of one hundred and twenty-three dual meets, and fourteen National Collegiate titles. For a while, his arch rival was Bob Beattie, who, before he became one of Willy's predecessors as National Ski Team coach, trained the ski team at the University of Colorado. Willy beat the pants off Bob. Most of the team did not appreciate Willy's authoritarian attitude toward ski racing. Willy smiled tightly at the photographer.

Standing next to him for the picture was his assistant coach, Hanspeter Rohr. He is twenty-six, and it was his first season as a coach. During the 1969–70 season, he was one of Switzerland's top downhillers until, in the Wengen, Switzerland, downhill, he crashed at 70 miles per hour and left a large splotch of blood on the snow, tore the ligaments in his left foot and leg, bent in the ankle bone, broke the right leg, dislocated his shoulder, broke his nose, injured his eye, scraped the skin off half of his face and tore the back shoulder muscle. Four operations later he decided his racing career was over. He hoped to make the Americans into good downhillers.

The women's coach, Hank Tauber, twenty-nine, wanted to pull the girls into the winning circle, and he also believed the route lay with regimentation. He had top racers in two sisters from Vermont, Marilyn and Barbara Ann Cochran, but the rest had to be trained and pushed.

The American ski racers had been tested psychologically, and the tests showed that they valued their independence highly. The tests also pointed out that the downhill racers were tense, assertive, and evaded rules. Craig Shanholtzer was a downhill specialist, and it was his first year on the circuit—the rookie. Bob Cochran was ranked thirteenth in the world in downhill and wanted to win a World Cup race. Hank Kashiwa, a three-year veteran, hoped to sort out things in his head and win a medal in the Olympics. He was developing downhill skills. Spider Sabich, who missed the picture session—he was off doing something else—preferred slalom. These young racers, and the rest of the team—there were no heroes among them, no super athletes—hoped to match the vast superiority of the French, Austrian, Italian, and Swiss skiers. Well, maybe in one race.

The team picture was taken at one-two hundred and fiftieth of a second, slightly less time than it took Rudd Pyles, a quiet Coloradoan who is a talented downhiller, to relax his face into an easy smile. A ski racer can win or lose in the time it takes to smile. In a downhill it takes just a little longer to crash and possibly smash your body to bits. No one thought about that. It was time to load into the Peugeot bus and head back to the Hotel Val d'Isère, shuck off the ski clothes, take a bath or sauna, and then go to the local pastry shop for something sweet, talk with racers from other national teams, perhaps make a new friend. Time is short for a ski racer during the season—a few hours in the afternoon after a day on the hill, then dinner at seven-thirty, and to bed early.

Rudd Pyles is a 6-footer, strongly built. His face is thick, heavy in the cheeks and jowls, but handsome in the American way—square-faced, long, full lips, a strong chin and well-proportioned nose. His gray-green eyes look directly into you, easily, and he blinks in a slow, measured cadence. He is a quiet person and chooses his words with care; no one could ever be flippant with Rudd. He would have been the team leader if there was such a thing; he felt honored to be on the American Ski Team, and it bothered him to see team members acting up when parading in their uniforms. He works hard at ski racing, but he enjoys it immensely. He wants to win. In 1969–70, his first tour of Europe, he started sixty-sixth in his first downhill race at Val d'Isère. He placed sixth, and at the World Championships in Val Gardena he finished eleventh. Rudd was the American team's best prospect to win a World Cup race.

The day after the American team had its photograph taken, Rudd was one of ninety-eight racers in training on the OK downhill, named after Henri Oreiller and Jean-Claude Killy, two of the famous native sons who helped to make Val d'Isère known as the resort of champions.

Willy Schaeffler was the American team coach in the early 1970s

The day was as clear and bright as mountain water. Rudd and his teammates rode the red, blue, and yellow gondolas of the Daille lift up above the timberline, past the mid-station, to the top of the Bellevarde. Each was to have another run down the course, and as they waited for their running number to be called they soaked in the sun. There was little wind.

The starting gate was a wooden structure that looked as hastily put together as a new outhouse. During the race, sophisticated Longines timing equipment would measure to one-hundredth of a second the time, from start to finish, of each racer. But in training, timing was in the hands of the team coaches and trainers, positioned at the start, halfway down the course, and at the finish. Each man was equipped with a stop watch and a walkie-talkie to measure the halfway and finish times of their racers and then compare these times with the times of the previous day's training, and with the times of those racers favored to win. Somewhere on the course, usually at different turns, were other trainers with their eyes locked into small videotape cameras. In the evenings the tapes would be played so the racers could hopefully pick out some flaw in their style or in the line they raced. The American team had one video camera, the French three.

Downhillers are as carefully dressed as matadors, perhaps not with so many frills and with more common sense. The racers are zipped into one-piece suits, usually colorful and as tight as snake skin. They were first developed by the French. The suit cuts down wind resistance and so increases the speed of the racer. The original version had one zipper and the racers found it was impractical. Now the suit has an additional zipper—a 4-inch horizontal affair at the crotch. A plastic helmet protects the head from wind, cold, and serious injury. It has a psychological effect too. Before racers were required to wear helmets, they wore wool caps. During the race the noise of the wind whistling into their ears because of high speed often caused fear. Now the helmets shut out the noise.

The American uniform is a sober two-tone blue, slightly iridescent. The helmet is red and blue and star speckled, as are the warm-up suits and sweaters. "This ski uniform, it is a scandal," yelped one of the French technicians. "Flags and stars on their shoulders, gloves, pants, helmets, maybe they have them on their underpants?" It is hard, in Europe, for an American to do anything right.

Rudd's mind was locked into the course. The previous day he had two fast runs that equaled the times of Henri Duvillard and Karl Cordin, France and Austria's two best downhillers, and he was confident. Four days earlier, at the season's first race in Sestriere, Italy, he had skied slowly in training, then gone all out in the race and crashed halfway down the course. "I really was a dumb bastard to go so fast," he commented to a friend, one of the few times he has been heard to swear. He had changed his technique for the Val d'Isère race—he was going all out in training, then would relax in the downhill. Rudd had not raced at over 55 miles per hour during a month of training in Aspen, Colorado, and he realized that his timing was not as sharp as it should have been. The French team had had 240 miles of downhill running since they went into training in July, and for ten days in early

December they had been running the OK downhill. They were up for the race.

"Beep!" the trainers chirped into their radios and Karl Cordin, Austria's youngest new star, was on the course. "Beep!" and World Cup champion Karl Schranz poled out of the starting gate a minute later. Then Henri Duvillard and the crazy, happy Malcolm Milne of Australia. Each racer was testing the course, searching for the perfect line and the speed that would carry him faster than the day before. "Beep!" and Bob Cochran was off.

Rudd's bindings were set to release at three hundred and ninety-six pounds, his 222-centimeter K2 skis, striped in red, white, and blue, were waxed with Swix green and paraffin. A good combination, thought Rudd; he had confidence in the skis—they were in top shape. "Beep!" and he was out of the gate, poling, skating, then dropping his body into an egg-shaped crouch that would lessen the wind resistance, so his skis would slide faster. He hit the first steep drop-off and was riding his skis lightly at 60 miles per hour, following the ribbon of carefully manicured snow that ended more than 2 miles below in the valley. The downhill trail, about 30 yards wide, was lined on each side by small red and white Evian flags. Thirty-one control gates were set on the course, and it is running through these gates that the racer hopes to find the fastest line to the finish. If he cuts the corners well, his time should be slightly over two minutes.

Speed, speed, speed, this is what makes a downhiller. He must love speed, the feeling of conquering a mountain with his skis, his body, his mind. The top speed of a downhill racer has been measured at 82.5 miles per hour. Yet downhillers who rely only on speed do not last long. They must have other qualities, particularly the strength and suppleness of a thoroughly trained body that can control speed. They must have a sense of what they call in France *glissement*—the ability to slide their skis well. They must know how to relax their ankles and knees so that both skis ride flat on the snow, which gives them more speed. They must predict the difficulties of speed in relation to turns and bumps. Some of this knowledge is acquired but much of the down-

Skier hurtling out of control on the race course sends flags flying

hiller's psyche is intuitive. And aggressive.

The psychological studies of the American racers supported the premise that the downhiller is an extrovert. This is not necessarily true; downhillers are usually lucid, calm individuals. They do not react with the quick movements of the slalom skier fighting for one-hundredth of a second on many turns; the downhiller gains split-seconds with a feeling of the whole race. Yet if he misses his line or slides a turn at a crucial point, he can blow the race. If he does not know his speed he may crash disastrously. The downhiller must always be on the edge between the highest speed and safety, riding the skis into the inner limits of danger. "You need guts to run downhill," said Karl Schranz, who was world champion two years in a row, "and not everyone has it."

Rudd—you could call him an introvert—was thinking only of speed after he poled onto the course and crouched his body into the egg position. He limbered his knees and ankles, softening them so he could feel contact between his feet, the skis, and snow—a feeling of riding the skis flatly, efficiently. His eyes were on the first steep drop-off; he would press low into this pitch to pick up speed for the flat below.

No trees cover this portion of the downhill; it is rolling, snow-covered terrain of thousands of acres barren of people save the racers and trainers, and a few recreational skiers, an undulating white desert dominated by the Grande Motte glacier. The racers glided through this scenery, as infinitesimal as the billions of snow crystals that compose the huge plateau.

The snow was soft and whispery, light and deep, but on the course it was packed very hard, almost icy. Very few bumps were in the trail; the snow was meticulously prepared for high speed. The upper part was smooth, flat and shiny. It sucked the speed out of Rudd and he could feel the exhilaration as he accelerated.

Rudd was always fast. At the age of five, he was racing on Chalk Mountain in the mining town of Climax, Colorado, on a slope his grandfather and a few friends spent seventy days clearing in 1932. Rudd's mother recalled that he was always the fastest among his friends, snowplow-

ing staight down the hill. During the dry, cold evenings he, his brother and the others would strap on their skis and chase rabbits down the mountain, through the forests, and sometimes they would play tag or hide and seek, their yells and laughter muffled by the pines and fir trees. Moments like these Rudd recalls fondly and with amusement. His desire to ski fast grew with him, and he practiced as a young racer at nearby Arapahoe Basin, where Willy Schaeffler, now his coach, was the ski school director; Willy remembers Rudd at that time as having a head that looked like an overgrown pumpkin, his racing helmet was so big. Rudd's racing progressed through a cracked ankle and two dislocated shoulders. He was named to the American Ski Team in 1969 and improved so quickly in downhill that he was appointed to the A Team and sent to Europe to race.

Inside his helmet Rudd heard nothing. There is not much noise to a downhill, just a whistling *swisssh* as the wind sucks past the racer. He glimpsed snow blurring him, yellowed by his goggles. He pressed his weight evenly onto the two skis, to move faster. Because there were no trees with which to judge speed and distance, Rudd concentrated on the first difficult obstacle in this section, a bump that he had to prejump— to lift up his weight just before the bump so that he would land quickly and not be thrown in the air and lose speed. Immediately afterwards there was another bump, a bigger one, which he also had to prejump. Below it lay a long flat that dipped into a chute; then the course curved past the mid-station of the gondola lift that he had ridden up that morning.

Shadows hid part of the trail, making vision difficult, and Rudd smoked onto the bump quicker than he expected. He jumped, pitching his body up and forward like a ski jumper; then he lowered it into a crouch and pressed his hands forward, so his body would follow and the weight would force the ski tips down. The wind would hit the top of the skis, pressing them even more quickly onto the snow. Then Rudd would repeat the process for the next bump.

But he did not land where he expected; his skis just kept going, skimming through the air toward the next bump. Rudd remained about 6 feet in the air over the snow, a rushing blur of motion aerodynamically balled up to reduce wind friction. Rudd subconsciously knew he was over-shooting the bump and the automatic reflexes that a downhiller develops started to function. Again he stood up on his skis, making a wind-check of his body to slow him down. But he re-mained airborne, hit the top of the next bump, and, like a stone skipped across a trout pool, was scaled higher into the air, over the hill, straight over the flat, 25 feet above the ground. His speed still produced the whistling swish as he hurtled through the air. He was no longer a ski racer in control of the mountain, he was a projectile.

During the previous day of training, Rudd had estimated his speed on this section at about 60 miles per hour. Overnight, the course had frozen harder, and the morning sun had not soft-ened the snow. Rudd had made his first prejump at about 75 miles an hour. It was one small mis-take, uncorrectable, that was leading him into a very high-speed crash and burn.

A spasm of fear, a clammy, cold wetness slammed into his stomach, then disappeared as Rudd tried to make a landing onto the flat. He kept his body stretched out vertically to break the wind, then prepared to absorb the shock of land-ing on the flat by folding his body, like an accor-dion. As his skis made contact with the snow, he used his body as a spring, folding his knees, then his back. But the force of gravity plus mass at 75 miles per hour was too much on the flat and his knees were forced into his chest, and his whole body was compacted, thrown forward. His face hit one of the ski tips and his jaw shattered in three places. Everything went black, and, like a dead rabbit worried by a hound dog, Rudd was shaken violently by the mountain.

As Rudd's jaw cracked and his face was mashed into the snow his body hyperextended in a flip. His skis arched above him, then slammed into the snow tails first. One buried itself and Rudd was whiplashed into the snow back first. Two vertebrae cracked. The ski cracked too, the sound of dry pine popping in a picnic fire. Rudd flipped again, then slithered loosely down the smooth course until the speed was dead and he lay still, a dark, collapsed lump on the sun-bright snow. He had gone over 200 feet in the air, 100 feet on the ground.

In the time it takes to smile.

Many team coaches were huddled at these bumps, timing their racers and checking their prejumps. Willy Schaeffler was there, a Longines stop watch in his hand, a Motorola radio slung across his shoulder. "God! He must be dead!" exclaimed Willy, and over the radio he called the team doctor, Rod Kirk, who was at the girls' sla-lom race. The young Canadian, Betsy Clifford, dressed in a red jump suit, was about to win her first World Cup race of the winter.

Stefano Anzi, the Italians' best downhiller, had also fallen at the same spot, but not seri-ously. He dragged Rudd to the side of the course so he would not be hit by the next racer. Stefano leaned over as Rudd regained consciousness and focused his eyes on the bright red-suited man with a pockmarked face. "Okay? You okay?" "Yeah," mumbled Rudd, and he got to his feet. Other racers had hurried onto the course and brought over his helmet, poles, gloves, and skis, all of which had been ripped from him during the crash. The next racer, Marcello Varallo, swished past, a blur of red—another shiny, red-suited Italian. The word had gone to the top—the course was fast, slow down.

Willy was on the radio with the doctor. "He's walking, I guess he's okay . . . No, he's walking in circles. Maybe he has a concussion. We meet you at the hotel." A Swiss doctor who knew the dangers of downhill training, and of this particular spot, examined Rudd, who felt he was all right. The doctor walked him several hun-dred yards to the mid-station gondola. Rudd rode it to the bottom and hitchhiked to his hotel, a five-minute walk from the mountain.

Betsy Clifford had won the girls' slalom and was surrounded at the bottom of the course by reporters and photographers. A gray silk scarf stuck out of her jump suit as she leaned over her poles. One hand moved nervously up and down the pole shaft but her face, smiling, happy, seemed to sparkle in the sunlight. Her eyes, gray and bright, darted from the reporters to the mountains, then back.

"Well, I almost blew it on the third gate of the first run . . . Yeah, I like to race, I see countries, learn languages . . . I hope to win the World Cup. Next year I think I can win three gold medals in the Olympics. Everybody does. Lot of pressure though, even if I win two . . ."

"Oh, she had an unbelievable second run," commented her coach, Peter Franzen. "She has plenty to go, she's only seventeen."

On her second run through the slalom course Betsy was unbelievably aggressive, fighting the gates, her mouth held in a sharp grimace, a pigtail streaming behind her. There is no doubt of her talent. She also plays the guitar, makes up lyrics, says and does what she likes. Some say she is a wild one. Her eyes never slow down, as nervous as a hummingbird, darting about. A few months before this race her younger brother was killed in a dune buggy accident.

As the press jotted down her comments Rudd lay on his bed. His back and jaw were beginning to hurt, and the doctor wanted an x-ray. The only machine big enough to photograph Rudd's back was in Bourg-St.-Maurice, 28 kilometers away. Rod Kirk drove Rudd down the winding road, past Lac de Tignes and into the valley. The doctor from Aspen, Colorado, who donated his time and paid his own way to Europe to be with the team, had his diagnosis confirmed—broken jaw and two compressed vertebrae. Six weeks of recuperation and you're lucky it's not serious.

They wheeled Rudd onto the third floor of the hospital at Bourg-St.-Maurice, past a tray full of crusty bread, into a bare room with a sink, a white tiled table, and two single beds with metal tubing hanging over the end, ready to support a traction break. The room looked like the morgue.

Rudd was on his back, an Ace bandage holding his jaw in place. The only sign of injury was his swollen lips. The jaw did not hurt as much as his back. The nurse doped him for pain. He lay there, flat on his back, sometimes reading Vonnegut's *Slaughterhouse Five,* until his arms ached from holding the book over his head. His teammates visited, bringing oranges and jokes and smiles. They did not stay long. A hospital is a creepy place for a ski racer.

During the rest of the winter this room would be occupied with injured skiers, the refuse from Val d'Isère and other nearby ski areas—Tignes, La Plagne, Les Arcs—tourist skiers with wrenched knees, broken legs and ankles, the result of unused muscles fighting with unfamiliar skis. If they had taken a spill as Rudd did, on the OK *piste* at 75 miles per hour, they could be crippled, or dead.

Rudd was not missed at Val d'Isère, except by the Americans, because who ever heard of Rudd Pyles? And if an American is hurt and misses the season, well . . . a shrug of the shoulders . . . "It's too bad, but . . . they're just a bunch of amateurs." Besides, there were cocktail parties to go to. One for the press was given by Martell and Black and White, two of France's better selling cognacs and scotches. Tiny, hot hors d'oeuvres were served by long-skirted, smiling hostesses.

The press in Europe is privileged and welcomed. Hotel rooms at various races are discounted for them, and if some do not get a room with a bath, they complain. The press invariably congregate at the finish line, as they had that morning at the girls' slalom, marking down times, listening for and promoting rumors. The winning racers are asked the same questions, race after race—"Did you have trouble on the course? . . . Was it fast? . . . Did you think you would have a chance to beat . . . ?" When the French skiers lose, the French press will invariably publish a statement saying why the French cannot win all the time. And the Austrians write about why the Austrians are not winning and talk about firing the coach, but they prefer to criticize the French, who usually do win. "And to what," minced Austria's leading ski journalist to French star Patrick Russel, after he took a spill in a slalom, "do you attribute your defeat?" There are the newspaper journalists, a middle-aged bourgeois group, and the TV people, who generally work hard, and the photographers, who spend much of their time hustling their pictures to the ski equipment people for advertisements. The press make heroes of winners and ignore losers.

They could care less about an unknown American who cracked his back in training just as Betsy Clifford won her first race of the season.

There was also a glamorous cocktail party hosted by the Evian people. It was the big event of the Val d'Isère races. Officials and politicians and coaches and beautiful women with beautiful clothes and ski equipment directors, presidents, vice-presidents, and even Jean-Claude Killy, mingled and drank scotch and gin-and-orange-juice and bit into the flaky hors d'oeuvres and made dates for dinner, a discotheque, and hopefully a common bed. It was as glamorous as the movies. But there were no racers at the party; none had been invited. Later, at Jean-Pierre's, a small pub that is quiet and serves three-franc beer, Killy shared drinks with three girls, one of them an old-time aficionado of the race circuit. Killy worked hard during the day, promoting Head skis. Ex-racers who win big are invited to all the cocktail parties.

While the parties were flashing, the lights were extinguished in the hospital room where Rudd lay still, staring into the darkness. Before sleep came, Rudd thought about his crash and injury and the circumstances that led to it, and about ski racing, and a lost season.

Downhill

by **JAMES SALTER**

The film, **Downhill Racer**, *released in 1970, was extraordinary from every point of view: the initial drive of the young and relatively unknown actor Robert Redford to get a credible story of downhill racing on the screen; the seminal collaboration with a film writer who also knew his skiing, James Salter; the unexpectedly warm critical reception of this first genuine, dramatic and serious ski film.*

*When Robert Redford began in 1967 to look for a writer whom he could seriously consider for the script of an authentic film about downhill racing, the name of James Salter, a resident of Aspen, immediately came to mind. He and Salter knew each other socially and shared a love of skiing. Redford's contract was with Paramount, which had already shown its interest by buying Oakley Hall's novel, **The Downhill Racers**. By 1967, several scripts had been written based on the book, all of which had been rejected. To pique Paramount anew, Redford spent a considerable sum of his own money filming the World Cup circuit prior to the 1968 Olympics at Grenoble ("the Killy Olympics"). Redford stitched some of the footage—particularly the incident involving Moose Barrow's spectacular fall of that season—and showed the film to Paramount, which said, "go ahead." He and Salter then collaborated for six weeks on a script. The collaboration included traveling together for several weeks on the World Cup circuit, absorbing the atmosphere and character of international racing.*

"My motivation," said Redford, "was to erase the bad feeling between Hollywood and the ski world. In the past, because Hollywood had never had good intentions about a ski film, skiing was used as the background for some sex thing or a dopey teen-age party film."

*By the time they were ready to write in 1968, both Redford and Salter had such strong ideas about ski racing that neither felt he had to read Hall's book or any of the scripts based on it. They felt competent to forge ahead toward what they both wanted, a film that laid out realistically the tough, lonely, pressured world of the downhill racer. They called the script **Downhill**.*

"The film," said Salter, "became the story of an American coach, Claire, whose lifelong ambition was to 'win' an Olympic gold. When his chosen weapon for this, Creech, is injured, he is forced to use a racer he detested, Chappellet, the Redford character."

The Salter script deftly sets up the opposition of Claire and Chappellet: two men with entirely different approaches to life. Claire is idealistic and fervent, a believer in the "justice of sport," in which a man's ability alone counts and where teammates help each other—all for one and one for all. Chappellet, more realistic, believes that ability alone is often foiled by politics and jealousy, that teammates can hurt as easily as help. He is, and remains, a loner, a skeptical man. Claire wants a racer in the "willing hero" mold. Chappellet does not fit. He is not a team player. He trains without a thought to the schedule. Then, to Claire's chagrin, Chappellet begins to win, beating even Creech. Salter's script tells what hap-

pens when the failed relationship between Claire and Chappellet is called upon to bear the stress of the ultimate race for the gold medal; you are left wondering what might have happened had the two accepted instead of fought each other.

Downhill Racer is more than a memorable, realistic film; it has a special meaning for skiing, since it was inspired by the world of skiing in the late 1960s, soon after Killy's Grenoble achievement.

Not only did Moose Barrow's spectacular fall help sell the picture to Paramount, but something of Killy's intransigent independence filtered into the Chappellet characterization. Both were loners, self-contained and terse. And the film proved prophetic when a loner, an American racer who trains on his own, Phil Mahre, became the world's Number 1 skier in 1981 and 1982.

This selection is from the last half of James Salter's Downhill *script. The hero, David Chappellet, and his teammates on the United States national squad are in Europe where Chappellet starts winning for the first time, much to the surprise of everyone including Claire, the coach, who never thought much of Chappellet or his chances. Creech, until now the Number 1 United States racer, is unbelieving, and so is Brumm, the top European ski correspondent. Even Max Meier, the European, favored to win the upcoming Olympic downhill, becomes curious about Chappellet's potential. Chappellet meets a Swiss industrialist and ski maker, Machet, and his stunning secretary, Carole. He begins an affair with Carole, even though she has a Swiss fiance. Then Chappellet returns, a hero, to his home town, Converse, Colorado.*

Chappellet flies to Europe, tries to recommence the affair with Carole and then after Creech is sidelined by injury, enters the Olympics, favored to win. Other characters are Mayo, the assistant United States coach; Bryan, Kipsmuth and Gabriel, members of the United States team; Ron Engel and Bruce Devore, TV sports announcers; and an unnamed racer, Chappellet's nemesis, coming down behind him on the Olympic course.

We pick up Salter's script in Morzine, France, a stop on the World Cup race circuit.

ALL in quick cuts: A racer crossing the finish line, the blur of his legs past the electric eye. The camera finds him com-ing to a stop, wearing number 20, unsmiling: CHAPPELLET.

The tote board, his name replacing the one in first place, the names dropping back a space.

Congratulations. Smiles. They are taking his picture. His face is serious. He's still trying to look up the hill a little. CHAPPELLET seems pleased but a bit wooden, unused to it.

A French announcer talking into a microphone, hastily describing the event.

ANNOUNCER: . . . *et puis, debout après sa victoire, sa victoire incroyable, le jeune Chappellet avec le calme d'un maître . . .*

30. Wengen. Another finish. There are more cameramen this time. They have been waiting for him. He is number 16.

The tote board has CHAPPELLET first, SIEGMAN second, CREECH third.

CREECH stands beside him this time. The delirium and excitement surrounding CHAPPELLET is less painful to him. He is third. The certainty of eventual victory still lives within him. It's in his calmness, his expression.

31. JEROME BRUMM, dressed like a crack skier himself, sitting at a table, smoking. CHAPPELLET arrives. He is more casually dressed, he almost looks like a delivery boy. BRUMM wants to know CHAPPELLET a little. CHAPPELLET is fully aware of who has finally decided to interview him. Fine, he is thinking, you didn't have time for me last year, you waited until I was winning . . . He's going to give BRUMM an interview but he's not going to be particularly nice.

BRUMM: Well, David, sit down. Would you like a tea or something?

CHAPPELLET shakes his head: no. BRUMM, who is clever, sizes him up.

BRUMM: The papers are filled with stories about you. There's a great affection here for an American champion, perhaps because there's never been one. At least up to now there's never been one.

CHAPPELLET smiles slightly. He's like a sullen boy, or at least a cautious one, listening to a lecture by his school principal.

BRUMM: It's ironic, isn't it? You came here a year ago, you were the same man you are now and practically the same skier. Nobody knew you were alive. You were one of scores of unknown boys . . .

CHAPPELLET: That's right.

BRUMM: Well, don't be suspicious. That's the way it always is. (Pause—there is no answer. He continues) Max Meier was even asking me about you.

CHAPPELLET still appears unimpressed.

BRUMM: In private. He never asks questions like that. (Pause) I told him I knew very little about you. (Pause again) David, what do you think of some of these other racers?

CHAPPELLET: Which ones?

BRUMM: Oh, Meier.

CHAPPELLET calmly takes a small cigar from BRUMM's tin and lights it. He blows the smoke out slowly. An act of extraordinary contempt but so carefully controlled that one is not sure. BRUMM watches.

CHAPPELLET: He's all right. He's getting a little old, isn't he?

BRUMM: He's twenty-seven.

CHAPPELLET: Is that all? I thought he was more. (He inhales once more)

Afterwards, alone in the corridor, he leans against the wall. The cigar has made him dizzy, almost ill. His face is damp.

32. In one of the big hotels, we follow a white-jacketed waiter with a tray to the table,

CLAIRE is having tea with some people in the salon. It's a vast, luxurious room, somewhat old-fashioned. They are a party of five. One of the men we have seen before. He is lean, balding. He was at the awards ceremony when CHAPPELLET won his first trophy the year before. He is ANDRE MACHET, about forty-five, with the faint tan of the rich on him, well groomed, comfortable. He's an industrialist whose money comes from textile companies. He makes one want to be forty-five. And with him, we now see her as MACHET leans forward, that same stunning girl. She's in a high-necked sweater. Opened on the chair—she is sitting on it—a marvelous, pony coat. CAROLE is her name. She is MACHET's secretary.

The waiter is setting down the tea things. We don't hear what they are talking about. The other two people are a man and a woman, both in their thirties. Friends of MACHET. Something amusing is said, they all laugh. CAROLE smiles. She is silent, she is not really a part of it, but how that silence compels.

CHAPPELLET comes in the door. He sees them. After a moment of hesitation, he walks over to the table. He stands there. MACHET looks up, then CLAIRE.

CLAIRE: Hello, David. (A questioning pause) I'd like to introduce you to Mr. Machet, Carole . . .

He has evidently forgotten the names of the other two people. MACHET supplies them.

MACHET: Monsieur and Madame Treler.

CHAPPELLET nods at the introductions. CLAIRE is looking at him as if to say, yes, what do you want? There is a moment of awkwardness which MACHET again clears up.

MACHET: Please join us. (He indicates a chair at another table)

CHAPPELLET sits down. MACHET has made a space for him beside himself. CHAPPELLET glances at CAROLE who shows modest interest. She awards him a faint smile. The sequence is

Downhill racer at high speed has to demonstrate smoothness as well as strength

shot like a brief dinner party: various faces, not always the ones speaking. It doesn't seek to give the whole, but rather the details of this encounter.

MACHET: Would you like some tea?

CHAPPELLET: Yes. Fine.

MACHET raises his hand and snaps his fingers. He then forgets about it, talking instead to CHAPPELLET while CAROLE attends to the request in the background—a glimpse of her speaking to the waiter, perhaps.

MACHET: I'm very pleased to meet you. Your coach is too secretive. He's keeping you a mystery to us all. (Smiles)

CLAIRE sits, not precisely unhappy but quite reserved.

MACHET: That was a brilliant victory at Wengen. What skis did you race on?

CHAPPELLET: Dynamics.

MACHET: Dynamics. Do you like them?

CHAPPELLET: (His interest is centered on CAROLE though he is unable to talk to her because of MACHET) They're all right.

MACHET: You know, I have a company that makes the best skis in the world.

CHAPPELLET: (After the briefest pause, as if

he hadn't been listening and now realizes . . .) Oh, yeah? I didn't know that.

MACHET: There are very few racers good enough to get the most out of them, though.

CHAPPELLET nods. A faint smile.

MACHET: I'd like to have you try a pair. (Smiles)
At the door, as they are leaving, just the two of them, CHAPPELLET and CLAIRE. Outside, CHAPPELLET looks back in, trying to see her.

CHAPPELLET: Who is she?

CLAIRE: You have very bad manners.

CHAPPELLET: (Still looking through the glass) You introduced me like I was some disease.

CLAIRE: You're getting a curious sense of your importance.

CHAPPELLET: Me? I couldn't be very important, you don't even talk about me. What's wrong, don't you like winning?

CLAIRE: (As he starts down the steps) Not too much.

33. CHAPPELLET, his nerviness gone, walking alone on a street of town. It's early evening, the dark winter hours, four-thirty, five. It is the portrait of the competitor the morning after. A kind of melancholy has taken hold of him, an indolence he cannot shake. Suddenly he stops, as if struck by a thought.
In a shop, buying pastry, she is standing. He has seen her. He enters the shop, comes up behind her.

CHAPPELLET: Hello.

She turns, not enough, it's almost a double take and then she rewards him with the most marvelous smile, a smile that says more than words. It's as unexpected as it is overwhelming.

CAROLE: Did you come to buy something?

CHAPPELLET: (Simply) No.

She has a slight Swiss accent. She is calm but very affecting. If there is an aura which surrounds people and which we react to automatically, without volition, as magnets attract or repel, then that is how these two, without explanation or frivolous gestures, interact.

CAROLE: I'm happy you stopped.

CHAPPELLET: Well . . . me, too.

She is paying the salesgirl. CHAPPELLET almost feels dizzy. A change has come over him, a moment almost of uncertainty.

They walk down the street together, a quiet street.

CAROLE: I've been reading articles about you.

CHAPPELLET: You have?

CAROLE: There are many.

CHAPPELLET: Really?

CAROLE: In all the papers.

They come into her hotel, the same one in which they were having tea. At a table which has eight or ten newspapers laid across it like flags, she picks one up. It's on one of those reading sticks. She begins to read, in German.

CHAPPELLET: What does . . .

CAROLE: (Before he can really ask she begins translating it)

CHAPPELLET listens. He likes to hear it, and he likes to hear her speaking German and then that wonderful, slightly strange English.

CHAPPELLET: Read it again. Do you live here?

CAROLE: No, I'm just here for the week. With my boss.

CHAPPELLET: He's your boss?

CAROLE: Yes, what did you think? (A little smile)

CHAPPELLET: Read it again.

34. In the morning at the cable car station. CHAPPELLET has made his first practice run. He walks, his skis in his hands, down an outside channel to the head of the line—the crowd is folded back five or six times inside the guide railings. Other racers entering too. Suddenly he stops. Near the end of the line he sees CAROLE. He motions to her: come on. She hesitates. He goes to her and lifts her skis over the rail.

CHAPPELLET: Come on.

They go to the head of the line together. The GUARD starts to question them, but CHAPPELLET bluffs her through.

They stand among the others on the platform waiting for the car. She is in a trim parka, three wide bands of color, the bottom blue, the middle rose, the top blue-violet. Slim pants. She could be a racer herself she looks so great. She is smiling, delighted to be there.

CAROLE: I saw you coming down yesterday.

The cable car is approaching.

CAROLE: You were like a bullet.

He looks at her. He doesn't smile. He is heroic: it is his day, his milieu, his very hour.

They are crushed close in the car. They talk in low voices we cannot hear.

At the top they put on their skis without a word. He is finished first. He watches her. And

off they go, CHAPPELLET leading. She skis very well, of course not so well as he. They are nearly alone, two figures on the open mountain, across flats, into corridors of trees. Finally he stops. She checks, out of breath, beside him. The sweet exhaustion, like the exhaustion of love.

CAROLE: I was afraid you would never stop.

CHAPPELLET: Are you tired?

CAROLE: A little. My legs.

CHAPPELLET: (Touching his upper leg) It's all here.

CAROLE: (Feeling) It's like iron.

He feels her leg.

CHAPPELLET: Not bad.

CAROLE: But not iron.

CHAPPELLET: No. (Slight smile)

On the downhill course, CLAIRE and MAYO standing together, MAYO with his stop watch.

CLAIRE: Where's Chappellet?

MAYO: He came down.

CLAIRE: I haven't seen him since that first time.

MAYO shrugs. CLAIRE looks uphill.

A long shot, a series of long shots of the two of them skiing, some of the most arresting and poetic in the film, in fact the *only* shots of that pure joy which is so often and so badly shown in "skiing" films. They must be the best one can imagine—more than one can imagine.

35. CLAIRE entering the hotel at night. It's late. Most of the lights are out. The NIGHT PORTER, an old man, gives him his key.

He enters a small writing room. He is star-

Downhill racers sometimes leave the snow for leaps of fifty or sixty feet

tled to see someone asleep, curled up in a chair. He looks closely. It's BRYAN.

CLAIRE touches him.

CLAIRE: Hey, DK . . .

BRYAN opens his eyes.

CLAIRE: What are you studying?

BRYAN is befuddled. He's not fully awake perhaps. He gives an embarrassed smile.

CLAIRE: What are you doing down here?

BRYAN: I must have fallen asleep. I guess I was reading.

Something in his voice makes CLAIRE curious. He looks, but sees no book, no paper.

CLAIRE: What are you reading?

BRYAN doesn't have a reply.

CLAIRE is rapidly mounting the stairs. He goes down the darkened corridor. Shoes set outside the doors. He knocks on a door. There is no answer. He knocks again.

CLAIRE: Chappellet? (He knocks a third time)

CHAPPELLET: (His voice muffled) Who is it?

CLAIRE: Open the door.

The door opens. CHAPPELLET's face looks sleepy, perhaps he is feigning it.

CLAIRE: Who's in there?

CHAPPELLET looks at him, then slowly begins to smile.

CLAIRE: Get her out of here.

CHAPPELLET: There's nobody here.

CLAIRE pushes his way in. He turns on the light. The room is empty. CHAPPELLET is looking at him with amusement and scorn.

CHAPPELLET: You didn't look in the bathroom.

CLAIRE: Who do you think you are? DK is sleeping in a chair downstairs.
CHAPPELLET: (Slight laugh) He just doesn't remember anything unless you write it down for him. I told him about an hour.

CLAIRE: No wonder they hate you.

It hurts. CLAIRE goes out, the door closes. CHAPPELLET is left standing there. His head lowers.
A light knock.
CHAPPELLET opens the door. It's BRYAN.

CHAPPELLET: (Not unkindly) What'd you do, fall asleep?

BRYAN squeezes past him, ashamed to answer, ashamed of himself and of being involved. Silent, unresponsive, he begins to brush his teeth.

37. MAX MEIER at the top, ready to start. CU. The picture of absolute determination. He leans forward. He looks like Schmeling jumping into Crete. His ability is great, his pride enormous.
CREECH and CHAPPELLET standing close together. CHAPPELLET is number 9, CREECH 14. They're running their skis back and forth in the snow. It's CHAPPELLET's turn soon. He starts to move off.

CREECH: (Not looking up) Okay, Giant-Killer.

CHAPPELLET grins.

CHAPPELLET: Hey, John. (His voice has a tone and intimacy that only comrades share) If not me, you. If not you, me.

Cut to the final, closeup rush of CHAPPELLET coming in to a stop at the finish and a great crowding, a wild elation around him. We hear no dialogue. Photographers pressing close, six or seven of them, men with microphones in their hands, the bulk of a film camera . . .
MEIER standing to the side, head down, not watching.
CLAIRE at the edge of the crowd around CHAPPELLET. Someone is shooting his picture, too. He appears very cold, very impassive. Events have proved more bitter than he dreamed. He has no further power over CHAPPELLET, he realizes that.
CHAPPELLET smiling with that tight, mirthless acceptance of champions. He's still being crowded. Someone has handed him a cup of Ovamaltine for publicity photos. He doesn't seem to realize it. He takes a sip, makes a face. They are trying to get him to say a few words into a microphone. He tosses the cup over his shoul-

der, some of it splashes on people behind him. He begins to ski away a bit so he can look up at the board.

38. A WAITER, serving, not knowing exactly the right words, congratulates CHAPPELLET.

WAITER: (Sincerely and touchingly) Eh, I could like to give congratulations, eh, I . . .

CHAPPELLET eating, looks up, nods. Yes, offers his hand. His teammates, not seeming to pay attention, hear it.

39. CHAPPELLET. CU. He is looking at himself in the mirror in his room. He sees, quite clearly, the champion of the world. The door opens. He quickly looks down, as if turning on the water in the sink. CREECH comes in. He leaves the door ajar. It's not easy for him to talk.

CREECH: Good race, Dave.

CHAPPELLET turns on the water. Nods. He rinses his hands. Dries them.

CREECH: I thought I was going to beat you today.

CHAPPELLET, a little soft snort. A half-smile.

CREECH: It's not so easy to do.

CHAPPELLET: I had a good run.
CREECH: You're the big man. There's no question about that now. You're the man to beat.

In a strange, almost awkward gesture, CREECH holds out his hand, practically full-length. CHAPPELLET, after a moment, a split moment of wonder, takes it. They shake. CREECH looking at CHAPPELLET and then dropping his glance, even his head a little. He is passing his primacy to CHAPPELLET. He is passing his rank.

40. Early spring. Switzerland, perhaps Montreux. In any case, on a lake in one of those old,

extraordinary hotels. Perhaps it's even Annecy.

A WAITER walking down the corridor carrying a tray. The many large doors. The creak of the floor underfoot. He stops. Knocks.

He comes into the room. The camera remains on him. He puts down the tray on a table, clearing away a magazine first, an ashtray, some other things. He is very discreet. He does not look at anything in the room.

WAITER: (Not looking) *Voilà, Madame.*

VOICE: *Merci.*

He closes the door. The voice was CAROLE'S. She is in bed.
A head appears at the door to the large bathroom. It's CHAPPELLET.
Outside, the silence of a cool morning. The lake is still. The rowboats creak in the smooth water. A lone dog walks on the lawn.
CAROLE preparing the breakfast. The camera coolly but tenderly recording every detail of the ritual. She looks in the pots to see which is tea and which is water. She unwraps the little packages of butter. She opens the *petit pain,* butters it, spreads on jam. The simplicity, the silence of this service is very touching. In her expression, which is not easy to read, is both disinterest in a simple task and a faint pleasure, amusement, because of the way he is watching. As for CHAPPELLET, he knows she is a girl he could never ordinarily have met, there simply would have been no way.
They have eaten. She is back under the covers. CHAPPELLET sits cross-legged, dressed only in pajama bottoms, on the bed. He's beautiful: flat-chested as a farmboy, lean, graceful, at least as beautiful in his way as she is. He's reading from a magazine, *Sports Illustrated,* which lies on the bed at his knees.

CHAPPELLET: Superbly calm, and with the absolute concentration the sport demands, a concentration which if it wavers for only an instant can mean the difference between victory and defeat or serious injury . . .

The camera has drifted to him. He likes

reading this. He continues.

CHAPPELLET: . . . a young American skier brought something to the dazzling runs of Europe this season which had not been seen for many years, if, in fact ever. David Chappellet, the fresh hope and dream of U.S. competitive skiing was . . .

A sound of her getting up. We don't see her but as he reads he watches her, the last sentence trailing off.

CHAPPELLET: . . . feared in Europe this year, feared and respected in a way reserved for the great heroes . . . of sport . . .

At the bathroom door. Her slow, pleased smile as she pauses there, against the jamb, looking at him, her face half-hidden. It is only her face, a bit of her neck, and then, perhaps, her bare forearm. One is suddenly certain she is naked.

41. They're at the top of the diving tower together. They've been swimming. She's very long-legged. She wears a one-piece suit. She's matching her nerve with his, walking out on the board though frightened, arms held close to her bosom. He's cruel. He's further out. He beckons her. She goes out more. He takes a little leap, making it vibrate. She cries out.

CHAPPELLET: (Stopping) Come on. (Stepping backward to make space) There's nothing to it. (Suddenly he has stepped off, it seems by mistake. He cries out as he falls) Aaah!

Down he goes, 20 feet. A great splash. He comes to the surface grinning. He was really clowning.

CHAPPELLET: (Calling to her) One, two . . .

CAROLE: Wait! (Pause, gathers her courage) All right.

CHAPPELLET: *Three!*

She jumps off and comes down not in a dive but standing up and maybe holding her nose. When she surfaces, she smiles. She's proud to have done it.

CHAPPELLET: One more.

CAROLE: No, that's enough. I proved I love you.

42. Lunch on the terrace in the sunlight, or at a window in the dining room. Only a few of the tables are occupied. It's still too early in the year.

CHAPPELLET: (While cutting something, his attention on the plate) Did you call today?

CAROLE: Ya. (That inhaled, German *ja*) I said the garage was having a lot of trouble getting the parts, but they would have them in a day or two. My brother wanted to come down and get me.

CHAPPELLET's eyes dart up.

CAROLE: (Not seeming to notice) But I said I was quite content . . .

CHAPPELLET: Content.

CAROLE: Yes. I told him I had met the man I was born for.

Sometimes she says things which are too poetic or overstated for him.

43. CU of him. He is doing something very slowly, as slow as taking adhesive plaster off a leg. In fact he's a little sleepy, perhaps it's the wine. He's undressing her. He's unfastening her necklace, her sleeveless dress. The deliberateness, the calm of his act is compelling.

CAROLE: (Submissive, her back to him) I told him not to tell my fiance.

CHAPPELLET: (Disinterestedly. He is opening the back of her dress, freeing it from her arms) You have one?

CAROLE: We've never made love.

CHAPPELLET: (Unfastening her brassiere) What's wrong with him?

The camera is on her face now. His actions in making her naked are reflected in it.

CAROLE: (Now he is touching her. Her eyes close. Her mouth parts) I don't know.

44. The sound of jet engines. CHAPPELLET in the airport corridors, glass-walled, talking to newsmen, two of them a TV team. He has an ease we have not seen before, the new poise of a movie star.

CHAPPELLET: Well, things have changed, I guess people know what it's all about. The first year I raced in the Nationals I came through New York, I had my skis in a case, and my boots. People would say, what are they? Skis. Skis, they'd say, well where are you jumping? It's a little different now. They say, hey, I saw your pictures in *Sports Illustrated.*

NEWSMAN: What are your immediate plans?

CHAPPELLET: Going home. They're having a sort of parade for me in my home town. (Grins)

NEWSMAN: Which is . . .

CHAPPELLET: Converse.

NEWSMAN: Converse.

CHAPPELLET: You've heard of Converse.

NEWSMAN TWO: They say you're a man of unconventional training methods.

CHAPPELLET: Oh, yeah? What does that mean?

NEWSMAN TWO: (Good-naturedly) That you don't train very hard.

CHAPPELLET: (A pause, like a politician who's been asked an awkward question) You just keep believing that.

45. A small Colorado town, some of it wretchedly modernized so that it's like all the small towns of America, hamburgers and milkshakes, cheap department store, drugs—some of it still in the Victorian past—the crumbling brick of a hotel or town hall, an old blockfront, unpainted houses. A town like a small Leadville. Carbondale. Marble.

Bunting in the streets. The marquee of the hotel has a banner which is folded over by the wind so one cannot read it. The barber shop has a printed sign CLOSED.

Ten or twelve cars parked in front of the town hall. One is a convertible (a 1966 Buick). It has bunting on it. Some of the others have signs and flags. A very homely assemblage. At the window of the building a few kids are looking in.

There are kids hanging around, too, at the doorway to what looks like it is the Town Council meeting room, now rearranged for a reception. About twenty or thirty people are inside, a third of them women, most of them weathered, plain, small-town Colorado. There are a few in their twenties. The average is older. One of the women is missing two front teeth.

A table is arranged in a sort of a buffet. Beer, Ritz crackers, pretzels, cheese. A cake which has been cut and on which only some fragments of DAVE CHAPPELLET, PRIDE OF CONVERSE, COLO., remain.

CHAPPELLET is found with a glass of beer in his hand. A YOUNG MAN, who probably works in the hardware store, is talking to him.

YOUNG MAN: It must be pretty exciting, Dave.

CHAPPELLET: Um.

YOUNG MAN: Racing in Europe and all.

The tedium of these conversations. An OLDER MAN is talking to CHAPPELLET'S FATHER who is gaunt, hard-faced, dressed like a workman on his day off.

OLDER MAN: I bet you never figured you'd see the day when Dave had a big celebration in town just for him.

FATHER: Don't think I did. (He's drinking beer, too)

OLDER MAN: Turned out to be a fine boy.

FATHER: I figured he'd end up in jail.

A WOMAN, about forty, is asking CHAPPELLET,

WOMAN: Do you plan on doing any more racing, now, David?

CHAPPELLET: (What can he answer?) Well . . . a little.

He's depressed by it all. They stand around, half in silence, not knowing exactly what to say to him. They are from a different world, these plain townspeople. The kids are whispering to each other at the door.

46. In his FATHER's house, an old frame house, bare as an orphanage. Worn-out linoleum on the kitchen floor. A wire fence outside, the iron posts are rusted.
His FATHER putting coffee on the stove. CHAPPELLET sits at the kitchen table. Silence.

FATHER: Want some coffee?

CHAPPELLET: Yeah.

Silence.

FATHER: I got your letter from France. (Pause) Sure takes a lot of stamps, don't it? (Silence. Still watching the coffee) I hear you been in all the magazines. You must of won a lot of races.

CHAPPELLET: I had a pretty good year. I won the Lauberhorn. Couple others.

FATHER: Win any money?

CHAPPELLET: Money? No. See, the thing is we have the Olympics next year . . .

FATHER: The Olympics ain't for money.

CHAPPELLET: No, but afterwards.

FATHER: Ah, yeah. (Takes coffee off. Pours) That's how it works, eh?

CHAPPELLET: Yeah. Well, it can.

FATHER: Hm. If it don't, you're going to end up asking yourself the same question, they're all the time asking me: what's he do it for?

CHAPPELLET: (Two big spoons of sugar. Three) Well, I'll be famous. I'll be a champion.

Silence. The old man's (he's fifty) whole life is in his dress, his voice.

FATHER: World's full of them.

47. In his white sweatsuit, his face grim. He's lying on the floor—it's the Aspen gym—doing leg raises. The scene widens. Four or five of them are there. A TRAINER is counting for them. The shouts are like statements of where it hurts.
They're skipping rope like boxers. The solid rhythm.
Bicycling—60 miles a day. Nothing of the picturesque in it. Their legs aching as they pump, pump, pump. CHAPPELLET isn't in front, he's in the pack.

48. In their room, CHAPPELLET reading a magazine article. He has the magazine folded back. He's sitting in a chair, his legs up on a table or the windowsill. CREECH and KIPSMUTH are sitting, listening, CREECH on the bed.

CHAPPELLET: . . . Although still lacking in the kind of solid depth that makes the French and Austrians so strong, still the situation has changed in a way that makes it brighter than ever before. The U.S. team now has not one, but two icy-nerved racers who might well be able to achieve the impossible. Never in history has an American man brought home a gold medal in the Alpine events. They are the Everest of skiing. But never in history have American chances begun to look so good . . .

CHAPPELLET grins, suddenly tosses the magazine across the room at CREECH.

They are doing arch-ups on the bed in the morning, face down, raising arms and legs.

And then, somewhere outside, just the legs—several cuts—running, running, running . . .

49. They arrive in Europe. They emerge from the plane one by one. The camera picks them up like pieces of a team photo or like a silent rehearsal of the appearance of former champions in the ring. They look calm, experienced—real contenders—CLAIRE is talking to someone, a NEWSMAN whose back is to us. CLAIRE walking slowly.

CLAIRE: . . . No, we don't have a strategy. (His skiers passing slowly behind him as he talks, some glancing, some not) Our strategy is to win. We don't want the early races. We're going for the gold.

50. A telephone rings, the instrument fills the screen. CHAPPELLET picks it up on the second ring. He doesn't like to talk on the phone in Europe, it's tinny and he can't understand half the time.

CHAPPELLET: Hello.

It's CAROLE. We only hear her voice at first.

CAROLE: How are you, my beloved lover?

CHAPPELLET: (A different voice, a different meaning) Hello.

CAROLE: I saw you arriving on television today.

CHAPPELLET: You did? Hey, I've missed you.

CAROLE: I have missed you.

CHAPPELLET: Have you been reading about me?

The camera goes to her, then begins to alternate.

CAROLE: Practically every day.

CHAPPELLET: You have, eh? You coming down here?

CAROLE: That would be marvelous.

CHAPPELLET: Can you? After the race we have a week off.

CAROLE: (In that low voice) Yes. I would sleep in your arms.

CHAPPELLET: We've got a lot of snow here.

CAROLE: Where are you staying?

CHAPPELLET: Some place. The Solage.

52. The waitresses arranging decorations in the dining room. It's all for the Christmas *fête*.

CHAPPELLET sitting alone in the reading room. It's early evening. He looks at his watch.

CHAPPELLET eating alone. The dining room has many people in it, but no one from the team. The ordeal of a solitary meal in public. The sound of every movement, every bite. The faint embarrassment at being without company.

At the desk,

CHAPPELLET: Any calls for me?

CLERK: No, sir. (Looking in box) Nothing.

CHAPPELLET looking around his room. He sits down, waits.

He's lying, eyes closed, on the bed. Suddenly he reaches over and takes the telephone.

CHAPPELLET: Hello. (Has to wait) Operator?

Hello. I'd like to call Switzerland.

A telephone rings in another room, the room of a richly lived-in house. Someone comes to pick it up, a dark, earnest looking young man of about twenty-eight, CAROLE'S BROTHER.

BROTHER: Hello . . . Yes, *oui.* (Waits) Hello. Yes. Who is calling? Ah, yes . . . No, this is her brother . . . No, she's here. One moment, please.

CAROLE with the phone in her hand. They've been talking after dinner.

CAROLE: Hello. (She then puts her hand over the mouthpiece for a moment while her brother leaves—she watches him, though we don't see him. Then she begins again) Hello, darling. Where are you? (Pause) Yes, but darling, I can't. My fiance is here.

The camera goes to CHAPPELLET now. And then cuts back and forth.

CHAPPELLET: Who? (He had forgotten. Everything is crashing)

CAROLE: My fiance. He's visiting us, I can't help it.

CHAPPELLET: What is this, a joke? You're meeting me here.
CAROLE: Darling, I'm sorry. Did you win the race? Tell me, I didn't hear.

CHAPPELLET: What about this week? I stayed here to see you.

CAROLE: (Simply and not at all coldly) Darling, I'm sorry, you're just not in my plans. I had to change them. (She stops abruptly)

He hangs up. He is furious, depressed. Without arrangements, without money. The phone rings back. He picks it up—it's the charges or asking if he's finished.

VOICE: Hello, David?

CHAPPELLET: Yes.

Cut to BRUMM on the other end, downstairs.

BRUMM: This is Jerome Brumm,

53. CHAPPELLET has had several drinks. He can feel them and one can see them in a certain irresolution he shows.

BRUMM: So, I thought you'd be gone away with everyone. Where are they?

CHAPPELLET: Geneva, mostly. I should have gone, too. I've been . . . eh . . . stood up.

BRUMM: Stood up?

CHAPPELLET: Yeah,

Silence.

CHAPPELLET: I was supposed to be meeting this great girl.

BRUMM: A girl. She didn't come?

CHAPPELLET: No.

BRUMM: (With a knowing little laugh) You'll have many after this season.

CHAPPELLET: Oh, yeah?

BRUMM: One must go without to really—when the time comes—know how sweet it can be.

CHAPPELLET's blank expression. Disinterest as he looks away. Philosophy means nothing to him.

BRUMM: Glory comes first. The women follow.

56. Cut to daylight and noise: Garmisch. A trio posing, as one sees them in the newspapers: CHAPPELLET, CREECH, and HAAS. HAAS seems a little uncertain, as if they were dancing and he

were out of step. Somebody has called something to him from the side. He looks. Shrugs. Someone else asking them to look his way . . . CREECH containing great joy.

57. In a crowded restaurant or *Keller,* CLAIRE and BRUMM. MAYO is at the table, too, although he is only glimpsed.

BRUMM seems changed. He is cooler. He is a man whose interest in CHAPPELLET is now to see him fall.

BRUMM: . . . You're not afraid of him peaking too soon?

CLAIRE: (Slight laugh) . . . That hasn't been one of our problems. But I'll tell you something: Creech is the boy who may surprise everybody.

BRUMM makes a motion with his eyebrows: doubtful.

CLAIRE: (Nodding) Believe me.

BRUMM: Yes, he has the experience . . .

CLAIRE: He has something else, he has a determination he never had before. You know, in a funny way for him it's a moral question. He has great character.

BRUMM: That's more than can be said for . . . all of them. (Pause) How will he do at Kitzbühel? Can he win?

CLAIRE: You know I never say that. I'll say one thing. It could be the crucial race of his life. If he won—he doesn't even have to win, if he did well, he'd go into the Games with a confidence that could mean everything.

BRUMM nods. He's thinking about it.

CLAIRE: Right, Alec?

MAYO: I think so.

58. Kitzbühel. The Hahnenkamm, where

long ago, in the first scenes of the film, it all started. It depends upon those first scenes; it is built upon certain elements which were seen then. A slowly rising electronic note of anticipation.

The crowd ascending.

The faces and gathering at the top. Prepared. Preparing.

Faces we recognize. No dialogue.

The crowd at the bottom.

The chanting.

A cut of a racer in full course.

Chanting.

CLAIRE, the radio over his shoulder—he's at the finish.

People's faces, looking upward, wondering.

MAYO.

The cold metal flower of a loudspeaker, the chilling voice. First in German. Then,

LOUDSPEAKER: Number 16 did not start. There has been an accident on the course.

People are already looking through their programs. The loudspeaker repeating in French. CLAIRE looking uphill.

People whispering in the crowd. Finally we think we hear the name. Then in German, the loudspeaker. After that,

LOUDSPEAKER: We have no information on number 16, John Creech. Number 17 is now on the course.

And repeating, in French. CLAIRE calling on the radio, we don't hear his voice.

59. Medium long shots, unhurried, bleak. CHAPPELLET in the corridors of the hospital. Climbing steps. Asking something of the nurse, we don't hear it, only the murmur of the voices. He continues on. Finally he comes to the room. He opens the door.

CREECH is in the bed, the covers tented over his injured leg and hip. He looks a little sleepy, even drugged. The sound of his head turning slightly on the cotton pillowcase.

Silence.

CHAPPELLET: I hear it's not too bad. About fifty pieces, that's all.

CREECH: (Faint smile which fades. Injuries are not serious to them) Yeah, it's not bad.

It's difficult to talk. There is no real sympathy in CHAPPELLET, no concern in the normal sense. He is only going through a protocol, yet at the same time he is moved. If he had an affection for any of them, it was for his rival.

CHAPPELLET: Well, you'll get 'em next year.

CREECH: (His eyes are closed) You mean four years from now?

Slight, automatic laugh from CHAPPELLET.

CREECH: No. No, this was my chance. (His eyes open, but he doesn't look at CHAPPELLET) I always knew I was going to win that medal, you know? The Olympic gold medal. I *knew* it. I went to bed with that dream for fifteen years.

The door opens silently. A NURSE looks in. A woman of about thirty. CHAPPELLET glances at her, his face hiding the hope she will interrupt them. And she does come in. She passes between them with a lowering of her head, a little smile. She attends to certain things in the room, the chart, the medicine on the bedside table. Her presence changes things slightly.

CREECH: How does it feel alone up there?

CHAPPELLET doesn't answer. He shrugs.

CHAPPELLET: Well, I sure wish you were . . .

CREECH: (Interrupting) Chappie. (The NURSE is adjusting the tent) You have to beat them.

CHAPPELLET doesn't want to return his look.

CREECH: If you don't . . . it means we've done it all for nothing.

CHAPPELLET doesn't know what to say. He's a little uncomfortable but he's been touched. His reply is casual, even a little callous.

CHAPPELLET: Don't worry.

The door again opens. A suspended moment as CLAIRE comes into the room. If he sees CHAPPELLET he gives no indication. He goes over to the bed. They don't say anything to one another. CREECH's mouth moves, but nothing comes out. Tears fill his eyes. He doesn't hide them.

CLAIRE: How is it?

CREECH turns his head away a little—he cannot answer. He nods, yes, all right. Silence. Finally he murmurs,

CREECH: Isn't it . . . stupid?

CLAIRE nods very slightly, very privately. He doesn't reply.

CREECH appears to want to speak, but he cannot. And CHAPPELLET, off in the corner, feels uncomfortable, embarrassed, like the lover with the husband present.

CREECH: (Finally) . . . remember how you . . . I was telling Chappie . . . we used to talk about the justice of sport . . .

CLAIRE: (Nods) The justice. Yes. Sure. Sacrifice without end.

CREECH: There is a justice.

CLAIRE: Well . . .

CREECH looks to CHAPPELLET. It is a kind of nomination, a plea.

CREECH: He'll prove it.

CHAPPELLET hesitates, lowers his head. CREECH is looking at him, tear-stained, willful, bitter as well. Now CLAIRE slowly turns to look at him for the first time. CHAPPELLET senses it. CLAIRE slowly nods.

60. And now the Olympics. (Sound is everything in this sequence) Into the great stadium, black with crowds, the last runner comes with the torch. He mounts the steps, perhaps as the French did at Grenoble, to the amplified beat of his own heart. He lights the brazier. The flame leaps up. Unforgettable, Promethean moment. The crowd applauds.

Cut right to the CU and XCU faces of athletes marching in and standing in ranks during the ceremonies, a gallery of faces, young, determined, sneaking glances. The somewhat martial, stirring anthems.

The hockey matches, XCU. The slamming of bodies. The roaring crowd. RON ENGEL and BRUCE DEVORE hard at work—we cannot really hear them as they cover the event.

All these images are large, newsreely. CLAIRE, his team filing behind him against the background of the side of a bus. Just a glimpse of him saying,

CLAIRE: No, I really can't say (fading) much at this . . . time . . . I . . .

The thunderous (highly amplified) cracking of the banners in the wind. All this noise, then, to silence. The camera slowly rising, traveling very close over the empty downhill course. Early morning. The small flags that mark the side of the trail are silent. The steep pitches are silent, glinting in the sunlight, the many difficult turns.

61. The CU, the sudden appearance in the manner of Godard, of a former champion, French, a man in his early thirties. He is hatless, the wind moves his soft hair. He's not a grinning ex-celebrity. He's a skinny loner, a man who knew one sole ascent to glory like BONLIEU, like VUARNET. He speaks to someone, a listener we do not see. A thoughtful, curiously naked monologue. A revelation. A confession.

FORMER CHAMPION: You can't compare it anymore with what we did. It's a different sport.

As for me, I can't imagine . . . I couldn't win if I were racing now. It's too disciplined. Too methodical. No, I belong to another era, one which has been surpassed. You know, the coach . . . the coach teaches you very little. What he does is make you learn. And of course, he makes you work. Most racers are lazy, they won't push themselves that hard. I was like that. I thought my talent was enough. I would have never won the medal if it weren't for him. I didn't know that then. You have to be merciless with yourself, you have to have a soul of iron. People ask me if I miss it. I don't miss it. It's a life that's passed. Sometimes I can't even imagine it. I'd be afraid of falling now. Falls didn't hurt me then. They showed me I could survive them. They gave me strength. I know one thing. You can't be a champion unless you give up everything else.

62. And then, their breath visible in the cold air as they work—but no sound, only electric silence—a group of twenty or thirty young soldiers. Small, dark figures, on the mountain, tamping down the course.

63. A large room, a reception room such as one finds at a press center. People are talking, attending to details. Gradually the camera closes in past, eliminates, most of them. In the corner sit CHAPPELLET and BRUMM in two chrome and black leatherette chairs. CHAPPELLET is facing us. He has one ski pole which he uses as he is talking, jabbing the rug with it. The point makes faint impressions. BRUMM is listening, with the detachment of a doctor. A suspicious feeling on both sides.

CHAPPELLET: Creech and I were great buddies, we were very close. (Pause) What am I talking about?

(Abandoning the deception, inwardly weary of it) Do you really want to know?

BRUMM: Yes, of course.

CHAPPELLET: (Still jabbing. Looks at BRUMM. Decides) No, you don't.

BRUMM is silent. Onlookers, other newsmen are watching them guardedly. CHAPPELLET jabs. He's like a schoolboy who has decided not to cooperate. He's closed. He's self-assured, sullen. Suddenly, surprisingly, he continues, a mixture of truth and lies, of performance and a sincerity despite himself.

CHAPPELLET: I gave up everything. I gave up . . . (Sighs, cannot say it) Claire did a great thing for me.

BRUMM: What thing, David?

CHAPPELLET: (Jabbing. Simply) He made me a man. When I came to him, I was a snapping dog. I was skinny, my ribs showed. I lived in the street. All I had was teeth. (Glances at BRUMM) You can't win with just teeth. It takes a lot more than that. It takes many qualities. If you don't have them . . . well, you have to get them.

BRUMM: Which qualities, David?

CHAPPELLET hesitates. He knows how BRUMM feels, recognizes the fine edge of contempt in his voice. Still he wants to talk. He shrugs lightly. Silence. Finally,

CHAPPELLET: I don't know. Whatever they are, he gave them to me.

BRUMM: No, he didn't.

CHAPPELLET: (Not listening) And if I win tomorrow . . . (Jabs at floor. A final statement) I came here to win.

BRUMM: Of course you did.

CHAPPELLET looks at him, a look of complete understanding of what BRUMM is, what it all is. A long, penetrating look. After all, he is the contender, BRUMM only observes.

CHAPPELLET: I promise you that.

One believes this cold vow. Beneath all the defects of character, despite the past, there is his belief in the holiness of that victory, the determination to win, one can read it in the quietness of his final words, one can see it in his face.

64. In the darkness before morning, as it will for fourteen days and nights, the Olympic flame burning above the city. Absolute silence.

The great peaks, massive, barely visible in the first, blue light. Majestic shots, and ominous. Images such as one might see of K-2, of the Eiger. Images from Scott's expedition, icy, reverence towards a cruel, unyielding Nature. Silence.

And almost in darkness, too, CHAPPELLET, CU, looking in the mirror. From this moment we follow him with a kind of fascination, a morbid interest one gives a suicide. His hair is uncombed, his face seems weak. The morning of the race—already he inhabits a world in which nothing exists except him and that act, that ordeal towards which he is slowly turning.

Gradually, as we watch, he begins to change himself into another man. A transformation, one not unlike that of an actor in his dressing room as he puts on makeup, strange clothes . . . This whole section is a small film in itself as he slowly sheds his mortality, detail by detail, the light slowly arriving, and becomes the athlete we have marveled at, trim, unemotional, cat-hard.

He begins to put on his clothes. His underclothes. Socks. Shirts. His pants, those tight, thrilling pants. His sweater. He combs his hair. (We don't see him shave)

He drinks orange juice at the table in silence. He doesn't feel like eating. He forces himself, eggs, something solid. The others eat silently, too.

They are in the bus. Still silence (though slowly, sound effects have entered the sequence by now). They drive. Outside the white world passing, one cannot make out details.

MAYO, looking colder, his mouth cold, head lowered, reporting on the conditions on top. They are in group near the bus—a parking lot empty of cars. CHAPPELLET, BRYAN, KIPSMUTH are listening, their expressions, poses, as if they were thinking of something else. As MAYO finishes GABRIEL comes into the group, at its edge. The racers all wear numbers. They carry their skis. CHAPPELLET is 11. (BRYAN 21, KIPSMUTH 38, GABRIEL 33).

MAYO: The long section at the top is grippy snow. The snow isn't blowing up on top anymore . . . It's all blown off.

They are walking across the parking lot to the cable car terminal. Several other individuals and groups walking, too. The TV cameramen are following MEIER in. They stop him just at the entrance. He gives like an astronaut, his last words to a short, gray-haired JOURNALIST who has stopped him. The cameramen are shooting some of the others. They spot CHAPPELLET. They shoot him. Two JOURNALISTS walk along talking to him, things we don't hear. His replies are brief or nonexistent. He shakes his head.

In the cable car, the CU faces. The silence and beat of an unmelodic music. ISTEL and BOYRIVEN are there. MEIER, of course. HINSCH. HAAS. SIEGMAN. Others. Among them, CHAPPELLET and CLAIRE.

At the top they put on their skis (some of them have carried them up with newspaper between the faces to protect the surface, the wax).

A military band playing in the snow at the bottom of the course.

CHAPPELLET doing loosening exercises. The racing bib, with its five entwining circles, is like heraldry. CLAIRE is massaging his legs.

The TV camera crews, six, seven, eight of them at various posts on the mountain, swinging their equipment, getting ready.

The crowd.

The official timers in their booths.

RON ENGEL and BRUCE DEVORE.

[in front of their microphones]

RON: We're only a few minutes now, ladies and gentlemen, from the start. This is *the* event of Alpine skiing. The course is in excellent condition, I would say. Bruce?

While they speak, as if the mind were wandering, the camera shows the crowd. CREECH is there, on crutches. BRUMM is at the bottom with his journalist's armband, his program . . .

BRUCE: Yes, Ron, it's a very good course. They've done a great job preparing it. There's almost no wind and the visibility is excellent. You know how important that is. The course here is long, even a little longer than the usual downhill, and in certain sections extremely steep. Keep your eye on a bumpy section . . .

BRUCE: Getting a little icy there now, but, Ron, oh, look at this! He's skiing a fantastic race perhaps the most brilliant of his career!

RON: Down the last pitch . . .

BRUCE: Here he is! The time . . .

RON: *2:20.85!*

His coach, admirers, the journalists are mobbing him. A gold medal for Maxl at last! MEIER, battered by the excitement, acclaim, is reluctant to say anything. He shakes his head, no, no. He looks up the hill, at the board to see what's happening.

BRUCE: Max Meier of Austria! Solidly in first place. He's looking up the hill and saying, no, wait. The race isn't over.

A shot of MAYO talking on his radio while all this is going on.

CHAPPELLET is two or three places away from the start. The depth of his commitment and concentration is written on his face. He is lost in his own world. He sees nothing except that which is immediately around him. He is beginning to take deep, ventilating breaths.

CLAIRE: (Beside him) Chappie . . .

CHAPPELLET gives him his attention without looking at him or changing his actions.

CLAIRE: Course is holding up all right, Alec says.

They are moving forward.

CLAIRE: It's a little icy near the farmhouse, the three turns. It's not bad, he says.

CHAPPELLET nods. Then,

CHAPPELLET: Who's ahead?

CLAIRE: Meier.

CHAPPELLET nods again.

CLAIRE: (Simply but fully) You can win.

The television announcers, the image of CHAPPELLET on the TV screen, entering the gate.

RON: Here is number 11, David Chappellet of the United States. Bruce, he's a great racer. Does he have a chance today?

BRUCE: He has a very good chance. He's the one Meier is waiting for. They're counting now. Two, one, he's off!

RON: He said something, he cried out something just before he left the gate. Did you hear what it was?

BRUCE: I couldn't quite hear it. We'll try and find out.

Everything that has been saved goes into this race. By now we know quite well what a race and a racer look like, but on this one everything is riding. Even the television announcers are emotionally involved.
CLAIRE's face as he watches from on top—he can only see a portion of the race.
MAYO's waiting for CHAPPELLET to appear.
The loudspeaker at the bottom announcing in German that number 11, CHAPPELLET of the United States, is on the course. As it is heard, CAROLE's face. CREECH's.
And he is plummeting down. It has never seemed less possible for a man to complete a run at such speed, on such terrain. The shots are long, long, head-on, the man alone on the mountain, becoming closer, panning, the background blurring past. Closer, the details of his legs, his face. He bursts over a bump at midpoint. He's in sight of MAYO now. A low hum of electronic sound, a music of time, of clocks flying, has begun—it slowly grows more important as CHAPPELLET descends.
He passes MAYO.

MAYO: (Into his radio. A thrill concealed in his voice) 1:09. Did you hear me?

CLAIRE: (Voice only), Yeah. 1:09. How does he look?

MAYO: Very strong.

The announcers.

BRUCE: (Yes, a little excited) His interval time is the fastest yet! I have it as 1:08.5.

The electric clocks running.
BRUMM's face, looking uphill. CREECH's. CAROLE's. The time begins (as it does sometimes in television) running now on the screen itself from here on. 1:25 and mounting. The film itself becomes a sort of race against time.

BRUCE: Ron, he's skiing an exceptionally fast race. He's always been a fast skier, but he wasn't steady. Today he looks like a rock.

RON: Here he is, coming to the Shambles . . .

Over the bumps. He looks marvelous, all one ever hoped for, all one's dreams. 1:38, the clock is flying. He looks hard as iron, his legs pound like pistons, his torso doesn't budge. Into the air for the last bump. He lands.
At the bottom the other racers looking up. Some don't care much, they're out of it. MEIER is looking up. ERB. BRUMM.
1:50. The camera on CHAPPELLET now. The tone is mounting.

RON: Bruce, what do you think?

BRUCE: Ron, he hasn't made a mistake yet that I could see. His time is very, very fast, at least on the first half. It depends on whether or not he can hold it all the way, whether he tires . . .

BRUCE is getting more emotional. 2:03 the clock says under his image.
CHAPPELLET plunging down.

RON: (Voice only) He has 2:20.85 to beat! 2:20.85.

The clock racing as CHAPPELLET goes over the final bump, lands; down the last pitch . . .

RON: Here he comes! It's going to be very close . . .

He crosses the finish, low, driving, still in a tuck to the end. The film here becomes a bit delirious, unable to keep up, the voices, images, confusion merging with the time, 2:20.34 frozen on the screen.

BRUCE: (Voice only, shouting) He beat him! He beat Meier!

CHAPPELLET coming to a stop, spent, out of breath, looking up at the board. A great noise from the crowd. Photographers running. Reporters. Teammates. It's a scene like Lindbergh's arrival. In the background the loudspeaker announcing in German, English . . . The frozen time disappears from the screen.
CHAPPELLET's face has that marvelous, accepting expression. He is being buffeted, he doesn't care. They are trying to ask questions. He cannot hear. He shakes his head, ignores them.
BRUMM is watching.
The Italian, French TV announcers feverishly explaining. CREECH, on crutches, trying to make his way through the crowd.
Other racers finishing. They are only glanced at. Their times are much higher.
MEIER trying to lean across and somewhat

grimly shake his hand. He cannot.
And now CLAIRE comes up. They embrace one another. In the passion of that crowded moment, CHAPPELLET is grinning. He is immortal. CLAIRE, too.
CREECH cannot reach them.
At the top of the hill a young skier, number 23. Very young, nineteen perhaps. A remarkable face, clear, Nordic, bone-hard. He is ready to start. Two, one . . .
Oh, the celebration of this event! They have moved to the side somewhat, or are trying to. Probably an official has asked them to move from the run-out area. CLAIRE is talking to CHAPPELLET. CHAPPELLET's head down, the classic pose of trainer and athlete, the young man listening. CHAPPELLET shakes his head as if to say no, no, it's unbelievable. He looks up then, grinning.
Down the mountain number 23 is coming. Silence compared to what is happening at the bottom. A dark, unknown figure. Grace. The scrape of skis.
A brief, almost prophetic glance of CHAPPELLET towards the slope. To relieve the audience of the feeling that anything is happening unknown to him. Now his strong, smiling face. He leans over to a microphone. He begins to talk. We hear nothing and then suddenly his voice as if it had just been switched on.

CHAPPELLET: . . . a long time for something like this, a real long time. I don't know what to say except we hoped for it, we knew we had a good chance . . .

INTERVIEWER: No American has ever been successful, no man, in winning . . .

BRUMM at the edge of the group reaching in to congratulate CLAIRE. "The cable! Get off the cable!" someone is crying.
Number 23 coming into the bumps. Like the stranger at the wedding feast who casts a pall.
The crowd, some members of it, looking at their programs. A murmur.
MAYO looking downhill.
A MAN in the crowd asking someone to him,

MAN: 1:08? Is that what they said.

A shrug. They're not sure. But like a wave spreading, more people look up. Faces turn towards the hill. Even some involved with CHAPPEL-LET. They glance upwards, turn back. Some keep looking . . .

CREECH looking uphill.

23 coming down the final schuss. A series of shots that are close, closer, extremely close so that one sees him crossing the finish only in his face—the change of expression. He curves around, comes to a stop.

That beautiful moment as he waits, almost indifferently, for his time.

We don't see that time at first. Our indication is by the first movement of a photographer, two of them. Where? Someone is saying.

CREECH trying to look.

The board which shows: 2:20.21.

They have discovered him. A disbelief as they throng, trying to see who it is, this new, younger, fresher, hungry-for-it-all, this un-known, this splendid champion. BRUMM seems excited. He is trying to see. His face is pleased.

The faces of CLAIRE. CHAPPELLET. Unwavering, naked shots like those in the pits at an auto race, like the crowd at an accident. In CLAIRE's, a decade of hope and struggle that has come to nothing, a great attempt that has failed.

And number 23 in the delirium, moving along in the adoring, curious crowd (fifteen minutes later, perhaps twenty). Beautiful images of his triumph. The crowning of a great, young king. A coronation of sport, confused, affecting. Over this, CLAIRE's voice through the muted noise, as if coming from afar.

CLAIRE: . . . it takes honesty. Sacrifice. Yes, and a kind of dedication that you . . . you've never dreamed of. And it takes humility. And then, if you're lucky . . . if you're lucky . . .

Final shots of it all.

CLAIRE: But we were not.

I Was the Irish Ski Team

by **ROBERT MCKEE**

Not all racers are backed by a bottomless national kitty. Here one enterprising skier tells how to increase your mileage per dollar on the World Cup circuit, at age forty-plus.

THIS is it. I set my poles on the other side of the wand and wait for the countdown. I'm standing in a small wooden starting shack that looks like an outhouse perched on the top of France—above the OK *piste* in Val d'Isère. I had just gone to the bathroom for the fifth time in twenty minutes. My mouth tastes like a big ball of cotton and I reach down for some snow and stuff it in my mouth. I take a last deep breath. I'm about to run my first World Cup downhill . . .

What is someone almost forty years old doing in a downhill race in the World Cup? Most guys my age are worrying about their hairlines and waistlines and here I am worrying about whether I'm going to get killed. I hadn't skied until I was twenty-five. I didn't race until I was thirty, an age when most racers have retired. I'm almost old enough to be the father of a lot of these guys I'm racing against.

"Ten seconds," monotones the starter. It's sunny. That will help. But I don't feel good about the race. It was very cold last night and the snow has really set up. Klammer has already won

the race and he was seven seconds faster than any training run. Jeez—seven seconds! When you run downhill you have to have confidence. And I didn't have it. I looked around at the start and everyone was gone. All the other racers, the coaches, the service reps, the hangers-on had left. Just me and the starter. It was a lonely feeling . . .

Nastar got me into all this. I was running a small inn in Stowe, Vermont, which had no Nastar race. After cooking breakfast, I would drive over to Wildcat, New Hampshire, to race, and then drive back to cook dinner for thirty guests. That was in 1970. I can't remember how I did in that first race, but I was sure bitten by racing. Since then I've raced in just about every kind of competition I could enter. I'm a regular competitor on the Eastern Senior circuit. I trained with the racers at Burke Mountain Academy, and I trained with the juniors at Mount Mansfield. Ski racing had become a passion—I fell in love with the sport. I sold my inn and went into real estate, so I would have time to race in the winter.

I poled out of the start and dropped into a tuck. After about 100 yards I thought I was going to crap my pants. I knew that it was going to be fast, but I had no idea it was going to be *this* fast— I must have been going 70 miles per hour! Collombin's Bump was coming up—where the Swiss downhiller broke his back two years in a row, the second time ending his career. . . .

296

During the first training run a few days ago, in fog and light-falling snow, I had made the bump okay. But the rest of the course was rough after ninety-five racers had run. My skis during that run were bouncing around like matchsticks. I was just hanging on. Then just before the Compression—WHOOMP—my right ski hit a hole and drove my knee right up into my jaw. I blacked out for an instant. The last thing I remembered was trees dead ahead. I came to in the middle of the Compression, still on my skis. Somehow I made it down the rest of the way, but in a state of shock. . . .

After my training run, the race jury told me they were kicking me out of the race. I was too slow, they said. I knew if they threw me out I probably wouldn't get in another downhill all year. So I told them I was just "testing skis." I said I could go faster and begged for another chance. I had come this far and was determined to show them I could do it. I was then humiliated in three different languages as the jury explained to the other team captains why the Irish racer and team captain was so slow. But they allowed me to race . . .

I'm really into the run now. The course is virtually straight. I'm in a low tuck and my back is as flat as possible. My skin-tight downhill suit cuts through the wind with hardly any resistance. The ground is just flying by and I can feel my skis going faster and faster. Collombin's Bump is just ahead and I know I'm not going to make it.

I came screaming onto Collombin's Bump. I wasn't ready . . . I flew off through the air for about a hundred feet. I never saw the ground. I hit the snow, bounced, somersaulted and landed on my feet. A patrolman brought me a ski that had come off. The other ski was still on my foot and looked like a banana that had been peeled back. A $500 pair of skis. "Thank God for that Irishman who works for Yamaha," I thought. I felt myself all over but could only feel disappointment. I wasn't hurt, but I wasn't going to finish either. . . .

I wasn't the only one who was disappointed. Dozens of newspapermen and photographers had been waiting at the bottom just to see me finish so they could make a story. The next day the *Wien Kurrier* ran a full-page picture of Robert McKee grinning out from under his crash helmet and holding the bent ski. Little did I know then that this was just the beginning of publicity that

by the end of the season would make me almost as well known in Europe as Franz Klammer and Ingemar Stenmark.

I have dual Irish-American citizenship. My wife Betty and I usually go to Ireland every spring and fall to our house that we built in Tipperary. A few years ago I met the people who had just organized the Ski Association of Ireland. The association had no racers at that time and asked if I would be interested in entering the British Championships for Ireland. I was. They issued me an FIS start license, which allowed me to participate in international events. (FIS rules allow each country to enter two racers in any race, regardless of FIS points, which I didn't have.) So I became Ireland's first and only ski racer. And also its only coach, trainer, service technician and financial backer—in every sense of the word, the only true "amateur" on the World Cup circuit.

I had planned to compete for Ireland in the 1976 Olympics at Innsbruck, but a knee operation canceled those hopes. Last year I decided to go for broke, racing on the World Cup and in the World Championships. It hadn't been easy telling Betty that I was going off to Europe for the winter to race on the World Cup—and compete on the same circuit with her son (by a previous marriage), Ron Biedermann, a member of the U.S. Ski Team. She thought I was crazy. However, she seemed satisfied at the time to come over for a month to travel around with me and be my "trainer." That meant she would bring down my warm-up clothes and training skis after a race. Any little bit would help. So in mid-October I closed down my real estate office in Stowe and headed for Europe to begin an odyssey that would cover over six months and 20,000 miles on the race circuit.

My first race had been in Tignes, the week before the opening of the World Cup circuit at Val d'Isère. I went over to see the U.S. Team and Ron. "What are you doing in Europe?" they asked. "Racing against you," I answered. They couldn't believe it. The U.S. Ski Team probably has more coaches, trainers, back-up people and money now than any other team, except perhaps the Austrians. The Irish Ski Team has the least.

While the Americans were bedded down luxuriously in Tignes, I was assigned a room outdoors up over a ski room. To get to it, I had to pull myself up with a rope while balancing on little stone steps. To enter, I had to duck down through a 4-foot-high doorway on which I always knocked my head. It looked like a small cell for a condemned man, only padded with wood. On the eve of my first European downhill I felt like it was my last day on earth. The room was about 8 feet long and 6 feet wide. In it there was a bed, a chair, and a toilet. The shower was outside, back down the rope and inside the hotel. The ceiling was about a quarter-inch higher than my 5 feet 8¾ inches.

I had heard that the big teams got the best accommodations and the smaller teams got whatever was left over, but this was ridiculous. The wind whistled through the crack in the door as I shivered and thought about the idea of going 70 miles per hour down a mountain for the first time. Somehow I felt that this room was all planned and they were trying to discourage me. I was going to start last in this race and probably finish last and I certainly had the last of the accommodations. It was as if they had stuffed away the bearded little Irishman in this French tree hut to make his last Act of Contrition.

As it was, I didn't finish last at Tignes. I beat one racer from Czechoslovakia.

There was hardly any snow. Just the little bit the army pulled out of the woods and mixed in with the dirt and rocks. The course was hard, icy, fast, and dangerous. There weren't any safety nets and the speeds averaged 70 miles per hour. Some eighty-five racers trained on the course. Seventy racers started and only fifty-two finished. There were numerous injuries and two broken backs. I was one of the fifteen racers who didn't start. I may be nuts about racing, but I'm not crazy. The newspapers said I got "cold feet" and started to refer to me as the "Odd Irishman" and the "Opa," which is German for Grandpa.

The downhill race at Wengen was canceled after several days of fog and high winds. When I got to Kitzbühel for the Hahnenkamm downhill, I found out that U.S. Alpine Director Hank Tauber, referee for the race, had pulled my card from the seeding board at the first team meeting. He said the downhill course was too difficult for me. Maybe he thought I might get killed in front of sixty thousand spectators and live TV coverage. Tauber was probably miffed because I was getting more press in Europe than the U.S. Team. I was pretty down at this point. I had hopes of making FIS points so that I could be seeded at the World Championships. I hadn't made any decent results and it looked like I was just going to have to run at the end with the Turks and the Greeks.

The FIS World Championships at Garmisch put the Irish Ski Team to the test—not so much in skiing, but just in coping. On arrival, I had to convince the officials that I was not the trainer but the competitor, and that Betty was the official trainer for the Irish Ski Team. Then we had a big hassle finding hotel space. We finally settled into a room over the kitchen at the Rheinisherhof. The race office never sent over the start numbers and armbands and all the information needed to find out when, and where, to train or race. The woman in charge at the race office just couldn't accept the idea that we wanted to be treated just like any other visiting team.

The first morning at the hotel I was doing my daily stretching exercises in the hall (there was no space in our tiny room). About 20 feet away a small dog was barking like crazy. On the other end of the hall a chambermaid was pushing a vacuum cleaner. Just then the manageress came upstairs and told me to stop immediately as I was making too much noise. I thought I was having a bad dream. When I didn't stop she told me to leave the hotel. I wouldn't. Then the maitre d'hotel wouldn't let me in the dining room with my training suit . . .

The word had gotten out to the press that an unusual older guy was entered in the World Championships. Everyone suddenly wanted an interview and the press began following me around. People came up to me on the street and asked for my autograph. I began getting fan mail. A local factory even put on a dinner for me. I was being portrayed as an antihero—the guy who leaves his office and goes off to make a sort of Walter Mitty-George Plimpton challenge against the best professionals in the world. But I wasn't out to escape my wife or make money. There were no tricks, no gimmicks—just me risking my neck and spending my own money to compete against guys who make hundreds of thousands of dollars a year in a multimillion-dollar sport. Of course, the fact that I had to buy my own equipment and pay my own expenses, prepare my own skis, train alone—as well as being an older, bearded Irishman—helped to complete the picture.

One morning I was called to the front desk to take a phone call.

"Hello, Robert. This is Jean-Claude Killy. We spoke at Kitzbühel. Do you remember me?"

Is he kidding? Remember Jean-Claude Killy? How could anyone not remember meeting him? I could quote all his records, every race he'd ever won—my idol.

"Oh sure. How are you, Jean-Claude?"

"I'm working with French-speaking Swiss TV here. We would like to do a story about you, portraying you as the opposite of Klammer. We would like to follow you around for a couple of days and film everything you do. I think it would be very interesting."

Imagine—Jean-Claude Killy wants to do a TV special about *me*. I thought it was a big deal when I just shook hands with him at Kitzbühel.

The next morning at 7 A.M. I opened the door of my room and was blinded by flashing lights. The film crew was all set up. I quickly went into my daily exercise routine and they started shooting. A few minutes later I went downstairs to take a phone call. When I turned around my mouth fell open as I saw the French TV director standing there with his equipment.

"If this is you here, who is that up there?" I said, pointing upstairs.

It turned out that the director of the German-speaking Swiss TV had overheard our conversation the night before. He had his crew sneak in early in the morning and set up their equipment. He told the French crew that he had made a private arrangement with me that only his crew could make the film.

The races at Garmisch were a struggle. I finished all three events and placed thirteenth—and last—in the combined. The newspapers, oddly, called my downhill run "sensational." After finishing last in every training run, I had managed to beat one person in the race.

Most people thought I was at Garmisch just to finish. At the slalom there were forty thousand spectators and it seemed like half of them were yelling my name. Some Swiss fans had erected a large sign that read, "The winner today will be Robert McKee."

When I staggered across the finish line after the second run, the PA system announced in three languages that I was forty-three years old. Every day they make me older. Next year it will be fifty.

I began to realize that coming in last had its value. After the giant slalom a ski company rep offered me a contract to ski on their skis next year, and another firm gave me a new downhill suit right on the spot. Maybe next year I could even race in the Irish colors—not that anyone would notice. In the opening ceremonies, I marched behind the Irish flag. It wasn't exactly the Irish colors, but I was probably the only one who noticed.

From Garmisch I drove to Chamonix in my leased Renault to race in the Arlberg-Kandahar, a combined World Cup downhill and slalom.

Notes from the last day . . . .

Both downhill and slalom are today. Weather has screwed us up. It seems the whole town is booked up and we've got to get out right after the race. TV won't hold over for another day. . . . There is fresh snow. I'm told to report to the finish area at 9 A.M. to see if the guys in the last seed will run first. There is no decision. I take the cable car to the top of La Houche and hang around. Almost a white-out up here—a lot of new snow. It looks like I'll be used as a snowplow. I take a few warm-up runs—it feels pretty good. This is my first time hanging out at the start at the beginning of a race. Plank, Grissman, Walcher, Klammer, Read—all the first-seed boys are standing around, waiting. And they are looking at me.

"The weather is bad—go slow," I yell to Klammer with a smile. "Maybe I will make FIS points."

"I will go as fast as possible!" he replies in sturdy, Teutonic fashion. It doesn't matter if he can't see—he knows the course. Besides, for him it is first or nothing. I like Klammer. He seems amused by me but otherwise treats me just like any other racer.

Because of the new snow, I'm starting third in the downhill. Damn! I'd rather go at the end and take my chances. I move into the starting gate. Klammer, Grissman and Gernsbichler crowd around me. This is a new experience for them to see the racer who usually runs last taking off ahead of them. As I get the countdown, Klammer grabs me around the waist. "Now McKee," he says with a chuckle. "Don't screw up the track."

I'm off into the fog, a bit tentative at first. The big jump comes up fast. I can't see the lip, only the scattered pine needles. I'm in the air and I can't see the landing. But I feel it. Shaky, but okay. I make the big right-hand turn and see the nets ahead. All night long I had laid awake thinking about this section. I see it over and over in my mind. If I don't take it right, I could snap a leg in two. I decide to prejump the bump instead of pressing it. Perfect—I make it! The best feeling I've had all year. Back in my tuck. Only small bumps, rolls and flats the rest of the way. I feel myself slowing down in the fresh snow. Concentration slips and a bump knocks an arm out. Come on! Hold the tuck to the finish. I cross the finish line and look up at the big electric scoreboard. The new snow has made me three seconds slower than my best training run. I'm disappointed but only for a moment. I watch the Russian racer split his skis and take a wicked fall on his face right at the finish line. Somehow he isn't hurt.

I beat Scott Kendall of New Zealand by eleven seconds. He's fit to be tied, but I feel great. I ran a downhill well for the first time. No one who started early is happy. Klammer finishes out of the top ten. Two Canadians finish first and second. The Canadian coaches are going out of their minds. Their jobs are secure for another year.

I hustle over to the cable car, ride to the top, find my clothes and training skis and ski down to the car. Grab Scott and head back to the hotel to change clothes, boots and skis for the slalom that starts at 2 P.M. at another area. Scott isn't going to do it. Too much in one day. Many other racers think the same thing. Me? I'm only here once.

Don't know where the slalom hill is. There's no lift. Somehow I find it and climb up for the inspection. The race has already started, but I keep on with my inspection anyhow. No one cares. This is France.

It's snowing hard and wet. I'm running last with number 59. Where the hell is everyone? The course is in excellent shape—few ruts and hard. Only one difficult gate and, of course, that's where I hook a tip. Koni Rupprechter, the British coach, yells at me. "Get up, McKee! Finish! The combined!" I climb back, go through the gate and finish, twenty-five seconds out. It's almost dark when I make my second run. No one at the finish. No one asking for autographs, no press, no photos, no World Cup atmosphere. It's 5 P.M. and I'm exhausted.

Phil Mahre won the race. The Americans are happy. A British spectator asks me, "What is your opinion of Alpine ski racing?" How do you answer a question like that?

I collect my gear and head back in the dark to the hotel to take a shower. Later that night I go up to the race office to pick up the results. A big crowd is down the end of the hall. The Canadian guys wave me over. There is an awards ceremony going on. Suddenly I hear, "Robert McKee, Ireland," over the loudspeaker. Applause and yelling. I'm pushed up to the stage. I receive handshakes, a trophy I can drink out of, a medal to go around my neck, and the Arlberg-Kandahar pin. Photographs, more applause. I have just come in third in the Alpine Combined of the Arlberg-Kandahar—one of the most prestigious races in the history of Alpine ski racing! My name goes in the record books, along with Zeno Colo, Emile Allais, Anderl Molterer, Karl Schranz, Jean-Claude Killy, and Gustavo Thoeni! There were only three finishers in the combined. A Swiss downhiller who also fell in the first run of slalom, an Iranian, and Robert McKee. Boy, am I embarrassed. Somehow, the way everyone is smiling at me, they look like they think I deserve it. I'd have felt better about it if I hadn't fallen in the first run. Bet this is the last year they give this award.

Still, I had not made any FIS points. FIS (International Ski Federation) points are a standard based on the amount of time a racer finishes behind the winner in a given race. I would have to earn less than one hundred FIS points to be recognized or seeded in a race. As long as I didn't have any FIS points, I would always run last, when the course was in the worst condition.

Stroke of luck! The Italian Ski Federation invited me to the Italian Championships, all expenses paid. I had the race of my life in the downhill—finishing just ten seconds behind the winner—good for sixty-six FIS points! When I crossed the finish line, Mario Cotelli, the robust director of the Italian team picked me up in a bear hug and shouted, "Robert! Ten seconds! Fantastico! You make FIS points."

I went on to make FIS points in the States, first in the downhill at the U.S. Championships and later at both World Cup giant slaloms at Stratton Mountain and Waterville Valley. I must, however, abandon slalom in the future. There is just no way I can make FIS points. I am just too old and too slow. What points I did earn I worked for harder than a lot of people will ever know.

It had been a long season. I had been on the road for six months and on skis for one hundred and fifteen days. In all, I had thirty-eight race starts. I had driven over 16,000 miles by car, flown another 6,500 miles and spent about $7,000. I was exhausted from filing skis until midnight, packing and unpacking, driving over mountain passes, putting chains on and off, and carrying around ski bags with over two hundred pounds of equipment. But none of that mattered now.

It was a hell of an experience. It sure is going to be hard going back to the office. Then again, I've been thinking . . . if I can just make a big sale in the next month or two, maybe I can get down to Chile this fall for some downhill training . . .

The TV Watcher's Guide

by WEEMS WESTFELDT

Seldom does a ski instructor write as fluidly as he skis; Weems Westfeldt is an exception: here he takes off on the subject of ski racing, a discipline surrounded by misunderstanding, much of it on the part of television announcers.

I T is the function and inalienable birthright of all sports fans to criticize. Since the sports fan cannot actually perform the feats he is seeing, it follows that he must compensate by knowing infinitely more than the sportscasters, coaches, referees, and competitors. A good fan not only knows the names and performance histories of the heroes and heroines, he should also be able to supply, on demand, an endless stream of commentary ranging from technique and strategy to the sordid, personal events and habits in the lives of the athletes. Merciless advice based on in-depth hearsay and first-hand innuendo is the essence of the complete sports fan.

Unfortunately, American fans are inept where ski racing is concerned. It's not nice to make such cultural generalizations, but, when it comes to watching, the Austrian ski racing fans win gold medals while the Americans don't even place. The Austrians know how to watch ski racing. It's their national sport. In America, we lack experience as spectators in under-standing, feeling, discriminating, and judging.

I contend, however, that with a minimum of training, we can make wild assertions and unfounded accusations with the best of them. This article is patriotically dedicated to that lofty goal.

TV Watching

To become first-class fans, we must learn to interpolate the reality through the medium. Television does not really tell it like it is. It is limited, like all media, to producing only approximate reality.

To its credit, ABC Sports has been constantly improving its coverage of ski racing over the years. We're now seeing much more sophisticated coverage because of expert use of slow-motion, stop action, and closeup color photography as well as more professionally prepared commentary. The sport of ski racing owes a debt (paid happily by the consumers, of course) to ABC Sports for its coverage. The increased awareness of real speed, danger, dynamic movement, drama, and suspense make the viewing worthwhile even for an inept fan. However, we must still look through and beyond the television to find our own version of the truth. The following hints about the realities of ski racing should help:

1. The snow is much harder than even the sportscasters indicate. Good ski racing snow is like fast granite and New England produces some of the best. If the snow is too soft, they will water it and let it freeze into solid ice. (However, soft snow is not a problem on an average down-East winter day.) Race courses should be damn-near bullet-proof so they hold up under the pressure of over one hundred racers. The hot rods learn to like the ice because of its freedom, speed, and predictability. (Perhaps, they like the pretty gray and blue hues also.) If it is not icy, it is considered grabby.

2. The racers are traveling much faster than they seem. TV has finally gotten a fair feeling for the speed of downhill by using wider shots and color to improve the texture and frame of reference. If you want to get a sense of just how fast they are going, look at the trees, spectators, fences, and other still objects. It makes you want to cry.

3. Slalom, giant slalom, and downhill are always editorially compared in terms of speed versus finesse. Slalom is considered to be the event of grace and precision; downhill, the event of mind-bending speed and strength; and, giant slalom, the marriage of the two. After this editorial preparation, watching the races through the eye of the camera can leave one with the distinct impression that slalom is slow, downhill is lacking in its demand for precision, and that giant slalom is both. GS tends to look boring in this light, while, it is, in fact, one of the most beautiful and exciting of ski races. When watching these events, you should keep in mind that slalom is much faster than most of us usually travel, while its line and rhythm are much more intricate. Downhill requires a poise, precision of timing and subtlety of response that is only possible for athletes who have tremendous reserves of strength, intelligence, and intuition. Giant slalom, of course, is the marriage of the two.

4. When they send the retired racer down the course with the helmet-mounted camera, so you can supposedly see it through the eyes of the racer, take a break for snacks, or beer, or yak-yak, or whatever. It doesn't look like that. Even to the guy wearing the helmet. The adjustability of the human eye is far superior to that of the helmet-camera.

5. Also, take a break during the postrace and prerace interviews. They generally go like this:

"Well, Wolfbait, what's your strategy for today?"

"Ja, I chust trry to shki fery faast und vin da rrace." Embarrassed silence.

" . . . yes, but Wolfbait, do you have any special plans about how to win today."

"Ja, I go fery, fery faast and make no miss takes."

Or, afterwards:

"Congratulations, Jean-Fred. That was a beautiful race. What made the difference for you today?

"Sank you, Bobe. I jus ski fastair zan zee ozairs, you know. I make no meestakes." (Aside.) "Quel con celui-la alors."

"You must be very happy after such a fine performance!"

"Yes, I am vairie 'appy."

"There you have it folks, a happy youngster and a fine young ski racer *and* the winner of today's slalom, Jean-Fred Gueule-de-poisson from Tignavoriaz-diserethorens, France. Now, back to you, Frank."

"Thank you, Bob. You're fired. Now over to the ice arena for more action.

6. When Bob Beattie starts talking so loud and fast that the words blur, something significant is happening. Act interested and find out what later.

7. In all fairness to the sportscasters, it is very difficult to make on-course analysis of racers because they don't want to commit themselves and then suddenly be made to appear foolish by the truth of the clocks. Also, the experts are still unskilled at translating their expertise into layman's terms. It is generally more useful to pay attention to their comments about time and strategy between races than to listen to their on-course comments concerning technique. Pay special attention to comparative stop-action and slow-motion. It is usually excellent. So don't schedule anything foolish like work, family activi-

ties, or skiing during the Olympics. You have some serious TV watching to do.

Now that we have considered some of the basics of interpreting the television coverage, we can talk about the events themselves. There are two ways to consider the Alpine events: from the point-of-view of "racing" and from the "skiing" point-of-view.

The Racing

As to the nature of the races and the racers themselves, the following information may be helpful:

1. There are three types of Alpine races. Slalom has the most turns and fewer miles per hour. Downhill has very few turns and very many miles per hour. A racer's time starts when he trips the timing wand in the starting shack and ends when he crosses the beam at the finish line. The racer with the fastest time wins, or as Jean-Fred and Wolfbait said, the major strategy is to go as fast as you can and make very few errors. It's pretty straightforward.

2. You can rest assured that you will be seeing some of the very best skiers in the world, and that, to arrive at this point, they have had to climb to the top of an awesome heap of talented racers. Do not look for one special hero to win. Any one of the top racers could win on any day if the breaks are right. But keep an eye out for fast-moving, Mosers, Nadigs, Nelsons, Kinshofers, Epples, Wenzels, Mahres, Heideggers, Hemmis, and Walchers.

3. The top three finishers in any event will probably come from the first seed (the first fifteen starters), because they have had the consistency to reach that group, and because the course generally begins to deteriorate after that point.

4. Races are measured to the thousandth of a second and it is not uncommon for the first ten racers to be within one second of each other. If someone like Stenmark wins by a margin of one-half second or more, he says, "What took you guys so long?"

5. The racers feel, that, since they are all so close, winning an Olympic medal is not nearly so great an achievement as winning in overall World Cup competition. It's just another stop along a rather difficult, but lucrative tour. However, there is a degree of inherent pressure in the Olympic situation, because, if a racer wins Olympic gold, his fame and marketability increase significantly. Also there is increased psychological pressure and reward for locals who do well in the Olympics. Rosie Mittermaier, in the 1978 FIS and Franz Klammer in Innsbruck in 1976 are examples. So, will members of the press kindly lay off Phil Mahre. His recently, and badly, broken leg gives him enough pressure.

Sportscaster: "Hi, Phil, how do you feel for today's slalom?"

P.M.: "Jus' great, Bob. Slept well and I feel ready."

Sportscaster: "How's your leg?"

P.M.: "Leg? My leg! Oh, Jesus, Oh God! My leg!! Aarrrggghhhh!"

The winner of the race will be victorious through a variety of factors. Obviously, the major factor will be athletic prowess. However, it is not uncommon to see some very fine skiing on some slow skis. Snow conditions can change from moment to moment and waxing, especially in downhill, can be an art. By listening and reading, you can sometimes get an inkling as to the varying psychological strengths and pressures each athlete contends with.

And finally there is the whole category of variables which have to be called "luck." It has to be there. The competitors are too good for one to win without it.

7. The question is always asked whether professional Dual Format racers or FIS Amateur Format racers are better. It is a difficult question to answer. Neither group has appeared at any of the races I compete in, so I can't give a first-hand comparison. (The fact that none of them has shown up to race against me can, of course, only be attributed to fear on their part, of the hopeless shame and humiliation to be endured after I administer a severe thrashing to them.)

The Skiing

One of the reasons why ski racing is so difficult to watch, is that the necessary ingredients to top performance are often very subtle and thus hidden to the eye of the average observer. In other words, it is damn hard to tell how a skier does unless he falls or wins. One of the ways to deal with this frustration is to momentarily ignore the results and watch the skiing itself. This is a fundamentally intelligent attitude anyway, since all of these skiers are superb and can trade victories daily. Below you will find some of the technical considerations which an untrained eye can apply to the situation in order to understand, evaluate, and enjoy the events.

World class racers, like other sportsmen, are subject to the vagaries of their emotional and physical environments. In other words, they make lots of mistakes. Since the racers are being timed to the thousandth of a second, minor errors are extremely costly. A series of minor errors will cost the race.

Errors in racing all have one thing in common. They cause the racer to lose overall speed along a given course. The obvious example is a fall. A fall always results in a radical loss of speed. You cannot win if you fall. Another example, somewhat more common, but less obvious, is air-time. In downhill, if you don't jump early enough before a sudden change of pitch, the lip will carry you into the air. Your forward speed will change into vertical speed and your landing will necessitate a recovery. Both of these results interrupt the free forward flow of the skis and will cause a loss of speed. So air-time, although spectacular, is bad form. Other errors are indicated by wild movements in the upper body. If the arms, hands, and torso suddenly begin to flail wildly, the racer is sending a clear message. He is saying that he has misjudged the speed-for-the-terrain. He has received kinesthetic signals from the snow to the effect that all is not well in the balance department and that, unless radical upper body response occurs, complete and sudden body-snow contact is imminent.

The best racers will be very clean and direct in their movements. Wildly aggressive recovery arts are kid stuff. You will often see them and sometimes they are useful. Look for the winners, however, among the calmer, more economical-looking athletes. Look for poise, confidence, smoothness, fluidity, rhythm, explosiveness, and

fearlessness. If you watch the body movements carefully, you can read out these qualities. Those who are going too slow often appear tense, jerky, and hesitant. They will demonstrate an easily noticeable physical defensiveness. Their body will appear stiff and the skis may seem to chatter excessively.

One other aid in differentiating fast from faster, is the sound. Billy Kidd told a group of ski instructors once that, on ice, he could always tell the faster of the two racers by the loudness. The skis of the slower racers make more grating and grinding noises as they brake and skid, while the faster ones seem to sneak across the ice.

But again, it's measured to the thousandth of a second and you can't see everything that happens. So do not come out with absurdities like, "I guess Stenmark's got the touch today!" after seeing the determination in his face at the starting gate. He could easily lose (if, say, he skied over a landmine or fell into a sniper's bullet), though he's the only other person as predictable as Annemarie Proell-Moser. If her skis are on pointy-end-forward and fast-side-down, she will usually win the downhill. But even she can be beaten. (I don't know by whom, but I have an open mind.)

Spectator Training

The best way to enjoy ski racing, as with most activities, is to experience it. I have had some fun at Bob Beattie's expense above. To balance that somewhat, it should be said that Bob Beattie, through the invention and successful marketing of National Standard Racing (Nastar) has done more than any other one person in the world to make ski racing available and desirable to the recreational skier. Through Nastar racing, any skier—including you—can now discover, at gut level, what it's like to race; to sidestep towards the start, to watch the other racers take off, to see their scintillating successes and terrifying failures, to step into the starting gate yourself, to adjust your poles and goggles, to stare intently down the course, to have every muscle twitching in anticipation, to have every nerve synapse exploding with awareness, to throw up all over your new racing outfit. (Actually, the butterflies are part of the game. They're good for you and show that you're ready.)

Experience is the key. It would be difficult for me to really appreciate football unless I had played a bit. (A very little bit.) Ski racing is like football, to that extent, in that, if you do it yourself, even occasionally, you will understand and enjoy watching it much better.

PART VII

THE SKIING LIFE

"I didn't talk to anyone much; I just skied and traveled. Everything was like cut-glass crystal: sharp, fine, pure. I'm not sure why it was like that. Maybe I had just forgotten what life was really like . . . . Perhaps life is really like that—crystalline."

—Bob Jamieson, *Me and Truck*

Ski Resorting, the Sport of _____

by ART BUCHWALD

The world champion humorist-skier, Art Buchwald, has been known to venture aboard skis only if supported on each side by a ravishing lady instructor in a one-piece, skin-tight racing suit. He was last seen slaloming down the entrance to the St. Moritz Palace on the tail of Suzy Chaffee. Herewith the bon mots _of the_ bon vivant.

SKI resorting, not to be confused with skiing at a resort, is one of the most popular pastimes in sports today. Most ski resorting takes place on the rocky bluffs or the intimate _pistes_ of hotel lobbies and bars in snowy areas. Since there is so much more interest in ski resorting than there is in resort skiing, we have borrowed the services of Aspen Piznair, the 1958 Olympic Ski Resort Champion, who now has a clinic in St. Moritz for people who are going downhill without any visible means of support. Mr. Piznair will answer questions about ski resorting and techniques in this column.

PROBLEM: _I am a beginner at ski resorting and wish to improve myself. But I find in the lobby of the Palace Hotel that so many of the women are more advanced than I am that when I try to sideslip I always fall on my face. How can I compete against all the ice in the lobby? I'm only a secretary. S.L._

ANSWER: Ski resorting takes confidence. The secret of success is not in how much ice there is in the lobby but how much body control you use. Hip swinging and body rotation are the keys to successful ski resorting. Stretch pants and a tight sweater can also be of help. Don't sit down but keep moving. Control the drift of your turn by maintaining an upright, relaxed body position. In no time at all you will be on equal footing with the more experienced ski resorters, and your shorthand days will be over.

PROBLEM: _I hate skiing, have always hated it, ever since my father beat me with a ski pole. But I like hot chocolate. (My mother used to give me hot chocolate after my father beat me.)_

Do you know of any place I can get hot chocolate outside of a ski resort? S.H.

ANSWER: No.

PROBLEM: _I just bought a new pair of ski boots with steel stays and twist-reinforced quarters and full length counters. I paid fifty-two dollars for them. Every afternoon my husband insists we go for a walk, but I don't want to because I'll get snow on them. Am I being unreasonable? F.G._

ANSWER: Absolutely not; it's your husband who is unreasonable. Wearing ski boots in the snow is the worst thing that you can do with them. Good ski boots are hard to come by and should only be used for dancing or bowling. If your husband insists on taking walks, make him buy you a pair of galoshes.

PROBLEM: *The other day a man in the lobby of the Suvretta House asked me to write something on his cast. I don't know him very well and I was at a loss as to what to say. I told him I'd think about it. Each day he keeps bothering me and says he is saving a good place for me just below his knee. What can I write? Miss S.P.*

ANSWER: Writing on a cast is a tricky business, particularly when you're not well acquainted with the leg. "I'd like to fall for you," or "The next time you're casting, give me a break," or "Set 'em up in the other alley" are all acceptable. Try to avoid sentimentality and don't put anything in writing that you'll be sorry for later. If you like the person you could put a return address on the shin.

PROBLEM: *I have been the photographer at the Corviglia Ski Club for twenty-five years. I am seventy-three years old. There is a rule in the club that I am not permitted to sit down. Do you think this is right? Dr. S.*

ANSWER: Yes, we do. As the club photographer, you have no right to sit down with the guests, and, after all, you're only seventy-three years old and should be able to stand on your own two feet. If we let you sit down, then the headwaiter would want to sit down, and the ski instructor would want to sit down and pretty soon no one would be on their toes. Perhaps on your eightieth birthday we'll let you *lean* against a wall, but sitting in a chair is out of the question.

A P.S. from St. Moritz:

ST. MORITZ—Tucked away in the Engadine Valley, shut in by snow-capped mountains and unspoiled by civilization, is a small town called St. Moritz. Here for over one hundred years the nomadic tribes of Europe have come for the winter to find grazing lands for their herds of Rolls-Royces, Cadillacs, and Mercedes-Benzes. These nomadic tribes are shy people by nature and avoid being interviewed by anthropologists and newspapermen. We are probably one of the few

anthropologists ever to get into their confidence, and we believe this is the first full report ever issued on this strange, yet amusing race of people.

The St. Moritzers, as we shall call them (the scientific name is E Pluribus Unum), have some very quaint customs. They live in dwellings called "hotel suites," sometimes as many as two to a room, and eat in community halls called "grill rooms" and "nightclubs."

The St. Moritzers are not cannibalistic by nature (though there have been cases known of one of them biting another's head off), and their main food staple is gray raw fish eggs which they call "caviar," and which they eat on slices of toast washed down with a bubbly drink made from grapes.

Instead of barter, the St. Moritzers use a currency called "money." Some of them save up this money all year long, then bale it and bring it with them. Each bale of money can be traded for one hot chocolate, which is a favorite drink.

If it is discovered one of the St. Moritzers does not have any money, he is taken by two or three of the elders in the village to the highest peak surrounding the Engadine Valley and pushed off.

Although this may sound primitive and cruel to the outsider, every St. Moritzer knows the risks he takes when he comes here, and if he is caught without money he usually accepts his fate quietly.

The women of St. Moritz are probably the most interesting. They are tall, well shaped and wear silk robes which they call Diors, Balmains, Desses, and Givenchys. They do not have to cook, sew, or clean (they have slaves known as "the Swiss people" for these things), and their sole purpose is to make their menfolk happy.

The mores of the St. Moritzers are such that each man may have one wife and one mistress but, unlike some Middle Eastern countries, the women are not allowed to live in the same dwelling. When a man takes to himself a wife or a mistress, he gives her a shiny stone called a "diamond." Some of the tribeswomen wear these stones around their necks, and others, on their

The epitome of the après-ski life is St. Moritz's Palace Hotel

fingers or on their bosoms, and still others hanging from their ears. The more stones they have, the higher their standing in the community. Other stones that the native women collect are called emeralds, sapphires, and rubies. (We tried to trade some packs of chewing gum for some of these stones, which we wanted to take back as samples, but apparently they have some religious significance because all the women refused.)

When a woman no longer wants to stay with her husband she gets what is called a "divorce." The husband must then pay the wife large sums of money (sometimes as much as two thousand bales) either monthly or all at once.

This is called "Ali Moanie," named after the most famous prophet of the tribe.

For recreation (that's about all the St. Moritzers are good for in the winter), they tie long sticks on their feet, and by holding two poles in their hands, they slide down snow slopes standing up. The object of the custom seems to be to see how fast they can go before they break a leg. When a native reaches the bottom of the slope in one piece, he turns around and goes right up again to do it once more. This has led many anthropologists to conclude that the St. Moritzers, by and large, are not an intelligent race, but rather creatures of habit.

This being true or not, we were still impressed by their friendliness, love of life, appreciation for material things, courage in the face of hardship (sometimes they don't catch a smoked salmon for days) and their ability to remain unchanged in a changing world. We hope the St. Moritzers will always remain the unspoiled, simple people they are today, and no well-meaning missionaries will invade the Engadine Valley to change their way of life.

Life with Stein, Leon, and the Chilean Crazies

by MARTIE STERLING

The indispensable aides de camp *of a major destination ski resort are the willing, able, stressproof psychiatrists, a.k.a. "the innkeepers." Martie Sterling of the Heatherbed in Aspen Highlands left the ranks of innkeepers* summa cum laude *and is now seeking to heal the wounds of war via typing-therapy—with nothing else in mind than an occasional best-seller.*

A generation ago skiers were *something.* I mean, skiing was treacherous, skis were lethal, and getting there was like kissing a woodpecker—tricky. Brides did not care to honeymoon in Arctic weather and long wool underwear. Movie stars could think of better ways to smear their mascara. Professional athletes were forbidden on the slopes. And I personally knew a Continental pilot who sneaked ski trips via TWA so he wouldn't have his ass fired right off his airline. He was a big investment and they wanted him locked up safe with the rest of their portfolio.

In my case, I had nothing to say about it. (I had plenty to say all right, but no one to listen.) I'd married a man, Iglook, sired by a deep-freeze and weaned on a rope tow, a man who didn't think it one bit daring when we came west in the Fifties, found Aspen, and threw in our lot with skiing forever.

The Aspen we found was a motley mixture of gingerbread and thermopane, garages and gazebos, farmers and cowboys. You felt sometimes the place had missed the turning of the century. Irrigation ditches flowed along Main Street. Sheep and cattle drives, which some wag frequently detoured through the Hotel Jerome lobby, moved to and from the mountainsides. There were more old-time ranchers and miners than skiers, but the whole population was so piddling you could take a daily headcount at the post office.

What's more, Aspen Mountain, with fourteen runs, represented the sum total of Aspen skiing. Or had, until 1958, when Aspen Highlands opened up next door. It was there, just past the town dump, beyond the paved road, that Iglook and I bought four untrammeled acres, cleared a site, winched out a poor dead, putrefying thousand-pound elk, and built our ski lodge—Heatherbed by name.

Building a ski lodge (and clientele) takes youth, guts, ignorance, a Ouija board, a large mortgage, and a good location. Our new Aspen friends thought our location was rotten and told us so. "You mean you're going way out there in the *country?*" they asked incredulously and often. "Way out there in the country" was six minutes flat from the heart of town, but I guess you could say we were an outpost of sorts. Buttermilk and Snowmass weren't even a gleam in someone's eye, and beyond us were only the T-Lazy-7 ranch, five mountain ranges and a couple of melting glaciers.

Our location may have been rotten but it had: (1) a breathtaking view of Pyramid Peak and the Maroon Bells above, (2) Maroon Creek tumbling below, (3) space for a summer dude-ranch operation. And (4), it had *Stein.*

Stein Eriksen was the first, possibly the greatest, of the all-time legendary skiing greats—a blazing blue-eyed, swivel-hipping 6-foot Norwegian who emerged from the post–World War II Winter Olympics wreathed in medals and dimpled smiles. Now, some five years after his sweep of the World Championships, here Stein was, the director of the brand-new Highlands ski school right next door.

I was such a greenhorn that first year that my principal interest was watching Norma Shearer float down the staircase of the Jerome Hotel in clouds of chiffon, followed at a worshipful distance by her ski instructor husband Marty Arrouge and ogled adoringly by me. We who are over forty will go to the grave remembering Norma as Marie Antoinette en route to the guillotine, every shining hair in place, sculpted head riding majestically above the clattering tumbril, eyes luminous with belladonna. She was every inch a queen, and the world was prostrate at her feet. Unless you count Iglook, who spent an unedifying childhood watching Hoot Gibson and Johnny Weismuller in Saturday afternoon serials. His constant rejoinder was: "Whoever heard of Norma Shearer?"

Well, *I'd* never heard of Stein Eriksen. And with the lodge booked solid, I was up to my eyeballs in bedding and bathmats, doing everything that first season but weave the carpets, too far gone to care. Naturally I hadn't so much as set a ski boot on those beckoning, snowy slopes.

The children, however, were under no such constraint. Aged two to ten, they weren't much help in a hotel, so they toddled right on over to the Highlands to get acquainted. As there were six of them, and only two of us, it was necessary to hold frequent roll calls. One harried holiday

afternoon when I scolded the whole crew for missing mealtime, Whit, our eight-year-old, said airily, "It's okay, mom, Stein bought us lunch and I had two hot dogs" and they all ran off to wax their skis.

As the only people who would possibly buy lunch for six ravenous kids were either dirty old men or a white slaver trading in plump children, I yelled after them, "Stein WHO?"

"Oh you know, *Stein,*" echoed down the hallway.

I didn't know then, but I did before long—and a lot more than I cared to. Fawning, swooning females (nowadays called groupies) started spilling over on our doorstep. Writers wrote wistfully: "Just once like Stein." Folksingers composed him paeans of praise. Whole families arrived, rushed to the front desk, and asked breathlessly, "Where do we see Stein?" Which, come to think of it, didn't bother me half so much as being asked what time the Maroon Bells rang.

If the world missed Stein on weekdays they could see him any Sunday at high noon, when he did his famous flip. With the elan of a Flying Wallenda, Stein would give a pat to the jumphill, a wave to the crowd, then climb to the top, pause dramatically, and at length roar down the course, hit the jump, stretch into a Swan, turn over in mid-air, and land to thunderous applause. (Go ahead, titter, all you freestylers out there. Just keep in mind that Stein was the first, and back then, the only. What's more, he did it on skis a whole lot bigger than a breadbox.)

But what the hell. All Stein really needed to do was enter a room. He got exactly the same effect: eyes glazed. Tongues tied. Stomachs rumbled. And when he swooped down a ski hill the "aaaaaaaaaaaaaaaahs" rose like dawn over Mandalay.

In time I grew used to having Stein in our laps, girls at our windows, and celebrities all over the place. Understand, we were no Hilton-West. What we offered was old-fashioned hospitality like mother used to make. Neither Iglook nor I played the zither or yodeled but we did acquire a modest reputation for open arms and a decent dry martini. We didn't give parties to flex our social muscles—they just seemed to happen—but after a while things started getting out of hand. Lodge owners all over Aspen were checking in guests and saying: "As soon as you're unpacked, go right on out to the Heatherbed—they're having a party."

It was thus, over the years, that we attracted crowds the size of Coxey's Army. And thus that I strolled into my own sauna to find Art Linkletter, Teddy Kennedy, and Jane Powell draped in towels and steaming their pores (none of us had met before) . . . or looked up from the canapes and into the eyes of Kim Novak, Hugh O'Brien, Lance Reventlow, Jill St. John, and Lana Turner.

In the days of which I write, Aspen was cozier than a neighborhood coffee klatch. It was not, after all, easy to get to, and once here people clung together like so much creeping clematis. Flying Cessna 310s, the young and brazen Aspen Airways brought in maybe twenty passengers a day, and didn't count for much in the transportation stakes. Thus most skiers faced two deleterious choices in getting here: they could drive a car over the top of the Rockies, braving blizzard and blight. Or they could catch the grand old D & R G Railroad to Glenwood Springs, arrive at midnight (all luggage lost), climb into rickety, freezing buses for the 40-mile drive to Aspen, be dumped unceremoniously at a dingy downtown bus depot (all luggage lost), and at 2 A.M. In the morning, having already encountered the seven stages of purgatory, be met by a fleet of idling station wagons and short-fused drivers bellowing, "Blue Spruce, over here! . . . Hillside, Hillside! . . . Anyone for the Heatherbed?" Lodge-owners lost a lot of sleep this way. And arriving skiers lost sleep, perspective, heart, and, frequently, all their luggage.

Which is how a whole lot of innocent, unwary flatlanders came to drive themselves in the dead of winter and the dark of night into the bowels of the Colorado ski mountains.

When writer Leon Uris knocked at our door one stormy December night he was ashen-faced and trembling, his voice reduced to a feeble croak. Lee was an ex-Marine who'd spent the war years crawling around a number of Pacific atolls under fire, but he was also a Baltimore boy who

had never driven a 12,000-foot mountain pass in a blizzard. Our treatment was standard—we thrust a strong drink into his lifeless hands.

Lee lived to overcome acrophobia, become our good friend, and fall in love with Aspen. Eventually he signed on forever and instead of commuting from Los Angeles to Aspen began building his own Red Mountain home and commuting from Aspen to the lodge. He spent a year with us writing *Armageddon,* which gave all the Sterlings a little corner on immortality. Since then he's progressed through *Topaz* and *QB VII* to the epic *Trinity,* and, I am happy to report, from being an indifferent skier to the superdeluxe A-1 bomber model.

Writers seemed to find us out. I, of course, was tickled. Alex Haley, in the days before *Roots,* created the *Playboy* Interview, and it was in the wake of an interviewee for that magazine that Alex came to the Heatherbed.

Twenty years ago Aspen was on its knees, begging skiers to somehow find their way to us. A lot of our friends fed themselves and their families on elk they'd shot, trout they'd caught, gardens they'd grown. Timmy Hayden, who taught for Stein with Iglook, ate trout sandwiches till I was sure he'd break out in speckles, and he and his wife Lynn slept with their feet on the family freezer-chest like it held the heirloom flatware. Given this state of bare survival, taking in a visiting ski team could be a hardship. Just the same we all did it.

I myself felt that people, like dogs, should be fed once a day. And since I was busier than a mustard paddle at a weenie roast, my meals, like premature babies, were often served up without any finishing touches. When the dinner table frequently expanded from ten to twenty what I did was either water the spaghetti or add beans to the chili.

I learned to make chili right and make it hot when the Chilean Olympic Ski Team, six-strong, moved in with us. The 1960 Olympics were due at Squaw Valley, but no one had notified the weatherman. So until snow fell out there, we, along with other Aspenites, welcomed any Olympians who wanted to train.

My only thoughts were of doing our duty

and possibly having someone around for the children to practice Spanish on. None of us had even heard of culture shock.

We felt our first tremor when the Chileans came barreling down our driveway in a borrowed Jeep, gears screaming, doing 50 in low gear. When they alighted we found them Latin to the core. They also possessed the very peculiar Latin death wish: they drove cars with feckess abandon and no regard for vehicular law, skied with an unconstraint that sent hackers scrambling for the trees, kissed every woman in sight (even if she looked like a hamster and was pushing seventy), woke guests singing loudly of heartbreak nights and joy-filled days.

Their battle cry, I'll tell you right off, was later banned from the Olympic site. Imagine, if you will, a sound composed of equal parts Yma Sumac, Comanche war cry, and the screech of tearing metal, and you have it. The cry originated with the boy Indio, who was not your routine Portillo or Santiago Chilean. He sprang from somewhere high in the Andes, was pure, unadulterated Incan, and didn't even speak Spanish.

Actually, Indio never spoke at all. He just looked alert, his button-black eyes moving from face to face and marking every exit. When Indio had needs the other boys divined them, probably through osmosis, and if he wished to vent a feeling or two, he simply broke into the high, mournful wail of the battle cry. Indio in full voice could single-throatedly set off an avalanche.

My mother arrived for her first visit from the East in time to hear The Cry issuing from forty throats in the upstairs lounge—the guests had picked it up in sheer self-defense—and immediately took to her bed with a three-day sinking spell and without, as I sniffled to Iglook, " . . . even one glance at our view!"

The Chileans plummeted up and down our driveway and all the ski runs, spilled hot wax the length and breadth of our dorms, used my steam iron to press their skis, leered shamefully at our prepubescent daughters, and triumphantly presented me with a housegift bouquet of live, unplucked chickens they'd wheedled out of a local rancher. The children, meanwhile, picked up a lot of Spanish, most of it unacceptable in polite homes, and followed the team everywhere. It was influences such as this which led to Dan, at the age of three, traveling the chairlift to 11,000 feet while his father and I rested secure in the thought that he was safely enrolled in kiddies' ski school down below.

The Chilean National Team may not have won any medals at Squaw Valley, but they sure left a lasting impression in Aspen.

It was our friend and neighbor Andy Mead Lawrence who made the impression at Squaw; she was the first pregnant Olympic torch-bearer. I heartily envied Andy, who gained three pounds per child, skied with undiminished zest, and gave birth at some convenient hour like right after lunch or in plenty of time for dinner.

Over the years Iglook and I housed, fed, and befriended Aussies, Canadians, Argentinians, Kiwis, Japanese, a few Czechs, half of Mexico, three Iranians, and a Pole. And then, of course, there were the Vikings.

I know this stretches credulity, but a few years back there were *not* hundreds of fast-skiing American kids vying in instructor clinics for a chance to teach. In fact, Stein, in desperation, had to import instructors. It was thus that the newest wave of Norsemen—farmboys, and sailors from Norway, Danish gymnasts, Icelandic sheepherders—hit Aspen. To our children the names of these skiing wonders—Ulfar, Magne, Steinthor, Finn-Eddy, Peder, Svein, Arnë—were at first uniformly unintelligible, so they simply lumped them all together as "the Vikings."

When Arnë Martinsson and Magne Nostdahl climbed off the boat and appeared at our door they were young, eager, apple-cheeked, and in for the shock of their lives. They'd expected gold and all they found was the same old snow. As an added blow, they discovered if they didn't teach they wouldn't eat. There were few guaranteed ski school salaries in those days, and an instructor really had to hustle. Hustling in Norwegian is as futile as pimping in the Gobi Desert, and until the Norwegians could learn English they lived on cafeteria leftovers, our largesse, and the Red Onion "Special." The Special cost $1.50 and fortunately fed a lumberjack, so

Magne and Arnë ordered one per sitting, alternating meat and salad one night, bread and vegetables the next.

After a few months Magne, who was fortunately dark-complected, got a night job as a Chinese waiter at Trader Ed's Restaurant. Ed himself was fighting off foreclosure at the time and operating his entire establishment on an extension cord plugged into an absentee owner's upstairs apartment. The place was consequently dark as a tomb (and almost as empty) and unsuspecting tourists, who couldn't be expected to detect the difference between a Mandarin and a Bergen accent, never even noticed Magne's suspiciously Occidental bone structure. This unfortunate confusion spilled over into the kitchen. So it was weeks before Magne discovered the Japanese cook's "asshole" was not a term of endearment, and the diners were treated to a spirited meat-cleaver chase among the tables and tiki torches.

Our children never picked up much Norwegian (nobody picks up Norwegian but other Norwegians) but they did spend some of their formative years trying to teach Magne and Arnë English.

"Listen, Arney, you're not supposed to say 'a lot of nail'—it's 'nails,' *plural!*"

"Gosh, Magne, why do you have to be such a spazz about an old 'J'? It's not pee-yam-muhs, it's pah-JAM-mahs!" Iglook insists all their efforts were in vain, because Arnë can't speak English to this day.

The Vikings married local girls, became citizens, successful businessmen, fathers of families. Iglook and I are crazy about them, except when they break out the aquavit. Stein used to whip up a punch of fruit juice, grain alcohol, aquavit, mead, and mayhem. On the days following we: visited in the hospital with Ulla Neilson, who'd broken both ankles in an obstacle race featuring the roof of Stein's house . . . bailed out Magne and Arnë after a cross-country auto race over Mrs. Paepcke's ranch, across town, and into a telephone pole . . . and soothed the hysterical members of a beginner's ski class which Magne, still roaring drunk, had ushered to the edge of a precipice and ordered, "Come now, we YUMP!"

Any hotel owner meets enough fascinating people to fill a book. Conrad Hilton managed three, between wives. I guess the ones I remember best are all the children. Word spread that we had this enormous family and would scarcely notice one more. On this mistaken theory parents sent us offspring by the score—ostensibly to learn to ski, in reality to get them out of the house. The kids mitered sheets, mucked out toilets, mastered skiing, hocked my silver. We helped rear a future race-car driver, a Texas department-store heir, an F. Scott Fitzgerald grandchild, seven school dropouts, two runaways, a navy orphan, and an army brat. By the time we were finished I had twenty-three children and a pale expression.

Our own children grew up thinking they were part of an institution and that ski mountains of Aspen were their personal property. Skiing became an integral part of their lives and eventually a ticket to every continent in the world. It was, we thought, the very best experience a child could have.

We were one of the last of the precondominium, old-time ski lodges. We dispensed Band-Aids, Alka-Seltzer, advice to the lovelorn, introductions to the lonely, 12,873 free meals and sixty-odd tank cars of *gluehwein.* We never made much money, but we gave our skiers everything we had—and got back more in return.

An era is gone. So are many of our wonderful skiers. I sometimes feel sad, sometimes sorry, but most of the time, I must admit, I just feel twenty years younger.

Heatherbedlam

by **LEON URIS**

Leon Uris, author of the bestseller Exodus, *is a sometime Aspen ski instructor. He remembers the town in its heyday of Stein and roses. Here are the good old ways.*

MARTHA JANE STERLING, mother of six and co-mortgagee of the Heatherbed Lodge in Aspen sat at the kitchen table, clamped a cigar in her teeth determinedly and pondered chestily over the copy for a new brochure. "The trouble," she said, "is to try to describe the Heatherbed in fifty words."

"Just call it the New York Met of the ski lodges," chortled her spouse, Poor Ken Sterling.

I made an appearance desperately seeking coffee and sympathy. It was the morning after an Aspen after-dark tour. I ended up in a loser-pay-all chug-a-lug contest at the Galena Street East having learned that aging ex-Marines should not contest the beer drinking capacity of wise-guy college kids and hope to win.

I managed a roquefort smile.

Poor Ken, noting my magenta shading, greeted me with a customary reverence for literary eminence. "Hey, Uris, your face looks like 20 miles of dirt road. How about having a greasy pork chop for breakfast?"

Encouraged by watching me change colors like a salamander he pressed on. "How about

lending me fifty 'till my brother straightens out . . . he's a hunchback." And after a slap on his own knee, "If you had a nose full of nickels you'd be richer than the Bank of America."

The phone interrupted Pa Kettle's soliloquy. "Heatherbedlam," he answered, "Poor Ken speaking."

I first got mixed up with this carnivorous bunch several years ago when a certain unmentionable Idaho resort blanked out my reservation a week before Christmas. In desperation I called my buddy, John Freiburg, the Tiki Torch king who had done the Aspen route.

"King," I said in the manner in which he likes to be addressed, "can you use your drag to get me into Aspen?"

"Let me phone the Heatherbed, boy," he answered, "they'll take anybody."

Old guests are apt to settle in their rooms wearily after driving through Loveland Pass in a blizzard to be suddenly greeted by a half-dozen "friends" in their bed wearing stocking masks and yelling "surprise, surprise" . . . or to find another old friend or two in their bathtub in long johns knocking out a Verdi duet.

The aforementioned Tiki John Freiburg is an habitual griper about the size of his room. Last year we made a final correction of this situation. With the help of MGM's wardrobe department I disguised myself as the house boy. When Tiki John and spouse Rosemary arrived, I took their bags to the sauna room, 8 by 10 feet in size, and furnished with a single iron cot. After letting their luggage come open I announced tersely, "Your room, sir. Pick up your clothing. I've got work to do." It is regrettable that the expression did not freeze on Tiki John's face for posterity.

Things always seem to happen at the Heatherbed. Things like the Norwegian wedding party which brought out all of Aspen's Scandinavian colony. They are a sentimental folk and, when potted, are given to overt weeping. While they drank and cried a series of disasters struck the Heatherbed. First the electricity went, then the hot water, then the cold water.

Poor Ken was crawling around under the lodge banging at pipes while up in the candle-lit lounge the happy bride opened her presents, cried, piled paper and tin foil in the fireplace and cried some more.

Somebody dropped an ash.

Scott Pierce, runaway socialite and typical Heatherbed chambermaid, whispered to M. J., "Don't panic, but like hurrysville, the roof's on fire."

Aspen's glorious volunteer fire department was more than up to the occasion. However, the alarm caught most of them in the middle of an Elk initiation dinner and they rushed to the scene in tuxedos and elks teeth.

With the fire under control, the grateful Norwegians prevailed upon the firemen to combine celebrations. The assistant chief caught the bridal bouquet and the bridegroom went the way of all flesh in a sea of aquavit. The kids, incidentally, had a swell time being driven up and down the driveway in Aspen's new hose and ladder truck.

Only Poor Ken sulked in a corner mumbling over and over, "Why didn't the damned place burn down all the way?"

Ken and Martie Sterling were well set economically and socially in Pennsylvania, then up and went West one day to keep from being drowned in suburbia. Despite minor and major disasters, the Heatherbed keeps growing in fact and legend—like the new corral and the six new hand-tooled rooms. Ken did most of the carpentry and the painting and M. J. designed them and made all the drapes and bedspreads.

If you need a friend in Aspen, you've got one. M. J. has developed a pair of cauliflower ears hearing out the woes of a gamut of lost souls, from unwed mothers to unemployed ski instructors.

That heckler she's married to serves not only as father, but doubles as ski instructor, wrangler, lumberjack, packtrip guide, maid, baker, carpenter, plumber, and occasional painter.

And the Heatherbed never runs out of those two essentials . . . love and martinis.

Another member of the Heatherbed crew is Dr. Harold Whitcomb, M. J.'s kid brother, president of the Aspen Ski Club and a Schweitzer of the Rockies, who has earned the title of "our beloved Dr. Whit."

Dr. Whit is a 6-foot-6 specimen who checks in at around two five zero. Last year one of his grateful patients gifted him with an ankle-length bearskin coat. Before the "bear" was fully identified, twenty some citizens had passed out cold and his car took six hits from the police who were determined to get that "crazy animal driving around in our streets."

Dr. Whit also beats a mean bass fiddle and occasionally sits in on a session at the Red Onion when he isn't "out there" stamping out disease. Last year Poor Ken and I fiendishly painted the fiddle a mandarin red for the New Year's party but carefully laid the blame on his partner, Dr. Bob Oden, who goes like 6-foot-7 and is twenty pounds heavier than the late Daddy Lipscomb. It is said that pro-football scouts have broken down and wept at the mere sight of him.

Whit and Bob form two-thirds of the Aspen Clinic. Last year when I was carted off the slopes, Whit deferred me to Oden, who is the bone specialist, and Oden applied my cast. Through my agony I could hear Whit's voice in reverence . . .

"You've done it again, Bob! Three minutes, twenty-six seconds. Close to the record! Bob, you're an artist, a Michelangelo."

Bob Oden cracked a plaster-caked smile, blushed and mumbled, "Nothing, Whit . . . nothing at all."

After a decade of battling high-rise zoning changes and freeway routes which usually ended up in my back yard I find myself looking more and more wistfully towards Aspen and the mountains.

There are two times in life when I feel I have a solitary piece of the world. One of the times is before daybreak. I would most likely be in Mexico, in Acapulco. I watch my fishing boat cross the bay to pick me up at La Concha. We load our gear aboard and head for the blue water just as the sun brings the dawn. It seems as though the whole world is asleep except for me, the skipper and crew, and my wife.

The other time I own a little of the world is the last run of the day on the ski slopes. I don't believe I have to try to explain that feeling.

But Aspen is more than a ski town. Over the tracks at the Meadows, the Aspen Institute of Humanities has gained international recognition. The first Aspen Prize, awarded last year to Benjamin Britten, begins an American Nobel tradition. The Music Association, its summer festival and camp, is the most important development of its kind in the western hemisphere.

Aspen has real artists. I don't mean the bearded beatniks but craftsmen of great skill who practice in unique forms as the iron forgers, the Valley Kiln wind bells, the nearly lost art of stained glass.

This town is a conglomeration of every level of the social, economic, educational, and intellectual scale. It is, indeed, a little Athens, with its warriors on skis and its thinkers at the Meadows.

It is not without the viciousness of small town politics, or its fair share of unreasonable characters, but the idea of Aspen is larger than anyone's ability to corrupt it. No one came to Aspen to make a bundle. They came, like the Sterlings and my family, because there was a certain way they wanted to live their lives. I would suspect there are few towns on earth so totally inhabited by people who love her.

I have been variously described as a poor man's Hemingway, both in talent and bank account. I suppose that is because I'm a ski bum and I love to fish for the big ones.

I'm writing in one of the Heatherbed rooms which I'll use as an office until the ski season starts. Below me, the Maroon Creek rushes by. Outside my window a billion aspen leaves have turned and they shimmer like gold doubloons. Down the valley, the jagged Pyramid peaks reach through a flawless blue sky for the heavens.

M. J. is a hell of a good writer and I'm prodding her to do a book about her misadventures as a lodge owner. She now has access to the old J. P. Marquand studio, near the Institute.

It is a real paradox. Every morning I get on my Honda and buzz out to the Heatherbed to write and generally pass M. J. in the guestmobile heading for the Marquand studio . . . to write.

Sun Valley Opens with a Bang and Skiing Hits Manhattan

by DORICE TAYLOR

For nearly twenty-five years, resident public relations director Dorice Taylor was Sun Valley to all the writers who came to Sun Valley Lodge. How did a nice girl from Manhattan end up with a job like that? It was through Steve Hannagan, the demon publicist who thought up the name Sun Valley on the theory that it was just the place to work on your preseason tan. Hannagan hated snow and hardly ever went there; Dorice loved snow and never left. Here is a selection from her recent autobiography.

IN spite of incredible difficulties and delays, Sun Valley Lodge opened on time. No markers said this or that would be built next year—it was a complete ski resort, as Steve Hannagan had advised.

The opening banquet was marked by an "interesting encounter." So said several metropolitan papers below a column of pictures of the participants. The donnybrook, the article said, was "between Charles F. Gore of Chicago, widely known investment banker (and from his picture in the papers a very handsome young man) and David O. Selznick, even more widely known producer."

Mr. and Mrs. Selznick, Gene Markey and his glamorous wife, Joan Bennett, and Dr. Joel Pressman and his equally glamorous wife, Claudette Colbert, were at a table together. Gore, reportedly, joined this table uninvited and asked one of the film stars to dance. Selznick promptly knocked Gore flat with a right or left to the eye. The management, their elegant and sophisticated housewarming ruined, removed the bloody Gore from the scene.

Someone thought to call Steve Hannagan in New York.

"What do you mean your party's ruined?" shouted Steve. "Not an editor in the country can resist this story." Then he sat down and wrote the headline himself—"Sun Valley Opens with a Bang."

Coming just after the Depression, the menu of the banquet must have been an eye-opener—Brioche au Caviar, Supreme of Sole au Champagne, Tournedos Saute Chatelaine.

The editor of the *Hailey Times,* the county weekly—making no mention of the fight—was ecstatic. "Seven months ago a small valley lay basking in the sun in peace and quietude. There it was tucked away in the heart of the hills, nameless and comparatively unknown with very little manmade things to mar its tranquillity. In just a brief time, Monday evening, December 21, 1936, the whole world heard the sound of music, speaking, sounds of revelry, broadcast from a mammoth hotel that stands majestically in the heart of what is known to the world as Sun Valley.

"This majestic structure that we have watched grow, wondering and incredulous, cost one and a half million dollars and has two hundred and twenty rooms . . . "

He goes on to say that "nothing has been spared to make the far easterner feel at home as well as to add to the comfort and pleasure of guests." And, "The hotel was opened by a formal dinner attended by a goodly representation of Idaho people and guests from the Far East."

The editor did not mean to insinuate that rice was being prepared to make far eastern guests in Oriental silks feel at home. To Idahoans at that time Omaha was "East," so that anything east of Chicago had to be "Far East."

It is a good guess, on the other hand, that half the eastern guests, unless they had just consulted a map, had no idea whether they were in the Dakotas or somewhere between Colorado and Mexico. Idaho was for many years one of the unknown states of the Union.

Just one thing was lacking at the opening. Snow. No snow on opening day, only a flurry at Christmas and New Year's, no real snow until January 9.

Averell Harriman handled his no-snow problem well. He sent a wire to all expected guests saying, "No snow here. If you are a good gambler, come on out and be our guest till it arrives." Then he went to Los Angeles and imported a group of starlets to pep things up. Pretty and full of fun, they were a great success.

Not quite so successful was another group of young ladies. Before the opening an ad was placed in the *Salt Lake Tribune* asking for maids. A group of girls from a laundry had applied en masse and were accepted. However, they soon showed much more interest in playing games between the sheets than in changing them. They were sent back to their laundry with the hope they would lead cleaner lives there, and new help was recruited from the housewives in Ketchum and Hailey.

Steve Hannagan sold *Life* magazine on the status of the resort, and photographers and writers rolled into the Valley to do a cover story. Big stuff—an eight-page spread headed, "East Goes West to Idaho's Sun Valley. Society's Newest Winter Playground."

The story says that "Since Christmas it has been packed, at from eight dollars to twenty-four dollars a day, with as fancy a crew of rich socialites as have ever been assembled under one roof in the U.S."

Among those pictured:

Lydia duPont, "of the Delaware duPonts." Lydia was to become a regular visitor until her death in an automobile accident many years later.

Count Felix. Shown high on a mountain in a great scenic.

Industrialist J. M. Studebaker III, who allowed himself to be photographed in a series of action pictures ending in a spill.

Averell and Marie Harriman. The photogenic couple are shown in an obviously fake doze outside a ski hut, wearing racing numbers while waiting for some competition to start.

Margaret Emerson McKim Vanderbilt Baker Amory smoking a cigarette in a deck chair. "Who," says the caption, "has $10 million mainly derived from her father's Bromo Seltzer."

Topping all of these is the picture of Gloria Baker, heiress to the ten millions, "who rests her pretty head in ski instructor Hauser's lap while 'sun-dozing'." Hans Hauser, handpicked by Count Schaffgotsch as head of the eight-man Austrian ski school, the Jean-Claude Killy of his day, was good-looking in spite of his gopher teeth, and Gloria was more than just pretty.

Steve Hannagan was pleased for there were two full pages of pictures with the Hannagan touch—bathing beauties, cocktails around the pool with snow-capped mountains in the distance, and skiers stripped to the waist.

When that issue of *Life*, with a skier riding the novel chairlift on the cover, hit the newsstands, Sun Valley took its place among the world's famous resorts.

But Hannagan had an even greater coup that first season. Paramount starred Claudette Colbert with Robert Young and Melvyn Douglas in a romantic winter tale involving a trip to a

Mt. Baldy's runs are easily among the world's best ski trails

Early customers at Sun Valley included Gary Cooper and Claudette Colbert

winter sports area. You can imagine what the title, *I Met Him in Paris,* and the setting, supposedly in the Alps, did to Hannagan's ulcers. But he managed to put out enough publicity to assure the public that the movie was made at the new resort in Idaho and it did benefit Sun Valley mightily.

Claudette had been in Sun Valley for the opening and was one of the lovelies involved in the fracas headlined "Sun Valley Opens with a Bang." The local paper listed her then as "the most looked-at of all." That was an achievement, since the competition included Constance Bennett, Madeleine Carrol, and Lili Damita, plus the bevy of sexy little starlets who were out to be noticed.

The Paramount crew rented sixty rooms in the Hotel Hiawatha in Hailey. This was the hotel with natural hot water plunge built by the Mellon interests. The most important mining financiers of that earlier era had been content to stay there without complaint. There was *one* "handsomely equipped toilet room," said the Hailey paper, "with porcelain lined bathtub with hot and cold water on each floor." The crew did complain— vociferously.

The principals of the movie stayed in the Lodge, but Jack Lane's store at the crossroads once again became a center of activity. Every member of the cast and crew had to sign in there whenever they went to the Casino or any other spot in Ketchum, so that they could be found on a moment's notice. The Casino bar, with its gambling tables, had become a favorite hangout of the cast.

Claudette, the vivacious star of the picture, was a natural for winter sports and did the skating for the picture herself, without the help of a double. She had never skied but started ski lessons with Hans Hauser, and in the years that followed became one of the best women skiers at Sun Valley.

The Tyrolean movie set was built in North Fork Canyon, a few miles north of Ketchum. It included a hotel with overhanging eaves and carved balustrades, and a little church perched on a steep hillside. A skating rink with a snow-topped gazebo had an ice bar, and skating waiters. Sleighs jingled past quaint chalets and the whole thing looked a lot more picturesque than the Union Pacific's big, spacious hotel sitting in the middle of its valley.

According to the art director, Ernest Fegte, the set was achieved with sweat, blood, and tears. Materials for the quaint church had to be hauled up the steep hill by block and tackle. Because of subterranean hot springs several spots on the skating rink would not freeze over no matter how much water was sprayed on. At the last minute before filming Fegte was inspired to build an ice bar around the holes and add skating waiters to the cast.

On the very night before the filming, snow came, 18 puffy inches of it. Great, but the next day the sky was leaden and shooting was impossible. However, a makeshift stage had been built behind the facade for just this contingency and director Wesley Ruggles decided to shoot the bedroom scenes.

Fine, only in the cold the camera picked up the breath of the actors as if they were snorting fire. Quickly, salamanders, those cannonball heaters filled with kerosene that you see along roads where construction work is going on, were brought to heat the stage. But the concentrated heat melted the snow on the roof and the mikes picked up the drip, drip, drip. Sawdust eventually halted the dripping sounds, but it didn't halt the melting of big patches of snow on the roof.

Fortunately it started to snow again in the late afternoon, covering the roofs once more, and the next day was perfect for shooting the outdoor scenes.

As Fegte, winner of one Oscar and several nominations for set designs, said philosophically, "Sway with the wind and you'll come out on top. The law of averages is on your side."

The filming stretched into early spring when the lambing season began. Claudette expressed the desire for a bum lamb and Jack Lane gave her one. A bum lamb is an orphan, and a pathetic little creature when no ewe will adopt it. Bottle-fed, it becomes a most affectionate pet, and the antics of Claudette's snow-white woolly baby generated a great deal of publicity.

There was only one mishap. A young member of the crew volunteered to take the actress's lamb back to Hollywood for her but then neglected to take along milk as he had been instructed.

In the night the lamb began to bleat from hunger and its escort made use of the only bottle available in the train compartment—a bottle of Johnnie Walker Black Label. Being a native of Idaho, the lamb took to the scotch with enthusiasm and proved a good drinking companion for its roommate. In the morning it was a bleary-eyed escort and an inebriated little lamb with rubber joints that met the waiting press.

The last of the Paramount crew left in April.

The picture was a great success—it is still delightful to see.

The only tangible remains of the filming is a chalet, moved into town from North Fork Canyon. It stands today on Highway 75 just south of Ketchum, as the office for the Andora Villa.

There was one far-reaching result of the filming of the picture. Averell Harriman planned another hotel at Sun Valley to provide for the young skiers who could not afford the Lodge. He envisioned a simple country inn to be called the Challenger Inn as a tie-in with the streamlined sit-up trains, the Challengers, economy versions of the luxury trains.

Harriman wanted a Tyrolean edifice but wasn't satisfied with the preliminary sketches of the architects in Washington, D.C. During the filming of *I Met Him in Paris* he admired the sets done by Fegte and asked him to do conception drawings to set a "style" for Sun Valley Village.

Fegte said the work was a "designer's delight" but when contractor Larry McNeil saw the plans he nearly lost his mind. Such boring considerations as necessary windows and other openings had been overlooked. "Strictly a movie set," McNeil groaned. Quite a scrap developed but with a little common sense and using as many of the Fegte ideas as possible, a compromise was made.

You can walk from one end of the Inn to the other, all inside a big boxlike structure, but the outside is divided into the Challenger Inn, the Ram, the Grand Hotel, and so on, each painted a different color to look like a separate building.

Artistic noses may go up and the owners cry "pseudo-Swiss" when they see the village square. But when the snow is on the eaves it's very pretty "pseudo" and sits snugly in the Valley as if the Valley had always been waiting for it.

The Challenger Inn and the Opera House were both built in the summer of 1937. Then a cottage for the Harrimans was started in October. It was built under a circus tent heated by salamanders and was ready when the family arrived from New York on the streamliner *City of Los Angeles* for Christmas.

The Taylors, my husband and I, paying our first visit to Sun Valley, were also on the *City of*

Los Angeles, which brought the Harrimans for their second Christmas visit.

Controlled skiing began in this country as early as 1929, when Sig Buchmayr, an Austrian skier, started his ski school at Peckett's on Sugar Hill in Franconia, New Hampshire. Lessons were a dollar. Lowell Thomas and Lowell, Jr., were in the first class. Sig Buchmayr chased the girls, and the teaching—at least 80 percent of it, according to Lowell—was done by a tall pro, Kurt Thalhammer, from Salzburg.

Rope tows and J-bars soon dotted New England, and ski trains pulled avid skiers to mountains in the Berkshires and the Adirondacks. But it was not until 1936, when the blizzard of publicity about the building of Sun Valley reached the East, that the skiing craze hit New York.

Pictures of Steve Hannagan's young, blond god, stripped to the waist, were everywhere. There was a sports show at Madison Square Garden that featured a giant slide sprayed with artificial ice. Hannes Schneider, founder of the Arlberg Ski School at St. Anton and a hero through all the Alpine countries, was present and demonstrated his turns on the slide.

Saks Fifth Avenue, soon to operate the ski shop at Sun Valley, had its windows decorated with huge murals of the new resort. They formed a background for new ski fashions designed especially for Sun Valley.

Saks also put in a borax slide, as did Macy's and Wanamaker's. At each store Austrian instructors were available to teach the controlled turns of the Arlberg system. It was on the slide at Saks that the chain of events began that brought me to Sun Valley to stay.

I was then teaching English at Miss Hewitt's Classes, a fashionable New York day school attended by such celebrities as Brenda Fraser and Cobina Wright, Jr. The school was housed in three delightful old brownstones on Seventy-ninth Street. It lacked a gymnasium, so the girls trooped down to the YWCA on Lexington Avenue for athletic activities. Using the logic that skiing was more of a social asset than basketball, I persuaded the heads of the school to accept it as an accredited sport and offered to chaperone.

Two pretty blond seniors signed up and off we went to the borax slide at Saks.

My reasons for introducing skiing to the school were almost entirely selfish. Growing up in DuBois, Pennsylvania, in the Alleghenies, I saw my first pair of skis at the age of eight. The brother of a friend had made them for her in the woodworking class at an eastern prep school. After one ride on my friend's skis, I had my own pair made at a wagon-wheel shop. They were fashioned of straight-grained hickory, about 4 inches wide, with a simple toe strap attached. I skied through my high-school days on a pair of Northlands made of ash and coated with cheap yellow varnish. These skis had some sort of heel straps, but they didn't work. At Smith College, I skied on Dippy Hill, so-called because of a state mental institution at its top, and not because of what nonskiing students thought about those of us who skied.

Despite those years devoted to skiing I had only skied straight downhill. Now I found myself for the first time learning the Austrian system of controlled skiing. The borax slide at Saks ended in the men's shoe department and my debutantes and I were an immediate sensation. Salesmen and customers alike formed an appreciative audience. The slide itself, covered with flannel and then sprinkled with borax, produced a skiing surface much like greased glass. Nevertheless I began to learn the rudiments of the snowplow and could exercise some control. My younger companions fared differently.

One would take off from the top competently enough. Halfway down, when she was supposed to go into her snowplow, she would let out an explosive squeal and sail out of control, usually managing to get one long, graceful leg over the barricade between the slide and the shoe department. The other member of our class usually rolled down the slide like a teddy bear. She changed that pattern on one occasion to bounce over the barricade skis and all and land in the lap of an elderly gentleman. A reporter happened to be there with a camera. He got a picture of the gentleman looking as surprised as J. P. Morgan with the midget.

The Hewitt School, in spite of its rather liberal attitude, decided it had had enough of my ideas about the social value of skiing and dropped the course from the curriculum. Nevertheless, I finished all the lessons. When they ended, I could make three linked turns on that impossible surface.

I had been married at this time for about five years. My husband, "Phez" Taylor,* although a Dartmouth man, had been on skis only once in his college years and had concluded that the sport was strictly for the birds. However, he was caught up in my enthusiasm and the general interest in skiing in New York. We gave each other skis for Christmas and waited for snow.

One Sunday morning in February, we woke to find that a foot of snow had blanketed the city. When I opened the closet in our small apartment to get the coffee pot, out fell the skis. I didn't bother to put them back. "Get up," I shouted to Phez. "We're going skiing in Central Park."

We had never heard of anyone skiing in the park, but when we neared Fifty-ninth Street, we found kindred souls coming from all directions. We tried the first little hill, but a cop promptly chased us off. We tried the next, where children were sledding. Again the cops. Then we walked all the way up to a hill at Seventy-ninth Street. There were a good many skiers there, and we had several good runs before the police caught up with us. We trudged to another hill, were chased off there, and went back to Seventy-ninth Street. We were enjoying the escape and evasion tactics thoroughly until a patrol car arrived full of cops who meant business. They rounded up all the skiers and herded us out of the park.

As we walked back down Fifth Avenue we found a group of skiers gathered in front of the Armory. They asked us to join them for a photograph as a protest against the exclusion of skiers from Central Park. For some reason I hesitated, but Phez, smoldering because we couldn't ski, rushed into the group. Next day, in the *New York Times,* there was my Republican husband, a lawyer with the City Bank Farmers Trust Company,

front and center in the photograph. The headline read, "Communists Protest Against New York Police."

By Washington's birthday, the only snow report that could be put out in the East was "Good Borax at Wanamaker's, Macy's, and Saks Fifth Avenue." Phez and I found a ski train to Montreal and the Laurentians, and called for reservations for the weekend. Ste. Marguerite was full, St. Saveur was full, Ste. Adele, and Ste. Agathe likewise. We finally found a room in a little inn at Val Morin. There we found wet snow falling like white rain in large drops. We struggled down the Maple Leaf Trail to Ste. Marguerite and made reservations for the next Christmas.

Planning ahead did us no good. The next December there was no snow in eastern Canada, and the inn where we had made reservations had burned down in the interim. My husband looked up one Sunday morning from the *New York Times.* "We'll go to Sun Valley," he announced.

I thought he was mad. You went to the Berkshires to ski, you went to the White Mountains to ski, you might even extravagantly go to the Canadian Laurentians to ski, but you didn't go west—*that* far west—just to ski. On my mental map, the continent between Chicago and California was a neutral-colored blank.

Phez handed over a full page advertisement saying that the *City of Los Angeles,* a new Union Pacific train, would make its maiden voyage to Sun Valley. "Very nice," I said, "but we can't afford it."

A week later, the *City of Los Angeles* was put on exhibition in Grand Central Station and Phez dragged me over to see it. It was the first streamlined passenger train ever seen in the East, and I had to admit it was impressive. Shiny, yellow, sleek. It would make its first run straight from New York to Sun Valley before settling down on its regular schedule from Chicago to Los Angeles.

The observation car at the rear of the train was the most comfortable and luxurious I'd ever seen, and the room cars were colorful and commodious. The "Little Nugget" was a bar car fitted up like the parlor of a Gay Nineties madam. The curtains and settees were red velvet, and the

---

*"Phez" is a Dartmouth nickname of obscure origin that followed him through Yale Law School. The older people in Hailey, Idaho, the site of his law office and the county seat near Sun Valley, call him Everett.

bartender had a tremendous mustache. Near the bar, a music box shaped like a bird cage played, "I'm Only a Bird in a Gilded Cage."

In the diner, we read the menu of what would be served on the trip. Free wine was included. I asked, "How much *would* it cost to go to Sun Valley?" We walked on through the train to the comfortable sit-up coaches in the front. "We could sit up," I suggested.

"We could, but we won't," Phez said.

I began to weaken: "Well, let's stop at the information booth and see how much it costs." We didn't need to make that stop. Phez had already made reservations.

When we later met Steve Hannagan and told him the story, he said, "I always wondered how in the hell that sign got there."

The second morning of that first trip on the *City of Los Angeles* we awakened in Pocatello, Idaho, where we were greeted by the Indian chief from the Blackfoot Reservation. When we left the main line at Shoshone, Idaho, and turned north on the branch line to Ketchum, Averell Harriman gave us permission to ride in the diesel cab.

Riding along looking out the diesel windows, we saw what seemed to us the most unlikely country in the world for a ski resort. Less than 60 miles from the skiing, we were traveling over a perfectly level sagebrush desert. We didn't know then that Sun Valley is more than 2,000 feet higher than Shoshone. The ascent is so gradual there seems to be no grade at all.

There was no snow in sight—far different from the picturesque Laurentians through which our train had wound its way the previous year. In that evil way wives have, I began to watch to see when my husband reached the lowest ebb of disappointment. Then I was going to raise my eyebrows and say, "So you wouldn't wait until there was snow in the Laurentians!"

But suddenly in the distance—suddenly, just like that, almost as if in a mirage—jagged snow-covered peaks gleamed against a blue sky.

Nothing you can say describes that mountain vista when it first appears except that it looks like Shangri-La. Everyone has been saying it for years. Because it does.

Among the many explanations for the name "Idaho," the prettiest is the legend that the Indian word means "shining mountains." These were the shining mountains at their best.

At the station in Ketchum a band was playing and dog teams and sleighs were waiting. There were even sleighs drawn by reindeer.

The reindeer proved to be costly window dressing. Sun Valley had held its first rodeo the summer before, and Bob Miles, one of the producers, had stayed on in charge of all Sun Valley sports. It was his idea to import reindeer from Alaska.

Meaner animals had never been seen in these parts. With them came several tons of moss, but the plan was to wean them gradually to hay. When the moss was gone, however, the reindeer went on a hunger strike and would have no part of hay. Several carloads of moss were imported at great speed and cost from Alaska, but just before it arrived the animals decided to give up their strike and start eating the hay. They never would take another mouthful of moss and the expensive fodder went untouched.

With the reindeer came Ernest Alsook, an Eskimo, who had no previous experience with reindeer.

Ernie became the bane of Bob Miles' existence. Ernie would go to Ketchum, get drunk, come home, and start wrecking the employees' chalet. Bob would be sent for and Ernie would burst into tears and weep on Bob's shoulders. Bob said that he could stand Ernie's getting drunk, he could stand him breaking up his furniture, but he could not stand that Eskimo blubbering in his arms.

When the first snows came, Ernie caught cold. Bob went to his room and found him huddled by the radiator with a Sears catalogue from which he wanted Bob to order him a pair of galoshes. No more mukluks for Ernie.

The end for Ernie came later that year when he took Bob's car, which had the radiator drained for the winter, and drove it to Hailey, burning out the motor. Ernie as usual got drunk, then obstreperous, and finally cried in Bob's arms—but to no avail. Bob shipped him back to Alaska.

First Sun Valley ski school had authentic Tyrolean uniforms

During our stay in the Valley we had the usual picture taken in a sleigh pulled by a reindeer. The technique was that Ernie would catch the reindeer by its huge horns and twist its head until the passengers were in the sleigh. The cameraman would get ready on the driveway. Then Ernie would let go the horns and jump into the sleigh, and as it went past, the cameraman would click his camera. The only trouble was that sometimes the reindeer would decide to chase the cameraman instead of passing him. Then the photographer had to jump into the snowbank and the whole scene had to be played over again.

On Christmas Eve one of the reindeer trotted under the clock tower of the Inn, pulling the sleigh with Santa Claus and his bag of gifts for the children. It was a picturesque and beautiful scene. Then, as Santa dismounted and stepped toward the little platform at the foot of the Christmas tree, the reindeer lowered his big antlers towards the seat of Santa's pants and chased him around the tree while children shrieked and mothers and fathers grabbed their offspring out of the way. It was the third lap before someone caught the reindeer's horns and stopped him.

I don't remember whether the reindeer lasted more than two seasons or not. Eventually Spike Spackman, who made the Sun Valley stables one of the show places of the resort—before he left to manage one of Bing Crosby's ranches—would put up with the mean monsters no more and shipped them off.

Not long afterwards, Bob Miles and a friend went down to the stable and started measuring and pacing off a corner. Spike watched suspiciously while they measured and paced and paced and measured and at last asked what they were up to. "Oh, we thought you knew," said Bob. "Since the reindeer are gone, we're having camels next Christmas and we're figuring where to put them." Since camels are even meaner animals than reindeer, and infinitely dirtier, Bob and his conspirator got out just ahead of Spike's pitchfork.

On the morning of our first arrival in Sun Valley we did not rate a ride from the station in a sleigh—reindeer or horse-drawn—nor did we rate a ride in a dogsled. We watched the celebrities taking off in these novel conveyances and then climbed into the more plebeian but faster bus. So it happened that we were the first guests to arrive at the new Challenger Inn.

Social Climbing on the Slopes

Gay Talese, later student of the Mafia (Honor Thy Father) and unsublimated sex (Thy Neighbor's Wife), here sharpens his claws on the eastern boilerplate in preparation for bigger game.

EACH Friday afternoon they gather along Park Avenue wearing their Aspen-raced ski parkas (mildew-proof, crease-resistant and allergy-free) and their slim, zippered stretch pants (pickpocket-proof), and wait for the chalet bus that will transport them up to a ski weekend at Sugarbush, Vermont—where they might break a leg.

Such grim possibilities do not haunt them. "If you ski, you're going to break something sooner or later," said Mary Baker, an attractive brunette, casually shrugging her shoulders under her black fur parka. "And besides, breaking a leg is no worse than having a baby."

Though she spoke with somewhat limited authority—she has had two babies, but so far has broken only an arm—her friends standing along the sidewalk quickly agreed. They were all young people of great energy and optimism; their only problem was that merely three months of ski weather remained, and the chalet bus was already five minutes late. Finally somebody yelled, "Here it comes," and a big vehicle, driven by

Johnny McBride, who used to chauffeur Count Basie's band, stopped and, amid a clatter of skis and a clinking of bottles, everybody hopped aboard.

"We've met somewhere," said a Wall Street broker to a slinky blond, sitting across the aisle. "Was it Squaw Valley?"

"No," she said demurely.

"Kitzbühel?"

"I don't think so."

"Wait!" he exclaimed. "It was at Bunnie's wedding."

"Oh, yes," the blond cried. Then the broker broke out a bottle of scotch and handed the blond a cup.

Meanwhile the bus moved on through suburbs and exurbs, dipped into the winding roads of smaller towns and, at last, climbed into the hills of New England, not stopping until, six hours and two hundred eighty-eight miles later, it had crossed into Vermont and reached that frosty joyland, Sugarbush.

Sugarbush is the most chic snow spa in the eastern portion of the United States. Opened in December, 1958, nicknamed "Mascara Mountain" and "El Morocco on the Rocks," it styles itself after the fashionable slopes of Europe. Its skiers, without having to risk a single hair blowing out of place, can ride to the summit of the

328

4,000-foot mountain within glass-enclosed, wind-proof gondolas which are globe-shaped and which look, as they hover over the white trails and trees, like an endless sky train of vari-colored apples on the stick.

Dior Provides the Pants

It was too late for skiing when the Park Avenue bus arrived that Friday night, but by ten the next morning the slopes were slippery with sophisticates. There were women in Christian Dior pants and parkas lined with Scottish fleece and rimmed with silver fox. There were men in Garmisch boots cut from the hides of sheltered Bavarian steers, and flamboyant, quilted parkas flapping with various cardboard tags indicating that either the parkas or the wearers—and possibly both—had skied in such storied European places as Chamonix, St. Moritz, or Cortina d'Ampezzo.

The slopes of Sugarbush are superbly conditioned for social climbing. At the very top, though the group numbers fewer than one hundred of the twenty-four hundred who ski Sugarbush on a busy day, is cafe society's heralded jet set, which does not come by bus. The jet set, which travels to Europe a great deal and insists on having to its parties at least one Greek shipowner, a Ferrari auto racer, and a cocktail of countesses, was not lured to Sugarbush through any enticement by the center's thirty-six-year-old president Damon Gadd, a congenial but not effusive Yale man. It came, rather, because it was seeking a new cold-weather playpen and because one of its very favorite people was Sugarbush's chief ski instructor, Peter Estin, a slim, rich, thirty-five-year-old former Dartmouth ski hero, a tennis player and winetaster, a linguist, a cartoonist and a climatehopping *bon vivant* whose current girl friend is a French baroness. Estin has had as many as three Greek shipowners to a single party.

With such credentials, Peter Estin had no difficulty getting the jet set to Sugarbush, and soon they decided that they liked the place so much they built their own small chalets on the mountain near Estin's. Sugarbush quickly

achieved its posh, cosmopolitan image. Each weekend this winter the mountainside has been climbed by rising new cliques, but the jet set remains the envy of many of those below.

For one thing, jet-set skiers sleep late in the morning. Inasmuch as they have their own chalets, they may rise late for breakfast and are not subjected, as are ski lodge guests, to the 9 A.M. closing of dining-room doors. On this particular Saturday morning the jet set was the last to appear on the slopes. They were casual and calm in slipping on their parkas and their Italian goggles. They walked slowly, confidently toward the gondolas. They *knew* they would get seats.

At lunchtime the jet set did not have to submit to the clatter of the cafeteria. They retired, instead, to a private club, Skiclub 10, within which some of the most slumberously sleek and exquisitely elegant women ever to have schussed through a ski boutique sat on the dark blue banquettes, amid the smoke of Turkish tobacco, surrounded by music from *La Dolce Vita*.

They do not possess the sweet, college-girl look of most of those in the cafeteria, girls whose confidence comes from a surfeit of attention from college boys. Skiclub 10 women are somewhat older, between twenty-seven and thirty-two, and, as F. Scott Fitzgerald said in another time, they are "nourished on subtler stuff" and "choose aperitifs wisely." There is just the slightest trace of boredom in their manner, just the right amount of challenging coolness. Nearly all of them are excellent skiers, but they ski only when conditions are good. Otherwise they spend the afternoon—such as this one—at Skiclub 10 sipping orange juice mixed with white wine and playing bridge or backgammon with the men.

The men are also very attractive—or, if not attractive, very rich; or, if not rich, very talented; or, if not talented, very useful to the club. Here, with the outside temperature close to zero, Nan Kempner, a delicate beauty in an ocelot parka, played cards with Louise Collins, a blond actress who is the widow of Peter Collins, the British racing driver. At an adjoining table, suffering slightly from a touch of frostbite on the ear, was the musician Skitch Henderson. Across from him was Carlos de Borbón, son of Spain's Don Juan, and John Bragonca, pretender to the Portuguese throne. Everyone was having fun—everyone except Harry Theodoracopulos, the Greek shipping scion, who was not doing anything.

"Har-r-r-ry," cooed a throaty redhead from across the room, "br-i-i-dge?"

Harry shook his curly head. He was thinking. He is a very serious man of twenty-nine, a big, broad-shouldered bachelor who says, "I do not share in this Anglo-Saxon belief that if you are involved with a girl, you should marry." He works hard in his family's business, plays hard at tennis, drives a sports car, and took up skiing a few years ago under the tutelage of Peter Estin. Harry learned quickly, but he does not need the prestige of a broken limb, so he holds himself back. "What slows me down is I cannot afford to get hurt," he says. "I have to go to the office."

Harry Theodoracopulos is a typical member of the jet set. He is not in the moody, restless tradition of the European playboy who cavorts all night and sleeps through most of the afternoon. He, like most other men in the set, takes work very seriously. He plays hard, works hard. He tries to keep ever on the move, jetting here and there, spiking his life whenever possible with lovely women, delectable food, and vivacious companions in fashionable places.

On the heels of the jet set is another rapid crowd of skiers. They are a little younger, a little less continental. While they are attractive and carefully dressed—a number of them came up to Sugarbush on the Park Avenue chartered bus on Friday night—they have not *yet* made it big in the professions and they are not *yet* ready to splurge on a private chalet on the mountain. They are, in a sense, still in the turboprop class, but they are formidable, up-and-coming types, sometimes called the "tourist-class jet set."

While they patronize the ski lodges and are forced to rise early before the breakfast room closes, they are always careful to be in the better lodges, such as the Alpen Inn, which is well equipped and friendly and which has in the kitchen some ski "bums" listed in *The Social Register*. Or tourist jet-setters may stay at the Sugarbush Inn, which is a bit more formal, with tea served in the afternoon and the guests usually dining at night in jackets and ties.

Not all, possibly not even most skiers at Sugarbush are trying to climb the hills solely for social status. Many are seeking higher status, to be sure, but it is not only social. It is also the status one enjoys when one is an excellent skier in fast company. This status has romantic ramifications. Girls who ski well like to date boys who ski well, and the other way around. Chalet romances frequently result in marriage.

Conversely, many a relationship has failed because of his (or her) inability on skis. One such case, pure frozen Freud, concerns a lovely Sugarbush belle named Ann McAlpin. Miss McAlpin is a superb skier—her mother was an Olympic skier, her father a fine amateur hockey player—but at twenty-two she has come to believe that before she can marry any man he probably will have to conquer her on the slopes—that is, he will have to ski as well as, or better than, she: she being Olympic material.

"It would be silly if I married a nonskier," she said, recalling a few uneventful relationships with ungainly boobs and snowplowers. "Last fall, I remember, I had a blind date with a very nice boy, and we hit it off right away and used to see each other every weekend at Yale or in Connecticut with his family. Then one day we went skiing. He was not," she said softly, "very good. Perhaps if our relationship had *really* been perfect, perhaps then he could have learned to ski better. I don't know. But, anyway, he got to hate skiing more and more, especially with me. He'd be in bad moods. So we stopped skiing together. Now it is over."

She recalled that a friend of her mother, a top skier on the 1936 Olympic team, once had much the same attitude, and today this woman is a spinster on a dude ranch in Wyoming. "I realize that if I do not learn to become less demanding," Miss McAlpin conceded, "the same thing could happen to me. But," she concluded, "if this has to be, this has to be."

While such a dedication to fine skiing is not uncommon, a high percentage of ski addicts find the sport irresistible for another reason—it offers escape. This, at least, is the opinion of a self-described escapist named Bob Pratt, twenty-eight, a graduate of Brown University, who said, during a late-afternoon recess from the snow, "You want the *real* lowdown on these people? Well, I'll tell you; a lot of them are simply running from the nine-to-five job, running from responsibility. This is especially true of the people who work all the time at ski resorts, the ski bums. This, in fact, is exactly what I've done.

"Look," he said, finishing his drink, "I'm a swinger. I got to have it all the time—kicks, I mean. It basically stems from a very deep lack of confidence in myself—*but not in my skiing ability.* In skiing, I probably am as good as the top 6 percent in the United States. I've gone as fast as 50 miles an hour. I'm a part-time instructor too, and in this kind of place the ski instructor is God. They know it too. They know that the girls are watching."

Also visible on the slopes of Sugarbush on this late Saturday afternoon was a small society of skiers who remained apart from the escapists or addicts, and yet who also stood aloof from the jet set. This group rebels against everything the jet set stands for. Composed mostly of college boys, its members bunk in the run-down ski lodges and often wear blue jeans instead of ski pants. There have been times when they've even skied at Sugarbush wearing long red underwear *over* their blue jeans.

But the college boys are fighting impossible odds. The world of high fashion has conquered the hills of Sugarbush, and so has the skier who wouldn't think of wearing the same fur parka two days in a row. Fur parkas, bushy fur hats, and other expensive ski clothes are so common at Sugarbush that the general manager, Jack Mur-phy, can appraise almost to the dollar the value of each ski outfit that passes. (This helps him make up his mind on whether or not to cash a skier's check, and so far Sugarbush has had only two checks—total: $17.50—bounce.)

Even the ski patrol's medical teams have become fashion-conscious. "At almost any other place, when a lady skier breaks a leg, they automatically cut right through the stretch pants to attend the wound," one medic said. "But at Sugarbush we try to be careful never to cut pants; or, if we must cut, we try to cut along the seam. Sugarbush wishes to keep *all* its skiers looking trim," he said, "even its casualties."

At night, especially Saturday night, the fashions are even more dazzling. In one new nightclub, once a barn where horses used to stomp and kick, are now shimmering shapes in twisting gold-lamé pants and sparkling après-ski jackets lined with French satin. And in the lodges, too, the skiers are lost in nightlife—snowplowing through the bars, trying to romance a snow bunny, listening to the Vermont farmboys talking in the corner:

"You shoulda seen those stretch pants twisting earlier—one was flesh-colored."

"That wasn't flesh-colored—that was *flesh!*"

Though everybody seemed to be up late, most of them were on the slopes again early the following morning, perhaps because it was Sunday. And because, in a few hours, after a few more desperate runs down the hill, it would be all over for a while—and then there would be only the long ride through the narrow roads, and finally back again to the indoor world of elevators and telephones and tension.

The Ski Bum
as an Endangered Species

by JEAN VALLELY

Pepper Gomes is a typical ski instructor in the same way that Ronald Reagan is a typical actor. Both, in a manner of speaking, got carried away a bit. Jean Vallely, a journalist with the finely honed instincts of a born storyteller, brings her portrait of Gomes to a high finish —a final collision of reality and fantasy.

THE first thing you notice about Pepper Gomes is his voice. It is marvelous: deep, rich, definitive. Everyone tells him he should be in broadcasting. Each Friday he hosts the hot-dog skiing contests and is known as the Voice of the Aspen Highlands. He has traveled around the country announcing some of the major contests. Pepper weighs one hundred and sixty pounds and is 5 feet 10 inches tall. A scar, shaped like a half-moon, takes up most of his right cheek (he was hit by a car when he was six), and another scar sprawls down his chin (he used to ride with a motorcycle gang, the Pagans; he locked handlebars with another bike and took a bad dump). His animated hazel eyes dart from side to side when he talks. He looks at once mean, sinister, sexy.

Pepper has traded in his cowboy hat for his ski instructor's jacket and swaggers through the Base Lodge with confidence. Almost everyone knows Pepper and calls out to him as he passes by. The few that don't, study him. They sense he is someone.

The night snow has left 6 inches of powder, and Pepper, who likes to teach one-hundred-dollar-a-day private lessons (fifty dollars of that goes to the ski school), snaps on his skis and heads for the lift. "Follow me," he yelps as he skis to the side of the mountain and powder up to his thighs. "Stay in my tracks," he screams. Pepper can ski. His strong body gently pushes the heavy snow around as if it were a cloud. He disappears into the trees. He reemerges, and his mustache is frozen. His eyes sparkle impishly as he heads out-of-bounds. Pepper is Peck's Bad Boy of the mountain and has been fired five times, mostly for pulling just such a stunt. One time he got caught in an avalanche and was pulled and tugged some 500 feet. Suddenly he's back, flies off a mogul, and glides, spread eagle, through the air. He lands laughing, and the next moment he is skiing down the mountain—backward. "You're skiing like garbage," he yells. "Go for it. It doesn't hurt when you fall in powder." Yeah, but what about all these trees? "Only sissies ski on the open trails." He smiles. "God, I love these mountains. Just when you think you've got them beat they reach out and knock you on your ass, just to remind you who's boss."

Life in Aspen is a fantasy; everything there

332

is a performance. Pepper is an actor playing a role. "I'll be exactly what you want, man," he says, bowing and affecting his most dramatic voice. "Yes, I am the golden-god ski instructor with the bronze tan. I am the man you came to see. I'm the instructor who's not only the greatest skier but the world's greatest lover. I know you've read the articles. Well, I'm him, man. I'm paid to enjoy life. I'm whatever you want me to be."

Ladies and gentlemen, meet Pepper Gomes, glamorous ski instructor, ultimate lover, who skis, drinks, dines, dances, makes love with the rich and famous. Pepper Gomes, who spends two weeks each spring in Mexico, travels all over the country, even in a private Lear Jet, gambles in Vegas, eats in the best restaurants in any city he visits.

Ladies and gentlemen, meet Pepper Gomes, the poor kid from Natick, Massachusetts, who works nights as a projectionist at the Isis Theatre, plants potatoes in the spring, runs the chairlift in the summer, harvests potatoes in the fall, and can barely pay his rent. Pepper Gomes, who works a total of seven months and in his best year in Aspen made $6,000. Sometimes grim reality intrudes on fantasy—even in Aspen. Pepper is having a hard time hanging on to his fantasy life.

Eleven years ago, Pepper Gomes had had it with the East Coast. It was as if some invisible machine had attached itself to him and were slowly sapping the juices that made Pepper Pepper. Each morning he got up and drove to his job at the telephone company in Washington, D.C. How he hated that drive: bumper-to-bumper traffic, all those defeated faces, inhaling that toxic exhaust. And how he hated his job. He had been at the telephone company for two years and in the army for three years before that. At least in the army he had been a member of The Old Guard and served in John F. Kennedy's funeral. That was special. Pepper had even been interviewed on a local television station in Boston. But now he was just another phone man. And his marriage was busting up.

For five years people had been telling Pepper Gomes what to do, and Pepper Gomes had never been good at taking orders. The only thing keeping him going was skiing. Each weekend he would strap his skis on top of his car, head for Pennsylvania and the hills, and teach skiing. On the mountain, Pepper Gomes was somebody. On the mountain, Pepper Gomes gave the orders. On the mountain, people listened to him. Back in high school, when Pepper taught skiing in New Hampshire, he had discovered that when they found out he was an instructor, the kids treated him differently, especially the girls, and if you lived in Natick and your name was Gomes and you were dirt poor, respect was hard to come by.

One day, his boss leaned a little too hard, and Pepper up and quit. He flipped through his Rand McNally atlas: Boston, New York, Washington—the whole East Coast looked like some web spun by a spider on acid. Highways crisscrossed every which way. He kept flipping the pages. Colorado. Ah, some room. Aspen. That's where he'd go. He had skied Aspen once before, and it was some of the best skiing he had ever done in this country. He kissed his wife and baby son good-bye, tied his skis to his 1960 Rambler American, grabbed his new girl friend, Patty, whom he had met skiing, and headed for Aspen.

Pepper laughs. "We pulled into town at four in the afternoon, headed for the Jerome Bar, and within hours someone had fixed us up with an 8-by-24-foot trailer in Woody Creek." When Pepper arrived in Aspen, it was a small, friendly place full of independent free spirits, refugees from the urban hassles; disparate folks bound together by their love of the mountains and skiing. They were the ski bums, content to ski all day and work in the bars and lodges at night. No one made a lot of money, but it didn't matter. You could eke out a living, but more important, you could be yourself. In a complicated world, Pepper and the other Aspenites felt as if they were in control of their own lives.

He and Patty settled into their trailer, and he did odd jobs and taught skiing to get by. It was a struggle, but it was fun. Pepper was his own man. Aspen was a wonderful community where everyone knew and supported everyone else. Patty wanted to have a baby, so she and Pepper were married in 1971. Things were perking along just fine—and then Pepper met Dorothy, the wife of a famous actor.

Dorothy wanted to learn to ski and heard Pepper was the man. She signed him up for a week. The famous actor was back in Hollywood. Dorothy signed Pepper up for another week. They soon settled into a cozy routine: days on the mountain, après-ski beers at the lodge, dinner at all those fancy places Pepper couldn't afford, and dancing in the discos until 2 A.M. Pepper and Dorothy were quite a pair. She had been a professional dancer, and Pepper, well, he was sort of a legend as a dancer in Aspen, winning all the local contests; Pepper was to Aspen what Tony Manero was to Brooklyn. Pepper and Dorothy would dance and the floor would clear. Then they would all go back to Dorothy's condominium and drink some more and talk. Pretty heady stuff. "Here I was," says Pepper, "this low-rent kid living this dream, man. Suddenly all these famous, rich people liked me, man. People you recognize on television wanted to hang out with me. And then the people in town started coming up to me and asking what all these people were like. They thought I was really something."

At 4 A.M., Pepper would struggle to his car and make his way back to his trailer, his wife, and infant baby girl in Woody Creek. Dorothy went back to Hollywood and her rich famous-actor husband, and Patty and the baby went home to Washington and her parents. Everything had changed. Pepper had had a taste of the fast life and liked it. But he promised Patty that at the end of the ski season he would sell the trailer and move back to Washington. He would leave Aspen and rejoin the real world. The lifts shut down, Pepper sold the trailer, packed his skis and black Labrador retriever into his Datsun pickup, and headed east. Suddenly Pepper made a U-turn and set off for California and Mammoth Mountain and one last week of skiing. He skied and thought about how Dorothy had told him that he should give her a call if he ever got to L.A.

Pepper pulled into Beverly Hills at midnight

and was immediately pulled over by the cops. He finally located Dorothy's house, eased his truck into her long driveway, and walked to the door. It was the biggest house Pepper had ever seen in his life. He rang the bell. The maid told Pepper that Dorothy and her husband were out but would be back soon. Pepper parked his truck across the street and waited. A few hours later, they came home. Pepper raced down to Sunset and called them. The famous actor answered the phone.

"Is Dorothy there?" asked Pepper.

"Who is this?" asked the famous actor.

"Pepper from Aspen." Pepper heard Dorothy gasp "Oh, my God" in the background. She asked him to come over the next morning. Pepper got back into his truck, parked on a side street, and went to sleep. Pepper's mornings generally begin at seven, but he waited until what he thought was a reasonable time—ten—and called. The famous actor answered the phone.

"Hi. This is Pepper. Is Dorothy there?"

"No," snapped the famous actor. "She took the kids to school."

"Well," said Pepper, "I hope I didn't wake you up."

"You did," growled the famous actor. "Call back later." Pepper waited until eleven and called back. The phone rang and rang.

"Who is this?" screamed the famous actor.

"It's Pepper. You told me to call back. Were you still in bed?"

"No, I was in the shower. Dorothy will be home at twelve." Pepper got into his truck, drove to the house, and once again parked across the street and waited. The famous actor went to work and Dorothy came home. Pepper spent the day with Dorothy, talking and drinking beer. "I couldn't believe it," says Pepper. "Here I am, Pepper Gomes, sitting in this beautiful house in Beverly Hills, smashed. I was so nervous." The famous actor came home, walked into the study, tripped over Pepper's dog, and fell flat on his face. "I almost died," recalls Pepper. The three sat down for dinner. There was a television on the counter, and the famous actor spent the entire dinner watching an old Gregory Peck movie.

Pepper hung out in Beverly Hills for a week,

spending his days with Dorothy lounging by the pool, eating lunches and dinners in the chic bistros of Hollywood, and sleeping in his truck at night. He became friends with the famous actor and promised to teach him to ski. The famous actor kept telling Pepper he had a fabulous voice and a future in television.

Reluctantly, Pepper said good-bye to Beverly Hills and headed east. He lasted in Washington for one week. He couldn't handle his in-laws or the city. The stargazing in Hollywood had gotten to him, so he headed for Miami, where a friend of Dorothy's was shooting a television series and just might have a part for Pepper. He arrived at the producer's office to find twenty other guys after the same part. "In Aspen, everyone is friendly," says Pepper, "but these guys were the worst. I tried to talk to them, but as soon as they found out I was there for the same part, they wanted nothing to do with me." Pepper split, cracked open the piggy bank he kept in his truck, and used the thirty dollars in pennies to drive to Washington. "I told Patty it was time to get back to Aspen," says Pepper. She said no way. Pepper worked construction for a few days, made sixty dollars, kissed Patty and his baby girl good-bye, and headed for Aspen. Pepper had taken another look at the real world and found he still didn't belong.

But now the Aspen dream—at least for Pepper—is crumbling. He and his friends, the people who give Aspen its wonderful flavor, its distinct character, who keep the town going, can't make it there much longer. Aspen has become a country club for the very rich. It is Beverly Hills in the mountains. Galena Street looks like Rodeo Drive. The Ute City Banque restaurant, with men and women decked out in mink parkas and Gucci accessories, looks like Ma Maison. You even hear people talking deals. And Aspen is 100 percent international; English is almost a second language.

Aspen is a beautiful old mining town a century old this year. No corporation swooped down and built this town in two weeks. Walking down the streets, one is overwhelmed by a sense of history. It has a population of eight thousand that swells to thirty-five thousand during ski season. There are four mountains to ski: Aspen, Aspen Highlands, Buttermilk, Snowmass. Aspen Mountain has some of the most challenging skiing in the world. A hundred years ago, the Ute Indians used Aspen as a summer retreat. It has been a booming mining town, a ghost town, a small ski resort, a haven for hippies. Now it is a chic club that only the very rich can afford—people like Jack Nicholson, Barry Diller, Diane von Furstenberg, the Eagles, Jimmy Buffet, Jann Wenner, Steve Martin, Jill St. John, George Hamilton, Teddy Kennedy and his children, Ethel Kennedy and her children, and Steve Smith (who is married to Jean Kennedy) and their children. The town is totally geared to the spending and making of money. Young families, the backbone of any community, have left. High-school enrollment is down. People now come to Aspen for sex, for drugs, to make money and be discovered. Aspen is the new Schwabs. "It used to be," says Pepper, "that anybody could make it in Aspen as long as you weren't a jerk. Now the town is full of them."

Aspen is like a movie set. Nothing is real or permanent. With its new malls, trendy little shops, expensive galleries, and restaurants, all with hanging plants, Aspen is beginning to look like one big boutique. The mountains loom majestically. Aspen is the place to be when the world ends—no one here will know about it until a week later. Each day skiers carve out huge moguls in the mountain and each night giant machines grind them smooth. The snow gives way to spring flowers that give way to fall leaves that give way to snow. On weekends, planes fly in and out of Aspen every half hour, all day. People check in and check out. Life in Aspen is a collection of moments, moments that disappear as quickly as a flake of new snow when it greets the sun. And Aspen is about money, lots of money.

Money is something Pepper Gomes doesn't have much of. He lives in Silverking, or Silver Slum, as he calls it. Silverking is a low-cost housing project geared to the locals. Or at least it has been. A developer bought Silverking and wants to turn the apartments into condominiums. That happens a lot in Aspen. A developer bought Smuggler Trailer Park, another stronghold for locals, and raised the monthly rent from $95 to $250.

Pepper and his new bride, Susan, live in a small one-bedroom apartment. There is room for a couch in the living room, and that's about it. They pay $335 a month. Pepper tosses a salad while Susan cooks burritos. Their good friend Leroy Finke joins us for dinner. Finke, who fled the pressures of Chicago four years ago, owns Car Trek, a garage that specializes in foreign cars. There are a lot of them in Aspen these days—Mercedes, BMWs, Porsches. Finke, like Pepper, foresees the time when he will move on. He is "making a living," but not much more than that.

Every Wednesday night, Pepper and his friends rent the Aspen Ice Garden and play hockey. We finish dinner, Pepper puts on his cowboy hat, and we all pile into his 1967 Chevy Impala (he paid one hundred dollars for it) and head for the rink. Only in Aspen could there be such a night: clear, cold, with a gentle snow just beginning to fall. The lights of the village do a dazzling tap dance with one another. Aspen looks make-believe. Aspen *is* make-believe. It's Disneyland for adults.

Pepper plays hockey with the kind of intensity with which he lives his life. He skates hard, fast, mean. *Whack!* He smashes the puck. *Pow!* He is creamed against the boards. *Crash!* He falls on the ice. This pick-up hockey team is made up of the guys who work as ski instructors, bartenders, construction workers, dishwashers. These are guys who serve the rich. They love and care for Aspen while the people in the $600,000 houses on Red Mountain are in their real homes back in Houston, New York, Chicago, Europe. None of the hockey players live on Red Mountain. Few, in fact, live in Aspen anymore. The high rents and lack of housing have forced them down valley, to places like Basalt, 20 miles away. Almost one-third of the labor force in Aspen commutes.

One of the hockey players lives in a trailer with three others. Another lives in a cabin with

no heat or electricity. One got lucky and is house-sitting for a rock-and-roll star. They talk about a ski instructor who has been living in the back of his VW bug and the six guys who share a two-bedroom apartment and the one guy who is renting and living in a large air-conditioning unit that is not used during the winter months. Most of them work two jobs. It used to be worth it, they say, because they loved the town, the people, and they could ski. But four years ago, Aspen Skiing Corporation eliminated the season pass, and now it costs fifteen dollars a day to ski. The dedicated skiers are going to other places, like Telluride. The skiing bond that held the community together is weakening. The bond is now money.

Michael Solheim stands quietly at the end of the bar and scans the room. He runs the Jerome Bar. It is a little after midnight, and the place is jammed. It is getting on to the two o'clock shuffle. If you haven't connected with someone on the slopes or during après-ski drinks at Little Nell's or discoing at The Paragon or the Tippler, this is your last shot. There is an unwritten rule in Aspen: you can't go home alone. Aspen is also about sex.

Solheim, a handsome man with a well-trimmed, gray-tinged beard, came to Aspen eleven years ago. He came for the skiing, the hiking, the fishing, and the cultural elements that make Aspen unique. "It used to be that people came here to ski," he says. "I would go over to Aspen Mountain and there would always be a group of friends to ski with. Now I go over to ski and I don't know anyone. We all took great pride in being local skiers. We loved skiing past a class and knowing that we were better than the instructors. Now the skiing is just too expensive."

Solheim managed Hunter Thompson's famous 1970 campaign for sheriff of Aspen. He wonders if they didn't make a mistake, inadvertently creating a monster that is now eating them alive. Thompson and his far-out platform lost, but in the process some very liberal thinkers got elected to city and county government. The result was a no-growth policy. (Two years ago it was modified to what is called a Growth Management Plan, which allows 3.5-percent growth each year.) "It seemed like a good idea at the time," says Solheim, "but then housing went through the roof. Next thing I know the town is full of people who can pay $350,000 for a second house and we're spending all this money on bike paths and horse trails. We live in the goddam Rockies. Who needs all that? It sounded so good—keep the quality of Aspen. Except now none of my friends live here anymore. They've been forced out."

Last call at the Jerome. The two o'clock shuffle is fierce. The place is so packed that it is almost impossible to move. The music is so loud that it is almost impossible to talk. "You're coming with me," drools a beautiful blond to the man on her left. His eyes light up like a Christmas tree as the pair disappears into the cold night. A handsome man slides his hand down the thigh of a woman sitting next to him. Her eyes acknowledge his hand. "Got any 'ludes?" asks a tall, thin woman. "Yes," answers a man nearby. "Then I'm your girl." A striking (everyone in Aspen is beautiful) young woman tells proudly how over Christmas she slept with Teddy Kennedy. She recounts how she called a friend the next day because Teddy had left his reading glasses in her room, and she was frantic to get them back to him—discreetly. "Don't worry," advised her friend. "He buys them by the gross." She tells how, when she's feeling frisky, she wears Teddy's glasses around town. In Aspen, people are granted a special dispensation. There are no parents. It's like a sailor's last night in port.

"A ski instructor is part of the scene," says Pepper. "The rich people want to hang out with us because we know what's happening. Some guy can come to me and be the biggest movie producer in Hollywood or the biggest rock-and-roll star or the president of a huge company. But when he gets into my class, man, he deals with Pepper. I'm the boss. He needs me. That puts me on his level. I've got his psyche and bones in my hands. And if he acts like some kind of big shot, well, I can just take him down a trail and show him he's no good. I'm the big shot. He has

to respect me. I'm the man. He can't tell me what to do. While he's on the mountain he has to listen to Pepper Gomes."

But all that glamour and power still doesn't pay the rent, so Pepper hustles. He is always on the lookout for someone in his class who can do something for him. The hustle is subtle, and he defends it. "It is not a businessman's hustle, where you screw your friends. Say I meet someone from L.A. who will take me to dinner, introduce me around, let me stay with him when I'm in town. Well, he does that only because I offer that person everything I have. I am willing to give up everything for that person. My time might not be worth as much as his, but it's all I got and I give it to him."

Pepper opens his mouth and shows me his teeth. They are nice teeth. Pepper taught a dentist from L.A. how to ski, showed him the town, where to hang out, what was happening. The dentist capped Pepper's teeth, a $2,000 job, free. The dentist returned to Aspen with a bunch of friends, and Pepper arranged for some of the instructors to ski with them for a few days. And there is a couple from Australia who come to Aspen every year and insist on taking Pepper out to dinner every night. And there is the doctor and his wife from Mexico City who take Pepper skiing with them at other resorts. And the couple from L.A. who bring Pepper along with them to Vegas to gamble. They like introducing Pepper as their ski instructor. "People do things for me," says Pepper, "because when they are in Aspen I show them the best goddam time Pepper Gomes can show them. I can go everywhere in this country and be royally treated. I work 100 percent max, and I am proud of the hustle."

Mostly Pepper hustles women. The ski instructor as the ultimate lover is an image Pepper not only thrives on but promotes. He has dated women from fifteen to fifty-five. He tells tales of wild parties, nights in Jacuzzis, love on diving boards. Pepper makes the most of his contacts in his classes. It is a tricky business. "A few years ago," says Pepper, "the ski school director used to say, 'Okay, guys, a whole new group this week, and a lot of the ladies aren't here to ski, so go out there and do your job,' so we had the okay of the bosses to hustle." Continues Pepper, "A smart instructor won't hustle on the mountain. Say you have four chicks and four guys in your class. They are all paying the same amount of money. You pick a chick, one who might take you out to dinner that night, one who might be able to do something for you. But you have to be careful not to pay too much attention to her because you don't want the guys to get pissed off and you don't want to alienate the other chicks. You want that tip at the end." Which can be as high as $500.

Pepper makes his move on the chairlift. He lets a woman know he is interested; if she responds, he makes plans with her then. Once he's back on the mountain and in front of the class he doesn't pay any more attention to her. Sometimes it gets complicated, like when both the mother and the daughter are hitting on him. "A few years ago," says Pepper, "you could meet someone in your class and just ask her out to dinner. But not now. It's too expensive. You want to be real sure, before you lay out fifty dollars, that you'll end up in bed."

Pepper sounds like a Beach Boys song when he talks about women. "Southern girls are the best, and they get everything they want. They are totally geared toward men. Girls from Boston have to be in at midnight, and they all wear baggy jeans and sweaters with shirts under them. L.A. girls are pretty, man, tall, in great shape, and if they want you, they just take you. New York girls will only talk to you to show you they are superior. It becomes a challenge the minute you meet them on the slope. It's 'If you want my britches, then you're going to have to work for them.' The poor eastern guys are so used to that shit that when they get out here and meet southern girls and L.A. girls, they go nuts."

Pepper rarely hustles in the bars—there, he is just part of the masses. There is a rule in Aspen that instructors can't wear their jackets after 6 P.M. "I feel lost without my jacket," says Pepper. "If I'm in a bar, sometimes I wear my instructor's sweater just so they notice. Then the girls know who I am, that I belong, that I know what's going on."

Those were the Aspen days that had no be-

ginning and no end. Pepper was in training, learning to get by on two hours' sleep. He skied all day, was at work at the theater by eight, met a date at ten-thirty, stayed out until two or three, caught a few hours' sleep, popped a Percodan, and was back on the mountain by nine. Mostly Pepper dated tourists. Tourists were always leaving in a few days. If he had a good time, he would visit the woman in the spring, and if not, she would always be back the next winter. "But the real beautiful thing about dating a tourist," says Pepper, "is that you don't have time to hurt each other. You are constantly laughing. You have a good time because you only have three days. I do everything she wants. You don't get involved on the level that you start picking faults. There is no reason to ever have a fight, except over what position you want to do it in."

"No," says Pepper, anticipating my next question, "it never gets boring because there is always someone new and different around the corner." That's what Aspen is all about—no matter how good today is, it will never be as good as tomorrow.

Andre Ulrych stands among the boards and nails and bricks that will soon be his new restaurant. Originally from Poland, Andre came to Aspen eleven years ago to escape the rat race of New York. "Aspen struck me as a small community that I would like to live in. It had a diverse population, natural beauty, and great skiing." He realized that there was no place to have breakfast after 11 A.M., so he opened Andre's. That was nine years ago, and it is still the place to be seen in the morning.

But now Andre is building a three-story extravaganza across the street. The kitchen will be in the basement, dining on the first floor and mezzanine, and a private club at the top. If you are not a member of the club, it will cost you fifteen dollars a clip just to walk through the door. The new Andre's will be the most expensive place in town. And there are a lot of expensive spots in Aspen.

"The people who are moving in here now and can afford these prices are a different breed than in the past. The town used to be full of kids taking a year off from college, willing to do anything as long as they could ski. And back then people—the locals—were not so involved in their businesses, in making money. I could always take time off to ski. In the last two years my business takes up all my time.''

Because of the elimination of the season pass, the high cost of living, and the lack of low-cost housing, the ski bum in Aspen has gone the way of the whooping crane. There is a severe shortage of workers. Every shop, lodge, and restaurant in Aspen has help-wanted signs in the windows. There is no one to do the menial jobs—dishwashing, making beds, shoveling snow. The employee situation became so critical last year that Andre imported three Vietnamese refugees. They agreed to work for him for two years, doing dishes, clean-up, and he housed them in a four-bedroom house with three others. The Gant and The Aspen Meadows (one a condominium, the other a hotel) also imported Vietnamese to do the menial jobs. Americans either won't do or can't do and survive in Aspen. "The Vietnamese are reliable and work hard," says Andre. When his new place opens, he will import five more. A glimpse of what Aspen will be like in the future—a town made up of the very rich and slaves who serve them?

Pepper remembers a time in Aspen when a man was as good as his handshake and says now there are all these people coming to town with accountants, lawyers, and contracts that must be signed. People used to help you out—now they try to screw you. Like the doctor who fixed Pepper's arm when he shattered it hang gliding. The doctor charged Pepper $400. He had $170 left to pay on the bill when the doctor removed the cast.

"My arm's crooked," said Pepper to the doctor. "You didn't fix it right. I'm not paying the rest of the bill."

"You have to pay the rest of the bill," the doctor told him.

"No, I don't," said Pepper. "You took my arm and left it crooked."

"I'll rebreak it and reset it," said the doctor.

"How much will that cost?" asked Pepper.

"A couple hundred dollars," said the doctor.

"So what you are talking about now," said Pepper, "is taking a $400 break and turning it into a $600 double break that may or may not work. Well, I'm still not paying. Four hundred dollars was the bill for a totally fixed arm, and my arm is crooked. I think I've paid you enough money for what was fixed." Then, says Pepper, "he sent the credit union after me, and he kept calling and calling. I finally went over to him and said, 'Look, you can arrest me, haul me to Denver, but don't call me anymore.' My credit ain't so good. But I borrowed $2,000 for my trailer and I paid that all back and I paid off my car. But don't go screwing me around telling me I have to pay for a goddam crooked arm. You buy a dozen eggs and if you get eleven; you don't pay for a dozen just because the box says twelve."

Jere Michaels sits at the bar of the Ute City Banque sipping coffee. It is the lull before the lunch storm. Ute City is the place to have lunch in Aspen. Michaels, who owns the Ute City and a country and western club called Chisholm's Saloon, came to Aspen ten years ago. He had worked in the theater back in New York and, like the others, was sick of the pressures; Aspen offered him the skiing and the kind of life-style he wanted. But Jere Michaels is depressed a lot these days. "My place at noon looks like the East Side of New York," he says. "I had to get a new pair of jeans to get into my own place. It is so social. That's not why I came to Aspen."

He shakes his head. "We were so uptight about growth. I think we did ourselves in. Aspen is passing us by. The no-growth policy made a lot of sense on paper. We were trying to prevent Aspen from becoming a Vail. I was for it. But we zapped the working class. We're not getting the people with all the spirit who used to come to Aspen. It's just too expensive. There is no place to live, unless you got an extra $300,000. And the employee problem is murder. I am totally at the mercy of my dishwashers. I've even had to do my own dishes. And I've had to raise my prices because I have to pay the help so much. The young people aren't coming anymore. They don't have the money. About the only way to make it in Aspen anymore, unless you have money to begin with, is real estate and drugs."

"Everyone talks about Aspen being the cocaine capital of the world," says Pepper. "If I ever scrape enough money together to buy a gram, by the time it gets to me it's been cut a thousand ways and has about the same effect as a sleeping pill. Cocaine, like everything else in Aspen, is for the rich."

Pepper met his new wife, Susan, last summer. She was a buyer for the May D & F stores in Denver and was on a holiday. Susan could be a model. She is tall, skinny, and quite beautiful. She looks like a young Audrey Hepburn. She wasn't sure she wanted to marry a ski instructor or live in Aspen for that matter, but when Pepper gave her an antique ruby ring, she said yes. Susan now works in a local ski clothing shop, the Aspen General Store. She is nervous. There is never enough money, and she wants to have a family. They can barely support themselves. Pepper and Susan never argue—except about leaving Aspen. And it is not easy to be married to a ski instructor in Aspen.

"It's hard to be married and keep up the image," says Pepper. "I try not to put myself in a position where women become available. Boy, it scares the living hell out of me. I let the women in my classes know I'm married. But then there are the women who prefer married men. I introduce my single ski instructor friends to the chicks, and if a woman still wants me, I just hope I can sneak around it." He pauses. "But, man, after ten years of eating hot-fudge sundaes and all of a sudden someone says you can't have them anymore, wow, suddenly you want one. I'm thirty-four now, and I love Susan. This is my third marriage, and I want it to work. I can still flirt, kiss them on the cheek, put my arm around them—that helps keep up the image. But God, it's harder now than ever before. Sex is part of the Aspen package. The trip wouldn't be complete without it. If a chick can go home and tell her friends, 'I had a great time, skied well, and ended up in bed with my ski instructor,' well, that would be it. There are women here just flat-ass

hitting on you. The only thing that counts in this town is enjoyment with the person you're with." He smiles. "You know we're really not such great lovers. We're human. It's just the training."

It's four o'clock, the lifts have closed down, and Little Nell's is the place to be for après-ski drinks. And to connect. The place is teeming. Men and women desperately check one another out. The key is to have an uninterested but interested look. Those who have been at it for a while have the look perfected. Larry, twenty-eight, stands against the bar. He is tall, thin, and very good-looking. Women parade in front of Larry. Some just look, some smile, others offer to buy him a beer. "This is a wild place," says Larry in a soft southern drawl. He is from Virginia, felt he was in a rut, and wanted some time to figure out what to do with his life. And he loves to ski. But Larry is thinking of moving on. He's been in Aspen for a month and cannot find a place to live. He grabbed *The Aspen Times* the minute it hit the streets, checked off ten ads that looked promising, called, and they were all gone. He had a chance to bunk in with three other guys in a small room for $40 a night. He also looked at an even smaller room in the attic of a house in downtown Aspen. The asking price: $900 a month. Larry thinks he'll head to Utah.

Doug is thirty-two, handsome, with a big, bushy mustache. He lived in Aspen for four years and moved to Fort Collins last spring. "Four years ago Aspen was full of people like me, ski bums. Now they are all jet-setters." Doug finally threw in the towel when his landlord doubled the rent on his small one-room apartment to $300 and he was forced to move into a trailer in Basalt, 20 miles away. "One day all these rich people will come to town and there will be no one left to serve them."

Two Germans, dressed in fancy Bogner outfits, belly up to the bar. It cost them $3,000 each just to get to Aspen, and each night they have sampled a different restaurant. They are rich and don't find Aspen particularly expensive. Back home, Aspen is noted for its skiing and wild party life. Each has lived up to expectations. Their only complaint is that the condominium complex where they are staying seems to be short of maids, so their place (two bedrooms, $2,000 a week) doesn't get cleaned up until late in the afternoon. The maid refuses to do the dishes or make the beds—all she will do is bring in fresh towels. It is just a minor irritation, they point out, and they have, in fact, extended their stay another week and plan to return for an even longer time next winter.

Donna Summer wails sex over the speakers. Mindless disco takes over. Red and blue lights flash hypnotically. Bodies move rhythmically. The sun disappears behind the mountain. One by one the Germans, Larry, and Doug leave Little Nell's—each with a pretty woman in tow.

Pepper threads the film of *The Wilderness Family* through his projection machine at the Isis. He makes ten dollars a night as a projectionist. He has seen every movie ever made in the last ten years and can quote dialogue from all of them. He looks tired. Keeping up the glamorous ski instructor's image and all that goes with it is getting harder and harder. Pepper is confused. He feels he has a stake in Aspen, that he has earned the right to live here. Some days he says he will fight and stay; other days he talks of going to Hollywood and becoming an actor. He'd like to play Clint Eastwood's sidekick.

Or maybe he'll go into sports announcing: "My knowledge of sports, my voice, my glibness—these are my big assets. I can get into any situation and make people laugh. I can get in front of my class and it is freezing cold and there is a blizzard going on, and I can make my class relax, laugh, have a good time. When I'm announcing the hot-dog contests and hear people laugh at my jokes, I just love it.

"I keep telling Susan that something is going to break. I keep thinking in the back of my mind, with all these people I am dealing with, that someone is going to see something in me they want and discover me. I'm an entertainer now on a minor scale." Continues Pepper, "It will be hard to leave Aspen. Here's Pepper Gomes from Natick, Massachusetts, hanging out with movie stars. I'm accepted by people from L.A., New York, Houston, Chicago, Dallas. I walk down the streets and people know me. And when I go places and people hear I'm from Aspen, they think I'm cool. I make Aspen cool. Why do I have to leave?

"But the struggle is too much. I work three jobs, and I am totally frustrated. Before, everyone worked three jobs and it didn't matter. But now all these super-rich people are here. I work hard, but I don't move up. I am beginning to feel burned out. When am I going to get a piece of the pie? I've paid my dues. There is no way I can buy a house. There is no way I can buy a goddam thing in Aspen. The glamour, the ski instructing, living in Aspen, just don't add up anymore. Why can't it be like it was?"

Me and Truck

by **BOB JAMIESON**

A recognized classic of ski writing, this story is about a boy and his truck and some powder snow and how it all fit to make a happy ending. Moral: for peace of mind, choose snow over women.

IT was love at first sight, really. It came rumbling down the road, its nose in the air, sorta lopsided, with this cool way of taking corners: a big, ugly, red '56 International, rusted, with 142,000 miles on it. A hundred dollars and it was mine. I fixed it up with a rear end, new tires, added a roof rack with a propane bottle and a beat-up jerry can. Inside, a heater, stove, bed, table, even a fridge. Then wall-to-wall carpet and ski posters. And the finishing touch—a little cubbyhole under my bed where I gently laid my skis.

I packed up on a cold December day, my last day in the big city, and headed west, out toward the Canadian Rockies. And man, I don't remember anything as pretty as those blue and silver peaks coming over the horizon. I stopped on the long hill leading out of Calgary and got out to check things. I looked back down into the smog-filled valley where I had spent the last four years of my life—all for a little piece of paper. Yeah. Kinda laughed at myself. I got back into Truck and turned the key. Dead silence. Again . . .

Nothing. Just fine. I got out and checked under the hood. Everything seemed okay. So, what to do? Well, for sure I was smarter than an old Truck, havin' a university degree and all. With a B.Sc. in biology, majoring in wildlife management, the least I could do was manage one wild Truck. I shoved into reverse, let the brake off, and rolled back downhill till the old boy turned over.

And that, ladies and gentlemen, was how I started my career as a ski bum: hanging out of an old Truck, rolling downhill backward, back into the smog-filled valley from whence I came.

Those first few weeks wandering around, I was in a sort of mega-world. I remember the minute details of all the troubles I had with Truck: frozen waterlines and dead batteries and sliding sideways down a patch of ice. I remember a tiny farmhouse, pastel blue and green, set against three tall, dark spruce. It was utterly quiet: wet snow drifting down, a few winter birds, a truck barely audible in the distance. I watched it for a long time. I didn't talk to anyone much; I just skied and traveled. Everything was like cut-glass crystal: sharp, fine, pure. I'm not sure why it was like that. Maybe I had just forgotten what life was really like after four years of monotone halls and lead-gray classrooms. Perhaps life is really like that—crystalline. Or perhaps it was just the supreme excitement of discovering freedom. I don't know. But I do know it was beautiful.

Then somewhere along the line, somewhere my eyes no longer opened quite so wide when the clouds parted and the sun came through so warm and golden. Somewhere I crawled out of Truck and sucked in a deep breath of morning—and it wasn't incredible anymore. It was, well, just sort of the way it was: out in an old Truck in a corner of an empty ski area parking lot, cooking dinner and watching the snow fall. It no longer was a strange silent movie; it was me. And "me" was a ski bum.

I took about a month running down to Vancouver, skiing all the little hills in the interior of B.C. Then I headed up to the big one—Garibaldi (Whistler Mountain to you Yanks). I didn't get there till dark, but the next morning I looked up an old buddy from Lake Louise and got a job on the patrol for meals and lift tickets, and got down to some serious skiing. It's one hell of a mountain. Like everybody tells you, it has the biggest lift-serviced vertical in North America. But hell, Squaw Jump, Saskatchewan, has lots of vertical. What they don't tell you about Garibaldi is that all that vertical is hanging by its tiptoes over the Pacific Ocean. It's steep, and it's beautiful. It's hard now to remember all the things we did; each day sort of folds into the next in my memory of Garibaldi. I remember the day we went jumping on avalanches and I got caught. And the day it snowed 2 feet of sweet, light powder, and we went wild. I remember the guy who lived up on the mountain and had this crazy dog called Yossarian. I remember the fog, learning the wonders of reaction skiing in the bumps that you never saw. And the cold. *Ooooooh,* do I remember the cold. Not nice dry old Rocky Mountain cold, but good West Coast, slopping-around-on-the-decks kind of cold. You'd be hunched over in a swaying chair, an icy mist whipping across you. I can actually remember wondering if it was all worth it. But it was. Laughing and being crazy, skiing with those incredible guys on the patrol there—probably some of the best crud-snow skiers anywhere.

Big G. is a great place to bum. Every day at four, they serve cheese fondue in the L'Apre. So you go in, buy one beer, stand by the fondue pot, and have dinner. After a week or so of a straight fondue diet, you get the runnies; but what the hell, if you survive the fondue, and get established as a resident, then you can buy a Monday–Friday resident's season ticket for eighty dollars. The place is empty during the week, so the skiing is great. Then you work on the weekends when the crowds arrive and there are plenty of jobs. So you get your ticket, rent a little log cabin down on Alta Lake (one hundred dollars for *all* winter), and install a coal-oil heater. Then around about December, you meet this very cool chick and you get along. She comes down to see your cabin and she stays for the night. She stays for another and another, and you find she can really cook. Paradise, man.

But not for me. I don't know why—too many far-off places on my mind, I guess. I stayed around the place about three weeks. I knew everybody and things were getting sort of regular. Then I looked around one day and discovered they *were* regular. The next day, I headed south.

It isn't hard to tell when you've arrived in Greene country. You drive over Nancy Greene Pass, rumble by Nancy Greene Lake, turn right, and you're in Nancy's town—Rossland, B.C.—and at the mountain that spawned that wild little woman. That was the first thing I noticed: Red Mountain. And some cat doing it up in the bumps, and doing them fast and French—very, very nice. He pulled into the lift line, and I realized that he was a kid about 3 feet tall. There oughta be a law . . . . I spent a couple of days there, skiing the bumps on Red and riding that old monster chairlift. One day I quit early and went down to town. The town is great, totally turned on to skiing. Whoever heard of ski posters in a hardware shop? And baby, are they proud of their little woman.

From Greene land I just wandered, skiing all the little hills down through southern B.C. and into Montana. Mostly, it was pretty poor—it hadn't snowed for weeks. But when I got down to Missoula, I finally picked up some good skiing. Their mountain is steep, very interesting. But the second morning I found a little tree to twist my ankle on, so I got moving again. A twisted ankle can still push a gas pedal. I drove up the Gunnison River past Lone Mountain, thinking about Huntley's planned extravaganza. It was snowing softly when I stopped in Driggs, Idaho, for some groceries. The man taking my money told me about a new place called Grand Targhee just out of town over the Wyoming border. I listened and went up.

Morning showed with 6 inches of new stuff and a pure blue sky. I had a chat with the manager and talked my way into a ticket. I rode their long, long chair up into the sky and unloaded in the high, bright sunshine, right up behind the Grand Teton. I was just across the range from Jackson Hole. I skied the main runs in the morning—big, wide slopes with lots of room. Then, just when the shadows were starting to stretch, I found this little patch of paradise: far off to the left, a protected little valley, with perfect little Alpine firs casting long blue shadows across the snow. Untouched. I just closed my eyes and let it go, sliding in and out of the shadows, listening to the soft hiss of *my* skis.

The next morning, I went over the ridge into Jackson. I hit the Jackson valley as the long afternoon shadows of the Tetons tripped across the meadows and through the woods that lead to Teton Village. And there it was, looking just the way it does in the posters, a tiny circle of lodges tucked up against the mountain. After dinner, I went out to take in the local goodies. First, a wild place called the Mangy Moose; then a little, not-so-quiet bar in one of the lodges. The barmaid was a Canadian, and (bless her little heart) she found a couple of the local girls to keep me company. I told them about Banff and Garibaldi and Rossland; they filled me in on Jackson.

Next morning, up the mountain, I got out of the cable car in the howling wind and hustled down to get the boards on. Then I slid down to where the mountain drops away and stopped to dig it. The bright sun, the wind whipping ice particles in your face, and below, a big bowl of wind-drifted moguls. And all around, country, stretched out as far as you can see. Wow! I took off, wandering down, sucking up the bumps and

playing with the drifts. Then cut off onto the cat track down and around the mountain. You sift along the track. You can feel the warmth of your exertion, relaxed, digging the sun, dipsy-doodling around the prune pickers, just digging it. And then . . . there is the place I remember. You come off the track into this beautiful little flush of bumps. In the afternoon with the sun behind you, doing them up, you can watch your shadow dance. Man, it's like making your own ski movie.

But Jackson is not a mountain for bumps. Jackson is deep powder and skiing Hoback and jumping off the cliffs. And it hadn't snowed for weeks. So I packed up and headed south again.

The next day, I hauled up in a little ski resort in the hills of northern Utah. A typical little hill: the lodge full, the slopes icy, and the skies gray. I sat and talked to the manager over coffee: a great little man full of big ideas for his hill. His eyes were bright with the excitement of having someone to listen to his dreams. We were in the middle of his 2-mile chairlift right to the top of the mountain, when a little flicker of white caught my eye. A snowflake. The first one in weeks. In a few minutes, it was coming down thick and gorgeous. I began to find it difficult to concentrate on the future of Schulkenberg's Hill, or whatever it is called. My feet started to do a tap dance. It looked like it was a general storm, a 2-footer, maybe a 4-footer. And if it was going to snow in Utah, then I didn't want to be on Schulkenberg's Hill. I said my good-byes as politely as possible, even turned down a free lift ticket. I got on the road and started moving. Truck complained a little, I was pushing him, but pretty soon we settled down to covering country. The snow was beautiful, pasted against the windows, floating down in quiet, sifting clouds.

I got down into the Salt Lake Valley, and it turned to sleet. It was dark and driving rain by the time I reached Salt Lake City. I sped through the night, squinting for a second at my map, then out through the rain at the road signs. I got lost. Other cars flashed by, leaving red blazes in the wet pavement; I fumbled along. Then, there they were, those four magic letters: A-L-T-A. I cut across four lanes of traffic, nearly causing a pile-up, and pulled off into a quiet, tree-lined suburban street. A few minutes later, I was into Cottonwood Canyon and climbing; in ten minutes, I was plowing through 2 feet of snow, following a single set of tire tracks up into the night. It got still deeper as we went, and I began to wonder if we were going to make it. We started to slip and slide, and once we had to stop and pull back and try again. We went higher and higher, the snow deeper and deeper.

Then, just a little farther, and I saw a turnoff and the shadow of a building. Then another—and a light. I crept along. A figure appeared out of the snow, skis on his shoulders. I pulled up, and he came over as I rolled down the window.

"Am I there?"

"What do you mean, are you . . . ?" Then he looked at Truck, at my tired eyes, and smiled.

"Yeah, you're there."

Alta gave me its special welcome early the next morning: the pounding of the avalanche guns. I ate a fast breakfast in the dark and dressed. Then I discovered that I had a problem: how to get out. The back door was jammed; so were the front doors. I rolled down a window. A few flakes fluttered down, and I was staring at a pale blue wall. I poked a hole in it up to my elbow, leaving a long, deep blue pipe. Hmmm. A silent avalanche? I poked another hole, this time at the top of the window. I retrieved my arm and found myself staring out into the early morning sunshine of Alta—*from snow level.* The snow went out level from halfway up Truck's window. Unreal. I tried the door again, frantically. But to no avail. So I accepted the inevitable. On with the gloves, zip up the jacket, pull down the cap—and out the window.

After a few minutes of floundering around, I poked my head out, pulled back my cap . . . and WOW!! It was just too much. They tell you about it, and you see it in the movies, but somehow you don't really think it exists. Well, man, it does. It's entirely above tree line (or so it seems after a big storm), a few lodges scattered around the lifts, and all this snow. All around. Everywhere. And then there is High Rustler. Man, you look at that mountain, and you know that God skis. It starts at the lodges and goes up and up and up, narrowing at the top into a chute between two rock ribs—all by itself, hanging over the valley like some angelic phallic symbol.

I just stood there and stared. But awe wastes time. I hustled my butt around back of Truck, got my skis, and headed for the lift. It was running, but no one was riding. The patrol was up the mountain, making sure that the snow wasn't too deep. One of them came into sight. He stops at the top, looking it over. Then he turns them on. One turn, then another, another—this cat can ski. Nothing but two arms and a smile, bobbing in and out of a white cloud. My heart was pounding. I couldn't stand still. I checked my bindings three times, then again; I checked out the chick bent over in front of me. I hardly noticed how tight her ski pants were. (But they were.) I looked up the mountain, checked the possibilities. Finally, I got on the lift.

Hours, days, *decades* later, I got off at the top. Free. And I knew what I wanted. That steep little mother under the chair. No ego trip; it was just the only run that I could check out on the way up. And the patrol *hadn't* checked it. I had to make a long traverse, slogging through the deep stuff. Finally I'm there, peering over the edge; eyes on the chair watching me. Ignore them, baby. Feel the snow. Yeah, soft. Relax . . . relax . . . *relax,* man. Let the sun in . . . feel it . . . easy . . . easy . . . yeah . . . settle down. Okay? Yeah. DO IT.

I let them slide, sitting back, picking up my balance, getting my speed. The tips pop out, making a cool little swirl in the snow; the snow sifts up to my waist, curling up behind me. I can feel pin-pricks of cold in the back of my neck. I bounce once and plant, watching my hand move out. Slow motion. I can feel the snow, the sun, the wind, and the eyes. The world stops. My hand inches out and cocks. My legs tense and unweight . . . ever so slowly. My tips dip and are gone. And I watch, wide-eyed, as the snow crawls up my chest, up my neck, into my mouth, and the sky, the trees, the skiers . . . everything disappears. Head-deep, man. HEAD-DEEP!

I reach out through the whiteness, plant, and start the next one—and back into the sunshine, jet-trails of snow streaming across my face. Up and around, then back down into that flowing white world. Out again. A tree flashes by. A voice: "Do it, man!" Down into oblivion. And out again, laughing, screaming, howling. Down again. Suddenly, the bottom drops out. The drop-off. I'd seen it on the way up but forgotten. Crashing down, struggling for balance; falter, catch it, lose it. Try again, almost . . . but you are gone. You can feel the strain in the front of your ankles, your upper body arching into the sunshine, the wind and the big eyes watching . . . then down and tumbling into a soft, blinding world of white. Over and over you go, an astronaut in white space, your lifeline cut, tumbling away into the stars.

Silence. Unmoving. No sound but your own heart. And deep, delirious laughter. Try to lie quietly for a moment. Man, it is just too much. And the cold creeps in, and you think of the next run. Roll over, take off the clogged goggles, and squint into that blue, perfect sky. And laugh, man, laugh and laugh and laugh and laugh. . . .

I was headed up for number two when I thought I heard someone call my name. I looked around, but there are a thousand Bobs in this world, and I was a long, long way from home. I bumped off the ramp and stopped at the edge. A little slope with no tracks. Why? One turn informs me. Buried bumps. I picked myself up and started over, feeling with my tips for the troughs. I got some speed and did a couple of good ones. Another and another, and I've got them going. Somebody is calling that cat Bob again. Then I heard it, clear as a bell:

"JAMIESON, YOU ----ING BUM!"

I crashed, nose between my tips—or rather, between my ears, since I was trying to look back up the hill. I straightened up out of a jungle of goggles, skis, bindings, and various twisted portions of my anatomy, and stared back up the hill. Two cats on the chair, yelling and waving. Who the hell . . . ? They got off and came bouncing down. Whoever they were, they could ski. They pull up. And it's two of my old buddies from Lake Louise! Laughing and back-slapping and "Get your skis on, bum!"

That was the beginning of a day that will never really end. Some of that day—of the snow,

the sky, the laughter, the companionship—will always be with me. Two years and 14,000 miles later, out on the African savanna, a hot breeze hits me, I close my eyes, and I'm back there: the three of us, jumping off the cliffs, plowing through the powder, going, going, going . . . .

They had been there for three weeks and had the place cased—every slope, every gully. They knew the spots where the warm afternoon sun couldn't reach. And the places where only the heroes went. The cliffs with the landings in the trees. The trees up left of Rustler. Thick and steep. Slow motion in the powder, elbowing by the twisted firs, then down into the steep little avalanche gullies, head-deep in cold, blue powder. It went on for weeks. It snowed, and we went wild. First day, ski anywhere. Second day, the steep gullies left over. Third day, ski the crud, see if you can handle it. Fourth day, jump off the cliffs. Egging each other on. You stand on top, looking down, shuffling your skis. And the bastards down below start to count. You took fourteen last time, but that was only 30 feet high. On the fifth day, the landings get packed out so you go out on the packed slopes and do tricks: crossovers, 360s, laybacks between each other's legs. And skiing the bumps, working on the French Technique. Then, you're up on the Rustler traverse, late in the afternoon. You look west, down the canyon out upon the dirty brown fields of the Salt Lake Valley. And far across the valley, along the horizon—are those clouds? Yep, sure are. Tomorrow we are back in the goodies. It starts about 7 P.M., and you sit at the window of the bar and watch it come down. You put a buck down on the local lottery: guess how many inches we are going to get. Next morning, it is still socked in, and you can't ski. You can't even leave the lodge. Cards all day, and just watch it come down. And the next morning, the Alta alarm clock goes off and you know that you're back in business again.

And so it went. There must have been bad days, but I don't remember them. I do remember the day I skied with Alf Engen and learned how to turn them inside-out in the powder. I remember the redhead from Boulder and the blond from Toronto, who had just spent three weeks with Gmoser in the Bugaboos. I remember the day I rode head-first down an avalanche chute, a mini-avalanche piling up behind me. And the day I hit the tree.

There were some special days—like the day another Canuck, Gordy Blake, showed up. And then we showed the Yanks how to turn them. That boy turns them *so sweet.* The day before Gordy left, it snowed a good one. Rustler didn't slide, and we chased the Snow Ranger up the mountain and across the traverse to the top of it. We waited on the rim while he tossed some bombs on the trigger-point. They blew, and nothing happened. He looked at it for a moment, then turned to us and said, cool as hell:

"Okay, boys."

And we ripped it up.

In March, my buddies ran out of money. I didn't have any so I couldn't run out of it. They headed home, and I headed east to Colorado. I took a look at Solitude, Brighton, Park City, etc., but they were short of snow—and after Alta, well . . . I headed out across the flatlands. I was watching a blaze-red sunset in the side-view mirror when the WELCOME TO COLORADO sign flashed by. About 9 P.M., the full moon came out; it was almost as bright as daytime. The road was empty, so I turned off my lights and drove through the moonlight. What a trip! Roaring down this straight black strip across the desert, a skiff of snow gleaming in the sagebrush.

The morning was beautiful—clear and snapping, smelling of wild sage. I headed into town looking for a new tire to replace one that had blown. The old guy in the Texaco helped me out. He started out kind of gruff; then we chatted for a while, and I gave him a tour of Truck. While I put the tire on, he asked me where I'd been, where I was going. Between grunts on the wrench, I gave him glimpses of what I had seen. I climbed in and started her up. He looked at me, sucking on his pipe, and I thanked him.

"Wish I'd done somethin' like this when I was a young feller." We looked at each other for a moment. In his eyes, I could see my own reflection. I don't know what he saw. As I pulled out he stood there a long time, his little garage and town behind him, slowly receding into my mirror.

Vail is Vail, the Calcutta of skiing—the richest and the poorest. All the beautiful people from out East in their condominiums and their big cars. Fat-cheeked blonds from Cincinnati wearing more money in Bogners and Obermeyers than I spend in a year. And then there are the bums.

I was wandering around, looking at things, getting the feel of the place, when I saw a ski hat with a maple leaf on it. So I said, "Hi, Canuck." He was from Toronto, had spent the winter at Vail, and knew the scene cold. We went over to his pad, listened to some great music, and had a little party. The next morning, I met the great bums of Vail. Everybody shows up at the lift early and gets a job for half a day, thereby getting a ticket for the next day. A great deal; enough bread to ski and survive (the bread comes from hustling the tickets). And if you don't show up one morning 'cause of the night before . . . well, nobody could give a damn.

I ended up doing a lot of skiing with a cat called Steve Quicksilver. We met up on the mountain one day. Didn't talk much—sometimes words just get in the way—and we went skiing. We discovered we had a couple of bad habits in common, like cliffs and trees. The trees were his thing. I never did figure out how he skied some places. He was one of the great bums. There may have been tricks he didn't know, but I doubt it. He knew all the lift operators, of course, and if one of the ornery ones was on the bottom lift . . . well, you walk up in the trees, then come careening down and crash into the lift line, thereby making it obvious that you have just come down the mountain, and therefore must have a ticket. Or, you look in the garbage cans and collect a huge wad of tickets. Make sure there is a big lineup. Then, when he asks for your ticket, start going through your wad, slowly. And always, always get in line in front of some long-legged bit of lift-operator attention distracter.

Ah, we had some good times, skiing the deep stuff in the back bowls, coming down all tired and cold, then sitting around in the delicatessen. Talking loud and consuming huge amounts of unpaid-for yogurt (I'll bet they haven't figured *that* one out yet). Then down to the Keg, get juiced—it's always cheaper on an empty stomach—and watch the six o'clock news. (They're talking about some other planet, man!) Then, since you're in before six, you don't have to pay the evening cover charge. You see, it's easy.

The only thing wrong with Vail is the skiing. It's tailored to the ladies from Cincinnati. Not that I blame the management; they know which side is buttered. There is one cool slope, though: Look-Ma. I don't know if Ma is looking, but when you come sifting over the edge of that one, everybody else is. It is short, steep, icy, mogulled, and right on top of the lift line. The bumps have no rhythm at all. You have to hump every bump, then extend *fast,* because the next one is right there. One day, I watched a chick do it up pretty as you please. We got together, doing linked crossovers, one behind the other—really diddling the tourists. Then we *really* got it on, skiing arm in arm and *turning* them. And it was only when I suggested that we try the same in the bumps that she decided maybe I was just a little *too* weird.

Aspen. I drove in slowly, taking it all in: the wild little purple house on the main road; an old, white-haired man in a huge gray coat, walking in the sun. I went up to the lift, parked, sat on the bumper, and watched the evening migration down off the mountain. Lots of the Beautiful People. Bogners and Bonne Bell. The instructors, with their skis hung ever so carelessly over their shoulders, so cool they're all frozen up. Some real heroes, still hyperventilating. A few Frenchmen, talking as always. The chicks, wearing their little sister's ski pants. And then the weirdos—the bums: Butch Cassidys on every lip; blue jeans and faded, stitched racers; a jungle jacket and a wet look, patched with denim; and of course, hair, long beautiful hair.

I got into Truck, followed the crowd downtown, and did a little of Aspen's second most important winter sport: fingering the merchandise. Grooving on the stuff that costs more than

it cost you to live last month. I was fingering one especially cool hat, an EASY hat (and God knows, I'm easy), when I heard the *pitter-patter* of little salesgirl feet. I turned around, expecting a frozen, Barbie-doll smile and a polite trip to the door. Instead, I got this beautiful, *real*, glad-to-meet-you kind of smile from one of the finest little women I have ever had the opportunity to meet. Like, I'd been on the road a long time, and here was this woman smiling at me. A small thing, perhaps, but after all those miles . . .

"Hi."

"Hi."

She proceeded to talk me into spending my last few cents on this EASY hat. I asked if she came with the hat, as accessories or something. It turned out she didn't. She was married, hubby was an instructor, and they had a little house with two Saint Bernards. They skied all winter and climbed all summer. Mountain people. She listened, smiling, as I told her about Garibaldi and Jackson and Alta. Then she sold me the hat and filled me in on the bumming procedures in Aspen. We walked to the door, and she gave me another of those smiles and a little wave. And I was alone again. But not for long. Two big, white huskies came up for a neck rub. We discussed Aspen from a dog's point of view for a while. Then I bought some bread and salami and had dinner with my two new friends.

A guy with pigtails came up and started rubbing the dogs' ears. I gave him a sandwich, too. We sat on Truck's bumper and talked about skiing. We got around to mountains in general and then to freedom. From there, we got on to love—and that, interestingly enough, brought us back to skiing. A chick he knew stopped to talk, and then she saw Truck. She looked in the windows and made all kinds of funny little noises. She came around front and started running her fingers over Truck's classic lines, caressing them. Poor Truck. I could see that he was getting turned on. *Then,* she started jumping up and down on his bumper. I tell you, I had to admire old Truck. He showed real self-control. I suggested that we go down to the bar so that she would stop titillating the old boy. We went down and had a few in this little bar full of patrolmen, instructors, and bums. Small, noisy, and crowded, a leftover from the mining days. There were two bullet holes in the ceiling—from a shoot-out between a patrolman and an instructor, they say.

Much later, I left my friends and toddled home. I stopped at the door and looked down the quiet, empty street. Four drunks, locked out of their car, were yelling and swearing. A little old lady who couldn't sleep was taking a walk. I felt great. I'd been here only a few hours, but a smile, two dogs, and some quiet talk, and Aspen was my town.

I had some good skiing at Snowmass, jumping over the cabin, and we had some good powder one day up at Highlands. I skied with the wild patrolmen up there (Christ, they *all* do flips), and they showed me some beautiful little hidden places where the snow hangs late. But it was the face of Bell that I got it on with—one sweet little hunk of mountain.

The snow was sticky now. I really didn't notice it at first. Up in Canada, we are used to a little longer season. But pretty soon, the wineskins and the bikinis appeared; I knew the end was in sight. I tried to forget it, skiing hard and wild in the spring slush. All the tourists were gone now, leaving the locals and the bums to tidy up the season. There was much celebration, as if the end was some joyous event. They had a flipping contest at Snowmass—into a swimming pool. Man, they have some weird people in that town. Doing flips is one thing, but into a small, I said *small,* swimming pool? Well . . .

And there was the night that one of the fancy restaurants discovered they had too much steak and lobster left over and had a two-for-one sale. We toddled down about 7 P.M. I opened the door, and what a sight! Every table was filled and the hallway was clogged with people. All the bums were there, all with a case of the blind munchies. I found a patch of floor and sat down to wait. I took it all in: the Beautiful People, the laughter, the good smell of grilled steaks and lobster—high society in Aspen.

But mostly I skied. I knew the end was coming. The last day, I went berserk trying to squeeze the last ounce of ecstasy out of myself and that mountain. I've never skied like I did that day. The bumps were incredible—chopped up and deadly. I slammed into them, too fast and too wild, canning out, doing body slams across the bumps.

As the shadows started to stretch I got on the lift and went right to the top. I slipped down and across the slope into the first patch of trees, and tucked myself up against a stump. A few minutes of silence; then the patrol came down, calling occasionally, slipping down the mountain. After they had gone, I started out of the trees—and almost ran into the tag-end patrolman. After he was gone, I sidestepped up to the top. I stood there for a long time, watching the sun dip down over the Maroon Bells. It was very quiet. The wind was cold and occasionally rattled snow pebbles across my skis. A raven drifted by and squawked when he saw me; I watched him drift down into the shadows over Aspen. I followed.

It was cold now; the snow was sharp and hard. I took it fast and wide, sweeping GS turns down into the valley. It seemed so fast, that run, yet so slow. I didn't really ski it. I was just there, and somewhere below me my legs and skis twisted and turned, finding their way down the mountain. I tucked down the smooth, wide-open valley in the center of Aspen Mountain, the rough ice whistling under me. I cut onto the cat track, and at the corner I cut in my edges and stopped . . . in a spray of ice and roaring skis.

Below me was Aspen—somehow very dirty and old in the evening shadows. The snow had long since left the roofs and streets. Patches of brown, and even a little green, showed through on the slope below me. Only a few people were in sight; only one was carrying skis. I looked back up the mountain, still silver, blue, and cold. I felt many things at that moment. Mostly sadness, but also ecstasy—a deeper, quieter kind—and even, I guess, a little relief. It was over. I took a deep breath, pushed off, and went down, listening to my skis rattle on the old, hard snow.

The Two Million Dollar Ski Man

by MORTEN LUND

On the list of skiers who gave back generously to their sport, Lowell Thomas' name leads all the rest. Skiing meant a lot to him and he contributed more to it than any other man in the history of the sport. This story originally appeared in abridged form as "So Long, Lowell" after Thomas' death in 1981 in Ski Magazine.

THE man, Lowell Thomas, is a rather strong and wiry eighty-eight-year-old who looks and acts a lively sixty-five. If you meet him in a casual way, he impresses as an extraordinarily mild yet wistfully witty man, with a body as alive and muscled as a badger's—big shoulders and arms (if you look) and a grip that leaves you feeling that if he just bothered to close his hand, your own would be left squeezed out like a damp washcloth. This is a man whose broadcast presence has provided America with its most familiar individual voice over the past fifty years, a voice that, like the man, carries qualities of the ideal embodiment of the American male—well liked, self-made, rich, adventurous, personable, modest, mellow, loyal, brave, popular, apolitical and—avidly—an outdoorsman. All that aside, there is an *airtight* case that Lowell Thomas is the foremost recreational skier of all time, if only in that he has spent more money at it than any other skier in history.

To make his extraordinary extravagance vis-a-vis skiing credible, we have to first sketch in with a few broad strokes the prominent aspects of the man's life. Otherwise everything else a journalist might write about Thomas has a tinge of the unbelievable.

Lowell Thomas' travels encompass a multiple crisscross of the known world: in sum, there is almost no remote corner where he has not been; his entertainments in radio, TV, film, and public speaking have engulfed (almost literally as in the case of Cinerama) the American audience; he has enthralled a goodly portion of the English-speaking world audience with fifty-plus books of adventure and information; on a human scale, his feats of prowess include some unbelievable expeditionary survivals, some monumentally dangerous pioneer flying, superb horsemanship, expert golf, world class mountaineering, and a marvelous devotion to skiing, beyond any call. And the whole edifice rests on the voice.

The Thomas voice—clear yet resonant, sonorous yet pleasing of timbre—was without peer in early radio, which is where Thomas' worldwide fame found its mainspring. Early radio rendered anything less than perfectly distinct into unintelligible speech—what with the loss of power, poor technical reception, and just plain static that afflicted radio in the decade of its emergence as a credible national phenomenon (the same as that of skiing): the 1930s.

Thomas' early training in voice (from his father, a surgeon in a lurid gold mining camp, a man of classical and inquisitive turn of mind) enabled Thomas—in the year 1930, when radio was barely out of the cat's-whisker-and-crystal stage—to convince the sponsoring *Literary Digest,* then the leading magazine of national opinion, that Thomas, as a potential commentator for its network news program, the first in the world, had just the voice the program wanted.

Though the *Literary Digest* later folded, Thomas picked up Sun Oil Company (and later Proctor and Gamble, then for twenty years General Motors) and went on and on and on and on—for forty-five years, live on radio, the longest single run of any regular public media figure, including Amos and Andy and Walter Cronkite. Thomas' final "So long, until tomorrow," went out over the airwaves in 1975—ending "Lowell Thomas and the News" as an American institution one-quarter as long-lived as the Constitution itself. (Thomas' taped, syndicated "The Best Years," however, is still going strong over the air after two hundred broadcasts.)

In those forty-five years of live radio, Thomas' total listening audience, figuring one listener for one program as a unit, reached the astronomical figure of a hundred *billion,* more audience than any other voice has reached in history, including all the popes reigning in that time taken together and throwing in Franklin Delano Roosevelt to boot. And as an historical footnote, during that time Thomas was more firmly associated with skiing than any other public figure of his era.

This brings us to Lowell Thomas and the skiing.

His first bout with skis was short-lived, consisting of walking around on crude unhandy 9-foot boards that served to bouy the *arditi,* the Italian Alpine troops, above the snow surface, on Monta Rosa on the mountainous front line in World War I. This was in 1917 when Thomas was twenty-five years old, already an independent journalist. Not until fifteen years later, dur-

ing his broadcasts from the 1932 Lake Placid Olympics did Thomas take up skiing in earnest, age forty.

This time he was inspired by Norwegians, the brothers Sigmund and Birger Ruud, who were, like Thomas, staying at the Lake Placid Club during the Games. The Ruud brothers would strap on their huge jumping skis in front of the club and go springing off across the snow, *sans* poles, headed for the Olympic jump at Intervale. Thomas signed up for lessons with the Placid pro, Erling Strom, another Norwegian (the 1930s was the last decade of the Norwegian instructor), on the snow-covered Lake Placid golf course.

Thenceforth, he was our leading pioneer consumer of skiing.

When Katherine Peckett in 1934 brought over the first of the Austrians from St. Anton to teach at Pecketts-on-Sugar-Hill, New Hampshire, Thomas was there. ("One of the Austrians," said Thomas, in his musing, amused, yet definitely enunciated way, "Harold Paumgarten, married a millionairess. Sig Buchmayr was busy entertaining the ladies, so Kurt Thalhammer did most of the teaching.")

When the first U.S. rope tow came in at Woodstock, Vermont, Thomas, within a winter or so, had one installed on "Strawberry Hill" at his Pawling, New York estate. (If you know Thomas' humor, you might suspect there was a reason *why* it was called "Strawberry Hill.") This was incidentally the first rope tow in New York State.

When Sun Valley opened, in the winter of 1937, Lowell Thomas was there, taking lessons from the then ski director, Hans Hauser, and, in later winters, from Sigi Engel, Otto Lang, and others; when in 1939 Hannes Schneider, the famous inventor of the Arlberg teaching method, was sprung from Nazi prison and ensconced on Mount Cranmore at North Conway, Thomas was there. When, in 1941, Fred Pabst opened his T-bars at Bromley, Vermont, and Snow Valley, Vermont, Thomas was there. He skied Mount Washington, New Hampshire when not many ventured up into its huge glacial cirque, Tuckerman's Ravine, in winter. He invested in and was on the board of directors of Stowe, Mad River, and Madonna in Vermont when they were founded. When Joe Ryan, the eventual developer, first skied Mount Tremblant, Quebec, before it had lifts, Thomas was skiing along with Ryan. Thomas was in more places with his skis than the ubiquitous "Kilroy" was with his face in the 1940s. If you skied, there was no escaping the track of Lowell Jackson Thomas.

And he managed this on less than one-tenth of 1 percent of the time he was awake and functional. Thomas had simultaneous full careers going in several of the following: film lecturing, adventure filmmaking, daily radio broadcasting, weekly newsreel commentary, producing and directing television series, writing books (as if there were no tomorrow), having a social life of considerable proportions (a hundred to dinner at Quaker Hill in Pawling was not out of the way), completing an enormous quota of travel (he once collapsed of jet lag after logging 50,000 air miles in two months), and surviving stunning adventures (cannibal cuisine, poison pigmy arrows, penetration of Tibet, expeditionary hunger and deprivation).

How could a man who, among all the other things, had to make a daily broadcast five times a week at 6:45 P.M. EST spend so much time skiing in the day before regular resort airline service?

Simple.

He took along (by rail or auto) a studio engineer, a telegraph operator, as well as his secretary, fittingly named Electra—still with him after forty-seven years—to type the scripts and time the program.

And what if such piddling (then) country towns as Aspen, Lake Placid, and Sun Valley—locations unimaginably remote in the popular mind in the 1930s and 1940s—did not have in place the requisite outgoing wires to transmit coast to coast? Well, Lowell Thomas had the wires strung at his own expense.

And that is where the extravagance came in.

Over the years, the total costs of the rewiring, wire charges for remote broadcast, travel, meals, and hotel for his crew came out to shocking sums, which fortunately, thanks to his wild and energetic pursuit of the popular taste, Thomas could well afford. "I figured it out one day," he told an audience of ski school directors last season, "and the total came to $2 million over the years." (It sounds better if you break it down into, say, forty ski seasons at $50,000 a season—still, a sum that would give pause to even an oil sheik.)

Thomas is an extraordinary man, a man of—in his own quiet way—gargantuan appetites.

The almost ferocious desire for action that he has exhibited steadily is coupled, beguilingly, with his infinite capacity for winning friends, giving time as needed (where he found it is hard to see) to cultivate same. In the course of our interchange, as required for this article, Thomas suddenly called me up out of the blue and spent fifteen minutes outlining an unrelated tip he thought that I might be able to make use of.

"Mort," he said over the phone from Pawling, "some years ago—it was 1919, that's a long time ago—sixty-one years—I was a guest at a dinner in Singapore, given in honor of a Chinese scholar, Dr. Lin Boon King, by a man who had made a huge fortune in discovering and selling "Tiger Balm." He had over two hundred people to dinner and each guest had his own waiter in white linen to remove and replace the plates during the meal. Later, I was told he actually changed his name to "Tiger Balm." Now he has been dead for years but yesterday, in front of the Waldorf, I ran into his daughter. She's from Hong Kong and is now head of the Tiger Balm empire that he left and she is, I would think, a good story for somebody at this time."

Now that was pure Lowell Thomas.

There was the concern for an acquaintance (myself), there was the nose for news, there was the fantastically accurate memory for names and dates, and the network of circumstances stretching back through the years that enables him to set events vibrating if he so chooses, by simply shaking the net a little.

Thomas' conversation sometimes seems to consist of a name leading to another and another and another. And, even in a field as special and insular as skiing can be, his overview is amazing. He is ahead of anybody in any crowd in any room, in any resort, with names and events and dates. *Ski people*—he knows them all. Moreover, he has skied with them all. Who else, for instance, has skied with both Peter Seibert at Camp Hale in the embryo days of the Tenth Mountain Division (Thomas is an investor in Seibert's new Snow Basin, Utah) *and* with Hans Hauser in Chile after he and his wife, Virginia Hill, had been chased out of the U.S. (by disclosures of Hill's involvement with organized crime, as a special friend of the notorious Buggsy Seigal)? Who else, for instance, has skied with an array of sometime notables such as Kurt Thalhammer, Benno Rybizka, Toni Matt, Jacques Charmoz, Sepp Ruchsp, Lionel Hayes, Kerr Sparks, Otto Hollaus, Bruce Fenn, Friedl Pfeiffer, Luggi Foeger, Sigi Engl, Otto Steiner, Wiggi Hasher, Sverre Engen, Steve Bradley, Bill Klein, Emil Allais, Sepp Froelich, Raider Anderson, Tom Murstad, Heinrich Harrer, Peter Gabriel, Johnny Litchfield, Michael Fursinger, Fritz Weissner, Sel Hannah, Mary Bird Young, Jim Parker, Gladys and Jack Sawyer. Not to mention "Iron Man" Bob Kehoe and Herman Smith-Johannsen. This represents a fraction of less than one one-thousandth of Thomas's ski acquaintances from the ski industry itself, yet who else even *knows* who they—even these few—all were or are?

Lowell Thomas' voracious and startling capacity for digesting work, travel, adventure, sport, friendships, and socializing is matched by an energy more than sufficient thereunto. The man's output is undeniable, impressive—a torrent. Even at eighty-eight. His longstanding friends, who may call him "Tommy," are to a man in awe of the dawn-to-dusk schedule, the film projects that are now current, the books that are underway, the board meetings scheduled, the dinner speeches in preparation—he's as dry and witty a raconteur as he is bland and creamy smooth on the air—with a talent for delicious understatement, a memory for the ridiculous, and a command of anecdote—speakable and unspeakable—that together enable him to break up an audience as easily as someone else may say, "Please pass the butter."

For all that, he is a very private man. He is, for some purposes, a "hard interview." The anecdotes come out, the memories roll on in a flood, and past worlds, hidden worlds come to light but Thomas' personal emotions, his opinions, his mystery—all remain carefully veiled. He has a reticence—and yet reticence—not the right word. His "World of Lowell Thomas" is a show screening out the ringmaster's personal. (He quotes General Allenby with approval, "Who am I to set the world aright?")

What we know about Thomas is the externals and they are dazzling. His first job was delivering newspapers in Victor, Colorado in the famous Cripple Creek mining district on the western slope of Pike's Peak (where when he threaded the gauntlet of saloons and whorehouses, he had to "walk tough") and from there, he progressed to working in the bowels of the Portland mine before becoming half the staff of the *Victor Record and News* and later the *Victor Daily* (after a bout with college studies during which he completed the five-year master's degree requirement at Valpariso in Indiana in two years), then to covering crime and passion in Chicago during the heyday of macho reporting (Ben Hecht, Charles McArthur of *Front Page*) for the *Chicago Journal,* and thence, in a typical Thomas segue, to writing promotional travel pieces and running the Whitehorse rapids in the Yukon, to dodging bullets while directing a film unit (*another* switch) commissioned to capture stories of the Allied effort in World War I, to filming General Edmund Allenby and Colonel T. E. Lawrence cleaning up the Turks in the Holy Land to getting a bullet shot through his hat in Berlin (he was reported killed in a dispatch to the U.S. And his wife, Frances, thought herself a widow for two weeks) during the postwar socialist uprising. And thence to breaching, camera in hand, the forbidden frontiers of Malaysia, India, Afghanistan, Nepal, Tibet, and New Guinea (where he interviewed gorged but not necessarily satiated cannibals, after having been advised to lose weight before the trip, so as to appear less appetizing).

How did he find the time to ski?

Or sit down? Eat?

He showed his first personally narrated film, *With Allenby in Palestine and Lawrence in Arabia,* at the Royal Opera House in Covent Gardens and Royal Albert Hall in London, in 1919 for over a year, getting a multimillion dollar gross and a million-person gate. Then he toured Britain and its empire with the film and, while in Malaysia, began filming his second show, *Through Romantic India and into Forbidden Afghanistan.* Lowell Thomas was off and running.

He wrote his first book, a best-seller that eventually ran through one hundred editions and a million copies in 1922, *With Lawrence in Arabia;* he wrote *Beyond the Khyber Pass* in 1925 and from then on averaged a book a year (some years none, some as many as *five*). His other careers include his five-day-a-week radio, his spark-plugging of Cinerama (the first wide screen process) and doing three Cinerama productions—(*This is Cinerama, Seven Wonders of the World, The Search for Paradise,* etc.) and included as well voice commentary for Fox Movietone newsreels (where he added another fifty billion to his audience total) and more than a thousand film projects as well as two television series, (one, "The World of Lowell Thomas," for BBC in London) and sundry syndicated radio programs, the most recent, "LT Remembers."

To fill up the idle hours left him by these, Thomas worked over the 100 square mile grounds of Quaker Hill in Pawling; now building his own private ski area with two slopes and three trails, now building a private twelve-hole golf course, now buying half a dozen houses in the neighborhood to refurbish and resell to *sympatico* people (e.g., Tom Dewey, then district attorney in New York), getting up backlot baseball teams to play against President Franklin Roosevelt's "Packers" (for *packing* the Supreme Court, get it?) from Hyde Park across the Hudson, now buying a used steam shovel to move a hill from one place to the next—boredom ever threatening was held off with ploys like these.

Not only was Thomas constantly embroiled in action, but he constantly found others whom he *then* likewise embroiled. If he started a dairy herd, he embroiled a dairyman; just so, his estate superintendent was suddenly commanded to build the then exotic ski lift; and when he signed for six books in one contract (getting the largest

advance in Doubleday's history), he found a writer to help out, Prosper Buranelli. (A "contra-ego," Buranelli was nonathletic, nonadventurous, a lovable, roly-poly polymath and barfly whose memory for the arcane and intellectual matched Thomas' for personal history, who was with Thomas for thirty-four years—until the day at Quaker Hill he died of a massive coronary, in the middle of an as-usual series of brilliant conversational gambits. One of a kind. But Thomas relished the *different* in character.)

When Thomas got into broadcasting, he hired two scriptwriters, three secretaries, and two teletypes, all of them installed in Rockefeller Center. His earliest "embroilee" was Harry Chase, wizard cameraman and projectionist who ran two film and one still projector simultaneously for Thomas' worldwide personal appearances and who was with Thomas for ten years.

His financial manager, Frank Smith, became an embroilee when Thomas, in 1946, in a spurt of excess energy, managed to make his entire visible fortune vanish. Smith, surveying the wreckage, commented to Thomas' lawyer, "It is my considered opinion that no man in the annals of humankind who has so little interest in gambling, strong drink, and fancy women has managed to unload as much money as LT."

(The other grand pronouncement on Thomas' life came from a former president of Sun Oil who, perhaps unnerved by years of Thomas' noncommittal radio commentary, sensed that Thomas was hiding something, possibly an antipathy to the established powers. Asked what he thought Thomas' politics *really* were, the executive replied, "I *think* he's an anarchist.")

At any rate, Smith within a few years created an interesting communications empire for Thomas which today is expressed as a major share of Capital Cities Communications, an outfit that owns the Fairchild publishing company (*Women's Wear Daily,* etc.), TV stations, and properties like the *Kansas City Star,* investments that are safe from even Thomas' energetic depredations.

Through it all, Thomas had the time to be a concerned caring family man, to marry and enjoy the marriage for fifty-eight years, to have with that wife, Frances, a single male child, Lowell, Jr. (formerly lieutenant governor of Alaska and a filmmaker, lecturer, and writer in his own right); and, when his first wife died, to remarry two years ago, at age eighty-six, a second wife, Marianna, a lovely lady who now presides over a house on high ground at Quaker Hill: Maintop.

But we were talking about skiing.

With the spare time left at Lowell's disposal from lighter preoccupations, he managed not only to get in a good deal of serious skiing with this one and that one, as noted, but to have deeper and more ongoing relationships with a good many skiers, particularly filmmaking skiers, to the extent of affecting their lives considerably. Among these the Marquis degli d'Albizzi, commander of the *arditi,* whom Lowell later hired as a "pro" to help rehabilitate U.S. Air Force men by teaching them skiing on Strawberry Hill), Dick Durrance (one-time U.S. champion, now a filmmaker), Chris Young, and Otto Lang.

Young was a futurist poet and Surrealist painter and filmmaker whom Thomas met in 1933 on the slopes of Mount Washington, making *Dr. Schlitz Climbs Mt. Washington,* a slapstick comedy on skis that also happened to be the first commercial ski film shot in the United States. Thomas, drawn to the unusual, took to Young immediately, helped him crank his camera (those were the days of the handcranked camera), and narrated the film in its final form—when it was finished three years later. On the strength of the finished film and Thomas' participation, Young next sold a film project to Warner Brothers and, marrying his star-to-be, took his bride, Mary Bird (aha, one of the names on the list), to Europe where he filmed her in *Ski Girl* which ran in 1919 as a short at Radio City Music Hall.

When Young—six years later—ended up doing duty in an underground darkroom in London for the U.S. Army, a situation he found stifling, then (naturally) Thomas rescued him by insisting that Young, and no other, be the cameraman for Thomas' tour of the Allied fronts in World War II. Young and Thomas thereupon produced *The Rover Boys Abroad* from the footage shot and Young was on his way to an eventual career as a film lecturer, like his mentor, successfully touring with ski and travel films.

Another ski-and-film talent, Otto Lang, was Thomas' favorite instructor at Sun Valley where Lang, befriended by another pupil, Darryl Zanuck, head of 20th Century Fox, was able to make his way in Hollywood, with Zanuck's help, into the ranks, first of directors and then producers, where he functions today, a long way from his beginnings as a ski instructor for Hannes Schneider in little St. Anton am Arlberg. Thomas, a small-town boy himself, made it a point to borrow Lang from Zanuck from time to time and carry Lang off to some far corner of the world, like Kashmir and Nepal for the Cinerama film *Search for Paradise.* (Thomas also brought along Chris Young to enact the part of an air force captain in the film.) And, another time to New Guinea, where he and Lang went eyeball to eyeball with the cannibals.

But if asked finally to pick his one most-treasured ski companion—since he is definitely not willing to do this publicly—his actions will have to speak for him here, to wit: "I ski at Alta, every year," said Thomas. "It's my favorite place." The fact that a comparative youngster named Alf Engen is, at seventy-one, still head of the Alta Ski School and still one of the fine powder skiers on the mountain has something to do with it.

And the fact that Thomas enjoys skiing with Egen isn't hurting Alta a bit.

In fact, wherever Lowell Thomas has skied, or skis, there's a positive effect. This was particularly true back in the 1930s and 1940s, when skiing as a sport needed to shake the elite, the "freak" image, and achieve solid bourgeois respectability. Thomas, a soothing, dependable image, broadcasting from Aspen, Sun Valley, or St. Jovite, thereby lent his mantle of the ordinary and familiar to the frightfully exotic new sport. After all, how dangerous and elite could a sport be when good old Lowell, forty and familiar, a family man, a reassuring bundle of commonplace virtues, would go out on the slopes day after day and come back alive and unhurt to tell about it?

(Anybody in the radio audience knowledgeable about the kinds of hair-raising scrapes Thomas was eminently likely to get into, year in and year out, would have been very *wary* of skiing.)

Not only skiing, but almost everything else tended to be fairly risky the way Thomas did it, usually. Radio newscasting from resorts was in itself chancy—not so much perilous because of the resort's remoteness as in the hasty makeshift of the technical situation; and, not so perilous in terms of blizzard and avalanche as in the possibilities of Thomas' catching cold. More than once, the ski boots of someone in the skier audience (sitting fascinated on the floor of some lodge watching Thomas broadcast) would insensibly encounter and unplug some vital connection between Thomas and the outside world. The closest and therefore most perilous of broadcast quarters was at St. Jovite where the only possible broadcast location was from the ladies' room of the Canadian Pacific Railroad station—a first. And once, at this same St. Jovite, after a day out in 40 below at Mount Tremblant, Thomas' celebrated vocal cords were suddenly immobilized three or four sentences into the script. Thomas simply shoved the mike and the script over to Lowell, Jr., who has a voice remarkably like Lowell, Sr.'s and the show went on with the change unnoticed by most of the radio listeners, as the audience was called.

One winter, that of 1942, had two star ski events, one of which was kept quiet. That one was Thomas's indiscreet run over the Headwall on Mount Washington—down into Tuckerman's Ravine via a 60-degree incline—in celebration of Thomas' fiftieth birthday. Thomas had no business being on the Headwall, and he soon found that out because, at the end of the first 200 vertical feet, he fell and slid, rolled and cartwheeled the next 800 vertical feet to the ravine floor, before he finally stopped, happily unhurt. The more positive event was his and Lowell, Jr.'s triumph in winning the national father-son slalom title at Snow Valley, Vermont, that year, the high point of Thomas' competitive skiing career. Now that (and not the other) was the kind of promotion that the sport could use.

In one other important respect, Thomas helped skiing.

He got more famous people to go into the sport than any other nonprofessional skier. So much so that the signal failures stand out. One of these, Tom Dewey, was a skeptic on skiing as a district attorney and as a governor, too. But he finally consented to come to Strawberry Hill to give it a whirl. It was a day when the hill was nothing but glare ice. "Dewey was down more than he was up," Thomas said in his faintly amused voice, "and he left and never came back to ski again."

Mark Hatfield was another governor with whom Thomas failed. He had finally gotten the Oregon politico onto a pair of skis, and they were walking across the flat when here came a ski patrol toboggan which stopped right at their feet. Hatfield gazed down upon the face of the Hatfield's family doctor who had been taken with a sudden case of spiral fracture. Hatfield quietly removed his skis and Thomas never got him back on them again.

The most dramatic failure of all resulted in backlash as well. This was the case of Tim Shane, the sports editor of *Colliers*, once a magazine of considerable national influence and audience. Shane—Irish, strong, fiery and fun to be with—was just the writer that Thomas had been evolving a plan for. The essence of the plan was to take a nonskiing writer and slowly teach him to ski, first a few lessons at Lake Placid, then a stem turn at Mount Tremblant, the stem-christie with Hannes Schneider at North Conway, and onward and upward until—as the writer's book evolved—at the climax, the writer would successfully ski down the Headwall. Unfortunately for Thomas' plan, on the third turn at Tremblant, Shane fell and broke a leg, and Thomas was unable to get word to the ski patrol—he had to leave Shane alone, and go for help. On getting back, he found that Shane, panic-stricken at the thought of being left alone on the mountain to die in the oncoming night, had desperately crawled into the woods seeking shelter. By the time he was located, Shane had developed a deep and abiding distaste for skiing.

Now Thomas never walks away from a friend. He kept calling Shane to make sure the leg was healing all right: Shane kept assuring Thomas everything was fine, but Thomas' intuition said otherwise. So, investigating and finding out that Shane was a Christian Scientist who had never even seen a doctor after he got home, Thomas evolved another plan: he promised Shane a terrific story if Shane would take the train with him to Franconia, New Hampshire. Upon reaching that destination, Shane was carted from the train to an ambulance, then to the hospital, there anesthetized—a waiting surgeon reset the leg and recast it. The leg healed, but not Shane's soul. He wrote an acid, lengthy, and intemperate piece for *Colliers,* implying that anyone who tied boards to his feet was fit candidate for a psychiatric evaluation.

Thomas himself was not what one might call a cautious skier, as noted, and he himself failed several times to come back unscathed. In the course of an interview, Thomas said, apropos skiing, "I broke the usual number of bones, you know." The breaks include both legs, both collarbones and an indeterminate number of ribs. The first leg went at Strawberry Hill. The collarbones at Tremblant and Bromley. The ribs at Cannon. The other day, Thomas uncharacteristically couldn't (or wouldn't) recall where the other leg was wasted. "It all happened in the East," said Thomas. "I know that. Never could handle glare ice very well."

None of this, however, could match in risk or ultimate seriousness the time in 1949 when, on his way back from Lhasa, going over a pass in the Himalayas, Thomas was thrown from a half-wild Tibetan pony who, just as Thomas was mounting, whirled and spun him over the side of the cliff. Thomas broke his hip in eight pieces. He was several weeks away from medical help and, as he said, "I had to face the fact that I might be having my last adventure." He nonetheless survived, thanks to Lowell, Jr., and the porters and his own willpower and strong constitution.

In fact, not twelve months later, Thomas was not only up and around but skiing blithely down glaciers in Alaska. This is a typical Thomas sequence, a fitting summation of the man.

One thing more has to be considered, however, and that is why Thomas' oftentimes too trusting challenges to obvious danger have been nevertheless lucky. As Napoleon said of one of his men, "I know he is a good general, but is he *lucky?*" Luck is an ability as much as a fall-out of chance.

Thomas, when asked if he thought he had been lucky in his life, said, with his usually fairly sober-faced expression breaking out into a full smile, "Yes. Yes. There had to be some of that."

The run of Thomas' luck goes through his life like a taut wire. To wit:

He was in love with Frances and she was at Denver University, and to afford to go there, Thomas promoted himself a western travel writing tour. *Because* he went West, he was invited to Alaska. *Because* he went to Alaska, he bought his first movie camera. *Because* he made a film, he lectured with this film around Princeton (where he was taking postgraduate work). *Because* he did that, he was invited by the U.S. Secretary of Interior to come to Washington, D.C., as part of a promotion called "See America First." *Because* of that, Thomas was able to get credentials from D.C. and go back to Chicago and raise $100,000 from meat-packing millionaires who owed him a favor (*because* he'd exposed a confidence man who was blackmailing the meat industrialists). *Because* he had the money, he could hire Harry Chase and head for Europe and World War I and, eventually, work his way to the Middle East where, *because* he was filming General Allenby, he got to know and film Lawrence, an authentic hero, as he and his camel-mounted Arabs were blowing up the Turkish trains all over Arabia. And thereby, Thomas had his handhold on fame, his subject for appearances on the platform all over the world.

And thereby he launched his career of public entertainment and information whose unparalleled success we have been describing here, and as a by-product, almost, his illustrious career as history's most ardent recreational skier.

Under Napoleon, Lowell Thomas would have been a full general.

But he's done well on his own, as things stand.

Suzy and Jill

by DINAH B. WITCHEL

Suzy Chaffee and Jill Kinmont, both racers, are a fascinating study in opposites. Suzy is a triumph of personality and promotional hoopla; she has been a national celebrity for more than a decade. Jill, by virtue of an indomitable spirit, iron determination and wondrous serenity, has been a celebrity even longer, heroine of both book and film, The Other Side of the Mountain. *The two women project the sport's deepest attractions and values, as attested here by Skiing Magazine's managing editor, Dinah Witchel, who has also been a force for women in skiing.*

IN the annual Women's Sports Foundation auction of celebrity memorabilia, a pair of ski boots and a poem donated by Suzy Chaffee brought in $300 to the Foundation. That's less than Dorothy Hamill's skates, but at the finish line with Billie Jean King's Wimbledon racquet, Joe DiMaggio's autographed baseball bat, Pele's soccer jersey, and about four times as much as a memento of Marilyn Monroe.

Now Suzy Chaffee is a skier who never won an Olympic medal, never was in the running for a World Cup, whose claim to being three-time World Freestyle Champion is suspect by some. Why should her cast-off ski boots bring the same price in the marketplace as equipment donated by legendary sports figures like Joe DiMaggio and Billie Jean King?

Because Suzy is probably the best known U.S. skier—of either sex—in this country. She is the skier who was a Revlon "Charlie" girl, the woman who made eating Dannon's yogurt seem X-rated, an Ultrabrite ("How's your love life?") star. She was co-host of last season's "Challenge of the Sexes" TV series, the subject of three pages in *People* magazine, the skier who posed nude on a Sun Valley summit for *Town & Country* magazine, the skier who corralled President Ford at Vail and got an invitation to a White House dinner.

She is also a vehement advocate of women's rights, ski racers' rights, health through sports, and free speech. At first meeting, it's difficult to know whether she is using her career to promote her causes or her causes to promote her career. Her conversation tumbles like a gymnast, somersaulting with a full twist from a recitation of personal glories and grievances to a provocative plan as to how the U.S. government can subsidize athletics. She's doing a handstand on the benefits of chiropractic while you're still struggling with subsidies and is straddling the possibility of a feature film and her own television show while you are trying to locate your coccyx.

It is not for nothing that she used to be called Daffy Chaffee. That was ten years ago and she was the 5-foot 9-inch blond and blue-eyed darling of the U.S. Women's Alpine Team, one of the best U.S. women downhillers to come along in quite a while.

She was naïve and charming with so much energy it exploded like buckshot, nicking interests that ranged from marine biology to photography from clothes to languages. But its target was ultimately skiing.

Suzy started skiing in Rutland, Vermont, when she was four (or three or two and a half, depending on your source) years old. She was the third child in a skiing family—her mother, Stevia, was an ex-racer; her older brothers, Kim and Rick, were to become racers, with Rick a member of the same national teams as his sister.

Even then, Suzy was persistent (or stubborn or competitive, depending on your source). Given her own skis when she was still in diapers, she would zoom up and down the slopes of nearby Pico Peak all day until her wet diapers were frozen. (Her mother tells that story—Suzy observes the air.)

She moved on to race in the Mid-Vermont Council coached by Joe Jones.

"She was very friendly," says Jones, "and a good racer. But no more than any other child."

That's not an attitude that sits well with Suzy. She was receiving neither the applause nor the encouragement that she thought she should.

"That's the first time I learned to turn negativism into I'll-show-em," says Suzy. When she finally arrived at the Olympic Games as a competitor, "I wanted to turn to the TV cameras and thumb my nose at Joe Jones."

With or without sufficient encouragement from Joe Jones, she moved up through the junior ranks, picking up a junior golf championship along the way, then set out for Denver, hoping to ski for the hot coaches of that day, Willy Schaeffler or Bob Beattie. Although she was enrolled at the University of Denver where Schaeffler coached, she was not allowed to ride with the men to practice because of what Suzy understood to be "insurance problems." Denver is a downtown university, and hitchhiking to the slopes became a burden even for a pretty and friendly girl—or perhaps more so for a pretty

and friendly girl. Beattie, at the University of Colorado at Boulder, said she could come work with him, but that was also a considerable commute.

Suzy finally discovered Dave McCoy of Mammoth Mountain, California, who was grooming a pride of female champions. She became one of the Mammoth women. She also switched to the University of Washington and when she wasn't skiing or pursuing her new-found interest in oceanography and photography, she won, as an alternate, a *Glamour* magazine best-dressed-coed contest.

She also won a place on the United States National Alpine Team. In 1966, nineteen years old, she took a fifth in the World Championship Women's Downhill. She spent 1967 on view as the top American woman downhiller—says her then coach Bob Beattie, "Maybe one of the two or three best downhillers in the world."

It was at the end of 1967 in a race at Vail that she crashed and dislocated her hip. It was a painful injury, long in healing. Because of her '67 record, her participation in the 1968 Winter Olympic Games was assured, but says Beattie, "The spark was gone."

She went to Grenoble for the Games, and if not the most successful racer there, she was certainly among the most photographed. That may have had something to do with the way her long frame filled the silver stretch suits which were the United States team's new uniform.

The photographers' flashbulbs ignited another spark in Suzy, and she moved from the summits of the French Alps to the canyons of New York City, intent on becoming a model and a movie star. She was scooped up by the fringes of the jet set, glamorized at parties, caught up in an affair with a millionaire. She did become a movie star of sorts—the star of Willy Bogner's imaginative series of ski films in which her balletic style of skiing began to develop. She also became a model, booked for print ads, TV commercials, and personal appearances.

It was at about that time that freestyle skiing was born. In the beginning, freestyle was a male enclave, but Suzy was there, wanting to be part of the scene. Either farsighted enough or hungry enough to see her future in freestyle, she insisted on competing with the men, sometimes the only woman among them.

Says Doug Pfeiffer, a man instrumental in getting freestyle off the ground and one who has weathered some stormy battles with Suzy: "Suzy is not a naturally talented skier, but she worked hard, she pushed, she improved as a performer.

"She had the nerve and the guts and the drive to stay with the men when no one else would help."

Now, prize money for women's freestyle is equal to and in some seasons tops the money for the men, and freestyle is one of the few sports where the ABC-TV cameras and the spectators rate the women's events over the men's. A good deal of the credit for that rightly belongs to Suzy.

Freestyle skiing is not Suzy's only cause. Her big battle, in fact, began back in 1971 when she realized that some of the amateur athletes were making more money under the table than she was in the public spotlight. She took on the International Olympic Committee in an effort either to purify the Olympics or preferably to permit professional athletes to compete in them. She is, according to her bio sheet, "the only athlete in history from whom Avery Brundage (then IOC president) tried to take away her medals for her reform activities, only she didn't have any."

Brundage (who made such threats to Killy, others) did not take away her nonexistent medals, but neither did he stop her crusade. With Olympic gold medal swimmer (now ABC sports commentator) Donna de Varona and sportsman, uncle-of-Princess Grace, Jack Kelly, she founded the World Sports Foundation, an organization dedicated to removing the barrier between amateur and professional and to bringing some of those under-the-table subsidies to the surface as legitimate aid to athletes.

It was probably the Karl Schranz fiasco at Sapporo in 1972 that did more than any single incident to move the IOC over a little, but Suzy was there early and noisily pushing on that recalcitrant body. She still proselytizes whoever will listen at public forums or in private conversations.

Suzy is a buttonholer. She attends commit-

tee meetings and braces delegates in corridors. She zeros in on influential voices at parties, occasionally leaving her victims breathless and confused, but impressed. Her well-publicized encounter with President Ford at Vail and her subsequent appearance at the White House was put to use to lobby the president for support on government money for athletes. More recently, she has been gleefully setting her sights on Vice-President Mondale and his wife since she learned they were skiers.

Suzy's penchant for saying what she thinks and asking for what she wants has not always made her numero uno among the powers of skiing. A conservative, low-profile group, the skiing establishment does not like skiers who swing or bump chairs literally or metaphorically. Suzy is a swinger and a bumper and she has created antagonisms, particularly among skiers who resent and/or find amusing her efforts at self-promotion.

"She was never captain of the U.S. Women's Team in 1968 (as she claims)," says one 1968 teammate with annoyance. "There was no captain of the women's team."

"Sure she was the world freestyle champion in '71-'72-'73 (as her publicity material states)," says another freestyler. "There wasn't anyone competing against her, and there wasn't even such a title."

"She's lost her femininity," says another (male) skier. "She just uses it to get what she wants."

There are those who mock her passion for clothes; a few, even, who take a kind of quiet pleasure in believing that Suzy is on her way out. After all, she lost out to skier Kiki Cutter in the women Superstars competition, lost out to Phyllis George as host for the second "Challenge of the Sexes," lost out to freestyler Marion Post as the female skier who's done the most for the sport; her freestyle standings have been slipping slowly for the past few seasons.

Given this profile, it is tempting to picture Suzy as a statuesque Don Quixote, idealistic but inept, entangled in the windmills of the world. She certainly identifies herself to some extent with the Knight of the Woeful Countenance. Her ballet performance begins with a dramatic whirling of ski poles (windmills? lances?) and is often accompanied by the music from *Man of La Mancha,* including "The Impossible Dream."

The temptation should be resisted. Take a closer look at the public Suzy: it's Suzy Chaffee Day at Great Gorge/Vernon Valley, New Jersey, a promotional effort to tie Suzy's title as director of skiing more firmly to the area.

At 10 P.M. the night before, she sweeps into the lobby of the Great Gorge Resort Hotel, cheerfully greets the small entourage that has been waiting for her, drops off her bags and an acid comment about the more sexist aspects of the hotel's Playboy Room, and heads out again to the area to check the jump she and Bill O'Leary will be using the next day. It doesn't suit her, much to the irritation of area personnel who will have to spend early morning hours rebuilding it.

Not in bed until after midnight, she's at the area early next morning, hair shining, face shining, swathed in the fox cape she designed herself for a *Town & Country* spread. It's raining. She and O'Leary head for the hill to practice. Skiers gradually begin to line the course, lured by the constant plugs over the loudspeaker. The two attractions warm up carelessly for a while; then Suzy huddles with O'Leary at the top of the small jumping hill. She steps into the track and begins to breathe—deep, controlled breaths, the kind of breathing you learn in TM and yoga, the kind of breathes that help you to take command of your body and your fears.

Suzy flips—and flips again and again, falling twice, taking long minutes before each flip to steady her nerve. O'Leary coaching and encouraging. She's oblivious to the crowd, to the few kids muttering, "Boy, she's really living on her name."

This was the first season Suzy had flipped. She considers it dangerous and no test of skiing skill, but pressure from younger competitors, more demanding audiences finally pushed her into the air upside-down.

Showtime approaches, the loudspeaker becomes more and more insistent, and more and more skiers drift over for the big event. It's still raining. Suzy appears at the top of the hill, and it's as if someone had plugged her into an electric outlet. Energy also visibly radiates from her. She whirls her ski poles and takes off in a run so full of showmanship that even the sticky snow and the short hill does not much dissipate it. It's star quality.

Bill O'Leary calls it less romantically: "Suzy's not the best skier, but she can control that adrenaline . . . she's always professional."

They chat with the kids briefly, O'Leary answering questions, Suzy amiably on standby. At the bottom of the hill, she's hustled off to a nearby condominium where she dries her hair, sprays her scuffed boots with whitener and returns to the rain so ABC-TV can film an interview. Maneuvering so the cameras will get a full view of the Great Gorge/Vernon Valley lodge over her shoulder, she gives them the interview they want: comments on her meeting with the president, a poem, some provocative quotes about the state of athletics in this country. Back to the condo for another hour of radio and print interviews, back into the rain for a photo session with a local photographer who's shown up too late for the freestyle demonstration. She stays on the hill to spend another hour and a half skiing with the local youngsters.

"Wow," she says, shaking off the rain as she comes back into the condominium. "They really helped me with my helicopter."

It's a remark that throws her listeners off-balance.

A star is not supposed to admit that she needs help with her helicopter, let alone that she got it from a group of adolescents.

It's a remark that in a way is very revealing of Suzy. She delights in throwing people off-balance. It helps her retain control and independence. But her pleasure in the time spent on the hill and the skill and commitment of the youngsters is also genuine.

People interested in defining the private Suzy often fall back on clues like that. It's not that Suzy is reticent.

She says, "I want to be as open as I can."

She will answer any question: "I made $70,000 last year. I want a house, I want to travel, but I don't care so much about the money. It's a satisfaction because it means something to society as a measure of my success, of what a woman can do."

She writes revealing poetry which she distributes indiscriminately to friends, press, fans. Poems about her love affairs: "You are the heir of the universe"; about her loneliness: "My loneliness, my loneliness"; about her brothers: "My brothers, what mothers." Poems like a John Denver song: "Yesterday's high dropped me so low . . . does anyone have the answer?"; joyous poems: "I'm alive, I'm alive"; mystic poems: "I am infinite, I am woman."

But despite her rather determined openness, there is a secret core to Suzy which deflects intimacy. It reveals itself more in what she does than in what she says: a series of involvements with men which suggest a hard-to-shake hostility more than an expression of freedom for women. Sensitive to criticism, she seems often to provoke it. She is impatient with those less committed to her causes than she is, impatient with those who counsel tact and time. She has been known to stalk from a meeting and fire off a vituperative personal attack when discussions or events veer from what she considers the right course.

It would be presumptuous to plunge into a deep analysis of why Suzy behaves as she does. Certainly hints of family conflicts which cover three generations and have the overtones of a soap opera are part of it.

Suzy has made great efforts to explore those conflicts and those areas of her psyche that cause her pain. She's been involved in Esalen, est, yoga, Silva Mind Control, and her latest enthusiasm—progressive chiropractic. When eyebrows raise over her spiritual mogul-hopping, she has the grace to laugh: "I get something from each of them and move on."

Probably more important ultimately in who Suzy is and what she will be are her remarkable energy and determination.

Says her brother Kim, head of the Student Ski Association, who considers himself "pretty close" to Suzy: "She's a hard act to precede. She looks for a cause and throws herself into it totally. And she's ahead of her time . . . she was on to women's lib before the ski industry even knew what it was."

Suzy turned thirty recently. Age doesn't seem to be slowing her down, but perhaps age, poetry, and progressive chiropractic are helping her come to terms with herself. "I want to be a writer," she said once, "but I guess I'm not really a writer. I think I'm at my best as a performer."

Involved in promotional assignments for Colgate, she's also flirting with a feature movie, a TV show, a radio show. She's been on the college lecture circuit, preaching and demonstrating health through exercise. And in case you are curious about what The Cause for the next decade will be, it's sports for the aging. That's those of us who, like Suzy, are over thirty.

Suzy's chimes are being rung by a slowly growing interest in something called the Senior Olympics.

"I'd rather call it the Cosmopolitan Olympics. I see freestyle for older skiers—we could do it in three categories, thirty to forty, forty to fifty, fifty to sixty years old. Concentrate on ballet—some of the other tricks are a little hard on the vertebrae. There's no reason why anybody can't learn some freestyle.

"That's what I see as my contribution—a thirty-year-old who's still active in athletics."

Suzywatchers give her more credit. The man who paid $300 for her used ski boots (he met her in passing in Israel, where he saw her buttonhole the Israeli Minister of Defense—before Entebbe—and deliver a lecture on how important it was for the troops to be involved in athletics, particularly in skiing) suggested: "Look up that Holmes quote about the passion of the times. That's what Suzy is all about."

It was Oliver Wendell Holmes Jr.:

Life is action and passion; therefore it is required of a man that he should share the passion and action of his time at peril of being judged not to have lived.

Suzy is not in peril.

The Other Side of the Mountain

Jill Kinmont's life is the stuff of which "B" movies are made. Twenty years ago, Jill Kinmont was a skier, said by some to have been the most promising young racer since Andrea Mead Lawrence. She was headed for a spot on the 1956 Olympic team, maybe even for an Olympic medal.

The scenario begins a few years earlier, when Jill and her best friend, Audra Jo Nicholson, were juniors in the Bishop, California, high school and new members of the ski team. They were coached by Dave McCoy, owner of Mammoth Mountain, whenever they could make the trek up to the mountain from Bishop. They were pretty, popular, secure; life was full, rich and promising.

Scene: Audra Jo contracts polio, which puts her in an iron lung and ultimately confines her to a wheelchair for life.

Scene: Jill carries on and, although racing does not come easily to her, soon proves she's a racer of national caliber. With the help of the press, a romance develops between Jill and the most promising male racer, Bud Werner of Steamboat Springs, Colorado, Sports Illustrated spends a week tagging after them at a Sun Valley, Idaho, race camp, features Jill on its January 31, 1955 cover.

Scene: January 30, 1955. The Snow Cup, Alta, Utah. This race will determine whether Jill gets to go East for the Olympic tryouts. Jill pushes off from the start, hurling down the first part of the course with a time that would give her an almost sure win, prejumps a knoll too late, and hurtles twisting into the air toward the trees and the spectators. She lands on her back. Her spine is broken. She will never ski, never walk again.

Scene: Months in hospitals, months in the California Rehabilitation Center where she learned to make the most of her limited movement. Her spine had been fractured at the fifth cervical vertebra, meaning she had no muscular control from slightly below her shoulders down, and only limited movement in her arms—she could raise them but had to let gravity lower them.

Scene: Visitors. Family, friends, lovers. Bud Werner writes frequently and visits occasionally, but as he realizes the extent of her injuries, visits and letters become less and less frequent, finally stop. Skier/pilot/adventurer Dick ("Mad Dog") Buek, an early skiing friend, comes roaring back into her life, taking her for a wild ride down Santa Monica Boulevard in her wheelchair, at one point blocking traffic in four directions when he stops in the middle of an intersection to give her a kiss on the nose.

Scene: Jill's recovery is good. She is enrolled at UCLA and is invited to stay at Buek's home in northern California so she can attend the Nationals. That summer, Buek flies down frequently to visit. He wants to marry her. He has already designed the house where they will live.

Scene: Buek is killed in a plane crash.

Scene: With the guidance and encouragement of a close friend, Lee Zadroga, she finishes college.

Scene: Lee Zadroga dies.

Scene: The family moves to Washington State, where her father has a new job. She writes to Bud Werner to congratulate and encourage him on his racing successes.

Scene: Bud Werner is killed in an avalanche.

Scene: Her father dies of a brain tumor.

Scene: A cousin, a childhood friend, now grown with six children of his own, falls from a tree and breaks his spine in almost the same place Jill did. He retains the use of both arms and one hand.

Scene: Through it all, Jill carries on, and as the music comes up and over, we see her wheeling off into the sunset, chin up, courage unflagging.

They did make a movie out of Jill Kinmont's life. It is called *The Other Side of the Mountain,* and it's not all bad. It stars a girl named Marilyn Hassett who, at one point in her career, was stepped on by an elephant and was herself paralyzed for more than six months. Perhaps because of that, she successfully avoids chewing the scenery—overdramatizing her role as Jill. The movie also stars Beau Bridges as Dick Buek. Bridges did a lot of research on the Buek character, including long conversations with Jill and old friends of Buek's such as Ed Scott of Sun Valley.

It features some, though not nearly enough, skiing sequences, notable mostly for what skiing was like in the fifties, including reindeer sweaters, headbands, long wooden skis, lots of stemming even on the race course, no lift lines—for that matter, not very many lifts—and lonely, empty mountains. (All of the skiing sequences were shot at Mammoth during nine days in April. Look at that April snow!)

It is not a *good* movie, either. The producers were unable to resist the temptation of turning Jill's life into a catalogue of tragedies and triumphs, a barren cliché of a pretty girl who overcomes her handicap and devotes her life to others. The film overlooks not so much the physical struggle involved in learning to live as a near-quadriplegic—although that too suffers from trite presentation—as the mental and emotional struggles that changed the girl crumpled at the bottom of the mountain to the independent, self-confident woman whose wheelchair seems merely a place for her to sit.

Jill said, after seeing a screening of the film, "I cried. We all cried—crew and everyone—for that poor girl up on the screen. But I had no sense that it was me."

The book upon which the movie is based, a biography of Jill by E. G. Valens originally titled *A Long Way Up,* now reissued in paperback as *The Other Side of the Mountain,* much more effectively resists sentimentality and, simply by piling chronological detail upon chronological detail, gives a better sense of what it was like to be a young ski racer and of what Jill's stubborn determination achieved and is achieving for her. The book also effectively avoids that climax which the moviemakers apparently could not resist: Yes, Jill literally wheels off into the sunset, an inspiration to us all.

The story of Jill Kinmont is indeed an inspiration to us all, but not for the sentimental reasons the movie suggests—the plucky girl who perseveres over her handicap. Jill has done much more than merely persevere: she was a girl who lived only for skiing; with skiing taken away from her, she carved out a rich, full life for herself, and

she has done it on her terms.

Early on, prodded by Buek, Audra Jo, and Andrea Lawrence, Jill rejected self-pity as a way to deal with her new condition. As soon as it was possible, she got out of the hospital and into the rehabilitation center, where she learned to make the most of what muscular control she had left. With the help of some ingenious devices invented by therapists at the center, she learned to feed herself, push her own wheelchair, paint and write. Anxious to break away from the isolated world of the handicapped at the rehabilitation center, she enrolled in two courses at UCLA: art and history.

Jill still kept in touch with her skiing friends, writing letters, visiting Bishop and Mammoth frequently. Dave McCoy offered her a job as manager of the Mammoth Mountain ski shop, and she accepted. What an appealing thought that must have been—a job that would keep her independent and self-sufficient but, at the same time, permit her to stay in the world of skiing where she was known and loved, to be at Mammoth which she loved. She would have been the center of attention, a mini-celebrity to the thousands of skiers who visit Mammoth.

Jill likes attention. She likes to see her picture in magazines, to read about herself in newspapers, to appear on television, and to have a movie made about her life. She has scrapbooks full of clippings which she will show to visitors without false modesty.

So Jill began to study business administration at UCLA, preparing herself to take over the Mammoth shop. But somewhere along the line, Jill changed. Experiencing her mind stretching and strengthening as her body used to do when she trained for races, enjoying the chore of tutoring two or three neighborhood children, Jill decided that what she really wanted to do was teach. Adjusting her course of study at UCLA was no problem; keeping her grades high meant only hard work. What Jill hadn't bargained on was the educational bureacracy.

To teach in California, she needed a certificate from the School of Education. That body turned her down flat; in order to teach in a Los Angeles public school, she would have to deal with stairs, and anyone could see she couldn't do that in a wheelchair. Since Jill had successfully dealt with all the stairs on the UCLA campus for more than four years, she was confused and annoyed. She struggled for more than two years with the Catch-22 maze which allowed that she couldn't teach without a certificate, that you couldn't get a certificate even if you had the promise of a job, because you couldn't get into the School of Education because you couldn't manage stairs which you had been managing for more than five years by now.

One of the things Jill is blessed with is quiet determination and a cool grasp of reality. She knew the things she could do and couldn't do. She couldn't drive a car and she couldn't bear children; she could write, paint, think and teach school. The determination had made her a skiing champion; the same determination made her, eventually, a certified teacher.

She has been, for nine years now, a teacher of remedial reading at an affluent Beverly Hills elementary school in affluent Beverly Hills. The school bypassed the problem of stairs by building a few ramps where they would be most useful.

There is an irony in the fact that Jill finally succeeded in getting her teaching job in one of the more prosperous neighborhoods in the United States. Because what she really wanted to do was teach underprivileged children.

She got around that, too. Able to make frequent visits to Bishop in the summer, she rediscovered the Paiute Indian Reservation near Bishop, discovered that many of the Indian children were dropping out of public school before they learned to read. With the cooperation of the Indian community, she started a summer school on the reservation, teaching reading to a group of children in a room in the Valley Presbyterian Church. So successful was the program that the enrollment rose from twenty children in the first year to seventy-five children last year and may, in fact, have succeeded itself out of existence. For this year, Jill has taken a leave of absence from her Beverly Hills school, leased her house in Los Angeles, and will work as a remedial-reading teacher in the Bishop school, teaching many of the Indian children who would be enrolled in her summer school. She'll live in the house that she and her mother bought from the proceeds of her work as technical advisor on the movie, and her spare time is being devoted to the establishment and administration of the Jill Kinmont Indian Education Fund to be used for the Indians of Owens Valley, where Bishop is located. A benefit premiere of the movie raised $6,000 for the fund; a Masonic auxiliary, the Rainbow Girls, raised $22,000 as a charitable project; and Jill herself is making personal appearances in many cities where the film is scheduled to open.

Her personal appearances should make quite an impression on luncheon and movie audiences. For Jill Kinmont is startlingly attractive. Startling because even though you have advance knowledge that she works every day, that she spends her summers in the Sierra, the expectation is that a person who is invalided will look like an invalid—pale, somewhat wistful, with a blanket over the lap and ruffles at the neck. Not Jill.

It was once said of her, "She didn't mind using a wheelchair, but she didn't intend to look as if she belonged in one." She has succeeded again. Jill wears shirts that occasionally dip to her cleavage, skirts that bare her legs above the knee; she has long shiny hair, startling blue eyes, and a California tan. Approaching forty, she looks in her twenties. Her movements are so graceful that it is only when she balances a cup of coffee on the back of her hand or brushes an imaginary strand of hair off her forehead—a habitual gesture—that you remember that she is not sitting in a wheelchair because she wants to.

More remarkable than her physical skills is Jill's freedom from self-pity and guilt. Of course, Jill did not win all these physical and emotional battles in a vacuum. Jill's family, for instance, is apparently as free from excess emotional baggage as she. It probably never occurred to her parents that the things they did to accommodate Jill's injuries—selling the ranch, turning their lives around to move to the city—were sacrifices. Jill was a daughter who had certain needs, as their two sons also had certain needs, and all those needs would be met to the best of the family's ability. Her friends—skiing friends, school friends, teaching friends—alternately prodded and encouraged her. To those people, feeling sorry for yourself or settling for less than you were capable of, whatever the circumstances, was simply not accepted behavior.

Almost every skier has known at least for a moment on the mountain that burst of clarity, when the silence and the expanse seem to put the world into perspective, when inflation, recession, détente, and your own personal ambitions and frustrations each find their proper niches in the universe, and it all does make sense after all. Perhaps all those years on the mountain have helped Jill Kinmont retain that kind of clear-headed perspective; perhaps it is that quality in her which permits skiing to continue to claim Jill as one of its own.

Truman Capote: An Interview

by **DICK NEEDHAM**

No one ever accused Truman Capote of understatement in describing himself. Here the author of In Cold Blood *and other honored books builds a tale while tattling through lunch at an exquisite New York restaurant. His wary foil is Dick Needham, long-time editor in chief of* Ski, *an artful dodger of the precipices of publishing.*

SOME people can humiliate you in the most charming, disarming way. When the charming, disarming humiliator is novelist Truman Capote, it even makes you feel good—because if you listen closely, he will tip you on the secrets of his craft . . .

"I prefer not to use a tape recorder," he told me as I meekly plugged in my tape recorder, "and I seldom take notes. When you have all the material on tape, your editorial selectivity isn't operating. It's like panning for gold. If you do what I do, the dross strains away and you remember only what you want to remember."

If you do what Capote does, you have someone read you the front page of *The New York Times,* then retire to the typewriter and record it—all without a missed word or beat.

"I've developed 95 percent recall. Several years ago I had a nine-hour conversation with Marlon Brando in Japan. I returned to New York the following day and wrote it up verbatim. It ran three hundred typewritten pages. The interview appeared in the *New Yorker.*"

So here I am, sitting at La Petite Marmite with the controversial and eccentric novelist/ reporter/playwright Truman Capote, brought to the lair of American literature's *enfant terrible* by Jacky Ruette, a mutual skiing friend who owns this restaurant where Capote and his gang often gather . . .

"But the material," Capote continues, "is not as important as the presentation. The use of sprung rhythms and unusual but legitimate punctuation are what make a story interesting." Good writing, he'll tell you, is really just a matter of style.

Capote is also a study in style—a style, he would have you believe, that he carries into his skiing. So with that, I switch on the tape recorder. (I do not have 95 percent recall and no one around *Ski* has yet volunteered the time to read aloud the front page of the *Times* to help me develop it.)

Truman Capote is fifty-six and he is short— 5 foot 3, the statisticians who record these things will tell you, with a pate of thinning, sandy hair, a prominent forehead, melancholy, basset-hound-shaped blue eyes and a head that seems too large for his body. His voice is nasal, high-pitched—he would say "sassy"—and he talks slowly in his Louisiana-native way, one sentence meandering into another without punctuation, like a layer of fog creeping down-mountain softly and silently blanketing everything in its path.

He is also an uncommonly conscious stylist: *Other Voices/Other Rooms, The Grass Harp, Breakfast at Tiffany's, The Muses Are Heard, In Cold Blood,* his recent *Music for Chameleons* and his now-in-progress *Answered Prayers* ("The protagonists are excellent skiers—one chapter takes place in St. Moritz")—his works are characterized by a unique inventiveness and psychological insight, what *New York Times* critic William Goyen called a "talent for catching the offbeat nature of people."

But it was in Capote's best-selling *In Cold Blood* that he departed from the genre, to a literary form that combined fictional techniques with journalism (Capote still believes that creative reporting—the nonfiction novel—will be the dominant literary form of the future). And it was to translate his six thousand pages of notes into *In Cold Blood* that he withdrew to his ski house in Verbier, Switzerland. An appropriate place to begin an interview with Truman Capote the Skier, so let's pick it up there . . .

What's your ski house in Verbier like?

My house is small, a cozy chalet way high on the mountain. I love it—I've spent as long as six months at a time there. You know, Verbier has grown so much. When I came there in 1956 there were perhaps forty chalets and only two small hotels. Then the Belgians lost the Congo—and ever since, Verbier has been bulging with Belgians . . . bulging Belgians.

Verbier is infinitely better than St. Mortiz or Gstaad. It's not chic, and it's not crowded. Gstaad is a joke. I often go to Gstaad because it's just across the valley. But Verbier has very long runs—I don't like to yo-yo, I don't like getting back up the mountain—and it is in sun all day long. Verbier also, unfortunately, attracts Italians. Last season I was hit by one. I was going slow—and this big Italian came around this turn . . . I don't think he had ever been on a pair of skis in his life . . . and slammed into me. I was black and blue for months.

Had you skied before your arrival in Verbier, before

Truman Capote, skiing in disguise, dons misleadingly plebian outfit

the Belgians and Italians had put out contracts on you?

My, I've skied just about everywhere—in Europe, in the United States, even in Japan. I've skied, you know, since I was twelve years old. I first skied in Colorado, with my father—who was then married to one or another of his seven wives. My father was mad about two things—motorcycles and Colorado. He loved Colorado. Steamboat is where we went, and I've been back there often. I've also skied at Vail, but Vail is Disneyland—it's not my kind of place.

I find skiing in Utah incredibly crude—it's like a second-rate boys' camp in the Adirondacks. All those Mormons running around in black clothes and black ties—it's like Chanel without jewelry.

The place I really like most is Sun Valley. And I like Grey Rocks in Quebec—but not in February. In fact, it's the coldest place I've ever been. When I was last there, I stayed for ten days—not for ten days of skiing but because I was so knocked out by the cold. I hate to ski in the cold.

The most interesting skiing I've found is in Japan, in Hokkaido. I love Japan, I love its cultural charm. The Japanese have more taste than the French—such attention to detail. When they do something, they do it right.

How do you rate yourself as a skier?

I have the perfect body for skiing. I'm short, my balance is excellent, and I have two very strong legs, which I've developed really through swimming—I still swim 2 miles a day. I can do just about anything on skis. I have a tremendous amount of endurance. Most people I know think I'm a very good skier.

I have a certain element of—well, courage really. I do things on skis that other people won't do.

How would you rate others you know as skiers—say Jacqueline Onassis, John Kenneth Galbraith, William Buckley?

Jackie? You know, that's funny . . . I've seen her ski often but I really can't describe the way she skis. She kind of cross-country skis. Cross-country—all that shuffling along and whatnot—bores me to death. I only do it with friends who can't ski. They get a kick out of it, but I perish of boredom.

Galbraith and Buckley are strictly Mutt and Jeff—an amusing cartoon. I saw Galbraith, all 6 foot 7 of him, on short skis at St. Moritz, and I wondered "What kind of freaks are they letting in here?"

You once said "The thing that's most important is style—not what I'm saying but how I'm saying it, manner over matter." Does this also translate to your skiing?

Absolutely. I can always tell a fine skier by the way he moves back. Bad skiers are always in a crouch—as if some horrible disaster is about to happen. They're always clutching their poles. Elegance in skiing is when you're not in a crouch, when you're leaning back, when you're in complete control, when you're using your poles as little as possible . . . That's the way I ski most of the time.

You also once said "Gregariousness is the enemy of art." How does someone as socially active as yourself live with that? Doesn't skiing really foster gregariousness?

When I do things on skis, I don't do them to show off—and I usually do them alone. I don't like to ski with other people because I don't want to be conscious of them. I don't want to be worried about being behind them, or ahead of them. Skiing gives me a terrific sense of freedom—and I would define that freedom as not having to be around other people.

What about autograph hounds, celebrity groupies, people who recognize you on the hill? Do you find them bothersome when you're skiing?

Recognition is not a problem. I wear a ski mask. I've got sun-sensitive skin.

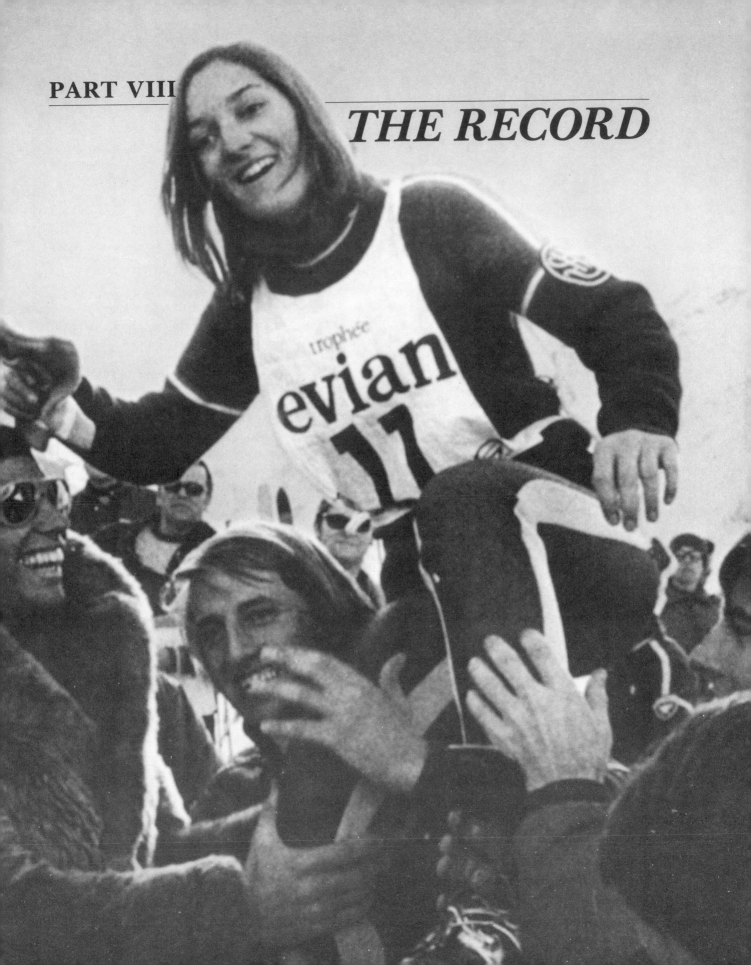

WINTER OLYMPIC GAMES

Although the ancient Greeks who staged history's earliest Olympic Games are not recorded as having displayed any interest in winter sports, the first site of the Games was an Alpine setting. The view from Mount Olympus was one of snow-clad peaks, wooded slopes, and wild valleys. Despite this prophetic setting, it was to take more than three thousand years before winter sports became part of the Olympic ceremonial. The modern Olympic era began with the Summer Games at Athens in 1896, but another twenty-eight years elapsed until the first Winter Games were staged at Chamonix, France, in 1924. Since then, the Winter Games have become a brilliant ornament in the Olympic tapestry, laced with great moments, drama, pageantry and spectacular individual performances.

The International Olympic Committee (IOC) makes no rules concerning any of the sports or individual events on the Olympic program. The rules of the international federation for each sport involved apply. Thus, the rules of the Fédération Internationale de Ski (FIS) govern the skiing events. However, the IOC does have rules defining amateurism (you are supposed to be one) and the number of entries permitted for each event. For skiing, that number is four per event per country, regardless of the number of high-ranking racers a nation may have. For this reason, the order of finish at Olympic races can be used only as an approximate indication of the ranking of the world's top ski racers and racing nations.

Here are the skiing champions and other records for the Winter Olympic Games from 1924 to 1980:

NORDIC EVENTS (Men)

Year	Champion	Runner-up	Third
15-kilometer Cross-country			
1956	Hallgeir Brenden Norway	Sixten Jernberg Sweden	Pavel Kolchin USSR
1960	Hallgeir Brenden Norway	Sixten Jernberg Sweden	Veikko Häkulinen Finland
1964	Eero Mäntyranta Finland	Harald Grönningen Norway	Sixten Jernberg Sweden
1968	Harald Grönningen Norway	Eero Mäntyranta Finland	Gunnar Larsson Sweden
1972	Sven-Ake Lundback Sweden	Fedor Smaschov USSR	Ivar Formo Norway
1976	N. Bajukov USSR	E. Beliaev USSR	A. Koivisto Finland
1980	Thomas Wassberg Sweden	Juha Mieto Finland	Ove Aunli Sweden

372

Year	Champion	Runner-up	Third

18-kilometer Cross-country

Year	Champion	Runner-up	Third
1924	Thorleif Haug Norway	Johan Grøttumsbraaten Norway	Tapani Niku Finland
1928	Johan Grøttumsbraaten Norway	Ole Hegge Norway	Reidar Ødegaard Norway
1932	Sven Utterström Sweden	Axel Vikström Sweden	Veli Saarinen Finland
1936	Erik-August Larsson Sweden	Oddbjørn Hagen Norway	Pekka Niemi Finland
1948	Martin Lundström Sweden	Nils Östensson Sweden	Gunnar Eriksson Sweden
1952	Hallgeir Brenden Norway	Tapio Makela Finland	Paavo Lonkila Finland

30-kilometer Cross-country

Year	Champion	Runner-up	Third
1956	Veikko Häkulinen Finland	Sixten Jernberg Sweden	Pavel Kolchin USSR
1960	Sixten Jernberg Sweden	Rolf Rämgärd Sweden	Nikolai Anikin USSR
1964	Eero Mäntyranta Finland	Harald Grönningen Norway	Igor Voronckiken USSR
1968	Franco Nones Italy	Odd Martinsen Norway	Eero Mäntyranta Finland
1972	Vyacheslav Vedenin USSR	Paal Tyldum Norway	John Haroviken Norway
1976	S. Saveliev USSR	Bill Koch USA	I. Garanin USSR
1980	Nikolai Zimyatov USSR	Vasily Rochev USSR	Ivan Lebanov Bulgaria

50-kilometer Cross-country

Year	Champion	Runner-up	Third
1924	Thorleif Haug Norway	Thoralf Strømstad Norway	Johan Grøttumsbraaten Norway
1928	Per Hedlund Sweden	Gustaf Jonsson Sweden	Volger Andersson Sweden
1932	Veli Saarinen Finland	Välnö Liikkanen Finland	Arne Rustadstuen Norway
1936	Elis Viklund Sweden	Axel Wikström Sweden	Nils Englund Sweden
1948	Nils Karlsson Sweden	Harald Erikkson Sweden	Benjamin Vanninen Finland
1952	Veikko Häkulinen Finland	Eero Kohlemainen Finland	Magnar Estenstad Norway
1956	Sixten Jernberg Sweden	Veikko Häkulinen Finland	Fydor Terentiev USSR
1960	Kalevi Hämälälnen Finland	Veikko Häkulinen Finland	Rolf Rämgärd Sweden
1964	Sixten Jernberg Sweden	Assar Rönnlund Sweden	Arto Tiainen Finland
1968	Ole Ellefsaeter Norway	Viatches Vedenine USSR	Josef Haas Switzerland
1972	Paal Tyldum Norway	Magne Myrmo Norway	Vyacheslav Vedenin USSR
1976	I. Formo Norway	G. D. Klause East Germany	B. Södergren Sweden
1980	Nikolai Zimyatov USSR	Juha Mieto Finland	Alexander Zavalov USSR

15-kilometer Combined

Year	Champion	Runner-up	Third
1972	Karl Luck East Germany	Urban Hettich West Germany	Ulrich Wehling East Germany

Year	Champion	Runner-up	Third
Nordic Combined (Cross-country and Jumping)			
1924	Thorleif Haug Norway	Thoralf Strømstad Norway	Johan Grøttumsbraaten Norway
1928	Johan Grøttumsbraaten Norway	Hans Vinjarengen Norway	John Snesrud Norway
1932	Johan Grøttumsbraaten Norway	Ole Stenen Norway	Hans Vinjarengen Norway
1936	Oddbjørn Hagen Norway	Olaf Hoffsbakken Norway	Sverre Brodahl Norway
1948	Heikku Hasu Finland	Martti Huhtala Finland	Sven Israelsson Sweden
1952	Simon Slattvik Norway	Heikku Hasu Finland	Sverre Stenerson Norway
1956	Sverre Stenerson Norway	Bengt Ericsson Sweden	Francis Gron-Gasienca Poland
1960	Georg Thoma Germany	Tormod Knutsen Norway	Nicolai Gusakov USSR
1964	Tormod Knutsen Norway	Nicolai Kiselev USSR	Georg Thoma Germany
1968	Franz Keller West Germany	A. Kaelin Sweden	A. Kunz Germany
1972	Ulrich Wehling East Germany	Rauno Miettinen Finland	Karl Luck East Germany
1976	U. Wehling East Germany	U. Hettich West Germany	K. Winkler East Germany
1980	U. Wehling East Germany	J. Karjalainen Finland	K. Winkler East Germany
Biathlon			
1960	Klas Lestander Sweden	Antti Tyrvainen Finland	Alexandr Privalov USSR
1964	Vladimir Melanin USSR	Olav Jordet Norway	Alexandr Privalov USSR
1968	A. Solberg Norway	V. Tikhonov USSR	A. Goundartsev USSR
1972	Maynar Solberg Norway	Hanyorg Knauthe East Germany	Lars-Goeran Arwidson Sweden
1976	Nikolai Kruglov USSR	Heikki Ikola Finland	Alek Elizarov USSR
Biatholon (20-kilometers)			
1980	Anatoly Alabyev USSR	Frank Ulrich East Germany	Eberhard Rosch East Germany
Biatholon (10-kilometers)			
1980	Frank Ulrich East Germany	Vladimir Aliken USSR	Anatoly Alabyev USSR
Jumping			
1924	Jacob Tullin-Thams Norway	Narve Bonna Norway	Thorleif Haug Norway
1928	Alf Andersen Norway	Sigmund Ruud Norway	Rudolf Purkert Czechoslovakia
1932	Birger Ruud Norway	Hans Beck Norway	Kaare Wahlberg Norway
1936	Birger Ruud Norway	Sven Eriksson Sweden	Reidar Andersen Norway
1948	Petter Hugsted Norway	Birger Ruud Norway	Thorleif Schjelderup Norway

Year	Champion	Runner-up	Third
1952	Arnfinn Bergmann Norway	Torbjorn Falkanger Norway	Karl Holmstrom Sweden
1956	Antti Hyvaringen Finland	Aulis Kellakorpi Finland	Harry Glass West Germany
1960	Helmut Recknagel West Germany	N. Halonen Finland	O. Leodolter Austria

Jumping ("Normal" Hill, 70 Meters)

Year	Champion	Runner-up	Third
1964	Veikko Kankkonen Finland	Toralf Engan Norway	Torgeir Brandtzaeg Norway
1968	Jiri Raska Czechoslovakia	Reinhold Bachler Austria	J. Preiml Austria
1972	Yukio Kasaya Japan	Akitsugu Konno Japan	Seijii Aochi Japan
1976	H. G. Aschenbach East Germany	J. Danneberg East Germany	K. Schnabl Austria
1980	A. Innauer Austria	Hirokazu Yagi (tie) Japan	Manfred Deckert (tie) East Germany

Jumping ("Big" Hill, 90 Meters)

Year	Champion	Runner-up	Third
1964	Toralf Engan Norway	Viekko Kankkonen Finland	Torgeir Brandtzaeg Norway
1968	Vladimir Beloussov USSR	Jiri Raska Czechoslovakia	Lars Grini Norway
1972	Wojciech Fortuna Poland	Walter Steiner Switzerland	Rainer Schmidt East Germany
1976	K. Schnabl Austria	A. Innauer Austria	H. Glass East Germany
1980	Joyko Tormanen Finland	Hubert Neuper Austria	Jari Puikkonen Finland

40-kilometer (4 × 10 Kilometers) Cross-country Relay

Year	Champion	Runner-up	Third
1936	Finland	Norway	Sweden
1948	Sweden	Finland	Norway
1952	Finland	Norway	Sweden
1956	USSR	Finland	Sweden
1960	Finland	Norway	USSR
1964	Sweden	Finland	USSR
1968	Norway	Sweden	Finland
1972	USSR	Norway	Switzerland
1976	East Germany	USSR	Norway
1980	USSR	Norway	Finland

30-kilometer (4 × 7.5 Kilometers) Biathlon Relay
(Each man skis 7.5 kilometers and shoots twice)

Year	Champion	Runner-up	Third
1968	USSR	Norway	Sweden
1972	USSR	Finland	East Germany
1976	USSR	Finland	East Germany
1980	USSR	East Germany	West Germany

ALPINE EVENTS (Men)

Year	Champion	Runner-up	Third

Downhill

Year	Champion	Runner-up	Third
1948	Henri Orellier France	Franz Gabl Austria	Karl Molitor Switzerland

Year	Champion	Runner-up	Third
1952	Zeno Colo Italy	Othmar Schneider Austria	Christian Pravda Austria
1956	Anton Sailer Austria	Raymond Fellay Switzerland	Andreas Molterer Austria
1960	Jean Vuarnet France	Hans Peter Lanig Germany	Guy Perillat France
1964	Egon Zimmerman Austria	Leo Lacroix France	Wolfgang Barteis Germany
1968	Jean-Claude Killy France	Guy Perillat France	Jean-Daniel Daetwyler Switzerland
1972	Bernhard Russi Switzerland	Roland Collombin Switzerland	Heinrich Nessner Austria
1976	Franz Klammer Austria	Bernhard Russi Switzerland	Herbert Plank Italy
1980	Leonard Stock Austria	Peter Wirnsberger Austria	Stephen Podborski Canada

Slalom

Year	Champion	Runner-up	Third
1948	Edi Reinalter Switzerland	James Couttet France	Henri Oreiller France
1952	Othmar Schneider Austria	Stein Eriksen Norway	Guttorm Berge Norway
1956	Anton Sailer Austria	Chiharu Igaya Japan	Stig Sollander Sweden
1960	Ernst Hinterseer Austria	Mathias Leitner Austria	Charles Bozon France
1964	Josef Stiegler Austria	William Kidd USA	Jimmy Heuga USA
1968	Jean-Claude Killy France	Herbert Huber Austria	Alfred Matt Austria
1972	Francisco Fernandez-Ochoa Spain	Gustavo Thoeni Italy	Rolando Thoeni Italy
1976	Piero Gros Italy	Gustavo Thoeni Italy	Willy Frommelt Liechtenstein
1980	Ingemar Stenmark Sweden	Phil Mahre USA	Jacques Leuthy Switzerland

Giant Slalom

Year	Champion	Runner-up	Third
1952	Stein Eriksen Norway	Christian Pravda Austria	Toni Spiss Austria
1956	Anton Sailer Austria	Andreas Molterer Austria	Walter Schuster Austria
1960	Roger Staub Switzerland	Josef Stiegler Austria	Ernst Hinterseer Austria
1964	François Bonlieu France	Karl Schranz Austria	Josef Stiegler Austria
1968	Jean-Claude Killy France	Willi Favre Switzerland	Heinrich Messner Austria
1972	Gustavo Thoeni Italy	Edmund Bruggmann Switzerland	Werner Mattle Switzerland
1976	Heini Hemmi Switzerland	Ernst Good Sweden	Ingemar Stenmark Sweden
1980	Ingemar Stenmark Sweden	Andreas Wenzel Liechtenstein	Hans Enn Austria

Alpine Combined*

Year	Champion	Runner-up	Third
1936	Franz Pfnür Germany	Gustav Lautschner Germany	Émile Allais France
1948	Henri Oreiller France	Karl Molitor Switzerland	James Couttet France

NORDIC EVENTS (Women)

Year	Champion	Runner-up	Third

5-kilometer Cross-country

Year	Champion	Runner-up	Third
1964	Claudia Boyarskikh USSR	Mirja Lehtonen Finland	Alevtina Koltjina USSR
1968	Toini Gustafsson Sweden	Galina Koulacova USSR	Alevtina Koltjina USSR
1972	Galina Koulacova USSR	Marjatta Kajosmaa Finland	Helena Sikolova Czechoslovakia
1976	H. Takalo Finland	R. Smetatina USSR	N. Baldycheva USSR
1980	R. Smetatina USSR	H. Riihivuori Finland	K. Jeriova Czechoslovakia

10-kilometer Cross-country

Year	Champion	Runner-up	Third
1952	Lydia Wideman Finland	Mirja Hietamies Finland	Siri Rantanen Finland
1956	Lyubov Kozyreva USSR	Radija Yeroshina USSR	Sonja Edstrom Sweden
1960	Maria Gusakova USSR	Lyubov Kozyreva USSR	Radija Yeroshina USSR
1964	Claudia Boyarskikh USSR	Eudokia Mekshilo USSR	Maria Gusakova USSR
1968	Toini Gustafsson Sweden	Berit Mördre Norway	Inger Aufles Norway
1972	Galina Koulacova USSR	Alevtina Olunina USSR	Marjatta Kajosmaa Finland
1976	R. Smetatina USSR	H. Takalo Finland	G. Kulakova USSR
1980	B. Petzold East Germany	H. Riihivuori Finland	H. Takalo Finland

15-kilometer (3 × 5 Kilometers) Cross-country Relay

Year	Champion	Runner-up	Third
1956	Finland	USSR	Sweden
1960	Sweden	USSR	Finland
1964	USSR	Sweden	Finland
1968	Norway	Sweden	USSR
1972	USSR	Finland	Norway

20-kilometer (4 × 5 kilometers) Cross-country Relay

Year	Champion	Runner-up	Third
1976	USSR	Finland	East Germany
1980	East Germany	USSR	Norway

ALPINE EVENTS (Women)

Year	Champion	Runner-up	Third

Downhill

Year	Champion	Runner-up	Third
1948	Hedi Schlunegger Switzerland	Trude Beiser Austria	Resi Hammerer Austria
1952	Trude Jochum-Beiser Austria	Annemarie Buchner Germany	Giuliana Minuzzo Italy

Year	Champion	Runner-up	Third
1956	Madeleine Berthod Switzerland	Frieda Dänzer Switzerland	Lucille Wheeler Canada
1960	Heidi Biebl Germany	Penny Pitou USA	Traudi Hecher Austria
1964	Christl Haas Austria	Edith Zimmermann Austria	Traudi Hecher Austria
1968	Olga Pall Austria	Isabelle Mir France	Christl Haas Austria
1972	Marie-Theres Nadig Switzerland	Annemarie Proell Austria	Susan Corrock USA
1976	Rosi Mittermaier West Germany	Brigitte Totsching Austria	Cindy Nelson USA
1980	Annemarie Proell-Moser Austria	Hanni Wenzel Liechtenstein	Marie-Theres Nadig Switzerland

Slalom

Year	Champion	Runner-up	Third
1948	Gretchen Fraser USA	Antoinette Meyer Switzerland	Erika Mahringer Austria
1952	Andrea Mead Lawrence USA	Ossi Reichert Germany	Annemarie Buchner Germany
1956	René Colliard Switzerland	Regina Schöpf Austria	Yevgeniya Sidorova USSR
1960	Anne Heggtveit Canada	Betsy Snite USA	Barbi Henneberger Germany
1964	Christine Goitschel France	Marielle Goitschel France	Jean Saubert USA
1968	Marielle Goitschel France	Nancy Greene Canada	Annie Famose France
1972	Barbara Cochran USA	Daniele Debernard France	Florence Steurer France
1976	Rossi Mittermaier West Germany	Claudia Giordani Italy	Hanni Wenzel Liechtenstein
1980	Hanni Wenzel Liechtenstein	Christa Kinhofer West Germany	Erika Hess Switzerland

Giant Slalom

Year	Champion	Runner-up	Third
1952	Andrea Mead Lawrence USA	Dagmar Rom Austria	Annemarie Buchner Germany
1956	Ossi Reichert Germany	Josefine Frandl Austria	Dorothea Hochleitner Austria
1960	Ivonne Rüegg Switzerland	Penny Pitou USA	C. Chenal-Minuzzo Italy
1964	Marielle Goitschel France	Christine Goitschel France Jean Saubert USA	
1968	Nancy Greene Canada	Annie Famose France	Fernande Bochatay Switzerland
1972	Marie-Theres Nadig Switzerland	Annemarie Proell Austria	Wiltrud Drexel Austria
1976	Kathy Kreiner Canada	Rossi Mittermaier West Germany	Danielle Debernard France
1980	Hanni Wenzel Liechtenstein	Irene Epple West Germany	Perrine Pelen France

Alpine Combined*

Year	Champion	Runner-up	Third
1936	Christl Cranz Germany	Kathe Grasegger Germany	Laila Schou-Nilsen Norway

Year	Champion	Runner-up	Third
1948	Trude Beiser Austria	Gretchen Fraser USA	Erika Mahringer Austria

*No medals awarded after 1948; the FIS, however, makes awards to winners since 1956 of the best combined score of the three Olympic Alpine events. The 1936 and 1948 Olympic Alpine combined events were based only on slalom and downhill races.

WINTER OLYMPIC GAMES SITES

I	Chamonix, France	1924
II	St. Moritz, Switzerland	1928
III	Lake Placid, New York, U.S.A.	1932
IV	Garmisch-Partenkirchen, Germany	1936
V	St. Moritz, Switzerland	1948
VI	Oslo, Norway	1952
VII	Cortina, Italy	1956
VIII	Squaw Valley, California, U.S.A.	1960
IX	Innsbruck, Austria	1964
X	Grenoble, France	1968
XI	Sapporo, Japan	1972
XII	Innsbruck, Austria	1976
XIII	Lake Placid, New York U.S.A.	1980
XIV	Sarajevo, Yugoslavia	1984

OLYMPIC GOLD MEDALS WON BY NATIONS YEAR BY YEAR

Year	Country	Men	Women	Total
1924	Norway	4		4
1928	Norway	3		3
	Sweden	1		1
1932	Norway	2		2
	Finland	1		1
	Sweden	1		1
1936	Norway	2	0	2
	Sweden	2	0	2
	Germany	1	1	2
	Finland	1	0	1
1948	Sweden	3	0	3
	France	2	0	2
	Switzerland	1	1	2
	Finland	1	0	1
	Norway	1	0	1
	Austria	0	1	1
	USA	0	1	1
1952	Norway	4	0	4
	Finland	2	1	3
	Austria	1	1	2
	USA	0	2	2
	Italy	1	0	1
1956	Austria	3	0	3
	Finland	2	1	3
	Norway	2	0	2
	USSR	1	1	2
	Switzerland	0	2	2
	Sweden	1	0	1
	Germany	0	1	1
1960	Sweden	2	1	3
	Germany	2	1	3
	Finland	2	0	2
	France	2	0	2
	Switzerland	1	1	2
	Norway	1	0	1
	Austria	1	0	1
	USSR	0	1	1
	Canada	0	1	1
1964	USSR	1	3	4
	Finland	3	0	3
	Austria	2	1	3
	France	1	2	3
	Sweden	2	0	2
	Norway	2	0	2
1968	Norway	4	1	5
	France	3	1	4
	USSR	2	0	2
	Sweden	0	2	2
	Italy	1	0	1

Year	Country			
	Germany	1	0	1
	Czechoslovakia	1	0	1
	Austria	0	1	1
	Canada	0	1	1
1972	USSR	3	3	6
	Switzerland	1	2	3
	Norway	2	0	2
	Germany	2	0	2
	Italy	1	0	1
	Japan	1	0	1
	Poland	1	0	1
	Sweden	1	0	1
	Spain	1	0	1
	USA	0	1	1
1976	USSR	4	2	6

Year	Country			
	W. Germany	0	3	3
	Austria	2	0	2
	Italy	2	0	2
	Finland	1	1	2
	E. Germany	2	0	2
	Norway	1	0	1
	Switzerland	1	0	1
	Canada	0	1	1
1980	USSR	5	1	6
	E. Germany	2	2	4
	Austria	2	1	3
	Sweden	3	0	3
	Liechtenstein	0	2	2
	Finland	1	0	1

WORLD CUP

The World Cup point scoring is necessarily complex because it seeks to be eminently fair in a complex situation. It starts by preselecting, before the start of the winter racing circuit, a series of meets in Austria, Germany, Switzerland, Italy, Sweden, Japan and North America, where competitors can win World Cup points. The fairly large number of qualifying races offers many opportunities to compete as well as enabling top racers to miss races owing to injuries or conflicting interests at home and school. It puts a high premium on first, second and third places because it seeks ski *champions,* not racers, who can accumulate a large number of points by consistently average performances. This feature of the World Cup is further accentuated by counting only the three best results of a racer in each Alpine specialty during the winter. It also prevents a competitor—who, for instance, is a specialized downhiller but only a mediocre slalom racer—from winning the overall World Cup by accumulating a huge total of points in one specialty or discipline.

Under the *original* scoring system, a racer wins 25 points for first place in an event, and can therefore gather a maximum of 75 points or three first places in a specialty during the season. The maximum total of 225 World Cup points can be won by three victories in each of the specialties.

WORLD CUP STANDINGS (MEN)

Year	Winner	Country	Total Points
1967	Jean-Claude Killy	France	225
	Heini Messner	Austria	114
	Guy Perillat	France	108
1968	Jean-Claude Killy	France	200
	Dumenc Giovanoll	Switzerland	119
	Herbert Huber	Austria	112
1969	Karl Schranz	Austria	182
	Jean-Noël Augert	France	123
	Reinhard Tritscher	Austria	108
1970	Karl Schranz	Austria	148
	Patrick Russel	France	145
	Gustavo Thoeni	Italy	140
1971	Gustavo Thoeni	Italy	155
	Henri Duvillard	France	135
	Patrick Russel	France	125
1972	Gustavo Thoeni	Italy	154

Year	Winner	Country	Total Points
	Henri Duvillard	France	142
	Edmund Bruggmann	Switzerland	140
1973	Gustavo Thoeni	Italy	165
	David Zwilling	Austria	151
	Roland Collombin	Switzerland	131
1974	Piero Gros	Italy	181
	Gustavo Thoeni	Italy	165
	Hans Hinterseer	Austria	162
1975	Gustavo Thoeni	Italy	250
	Ingemar Stenmark	Sweden	245
	Franz Klammer	Austria	240
1976	Ingemar Stenmark	Sweden	249
	Piero Gros	Italy	205
	Gustavo Thoeni	Italy	190
1977	Ingemar Stenmark	Sweden	339
	Klaus Heidegger	Austria	250
	Franz Klammer	Austria	203
1978	Ingemar Stenmark	Sweden	150
	Phil Mahre	USA	116
	Andreas Wenzel	Liechtenstein	100
1979	Peter Luescher	Switzerland	186
	Leonhard Stock	Austria	163
	Phil Mahre	USA	155
1980	Andreas Wenzel	Liechtenstein	204
	Ingemar Stenmark	Sweden	200
	Phil Mahre	USA	132

WORLD CUP STANDINGS (WOMEN)

Year	Winner	Country	Total Points
1967	Nancy Greene	Canada	176
	Marielle Goitschel	France	172
	Annie Famose	France	158
1968	Nancy Greene	Canada	191
	Isabelle Mir	France	159
	Florence Steurer	France	153
1969	Gertrude Gabl	Austria	131
	Florence Steurer	France	112
	Wiltrud Drexel	Austria	111
1970	Michèle Jacot	France	180
	Françoise Macchi	France	145
	Florence Steurer	France	133
1971	Annemarie Proell	Austria	210
	Michèle Jacot	France	177
	Isabelle Mir	France	133
1972	Annemarie Proell	Austria	269
	Françoise Macchi	France	187
	Britt Lafforgue	France	128
1973	Annemarie Proell	Austria	225
	Monika Kaserer	Austria	205
	Patricia Emonet	France	162
1974	Annemarie Proell	Austria	268
	Monika Kaserer	Austria	153
	Hanni Wenzel	Liechtenstein	144
1975	Annemarie Proell	Austria	305
	Hanni Wenzel	Liechtenstein	199

Year	Winner	Country	Total Points
	Rosi Mittermaier	West Germany	166
1976	Rosi Mittermaier	West Germany	281
	Lise-Marie Morerod	Switzerland	214
	Monika Kaserer	Austria	171
1977	Lise-Marie Morerod	Switzerland	319
	Annemarie Moser-Proell	Austria	246
	Monika Kaserer	Austria	196
1978	Hanni Wenzel	Liechtenstein	154
	Annemarie Moser-Proell	Austria	147
	Lise-Marie Morerod	Switzerland	135
1979	Annemarie Moser-Proell	Austria	243
	Hanni Wenzel	Liechtenstein	240
	Irene Epple	West Germany	189
1980	Hanni Wenzel	Liechtenstein	311
	Annemarie Moser-Proell	Austria	259
	Marie-Theres Nadig	Switzerland	221

NATIONS CUP

The Nations Cup, donated by Ski Magazine, is based on the aggregate of World Cup points earned by individual competitors—both men and women—from each Alpine skiing nation. While the World Cup goes to the top racers, the Nations Cup is presented to the coaches of the winning national team. The point totals reflect the work of the coaches in creating broad strength in their national teams.

NATION'S CUP STANDINGS

Year	World Cup Country	Total Points	Year	World Cup Country	Total Points
1967	France	1,260	1974	Austria	1,315
	Austria	597		Italy	766
	Switzerland	261		Switzerland	495
1968	France	1,165	1975	Austria	1,274
	Austria	887		Switzerland	790
	Switzerland	536		Italy	772
1969	Austria	1,120	1976	Austria	1,123
	France	1,050		Switzerland	992
	United States	542		Italy	782
1970	France	1,631	1977	Austria	1,998
	Austria	889		Switzerland	1,175
	United States	581		Italy	703
1971	France	1,333	1978	Austria	906
	Austria	892		Switzerland	517
	Switzerland	396		United States	411
1972	France	1,145	1979	Austria	1,763
	Austria	834		Switzerland	1,251
	Switzerland	660		Italy	996
1973	Austria	1,526	1980	Austria	1,314
	France	716		Switzerland	921
	Switzerland	585		United States	719